D0203169

Skilled interpersonal communication

Fourth edition

Skilled interpersonal communication

Research, theory and practice

Fourth edition

Owen Hargie and David Dickson

Routledge
Taylor & Francis Group

LONDON AND NEW YORK

First published 2004 by Routledge
27 Church Road, Hove, East Sussex,
BN3 2FA

Simultaneously published in the USA
and Canada
by Routledge
29 West 35th Street, New York, NY
10001

*Routledge is an imprint of the Taylor
& Francis Group*

© 2004 Owen Hargie and David
Dickson

Typeset in Century Old Style by
RefineCatch Limited, Bungay, Suffolk
Printed and bound in Great Britain by
MPG Books Ltd, Bodmin, Cornwall

*British Library Cataloguing in
Publication Data*
A catalogue record for this book is
available from the British Library

*Library of Congress Cataloging in
Publication Data*
Hargie, Owen.
    Skilled interpersonal
communication : research, theory, and
practice / by Owen Hargie and David
Dickson.— [Rev. and updated ed.].
        p.   cm.
Includes bibliographical references
and index.
    ISBN 0–415–22720–8 (pbk)
    ISBN 0–415–22719–4 (hbk)
    1. Interpersonal communication.
I. Dickson, David, 1950–   .
II. Title.
    BF637.C45   H33   2003
    302.3′4—dc21   2002153984

ISBN 0–415–22719–4 (hbk)
ISBN 0–415–22720–8 (pbk)

For our late colleague, co-author and dear friend, Christine Saunders

Contents

Figures

Boxes

Preface to the fourth edition

The contribution of effective interpersonal communication to success in both personal and professional contexts is now widely recognised. This topic is studied in its own right on many further and higher education programmes. Interpersonal training programmes have also been reported in the literature for every professional group, and the contribution of communication to social and personal well-being has been well researched. It is clear that the ability to communicate effectively at an interpersonal level is a vital part of the human condition. As such, knowledge of various types of skills, and of their effects in social interaction, is crucial for interpersonal functioning. It is for this reason that interest in the study of skilled communication has mushroomed in the past few years.

The present text emerged from our earlier book *Social skills in interpersonal communication*. It is eight years since the third edition of this book was published, and during this time we have received a considerable amount of feedback from tutors and trainees involved in interpersonal skills programmes, as well as from practising professionals. The result of this feedback has developed and shaped the current text. For example, the term 'social skill' tends to predominate within clinical contexts and in developmental/elementary educational fields. In academic and professional spheres, the more common usage now tends to be 'interpersonal skill' or 'communication skill' (Dickson *et al.*, 1997). The changed title of this new edition reflects the fact that its heartland lies in the academic domain of interpersonal communication, as applied to higher-order contexts. It also reflects the fact that the treatment of skill in the book encompasses a comprehensive review of research findings and analyses of theoretical perspectives, as well as direct applications to practice in a range of social settings.

The function of the book is to provide a key reference for the study of interpersonal communication *per se*. It is concerned with the identification, analysis and evaluation of a range of skills that are employed widely in interaction. As such, this text will be of interest both to students of interpersonal communication in general, and to qualified personnel and trainees in many fields in particular. Detailed accounts are provided of fourteen areas, namely: nonverbal communication; reinforcement; questioning; reflecting; listening; explaining; self-disclosure; set induction; closure; assertiveness; influencing; negotiating; and interacting in, and leading, group discussions.

However, from our personal perspective, the most significant change is the absence of our former co-author, colleague, and close friend, Christine Saunders, who passed away on 9 August 2002. We worked with Christine for over a quarter of a century and she was a constant source of inspiration, wisdom, support, creativity and unending good humour. Her untimely death meant that her absence was particularly deeply felt as we put together this new text.

We would also like to acknowledge the assistance provided by the School of Communication and Faculty of Social Sciences, University of Ulster. Thanks also to all those members of staff at the University, and at other centres, who have been involved in, and contributed to, the evolution of our communication programmes. The support, advice and encouragement of these colleagues are reflected throughout this book. The stimulation and invaluable feedback provided by trainees enrolled on our skills programmes are also recognised.

A special word of thanks is given to the editorial staff at Routledge, for all their help, support and expertise. Words of appreciation are due to Philip Burch, Graphic Design Technician in the School of Communication at the University of Ulster, Jordanstown for his skill in producing some of the more intricate diagrams. Finally, we are indebted to our families who provided the necessary motivation and love to sustain us throughout the production of this text.

Owen Hargie and David Dickson
Jordanstown, 2004

Chapter 1

Introduction:
The importance of
interpersonal skills

INTRODUCTION

THERE IS A FUNDAMENTAL, powerful, and universal need or desire among humans to interact with others. As expressed by Afifi and Guerrero (2000: 170): 'There is a long history of research establishing the importance that individuals place on connectedness ... individuals' needs for initiating, developing and maintaining social ties, especially close ones, is reflected in a litany of studies and a host of theories.' The mere presence of another has been shown to be arousing and motivating and this in turn influences our behaviour – a process termed *compresence* (Burgoon *et al.*, 1996). We behave differently in the company of another person from when alone. When we meet others we are 'onstage' and so give a performance that differs from how we behave 'offstage'.

We also enjoy interacting, and indeed the act of engaging in facilitative interpersonal communication has been shown to contribute to positive changes in emotional state (Gable and Shean, 2000). While our dealings with others can sometimes be problematic or even contentious, we also seek, relish, and obtain great reward from social interaction. Conversely, if we are unable to engage meaningfully with others, or are ostracised by them, the result is often loneliness, unhappiness and depression (Williams and Zadiro, 2001). This seemingly innate need for relationships with others has been termed *sociation* (Wolff, 1950). As Ryff and Singer (2000: 31) put it: 'Across time and settings, people everywhere have subscribed to the view that close, meaningful ties to others is an essential feature of what it means to be fully human.' In other words, individuals need to commune with others.

One hypothesised reason for this is that our early ancestors who lived in groups were more likely to survive than those who lived alone, and so the skills involved in developing and maintaining social bonds assumed a central role in human evolution (Leary, 2001). Thus, Forgas and Williams (2001: 7) noted that: 'Homo sapiens is a highly sociable species . . . our impressive record of achievements owes a great deal to the highly elaborate strategies we have developed for getting along with each other and co-ordinating our interpersonal behaviors.'

Another part of the reason for sociation is that: 'The essence of communication is the formation and expression of an identity. The formation of the self is not an independent event generated by an autonomous actor. Rather, the self emerges through social interaction' (Coover and Murphy, 2000: 125). In other words, we become the people we are as a result of our interchanges with others (this issue is discussed further in Chapter 2 and explored in more detail in Chapter 9). Interaction is therefore the essential nutrient that nurtures and sustains the social milieu. Furthermore, since communication is a prerequisite for learning, without the capacity for sophisticated methods and channels for sharing knowledge, both within and between generations, our advanced human civilisation would simply not exist. Communication therefore represents the very essence of the human condition. Indeed, one of the harshest punishments available within most penal systems is that of solitary confinement – the removal of any possibility of interpersonal contact.

Thus people have a deep-seated need to communicate, and the better able they are to do so, the more satisfying and rewarding will be their existence. Research by Segrin and Flora (2000: 490) has shown how 'good communication, or social, skills pay many dividends in people's lives'. Those with higher levels of skill have been found to cope more readily with stress, to adapt and adjust better to major life transitions, and to be less likely to suffer from depression, loneliness or anxiety. They also have higher levels of satisfaction in relation to their close personal relationships (Miczo *et al.*, 2001). In a review of research, Segrin (2000) concluded that interactive skills have a 'prophylactic effect' in that socially competent people are resilient to the ill effects of life crises, whereas individuals with poor skills experience a worsening of psycho-social problems when faced with stressors in life. In reviewing the development and contribution of the skills approach to interpersonal communication, Argyle (1999: 142) concluded: 'skills training is now given for many occupations . . . I wish it were more widely available for the general public – we now know that being socially skilled is a source of happiness'. Continuing this theme, Hybels and Weaver (1998: 5) succinctly summarised the position: 'To live, then, is to communicate. To communicate effectively is to enjoy life more fully.'

But there are more tangible rewards to be gained from developing an effective interpersonal skill repertoire. These begin from an early age, since it is now clear that children who develop good interactive skills also perform better academically. As summarised by Brigman *et al.* (1999: 323), 'Numerous studies have identified attending skills, listening skills and social skills as being most predictive of long-term school success.' The benefits then continue in many walks of life after school.

In the business sphere there are considerable advantages to be gained from good communication (Hargie and Tourish, 2000), and effective managers have been shown to have a strong repertoire of interpersonal skills (Clampitt, 2001). Baron and Markman (2000) used the term *social capital* to refer to the benefits that accrue from having a large network of contacts, being an effective interactor, and developing a good social reputation. They compared the relationship between social capital and interpersonal skill to that between resource stock and resource flows in organisations, and argued that 'Social capital can be viewed as an accumulated asset, while skills in interacting with others are one factor that influences the level of this asset' (p. 107). They also showed how those entrepreneurs who possess high levels of interpersonal skill have advantages in a range of areas, such as obtaining funding, attracting quality employees, maintaining good relationships with co-founders of the business, and producing better results from customers and suppliers.

Likewise, in health care, the importance for health professionals of having a 'good bedside manner' has long been realised. In 400 BC, Hippocrates noted how the patient 'may recover his health simply through his contentment with the goodness of the physician'. In recent years, this belief in the power of communication to contribute to the healing process has been borne out by research. Di Blasi *et al.* (2001) carried out a systematic review of studies in Europe, the USA and Canada that investigated the effects of doctor–patient relationships. This covered a wide range of conditions including high blood pressure, asthma and pain. Di Blasi *et al.* found that good practitioner interpersonal skills do make a significant difference to patient well-being, concluding that, 'Practitioners who attempted to form a warm and friendly relationship with their patients, and reassured them that they would soon be better, were found to be more effective than practitioners who kept their consultations impersonal, formal, or uncertain' (p. 760).

Thus interpersonal skills are at the very epicentre of our social existence. We ignore them at our peril. But the good news is that we can improve our ability to communicate. A great deal is now known about the key constituents of the DNA of interactive life. Indeed, the academic study of interpersonal communication has a very long and rich tradition, spanning some 5,000 years. Pedagogical Luddites of today who complain about the introduction of the 'new' discipline of communication should pay attention to history. The oldest essay ever discovered, written about 3,000 BC, consisted of advice to Kagemni, the eldest son of Pharaoh Huni, on speaking effectively in public. Similarly, the oldest book, the *Precepts*, written in Egypt by Ptah-Hotep, circa 2,675 BC, is a treatise on effective communication. Given this early focus, it is perhaps surprising that this area was subsequently largely neglected in terms of academic study in higher education, until its resurgence in the late twentieth century. As noted by Bull (2002: vii), 'Communication is of central importance to many aspects of human life, yet it is only in recent years that it has become the focus of scientific investigation.' For example, it was not until 1960 that the notion of communication as a form of *skilled activity* was first suggested (Hargie, 1997a).

In the intervening years, the fairly obvious observation that some individuals are better social interactors than others led to carefully formulated and systematic investigations into the nature and function of interpersonal interaction. Indeed Segrin (1992: 89) illustrated how: 'The concept of social skill has touched the interests of researchers working in virtually all fields of social science.' This has occurred at three levels.

1. Theoretical analyses of how and why people behave as they do have resulted in various conceptualisations of skilled behaviour (see Hargie and Tourish, 1999).

2. Research has been conducted into the identification and effects of different types of social behaviour. It is this level that the present book addresses.
3. Several approaches to training in communication skills have been introduced in order to ascertain whether it is possible to improve the social performance of the individual (for a review of these see Dickson *et al.*, 1997).

Over the past twenty years there has been a vast outpouring of research in this field. An important part of this research and scholarship has involved an analysis of the exact nature of the skills process.

THE NATURE OF INTERPERSONAL SKILLS

In terms of nomenclature, different terms are used synonymously to describe this area. The terms 'social skills', 'interpersonal skills' and 'communication skills' are often used interchangeably. The latter, however, can encompass written as well as interpersonal skills, while the former is generally used to refer to developmental or clinical applications. In this text we will employ all three terms interchangeably but will tend to concentrate on the 'interpersonal' descriptor. Thus interpersonal skills, in a global sense, can be defined as the skills we employ when interacting with other people. This definition is not very informative, however, since it really indicates what skills are *used for* rather than what they *are*. It is rather like defining an aeroplane as something that gets you from one country to another.

Attempts to define the term 'interpersonal skill' proliferate within the literature. In order to illustrate this point it is useful to examine some of the definitions that have been put forward by different theorists. Phillips (1978: 13), in reviewing a number of approaches, concluded that a person is skilled according to:

> the extent to which he or she can communicate with others, in a manner that fulfils one's rights, requirements, satisfactions, or obligations to a reasonable degree without damaging the other person's similar rights, requirements, satisfactions, or obligations, and hopefully shares these rights etc. with others in free and open exchange.

This definition emphasises the macro-elements of social encounters, in terms of reciprocation between participants. This theme is also found in the definition given by Schlundt and McFall (1985: 23), who defined social skills as: 'the specific component processes that enable an individual to behave in a manner that will be judged as "competent". Skills are the abilities necessary for producing behavior that will accomplish the objectives of a task.'

These definitions tend to view skill as an *ability* that the individual may possess to a greater or lesser extent. A somewhat different focus has been offered by other theorists, who define skill in terms of the *behaviour* of the individual. For example, Robbins and Hunsaker (1996: 7) iterated that 'a skill is a system of behavior that can be applied in a wide range of situations', while Cameron (2000: 86) stated that 'The term *skill* connotes *practical expertise*, the ability to *do* something.' Proctor and Dutta (1995: 18) extended this behavioural emphasis to encompass the *goals* of the individual: 'Skill is goal-directed, well-organized behavior', while Kelly (1982: 3) emphasised the dimension of *learning* by defining skills as 'those identifiable, learned behaviors that individuals use in interpersonal situations to obtain or maintain reinforcement from their environment'.

These elements were summarised by Robbins and Hunsaker (1996: 7–8):

> To become competent at any skill, a person needs to understand it both conceptually and behaviorally; have opportunities to practice it; get feedback on how well he or she is performing the skill; and use the skill often enough so that it becomes integrated with his or her behavioral repertoire.

In his review of definitions of skilled behaviour, Hargie (1997a: 12) defined interpersonal skill as: 'the process whereby the individual implements a set of goal-directed, inter-related, situationally appropriate social behaviours which are learned and controlled'. This is the definition adopted in this book. It emphasises seven separate components of skill.

First, as will be discussed more fully in Chapter 2, skilled performance is a *process* that involves:

- formulating goals and related action plans;
- implementing these plans;
- monitoring the effects of behaviour;
- adjusting, adapting or abandoning goals and responses in the light of outcomes;
- taking cognisance of other people and the context in which interaction occurs.

Second, skilled behaviours are *goal-directed*. They are those behaviours the individual employs in order to achieve a desired outcome, and are therefore purposeful, as opposed to chance, or unintentional. As Huang (2000: 111) noted, 'the purposes people bring into communication have important consequences on communication processes'. For example, if A wishes to encourage B to talk freely, A will look at B, use head nods when B speaks, refrain from interrupting B, and utter 'guggles' ('hmm hmm'; 'uh, hu'; etc.) periodically. In this instance these *behaviours* are *directed* towards the *goal* of encouraging participation.

The goals we pursue are not always conscious, and indeed one feature of skilled performance is that behaviour is often executed automatically. Once responses are learned they tend to become hard-wired or habitual. When we know how to drive, we no longer have to think about actions such as how to start the car, brake, reverse, and so on. Yet, when learning to drive, these actions are consciously monitored as they are performed. In the successful learning of new skills we move through the stages of *conscious incompetence* (we know what we should be doing and we know we are not doing it very well), *conscious competence* (we know we are performing at a satisfactory level), and finally *unconscious competence* (we just do it without thinking about it and we succeed). This is also true of interpersonal skills. During free-flowing social encounters, less than 200 milliseconds typically elapse between the responses of speakers and rarely do conversational pauses reach three seconds. As a result certain elements, such as the exact choice of words used and the use of gestures, almost always occur without conscious reflection (Wilson *et al.*, 2000). In relation to the negotiation context, McRae (1998: 123) explained how: 'Expert negotiators become so proficient at certain skills in the negotiating process that they do not have to consciously think about using these skills. It's as if the response becomes second nature.' However, an awareness of relevant goals does not ensure success. As expressed by J. Greene (2000: 147):

> action may not be so readily instantiated in overt behavior . . . the inept athlete, dancer, actor or public speaker may well have a perfectly adequate abstract representation of what he or she needs to do, but what actually gets enacted is rather divergent from his or her image of that action.

Thus skill involves not just the ability to formulate appropriate goals, but being able to implement them successfully in practice. In other words, '*skill* refers to the degree to which a performed behavior proves successful' (Miczo *et al.*, 2001: 40).

Third, skilled behaviours must be *interrelated*, in that they are synchronised in order to achieve a particular goal. Thus the individual will employ two or more behaviours at the same time. For example, as mentioned previously, when encouraging B to talk, A may smile, use head nods, look directly at B, and utter guggles, and each of these signals will be interpreted by B as a sign of encouragement to continue speaking. Each behaviour relates to this common goal, and so the behaviours are in this way interrelated and synchronised.

Fourth, skills should be *appropriate* to the *situation* in which they are being used. The skilled individual adapts behaviours to meet the demands of particular people in specific contexts. Dickson (2001) referred to this aspect of skilled performance as *contextual propriety*. In their review of this area, White and Burgoon (2001: 9) concluded that, 'the most essential feature of human interaction is that it involves adaptation'. Indeed, linguistic conceptualisations purport that skill is mutually constructed through dialogue and so can only be understood by an interpretation of how narratives develop in any particular context (Holman, 2000).

From an interpersonal communication perspective, Wilson *et al.* (2000: 136–7) illustrated how effective interaction involves adaptation at all levels:

> Speakers coordinate their own behavior with that of their interactive partner. Interparty coordination is evident at microlevels, such as in the timing of mutual smiles . . . [and] . . . at more macrolevels, such as in the adjustment of one's own plans to the apparent plans of one's conversational partner.

In many routine situations, such as filling stations or fast food counters, participants have a good idea of one another's goals and so adaptation is easy. However, in more complex contexts, such as psychotherapy or negotiation, the interactors have to spend considerable time establishing one another's agendas and agreeing mutual goals for the encounter, so that they can adjust and adapt their responses accordingly (Berger, 2000).

Fifth, skills are defined in terms of identifiable units of *behaviour*. In this way, 'Skill is reflected in the performance of communicative behaviors. It is the *enactment* of knowledge and motivation' (Cupach and Canary, 1997: 28). We judge whether or not people are skilled based on how they actually *behave*. Verbal and nonverbal behaviour therefore represent the oxygen of the communicating organism. Skilled responses are hierarchically organised in such a way that large elements, like being interviewed, are composed of smaller behavioural units such as looking at the interviewer and answering questions. The development of interpersonal skills can be facilitated by training the individual to acquire these smaller responses before combining them into larger repertoires (Dickson *et al.*, 1997). Indeed, this technique is also used in the learning of many motor skills.

The sixth aspect of the definition is that behaviours are *learned*. It is now generally accepted that most forms of behaviour displayed in social contexts are learned. From the day of their birth, infants are communicated with as if they can understand. Parents and other carers talk to them and ascribe intentionality to their behaviour (e.g. 'You are hungry and are looking for some milk, aren't you?' 'There, you wanted your rattle, didn't you?'). The function here is to bring the infant into 'personhood' by treating it as a communicating being (Penman, 2000). This is a very important step in the social development of the individual. For example, as the child grows it is taught to read. This begins with the social process of slowly reading and speaking the words aloud, which eventually results in the child learning to read silently. The skill of talking to oneself in silence takes time to master, and is predicated on the earlier social dynamic of reading with others. In this way, communication is central to the development of cognitive abilities.

Children reared in isolation miss out on these essential learning experiences. As a result they display distorted, socially unacceptable forms of behaviour (Newton, 2002). At a less extreme level, there is evidence to indicate that children from culturally richer home environments tend to develop more appropriate social behaviours than those from socially deprived backgrounds (Messer, 1995). Bandura's (1986) social cognitive theory purports that all repertoires of behaviour, with the exception of elementary reflexes (such as eye blinks), are learned. This process of social learning involves the *modelling* and *imitation* of the behaviour of significant others, such as parents, teachers, siblings or peers. By this process, from an early age, children may walk, talk and act like their same-sex parent. At a later stage, however, the child may develop the accent of his, or her, peers and begin to talk in a similar fashion – despite the accent of parents.

In addition to modelling and imitation, a second major element in the learning of social behaviour is the *reinforcement*, by significant others, of these behaviours when displayed by the individual. In childhood, for example, parents encourage, discourage or ignore various behaviours that the child displays. As a general rule, the child learns, and employs more frequently, those behaviours that are encouraged, while tending to display less often those that are discouraged or ignored. In this sense, feedback is crucial to effective performance (see Chapter 4 for a full discussion of reinforcement).

The final element in the definition of skills, and another feature of social cognitive theory, is that they should be under the cognitive *control* of the individual. As expressed by Cameron (2000: 86):

> A 'skilled' person does not only know how to do certain things, but also understands *why* those things are done the way they are. S/he is acquainted with the

general principles of the activity s/he is skilled in, and so is able to modify what s/he does in response to the exigencies of any specific situation.

Thus a socially inadequate individual may have learned the basic elements of skills but may not have developed the appropriate thought processes necessary to control the utilisation of these elements in interpersonal encounters. An important dimension of control relates to the timing of behaviours. If the use of a skill is to achieve its desired effect, then the timing of behaviour is a very important consideration, in that skilled behaviours need to be employed at the most suitable juncture. Learning *when* to employ behaviours is just as crucial as learning *what* these behaviours are and *how* to use them. As expressed by Wolvin and Coakley (1996: 52), 'Communication skills combine with communicator *knowledge* – information and understanding – to influence the entire process.'

Zimmerman (2000) identified four key stages in the learning of skills.

1. *Observation.* Here the person watches others perform the skill, and also pays attention to other dimensions, such as the motivational orientation, values and performance standards of the actors, as well as how the repertoires used vary across target persons.
2. *Emulation.* At this stage the individual is able to execute a behavioural display to approximate that observed. The display is emulated but not replicated. For example, the *style* of praise used may be similar but the *actual words used* will differ.
3. *Self-control.* This involves the actor beginning to *master* the skill. Thus the tennis player will practise serving until this is fully developed, while a barrister will likewise practise questioning technique.
4. *Self-regulation.* Finally, the person learns to use the skill appropriately across different personal and contextual conditions. To continue the analogies, here the tennis player is concerned with placing the serve where it is likely to find the opponent's weak point, while the barrister will consider appropriate questions to achieve the best outcomes from different witnesses.

The acronym CLIPS is useful for remembering the key features of interpersonal skill. Skilled performance is:

- Controlled by the individual;
- Learned behaviour that improves with practice and feedback;
- Integrated and interrelated verbal and nonverbal responses;
- Purposive and goal-directed;
- Smooth in the manner in which the performance is executed.

OVERVIEW

Simon (1999: 66) illustrated how 'people's own identity and meaningful existence depend on finding a place in the social world'. The ability to achieve this 'place', in turn, depends to a very large extent on one's interactive skills. The fluent application of skill is a crucial feature of effective social interaction. In Chapter 2 a model is presented, which sets the study of skill within the wider context of the social milieu. This illustrates how the appropriateness of behaviour is determined by a number of variables relating to the context of the interaction, the roles of those involved and their goals, as well as personal features of the interactors (age, sex, personality, etc.). It is therefore impossible to legislate in advance for every situation, in terms of what behaviours will be most successful to employ. The information about skills contained in this book should rather be regarded as providing resource material for the reader. How these resources are employed is a decision for the reader, given the situation in which any particular interaction is taking place.

There are fourteen main skill areas covered in this text, beginning with non-verbal communication in Chapter 3. This aspect of interaction is the first to be examined, since all the areas that follow contain nonverbal elements and so an under-standing of the main facets of this channel facilitates the examination of all the other skills. Chapter 4 incorporates an analysis of reinforcement, while questioning is reviewed in Chapter 5. In Chapter 6, an alternative strategy to questioning, namely reflecting, is investigated. Reflection consists of concentrating on what another person is saying and reflecting back the central elements of that person's statements. The skill of listening is explored in Chapter 7, where the active nature of listening is emphasised, while explaining is focused on in Chapter 8. In Chapter 9, self-disclosure is examined from two perspectives: first, the appropriateness of self-disclosure by the professional, and second, methods for promoting maximum self-disclosure from clients. Two important episodes in any action – the opening and closing sequences – are reviewed in Chapter 10. Techniques for protecting personal rights are discussed in Chapter 11 in terms of the skill of assertiveness. The skill area of influencing and persuading has attracted growing interest in recent years and this is covered in Chapter 12. A related skill, namely negotiation, not included in earlier editions of this text, is addressed in Chapter 13. Finally, in Chapter 14 the skills involved in interacting in, and leading, small group discussions are examined.

It should be realised that research in the field of social interaction is progressing rapidly and it is anticipated that, as our knowledge of this area increases, other important skill areas may be identified. The skills contained in this book do not represent a completely comprehensive list, but they are generally regarded as being the central aspects of interpersonal communication. In addition, it is recognised that, while these skills are studied separately, in practice they overlap and complement one another. What is definitely the case is that knowledge of the repertoire of skilled behaviours covered in this text will enable readers to extend and refine their own pattern or style of interaction.

Chapter 2

Interpersonal communication: A skill-based model

INTRODUCTION

THE COMMUNICATION PROCESS IS explicable from within a range of contrasting theoretical frameworks (see Griffin, 2000). What happens when two people meet and initiate a social encounter can be accounted for, as we have seen in Chapter 1, in terms of each behaving skilfully in order to accomplish sought-after goals. Several features of skill in this sense were also outlined in the last chapter. In sum, this type of behaviour may be thought of as an efficient and effective way of achieving warrantable outcomes. Furthermore, behaving in this manner should be in keeping with the rules and conventions governing acceptable conduct in that particular context. A televised advertisement for a digital television company specialising in sport depicts a young man at the end of a panel selection interview. He gets up, goes over to the members and, in turn, ruffles hair and pinches cheeks as he would were he with his football friends. While this form of leave-taking might be perfectly acceptable in that situation, it is an embarrassingly inappropriate way to finish off a rather formal interview. Skilled behaviour must be appropriate to situational expectations.

But what precisely is communication, in any case? The first part of this chapter will be given over to addressing this question. Having done so, it will develop a skill-based, theoretical model of the communicative process which highlights its transactional nature. What takes place when two people interact is presented as being undergirded by a complex of perceptual, cognitive, affective and performative factors operating within a person–situation framework. The activity is held to be energised and given direction by the desire to achieve set goals and

is accomplished by the ongoing monitoring of both personal and environmental circumstances, including, of course, those represented by the other interactor sharing the encounter. Before proceeding with the model, however, we need to give more careful thought to the notion of communication, and interpersonal communication in particular.

COMMUNICATION AND INTERPERSONAL COMMUNICATION

As a concept, communication is notoriously difficult to pin down (Heath and Bryant, 2000). It represents a phenomenon that is at one and the same time ubiquitous yet elusive, prosaic yet mysterious, straightforward yet frustratingly prone to failure. It has been portrayed as 'both complex and brittle, composed of several series of sometimes very subtle actions and behaviours, which as a rule are felicitous but quite often less than completely successful' (Rosengren, 2000: 37). Ellis and Beattie (1986) described communication as a 'fuzzy' concept, with boundaries that are blurred and not altogether certain. This has created difficulties when it comes to reaching agreement over matters of formal definition. Holli and Calabrese (1998) attributed the problem to the vast range of activities that can legitimately be subsumed under this label and pointed out that the *Journal of Communication* has published no fewer than fifteen different working definitions of human communication. Some practical, day-to-day examples of communication at work are given in Box 2.1.

Traced back to its Latin roots the verb 'to communicate' means 'to share', 'to make common', meanings reflected in many of the definitions available in the current

---

Box 2.1 Mr Topman keeps in touch

Communication and effective management go hand in hand. Consider part of the working day of Mr Topman, the managing director of a light engineering firm. His first task, on arrival at work, is spent with his PA dealing with the morning's mail and e-mail. He then dictates letters on matters arising, faxes some urgent material to suppliers in the USA, and makes several telephone calls before chairing the first meeting of the day with his executive team. After lunch, he and his financial adviser discuss the quarterly financial statement. At 2.30 pm, his personal assistant informs him that the sales manager has just arrived for his appraisal interview. That over, he meets with Ms Brightside who looks after the firm's public relations. An article that he read in the local paper on his way to work that morning had troubled him. It hinted that the firm may be on the verge of shedding up to 25 per cent of its workforce with devastating effects for the local community. A press release is prepared and it is decided that Mr Topman should go on local TV that evening to quash the rumour. Before leaving he prepares for a video-conferenced meeting that he will chair first thing next morning with members of the National Group of Management Engineers. A truly busy day and all of it communication centred – but communication in many and diverse forms.

---

literature. From the plethora of options available, two central themes have been distilled (Hewes and Planalp, 1987; Hewes, 1995):

1   *intersubjectivity* – which has to do with striving to understand others and being understood in turn, and
2   *impact* – which represents the extent to which a message brings about change in thoughts, feelings, or behaviour.

In this book our interest is largely restricted to *interpersonal communication*. As viewed by Hartley (1999), this sub-type concentrates on communication that:

- is essentially non-mediated (or face-to-face);
- takes place in a dyadic (one-to-one) or small group setting;
- in form and content is shaped by, and conveys something of, the personal qualities of the interactors as well as their social roles and relationships.

Adler *et al.* (1998b), thinking particularly of relational applications, added that this sub-category of communication accentuates the:

- uniqueness of each interpersonal exchange – people are dealt with as individuals;
- irreplaceability of the relationship that results;
- interdependence of the interactors;
- self-disclosure that ensues;
- intrinsic nature of rewards stemming from true person-to-person contact.

In simple terms, Brooks and Heath (1993: 7) defined interpersonal communication as, 'the process by which information, meanings and feelings are shared by persons through the exchange of verbal and nonverbal messages'. (We will return to definitional issues later in this sub-section.) With this in mind, and returning to Mr Topman in Box 2.1, we can therefore largely disregard letters, reports, newspapers, files, e-mail, TV, etc., as examples. It is the sorts of processes that characterised his encounters with his financial adviser, sales manager and public relations officer with which we are concerned.

Communication is a process

Craig (1999) commented on a distinct tradition within communication theory of conceptualising communication as a process of sending and receiving messages. Thinking in this way of what takes place when two people share meaning is also strongly endorsed by Heath and Bryant (2000), among others. Communication requires that at least two contribute to the ongoing and dynamic sequence of events in which each affects and is affected by the other in a system of reciprocal determination. As we shall see shortly, each at the same time perceives the other in context, makes some sort of sense of what is happening, comes to a decision as to how to react and responds accordingly.

SKILLED INTERPERSONAL COMMUNICATION

Being more specific, the components of the communicative process, in its simplest form, have been identified as including communicators, message, medium, channel, noise, feedback and context (Gudykunst, 1991; Adler and Towne, 1996). Each of these will be looked at in turn.

Communicators

The indispensability of communicators to the process is fairly obvious. In early models of how communication took place (e.g. Shannon and Weaver, 1949), one was designated the *Source*, the other the *Receiver*, and the process was held to commence when the former transmitted a message to the latter. This is a good example of what Clampitt (2001) called 'Arrow' communication, that is, communication that goes in one direction only. More recently the over-simplicity of this thinking about face-to-face interaction has been recognised. Communicators are, at one and the same time, senders and receivers of messages. While person A speaks, the effects of the utterance are also typically monitored by A, requiring information from B to be simultaneously received. Correspondingly, person B, in listening to A, is also reacting to A's contribution. The notion of 'source–receiver' is therefore a more accurate representation of the role of each participant (DeVito, 1998).

Message

The message can be thought of as the content of communication embodying whatever it is that communicators wish to share. Gouran (1990: 6) described it as, 'a pattern of thought, configuration of ideas, or other response to internal conditions about which individuals express themselves'. Such expression, however, presupposes some form of behavioural manifestation: thoughts and feelings, to be made known, must be encoded or organised into a physical form capable of being transmitted to others. Decoding is the counterpart of encoding whereby recipients attach meaning to what they have just experienced (O'Hair *et al.*, 1998).

Medium

The medium is the particular means of conveying the message. Fiske (1990) described three types of media.

1   *Presentational* – e.g. the voice, face, body.
2   *Representational* – e.g. books, paintings, architecture, photographs.
3   *Technological/mechanical* – e.g. television, radio, CD, telephone.

The first of these is pivotal to interpersonal communication. Media differ in the levels of *social presence* afforded. As explained by Straub and Karahanna (1998: 161) this is the degree to which 'a medium enables a communicator to experience communication partners as being psychologically present'. *Media richness* is a similar concept, suggesting that media differ in the richness of information that they carry. Actually talking to someone face to face provides a greater richness of social cues and a fuller experience of the individual than e-mailing, for instance. Choices as to the most suitable medium to use depend on factors such as the task in hand (Westmyer and Rubin, 1998; Harwood, 2000; O'Sullivan, 2000). In organisations generally, Rice (1993) reported that face-to-face communication was regarded as more appropriate than telephone, meetings, voice mail and e-mail.

Channel

Differences between this and the notion of medium are sometimes blurred in the literature, and indeed the two terms are often used interchangeably. 'Channel' refers to that which 'connects' communicators and accommodates the medium. DeVito (1998: 16) described it as operating like a 'bridge connecting source and receiver'. Fiske (1990) gave as examples light waves, sound waves, radio waves as well as cables of different types, capable of carrying pulses of light or electrical energy. Likewise, DeVito (1998) talked about the:

- *vocal–auditory* channel which carries speech;
- *gestural–visual* channel which facilitates much nonverbal communication;
- *chemical–olfactory* channel accommodating smell;
- *cutaneous–tactile* channel which enables us to make interpersonal use of touch.

These different channels are typically utilised simultaneously in the course of face-to-face communication.

Code

A code is a system of meaning shared by a group. It designates signs and symbols peculiar to that code and specifies rules and conventions for their use. The English language, for example, is a code in accordance with which the accepted meaning of 'dog' is an animal with four legs that barks. Other codes are Morse, French, Braille, etc.

Noise

In this sense the word has a rather special meaning which is more than mere sound. It refers to any interference with the success of the communicative act thereby distorting or degrading the message so that the meaning gained is not that intended. As such, noise may originate in the source, the channel, the receiver, or the context within which participants interact. It may be external and take the form of intrusive sound, which masks what is being said, or it may be internal, stemming from the unique life experiences of the participants. Where ethnic or cultural differences intrude, meanings attached to particular choices of word or forms of expression can

15

vary considerably, causing unintended confusion, misunderstanding, insult or hurt (Gudykunst and Ting-Toomey, 1996).

Feedback

By means of feedback, the sender is able to judge the extent to which the message has been successfully received and the impact that it has had. Monitoring receiver reactions enables subsequent communications to be adapted and regulated to achieve a desired effect. Feedback, therefore, is vitally important to successful social outcomes. It plays a central role in the model of skilful interaction to be elaborated in the second half of the chapter and more will be said about it then.

Context

All communication takes place within a context and is crucially influenced by it (Rosengren, 2000). To be more accurate, communication takes place within inter-meshing frameworks. An inescapable instance, geographical location, provides a physical setting for what takes place. To take one example, people in lifts often behave in rather restrained ways that match the physical constraints of their surroundings.

Then again, all encounters occur within a temporal context. A class may be held late on Friday afternoon or early on Monday morning and the vigour and enthusiasm of the discussion can be influenced as a result. Relationship provides a further frame-work for interaction. In a fascinating study of touch among opposite sex couples in public, Willis and Briggs (1992) found that males tended to initiate touch during courtship while, among married couples, females were more inclined to take the initiative. We can additionally think of a range of psychosocial factors such as status relationship, that constitute a different, but equally significant framework for communication.

So far, context has been depicted as exerting an influence on communication. But it should not be overlooked that, in many respects, interactors can also serve to shape aspects of their situation through communication. The concept of context features prominently in the model to be developed shortly and will be returned to there.

Communication is transactional

As mentioned, early theorists such as Shannon and Weaver (1949) viewed communication as a fundamentally linear process. A message is formulated by the source and sent to the receiver. This view has given way to a more transactional conceptualisation that stresses the dynamic and changing nature of the process. Communicators affect, and are affected by each other, in a system of reciprocal influence (Adler et al., 1998b).

Communication is inevitable

This is a contentious point. Communication has long been held, by those theorists who adopt a broad view of what constitutes the phenomenon (e.g. Watzlawick *et al.*, 1967; Scheflen, 1974), to be inevitable in social situations where each is aware of each other's presence and is influenced in what is done as a result. Watzlawick *et al.* (1967: 49) are responsible for the much quoted maxim that, in such circumstances, 'one cannot *not* communicate'. Imagine the situation where shy boy and attractive girl are seated opposite each other in the railway carriage. Attractive girl 'catches' shy boy eyeing her legs. She eases her skirt over her knees. Their eyes meet, shy boy blushes and they both look away in embarrassment. Has communication taken place between them, or can their reactions be at best described as merely expressive or informative? Are all actions communication? What if I display behaviour that I have little control over and do not mean to perform; am I communicating?

For some, unless we impose some conditions then all behaviour becomes communication, so rendering the term 'communication' largely redundant (Trenholm and Jensen, 2000). Even Bavelas who co-authored *Pragmatics of human communication* (Watzlawick *et al.*, 1967) later came to accept that some nonverbal behaviour was best described as informative rather than communicative (Bavelas, 1992). The debate concerns issues such as communicative behaviour being intentional, done with conscious awareness, and being code-based (Knapp and Hall, 1997). Applying such conditions in their most extreme form would confine communication to those acts, in each and every instance:

- performed with the intention of sharing meaning;
- perceived as such by the recipient;
- done by both in the full glare of conscious awareness;
- accomplished by means of a shared arbitrary code. Arbitrary in this sense means that the relationship between the behaviour and what it represents is entirely a matter of agreed convention.

But does the encoder have to be consciously aware of the intention? What if the decoder fails to recognise that the witnessed behaviour was enacted intentionally and reacts (or fails to act) accordingly?

For many these impositions are too extreme and create particular problems for the concept of *nonverbal* communication. Different sets of more relaxed restrictions have been suggested. Burgoon *et al.* (1996: 13–14), for instance, advocated that those actions be accepted as communicative that '(a) are typically sent with intent, (b) are used with regularity among members of a given social community, society or culture, (c) are typically interpreted as intentional, and (d) have consensually recognised meaning'. As such, any particular instance of an unconscious, unintentional facial expression, let us say, could still be accepted as communicative. Remland (2000) additionally argued that communication does not have to rely on an arbitrary code. Such codes are made up of symbols whose relationship to the thing in the world that they represent is merely a matter of agreed convention. There is no obvious reason why 'dog', for instance, should be the word symbol that represents the animal to which it refers. Indeed the French use 'chien'. Intrinsic codes that are biologically rather than socially based are also acceptable. This would include, for example, blushes being recognised as symptoms of embarrassment, despite the fact that they do not share this same type of arbitrary relationship.

Communication is purposeful

Another commonly cited characteristic of communication is its purposefulness (Dickson, 2001). Those who take part do so with some end in mind; they want to effect some desired outcome. According to this functional view of the phenomenon, communication is far from idle or aimless but is conducted to make something happen – to achieve a goal of some sort. As put by Westmyer and Rubin (1998: 28):

> To understand why people engage in interpersonal communication, we must remember that communication is goal directed. Interpersonal needs establish expectations for communication behaviour. Communicators are mindful in that they are capable of acknowledging their needs and motives, and realize that they can choose particular communication behaviors to fulfil these needs.

It is this that both adds impetus and provides direction to the transaction.

A pivotal implication of casting communication as purposeful activity is, according to Kellermann (1992), that it must also be thought of as what she called 'adjusted'. That is, communicators fashion what they say and do, on an ongoing basis, in response to the goals that they are pursuing and within the constraints that are operative. Both Hewes (1995) and Berger (1995) argued a similar point. Adjusted performance presupposes the possibility of selection and choice among alternative courses of action. Communication is a strategic enterprise, in other words. Dillard (1998) claimed that even the affective dimension of communication is in some respects managed strategically. While not denying an expressive element that may be more difficult to control, Planalp (1998: 44) agreed. She maintained that:

> people communicate their emotions to others for some purpose, whether intentionally or unintentionally. They may want to let the other know how much they care . . . perhaps asking in subtle ways for forgiveness and for another chance at connection. They may want to persuade (coerce) the other into a different course of action . . . threatening social disruption in the bargain. They may communicate emotion in order to get support (e.g. sadness, loneliness), negotiate social roles (anger, jealousy), deflect criticism (shame, embarrassment), reinforce social bonds (love), or for any number of other reasons.

Does attributing purposefulness to the communicative act presuppose consciousness? For some the answer is in the affirmative; purposive behaviour implies conscious awareness. Klinger *et al.* (1981: 171) believed that convictions of the existence of unconscious goals do not match the evidence, concluding that 'life would be far more chaotic than it is if substantial portions of people's goal strivings were for goals about which the striver was unconscious'. Emmons (1989) summarised this thinking by suggesting that it is commonly accepted that people have considerable access to their goals and can readily report them but are less aware of the underlying motivational basis on which they are founded.

On the other hand it has been argued that much of communication is 'mindless', to use the term employed by Langer *et al.* (1978). They distinguished between *mindful* activity where 'people attend to their world and derive behavioral strategies based upon current incoming information' and *mindlessness* where 'new information is not actually being processed. Instead prior scripts, written when similar information was once new, are stereotypically reenacted' (p. 636). Burgoon and Langer (1995) explored the various ways in which language itself can predispose to mindlessness in its capacity to mould thought. Similarly, Monahan (1998) demonstrated how inter-actors' evaluations of others can be influenced by nonconscious feelings derived from information sources of which they have little awareness. Consistent with this thesis, Kellermann (1992) argued vigorously that communication is at one and the same time purposeful/strategic *and* also primarily automatic. It is possible, she maintained, for intentional behaviour to be monitored outwith the stream of conscious awareness. Indeed, this is a feature of interpersonal skill, as discussed in Chapter 1.

Circumstances outlined by Motley (1992) and Burgoon and Langer (1995), in which we tend to become aware of customarily nonconscious encoding decisions include:

- novel situations;
- situations where carrying out a routinely scripted performance becomes effortful;
- conflict between two or more message goals;
- anticipations of undesirable consequences for a formulated or preformulated version of a message, thus requiring reformulation;
- some unexpected intervention (perhaps due to a failed attempt to 'take the floor' or experiencing the 'tip-of-the-tongue' phenomenon) between the initial decision to transmit a message and the opportunity so to do;
- the goals of the communication being difficult to actualise or the situation being troublesome in some other way.

In sum, describing communication as purposeful does not imply that the entirety of the communicative act must necessarily be prominent in the ongoing stream of consciousness. While intention, control and awareness are central to general conceptualisations of communication as skilled activity, it seems that many well-rehearsed sequences can be run off with only limited awareness. When skills are well honed, they can often be executed on the 'back burner' of conscious thought. But the success of an encounter may be compromised as a result.

Communication is multi-dimensional

Another significant feature of communication is its multi-dimensionality – messages exchanged are seldom unitary or discrete. Communication scholars broadly concur that there are two separate but interrelated levels to the process (Watzlawick *et al.*, 1967; Ellis, 2000). One concerns *content* and has to do with substantive matters (e.g. discussing last night's TV programme; explaining the Theory of Relativity). These issues form the topic of conversation and usually spring to mind when we think of what we do when communicating. But this is seldom, if ever, *all* that we do when communicating. Another level, although less conspicuous, addresses the *relationship* between the interactors. Furthermore such matters as identity projection and confirmation are also part and parcel of the interchange.

Identity projection and confirmation

In their choice of topic for discussion (and topics avoided), particular words and forms of expression adopted, manicured accents, speed of speech and a whole complex of nonverbal behaviours and characteristics, interactors work at sending messages about themselves. These messages are to do with who and what they are, and how they wish to be received and reacted to by others. According to Wetherell (1996: 305) 'As people live their lives they are continually making themselves as characters or personalities through the ways in which they reconcile and work with the raw material of their social situation.' Communication is at the forefront of this endeavour. As expressed by Coover and Murphy (2000: 125): 'Communication, then, is integral to the ongoing negotiation of self, a process during which individuals are defined by others as they, in turn, define and redefine themselves.'

In this sense, identity is not only something that we convey but a reality that is created in our dealings with others (this is discussed further in Chapter 9). *Impression management* or *self-presentation* is the term used to refer to the process of behaving in such a way as to get others to ratify the particular image of self offered (Giles and Street, 1994). A direct approach is talking about oneself and strategies for introducing self as a topic into conversation have been analysed by Bangerter (2000). For the quest to be successful, however, it has to be carried out with subtlety. Being seen as boastful and self-opinionated could well spoil the effect. Less conspicuous ways are therefore frequently utilised, often relying on the nonverbal channel (see Chapter 3). If the attempt is seen (or seen through) as a flagrant attempt at self-aggrandisement or ingratiation, it will backfire and a less than attractive impression be created (the topic of self-disclosure is fully discussed in Chapter 9).

Succeeding in conveying the right impression can confer several sorts of possible advantage (Leary, 1996). It can lead to material rewards as well as social benefits such as approval, friendship and power. Goffman (1959) emphasised the importance of social actors maintaining *face*, which can be thought of as a statement of the positive value claimed for self – a public expression of self-worth. He observed that actors characteristically engage not only in self-focused facework but are careful not to invalidate the face being presented by their partner. In a highly influential book chapter, Brown and Levinson (1978) analysed how politeness operates as a strategy intended to reduce the likelihood of this being thought to have happened. Giving criticism is an example of a face-threatening situation. Trees and Manusov (1998) outlined how both verbal and nonverbal cues are used in this situation to mitigate negative effects.

Relationship negotiation

Communication also serves relational ends in other ways by helping to determine how participants define their association. It is widely agreed that relationships are shaped around two main dimensions that have to do with *affiliation* (or liking) and *dominance*, although a third concerning level of involvement or the *intensity* of the association also seems to be important (Tusing and Dillard, 2000). Status differences are often negotiated and maintained by subtle (and not so subtle) means. The two directives, 'Pass the salt' and 'I wonder would you mind passing the salt, please' are functionally equivalent on the content dimension (i.e. the speaker obviously wishes the person addressed to make the salt available) but a different type of relationship is presupposed in each case.

Power is also implicated. When people with relatively little social power, occupying inferior status positions, interact with those enjoying power over them, the former have been shown (Berger, 1994; Burgoon *et al.*, 1996) to manifest their increased 'accessibility' by, among other things:

- initiating fewer topics for discussion;
- being more hesitant in what they say;
- being asked more questions;
- providing more self-disclosures;
- engaging in less eye-contact while speaking;
- using politer forms of address;
- using more restrained touch.

Sets of expectations are constructed around these parameters. It is not only the case that people with little power behave in these ways; there are norms or implicit expectations, that they *should* do so.

These two communicative dimensions, content and relationship, are complexly interwoven and interrelated (Knapp and Vangelisti, 2000). Statements have relational significance and the orchestrating of relationships is typically achieved in this 'indirect' way. As expressed by Hanna and Wilson (1998: 10) 'every communication event has some definition of the relationship'. While the relationship may become the topic of conversation (i.e. form the content of talk), this seldom happens. We will extend this line of thought when we come shortly to discuss the concept of goals.

Communication is irreversible

Simply put, once something is said it cannot be 'taken back'. It could be perhaps a confidence that was broken by a secret being revealed, but once that revelation has taken place it cannot be undone. This is not to deny that the personal and relational consequences of the act can be retrieved. We can work at redefining what has taken place in order to make it more palatable and ourselves less blameworthy. The *account* is one mechanism used to this end. Accounts in this sense can be regarded as explanations for troublesome acts (Cody and McLaughlin, 1988; Buttny and Morris, 2001). Possibilities include apologies, justifications, and excuses. In the case of the latter the untoward action is attributed to the intervention of some external influence (e.g. that the information was extracted under threat or torture). Nevertheless, once information is in the public domain it cannot be re-privatised.

A SKILL MODEL OF INTERPERSONAL COMMUNICATION

Having spent some time outlining key characteristics of interpersonal communication, we will continue by exploring the crucial components and processes underpinning skilled dyadic (two-person) interaction. In so doing, we will build on a conceptual model put forward by Hargie and Marshall (1986), Hargie (1997b) and Dickson *et al.* (1997), based on earlier theorising by Argyle (1983b).

The model presented in Figure 2.1 identifies six elements of skilled interpersonal interaction. These are:

1   person–situation context
2   goal
3   mediating processes
4   response
5   feedback
6   perception.

By way of an overview, the model rests on three basic assumptions. The first is that, as has already been claimed, people act purposefully; second, that they are sensitive to the effects of their action; and, third, that they take steps to modify subsequent action in the light of this information. In keeping with the model, dyadic interaction is depicted within a person–situation framework. What takes place when people come together and engage in communication is partly a feature of the particular attributes and characteristics that make each a unique individual, and partly due to the parameters of the shared situation within which they find themselves.

A widely agreed feature of social activity is that it is goal-directed (Fussell and Kreuz, 1998). People establish and pursue goals in the situations within which they interact. What transpires is entered into in order to achieve some end-state, even if this amounts to little more than the pleasure to be had from conversing. In a quest to realise the adopted goal, mediating processes are operationalised. Accordingly, possible strategies for actualising these outcomes may be formulated, their projected effects evaluated, and a decision on a plan of action derived. The implementation of this course of action will, in turn, be acted out in the responses made. The interactive nature of the process is such that each interactor, in reacting to the other, provides as feedback information of relevance in arriving at decisions on goal attainment. Additional to this mediated facility, each has a direct channel of feedback on performance, enabling monitoring of self to take place.

While feedback makes information available, it can only be acted on if it is actually received by the recipient. Perception is therefore central to skilful interaction, yet its intrinsically selective and subjective nature often results in perceptual inaccuracy and miscommunication (Hinton, 1993; Hanna and Wilson, 1998). Notwithstanding, and to recapitulate, information stemming from perceptions of self, the

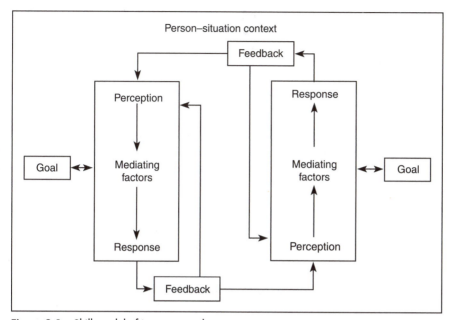

Figure 2.1 Skill model of interpersonal communication

situation and the other interactor is considered in accordance with a complex of mediating processes the outcome of which is a plan to govern action. This plan of action, deemed to maximise opportunities for goal attainment in the prevailing circumstances, is represented in strategies to be actioned, thereby determining individual responses.

To sum up, and in keeping with cognitive theories of interpersonal communication in general, 'people are assumed to be actors and to have goals . . . these actors are endowed with complex mental machinery. The machinery is deployed in pursuit of those goals' (Hewes, 1995: 164). It should be remembered that:

- due to the dynamic and changing character of communication, both participants are, at one and the same time, senders and receivers of information. Each is, even when silent, acting and reacting to the other; and
- potential barriers to successful communication exist at each of the different stages outlined (Dickson, 1999a).

A more detailed consideration of each of these components of the model will now be presented. Further information can be found in Hargie (1997b), Dickson *et al.* (1997), Hargie and Tourish (1999) and Dickson (2001).

Person–situation context

As mentioned, what takes place during interaction is partly due to participants and the personal 'baggage' that they bring to the encounter. It includes their knowledge, motives, values, emotions, attitudes, expectations and dispositions. The way in which they have come to regard themselves (*self-concept*) and the beliefs that they have formed about their abilities to succeed in various types of enterprise (*self-efficacy*) will also determine the sorts of encounters contemplated, goals selected, how these are pursued, and anticipated rewards derivable from them.

Interaction is also co-determined by parameters of the situation within which individuals find themselves, including role demands and the rules that pertain. Take, for example, a priest and a parishioner in the confessional. Each is personally unique, yet the respective roles offered by this highly restricted situation mean that, regardless of the individuals involved, much the same sort of activity will be entered into by priests, on the one hand, and parishioners, on the other. Again, the implicit rules dictating how both parties should conduct themselves in these circumstances will, by condoning certain actions and condemning others, regulate the interaction that unfolds.

The physical setting is a further constraining feature of the environment that has potential effects on interaction. How space is organised and adorned can exert a significant influence on the communicative process (Kaya and Erkip, 1999; Demirbas and Dermirkan, 2000).

These sources of influence are bi-directional. It is not only the case that personal characteristics and situational factors have a bearing on behaviour. What transpires during social contact can also effect changes in interactors. Involvement with others can lead to modifications in individual knowledge, beliefs and attitudes (indeed the success of educational and counselling interventions depends on it) and can also, within limits, serve to redefine the social situation. Thus participants may decide to dispense with the customary formality surrounding certain situations such as the selection interview, summit meetings, etc., and turn them into a much more relaxed occasion. The 'walk in the woods' approach adopted by Reagan and Gorbachev that ultimately led to the end of the 'Cold War' was in stark contrast to the type of formal summit meeting that typified international relations.

Personal characteristics

A complex of personal factors including knowledge, motives, personality, attitudes and emotions shape the interactive process in respect of goals pursued, perceptions, and interaction patterns.

Knowledge

We can distinguish between what is known, on the one hand, and the cognitive processes by means of which information is decoded, stored and retrieved from memory, on the other (Hewes and Planalp, 1987; Greene, 1995; Meyer, 1997). While they are closely interrelated, it is only the former that is relevant at this point. We will address the latter when we come to discuss mediating processes.

Knowledge of our social world and how it operates, of people and the circumstances in which they find themselves, together with shared communication codes, is fundamental to any contemplation of skilled interpersonal activity. Having relevant information on which to draw is invaluable when deciding courses of action and pursuing them. Indeed, it is drawn on at every stage of the communication process from identifying goals that are likely to be within reach, through making sense of the situation and the actions of the other, to selecting and implementing a considered strategy.

Psychologists and scholars of communication have made use of the notion of *schema* in explaining how information is organised into a framework representing the world as experienced by the individual, and used to interpret current events. A schema can be thought of as a 'mental structure which contains general expectations and knowledge of the world. This may include general expectations about people, social roles, events and how to behave in certain situations' (Augoustinos and Walker, 1995: 32). Different types of schema (or schemata) have been identified (Fiske and Taylor, 1991). These include:

- *self-schemas* – having to do with our knowledge of ourselves;
- *event schemas* or *scripts* – representing the sequences of events that characterise particular, frequently encountered, social occasions such as ordering a meal or buying a newspaper;
- *role schemas* – involving concepts according to which we expect people, based on occupation, gender, race and so forth, to abide by certain norms and behave within set parameters of appropriate conduct;
- *causal schemas* – enabling us to form judgements about cause–effect relationships in our physical and social environment, and to adopt courses of action based on the anticipations which such schemata make possible;
- *person schemas* – facilitating, as organised sets of knowledge about features and characteristics, the social categorisation of others.

The related concept of *category* has also been used to explain how we structure information about others and impose meaning on the social world in which we operate. Fiedler and Bless (2001: 123) defined a category as a 'grouping of two or more distinguishable objects that are treated in a similar way'. 'Party', for instance, is a category that you may use to group particular social events with features that distinguish them in important ways from other social events such as lectures, concerts or public meetings. The complexity of our social worlds makes categorising people, occasions, and happenings inescapable. It would simply be chaotically overwhelming to treat everything we encountered in life as separate, uniquely different and distinct. We would find it impossible to function in this way (Brown, 2000). Categorising others, and our social world, is therefore inevitable. Some people though have more highly elaborated category systems than others to represent areas of their social lives.

But placing people in categories can have a negative side. It can lead to the application of *stereotypes*, whereby individual characteristics are neglected and all members of the group are regarded, unjustifiably, in an undifferentiated manner, as sharing a set of generalised attributes (Oakes *et al.*, 1994). In these circumstances individuality suffers and people or events are regarded as being largely interchangeable. The cost of this type of generalising, 'is that we fail to appreciate the complete uniqueness of the whole person, ensuring that our stereotypes sometimes lead us into judgements that are both erroneous and biased' (Tourish, 1999: 193).

Such stereotypes may be widely held (social stereotypes) or peculiar to an individual (personal stereotypes). Stereotypes can also become self-fulfilling. If we regard all red-haired people as aggressive we may act towards them in a belligerent way, and so precipitate an aggressive reaction that confirms our stereotype (this is discussed further in Chapter 10).

Motives

Why do people do all the things suggested, as we have elaborated this model of skilled interaction? Why, indeed, take part in interaction at all? A full consideration of these matters would take us well beyond the scope of this chapter. For our purposes, however, they can be scaled down to two vital and related issues:

1   Why do people adopt the goals that they do?
2   Having done so, why do they continue to behave in accordance with them?

The second question is probably easier to answer than the first. Goals are taken to contribute both direction and impetus to the interactive process and therefore have inherent motivational implications (Maes and Gebhardt, 2000). They have been described as 'attractors' by Carver and Scheier (2000: 70), who go on to explain that 'people spend much of their time doing things that keep their behaviour in close proximity to their goals'. Persistence to achievement is an important characteristic of goal-directed behaviour and this motivational effect is perhaps the one that has received most attention from researchers.

Not all goal aspirations, of course, are necessarily translated into action. Whether or not they are depends on an appreciation of a variety of external and internal factors. They include assessments of how conducive environmental circumstances are at that time to goal achievement together with judgements of self-efficacy (Bandura, 1997), which determine the extent to which individuals concerned believe that they have the abilities and resources at hand to succeed.

We have already touched on some of the proposed reasons why goals are formulated in the first place. Many accounts refer to the notion of need (e.g. Ryan *et al.*, 1996). Guirdham (1996) regarded motives as the internal responses to needs. Dillard (1990) believed, in turn, that goals reflect broad underlying motives. But what are these underlying needs that impel us to establish goals in directing our activities with others? Three enduring concerns have been highlighted (Deci, 1992; Aronson, 1999) having to do with the need to:

*   feel in control and to be able to predict events of which one is part;
*   have a sense of belonging and intimate involvement with others, making possible approval from them;
*   exercise mastery and display competence in one's strivings, thereby experiencing a sense of self-worth.

On a broader front, a range of physiological and safety needs can also be thought of as determining what we seek from our environment (Maslow, 1954). We are obviously motivated to meet our biological needs for food, drink, sex, etc., and to protect ourselves from physical harm.

Attitudes

Our attitudes are another highly significant personal characteristic that impacts on interaction. Just how these attitudes are structured (van Harreveld *et al.*, 2000) and the extent to which they determine what we do (Terry *et al.*, 2000) are topics of ongoing debate. A long-standing way of thinking about attitudes (Katz and Stotland, 1959) is in terms of three constituent elements:

1   *cognitive* – contributing knowledge or beliefs about the target in question which may be a person, object, event or indeed any attribute of these;
2   *affective* – reflecting how one feels about the target, either positive or negative, in liking or disliking. Indeed for some this is the most important attribute; and
3   *behavioural* – having to do with one's predisposition to behave in a certain way towards the target.

For example, I may have a particular attitude towards my next-door neighbour such that I believe he is jealous of me and out to do me down (cognitive) which makes me dislike him (affective) so I avoid his company (behavioural). Note, however, that attitudes only define a tendency to behave in a particular way in respect of an attitude object. According to the *theory of planned behaviour* (Ajzen, 1991), additional considerations such as perceived *behavioural control* (the ease with which we feel we can accomplish the behaviour) and *subjective norms* (our appreciation of the prevailing expectations regarding that behaviour and our motivation to comply) are likely to shape our intentions to behave accordingly. It is these intentions that directly lead to behaviour in line with attitudes (we will further examine the relationship between attitudes and behaviour in Chapter 12).

In any situation, therefore, there may not be a direct correspondence between attitude and actual behaviour. Attitudes interact with other personal characteristics including motives, values and other attitudes, together with situational forces, to influence behaviour (Brigham, 1991). Furthermore, not all attitudes are equally accessible or held with the same strength of feeling (Bohner, 2001).

Personality

Personality is the complex of unique traits and characteristics of an individual that shapes interaction with the environment and the ability to relate to oneself and others. A large number of personality traits have been identified. For example, extroversion–introversion is one dimension along which individuals can be placed that has implications for communicative behaviour. There is some evidence that introverts tend to speak less, make more frequent use of pauses, engage in lower frequencies of gaze at their partners, are less accurate at encoding emotion and prefer to interact at greater interpersonal distances (Giles and Street, 1994; Knapp and Hall, 1997).

To take a second example, what are known as 'Type A' personalities may be revealed through vocal cues. These people tend to be hard-driven, competitive, time conscious, impatient and aggressive. An element of hostility in this complex also predisposes to coronary heart disease (Stroebe, 2000). Some research findings have suggested that Type As have a typical speech style that is fast, uneven with short pauses and a hard, staccato, loud voice (Remland, 2000).

Emotion

So far it might seem that our view of interactors is largely of completely rational, information-processing automatons, completely devoid of any sort of emotional dimension to their existence. Berger (1995: 163) is adamant though that any attempts 'to explain the relationship between cognitive processes and social interaction give serious attention to the relationships among cognition, affect and action'. Affect is obviously central to interpersonal life and has attracted considerable attention from scholars of communication (Andersen and Guerrero, 1998; Planalp, 1999). Just how emotion operates though, and the contributions of, for instance, physiological constituents, on the one hand, and social, moral and cultural determinants, on the other, is a matter of ongoing debate (Metts and Bower, 1994; Porter and Samovar, 1998; Kupperbusch *et al.*, 1999). Regardless, it is widely acknowledged that we cannot completely separate the affective and the cognitive – how we feel from how and what we think. As put by Bless (2001: 392) 'Affective states have been shown to influence encoding, storage, retrieval, judgmental processes, and style of information processing. These processes are, of course, highly intertwined.'

Dillard (1998) identified three ways in which emotions can be involved in the communication process, namely through:

1   *Emotion-motivated* communication – including behaviour driven by underlying emotion (e.g. one driver swears at another and acts threateningly in a fit of road rage).
2   *Emotion-manifesting* communication – providing insights into a person's under-lying emotional state (e.g. a patient's downcast look enables the nurse to make judgements about that person's 'spirits').
3   *Emotion-inducing* communication – involving words and actions that trigger emotion in others (e.g. a person cries after being told a sad story).

Age

The relative ages of participants will influence their behaviour and the expectations that each has of the other. Particular ways in which communication is used by and towards older people and issues surrounding inter-generation talk has attracted con-siderable research interest (for example, Nussbaum and Coupland, 1995). The elderly are frequently subjected to simplified forms of speech that can be seen as patronising.

Box 2.2 Examples of patronising communication with the elderly

- *Simplification strategies* – using a simplified register as one might with a child (e.g. basic vocabulary, short sentences, simple sentence structure, more restricted range of sentence patterns).
- *Clarification strategies* – ways of making yourself heard and understood (e.g. speaking more loudly, slowly, and with exaggerated intonation; using repetition).
- *Diminutives* – being dismissively familiar or patronising; includes calling the person 'honey', 'love' or 'dear', etc., or describing some thing or event, such as a nap, as 'little' (e.g. 'It's time for a little nap, dear').
- *Demeaning emotional tone* – acting superciliously.
- *Secondary baby talk* – talking as one would to a baby (e.g. 'Just a teensy-weensy bit more?').
- *Avoidance* – discussing the older person, in their presence, with a relative rather than addressing them directly.
- *Overly controlling* – being impatient or assuming the person's needs are already known.

Hummert *et al.* (1998) and Dickson (1999b) have described some of these features (see Box 2.2 for examples).

Negative stereotypes of older people seem to be at the bottom of this way of relating. Picking up on cues denoting advanced years can activate a stereotype suggesting incompetence, decline or senility, such that younger speakers may tailor what they say in keeping with this set of beliefs: one example of this is a tendency to use simplified or patronising talk with mature adults. Older people tend to have frequent contact with health workers. Does communication in this context, therefore, reveal these same trends? In working with institutionalised older people, secondary baby talk (BT) has been found to be a feature of carers' communication, often regardless of the level of personal competence of the receiver (Grainger, 1995). A related finding was that while recognising the positive affect message often intended, recipients themselves felt that BT was more appropriate for those with limited independence. Likewise, La Tourette and Meeks (2000) discovered that elderly both in the community and in nursing homes rated the nurse more favourably when non-patronising speech was used, but that levels of cognitive ability of the elderly were also influential in making these judgements.

Gender

Differences in how males and females communicate verbally and nonverbally have been documented (Ng and Bradac, 1993; Knapp and Hall, 1997). These, however, should not be overstated, nor should it be assumed that they apply to each and every individual (Coates and Johnson, 2001). With that in mind (and other things being equal), females compared with males, typically:

- interact at closer interpersonal distances;
- are more tolerant of spatial intrusion;
- make greater use of eye-contact and touch;
- smile more and are more facially, gesticularly and vocally expressive;
- are more adept at both encoding and decoding nonverbal messages;
- have deeper insights into their relational goals (Burgoon, 1994; Honeycutt *et al.* 1998).

Summing up, Argyle (1995: 87) asserted that:

> women score higher on most of the other [apart from assertiveness] components of social competence; they score much higher on empathy, and on measures of co-operativeness . . . Women are found to be more rewarding, they have better verbal skills (more fluent, better grammar, more educated accents), and are more expressive nonverbally (smile a lot more, gaze more, finer gestures).

Of course one must be careful with such bald generalities.

Males and females express themselves differently in language. As encapsulated by Dimbleby and Burton (1998: 64):

> many women like to talk about feelings; men do not. Many men like to talk about things, such as cars; women are not as interested in such things. Men like to talk about themselves, about their achievements; women listen to this when as they have admitted in surveys, they would rather not.

These findings resonate with work published by Tannen (1995) who analysed how males and females typically respond to 'trouble talk' – being told about some personal problem or difficulty. When women disclose personal predicaments, they primarily expect (and tend to get from other women) a listening ear, confirmation of their concerns and an understanding reaction. Indeed this type of talk serves, in part, to strengthen interpersonal bonds between friends. Men, however, instinctively respond by tackling the problem head-on in an attempt to solve it through giving information or offering advice. Miscommunication is such that men see women wallowing in their problems rather than discussing practical steps to solve them, as men do. Women, on the other hand, feel that men don't understand them and are not prepared to make the effort to do so. Frustration is shared equally. We will return to this issue of gender differences in several chapters, particularly Chapter 9.

Situational factors

It will be recalled that personal characteristics and situational factors operate to provide a contextual backdrop for communication. Acting conjointly they determine how people conceive of social episodes, formulate goals, attach meanings to events, and exchange patterns of conduct. Both features of the person and the situation may, within limits, be subject to change as a result of interaction. Having identified a number of key personal features that operate, we will now turn our attention to an analysis of the situation.

Several attempts have been made to delineate the essential constituents of situations (Miller *et al.*, 1994). Perhaps the simplest is that by Pervin (1978) who proposed that the key constituents are:

* who is involved;
* what is happening;
* where the action is taking place.

A more highly differentiated analysis of social situations, derived from extensive research, is that offered by Argyle *et al.* (1981) and elaborated by Hargie (1997b). They identified no fewer than eight key features of the situations within which people interact. Many of these will be familiar, however, from what has already been said about the personal characteristics of situated individuals, again emphasising the close interrelationship between these two dimensions. The elements delineated by Argyle *et al.* (1981) will now be briefly outlined.

1   *Goal structure.* Situations have goal implications. Not only do we seek out situations with goal satisfaction in mind, but particular situations will also place constraints on the goals that can be legitimately pursued.
2   *Roles.* In most situations individuals act in accordance with more or less clearly recognised sets of expectations centring on their social position and status (see Chapter 11 for further information on roles).
3   *Rules.* Situations are rule-governed. There are (often implicit) stipulations that govern what is acceptable conduct for participants. It is perfectly acceptable for two friends at a night club to wear revealing clothes, sing, dance and shout. Were such behaviour transferred to a lecture it would be in strict contravention of the contrasting rules that pertain in that situation.
4   *Repertoire of elements.* This refers to the range of behaviours that may be called on for the situation to be competently handled.
5   *Sequences of behaviour.* In many situations interaction may unfold in a quite predictable sequence of acts on the part of participants. We have already mentioned how people often function in highly routine instances according to scripts.
6   *Situational concepts.* Again we have discussed this basic idea of individuals possessing knowledge which enables them to make sense of situations and perform appropriately in them, when we introduced the notion of a schema.
7   *Language and speech.* There are linguistic variations associated with social situations. Some, for example public speaking, require a more formal speech style than others, such as having a casual conversation.
8   *Physical environment.* The physical setting including furniture, décor, lighting, layout, etc., often influences who talks to whom, how they feel, how much they say and how the talk is regulated (Richmond and McCroskey, 2000).

Culture

At a broader level, cultural background is a highly significant contextualising factor. Culture can be regarded as the way of life, customs and script of a group of people. Cultural and sub-cultural variables have a bearing on the different features of the communicative process. In turn communication shapes culture (Gudykunst and Ting-Toomey, 1996). Inter-cultural differences therefore run much deeper than possible differences in language, encompassing not only much of the nonverbal channel of communication but beyond to the underlying social order itself and the meanings and values that give it form. When two people from radically different cultures come together, it is not only that they may be attempting to use different language codes to represent a shared world. Respective social worlds themselves may overlap only marginally. Gao (1996) outlined how concepts like self, and the relationship between self and other, are quite different in China compared with western countries.

Cultural influences permeate values, beliefs and cherished practices. Indeed so pervasive are cultural effects that they can be thought to shape individuals' entire understanding of their social worlds. A classic study conducted by Hofstede (1980) exposed four underlying dimensions along which a large sample of different national groups could be plotted in respect of fundamental values espoused. These dimensions were:

- *power distance* – the amount of respect and deference displayed by those in different positions on a status hierarchy;
- *individualism–collectivism* – the extent to which one's identity is shaped by individual choices and achievements or a feature of the collective group to which one belongs;
- *uncertainty avoidance* – the degree to which life's uncertainties can be controlled through planning and foresight;
- *masculinity–femininity* – this has to do with the relative focus on competitive, task-centred achievement versus co-operation and harmonious relationships.

European and North American cultures score high on individualism and low on power distance, while those from Latin American and Asian countries are low on individualism but high on power distance. Gudykunst and Matsumoto (1996) discussed the myriad ways in which these cultural dimensions influence communication.

At another level, culturally prescribed norms govern how people conduct themselves in interaction with others. These norms determine punctuality, interpersonal distance, touch, use of gestures, facial expressions, gaze patterns – indeed all the nonverbal codes (Burgoon, 1994; Rector and Neiva, 1996; Remland, 2000). Machismo in Hispanic cultures, for example, imposes display rules that forbid male expressions of pain. In Muslim cultures there may be gender difficulties surrounding touch by a male health worker, let's say, in the course of a physical examination of a female patient. We will return to aspects of culture in future chapters, but particularly in Chapter 11.

Having considered the person–situation context of communication in some detail, it is time to move on to explore the other components of the model.

Goals

This concept has already been introduced in relation to motives. Here we will extend that discussion. Following Berger (1995: 143), we can think of goals quite simply as 'desired end states towards which people strive'. Put another way, the goals that we have in mind are mental representations of future end-states that we would like to make happen. Oettingen and Gollwitzer (2001) pointed out three telltale qualities of behaviour in pursuit of such outcomes.

* *Persistence* – a course of action will be continued until the goal is achieved (or abandoned, under exceptional circumstances).
* *Appropriateness* – courses of action adopted are ones likely to reduce the difference between existing and desired states and effect a successful outcome.
* *Selectivity* – the individual is attuned to stimuli associated with the goal in initiating and directing behaviour.

Different ways of analysing and categorising human goals have been suggested (e.g. Ford, 1992; Austin and Vancouver, 1996). Some of the most significant elements will now be considered.

Content and process elements

Maes and Gebhardt (2000) specified that goals have *content* and *process* properties. The former defines *what* is to be attained, the latter addresses *how* this is to be effected and commitment to the objective.

Task and relational goals

One of the assumptions underlying many goal-based accounts of human endeavour is that individuals are typically striving to actualise a multiplicity of outcomes in their dealings with their material and interpersonal environs, and often concurrently (Dillard, 1997). Austin and Vancouver (1996: 338), in their comprehensive review, argued that 'single goals cannot be understood when isolated from other goals'. Indeed, Samp and Solomon (1998) identified seven categories of goal behind communicative responses to problematic events in close relationships. These are to:

1   maintain the relationship;
2   accept fault for the event;
3   ensure positive face;
4   avoid addressing the event;
5   manage the conversation;
6   cope with emotion;
7   restore negative face.

Referring back to what was said earlier about the multi-dimensionality of communication, Tracy and Coupland (1990) believed that one of the most basic distinctions is that between *task goals* and *face goals* or *relational goals*. In certain situations it may be difficult to satisfy both and yet be vitally important to do so. Health care presents a myriad of occasions when face can be compromised, resulting in shame or embarrassment. Instances of humour being used, as a face-giving strategy, to stave off awkward embarrassment have been reported during gynaecological examinations (Ragan, 1990), and neuropsychological investigations of patients with dementia and other forms of cognitive impairment attending a memory clinic (Saunders, 1998). Additional issues around the handling of embarrassment in fertility treatment are discussed by Meerabeau (1999). As aptly summarised by Lawler (1991: 195) 'Skill is required by the nurse to construct a context in which it is permissible to see other people's nakedness and genitalia, to undress others, and to handle other people's bodies.'

Instrumental and consummatory goals

Along similar lines, Ruffner and Burgoon (1981) talked of goals that are *instrumental* and those that are *consummatory*. Instrumental goals are carried out in order to achieve some further outcome (e.g. a supervisor may reward effort to increase productivity). Consummatory communication, on the other hand, satisfies the communicator's goal without the *active* intervention of another: e.g. the supervisor may reward in order to experience the feeling of satisfaction when distributing largesse.

Implicit and explicit goals

Some of the goals that we try to achieve in interaction are readily available to us. We are consciously aware of them and, if asked, could articulate them with little effort. Not all goals are like this but rather operate in a reflexive, automatic manner (Bargh *et al.*, 1999). While influential in what we do, we would find these more difficult to account for. As explained by Berger (1995: 144):

> Given that conscious awareness is a relatively scarce cognitive resource, it is almost a certainty that, in any social-interaction situation, several goals will be implicit for the actors involved, and that goals at the focal point of conscious awareness will change during the course of most social-interaction episodes.

Furthermore, Carver and Scheier (1999) suggested that we may even be pre-programmed to automatically follow certain courses of action when faced with particular sets of circumstances, as a default option. What communication scholars need to address, Dillard (1997: 51) recommended, are issues of 'when goals exist in consciousness, how they arrive there, how long they stay, and by what mechanisms this movement occurs'. At the moment we have few answers to such questions.

Hierarchical organisation

Goals are hierarchically structured, with some being more widely encompassing than others (Oettingen and Gollwitzer, 2001). This theme is common in the literature although some authors have countenanced more complex arrangements than others. Dillard (1990) believed that a three-level structure was adequate, with broad motives leading to goals that, in turn, governed sub-goals. Berger (1995) also identified *metagoals* that over-arch more specific instances. These include quests for:

- *efficiency* – a requirement to achieve the objective by the most economical means, and
- *social appropriateness* – a stipulation not to violate prevailing norms and expectations.

Furthermore, primary and secondary goals may be at work in specific interactive episodes (Dillard, 1990: Wilson *et al.*, 1998). *Primary goals* are the ostensible reason for the interaction taking place, giving it meaning and setting expectations and responsibilities. *Secondary goals* span different episodes, shaping and placing constraints around the pursuit of primary goals (e.g. maintaining face).

Goal importance

Austin and Vancouver (1996) mentioned importance and commitment as factors taken into account in goal setting. More weight is attached to some goals than others. It is these that have most impact on action at any particular juncture. Decisions reached about goal selection and commitment depend very much on the psychological value attached to the accomplishment of that outcome, estimates of the likelihood of various anticipated courses of action being successful in this respect, projected immediacy of gratification, possible costs which may ensue, and so on (Locke and Latham, 1990; Shah and Kruglanski, 2000). The value or valence of an outcome, as has been suggested, is ultimately a feature of the anticipated satisfaction of particular motives and the needs that give rise to them.

One implication of recognising that goals differ in importance, coupled with the assertion that interactors are typically pursuing several goals at the same time, is the need for a prioritising mechanism to regulate goal selection. There must be some form of ongoing assessment and reprioritising as certain outcomes are achieved, others possibly abandoned or alternative means contemplated, and as circumstances alter (Bandura, 1997; Shah and Kruglanski, 2000). These circumstances, of course, include the participation of the interactive partner. In their investigation of goal management during contrived conversations between mainly strangers, one of the most striking outcomes reported by Waldron *et al.* (1990) was the greater importance of ongoing adjustment to changing circumstances rather than the deployment of fixed, predetermined plans.

Temporal perspective

Dillard (1997) mentioned a temporal dimension to goals. This, together with hierarchical orderings, is in keeping with the views of Hargie (1997a) when talking about long-term and short-term goals. The example given is of a personnel officer interviewing a job applicant. The principal goal directing this activity is, of course, to reach a proper decision as to the suitability of the interviewee. An appropriate short-term goal might be to welcome the candidate, make introductions and ask relevant questions. Actions are generally under the immediate control of goals at this level although long-term goals must not be lost sight of.

Level of precision

Carver and Scheier (2000) noted that goals differ in their level of concreteness/abstraction. Some may be quite specific and precise, others vague and indeterminate. Thus a junior nurse may have as a goal to be more assertive in transactions with other staff, or to politely but firmly refuse to swap shifts with Jo the next time the request is made. In the context of the identification of objectives for educational or therapeutic interventions, one of the commonly accepted recommendations is that they be precisely articulated in assessable terms (Millar *et al.*, 1992).

Goal compatibility

How the goals of interactors relate has obvious and extremely important implications for the encounter and what transpires. Goals may be either:

- *similar* – here both are striving to achieve the same or similar goal but in so doing each may coincidentally thwart the other (e.g. both friends want to off-load about their partner trouble);
- *complementary* – here goals are compatible (e.g. one wants to off-load, the other to listen);
- *opposed* – one's goal may be in direct opposition to that of the other (e.g. A wants to find out about B's romantic problems while B is determined not to self-disclose on the topic).

In terms of the individual, conflict can also take place between goals at a similar level and between goals at one hierarchical level and the next (Maes and Gebhardt, 2000). In discussing metagoals in relation to the strategic management of embarrassment, for example, Bradford and Petronio (1998) explained how social appropriateness is forfeited in favour of efficiency.

Mediating processes

These processes mediate between the goal being pursued, our perceptions of events and what we decide to do about them. They also, as we have seen, play a part in the formulation of goals, influence how people and events are perceived and reflect the capacity of the individual to assimilate, deal with and respond to the circumstances of social encounters. It will be recalled that, in keeping with the thinking of Hewes and Planalp (1987) and Greene (1995), we differentiated between these processes and the sorts of knowledge structures discussed in the earlier section as instances of personal characteristics.

Cognitive processes

Discussions of the cognitive processes that make interpersonal communication possible can be readily found in the literature (e.g. Kreps, 1988; Hewes and Planalp, 1987; Wyer and Gruenfeld, 1995; and Jordan, 1998). In the sequence of steps leading to a particular course of action being generated, Kreps (1988) outlined information organisation, processing and evaluation; decision-making; and the selecting of action strategies. It is these action strategies, or plans for action, that Argyle (1994) regarded as the essential contribution of this stage to interaction.

Wyer and Gruenfeld (1995) have deliberated on the cognitive operations that enable strategic action to be undertaken. There are five sub-processes leading to an interpersonal response that they regard as particularly salient.

1   *Semantic encoding* – the interpretation of messages in keeping with available semantic concepts and structures.
2   *Organisation* – the arranging of information into mental representations of the person, thing, or event.
3   *Storage and retrieval* – the storage of these representations in memory and their subsequent selective access as and when required.
4   *Inference processes* – decisions to respond are shaped by inferences about the implications and consequences of that action. Assumptions and implications about the nature of the encounter, the communicators and their relationship are also important.
5   *Response generation* – of overriding importance here are the strategies selected to bring about targeted goals and objectives. Possibilities of responses some-times being 'mindless' must also be acknowledged, as must the influence of emotion on performance.

The processes that lead to the pursuit of a certain course of action are some-times more cognitively demanding than others. Those involving 'mindful' problem-solving or decision-making are particularly challenging, and deserve further attention. We can distinguish between descriptive and prescriptive models of problem-solving and decision-making, or between how decisions are arrived at and how they should be arrived at. Nelson-Jones (1996) recommended a rational approach. The key steps to be followed are:

1   *Confront* – this includes recognising the need for a decision to be taken, clarifying what exactly it is that is hoped to be achieved, and being open to the circumstances, both internal and external, of the decision.

2   *Generate options and gather information* – try to think of as many options as possible, without any attempt at this point to evaluate their chances of success. This may involve, time permitting, gathering additional information which can be drawn on.

3   *Select an option* – this should be done with consideration for the anticipated consequences if each were selected. Projected advantages and disadvantages of each need to be thought through. One important consequence, of course, is the probability of that course of action successfully achieving the goal being pursued. Others have to do with judgements of self-efficacy – the belief in one's ability to successfully implement that strategy; implications for face – how one might be seen by the other or others; and personal costs – including the amount of difficulty and effort required. By reflecting on the positive and negative features of each option according to these criteria, the best option in the circumstances can be logically and systematically revealed.

4   *Commit to the decision* – here resolve to the course of action selected should be strengthened.

5   *Plan how to implement the decision* – a plan should be formulated in which goals and sub-goals are clearly stated, constituent tasks broken down, difficulties anticipated, and sources of support identified.

6   *Implement the decision* – timing of implementation is one of the important factors to bear in mind. Other features of implementation will be taken up when we move on to consider the *response* element of the model.

7   *Assess consequences of implementation* – reflecting on outcomes leads to improved future performance.

The complexities involved at this stage of cognitive processing are still the subject of much speculation. In any case, we can be sure that they are under-represented in this brief overview. For instance, *metacognitions* play a part. In order to interact successfully we must be able to think about and form an opinion on how others think and how they go about making sense of the world that they experience. The way in which messages are encoded by skilled communicators will reflect judgements along these lines.

Affective processes

Hargie and Tourish (1999) discussed both cognitive and affective elements that serve a mediating capacity in interaction, while acknowledging the close interrelationship between the two systems. Andersen and Guerrero (1998) explored various theoretical perspectives on how and when emotion is experienced and the role of interpersonal schemata in the process. For example, the meanings that we attach to events may be coloured by how we feel at the time. Forgas (1994) discovered that people who were happy tended to locate causes of relational conflict in external and unstable sources while those who were sad looked to internal and stable alternatives. The former responded with active strategies for coping while the latter were more passive. A further mediating role of emotion on behaviour identified by Wyer and Gruenfeld (1995: 38) is that of reciprocity. By this they mean that 'individuals appear to reciprocate the affect or emotion that they perceive a communicator has conveyed to them'.

While the important end product of mediating processes is a strategy or plan of action designed with goal achievement in mind, this plan must always be tentative and open to revision. Given the inherent fluidity of interaction, Berger (1995: 149) argued persuasively that, 'reducing the actions necessary to reach social goals to a rigid, script-like formula may produce relatively ineffective social action'. Unfortunately this is what sometimes characterises encounters with professionals, for instance, where interactions become ossified in repetitive, stereotyped rituals, merely carried out in the presence of the patient or client. Skilled communication must always be adaptively and reflexively responsive to the other (Dickson, 1999b).

Responses

Plans and strategies decided on are implemented at this stage. There can be no guarantee, of course, that their translation into action will be flawless or indeed successful. Jordan (1998) described slips and lapses as errors that can occur. *Slips* are actions that are not part of the plan, or actions that are planned but performed out of sequence; and *lapses* are planned actions that are left out rather than enacted. According to the *hierarchy principle*, when people fail to achieve an interactional goal, but persist, they tend first to adjust low-level elements of the plan (e.g. volume or speed of speech) rather than more abstract higher-order elements (e.g. general strategy) (Knowlton and Berger, 1997).

A common categorisation of social action, and one that has already been referred to, is that which identifies the *verbal* and the *nonverbal*. While closely connected, verbal communication has to do with the purely linguistic message, with the actual words used. Nonverbal behaviour encompasses a whole range of body movements and facial expressions, together with vocal aspects of speech. (A fuller discussion of nonverbal communication will be given in the next chapter.)

Feedback

Feedback is a fundamental feature of communication and without it prospects of skilled engagement are denied. DeVito (1998: 14) defined it as 'messages sent back to the speaker concerning reactions to what is said'. For Heath and Bryant (2000: 76), who emphasised the interpretive dimension of the process, 'Feedback stresses the strategic and interactive nature of communication'. Having acted, individuals rely on knowledge of their performance together with outcomes that may have accrued in order to reach decisions as to what to do next and alter subsequent responses accordingly.

In the model presented in Figure 2.1, two sources of feedback are depicted. The more direct channel acknowledges that we have access, through internal receptors in muscles and joints, as well as visually (to a certain extent) and aurally (albeit with distortion), to what we do and say when communicating with others. As interaction takes place, each member in pursing personal goals for the exchange is, at the same time, in what they say and do, providing the other with information which can act as feedback relevant to that other's goal quests. For Gudykunst (1991) convergence towards mutual understanding and shared meaning is proportional to the degree to which feedback is put to effective use. Limited provision and/or reception increase the chances of divergence and misunderstanding.

Corresponding to the different aspects of responding, feedback can be provided verbally or nonverbally, the latter in nonvocal and vocal forms. Although both are typically implicated, nonverbal modes may be particularly salient when it comes to affective or evaluative matters, while cognitive or substantive feedback relies more heavily on the verbal.

Perception

Not all information potentially available via feedback is perceived; not all information received is perceived accurately. But it is only through the perceptual apparatus that information about the internal and external environment, including other people and the messages that they transmit, can be decoded and acted on through making judgements and decisions in relation to the goals being sought.

How we perceive others is fundamental to skilful interaction yet is a profoundly precarious activity. Generally speaking, perception can be thought of, perhaps counter-intuitively, as being an *active* and highly *selective* process (Eysenck, 1998). These qualities tend to be emphasised in particular with reference to social interaction. We are actively involved in the perceptions that we make, rather than being merely passive recipients. Furthermore, we seldom attend to all that we might in any situation but tend to filter out the less conspicuous, less interesting or less personally involving elements. As such perception is inherently personal and ultimately subjective. Despite naive assumptions, the belief that we perceive and observe other people in a correct, factual, unbiased, objective way is a myth. Rather, what we observe typically owes as much, if not more, to ourselves in perceiving as it does to the other person in being perceived. As put by Wilmot (1995: 150):

> There is no 'immutable reality' of the other person awaiting our discovery. We attribute qualities to the other based on the cues we have available, and the unique way we interpret them. Our perception of the other, while seeming certain, is grounded in permanent uncertainty.

A consequence of the essentially selective and inferential nature of social perception and its heavy dependence on the knowledge structures, expectations and attributional processes of the perceiver results, in many instances, in perceptual inaccuracy and hence miscommunication (Hinton, 1993).

In addition to perceptions of others, skilled interpersonal behaviour also requires accurate perceptions of self and of how one is being perceived (or *metaperception*). Being mindful of the public image portrayed must not be overlooked. We have already touched on this point in relation to self-presentation and impression management. People differ in the extent to which they monitor their performance and under what conditions (Snyder, 1987). While high self-monitors endeavour to create and maintain an impression in keeping with the situation and to earn approval, low self-monitors are much less preoccupied by these concerns. Nevertheless, lax self-monitoring is likely to diminish one's communicative effectiveness (Adler *et al.*, 1998b).

CONCLUSION

The ability to communicate is not unique to humans, but we have a sophistication that far surpasses all other species. It enables us to move beyond events taking place at this time. We can share knowledge, beliefs and opinions about happenings in the distant past and possibilities for the future; about events here or in some other place; about the particular or the general; the concrete or the abstract. It also enables us to make meaningful contact with others through establishing, maintaining and terminating relationships.

Despite its significance, communication is a notoriously difficult concept to define precisely. Nevertheless, a number of attributes are readily recognised by many, if not all, of those who have deliberated on the topic. Interpersonal communication can be thought of as a process that is transactional, purposeful, multi-dimensional, irreversible and (possibly) inevitable.

Skilled interpersonal involvement can be accounted for accordingly in terms of notions of person–situation context, goals, mediating processes, responses, feed-back and perception. All communication is context bound. We can think of spatial, temporal, relational and sometimes organisational frameworks within which it is embedded. The personal characteristics of the participants together with features of the shared situation act to shape the interaction that transpires and both may be influenced, to some extent, in consequence. Likewise, goals pursued are determined by personal and situational factors. Plans and strategies to accomplish these derive from mediating processes and resulting tactics are enacted in manifested responses. A central premise of the model outlined is that, in interactive arrangements, participants are at one and the same time, in what they say and do, providing each other with information of relevance to decisions about the extent of goal attainment. Without such feedback, skilled interaction would be impossible but it can only be acted on if it is perceived. As we have seen personal perception, in particular, although inherently subjective, plays a pivotal role in interpersonal transactions. Throughout the remaining chapters of this book, we will examine the central features of each skill area under focus, in terms of goals, mediating factors, response repertoires, feedback, perception, and central elements of the person–situation context.

Chapter 3

Nonverbal communication

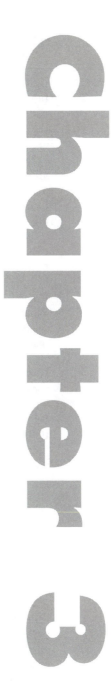

INTRODUCTION

T HIS CHAPTER IS CONCERNED with those forms and functions of face-to-face interaction that do not rely primarily on the content of what we say. Here we are concerned with how we make ourselves known through, for example, a look, gesture, postural shift or trembling voice. At the very outset, however, it should be stressed that distinguishing between verbal and nonverbal communication is not as conceptually straightforward as it might at first seem. Neither are the two operationally discrete (Bull, 2001a). For the most part in our everyday social contact verbal and nonverbal codes are complexly intertwined, each to varying degrees defining the other in the overall process of carrying meaning. That said, it is undoubtedly the case that, were we to step back from what we do when communicating, sufficient to bring the process into sharper focus, we would concentrate on those things *said*. As Benjamin Disraeli mused, 'With words we govern man'. The look on our faces as those words are uttered, the glint in our eyes, dismissive gestures of the hand, the tension in our bodies, and such like, will most probably be overlooked. It is unlikely though that our listeners neglect these nonverbal nuances. Often nonverbal communication (NVC) proves decisive in conveying information and making judgements about others. Relating successfully to others demands the ability to display appropriate nonverbal behaviour but also to be sensitive to the nonverbal messages of others.

Fascination with nonverbal aspects of social intercourse can be traced back at least to Aristotle. In the teaching of rhetoric in classical and medieval times, forms of specific gesture were identified along with their planned effects on an audience (Rozelle *et al.*, 1997). It is only relatively recently though that social scientists have devoted much concerted attention to nonverbal matters. This followed a long period during which the topic was depreciated, being regarded as inconsequential, and those interested in it as academically suspect. For example, Aldous Huxley (1954: 77) described nonverbal education as a subject which is, 'for academic and ecclesiastical purposes, non-existent and may be safely ignored altogether or left, with a patronising smile, to those whom the Pharisees of verbal orthodoxy call cranks, quacks, charlatans and unqualified amateurs'. Such milestones in the evolution of the subject as Charles Darwin's *The expression of emotion in man and animals* (Darwin, 1872/1955) only began to receive serious social scientific recognition in the last few decades (Ekman and Keltner, 1997). During this time, though, growth of interest has burgeoned leading to significant theoretical, conceptual and empirical advances in the field as witnessed by countless publications of books, book chapters and articles. There is even a well-established journal, the *Journal of Nonverbal Behavior*, now devoted to disseminating major work in this area. What was once described by Burgoon (1980: 179) as the 'foundling child of the social sciences – disdained, neglected, even nameless', has found its place as a respected member of the family.

Indeed the multi-faceted study of NVC now draws inspiration from disciplines beyond the established boundaries of social science. As well as contributions from social psychology, anthropology, sociology and psychiatry, perspectives are being offered from, for instance, ethology and neurophysiology. Here is a rich seam being worked by what traditionally has been in many ways two quite distinct types of miner, the social and the natural scientist, each with different sets of tools used to exploit individually appraised pay-dirt. In NVC it seems that both have found a common area of fascination and are beginning to become aware of and appreciate the contributions of the other. Segerstrale and Molnar (1997) believe that NVC is currently one of the foremost sites of a rapprochement between biology and social science as respective researchers investigate such fundamental issues as the extent to which nonverbal behaviour is culturally prescribed or naturally determined.

LOCATING NONVERBAL COMMUNICATION

Although the division between verbal and nonverbal communication defies any sharp delineation, NVC can be thought of broadly as all forms of direct communication not exclusively relying on the use of words, written or spoken. Some consideration has already been given in Chapter 2 to definitional issues surrounding communication in general, and will not be repeated. Rather we will focus here on the 'nonverbal' rather than the 'communication' element of NVC. At first sight, crafting a sharp definition of 'nonverbal' might seem like an easier task, but even here things are less than straightforward.

In a piece of early but still influential work, Laver and Hutcheson (1972) distinguished between verbal and nonverbal, and vocal and nonvocal communication. Vocal behaviour refers to all aspects of speech including language content and accompanying expressions such as tone of voice, rate of speech and accent, etc. Nonvocal behaviour, in contrast, refers to all other bodily activities that have a communicative function such as facial expressions, gestures and movements. These are sometimes referred to as body language. Verbal behaviour, on the other hand, is taken to mean the actual words and language used while nonverbal behaviour refers to all vocal and nonvocal behaviour that is not verbal in the sense defined above. This system seems therefore to insert a sharp and clearly recognisable dividing line between the verbal and the nonverbal, until it is realised that verbal communication has a nonvocal element. It encompasses types of gestural communication such as formal sign language that one may have expected to find listed as nonverbal. According to Richmond and McCroskey (2000) precise definitions that introduce hard and fast distinctions between verbal and nonverbal communication are illusory. Instead they suggested teasing the two forms apart by pointing up broad differences. As such, by comparison, verbal messages:

- rely much more heavily on symbols (i.e. words) as part of an arbitrary code;
- tend to be discretely packaged in separate words rather than represented in continuous behaviour, as in gaze;
- carry more meaning explicitly rather than implicitly;
- typically address cognitive/propositional rather than emotional/relational matters.

Remland (2000) further noted that verbal interchanges must take place sequentially (i.e. participants must take turns) but interactors can communicate simultaneously using a nonverbal code.

In this chapter, therefore, we concentrate on communication by, for instance, tone of voice, talk speed, volume of speech and intonation. In addition to these nonverbal aspects of speech, information is transmitted and received through a whole range of body movements such as the posture adopted when sitting in a chair – is it stiff, upright and symmetrical suggesting tension or anxiety or is the person sprawled down in the chair suggesting a feeling of relaxation or familiarity? Faces, too, play an important role in social encounters by at times giving some expression to our inner thoughts, such as showing delight when presented with an unexpected gift or displaying sadness when told about the death of a close friend. A smile can also suggest approachability and availability for friendly relational contact.

Before we open our mouths to speak our physical appearance conveys a great deal of information about our age, sex, occupation, status (if a certain uniform is worn) and personality. For someone with the unnerving perceptual acuity of a Sherlock Holmes in matters of social observation, such cues may become the veritable words of biography. In *The adventures of Sherlock Holmes*, Arthur Conan Doyle placed the following words in the mouth of the great sleuth:

> By a man's finger-nails, by his coat-sleeve, by his boot, by his trouser-knees, by the callosities of his forefinger and thumb, by his expression, by his shirt-cuffs – by each of these things a man's calling is plainly revealed.

As a manifestation of physical attraction, the powerful effects of appearance on favourable judgements of such attributes as intelligence, warmth, friendliness and social confidence are well documented (Smith and Mackie, 2000).

Not only are we concerned with the appearance and behaviour of the person involved in communication but, in addition, environmental factors such as architecture, furniture, decoration, smells, colour, texture and noise can reflect on the person inhabiting that space and shape interpersonal contact. These examples give some idea of the categories to which nonverbal behaviour attends. A more comprehensive range will be presented later in the chapter.

THE IMPORTANCE OF NONVERBAL COMMUNICATION

Talk of NVC, especially in the context of improving social relations, typically provokes one of two contrasting and equally extreme reactions. Some, the 'disciples', prepare themselves for a quasi-mystical experience during which will be revealed the great lexicon by means of which all man's (including woman's) deepest (and often darkest) secrets can be deciphered. In the diametrically opposed camp are the 'cynics' who tend to hold the line that all such talk is at best both pretty obvious to anyone with a modicum of social intelligence and decidedly over-rated; at worst, it is so much 'hocus pocus'. Reality unquestionably lies somewhere between these poles. While NVC should not be regarded as the holy grail of interpersonal involvement, neither can it be dismissed as a wholly discredited relic. Birdwhistell (1970), one of the earliest authorities in the field, persuasively argued the importance of appreciating the key role of nonverbal processes in communication. He claimed that the average person actually speaks for a total of only ten to eleven minutes daily; the standard spoken sentence taking only about 2.5 seconds. There can be little prospect of successful face-to-face interaction in situations where interactors have little appreciation of their own NVC or sensitivity to that of the other. This is equally true in everyday situations and in those of professional practice. The role of NVC has been acknowledged for instance in management (Hargie *et al.*, 1999), education (Miller, 2000), nursing (Caris-Verhallen *et al.*, 1999), law (Brodsky *et al.*, 1999) and medicine (Rosenblum *et al.*, 1994). In the latter study, the research team was able to predict the academic grades assigned to medical students by their clinical supervisors by rating a sample of students' nonverbal behaviour while interacting with patients in a paediatric setting. Riggio (1992) proposed that being nonverbally skilful involved an expressive element, an element of sensitivity, and one of control over performance.

Relative contribution of NVC and verbal communication

Difficulties in cleanly separating the verbal and the nonverbal have already been noted. Attempting to treat each as distinct and independent with a view to making differential judgements about relative value is not particularly fruitful. Nevertheless, the verbal medium has often been set as a benchmark for assessing the significance of the nonverbal. Consider a situation where a person is saying something but conveying an altogether different message through NVC. Which holds sway? What are the relative contributions of the two to the overall message received? In early research by the psychologist Albert Mehrabian, still frequently cited, he estimated that overall communication is made up of body language (55 per cent), paralanguage (the nonverbal aspects of speech) (38 per cent) and the verbal (7 per cent) (Mehrabian, 1972). It may come as something of a surprise to learn that *what* we say contributes a mere 7 per cent to the overall message received. These proportions, however, should not be regarded as absolute and seriously under-represent the contribution of verbal communication in circumstances where information from all three channels is largely congruent. While questioning the veracity of Mehrabian's figures, the review by Burgoon *et al.* (1996) still identified a general trend favouring the primacy of meaning carried nonverbally, with a particular reliance on visual cues. But qualifying conditions apply. The finding holds more for adults, in situations of message incongruity and where the message has to do with emotional, relational or impression-forming outcomes. It should also be emphasised, of course, that in any case NVC does not have to be shown to be *more* important than the verbal in order to have its import acknowledged.

Trustworthiness and NVC

We tend to be less aware of the nonverbal accompaniment to much of what we say, than we are of the actual words spoken. While we often carefully monitor what is said to achieve the desired effect, how we are saying it may escape censor such that the reality of the situation is 'leaked' despite our best efforts. In other words, NVC can be thought of as a more 'truthful' form of communication through the insights that it affords into what may lie behind the verbal message. This is the 'window on the soul' assumption. It is only true to a point. Even in the case of facial expressions, it would be wrong to assume a simple, direct and unerring cause–effect relationship with underlying emotional states. Certain facial displays are regulated in keeping with the social context, making them more or less likely to be exhibited perhaps in exaggerated form (Chovil, 1997). Social intentions and motives can be at the root of such expressions rather than blind emotional states (Izard, 1997). Skilled interactors can learn to control what their bodies say as well as the messages sent in words. The work of 'spin doctors' with politicians and other influential people in the public eye does not stop merely at verbal manicure. Appropriate facial expressions, looks, gestures, and tones of voice are all included in the packaged end-product. Part of the 'repackaging' of Mrs Thatcher, as she became one of the most formidable politicians of her generation, included the use of a somewhat lower vocal register. Formerly, her rather high-pitched voice was thought to create an unfavourable impression of feminine hysteria rather than the assured gravitas of an esteemed, international statesperson.

Phylogeny and NVC

Phylogeny concerns the evolution of a species. Taking an evolutionary view of our origins, NVC is undoubtedly an earlier, more primitive form of communication than language. According to Leakey (1994) particularly telling evolutionary changes took place during a period stretching from half a million to 35,000 years ago, and leading to modern mankind. The outcome was people with similar appearances and abilities to those we see around us today. The precise point at which language emerged and whether it developed rapidly or more slowly over a period extending beyond half a million years ago need not detain us. What does matter is that its emergence seems to have been associated with an increase in brain size, advances in tool-making skills, the first appearance of art, and in group living. A complex and sophisticated system of communication enabled individuals to become part of larger collectives and to successfully plan and execute collaborative projects such as hunting. Indeed this ability has been mooted as one reason behind the eventual displacement of Neanderthal in Europe by Homo sapiens, about 30,000 years ago (Pitts and Roberts, 1997).

Earlier hominid species would, of course, have had basic ways of making themselves known. Some suggest that this was most likely to have been in the form of body movements together with a range of vocalisations similar perhaps to those of the present-day, non-human primates such as chimpanzees. Lieberman (1998: 84–5) speculated that, 'the earliest form of protolanguage used manual gestures, facial expressions (grin, lip protrusion, etc.) and posture – a sort of body language'. As such, it would essentially be restricted to expressing emotional states such as anger or fear, and perhaps fixing relational bonds as in grooming. But the fossil record shows that these hominids would not have been anatomically equipped to command spoken language in the way that we do. Here, therefore, we have NVC enabling our early ancestors to regulate social life in small groups, albeit in less sophisticated ways than those made possible by the advent of modern language.

Ontogeny and NVC

Ontogeny refers to the development of the individual, and here again we find NVC pre-dating language as a rudimentary means of making contact with others. Important early interaction between mother and child takes place not only though touch but also through synchronised exchanges of patterns of gaze and vocalisation. Researching early social interaction between carers and infants has led to a re-evaluation of the view that the latter are basically passive and receptive. As put by Papousek and Papousek (1997: 100),

> The standard view of infants as mere recipients of parental stimulation and the notion that they simply have to adapt to the social environment cannot hold any more ... infants do not only adapt, but also function as very successful and autonomous elicitors of the caregivers' adaptations.

In addition to synchronising early vocal exchanges with carers in ways that mimic conversational turn-taking, infants a few months old display facial expressions that closely resemble those of adults in conveying emotions such as joy, surprise and interest, but especially pain (Oster *et al.*, 1992). Once again we rely on NVC when language is unavailable, this time in the evolution of the individual rather than the species.

Substance of nonverbal messages

Language is particularly suited to conveying ideas and information about our environment, together with our understandings and intentions in respect of it. Through the use of language Homo sapiens has succeeded in such spectacular feats of joint endeavour as building the pyramids and putting a man on the moon. Only through language can we access and discuss the philosophy of Wittgenstein, plays of Chekov or novels of Proust. Nonverbal behaviour, in contrast, tends to convey information of a different type (although not exclusively so) to do with such matters as feelings and attitudes towards those whom we meet. Included are impression management and the projection of personal and social identity. It is largely on this sort of detail that interpersonal relationships are built, sustained and sometimes terminated. These relationships, in turn, are the bedrock of institutions such as marriage, family, work, etc., which go to make up society as we know it.

Universality of NVC

We can often make ourselves known in a rudimentary way through signs and gestures when communicating with people from differing cultural backgrounds who do not share a common language. NVC has therefore a greater universality than language. This is true but only to a certain extent. Failure to appreciate the nonverbal nuances of cultural diversity can lead to miscommunication and interaction breakdown, which is just as real as failure to use the proper words. A range of examples are provided by Axtell (1991) of the myriad ways in which body language and gestures are used in dramatically different forms as we move from culture to culture. Many beginning a career in international business lack such knowledge at their cost (Morrison *et al.*, 1994). For instance, while in most of Europe and North America shaking the head signals refusal and disagreement, in parts of India it indicates the opposite. There nodding the head means 'No'. However in Japan nodding the head may mean neither agreement nor disagreement, only ongoing attention to the speaker.

PURPOSES OF NONVERBAL COMMUNICATION

Just why we should make use of NVC is a very legitimate question. We are the only species with this marvellously abstract and sophisticated means of communicating that we call language. Other species display various forms of nonverbal behaviour. Through changes in, for example, real or apparent size, posture and movement, odour and skin colour, and with a myriad of grunts, screams and roars, they convey information about bodily and emotional states, social status and territorial ownership. But language is different. It frees us from the here and now, from the physical and actual. Without it we would find it difficult or impossible to refer to, never mind take into account, abstract concepts such as love, loyalty or honour; happenings at this point in time in another place; happenings in the past; happenings in the future; things that have never happened and probably never will (including the whole literary genre of fiction).

The remainder of the chapter will be devoted to a brief mapping of different forms that nonverbal behaviour can take. Before doing so, however, we will extend some of the points raised in the previous section by taking a look at the uses to which NVC is put (Argyle, 1994; Bull and Frederikson, 1995; Knapp and Hall, 1997; Richmond and McCroskey, 2000). These are outlined in Box 3.1.

Replacing verbal communication

Some NVC, especially in the form of gestures, is used as a direct substitute for words in circumstances where speech is either not feasible or not desirable. It may be that interactors have neither hearing nor speech, relying entirely on the use of hand, arm or mouth movements as part of recognised signing systems allowing communication to take place. Sometimes, on the other hand, individuals are temporarily denied a suitable channel to facilitate speech, and so resort to some form of gesture-based contact. This is particularly evident among deep-sea divers, for instance, when working under water. In other situations, excessive ambient noise may make talking impossible. Alternatively, interactors may find themselves too far apart to have a normal conversation necessitating some alternative such as semaphore or the tick-tack system of signalling used by racecourse bookmakers. Secrecy may be a further reason for not wishing to talk publicly. In different sports, team members can be seen using nonverbal cues to call the proposed play at different stages of the game.

Complementing the spoken word

Nonverbal behaviour is often used alongside what is said in a way that is consistent with it. In so doing, the verbal message may be clarified, extended or enhanced. In an analysis of college lecturers' deliveries, Corts and Pollio (1999) found that bursts of figurative language and spontaneous pictorial gestures tended to occur at points

---

Box 3.1 Purposes of nonverbal communication

NVC is used to:

1 *Replace verbal communication* in situations where it may be impossible or inappropriate to talk.
2 *Complement verbal communication,* thereby enhancing the overall message.
3 *Modify the spoken word.*
4 *Contradict,* either intentionally or unintentionally, what is said.
5 *Regulate conversation* by helping to mark speech turns.
6 *Express emotions and interpersonal attitudes.*
7 *Negotiate relationships* in respect of, for instance, dominance, control and liking.
8 *Convey personal and social identity* through such features as dress and adornments.
9 *Contextualise interaction* by creating a particular social setting.

---

where the lecturer dealt with material beyond the students' normal experience or offered a different interpretation of a familiar topic. When both modes overlapped, gestures served to augment the metaphoric.

Some material, such as giving elaborate directions, or describing an irregular shape, can be difficult to get across in words alone. In order to facilitate the overall message an imaginary map or outline is sometimes drawn in the air while describing the route or object. Friesen *et al.* (1980) referred to these gestural acts as illustrators and they will be examined later in the chapter when discussing gestures. By observing people in conversations it can be noted that these accompanying movements actually facilitate speech where it is difficult to describe aspects of space and shape in purely verbal terms. They may also assist in the tasks of learning and remembering (Goldin-Meadow, 1997). In research carried out by Church *et al.* (1999), participants watched video recordings of children speaking and gesturing about the concept featured in the conversation and were then tested for immediate recognition of information carried verbally and by gesture. Nine- and ten-year-old children, tested in this way, performed poorly in processing contradictory messages resulting from a mismatch between the verbal and gestural. Interestingly, 7–8 year olds and college students were more successful.

A significant age effect was also reported by McNeil *et al.* (2000), but the complexity of the verbal message played a part as well. They discovered that accompanying gestures that complemented instructions aided comprehension for pre-school children but not those in kindergarten. Likewise gestures at odds with the verbal information were detrimental for kindergarten but not pre-school children. This effect disappeared, though, when the verbal message was simplified.

Nonverbal cues can also complement language in other ways involving propositional and emotional messages. Sympathising with someone is done much more convincingly when the sympathiser's overall demeanour mirrors what is said.

Modifying talk

The verbally delivered message can be either accentuated or attenuated nonverbally. This is a further example of accompanying nonverbal cues serving to qualify what is said. Such behaviour can sometimes help to emphasise parts of the verbal messages. When a speaker puts more stress on certain words than others, uses pauses between words to convey gravity or interest, or varies the tone and speed of utterances, the importance of certain words or phrases is underlined in the mind of the listener. In a sense it is analogous to the writer who puts words in italics, underlines them or gives chapter headings. In addition, body movements are frequently used to add more weight to the verbal message. Take, for example, the mother who wants to ensure that her son is listening closely and taking seriously what she is saying who may, in addition to the words, 'Listen to me', swing him round to face her closely and put both arms on his shoulders. These actions are all designed to add weight to the verbal message. Alternatively, a sympathetic smile may temper the overall message received in the context of a stern parental rebuke. All are examples of NVC working to deliver a more or less extreme message.

Contradicting the spoken word

There may be occasions where a person says one thing but conveys an incongruous message nonverbally: where the two modes are at odds. This may or may not be done intentionally. Devices of discourse ranging from sarcasm to humour often rely on something being said 'in a particular way'. The words suggest one interpretation but tone of voice and body language something different. The NVC, as it were, provides a frame for interpreting what was said. Such subtlety may, however, be missed by children who have been found, when compared with adults, to place a more negative interpretation on a critical comment said with a smile by an adult (Knapp and Hall, 1997).

According to Leathers (1979) when exposed to contradictory verbal and nonverbal signals, we typically become confused and uncertain, then we look for extra information to resolve the discrepancy and finally, if unsuccessful, we react negatively with displeasure or withdrawal. When it is assumed that the discrepancy is unintentional, it may be construed as an attempt to deceive.

Deception and nonverbal cues

Despite popular belief, there is no unique pattern of cues that unambiguously signals deception. As put by Vrij *et al.* (2000: 241) 'there is nothing like Pinocchio's nose'. What we do have are indices of underlying internal processes associated with deceptive behaviour. Lying can manifest itself in different ways including increased physiological arousal suggesting heightened stress (e.g. raised heart rate and sweating); conspicuous attempts to control performance (e.g. appearing wooden or slow deliberate delivery); displaying emotion which may be either caused by the deception (e.g. signs of anxiety and guilt) or the basis of it (e.g. pretending to be happy when sad); and increased cognitive processing of information (e.g. more concentrated thinking revealed perhaps in gaze avoidance).

Buller and Burgoon (1998) stressed that deceiving successfully is a cognitively demanding task that, at times, can over-stretch the processing resources of the individual. When this happens part of the communicative act may 'escape attention'. This non-strategic behaviour can be thought of as nonverbal 'leakage' and serve to arouse suspicion. Witness the political leader who announces every confidence in the measures taken for the good of the nation, while at the same time displaying a stream of nonverbal behaviour indicating anxiety and lack of confidence. Where this contradiction exists listeners often place greater credence on the nonverbal when it is regarded as a more credible source of information and harder to falsify (Ekman *et al.*, 1991).

Interestingly, cues that have been found to be more accurate and reliable indicators of deception do not correspond precisely with those of folk wisdom. Research evidence has not consistently backed up particular gaze patterns, facial expressions and rates of speech as the sure-fire signs of dissembling that they are often thought to be (Hartley, 1999). Again Machiavellian types are extremely proficient at most forms of nonverbal deception and tend, for instance, not to avoid gaze when being untruthful (Anderson, *et al.*, 1999). The complex relationship between deception and its nonverbal manifestation is pointed out by Vrij (2001) as involving mediating circumstantial factors (e.g. perceived consequences of being found out) and personal considerations (e.g. skill in carrying the deception attempt off). We shall return to this fascinating topic of deception in Chapter 9.

Regulating conversations

How do we manage to conduct conversations so that we don't keep interrupting each other but at the same time there are no awkward silences between speech turns? Detailed analyses have revealed some of the strategies used to prevent over-talk, handle it when it occurs, and generally manage turn-taking (Schegloff, 2000). NVC is used, in part, in this process. Conversationalists are able to anticipate when they will have an opportunity to take the floor. The next time you are talking to someone, think of the cues they provide that suggest to you that it would be acceptable for you to speak at a particular point. You will probably note tone of voice, gestures and eye-contact. Duncan and Fiske (1977) identified a number of nonverbal cues that offer a speaking turn to the other person. These are a rise or fall in pitch at the end of a clause, a drop in voice volume, termination of hand gestures and change in gaze pattern. In addition, they found that if a speaker continued to use gestures such as hand gesticulation, it essentially eliminated attempts by the listener to take over the turn.

Hence someone (but depending on their culture) coming to the end of a speech-turn will typically introduce a downward vocal inflection (unless they have just asked a question), stop gesticulating and look at their partner (Argyle, 1994). This information can, of course, be made use of in situations where one is keen not to hand over the floor. Since high status and interpersonal influence are usually positively correlated with extent of verbal contribution, there may be occasions where this pattern could form part of impression-management tactics.

Nonverbal cues have also been implicated in the broader work of organising the interactive episode. In a detailed analysis of doctor–patient consultations in a general-practice setting, Robinson (1998) revealed how gaze and shifts in body orientation were used to mark sequences of engagement with and disengagement from particular tasks, in preparation for patients' disclosure of the complaints that brought them along.

Emotions and interpersonal attitudes

NVC is a crucial source of information on how we feel, and how we feel about others. Again the extent to which this is done intentionally and with awareness can vary (Bull, 2002). Some emotional cues such as pupil dilation in response to heightened arousal are largely outwith our control. Others suggesting anger or sadness are more manageable. Facial expressions are an important emotional signalling system although body movements and gestures are also implicated (Montepare et al., 1999). Six basic emotional states that can be read from facial patterns are sadness, anger, disgust, fear, surprise and happiness (Ekman and Friesen, 1975). Contempt may be a possible seventh. A substantial body of evidence claimed, following the earlier work of Charles Darwin, that these are reasonably universal across cultures (Ekman and O'Sullivan, 1991). Nevertheless, more recent work has questioned the extent to which facial expressions can be thought of as the direct products of underlying affective states, untrammelled by social and cultural influences in not only pattern, but also perception and interpretation (Kupperbusch *et al.*, 1999). An alternative way of viewing them is as a means of signalling behavioural intent. This issue will be returned to later when we consider facial expressions in further detail.

We also reveal attitudes about others in our nonverbal behaviour towards them. As described by Argyle (1994: 46), liking someone is usually signalled by 'higher levels of (1) smiling, (2) gaze, (3) proximity and (4) touch; (5) posture with arms open, not on hips or folded; and (6) voice with higher pitch, upward pitch contour, purer tone'. Such attitudes predispose to a particular type of relationship.

Negotiating relationships

Communication is a multi-faceted activity as was emphasised in Chapter 2. Two people discussing an issue are doing other interpersonal things at the same time, both in what they say and how they say it. One of these 'other things' that can become the topic of conversation, but seldom does outside of intimate partnerships, has to do with the type of association shared. Judgements of dominance and affiliation can be relayed through nonverbal channels. Typical manifestations of dominance include:

- speaking in a louder voice;
- talking for a longer time;
- choosing a focal position in a room;
- standing on a raised dais;
- sitting behind a desk;
- taking up position at the head of the table;
- occupying a more impressive chair;
- interrupting successfully when another person talks;
- looking while speaking and using long glances to establish a dominant relationship.

In all these ways 'actions can speak louder than words'.

In largely nonverbal ways, both parties establish, sustain or indeed terminate a relational position, one with the other. This can be done on an ongoing basis, as adjustments are made to ensure that levels of involvement are acceptable. *Immediacy* or psychological closeness is a feature of interaction that is regulated in part nonverbally. It has to do with the depth of involvement or degree of intensity characterising a conversation. Violating expectations in respect of, for example, interpersonal distance, eye-contact, posture or orientation (bodily angles of interactors) by coming too close, gazing too much, leaning too far forward or orienting too directly leads, under certain circumstances, to discomfort and compensatory shifts by the other. These behavioural adjustments establish the status quo thereby maintaining a level of involvement that is both expected and comfortable (Andersen *et al.*, 1998).

Relationships also have to be managed on a more long-term basis and again NVC plays a part (Hinde, 1997). The rather bleak comment is sometimes made that it is always easy to tell the long-established married, from as yet unmarried couples, in restaurants from body language alone. The unmarrieds tend to be the ones lost in each other's eyes, leaning over the table towards one another, and so on.

When individuals are actively managing personal relationships it would often be too disturbing for one to state openly that the other was not liked or thought to be inferior. Nonverbal cues can be exchanged about these states but without the message ever being made explicit. In addition, initial relationships can change over time so that an original dominant–submissive relationship can become more equal in nature. Change would not come about as readily if persons had explicitly stated at the beginning how they felt towards each other.

Conveying personal and social identity

In a complex of ways involving habitat, dress, deportment, accent, etc., we send messages about ourselves and the groups to which we belong. Here we have a further use to which NVC is put (Hartley, 1999). While not all nonverbal behaviour is strategically deployed in this quest, among those cues that are, those promoting judgements of physical attractiveness, warmth and pleasantness, likeability, credibility and power are particularly salient. In business organisations with steep hierarchical structures of authority, projecting suitable images of status forms an inevitable part of dealings with others both within and outwith the company. Features such as size of office space and opulence of furnishings take on a special significance in this process. Many organisations have standards stipulating the minimum size and type of office for employees at a particular level in the management pecking order.

Contextualising interaction

Finally, in the ways that people interact and communicate they create social situations. Again NVC has an indispensable part to play. Through chosen dress code, layout of office space, and so on, opportunities are created for a meeting to become a very formal interview or a more casual chit-chat. As we shall see later, some managers organise their offices to include formal workspace and social areas more conducive to informality. Appropriate forms of conduct will be correspondingly suggested. All social settings, from the familiar, such as Sunday lunch, staff meeting, or a visit to the dentist, to the more elaborate, such as a graduation ceremony, or a funeral, carry with them acceptable codes of conduct. Someone who deviates from these common patterns of behaviour and so upsets the social scene may be called on either to apologise or to offer an excuse or explanation for the deviant behaviour.

These various functions of NVC do not always occur independently nor are they separately served by specific behavioural cues. It is quite possible for several to be exercised simultaneously. It is also important to note that typically these functions are satisfied by complex patterns of nonverbal behaviour closely interwoven with language.

Box 3.2: Types of nonverbal communication

NVC can take the following forms:

Haptics – communication through physical touch.

Kinesics – communication through body movement (e.g. gestures, head nods, posture, eye-contact, facial expression).

Proxemics – messages conveyed through the perception and use of personal and social space (e.g. interpersonal distance, territoriality).

Physical characteristics – information revealed through body shape, size and adornments.

Environmental factors – messages carried by features of the social surroundings such as furniture, décor and lighting.

Vocalics – communication by means of the nonverbal elements of speech (e.g. voice pitch, resonance, and so on).

The rest of this chapter will look more closely at the various forms that nonverbal behaviour can take. These are presented in Box 3.2.

HAPTICS

Touch is a primitive form of communication in respect of both evolutionary (phylogenic) and personal (ontogenic) development. It is one of the earliest and most basic forms of stimulation that we experience, even when still in the womb. Calling it basic and primitive should not detract from its potential impact. It is widely recognised that physical contact is crucial to the psychological and biological well-being of infants and to their subsequent social and intellectual development (Richmond and McCroskey, 2000). A profound lack of touch can even lead to early death. This was evidenced around the turn of the century when a condition called *marasmus* (translated from the Greek meaning 'wasting away') resulted in high mortality rates among institutionalised babies who were generally well cared for as far as bodily needs were concerned. Their inability to thrive was attributed to the fact that they had little physical contact with their carers: they were not lifted, fondled and cuddled in the normal way (Adler and Towne, 1996).

More recently, the benefits of massage in accelerating growth and weight gain among premature babies has been reported (Adler, 1993). The profound effects of tactile stimulation extend into adulthood. Apart from its specialised therapeutic ('laying on of hands') use in a health context, touch has been found to affect heart rate, blood pressure and nutritional intake of patients. It can also have a comforting or calming effect (Routasalo, 1999). Touch also has a long pedigree as part of psychotherapeutic practice, being used to encourage patients to talk about their concerns, elicit affect, offer support and nurture, and bring about therapeutic change (Smith, 1999). In more everyday situations a number of beneficial outcomes have been documented from research studies. In situations where it is used appropriately, the person touching is likely to:

- be more positively evaluated (Burgoon *et al.*, 1992);
- have others comply with their request (Willis and Hamm, 1980);
- have money returned (Kleinke, 1977);
- receive more tips from customers when waiting at table (Crusco and Wetzel, 1984).

But tactile contact is not always well received. For a start it can be an extremely ambiguous act frequently suffused with sexual possibilities. Probably for this reason it is strictly rule-bound (Argyle, 1988). One cannot go touching anyone, anywhere, at any time, in any place – at least not without getting into trouble. In an early and frequently cited study, students reported that they were touched most often on the hands and arms, although who was doing the touching made a difference (Jourard, 1966). Replicated a decade later, it seemed that opposite-sex contact by friends had become more intimate in terms of accessible body areas (Rosenfeld *et al.*, 1976).

Touching serves a number of functions relating to both the context in which it occurs and the relationship of the interactors. Heslin and Alper (1983) identified five such functions as: functional/professional, social/polite, friendship/warmth, love/intimacy and sexual arousal.

- *Functional/professional.* A number of professionals touch people in the normal course of their work: nurses, dentists, doctors, physical education teachers, health visitors, hairdressers and physiotherapists, to name but a few. A common distinction here is between *instrumental* and *expressive* touch (Tutton, 1991; Dickson *et al.*, 1997). The former happens in the normal course of carrying out a task and does not carry any further connotations (e.g. nurse taking a patient's pulse). Expressive touching, on the other hand, conveys interpersonal messages to do with emotion, attitude or association (e.g. nurse holding patient's hand during uncomfortable procedure conducted by the doctor).
- *Social/polite.* We have different culturally prescribed forms of contact used as part of the greeting ritual. They serve to acknowledge the other and ascribe to them a social involvement. In western culture a handshake is typically used, at least in formal situations. In other cultures kissing, embracing or nose rubbing may be more common. Being in direct, ongoing contact may also signal to others that these two are together: that they form a pair (or couple). Examples of these *tie signs* include linking arms and holding hands.
- *Friendship/warmth.* This includes contacts such as a friendly pat, arm linking, or a comforting touch on the hand, aimed at establishing amicable relationships. It is a way of showing interest in others and positive feelings towards them. This can be very rewarding in terms of giving encouragement, expressing care and concern, and showing emotional support and understanding. It has been pointed out by Richmond and McCroskey (2000) that in standard western culture friends are unlikely to engage in much touching when alone, because it tends to be associated more with sexual motives.
- *Love/intimacy.* In close relationships touching is a very profound way of conveying depth of feeling. This love of course may be that of a mother for a child, or love for a husband or parent. Even with a partner, love can take on different guises from the passion of early romance to the enduring commitment of old

age (Sternberg, 1988). Each set of circumstances will be marked quite differently through type and extent of physical contact. Again there may be close friendships that we could describe as intimate but not necessarily involving love, as such. Once more, touching will be likely to be one of the features that sets them apart from mere acqaintanceships.

- *Sexual arousal.* The famous sex therapists Masters and Johnston reputedly claimed that effective sex is the ultimate form of communication. Here we have touch being used in its most intense form involving parts of the body only accessible to certain others and typically when in private. There are other occasions when what was intended as friendship or even support is interpreted as having sexual intent. In the extreme such cases may well end up in court, especially when involving a professional relationship such as that of teacher–pupil or doctor–patient. Milakovich (1999) reported that for this reason some psychotherapists do not use touch.

To the above classification can be added several other types of contact identified by Jones and Yarbrough (1985) and Jones (1999). They include touch:

- in the context of play (e.g. tickling);
- as an expression of negative feelings (e.g. hitting or slapping);
- as a way of managing interaction (e.g. placing a hand on someone's shoulder to get attention);
- to gain influence and control (e.g. touching someone lightly as we ask a favour);
- as a symbolic or ritualistic act (e.g. two heads of state shaking hands to symbolise accord between their nations);
- that is accidental.

Various factors, including culture, status, gender and age, influence how haptic communication is deployed. Touch features much more extensively in some parts of the world than others. So-called *contact* cultures where touching features extensively include southern Europe, the Middle East and Central America, while among *noncontact* counterparts can be listed northern Europe, North America and Japan.

Issues of status also shape touching. People who touch, especially in situations where it is not reciprocated, tend to have higher ratings of power and dominance accorded to them than the recipients of that contact (Major and Heslin, 1982). In a later study by Hall (1996) of actual touching at academic meetings, while there was no evidence that high-status participants touched low-status participants with greater frequency than vice versa, differences did emerge in the type of contact initiated. High-status academics tended to touch arms and shoulders in what was judged to be a sign of affection. Low-status counterparts were more likely to shake hands, which was regarded as essentially a formal expression. Implications of power and control could also be the basis of some findings suggesting that female patients react more favourably than males to expressive touch by nurses (Dickson, 1999b).

Males and females differ in how they communicate by tactile means, at least in

North American and European societies. Generally men are less touch-oriented. This extends to professional interaction with male nurses touching less and male patients being touched less (Routasalo, 1999). In certain societies one man touching another in public may be associated with suggestions of homosexuality. In other cultures such norms do not prevail. Thus in the Middle East same-sex touching by heterosexual men in public is commonplace (DeVito, 1995). However, Roese *et al.* (1992) discovered that individuals who liked same-sex touching least had the highest scores on a scale measuring homophobia.

Finally, haptic communication seems to change across the lifespan (McCann and McKenna, 1993). From high levels in early childhood, it plays a less prominent part as adolescence is reached. In old age, touch re-emerges although it is not altogether clear whether merely for functional/professional reasons associated with increasing poor health and infirmity. When hospitalised, there is evidence that the elderly receive the least amount of tactile contact. Their perception of being touched was found, by Hollinger and Buschmann (1993), to be most positive when it:

- was appropriate to the situation;
- did not impose a greater level of intimacy than desired;
- was not condescending;
- did not detract from their sense of independence and autonomy.

KINESICS

Kinesics, as the name suggests, addresses communication through body motion. It includes all those movements of the body such as hand gestures, limb movements, head nods, facial expressions, eye gaze and posture. When we look carefully at individuals or groups interacting we are often struck by the sheer dynamism of what goes on. Even if seated, arms and hands are typically busy; heads and perhaps bodies turning to follow the conversation; eyes darting from one to another in the group, lingering here and there, or even signalling withdrawal at times; and all the while facial expressions conveying continued interest, boredom, or liking. The five main areas of kinesics to be focused on in this section are gestures, posture, head nods, eye gaze, and facial expression.

Gesture

Here we will concentrate on movements of hands and arms. The extent to which hand gestures are utilised varies depending on such factors as culture and situation. Italians are notorious users while British newscasters, it would seem, find little need for them at all. One of the basic divisions is between gestures that are independent of speech and those that are related to it (Kendon, 1989). A more fine-grained and widely used categorisation is that introduced by Ekman and Friesen (1969) who identified five main types, *emblems, illustrators, affect displays, regulators and adaptors*.

Emblems

Emblems are one of the few nonverbal cues that function, to all intents and purposes, like words. They include the signs used by policemen to direct the flow of traffic, by those communicating with the deaf, and by producers of TV programmes, to name but a few. Here we have probably the best example of NVC being used to replace speech, which is of course one of its functions, as previously noted. In all instances these gestures have a direct verbal translation which can differ, of course, from culture to culture. Since some have obscene meanings, one must be careful. The sign with the thumb touching the tip of the index finger forming a ring, palm facing out, that to some means exquisite and may, for example, be used to complement the chef, in France and Belgium means that the thing referred to is worthless. In Turkey and Malta the gesture is an obscene insult with the ring representing an orifice – invariably the anus. Further examples of emblems from around the world are well documented (e.g. Axtell, 1991).

Illustrators

These accompany speech, and are linked to it. On their own, however, they make little sense. Such hand gestures, in a variety of forms, can be used to enhance and facilitate what is said (McNeil, 1995). Providing emphasis is one example. Teachers, when they are asking pupils to remember some important information, may enumerate with their fingers the number of points to be remembered. This is borne out by research into teachers' use of nonverbal skills in the classroom where it was shown that gazing, mild facial expressions and hand gestures were the most commonly used non-verbal behaviours (Kadunc, 1991). It was also found that teachers most often utilised illustrators and least often used emblems.

In addition, hand gestures can provide illustrations of the verbal content of a message. These illustrations can take the form of *ideographic gestures* as when enunciating some abstract concept or idea (e.g. cupped hands when explaining love). Similarly, *iconographic gestures* help describe some happening, place or thing (e.g. describing an action sequence from a film; the layout of an office; or an irregular shape). On the other hand, pointing to an object or place while referring to it involves *deictic gestures*.

Regulators

These orchestrate conversation and ensure that turn-taking is switched smoothly. As speakers finish a speech-turn they will probably drop their hand as they bring a gesture to an end. Not to do so, despite the fact that they may have stopped speaking is usually enough to signal that they still have something left to say and have not conceded the floor. *Baton gestures* are a slightly different type used by the speaker, among other things, to mark out the beat of the delivery. They can be thought of as regulating an individual's contributions rather than the to-and-fro of exchange. It is as if the speaker is conducting the orchestra of his or her own voice with an invisible baton.

Affect displays

Hand movements can also convey emotional states, although the face is a richer source of such information. Gestures can reveal emotional dispositions such as embarrassment (e.g. hand over the mouth); anger (e.g. white knuckles); aggression (e.g. fist clenching); shame (e.g. hands covering the eyes); nervousness (e.g. nail and finger biting); boredom (e.g. hair preening); despair (e.g. hand wringing). Professionals should be sensitive to these hand signals which, because of their often spontaneous nature, may reveal more about the client's feelings than words would permit.

Adaptors

Feldman *et al.* (1991) distinguished between gestures that are linked with speech (illustrators) and directed towards objects or events, and those which are oriented towards the self. The latter act as a form of tension release. These are also called self-manipulative gestures and include such things as scratching, rubbing, hand wringing, hair preening, etc., which are characteristically unintentional and done with little awareness. Adaptors are thought to be the echoes of early childhood attempts to satisfy needs. One school of thought suggests that they are signs of anxiety or unease. Knapp and Hall (1997) claimed some evidence that they are associated with negative feelings toward self or others.

Those who supplement their dialogue with good use of hand and arm movements usually arouse and maintain the attention of their listeners, indicate their interest and enthusiasm, and tend to make the interaction sequence a stimulating and enjoyable experience for all participants. Kendon (1984) focused on the various conditions in which individuals use the gestural expressive mode and concluded that the speaker divides the task of conveying meaning between words and gestures in such a way as to achieve either economy of expression or a particular effect on the listener. For instance, a gesture can be used as a device for completing a sentence that, if spoken, might prove embarrassing to the speaker. It can also be used as a means of telescoping what one wants to say, when the available turn space is smaller than one would like. Alternatively, gestures can be employed to clarify some potentially ambiguous word or as an additional component when the verbal account is inadequate to truly represent the information being shared. Feyereisen and Havard (1999) discovered that adults made greater use of representational gestures when responding to questions requiring them to draw on mental images that were motor rather than visual.

Further evidence that clarity and comprehension of an explanation or description can be increased by the use of gestural cues comes from an early study by Rogers (1978). In it eight male and female students were asked to view various actions on a silent film, such as a tennis ball bouncing, or a car swerving, and then describe them to another person who was unable to view the film. These descriptions were subsequently video-taped and shown to another group of students either with sound and vision or with sound only. Results showed that comprehension was significantly increased in the audiovisual as opposed to the sound only condition.

Evidence that accuracy of understanding can be increased when gestural acts are used to complement the spoken word was provided in three studies by Riseborough (1981). First, she showed that persons were more able to identify objects from descriptions accompanied by appropriate gestures than those without gestures. Second, she found that subjects could recall a story more accurately when accompanying gestural behaviours were employed. Third, when the sound channel was obstructed by white noise, illustrative gestures increased comprehension

Head nods

Head movements are a particular form of gesture and as such can replace or be associated with talk. Head-nodding and shaking are a ubiquitous feature of the interactive process and are related to the role of both speaker and listener in quite involved ways (McClave, 2000). In relation to the listener's role, interest shown towards a speaker can be communicated by a tilting of the head to one side. Conversely, in work with marriage partners in conflict, Feeney *et al.* (1999) discovered that periods of withdrawal from discussion of issues that primarily exercised their partners were marked by the head being down. Husbands also turned the head away during these phases. In keeping with this finding, head-nodding is an important 'back-channel' signal to continue talking.

As mentioned earlier, NVC serves to regulate turn-taking during conversation. Examining the role of the speaker, Duncan and Fiske (1977) found that two cues – turning the head away from the other person and beginning to gesture – were significantly associated with taking the role of speaker. This was confirmed by Thomas and Bull (1981), examining conversations between mixed-sex pairs of British students, who found that prior to asking a question the students typically either raised the head or turned the head towards the listener. Just before answering a question the speaker turned the head away from the listener. This last finding may be due to the effects of cognitive planning on the part of the listener prior to taking up the speaker's role.

Posture

Posture can be revealing of status, emotion, interpersonal attitudes and gender. Heller (1997) mentioned four main categories of human posture: standing, sitting, squatting, and lying. In terms of everyday interpersonal communication we are predominantly concerned with the first two.

Status

Posture is one of the cues used to make decisions about the relative status of those we observe and deal with. The degree of relaxation exuded seems to be a telling feature (Argyle, 1994). High-status individuals characteristically adopt a more relaxed position when they are seated (e.g. body tilting sideways; lying slumped in a chair) than low-status subjects who are more upright and rigid. When standing, people in a position of power and influence again appear more relaxed, often with arms crossed or hands in pockets, than those in subordinate positions who are generally 'straighter' and 'stiffer'. The high-status also tend to take up more expansive postures, standing at their full height, chest expanded and with hands on hips (Argyle, 1988). More upright postural positions or 'reduced reclining angles' along with intensity of voice and increased head-nodding were found to be instrumental in achieving persuasive impact on others (Washburn and Hakel, 1973).

Interpersonal attitudes

A seated person who leans forward towards the other is deemed to have a more positive attitude towards both the subject and the topic under discussion than when leaning backwards, away from the person addressed (Siegel, 1980). The reason is probably that forward leaning is a component of this complex of interpersonal behaviour, already mentioned, called immediacy that signals close psychological contact (Andersen et al., 1998). It is also interesting to note that most prolonged interactions are conducted with both participants either sitting or standing, rather than one standing, and the other sitting. Where this situation does occur, communication usually is cursory (e.g. information desks) or strained (e.g. interrogation sessions).

Relative postures adopted is regarded as a further and very significant marker of how those interactors feel about each other and what is happening between them. *Postural congruence* or *mirroring* happens when similar or mirror-image postures are taken up, with ongoing adjustments to maintain synchrony. This is taken as a positive sign that the exchange is harmonious. A review of work on this topic found evidence that postural congruence between therapist and client indicated rapport. Based on client evaluations, these therapists are perceived as affiliative, empathic and promote verbal disclosure (Hess et al., 1999). In neuro-linguistic programming circles intentionally matching and mirroring the postural cues of the other is seen as a way of establishing rapport and is recommended to improve professional communication (Bixler, 1997). Such common matched behaviour involves crossing the legs, leaning forward, head-propping and arm-crossing.

Emotions

Based on earlier findings, bodily posture was thought to reveal the degree of intensity of emotion, rather than the specific emotional state which was held to be the domain of facial expressions (Ekman, 1985). In a series of experiments Bull and Frederikson (1995) illustrated how particular listener attitudes and emotions are encoded in this way, so that boredom was shown to be associated with a backward lean, legs outstretched, and head dropped and supported on one hand. Adults have also been found to successfully identify emotions depicted by actors playing emotional scenes on video-tape, even when facial and voice cues were denied them (Montepare et al., 1999). Approached from the opposite direction, there are fascinating findings to suggest that manipulating expressive behaviour such as posture and facial expressions can influence subsequent emotional feelings (Flack et al., 1999).

Personality

Extreme depression, for instance, can be shown in a drooping, listless pose, while anxiety can be seen in the muscularly tense, stiff, upright person. Focusing on patient behaviour, Fisch *et al.* (1983) found that posture was a significant indicator when differentiating between severely depressed and nearly recovered patients during doctor–patient interviews.

Eye gaze

Obsession with the eyes and their potent effects on human behaviour has been graphically documented down through the ages, epitomised in the celebrated eye gaze of the Mona Lisa that has fascinated viewers for centuries. Aphorisms such as 'The eyes are the windows of the soul' and expressions such as 'If looks could kill', also come to mind. By gaze we mean looking at another especially in the facial area. *Mutual gaze* happens when the other reciprocates. This is sometimes also referred to as *eye-contact* when the eyes are the specific target, although just how accurately we can judge whether someone is looking us directly in the eye or merely in that region of the face is open to debate. Associated terms are *gaze omission* where gaze is absent and *gaze avoidance* where it is intentionally being withheld. When gaze becomes fixed and focused in an intrusive way that may infringe norms of politeness, it becomes a *stare*.

Gazing during social interaction can serve a variety of functions. Kendon (1967), in making one of the first contributions to the literature, suggested these were primarily threefold:

1   expressing personal information;
2   regulating interaction;
3   monitoring feedback from the other.

Recent classifications (e.g. Knapp and Hall, 1997; Richmond and McCroskey, 2000) tend to be more elaborate differentiations of these core purposes.

Expressing information about personal states and dispositions

Here we are thinking particularly of emotions, interpersonal attitudes, relationships, and cognitive activity. The region of the eyes was found to be a particularly significant part of the face when it comes to expressing fear and surprise (Ekman and Friesen, 1975). Prkachin (1997) reported that closing the eyes was a consistent revelation of pain in an experiment with students using four different procedures: electric shock, cold, pressure and muscle ischaemia. Narrowing of the eyes and blinking were other signals to emerge from the research reviewed.

We appear to make more and longer eye-contact with people we regard positively and from whom we expect a positive reaction, as borne out by a number of early studies. These are summarised by Argyle (1988: 162) in the claim that, 'People look more at those they like'. Professionals such as counsellors are encouraged to make use of eye-contact to signal not only positive affect but also attention to and interest in the client (Ivey and Ivey, 1999). Reduced levels of eye-contact among couples can be variously interpreted as disapproval, less power and dominance, or lowered levels of intimacy, depending on the immediate context (Feeney *et al.*, 1999). Paradoxically, we also sometimes look extensively at those with whom we are in conflict. Noller (1980) documented how marital couples in conflict gazed more at each other during episodes of disagreement. While those showing a great deal of both hostility and love may persist in long periods of mutual gaze, it is usually easy to distinguish the two kinds of encounter based on co-lateral NVC and other circumstantial differences.

In addition to conveying relational information in respect of liking, affiliation and interest, gaze also signals differences in status, power and dominance. High-status, influential people indulge more extensively in this type of eye behaviour, especially when speaking (Argyle, 1994) and particularly at the end of utterances (Kalma, 1992), and have longer gaze patterns (Dovidio *et al.*, 1988). Finally, what we do with our eyes can reveal how cognitively taxed we are. We tend to avoid gaze when processing difficult material.

Initiating and regulating conversation

Catching someone's eye is the first step to opening up channels of communication and seeking contact with them. In a group discussion, patterns of gazing are used to orchestrate the flow of conversation, with members being brought into play at particular points. In dyads, a typical interactive sequence would be person A coming towards the end of an utterance looking at person B to signal that it is B's turn to speak. B, in turn, looks away after a short period of mutual gaze to begin responding, especially if intending to speak for a long time, or if the message is difficult to formulate in words. Person A will continue to look reasonably consistently while B, as speaker, will have a more broken pattern of glances (Argyle, 1994).

Monitoring feedback

Kleinke (1986) found that, in general, people looked more as they listened than as they spoke, and the duration of looking was longer during listening than talking. Indeed this imbalance could be up to twice as much when listening (Argyle, 1988). But speakers gaze periodically to obtain feedback and make judgements about how their message is being received and adjustments that may need to be made.

Culture and gender are two highly significant determinants of levels and patterns of social looking. Several studies (Hall, 1984; Bente *et al.*, 1998) have confirmed that women tend to look and be looked at more than men. Two possible explanations for this phenomenon are that women display a greater need for inclusion and affiliation than do men, and that desire for affiliation promotes more looking (Argyle and Cook, 1976). Alternatively, it is contended that eye-contact is seen as less threatening to women than men, with the result they are less likely to break eye-contact in similar situations. Culture likewise helps to shape expectations of eye behaviour, especially the frequency and target of gazing, although duration may also be pertinent. While Swedes gaze less frequently than the English, they do so for longer. At a general level, Arab culture tends to be more gaze-oriented than either English or North American. Even within the latter it seems that Afro-Americans, compared with Whites, look more while speaking and away when listening. In India gaze avoidance is a mark of deference when talking to someone much higher in status (Knapp and Hall, 1997).

Facial expressions

The face as a source of nonverbal information currently attracts more research and scholarly debate than probably any other aspect of NVC, with several books devoted solely to the topic published in the past few years alone. Over twenty different muscles responsible for producing in excess of 1,000 distinct expressions make the face a rich source of detail, particularly to do with emotion. There are three key parts: the brows and forehead; the eyes and bridge of the nose; and the cheeks and mouth. Variations here are highly salient even in schematic facial representations as in Figure 3.1. The traditional view that can be traced back to Charles Darwin emphasises facial *affect displays* as biologically based, direct expressions of underlying emotional states, that have some sort of adaptive value. He wrote, 'that in the case of the chief expressive actions they are not learned but are present from the earliest days and throughout life are quite beyond our control' (Darwin, 1872/1955: 352).

Consistent with this thinking is an emphasis on the universality of emotional expression: people reveal and recognise the same states in the same way regardless of where they live. As previously mentioned, the six basic emotions consistently decodable are sadness, anger, disgust, fear, surprise, and happiness, with contempt as a possible seventh. There is evidence that we may be specially attuned to process certain types of emotional information leading to the rapid recognition of anger and threat (Esteves, 1999; Fox *et al.*, 2000a). Of course our emotional experiences are not confined to the above seven. How shame, guilt and pride are depicted has also attracted considerable interest and Keltner (1997) has detailed the features of embarrassment and amusement. Some of these states may be revealed in fleeting, *micromomentary expressions* that pass with little conscious awareness in a fraction of a second and are particularly difficult to control. The complexity of the face is also witnessed in *affect blends* or configurations that convey more than one basic emotion at the same time: the mouth may be smiling while the eyes are sad.

More recently the orthodox view of the face as mainly a direct, biological signalling system of emotion has been challenged (Russell and Fernandez-Dols, 1997). Rather than the primacy of discrete categories of emotion (e.g. sadness, anger, etc.), Russell (1997) advanced a view that we first process emotional NVC in terms of the dimensions of pleasure and arousal. Any specific emotions attributed are secondary and in keeping with situational and additional detail about the person observed. Recent developments in this area also accentuate social coding over the biological. A view of facial expressions as culturally determined, circumstantially sensitive ways

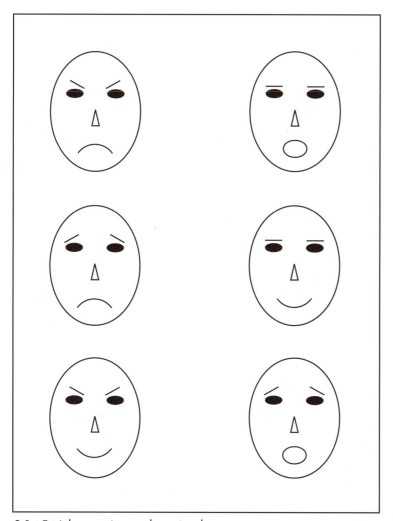

Figure 3.1 Facial expressions and emotional states

of communicating that are shaped by social motives and intentions has been proposed (Fridlund, 1997; Kupperbusch *et al.*, 1999). An experiment by Yik and Russell (1999), involving Canadian, Chinese and Japanese subjects, revealed that they could decode social intention and emotional state with equal accuracy from facial photographs. Perhaps both views can be accommodated. Buck (1994) argued that spontaneous and deliberate (symbolic) expressions represent two parallel systems, both of which are important.

The fact that showing emotion on the face is regulated by *display rules* is well established. Social pressures may mean that it is not always acceptable to reveal what we really feel. The inscrutable face is often a characteristic of the Japanese. In an often-cited experiment, Friesen (1972) had American and Japanese students watch alone a gruesome piece of film while being video-taped. Similar expressions of disgust, etc., were revealed but when later asked about the film, only the American students persisted with these negative facial displays. Japanese are also less approving of showing disgust and sadness in the company of close friends (Matsumoto, 1990). Apart from cross-cultural differences in display rules, Craig *et al.* (1997) found that patients with chronic lower-back trouble attenuated the expression of pain in the presence of the physiotherapist even when told not to.

Emotional contagion, a process whereby emotion spreads from one person to another, is a further interesting interpersonal feature of facial signalling. Laughing is infectious, it is said. When you see someone smiling, do you tend to do likewise? Do you feel happier as a result? One view of emotional contagion (Hatfield *et al.*, 1994) suggests a two-step process whereby we first mimic the expression of the other. People who interact with schizophrenics (expressively inhibited) are themselves less expressive than when interacting with other normal persons (Krause *et al.*, 1989). In addition, Jones *et al.* (1991) claimed that even infants appear to be more expressive when their mothers are facially expressive rather than when they are reserved. Such mimicking can be carried out automatically. Dimberg *et al.* (2000) found that subjects who were not conscious of being exposed to happy and sad faces still registered reactions in the facial muscles corresponding to happy and sad configurations. Second, feedback from our facial (and other) muscles leads to experiences of those corresponding emotions (Blairy *et al.*, 1999). We feel as the other person feels.

Smiles

These are one of the most common and easily recognised forms of facial expression, yet they have many and diverse meanings (LaFrance and Hecht, 1999). While enjoyment may be interpreted, smiling may also signal appeasement or even contempt. Spontaneous and contrived smiles can be readily distinguished with the former, *Duchenne* smile, involving not only the mouth but also the eyes. Apart from signalling enjoyment, smiling is influenced by gender and status in that females do more of it and low-status people seem more pressured to behave in this way (Hecht and LaFrance, 1998). Gender and information on job status of the person have also been found to have a significant impact on interpretations of facial expressions of emotion (Algoe *et al.*, 2000). Among men, there is some evidence that those with higher testosterone levels have less pronounced smiles (Dabbs, 1997).

While this sub-section has been about the fluidity of the face as a means of communicating, fixed features can also be informative and influential. A key factor in recognising gender from photographs is the distance from eyelid to brow, which is smaller in men (Campbell *et al.*, 1999). Additionally, personality attributes can be made from features etched in the face. Size of eyes was found by Paunonen *at al.* (1999) to be associated with judged personality traits based mainly on perceptions of masculinity/ femininity, babyfacedness and to a lesser extent attractiveness. Finally, symmetrical faces seem to be regarded as more attractive in both males and females (Perrett *et al.*, 1999).

PROXEMICS

Proxemics refers to the communicative significance of how we perceive and make use of personal and social space. In particular there are three broad aspects, namely territoriality; personal space and interpersonal distance; and orientation and seating arrangements. All of these have a direct bearing on the interactive process, and each will be discussed in turn.

Territoriality

Territory refers to a geographical area over which individuals claim some particular set of rights by way of access, occupancy or utilisation, for a period of time. It invokes associated concepts such as encroachment, invasion and defence.

- *Primary territory* is associated with the occupier who has exclusive use of it. This could be a house or just a bedroom which others may not enter without seeking permission and through invitation. It is an area of privacy that one can retreat to and where one has control. Omata (1996) reported that few Japanese women could lay claim to spaces at home that were exclusively theirs although most had personalised areas where they could go to be alone, relax or entertain friends. Those that had such private space showed better levels of adaptation. Gress and Heft (1998) associated an increase in the number of students sharing a room with more territorial behaviour, including creating barriers and arranging the room to make it less amenable to open interaction. Similarly, Sinha and Mukherjee (1996) discovered that students in these conditions of increased crowding required larger personal space and disliked the sharing arrangement more, although these effects were attenuated somewhat when room-mates were all highly co-operative. It is also possible to get an idea of levels of territorial commitment in a neighbourhood from the exteriors of homes and the pride taken in their up-keep (Harris and Brown, 1998).
- *Secondary territory* is less strongly linked with an individual or group. People may, out of habit, tend to sit in the same seat on the train or in the pub, and be looked for there, but this cannot be backed up by claims of 'ownership' and exclusivity.
- *Public territory* is space that is available to all to make use of for limited periods of time and is therefore particularly difficult to control. Park benches, library seats and parking spaces are examples. Nevertheless, we have a tendency to claim more rights here than we are entitled to: we often relinquish our occupancy begrudgingly. Ruback and Juieng (1997) watched drivers leave a car park and noted that they took longer when another car was waiting for their place – especially when the other car's horn was used. Males left sooner, though, if the other was a higher-status vehicle. Leaving *markers* is one way of defending our 'patch' and preventing others taking over. Examples include personal artefacts such as items of clothing or books left on library desks.
- *Interaction territory* is a special type of space that is created by others when interacting (e.g. a group having a conversation on the footpath). It lasts only as

long as the interaction but during that period others tend to walk around rather than through the gathering. Schiavo *et al.* (1995) noted though that this may be more likely in the overall context of public space (e.g. students in conversation in a corridor in the library) rather than secondary territory to which the interactors have limited claims (e.g. non-resident students in conversation in the corridor of the halls of residence). In the later case, resident students were less likely to acknowledge the non-residents' interaction territory.

Personal space and interpersonal distance

Personal space is that envelope immediately surrounding the body, within which we move around. In this sense it is like a permanent but mobile personal territory. It can grow or shrink depending on our personality, the situation in which we find ourselves or our relationship with the person with whom we are dealing. Introverts, violent offenders, Type A personalities (i.e. very driven, time conscious, competitive individuals), and the highly anxious tend to claim larger personal spaces (Argyle, 1988), although no significant sex differences seem to have been found (Akande, 1997). Violations of personal space may not only be disturbing but adversely affect our ability to function effectively. For example, those with a larger personal space were most negatively affected by high social density conditions on recall performance in a task requiring high levels of information processing (Sinha *et al.*, 1999).

Linked to personal space is interpersonal distance. This is the distance that interactors maintain when having a conversation: do they stand close together or far apart? The possibilities extend from a situation of touching to the limits of hearing. Within this range a particular distance will be established which may be thought to be a completely arbitrary factor of no particular significance. However this would be mistaken on both counts. Interpersonal distance is shaped by a nexus of factors such as culture, gender, age, status, topic of conversation, relationship shared and physical features of interactors. In turn it has implications for how comfortable we feel about the encounter, and our interpersonal attitudes towards, and relationship with the other (Knapp and Hall, 1997). Contact cultures, as well as engaging in more haptic communication, tend to sanction closer interpersonal distances. Females also are more likely to get closer when having a conversation in normal circumstances. When hints of threat or discomfort are introduced, though, larger distances than males may be taken up (Hall, 1984). This could possibly account for the finding by Kaya and Erkip (1999), when observing automatic teller machine users, that waiting females approached males less closely than vice versa. Interpersonal distance has also been found to be shorter in same-sex interactions (Jacobson, 1999; Kaya and Erkip, 1999).

Young children tend to pay scant regard to interpersonal distance conventions but will be looked on more negatively when older if they are still negligent. A generalisation cited by Richmond and McCroskey (2000) is that we probably interact at closer distances with people of the same age, although they caution that little systematic research has been conducted. In addition, both status differences and what is being talked about must be taken into account here. People of equal status tend to take up a closer distance between each other than people of unequal status

(Zahn, 1991). In fact, where a status differential exists the lower-status individual will allow the higher-status individual to approach quite closely, but will rarely approach the high-status individual with the same degree of closeness. As the topic of conversation shifts to become more intimate than is comfortable for the other, that person may increase distance either by taking a step back or by leaning back in the chair. As such, interpersonal distance is part of this dynamic of nonverbal cues, including gaze and orientation, that serves to regulate levels of intimacy and involvement.

Relationships shared have a further determining role in marking out physical closeness in situations. The anthropologist Hall, whose work in this area is seminal, found that four distinct categories of distance characterised the range of inter-personal contacts engaged in by predominantly white, middle-class American males from business and professional backgrounds (Hall, 1966). These are:

- *Intimate* (ranging from touching to about 18 inches). Reserved for very close friends and family.
- *Casual-personal* (from 18 inches to 4 feet). Typifies informal conversations with friends and acquaintances.
- *Social-consultative* (from 4 to 12 feet). Used for more impersonal professional transactions.
- *Public* (from 12 feet to the range of sound and vision). Used for making speeches and addressing large groups at formal gatherings.

Finally, physical characteristics of participants also, to some extent, determine the amount of distance between interactors. Kleck and Strenta (1985), for example, found that persons communicating with physically deformed individuals chose a greater initial distance.

Orientation and seating arrangements

Orientation refers to body angles adopted when people talk, such as directly facing or shoulder-to-shoulder. As such it concerns the position of the trunk, rather than head, and marks the degree of intimacy in the conversation and levels of friendship. It is useful to look at proximity and orientation together since it has been found that there can be an inverse relationship between them – that is, direct face-to-face alignment is linked to greater interpersonal distance and sideways angling to closer distance. This would be expected in situations where orientation was being used to compensate for excessive closeness (Andersen *et al.*, 1998). Orientation can also be used to include or exclude others from the group during discussion.

Early studies of seating behaviour by Sommer (1969) in North America, replicated by Cook (1970) in the UK, point to some interesting differences in seating arrangements if individuals are given a choice of where to sit when involved in different sorts of activities. Cook asked a sample including civil servants, school teachers and secretaries how they would position themselves at a rectangular table with six chairs if asked to carry out a series of tasks with a friend of the same sex. The tasks were:

- *conversation* (sitting chatting for a few minutes before work);
- *co-operation* (sitting doing a crossword or such like);
- *co-action* (sitting at the same table individually reading);
- *competition* (competing to see who would be first to solve a number of puzzles).

As Figure 3.2 shows, a side-by-side position was considered to be co-operative in nature, while a face-to-face orientation can carry intonations of competition. A 90° angle in relation to each other seems good for conversations. At the same time, co-action can be a more conducive situation for studying or for children working independently at a task in the classroom.

Finally, seating can be arranged in such a way as to encourage or discourage interaction. A layout that promotes interchange is called *sociopetal*; one that has the

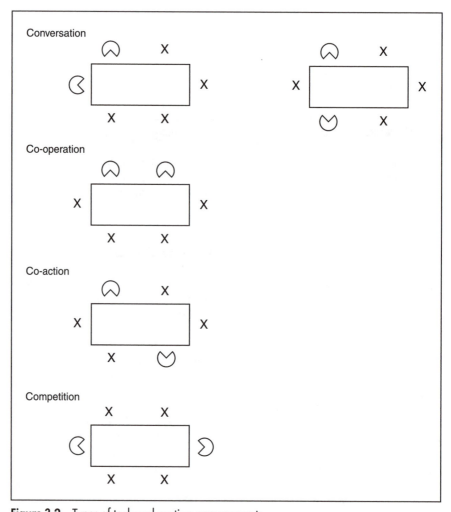

Figure 3.2 Types of task and seating arrangements

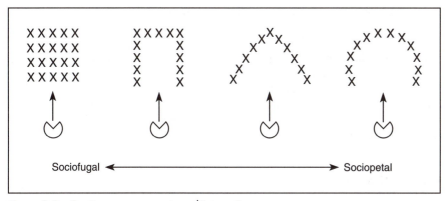

Figure 3.3 Seating arrangements and interaction

opposite effect, *sociofugal*. It is imperative, therefore, that seating for a group discussion be arranged accordingly by, let's say, using a sociopetal pattern to make it easier for open interchange and sharing. On the other hand, a sociofugal variant would be more suited if the intention is for a presenter to play a centrally dominant role by making more use of one-way communication. Examples of types of seating varying along the sociopetal–sociofugal dimension can be found in Figure 3.3. Further elements of spatial arrangement in respect of office design will be presented later in the section on environmental factors.

PHYSICAL CHARACTERISTICS

Here we can include a vast array of bodily features some of which are more easily altered than others, but all of which are used to make judgements about the person in respect of ethnicity, gender, age, occupation, status, etc., and influence interaction. It can include body shape and size, height, hair colour and style, dress, and adornments such as jewellery. Physical characteristics, as a potent aspect of the nonverbal channel, cannot be over-emphasised, particularly in initiating some form of social contact. As will be discussed in more detail in Chapter 10, before we even know what people sound like or what they have to say we begin to form impressions based on physical appearance. At the centre of most of these will be evaluations of physical attractiveness. In our society physical attractiveness is one of the key dimensions of appearance, although we also manipulate our appearance on occasions to signify a particular occupation, status, or personality type, or project a desired image.

The importance of physical attractiveness is abundantly evident in both the amount and variety of artefacts, such as designer clothes, jewellery, false nails, perfume, after-shave, expensive shoes, and so on, sold annually. The potency of attractiveness is well documented. To the extent that we can make ourselves more attractive in the way that we present ourselves, we have a distinct advantage in most walks of life. Physically attractive people are seen as more personable, popular, intelligent, persuasive, happy, interesting, confident, and outgoing (Hargie *et al.*, 1999; Wilson and Nias, 1999). This has important implications for professionals involved in day-to-day evaluative decisions about the quality of people's work or their suitability for selection. Here bias may favour the attractive, especially in situations of little protracted contact with that person. Mehrabian and Blum (1997) derived five main factors to account for ratings of physical attraction by both males and females from photographs of young adults of both sexes. These factors were *masculinity* (determined by features to do with strength, larger chest, broader chin), *femininity* (based on longer hair, make-up, larger and rounder eyes), *self-care* (suggested by shapely figure, well groomed, well-fitting clothes), *pleasantness* (based on perceptions of friendliness, happiness, babyish features), and *ethnicity*.

Body size and shape

Fatism seems rampant in estimations of physical attraction based on body size and shape. In a study by Singh and Young (1996) involving ratings given by male undergraduates of female figures, larger body size, high waist-to-hip ratio, and larger hips were associated with lower estimations of attraction and desirability. According to Margo (1997) 'Barbie Doll' features are universally beautiful and represent stereotyped features of the human form that have become more prevalent during recent evolutionary history. Being underweight seems an attractive feature in men as well as women (Henss, 1996).

But perhaps this preference has a larger cultural component than has been suggested. While it has often been reported that men favour women with an ideal waist-to-hip ratio (WHR) of 0.7, this could be more typical of affluent western society. Marlowe and Westman (2001) found that Hazda men in Tanzania, who are hunter-gatherers, preferred heavier women with higher WHRs (i.e. with fuller waists). These researches argued that in subsistence situations such as these where women's work is physically demanding and energy-sapping, thinness could indicate poor health or inability to cope with the harsh conditions. From an evolutionary point of view such women would be less likely to conceive and successfully raise children.

WHR is one gender marker: baldness is another. While not restricted to men, of course, it is a more prevalent male characteristic. No significant differences were found by Butler *et al.* (1998) in attraction between a photo of a naturally bald man and an alternative version in which his hair was 'restored' through computer-manipulation. However, undergraduates regarded the full-hair photo as more dominant, dynamic and masculine.

Height

It is well established that tall people are perceived more positively than short people (Hensley and Cooper, 1987) and these expectations may reinforce behaviours associated with success in the workplace, increasing the likelihood of promotion. Melamed and Bozionelos (1992) examined the relationship between physical height and managerial promotion among 132 British managers from the civil service. The results indicated that even taking into account the personality traits of the managers, height was a more potent factor in determining who attained promotion. Furthermore,

Young and French (1996) reported that those US presidents polled as being the greatest were almost four inches taller on average than the five regarded as failures.

Dress

In addition to attractiveness, we make assumptions about, for example, occupation and status from how someone is dressed. Several studies have shown that people are more inclined to take orders from, accept the lead given by, and comply with requests made by someone wearing 'high-status' clothing (Adler and Towne, 1996). Despite the vagaries of fashion, Molloy (1975) believed men in business and managerial positions commanded greatest credibility when wearing ideally a dark-blue suit. In the often-cited television debate between Richard Nixon and John Kennedy as part of the 1960 presidential campaign, Nixon appeared in a grey suit that contrasted poorly with the drab grey background of the studio. Kennedy, on the other hand, wore a stylish dark suit. While Nixon's failure to win the battle of image in this debate has been commonly put down to his infamous 'seven o'clock shadow', this sartorial contrast is also thought to have played a big part. Likewise, Golden (1986) claimed that the darker the suit, the greater the authority suggested.

As far as women are concerned, dress choices at work are more complex and possible interpretations more varied than with men (Kaiser, 1999). Suitability will probably depend ultimately on the type of profession and the corresponding image cultivated. Wallach (1986) suggested three categories.

- *Corporate.* The corporate woman wants to be seen as competent, rational and objective (e.g. banker, accountant, lawyer). Women wearing a jacket rather than a dress or skirt and blouse were viewed as more powerful, in a piece of research reported by Temple and Loewen (1993).
- *Communicator.* This woman wants to project an image of warmth, sincerity and approachability (e.g. reporter, teacher, social worker, media person).
- *Creative.* Here the image is one of flair, originality and innovation (e.g. musician, artist, writer, fashion designer).

Before leaving this section, it should again be repeated that the effects of physical attraction are more pronounced in situations where there have been few opportunities to interact with the target person over an extended period. Riggio and Friedman (1986) identified those nonverbal and verbal cues that determined likeability, confidence and competence when persons were engaged in public speaking. They found that physical attractiveness, although initially important, in the long term was less important than other social skills such as expressive facial behaviours and speech and gestural fluency.

Environmental factors

The physical setting can influence our mood, how we perceive the social situation, and judgements about the person who occupies, or has responsibility for that space. It can also help determine our likelihood of interacting with others, the form that interaction will take, and how long it is likely to last. Hall (1966) distinguished between *fixed-feature* and *semifixed-feature* elements of the environment. The former include everything that is relatively permanent or not easily changed, like the architectural layout of a house, size and shape of rooms, and materials used in their construction. Semifixed-features are much easier to move around or modify, and include furniture, lighting, temperature and colour of décor. Based on such characteristics, we form impressions of our surroundings organised around six dimensions, according to Knapp and Hall (1997). These are:

1 *Formality* – concerns cues leading to decisions about how casual one can be in what is said and done or if a more ritualised or stylised performance is demanded.
2 *Warmth* – here one feels more-or-less comfortable, secure, and at ease in what are regarded as convivial surroundings.
3 *Privacy* – has to do with the extent to which interactors feel that they have the space to themselves or whether others may intrude or eavesdrop.
4 *Familiarity* – involves impressions of having encountered this type of setting before and knowing how to deal with it (or not, as the case may be).
5 *Constraint* – concerns perceptions of how easy it is to enter and leave the situation.
6 *Distance* – addresses how close, either physically or psychologically, we feel to those with whom we share the space.

These perceptions will, in turn, shape the types of interaction we engage in and how we experience them. The ways in which work space is arranged and utilised can send strong signals about the status and authority of occupants, the sorts of tasks and activities being implicitly proposed, indeed the desirability and appropriateness of focused communication in that situation.

Those in authority and control in organisations commonly have their status acknowledged by the way that they position themselves *vis-à-vis* others with whom they associate. As a rule they tend to adopt positions that are more elevated, isolated and 'head-of-table' than their lesser ranking colleagues. Indeed it is common for the seats of power in organisations to be located on the top floors of buildings. It was said of Harry Cohen, the one-time president of Columbia Pictures, that he had his desk placed on a raised platform at the far end of a long, spacious room as a way of not only marking status but intimidating those who came to do business with him.

How office design conveys messages about the position and personality of the manager deserves further attention. According to Korda (1975), one of the factors that determines the power afforded by an office arrangement is the extent to which the manager can control space and readily restrict access to visitors. Furthermore, he believed that the organisation and use of office space has more impact in this sense than the size of the office *per se* or how it is furnished. Other factors such as not being exposed, being able to look directly at visitors, seeing visitors before being seen, and having access monitored on one's behalf by someone of lesser status, such as a gate-keeping secretary, are also held to be important. From the office plans in Figure 3.4, it can be seen that A communicates most power, B next, with C the least power.

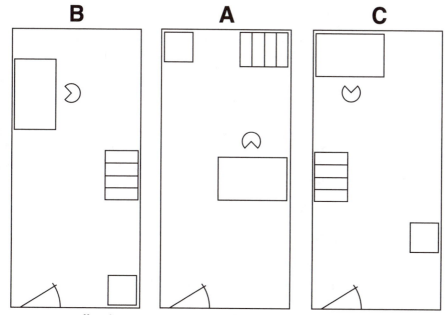

Figure 3.4 Office designs communicating power

In larger offices, separate areas are often set side for distinct purposes, enabling temporary adjustments to be made to suggest power and control. What Korda (1975) called the *pressure area* is centred around the desk and is the site of formal business transactions. It is here that hard bargaining and difficult decision-making takes place. The *semisocial area* is furnished differently with, for example, a sofa or easy chairs, coffee table, drinks cabinet, etc., and can be used to stall, ingratiate or mollify a visitor, as necessary.

Furthermore, it seems that apart from impressions of power and authority, personality judgements are frequently based on how office space is made use of. Comfort in dealing with others, friendliness and extroversion tend to be attributed to occupants of more *open* office arrangements in which, for example, the desk is moved against a wall rather than used as a barrier (Hargie *et al.*, 1999). The more effective professional will select that area of the office more appropriate to the task to be carried out with a particular client or colleague. Additionally, variations in the arrangements of environmental factors such as architectural style, interior décor, lighting conditions, colours, sounds, and so on, can be extremely influential on the outcome of interpersonal communication (Burgoon *et al.*, 1996; Pollack, 1998). (See Chapter 10 for further information on the effects of the environment on initial perceptions.)

VOCALICS

Nonverbal communication, it will be recalled, includes aspects of speech as well as body language. These are the parts that accompany the spoken word, but are not verbal. The general term *paralinguistics* includes such features as speech rate and intensity; pitch, modulation and quality of voice; and vocal lip, articulation and rhythm control. Other nonverbal sounds like moaning and sighing, speech dysfluencies, and vocalisations such as 'uh-huh', 'er' and 'ahh' are also included. Using the acronym VAPER, Nelson-Jones (1997) cited five nonverbal dimensions of voice messages, namely, *v*olume, *a*rticulation, *p*itch, *e*mphasis and *r*ate, as important for counsellors in helping interviews.

Prosody is the term used to refer to those vocal variations associated with the words that serve to actually change the meaning of what was said. This can be exemplified in the following statement: 'John's lending me his CD'. If we decide to place more vocal emphasis on certain words we can alter its meaning:

1   JOHN's lending me his CD.
     (*John* is the one giving the CD; no one else)
2   John's LENDING me his CD.
     (John's *lending*, not giving, swapping or selling his CD)
3   John's lending ME his CD.
     (*I* am the borrower and no one else)
4   John's lending me HIS CD.
     (The CD being lent does not belong to anyone but *John*)
5   John's lending me his *CD*.
     (Nothing else is being loaned, only his *CD*).

Extralinguistics is about, for example, variations in accent. This is an important marker of social identity and a rich source of opinions and value judgements about people. It is a readily accessible cue that can be used to place an individual in a particular social category. As explained by Wigboldus *et al.* (1999: 153) 'Even when communicating with a total stranger, information about a recipient's most relevant social category memberships, such as gender, age and origin, is mostly directly available from the recipient's tone of voice, looks or accent.' Once a person is located, by accent, according to ethnic background, culture or class, corresponding stereotypes are triggered that in turn can evoke favourable or unfavourable attributions. Accent can indeed be a powerful catalyst for prejudice on some occasions, so, allegedly, Glaswegians are aggressive, Yorkshire men doggedly determined but unimaginative, Essex women stupid, Irish drunken, and so on!

Accent is a speech characteristic that we sometimes modify to make more or less distinct from that of our conversational partner. According to *communication accommodation theory* we tend to bring our speech more into line with that of our partner when we are seeking approval, signalling in-group membership, and making communication as comprehensible as possible. Willemyns *et al.* (1997), in an Australian study, found that interviewees used broader accents when interviewed by someone with a broad Australian English rather than a more cultivated accent.

Knapp and Hall (1997) reviewed evidence that judgements are made from paralanguage (with varying degrees of accuracy) about different elements of the communication process. These have to do with the speaker, how the message is presented and how it should be received.

The speaker

From accompanying vocalic indices, impressions can be formed, with varying accuracy, about the speaker's age, gender, size, personality, emotional state, and to some extent occupation. Scherer (1979) claimed that rate of speech can be directly related to anger: 'hot' anger has a notably fast tempo while 'cool' anger is more moderate in pace. In addition, Scherer (1979: 251) also noted that 'Extreme pitch variation and up contours produce ratings of highly pleasant active, and potent emotions such as happiness, interest, surprise and also fear. Down contours have similar effects but do not seem to contain elements of surprise or uncertainty'. Mean amplitude (associated closely with loudness) was discovered by Tusing and Dillard (2000) to be positively related to perceived dominance of the speaker. Speech rate on the other hand, was negatively associated (i.e. the faster the rate the lower the estimation of dominance).

Anxiety is an emotional state likely to produce speech errors. In the early stages of interaction with others, participants can be beset by speech dysfluencies. However, as the participants become more familiar with the situation, the frequency of speech errors decreases (Scott *et al.*, 1978).

The presentation of the message

Decisions are taken about the message, in respect of levels of enthusiasm, excitement or competence, from the paralanguage. We have all had experience of speeches delivered in such a dreary monotone that the most interesting material seems boring. Conversely, quite boring material can become interesting if delivered by someone who stimulates interest, through changing the pitch, tone, speed and volume of vocal pattern. Politicians and good public speakers use these vocal techniques in order to emphasise points, stimulate feelings and generally obtain and sustain the interest of their audiences.

How the message should be received

The vocalics sometimes contain a metamessage that lets the listener know how the verbal content is to be taken (e.g. 'tongue in cheek', soberly, respectfully, etc.). In *The selling of the president 1968*, it is related how before a broadcast, the announcer who was about to do the introduction asked if his voice was too shrill. 'Yeah, we don't want it like a quiz show', he was told, 'He's going to be presidential tonight so announce presidentially' (McGinniss, 1969).

But it isn't just about image and personal impressions. How information is delivered paralinguistically has important consequences for how much of the message is understood, recalled and acted on. For example, verbal fluency was one of two strongest predictors of persuasiveness to emerge from a study by Burgoon *et al.* (1990).

OVERVIEW

When we think about the communicative process and how it operates, the nonverbal tends to be overshadowed by the verbal. Little wonder that the contribution of non-verbal elements is often downplayed in our estimation of their role in the overall activity. Their very ubiquity and prosaic quality often, and paradoxically, render them in many respects invisible to the eyes of the naive observer looking in on interaction from the outside. The case is very different on the inside for those who are actually acting and reacting to one another. Much of what they do is nonverbal and is in response to nonverbal cues picked up from the other. Yet it would be mistaken to assume that the verbal and nonverbal are two distinct systems of communication. Nothing could be further from the truth. As stressed by Wagner and Lee (1999: 262) 'nonverbal behavior in real settings is inextricably bound up with the verbal behavior that it usually accompanies and cannot be understood without reference to that verbal behavior'. Even reaching neatly defined conceptual distinctions is difficult. In broad terms, though, NVC compared with language tends to rely less on a symbolic code, is often represented in continuous behaviour, carries meaning less explicitly, and typically conveys emotional/relational rather than cognitive/propositional information.

By means of NVC, we can replace, complement, modify or contradict the spoken word. When it is suspected that the latter was done unintentionally and deceit is possible, nonverbal cues are often regarded as more truthful. We also regulate conversations through gestures, gaze, and vocal inflection. Revealing emotions and interpersonal attitudes, negotiating relationships, signalling personal and social identity and contextualising interaction are further uses served by means of haptics, proxemics, kinesics, and vocalics, together with physical characteristics of the person and the environment. We need information about other people's qualities, attributes, attitudes and values in order to know how to deal with them. We often infer personality, attitudes, emotions and social status from the behavioural cues presented to us. Of course the situation also works in reverse; not only do we gather information about others from the way they present themselves to us, but we ourselves go to great lengths to present others with a certain type of picture of ourselves.

The potency of the nonverbal aspects of interaction must be recognised by professionals who should be sensitive to the kind of atmosphere they are creating, the scene they are setting, and the parameters they are placing on an interaction, often before they even begin to speak. Knowledge of the various facets of nonverbal com-munication, and of their effects in social interaction, can enable us to improve our ability to deal successfully with others. The skilled use of nonverbal behaviour is a key facet of success in interpersonal encounters. It must also be stressed, however, that much of nonverbal meaning is inferred and can easily be misconstrued. It only suggests possibilities and must be interpreted in the overall context of not only verbal but also personal and circumstantial information. Many of the elements of nonverbal communication that have been discussed in this chapter will recur in the remaining chapters of this book.

Chapter 4

Rewarding and reinforcing

INTRODUCTION

A BASIC PRINCIPLE GOVERNING behaviour is that people tend to do things associated with positively valued outcomes for them. In contrast, they usually do not persist with alternative actions that from past experience have produced little of consequence, or even unwanted effects. Positively valued outcomes can of course take many forms. Some (e.g. obtaining food, water, and shelter) are necessary for physical survival, while others (e.g. attractive company) are less basic but still important. Events that are even less tangible, yet highly valued just the same, include positive features of interpersonal contact mentioned as examples in Box 4.1. A friendly smile, a word of praise, warm congratulations, generous applause or enthusiastic response from an attentive listener are all reactions that we, from time to time, find appealing. Not only do we find them appealing, we tend to act in ways that bring them about. The fact that such reactions can influence what we do in this manner, by making it more likely that we will engage in certain behaviours in preference to others, is central to the concept of reinforcement as an interpersonal skill.

As mentioned in Chapter 1, the ability to get and give rewards features prominently in attempts to define interpersonal skill. Deficits in this respect can have grave personal and interpersonal consequences. In a review of the area, Segrin and Flora (2000) found evidence linking poor social skills, inability to gain positive reinforcement and depression. Social inadequacy also seems to be associated with loneliness and social anxiety. Having the potential to reward (i.e. rewardingness) is therefore a key dimension of interpersonal interaction that plays a

---

Box 4.1 Everyday examples of reinforcement

- The striker for the home team scores a goal and the frenetic fans chant his name in exultation.
- Someone in the group tells a funny story and the rest erupt in gales of laughter.
- An infant makes its first attempt at 'Mummy' and the adoring mother responds with enraptured smiles, hugs and kisses.
- A pupil who has been struggling with quadratic equations gets them all right for the first time and the attentive teacher lavishes generous praise.
- A sales executive beats the monthly target and earns the heart-felt congratulations of the collective team.
- A learner driver manages to reverse around a corner for the first time without touching the kerb and the instructor smiles in recognition.
- A young swimmer makes it to the end of the pool for a first full length, and wins the admiration of the rest of the class.

In all of these cases it is likely that the person reacted to in each of these positive ways will be influenced subsequently to strive to do similar things in future situations. When they do so their actions (be it scoring goals, telling funny stories, saying 'Mummy', etc.) are said to have been reinforced.

---

central role in friendship formation and personal attraction (Hinde, 1997; Smith and Mackie, 2000). Faraone and Hurtig (1985) examined what those regarded as highly socially skilled actually did, compared with their low social skill counterparts, when in conversation with a stranger of the opposite sex. The highly skilled were more rewarding in the way in which they reduced uncertainty, and therefore possible unease in the situation, and were more positive towards the other through what was said and topics introduced. Commenting along similar lines, Argyle (1995: 82) asserted that rewards in social situations serve 'to keep others in the relationship, to increase the other's attraction to ego, and to make greater influence possible, when reinforcement is contingent upon the desired behaviour'. Likewise in professional circles, the ability to reward and reinforce effectively during dealings with those availing themselves of the service on offer has been heavily stressed.

REINFORCEMENT AND PROFESSIONAL PRACTICE

A core skill common to professional practice in a range of settings involves responding positively to those engaged so as to reward and reinforce appropriately. In education, for instance, reinforcement is seen as a potentially powerful tool to be used by teachers to improve pupils' social behaviour in class and promote academic achievement (McCowan *et al.*, 1995; Sutherland and Wehby, 2001). Indeed, Turney *et al.* (1983a) included reinforcement in their list of basic teaching skills. They described how teachers can increase pupils' attention and motivation, improve classroom behaviour and promote achievement by various verbal and nonverbal means including:

* praise and encouragement;
* touch;
* gestures;
* adjusting physical proximity;
* opportunities to take part in other activities such as playing class games with peers.

Shifting the focus from teaching to psychotherapy, a view has been advanced of the psychotherapist as a powerful source of social reinforcement used during the consultation to shape change (Follette *et al.*, 1996). For Beier and Young (1998), while clients' maladaptive patterns of relating may elicit painful responses from others, those same patterns may also meet a more compelling need for predictability and consistency in dealings with them. In this way dysfunctional behaviour is sustained through interpersonal reinforcement. The therapist's task is to reshape more productive and satisfying styles of interaction. Likewise, Borrego and Urquiza (1998) discussed the crucial role of the therapist as a purveyor of reinforcement during parent–child interaction therapy.

In the related field of counselling, Ivey and Ivey (1999) attributed special status to 'attending' and 'listening' in their taxonomy of constituent microskills. Attending in this sense to the client involves:

* following the conversational lead offered;
* adopting appropriate body language;
* engaging visually;
* being vocally responsive.

Ivey and Ivey (1999: 27) established this skill as the foundation for all further productive work and advised that:

> Attending behaviour encourages the client to talk. You will want to use attending behaviour to help clients tell their stories and to reduce interviewer talk. Conversely, their lack of attending behaviour can also serve a useful function. Through non-attention you can help other people talk less about topics that are destructive or nonproductive.

Based on the premise that people will only talk about what others are prepared to listen to, clients can be encouraged to disclose issues of concern through the judicious use of attending behaviour and the reinforcing effects of selective listening on the part of the counsellor or interviewer. (See Chapter 7 for further information on listening.)

Reinforcement was also identified as playing a prominent role in physiotherapists' interactions with patients (Adams *et al.*, 1994). In this study, physiotherapy sessions involving both adults and children in out-patient, obstetrics and gynaecology, neurology, and paediatric departments were video-taped for fine-grained analysis and evaluation by colleagues. From isolated positive and negative instances of practitioner–patient episodes, the object was to reach consensus on a set of behavioural categories of effective communication in the clinical setting. Reinforcement was identified as an important element of the task-oriented dimension of practice. It featured in work with both adults and children and comprised, for example, praise, acknowledging increased effort, positive feedback, smiling, and eye-contact. When employed with children, using an excited tone of voice, and holding and cuddling, were further instances recorded.

The piece of research just described was closely based on earlier work by Saunders and Caves (1986) who adopted this constitutive ethnographic methodology to unearth the key communication skills of a different professional group – speech and language therapists. 'Using positive reinforcement' was one of the categories to emerge from interactions with children and adults. Verbal and nonverbal sub-types were specified. Using the same approach, Hargie *et al.* (2000) not only established key communication skills of the community pharmacist, but asked participants to differentiate in terms of importance between the eleven types to emerge. Reinforcement in the context of explaining was rank-ordered second, after rapport-building.

In other areas of health care, health-worker social rewards in the form of attention, praise, approval, compliments, and such, can increase, for example, patient satisfaction and improve adherence to prescribed drug regimens and recommended courses of action. This may include sticking to a set diet and maintaining healthy eating patterns (Holli and Calabrese, 1998). By taking steps to monitor patient behaviour and reinforce adherence when it does take place, health workers can go some way to ensuring that patients co-operate fully in their treatment. This may have particular impact in cases of difficult or unpleasant courses of action. In controlling diabetes mellitus, according to Warren and Hixenbaugh (1998: 441):

> It is the role of the doctor to convince the patient that the discomfort or inconvenience in the short-term will bring rewards (by avoiding complications) in the long-term . . . In order to achieve this, reinforcements, such as praise for appropriate behaviour, must be immediate.

Raven (1988) emphasised that influencing change along these lines pre-supposes the establishment of a relationship of trust, acceptance and respect. It is only in this context that praise and approval are likely to be valued. Extending this thinking, Buckmann (1997) argued that using rewards like selective positive feedback, benevolent behaviour, and acceptance statements that convey to patients that they are held in high regard, can act indirectly to enhance adherence. These ways of relating strengthen health professionals' referent power (i.e. the social power bestowed on them as people to be identified with or 'looked up to'). This, together with their expert power (i.e. the influence they command due to their expertise), serves to strengthen patients' self-esteem and sense of self-efficacy (these aspects of influence are further addressed in Chapter 12). Following the argument through, patients who have a better sense of their own worth and a greater belief in their ability to succeed in the task are more likely to co-operate in their treatment.

Rewards, including praise, make a potentially beneficial contribution to other and diverse areas of professional activity such as management and organisational operations. Those intent on building effectively functioning teams in the workplace have been advised by Hargie *et al.* (1999) to be particularly attentive to the power of social rewards. When systematically applied, improvements in staff absenteeism, motivation, job satisfaction, productivity and safety can result (for reviews see, for example, Poling *et al.*, 2000; Alavosius *et al.*, 2000). The findings are summarised by Reid and Parsons (2000: 281), with reference to human service settings, as follows:

> A variety of consequences have been demonstrated through OBM [Organizational Behavior Management] research to have reinforcing effects on desired staff performance including, for example, money, free meals, commercial trading stamps, discount coupons, and work duties, trips away from the work site, and special recognition ceremonies.

But reinforcement in the workplace works both ways. In a fascinating juxtaposition of direction of influence, Green and Knippen (1999: 103) contended that reinforcement is also a potent means whereby *employees* can shape management practice: 'Employees can utilize positive reinforcement to change an undesirable behaviour of their manager into one that is desirable.'

Finally, sports coaches who employ rewarding techniques have been found to be popular, especially with younger competitors. They have also been shown to enhance levels of skill and to improve results (Smith and Smoll, 1990). Furthermore, Justine and Howe (1998) reported that among adolescent female field hockey players, frequent praise from the coach was associated with greater perceptions of self-competence and satisfaction with both the coach and general team involvement.

BEHAVIOUR AND ITS CONSEQUENCES

Since Ivan Pavlov, the eminent Russian physiologist, introduced the term (Pavlov, 1927), the concept of reinforcement has been the subject of much heated debate in psychology. One psychologist who was at the forefront of much of this during his long and highly active academic life was B.F. Skinner (1953). The application of reinforcement procedures in keeping with Skinnerian principles is known as *instrumental* or *operant conditioning*. The central tenet of this process focuses on the ability of the consequences of behaviour to increase the probability of subsequent manifestations of that behaviour, relative to some preconditioned level (Lieberman, 2000).

For any particular piece of behaviour, we can think, first, of environmental stimuli that precede or accompany it and, second, of others taking place subsequently. Consider the classroom example of a teacher asking the class a question to which Mary raises her hand. As far as the child's act is concerned, the most conspicuous antecedent stimulus is obviously the posed question. The pupil's response also takes place within the context of a plethora of accompanying stimuli which constitute the classroom environment. Other stimuli follow on from it and are made available as a consequence of the behaviour having been performed (e.g. the teacher may react enthusiastically, the child may be offered the opportunity to display knowledge by answering, other classmates may marvel at her brilliance, etc.). Further significant factors have to do with, for instance, how hungry Mary is for this sort of attention. The role of antecedent stimuli will be returned to, but for the moment we will stay with the outcomes of performance.

In broadest terms, the relationship between a response and its consequences may lead to that response subsequently being either: (1) increased in frequency; (2) decreased in frequency; or (3) left largely unaffected. As to the first of these eventualities, reinforcement is the process taking place. Reinforcers serve to make preceding actions more likely to recur. Reinforcement can take a positive or a negative form, as will be explained shortly. Before doing so though, we will consider outcomes that serve to reduce the likelihood of similar future actions. (Skinner preferred the term 'reinforcement' to 'reward' due to the greater semantic precision which it afforded, together with its lack of mentalistic trappings. As such, a reinforcer, by definition, has the effect of increasing the probability of the preceding behaviour.)

Punishment

Punishment has the effect of suppressing behaviour so that it is less likely that those acts leading to it will be repeated. Indeed, it too can operate in either a positive or a negative way.

- *Positive punishment* – involves the introduction of something unpleasant (a noxious stimulus) such as a physical blow or stinging criticism, contingent on the appearance of the targeted behaviour.
- *Negative punishment* – requires withdrawing some benefit that, had the individual not acted in that way, would have continued to be enjoyed. Removing privileges such as access to TV or Internet, is an example.

Attempts at control and influence through punishment are common in everyday interaction and may be subtly exercised. They can involve sarcasm, ridicule, derision, reprimands and threats, to specify but a few. However, a number of undesirable side-effects have been associated with punishment (Leslie and O'Reilly, 1999). It can produce negative emotional reactions such as fear and avoidance, which may generalise beyond the response being punished to the punishing agent, say to a teacher, and then have a further dysfunctional impact on attitude to the subject taught and even to school itself.

Extinction

When actions previously reinforced cease, for whatever reason, to produce customary outcomes that are positively valued, the likely long-term effect will also be a reduction in those activities. This occurs through the phenomenon of extinction. Thus while there are important differences between punishment and extinction, both serve to reduce the likelihood of a response (Sarafino, 1996).

Positive reinforcement

Reinforcement, as noted, can be engineered through positive or negative means. Positive reinforcement has been formally defined by Maag (1999: 71) as referring, 'to any stimulus, when presented after the occurrence of a behavior, that increases the future occurrence of the behavior'. He goes on to describe it as 'the most powerful and effective method for increasing or maintaining appropriate behavior' (p. 278). Mary, the pupil in the earlier example, may have had her contribution to the lesson enthusiastically endorsed by the teacher making her more prepared to offer further contributions, given the opportunity. It is positive reinforcement and rewards that are commonly acknowledged when reinforcement is talked of as a social skill, and it is therefore this type around which much of the chapter will be based.

Before moving on, the relationship between positive reinforcement and reward needs to be clarified. For some, such as Martin and Pear (1999), the terms are roughly synonymous. Indeed Nelson-Jones (1997), operating within a counselling framework, declared a preference for 'reward', believing it to be more in keeping with the language of helping. Technically speaking, however, a reinforcer must, by definition, act to increase the frequency of the behaviour on which it is contingent. For Kazdin (1994) a reward, in contrast, is something given and received in return for something done. While it may act as a reinforcer, whether or not it actually does is an empirical question. On this point, and in the classroom context, Zirpoli and Melloy (2001: 165) stressed that 'teachers cannot assume that an item, activity, or other stimulus will be reinforcing to a student'. Kazdin further acknowledged, however, that practically speaking many rewards or events that a person enjoys serve as reinforcers.

Negative reinforcement

Here an act is associated with the avoidance, termination or reduction of an aversive stimulus that would have either occurred or continued at some existing level had the response not taken place. Negative reinforcement and punishment must not be confused (Sarafino, 1996). Although both involve aversive states, in the case of punishment this state is made contingent on the occurrence of the behaviour under focus and has the effect of making that behaviour *less* likely to recur. With negative reinforcement, behaviour resulting in the noxious stimulus being reduced, eliminated or avoided will be *more* probable in future.

Examples of negative reinforcement in everyday life are common. We have a headache, take FeelFine analgesic and the pain disappears, making it more likely that we will take FeelFine the next time a headache strikes. The TV becomes uncomfortably loud when the adverts come on, spurring us to grab the remote control.

One theory is that habit-forming behaviours like drinking alcohol or smoking are maintained through their effect on reducing tension (Stroebe, 2000). Experimental evidence was produced by Craighead *et al.* (1996) that college women with bulimia nervosa and past depression had higher rates of learning on a computerised mental maze task when provided with negative social feedback for errors made, rather than positive feedback for correct responses. It was thought that avoidance or minimisation of negative reactions was the key factor.

No doubt much of our interpersonal interaction is shaped in a similar way through negative reinforcement. Bringing to an end as quickly as possible an interchange with someone found unpleasant, uninteresting or just difficult to relate to, could be accounted for in this way (Cipani, 1990). A similar explanation may be given for why we speak back in defence of our position in conversations where it has been challenged. An argument can be thought of as a logical, reasoned debate or, alternatively, as a quarrel between two people each of whom is out to vanquish the other (Billing, 2001). For Tannen (1998), thinking particularly of the latter, contemporary society increasingly typifies an 'argument culture', with associated confrontation and threats to face. As such, disagreement with our point of view and the prospect of being shown to be wrong can make us feel vulnerable, threatened and humiliated. Having the chance to successfully defend our beliefs and opinions often brings relief and therefore makes responding more likely.

Conversational repair is a further feature of talk (Grove, 1995). Corrections, apologies and disclaimers are brought into play when participants unwittingly break a conversational or societal rule, thereby running the risk of causing confusion or even losing face (Bull, 2002). Viewed as the application of negative reinforcement, breaking the rule may cause embarrassment or discomfort, assuaged by an apology or disclaimer, thereby making it likely that these forms of repair will be relied on again in similar situations.

Allen and Stokes (1987) reported a more formal application of negative reinforcement in managing the disruptive and uncooperative behaviour of children receiving restorative dental treatment. In this case, children were asked to be 'Big Helpers' by lying still and being quiet while the dentist worked. This led to the temporary suspension of treatment. Gradually children had to be 'Big Helpers' for longer periods of time in order to have the dentist suspend treatment for a period. Not only were children markedly more compliant by the last visit but, from readings of heart rate and blood pressure, were significantly less stressed by the experience.

The different types of behavioural consequence outlined in this section are summarised in Box 4.2.

CATEGORIES OF POSITIVE REINFORCEMENT

The vast range of things that we do as we go about our daily lives gives rise to a multiplicity of differing outcomes, both physical and social. Many of these exert a controlling influence through the operation of positive reinforcement. Psychologists have proposed different systems of classification. For Martin and Pear (1999), positive reinforcers can be (1) consumables, (2) activities, (3) manipulative, (4) possessional,

---

Box 4.2 Consequences of behaviour

- *Punishment* – suppresses targeted behaviour:
  - *Positive punishment* – involves the introduction of something unpleasant (e.g. being scolded, slapped, made to feel uncomfortable, etc.).
  - *Negative punishment* – involves the removal of something desired (e.g. TV confiscated, credit card withdrawn, car keys taken away, etc.).
- *Extinction* – eliminates targeted behaviour (e.g. you will stop putting a coin in a particular dispensing machine that consistently fails to deliver a can of soft drink).
- *Reinforcement* – promotes targeted behaviour:
  - *Positive reinforcement* – involves the introduction of something pleasant (e.g. receiving praise, chocolate, attention, money; playing a favourite computer game, etc.).
  - *Negative reinforcement* – involves the removal of something undesirable (e.g. stopping pain, boredom, embarrassment, stress, etc.).

---

and (5) social. Sherman (1990) suggests five similar categories, outlined in Box 4.3, to which we now turn.

Box 4.3 Types of positive reinforcement

- *Primary* – stimuli that are inherently valued (e.g. food, shelter, air, water, sex, etc.).
- *Conditioned* – stimuli that we learn to value (e.g. money, tokens, medals, badges, etc.).
- *Social* – made available through social contact (e.g. praise, attention, approval, confirmation, etc.).
- *Sensory* –based on exposure to certain sounds, sights, smells, tastes, or touches (e.g. music, film, opera, sporting events, etc.)
- *Activity* – being permitted to engage in particular enjoyed activities (e.g. swimming, walking, gardening and other hobbies).

Primary reinforcers

These can be thought of as stimuli, the positive value and reinforcing potential of which do not rely on a process of prior learning. Ones that spring most readily to mind include food, drink, sex, and so on. These are things that we depend on for survival, due to our biological make-up. Despite their fundamental indispensability, the limitations of these as a direct means of influencing the complexities of everyday person-to-person contact will be quickly appreciated. Here the rewards tend to be more subtle.

SKILLED INTERPERSONAL COMMUNICATION

Conditioned reinforcers

This grouping, also called *secondary* reinforcers, is in sharp contrast to the previous. It includes events that have no intrinsic worth but whose power to control behaviour is ultimately derived from an earlier association with primary reinforcers. We have *learned* to value conditioned reinforcers (Sarafino, 1996). Tokens, stickers, vouchers, stamps, badges, stars, and such like, have been incorporated into organised programmes called *token economies* where they are earned for engaging in certain tasks and subsequently exchanged for more basic back-up reinforcers (Kazdin, 1994). In certain circumstances, an originally neutral stimulus can become associated with a number of primary reinforcers. Money, to cite one example, can be used to obtain food, drink, heat, sex, etc. Skinner (1953) called this special class *generalised reinforcers*. Since these are particularly applicable in relation to social reinforcement we will discuss them further under the next sub-heading.

Social reinforcers

Lieberman (2000: 208) defined social reinforcers, in broad terms, as 'stimuli whose reinforcing properties derive uniquely from the behaviour of other members of the same species'. Social behaviour, by definition, pre-supposes the involvement of other people. In the main, the types of rewards that govern and shape it are also contributed by those with whom we mix and intermingle and are a powerful, though often subtle, influence on our actions. Buss (1983) suggested that these rewards can be thought of as either process or content.

Social process rewards

These are an inherent part of interpersonal contact and include, in order of increasing potency, the mere presence of others, attention from them, and their conversational responsivity. An interesting observation is that too much or too little of these activities can be aversive; it is only at a notional intermediate level that they become reinforcing. The attention given by a teacher to a pupil in the same environment may well change from being reinforcing to punishing if it is either withdrawn totally or, at the other extreme, becomes intrusively persistent.

Social content rewards

What takes place within interaction has also rewarding ramifications. Here Buss paid particular heed to the acts of showing deference, praising, extending sympathy and expressing affection. Unlike their process equivalents, these operate along unipolar dimensions and, additionally, pre-suppose a certain type of interpersonal relationship to be relevant and effective. We seldom praise or show affection to complete strangers, for instance.

As well as process and content rewards, individuals can find variously reinforcing, opportunities to compare themselves to others, compete, dominate or self-disclose, and may seek out situations and occasions to indulge themselves accordingly.

Generalised reinforcers

Individuals are moulded as social beings through the influence of the social milieu of which they are a part. As we have seen, the subtleties of the process make use of the judicious distribution, by significant others, of such mechanisms as attention, interest, approval and affection. It is these sorts of activities that lie at the heart of positive responding conceived of as an interpersonal skill. Through them one person can determine what another does without using actual or threatened physical force.

According to Skinner, positive social reactions can be used to shape interpersonal behaviour because they serve as generalised reinforcers. The approval and attention of others are examples. Of approval, he wrote, 'A common generalised reinforcer is approval. . . . It may be little more than a nod of the head or a smile on the part of someone who characteristically supplies a variety of reinforcers. Sometimes . . . it has a verbal form "Right!" or "Good!"' (Skinner, 1957: 53). In the case of attention, he claimed that, 'The attention of people is reinforcing because it is a necessary condition for other reinforcements from them. In general, only those who are attending to us reinforce our behaviour' (Skinner, 1953: 78).

For Lieberman (2000), among others, these aspects of social performance, in that they can be thought of at all as reinforcers in the Skinnerian sense, embrace both learned and unlearned dimensions. To be more specific, the suggestion is that some of the nonverbal features, such as smiles and hugs, may *not* depend on prior experience to be positively valued. In other words, they are a blend of primary and conditioned reinforcers.

Sensory reinforcers

Listening to beautiful music, looking at a striking painting, attending the theatre or watching an exciting sporting event are all attractive possibilities, albeit to varying extents for different individuals. We need only think of the costs and inconveniences that devotees will endure to indulge themselves in these ways, to appreciate that certain quantities and qualities of sensory stimulation can be rewarding.

This fact was exploited by Mizes (1985) in treating an adolescent girl who was hospitalised following complaints of chronic lower-back pain. The extent of this pain was such that she was virtually bed-ridden. Tests and examinations failed to locate any physical cause, and the case was treated as an abnormal behaviour disorder which was being inadvertently held in place through operant conditioning. When opportunities to watch TV, have access to the telephone and receive parental visits were made conditional on demonstrably increased mobility, symptoms gradually subsided.

Activity reinforcers

For Premack (1965), activities rather than things are reinforcing. It is eating and drinking that is of significance, rather than food or drink, as such. Stated formally, the 'Premack principle', as it is commonly known, proposes that activities of low probability can be increased in likelihood if activities of high probability are made contingent on them.

Activity reinforcement can be a powerful means of organising work routines and maximising commitment in a diversity of professional settings including management, health care, sport and education. Williams (1999) pointed out the benefits in the management of patients with eating disorders of walking, gardening or reading (or whatever the client finds attractive) as rewards to be earned by sticking to agreed dietary habits. In sport, the example is give by Martin and Pear (1999) of a swimming coach who produced a 150 per cent improvement in the practice of racing turns at both ends of the pool together with the number of swimming sets completed without stopping. The reinforcing activity was being allowed to take part in a final 10-minute fun activity in the pool, which was made contingent on these elements of training.

In school, pupils may prefer, for example, more practical classes to didactic instruction. Lessons can be arranged in such a way that to get to do practical activities the theory must be understood. The 'Good Behaviour Game', for use with younger pupils, is described by Maag (1999) as a way of improving behaviour in class. If the group record fewer than, say, five tally marks for breaking classroom rules during the day, they win privileges such as a period of 'free time' before going home. More generally, Burden and Byrd (1999) pointed out that being permitted to carry out classroom tasks, such as operating equipment, taking a note to the office, or checking attendance, can be prized activities in some instances. Working on the computer can be a massive incentive.

The potential for these principles to enhance managerial effectiveness and raise output has been recognised for some time (e.g. Komaki, 1982). Increasing productivity was demonstrated, in an early study by Gupton and LeBow (1971), through an internal rearrangement of the various types of task that workers carried out. In this case the workers were part-time telephone sales personnel in industry who sold both new and renewed service contracts. On average, the success rate for attempts at renewals was more than twice that for new sales, so sales personnel tended to devote most of their energies to the former. As far as the firm was concerned this resulted in a general failure to attract new customers. A new regime was imposed whereby five new calls were required before the representatives had an opportunity to make attempts at renewal sales. This contingency resulted in a substantial increase, not only in the number of new contracts sold, but in renewals as well.

It should not be assumed, however, that only certain activities can reinforce. Premack stressed that any behaviour can increase the likelihood of any other provided that the former tends to occur more frequently and, in order to perform it, the latter has to be carried out. In a subsequent modification of this principle, though, Timberlake and Allison (1974) produced evidence in support of their *Response Deprivation Hypothesis*. Thought of in this light, it is having been prevented from engaging in an activity at its optimum level that bestows reinforcing potential on it. The more we have been deprived of an activity in this way, the more powerful it will become.

STIMULUS CONTROL

It was mentioned earlier in the chapter that behaviour can be set in a context of, on the one hand, preceding and accompanying stimuli and, on the other, consequent events. When a certain action only succeeds in eliciting reinforcement in the presence of particular accompanying stimuli then that piece of behaviour is said to be under *stimulus control* (Leslie and O'Reilly, 1999) and those stimuli have become *discriminating stimuli* in respect of it. They signal the availability of a reinforcer for behaving in that way. When the overall context acts in this way then *contextual control* is in operation (Sarafino, 1996).

Many examples of stimulus control spring to mind. The doctor–patient consultation is traditionally a one-sided affair, especially with male doctors (Dickson, 1999b; Street, 2001). This high-control style 'involves behaviors such as asking many questions and interrupting frequently' (Ong *et al.*, 1995: 909). Here blatant attempts by patients to negotiate their own agendas meet with little success. In this setting, doctors' questions perhaps serve as discriminative stimuli indicating to patients when their contributions will be welcomed and when not. Hooper (1995) analysed differences between expert and novice nurses when taking the pulse and blood pressure of senior citizens. She discovered that discriminative stimuli such as casual conversation, client comfort and health-related information differentiated between the two groups in respect of such elements of practice as eye-contact, verbal interaction, use of touch, attending to the client and obtaining the measurement. The perspicacious employee who learns to read the subtle cues that suggest the likelihood of the manager being receptive to new ideas, and accordingly picks an opportunity to propose some innovation, is also being influenced by stimulus control.

Discriminative stimuli, therefore, signal the occasion for particular behaviours to be reinforced and must not be confused with reinforcing stimuli. The latter always function as a *consequence* of the targeted behaviour.

VICARIOUS REINFORCERS

So far we have discussed the direct impact of positive outcome on the acquisition and regulation of the behaviour that brought it about. But the influence of rewards is more wide-ranging. Through observing our actions others learn not only what to do, but how to do it; they benefit from our successes. Kazdin (1994: 244) stated that, 'Individuals are more likely to engage in certain behavior after observing others (models) receiving reinforcing consequences for engaging in those behaviors.'

The implications of this fact for professional practice are far-reaching. A teacher, in a large and busy classroom, may find difficulty providing reinforcement on an individual basis, for appropriate behaviour and accomplishments. In these circumstances much of the teacher-based reinforcement that a pupil receives is likely to be vicarious.

In relation to management, the maxim of 'praise publicly–punish privately', cited by Prue and Fairbank (1981), articulates the potentially vicarious benefits of bestowing rewards in the presence of others. This practice was used effectively by O'Reilly and Puffer (1989) to enhance expressed motivation, satisfaction and productivity among a group of retail sales clerks, when the basis of reward allocation was seen to be fair. On a more cautionary note, however, it should be recognised that:

- praising in public can cause embarrassment for some and, if so, may produce negative rather than positive effects (Giacolone and Rosenfeld, 1987);
- watching others persistently rewarded for something that the observer has done equally competently, but without comparable recompense, may cause resentment and de-motivation. The latter has been referred to as the implicit effects of observed consequences and, as such, distinguished from vicarious facets, by Bandura (1986).

Rewards, vicariously experienced, can influence learning, motivation and emotions. Seeing others rewarded for some action or behaviour can, therefore, act as a strong inducement for the observer to do likewise, when it is inferred that similar outcomes will accrue. Furthermore, when the consequences of actions are socially mediated, a basis is established for reassessing the attractiveness of experienced outcomes through witnessing what happens to others under comparable conditions. Receiving recognition from a supervisor will probably mean much more once it is realised, from observations of interactions with others, that this person rarely acknowledges effort.

Receiving rewards and punishments is associated with the creation of pleasant and unpleasant emotional states. Awareness of these states and circumstances in other people can be emotionally arousing and this facility is believed to account for empathic responsivity to them (Bandura, 1986). The ability to engage empathically with others is, of course, fundamental to effective counselling (Egan, 2001).

INTERPERSONAL EFFECTS OF SOCIAL REWARDS AND REINFORCERS

As shown in Box 4.4, a range of outcomes tends to be associated with social rewards and reinforcers (Dickson *et al.*, 1993; Cairns, 1997). We will now examine the main functions of reinforcement during interpersonal encounters.

Box 4.4 Effects of social rewards and reinforcers

1 Promoting interaction and maintaining relationships.
2 Increasing the involvement of the interactive partner.
3 Influencing the nature and content of the contribution of the other person.
4 Demonstrating a genuine interest in the ideas, thoughts and feelings of the other.
5 Making interaction interesting and enjoyable.
6 Creating an impression of warmth and understanding.
7 Increasing the social attractiveness of the source of rewards.
8 Improving the confidence and self-esteem of the recipient.
9 Manifesting power.

Promoting interaction and maintaining relationships

During social encounters we not only welcome but demand a certain basic level of reward. If it is not forthcoming we may treat this as sufficient grounds for abandoning the relationship in favour of more attractive alternatives. In a review of friendship and peer relations in children by Erwin (1993), characteristics that set popular and unpopular children apart included being rewarding and supportive. Conversely, Jones *et al.* (1982) discovered that college students who were lonely, in comparison with their more gregarious peers, were found to be strikingly less attentive to conversational partners. More extremely, Argyle (1995) noted the marked lack of reinforcement typifying the interpersonal performance of certain categories of patients with mental disorders, such as schizophrenia and depression. He described such patients as unrewarding to the point of being 'socially bankrupt'. Actual conversational deficits of depressives include less fluent, more monotonous speech and poor eye-contact. These individuals, it is argued, 'Fail to engage others and respond with interest and attention, so that interacting with them is aversive and unrewarding' (Hammen, 1997: 118). Impoverished social contact may produce a further deterioration in mental state with fewer opportunities for interpersonal involvement, thus creating a debilitating downward spiral: 'As the individual becomes more depressed, social avoidance leads to further reductions in exposure to positive reinforcement and the problem is compounded' (Walker, 2001: 162).

Increasing active involvement of the interactive partner

For professionals who work mainly with other people, it is important that recipients of the service are encouraged to be fully involved in what takes place, if the goals of the encounter are to be achieved. Promoting active participation in the classroom is a good example. Costs incurred by pupils, in the form of energy expended, lack of opportunity to devote time to competing activities, and fear of getting it wrong, among others, must be offset by the availability of rewards. In some learning situations (e.g. acquiring a novel skill), intrinsic rewards from efficient task performance may be initially limited. Teacher reinforcement is therefore one method of increasing pupil commitment to what is taking place.

Influencing the nature and content of the contribution

Apart from extending the general level of participation, rewards can be administered in a planned and systematic fashion to selectively reinforce and shape contributions along particular lines. When interviewing, the interviewee can be influenced in this way to continue with the detailed exploration of certain topics or issues to the exclusion of others regarded by the interviewer as being of lesser relevance or even counterproductive. In a medical setting, for instance, White and Sanders (1986) demonstrated how patients suffering from chronic pain focused more on their condition in conversation when the interviewer responded to that topic with attention and praise. Selectively reinforcing 'well talk', on the other hand, had the opposite effect, with patients placing less emphasis on their suffering in favour of more positive aspects of their condition.

Martin and Pear (1999) gave a more spectacular example of a young girl who began complaining of headaches. This attracted considerable attention in the form of concern from parents and eventually, as the migraine-like condition worsened, from health workers. No organic cause could be found for her complaint. A behaviour treatment programme was introduced in which all those with whom she came in contact agreed to ignore 'pain behaviour' (e.g. complaining, taking tablets, going to bed, etc.) and praise 'well behaviour' whenever it was manifested. Over a twelve-week period, the mean number of pain behaviours dropped from eight to less than one per day. Using the same principles, teachers can increase the incidence of appropriate pupil behaviour in class (Woolfolk, 1998; Zirpoli and Melloy, 2001).

Before progressing, it should be acknowledged that, when worded in this way, there is little which is either original or profound in the proposition that people are inclined to do things that lead to positive outcomes and avoid other courses of action that produce unwanted consequences. This much is widely known. Indeed the statement may seem so obvious as to be trivial. But Lieberman (2000) makes the telling observation that, despite this general awareness, individuals are often remarkably unsuccessful in bringing about behavioural change both in themselves and in other people. Indeed it has been found that partners of drug abusers often unwittingly encourage the very behaviour that they are trying to eliminate through their inconsistent use of reinforcement and punishment (LePoire et al., 2000). The conclusion drawn by Lieberman (2000: 193) is that, 'Clearly the principle of reward cannot be quite as simple as it sounds'.

Many professionals make surprisingly poor use of this interpersonal skill. Cannell et al. (1977), investigating the performance of survey interviewers, disclosed that adequate or appropriate responses received proportionately less positive interviewer reinforcement than did less desirable reactions. Refusal to respond, the least desirable response, received proportionately the highest levels of reinforcement. Furthermore during investigative interviews, interviewer reinforcement can distort the information-gathering process, leading to false accounts of what took place (Milne and Bull, 1999). For example, Garven et al. (1998) analysed several hundred interview transcripts conducted with children as part of an inquiry into alleged child abuse by seven Californian teachers. They found evidence of several suggestive techniques employed, including praising or rewarding children when they said or did something that fitted in with interviewers' assumptions.

Teachers also have been criticised for failing to make proper use of praise in the classroom. Reviewing a number of studies, Brophy (1981: 8) concluded that its use is 'typically infrequent, noncontingent, global rather than specific, and determined more by students' personal qualities or teachers' perceptions of students' need for praise than by the quality of student conduct or achievement'. Likewise they have been accused of praising on the basis of answers they expect to receive rather than those actually given (Eggen and Kauchak, 1999).

Conveying information about the source: interpersonal attraction

In addition to influencing what recipients say or do, bestowing rewards also conveys information about the giver. Providers of substantial amounts of social reinforcement are usually perceived to be keenly interested in those with whom they interact and what they have to say. They also typically create an impression of being warm, accepting and understanding. Teacher praise and encouragement have been associated with pupil ratings of teacher attraction, trustworthiness, expertness and potency (Kelly and Daniels, 1997) and of satisfaction with the course (Worland, 1998). By contrast, those who dispense few social rewards are often regarded as cold, aloof, depressed, bored or even boring.

Extending this thinking, some investigators, including Clore and Byrne (1974), have made use of the concept of reinforcement in attempting to account for interpersonal attraction. Responses and pleasurable feelings that stem from receiving rewards become associated, it is proposed, with the provider, or even with a third party who happens to be consistently present when they are dispensed. Such attraction, however, is neither universal nor unconditional, depending as it does on how what is taking place is construed by the recipient. The source is more likely to be found to be attractive if the action being praised is regarded by the recipient as praiseworthy; praise from that individual is valued; and if it reflects a change from a more negative disposition by the source towards the recipient (Raven and Rubin, 1983). If, on the other hand, it is suspected that there are ulterior motives for lavish praise or compliments, and ingratiation or manipulation are suspected, liking for the source will suffer (Aronson, 1999).

Influencing perceptions of self

Positive reactions may not only produce more favourable impressions towards those who offer them (in certain conditions), but arguably also result in heightened feelings of self-esteem and self-efficacy in the recipient. Self-esteem refers to the sense of personal worth that an individual entertains, ranging from love and acceptance to hate and rejection. Self-efficacy is a belief in one's ability to successfully accomplish a task or reach a goal (Bandura, 1997). Being given positive information about levels of skill possessed can make us think differently about tackling some task drawing on that capacity. More generally, Sullivan (1953) believed that one's concept of self develops out of the reflected appraisals of significant others. Thus positive rewarding experiences with parents and other key adults lead to positive views of self, while experienced negativity, including blame, constant reprimands, and ridicule, results in feelings of worthlessness. Does this mean then that those receiving praise invariably assume that they are better or more able than those who don't? This is an important question to be returned to shortly.

Self-enhancement versus self-verification

People are not merely passive recipients of the reactions of others. Rather they often make a deliberate effort to present themselves in such a way as to attract a particular type of evaluative response. One motive for this is *self-enhancement*. Through a process of *impression management* or *self-presentation* (Tedeschi, 1981; Leary, 1996) individuals go out of their way to make themselves as appealing as possible to others. The importance of promoting a positive assessment of self, in this way, and being looked on favourably, has been stressed (Pilkington and Smith, 2000; Tesser, 2001). Attention, praise, approval and various other rewards already mentioned, will be valued on these grounds. But what if such reactions clash with our existing perceptions of self and the suggested positive self-evaluations are inconsistent with how we already see ourselves? For some, in certain circumstances, *self-verification* rather than self-enhancement is what counts (Swann *et al.* 1990). It is not necessarily a positive evaluation that is being sought, they reason, but rather one that is consistent with the individual's existing self-referenced views and beliefs. According to Taylor *et al.* (1995), a range of factors including personality and culture, as well as situational aspects, will make self-enhancement rather than self-verification salient. For those with negative views of themselves, receiving information from others that backs up these perceptions (i.e. self-verification) seems to be stressed (Swann, 1997). These findings have interesting and significant ramifications for rewarding and reinforcing. For those with a poor self-concept and low self-esteem, praise, and other positive reactions incongruent with how they regard themselves, may not be appreciated and fail to have a reinforcing influence. Indeed the opposite may be the case. Before leaving the topic, though, it should be mentioned that people vary, more generally, in the extent to which their sense of self-esteem is contingent on external factors such as praise or criticism (Crocker and Wolfe, 1998).

Locus of control

A further dimension of personality that is of functional relevance to social rewards is *locus of control*. While subtle changes in conceptualisation have taken place over the years, this term refers to the extent to which individuals regard themselves, rather than powerful others or mere chance, as having control over what happens to them (Walker, 2001). Those who espouse internal control have the opinion that rewards gained are contingent on their own performance and a reflection of their relatively enduring characteristics and qualities. At the other extreme, an external locus of control is typified by the idea that successes that may occasionally happen are due largely to chance, luck or some external influence. Kennelly and Mount (1985) reported an association between internal control and good academic performance.

Manifesting power

Finally, the possibility of the distribution of rewards as an exercise in power and authority should not be overlooked. Being in a position to determine whether or not another receives something valued confers on the bestower the ability to exert influence and determine the conditions in which rewards will be bestowed. When the giving of rewards is interpreted as an attempt at control, however, resistance to such manipulation may be provoked. This may be a manifestation of *psychological reactance*, or the attempt to assert personal freedom and autonomy when these are thought to be violated (see Chapter 12 for a fuller discussion of the role of power).

BEHAVIOURAL COMPONENTS OF SOCIAL REINFORCEMENT

It will be recalled that, in theory, anything that increases the frequency of the preceding piece of behaviour can be considered a reinforcer. Even if this list is restricted to elements of interpersonal behaviour, the resulting number of potential reinforcers could be extensive. We will therefore restrict coverage to the more widely recognised elements featured in the literature. In doing so, a conceptual distinction will be made between components that are essentially verbal and those that are nonverbal. While this is a convenient way of structuring the section, as noted in Chapter 3 in practice these two channels are closely interwoven.

Verbal components

The verbal channel of communication is a powerful source of social reinforcement. Things said can provide feedback, validate self-views and strengthen feelings of self-esteem and self-worth, or have the opposite effect. Verbal components of reinforcement range in sophistication from simple expressions such as 'OK', to more elaborate responses that relate to some aspect of the functioning of the other.

Acknowledgement/confirmation

This category contains expressions, words, and phrases that acknowledge, confirm or agree with what has been said or done. Examples include verbalisations such as 'OK', 'Yes', 'Right', 'Fine', 'I see', 'That's it', as well as non-lexical vocalisations like 'mm-hmm' and 'uh-huh'. (Strictly speaking the latter would be more appropriately listed under the nonverbal heading but, since they have often been grouped with the other verbal utterances exemplified, it is more convenient to include them here.) These listener responses are a common feature of conversations. It seems that they signal 'that the listener is involved and following the speaker's thoughts' (Brownell, 1995: 183). They have also been shown to be crucial to the regulation of interaction when people talk over the telephone (Hargie *et al.*, 1999).

From a counselling perspective, Ivey and Ivey (1999) referred to these limited listener responses as *minimal encouragements*. They emphasised their role as part of a complex of basic, culturally prescribed attending skills that help the client to continue exploring areas of personal concern during the interview.

The reinforcing consequences of these attending utterances have been revealed in a number of classic experimental investigations, one of the most widely reported of which was that conducted by Greenspoon (1955). This researcher simply asked subjects to produce as many individual words as they could think of. By responding with 'mm-hmm', each time a subject gave a plural noun and ignoring all other types of words, the number of plural nouns mentioned by subjects increased considerably over the course of the experiment.

Not all subsequent investigations, though, have produced such positive outcomes. Rosenfeld (1987) suggests that at least some of these failures could be accounted for by the fact that social reinforcers were administered on a non-contingent basis (subjects were exposed to them regardless of whether they were engaging in the targeted behaviour). For a stimulus to serve as a reinforcer for any specific piece of behaviour and conditioning to take place, it must occur in conjunction with that behaviour (Lieberman, 2000). Incidentally, the lack of contingent application was also one of the reasons offered by Nelson-Gray *et al.* (1989) in explaining why, in their experimental investigation, no discernible increase in interviewee problem-related statements was brought about by increasing the frequency of interviewer minimal encouragements.

Praise/encouragement

Unlike the previous category, here listener reactions go beyond the simple acknowledgement and confirmation of, or agreement with, what has been said or done to express praise or support. Instances of this category of verbal reward range from one-word utterances, e.g. 'Good', 'Excellent' (and various other superlatives), through phrases like 'Well done', 'How interesting', 'Keep it up', to more elaborate avowals of appreciation, as circumstances warrant. These are commonly employed by a broad spectrum of professionals when interacting with those to whom a service is offered. When appropriately administered, reinforcing consequences can be achieved. Professional areas where such effects have been examined are as diverse as organisational management, interviewing and coaching. Martin and Pear (1999) presented, as an example, the case of a basketball coach who used praise to increase the number of supportive comments made by players to other team members, thereby strengthening team spirit. Practice drills were also enhanced in this way. Alternatively, Thompson and Born (1999) demonstrated how praise and verbal prompting could be effective with elderly people suffering from dementia or brain injury in getting them to take part correctly in exercise sessions while attending an adult day-care programme.

Teaching is an activity where opportunities abound for putting praise and approval to good use in rewarding effort and accomplishment in the classroom (Zirpoli and Melloy, 2001). It represents probably the most extensively researched area of application of this type of social reinforcer and several reviews are available (Brophy, 1981; Wheldall and Glynn, 1989; Cameron and Pierce, 1996; Cairns, 1997;

Hancock, 2000). Generally speaking it would seem that significant and beneficial changes can indeed be brought about in:

- student attentiveness (Taylor, 1997);
- on-task behaviour in class (Sutherland *et al.*, 2000);
- student time spent on homework assignments (Hancock, 2000);
- motivation to learn (particularly when good performance is linked to effort rather than intelligence or ability) (Mueller and Dweck, 1998);
- levels of academic achievement (McCowan *et al.*, 1995; Merrett and Thorpe, 1996);
- pupils' and students' evaluations of praise (Elwell and Tiberio, 1994; Bardine, 1999) and the teachers who use it (Kelly and Daniels, 1997). (It should also be mentioned, though, that in the latter study, teacher use of encouragement was better received than praise.)

As a general conclusion therefore it would appear that praise in the classroom can pay dividends. In practice through, there is evidence that:

- teachers put praise to a number of uses apart from rewarding and reinforcing;
- pupils are aware of this;
- praise is not always administered effectively;
- some pupils are more appreciative than others of praise and respond to it differentially.

Brophy (1981) questioned the extent to which techniques such as praise are a prominent feature of the day-to-day classroom discourse of teachers and are used with reinforcing effect. Alternative functions of praise were found to include encouraging, directing, and gaining rapport. Whether praise acts as an effective reinforcer depends on a number of qualifying variables, including:

- features of the pupils, such as reinforcement history;
- the type of task undertaken;
- the nature of the praise;
- the manner in which praise is administered;
- characteristics of the source.

Pupils are also sensitive to a plurality of uses to which teachers put praise and interpret it accordingly. Taylor (1997) found that they applied labels such as 'deserved' (when the performance was good) versus 'instructional'. The latter included (1) encouraging, (2) signalling to others to do the same, and (3) increasing co-operation and participation.

The success of praise as a reinforcer can be increased, according to Hancock (2000) and Burden and Byrd (1999), by ensuring that it:

- is applied contingently;
- specifies clearly the particular behaviour being reinforced;
- is offered soon after the targeted behaviour;
- is believable to the recipient;
- is restricted to those students who respond best to it. Not all do, with some finding this type of reward patronising or embarrassing when delivered in the presence of peers.

Praise and children's socioeconomic status

The influence of such factors as race, gender, age and socioeconomic status on children's susceptibility to reinforcers has been the subject of concerted enquiry. Socioeconomic status attracted the attention of researchers some years ago, leading Russell (1971: 39) to conclude that, 'One of the most consistent findings is that there is a social class difference in response to reinforcement.' Middle-class children have been held to respond better to less tangible reinforcers, including praise and approval, when compared with their lower-class compatriots. The latter, it is assumed, are less likely to be exposed to this type of reinforcement, especially for academic achievement, and are therefore unlikely to attach much value to it, favouring instead tangible rewards like money, food or toys. However, Schultz and Sherman (1976), having undertaken a comprehensive review of the area, were quite adamant that this view was ill-founded.

Relationships between these variables, if they do exist, are likely to be much more convoluted than those intimated by Russell. Miller and Eller (1985), for instance, reported significant increases in subsequent intelligence test scores among lower- and middle-class white children following the praising of initial test performance, but gender differences played a part as well. Thus middle-class, white females were more susceptible than their male counterparts. Praise also improved the performance of lower-class white males, but not females. Elwell and Tiberio (1994) reported that male pupils expressed a greater preference for teachers to praise 'all the time' and 'praise loudly'. With the growing classlessness of much of contemporary society, there seems to have been a reduced interest in this line of research in recent years.

Praise and age

As far as Marisi and Helmy (1984) are concerned, age differences are implicated in determining how praise is reacted to. Comparing the effects of this incentive on performances of 6-year old boys with those of 11 and 17 years on a motor task, they discovered that it was only with the youngest group that praise proved beneficial. Likewise, Campanella Bracken (2001) reported computer-mediated praise leading to enhanced learning in young children. Shifting the focus to perceptions and attitudes towards the praised, Miller and Hom (1997) replicated some earlier findings to the effect that older pupils (8th grade) compared with younger (4th and 6th grades) generally see praised children as being less able. On the other hand, Wheldall and Glynn (1989) have shown that the behaviour of adolescents in class can be effectively managed by the teacher praising acceptable conduct in keeping with rules previously agreed by members, and largely ignoring minor infringements. Here, however, praise was contingently administered, unlike the procedure followed by Marisi and Helmy (1984). Differences in the nature of the behaviour focused on should also be appreciated. The boys in the study by Marisi and Helmy were engaged in the acquisition of a motor skill.

Praise and personality

Several personality factors have been found to mediate the reinforcing impact of praise. The first of these is pupils' locus of control (Kennelly and Mount, 1985). As previously mentioned, people who are essentially internally set hold a belief in their own ability to extract reinforcers from the environment, whereas externals are inclined to put rewards that do come their way down to chance or luck. Internality of control, and an appreciation of the contingency of teacher rewards, was predictive of good academic achievement and teacher ratings of pupil competence in an investigation by Kennelly and Mount (1985). Alternatively, Baron *et al.* (1974) and Henry *et al.* (1979) associated an *external* orientation with receptivity to verbal reinforcement.

Self-efficacy, it will be remembered, refers to a belief in one's ability to succeed at some task or undertaking. Kang (1998) reported a complex relationship between praise, age, gender, academic status and self-efficacy. Praise was positively related to self-efficacy among regular students but negatively so for those at the bottom end in classes with a large spread of ability. This pattern was reversed in groups with a narrow spread of ability. Generally, girls and students at the bottom of the class had lower levels of self-efficacy.

There is good reason to believe, at least with older individuals, that the personality dimension extraversion/introversion may play a further salient role. In particular it seems that extroverts may be more receptive to the effects of praise, while for introverts the punishment of inappropriate responses can produce better results (Boddy *et al.*, 1986; Gupta and Shukla, 1989). Susceptibility to such interpersonal rewards from others seems to be strengthened among those who display a heightened need for approval, and therefore have a predilection to act in ways that will increase the chances of others reacting favourably towards them.

Praise: a possible downside

So far we have painted a consistently positive picture of rewards in general and praise in particular. Being favoured in this way boosts motivation for the rewarded activity, results in more of it, promotes learning, and improves self-image. However, these claims have been challenged (Ryan and Deci, 1996; Lepper *et al.*, 1996). Intrinsic motivation to engage in a task may suffer when external rewards are offered. By having the motivational basis for completing an activity switched from an intrinsic interest in it to some external gratuity such as money, we may gradually come to carry out that activity only for the money. Intrinsic motivation is a powerful impellent to action and anything that minimises its influence can seriously undermine commitment. Consider the scenario in Box 4.5.

Pupils' understanding of the reason for praise being given will determine what they make of it. So far we have assumed that praise, among other things, strengthens belief in ability and promotes self-esteem. Meyer *et al.* (1986) argued that just the opposite may sometimes occur and showed that those subjects praised for success at an easy task and not blamed for failure at a difficult task inferred that their ability for that type of work was low, when they had few other cues on which to base

---

Box 4.5 Intrinsic rewards have it

A group of cross-country runners meet up each lunchtime to cover a four-mile course before getting quickly showered and returning to work. It means that they have only time to grab a quick snack and the free hour is one endless rush – but they enjoy it. One winter's day they meet up as usual. By the end of the second mile, the weather quickly changes and they find themselves facing driving sleet while underfoot the freezing mud is ankle deep. The usual banter gradually dies as the group struggles up a steep rise with several miles still to go. They begin to get colder, wetter, more exhausted and decidedly miserable. One of the runners is finally heard to grumble through chattering teeth, 'If I was being paid to do this, I would resign!'

---

judgements. When praise for success at the easy task was withheld and failure at the difficult task blamed, subjects assessed their ability as being much higher. Similar findings have also been reported suggesting that children can attribute teacher praise to low ability on their part (Miller and Hom, 1997). Black students who were praised for a good academic performance by a white evaluator, who lacked knowledge of their level, assumed that the evaluator had lower expectations of them. They also rated the evaluator less favourably than black students not praised (Lawrence, 2001). Furthermore, Derevensky and Leckerman (1997) discovered that pupils in special education classes tended to receive more praise and positive reinforcement than those in regular classes. Praise does not always carry positive messages, therefore, as far as inferences about ability levels are concerned. Two important and related considerations are: (1) what precisely is praised?, and (2) to what does the recipient attribute its receipt?

Henderlong (2001) and Dweck (2000) pointed out that praise can be:

- of the total person for some particular trait that they possess (person) (e.g. 'What an intelligent boy');
- for what they have done (outcome) (e.g. 'Your essay is excellent');
- for effort or strategy displayed (process) (e.g. 'I'm really impressed with the amount of work you've put into this').

Muller and Dweck (1998) found that children praised for their intelligence, rather than effort, were less likely to want to tackle tasks that would have greater learning potential but would not guarantee success, in favour of those that they knew they could do successfully. Praising ability created vulnerability. When faced with failure such children expressed least enjoyment with the activity, showed less perseverance, and found the experience most aversive. Similarly, Henderlong (2001) discovered that process-focused (compared with person-focused) praise created less adaptive ways of dealing with failure. Moreover, children who attributed praise to their ability levels, rather than hard work, came to see intelligence as a fixed trait rather than something that could be improved (Mueller, 1997).

The extent to which praise can undermine intrinsic motivation and be detrimental to performance is, however, open to debate. In a centrally important article, Cameron and Pierce (1994: 394) carried out an extensive review of some 100 experiments and concluded that 'our overall findings suggest that there is no detrimental effect [of extrinsic rewards] on intrinsic motivation'. Nevertheless, Good and Brophy (1997) cautioned that in the classroom reinforcement must always be applied in such a way as to complement natural outcomes of performance and not undermine intrinsic interest. According to Lieberman (2000), praise and other social rewards are less likely to have this negative effect than are material alternatives.

Response development

There is, in a sense, a progressive sequence of increasing involvement and acceptance which commences with the mere acknowledgement of a response, continues with the positive evaluation of it through praise, and proceeds to the further exploration and development of the content. In this way, having an idea or action form part of the agenda for the ongoing discourse may be looked on as the highest form of praise. It is quite easy for a teacher, manager, interviewer or coach to express a few perfunctory words of acknowledgement or commendation before continuing on a completely different tack. However, the development of a response indicates (1) that the listener must have been carefully attending, and (2) that the content must have been considered worthy of the listener's time and effort to make it part of 'the talk'.

A response can be developed in a number of ways. In the classroom, Burden and Byrd (1999: 95) described how teachers may follow up pupils' contributions by encouraging them to 'clarify initial responses, expand their responses, lift thought to higher levels, and support a point of view or opinion'. Here is a powerful means of providing reinforcement during a lesson, even if it is less frequently used than alternatives already considered. On the other hand, teachers may develop a pupil's contribution by elaborating on it themselves. The potential reward for pupils of having their ideas form part of the lesson will be readily appreciated. In a group, members may be asked to contribute their suggestions and be reinforced by having their responses further explored by other members. In a coaching context, certain individuals can be selected to demonstrate a skill or technique to the other participants for them to develop. If tactfully handled, this form of response development can be highly motivating and positively valued.

Clearly there is a whole range of possibilities for developing responses. Dickson *et al.* (1993), in reviewing some conditioning-type studies, suggested that reflective statements (see Chapter 6) and self-disclosures (see Chapter 9) may function in this way. In general though, research concerning the reinforcing effects of response development is less prevalent than that involving reinforcers included in the previous two categories.

Nonverbal components

The administration of reinforcement is not solely dependent on the verbal channel of communication. It has been established that a number of nonverbal behaviours, such as a warm smile or an enthusiastic nod of the head, can also have reinforcing impact on the behaviour of the other person during interaction. For instance, Rosenfarb (1992:

343) believed that positive change in client behaviour during psychotherapy can be accounted for in this way. He explained how this might operate as follows:

> Often, subtle therapeutic cues serve to reinforce selected aspects of client behavior. A therapist's turn of the head, a change in eye contact, or a change in voice tone may reinforce selected client behavior. . . . One therapist, for example, may lean forward in her chair whenever a client begins to discuss interpersonal difficulties with his mother. Another therapist may begin to nod his head as clients begin to discuss such material. A third may maintain more eye contact. In all three cases, each therapist's behavior may be serving as both a reinforcing stimulus for previous client behavior and as a discriminative stimulus for the further discussion of such relevant material.

Leslie and O'Reilly (1999) also outlined how, in this way, the contribution of inter-actors can serve in turn as discriminative and reinforcing stimuli, although they had verbal rather than nonverbal contributions in mind.

The fact that nonverbal cues can operate to so influence behaviour should not surprise us unduly if it is remembered (see Chapter 3) that the nonverbal channel of communication is frequently more important than the verbal channel with regard to the conveying of information of an emotional or attitudinal nature. Indeed, when information of this type resulting from one channel contradicts that carried by means of the other, greater credence is often placed on the nonverbal message. It would, therefore, seem that the nonverbal channel is particularly adept at communicating states and attitudes such as friendliness, interest, warmth and involvement.

Gestural reinforcement

This category includes relatively small movements of specific parts of the body. 'Gestural' in this sense is broadly defined to encompass not only movements of the hands, arms and head, but also the facial region. Concerning the latter, two of the most frequently identified reinforcers are smiles and eye-contact.

Smiles

In carrying out a satisfaction survey of the quality of school life, Furst and Criste (1997) noted that the boys who took part valued teacher smiles. Some research evidence also suggests that smiles can have a reinforcing effect. In one experiment, Showalter (1974) succeeded in conditioning affect statements through the selective use of smiles by the interviewer. Many studies have combined smiles with other nonverbal and verbal reinforcers. Krasner (1958) combined smiles with head nods and 'mm-hmm' to increase the use of the word 'mother' by subjects. Pansa (1979) increased the incidence of self-referenced affect statements provided by a group of reactive schizophrenics, using a comparable procedure, although Saigh (1981) obtained less positive results. This lack of consistency could be due to smiles being interpreted differently by subjects. LaFrance and Hecht (1999: 45) stated that 'There may be no gesture with more diverse meanings and more varied forms than the human smile. Smiles convey delight and happiness, but people also smile when they feel anything but enjoyment.'

Eye-contact

This is an important element of interpersonal interaction. The establishment of eye-contact is usually a preparatory step when initiating interaction. During a conversation, continued use of this behaviour may indicate our responsiveness to the other, and level of involvement in the exchange (Grove, 1995). Its selective use can, therefore, have reinforcing potential. A positive relationship between interviewer eye-contact and subjects' verbal productivity was documented by O'Brien and Holborn (1979). Goldman (1980) also reported that verbal encouragement could be used to reinforce expressed attitudes more effectively when coupled with eye-contact. The overuse of eye-contact or gaze, though, can also be threatening and cause discomfort or distress.

Gestures

Certain movements of the hands and arms can signal appreciation and approval. Probably the most frequently used gestures of this type in our society are applause and the 'thumbs-up' sign. Head nods are gestures that have a wider relevance. Their frequent use can be seen during practically any interactive episode, being commonly used to indicate acknowledgement, agreement and understanding. As such, they belong to a group of attention-giving behaviours known as 'back-channel' communication (Grove, 1995). Matarazzo and Wiens (1972) found that the use of head nods by an interviewer had the effect of increasing the average duration of utterance given by an interviewee. Although total verbal output of subjects increased significantly, Scofield (1977) obtained a disproportionately higher number of self-referenced statements following contingent application of interviewer head nods combined with a paraphrase, restatement or verbal encouragement.

Proximity reinforcement

Unlike the previous category, the present one includes gross movements of the whole body or substantial parts of it. Proximity reinforcement refers to potential reinforcing effects that can accrue from altering the distance between oneself and another during interaction. A reduction in interpersonal distance usually accompanies a desire for greater intimacy and involvement. However, while someone who adopts a position at some distance from the other participant may be seen as being unreceptive and detached, a person who approaches too closely may be regarded as over-familiar, dominant or even threatening. In the study by Goldman (1980), already referred to, attitudes of subjects were more successfully modified by means of verbal reinforcers when the interviewer stood at a moderate (4 to 5 feet) rather than a close interpersonal distance (2 to 3 feet).

With participants who are seated, as professionals often are during encounters, it is obviously much more difficult to effect sizeable variations in interpersonal distance. However, this can be accomplished, to a certain extent, by adopting forward or backward leaning postures. Mehrabian (1972) reported that a forward leaning posture was one component of a complex of behaviours that he labelled 'immediacy' and which denotes a positive attitude towards the other person. Similarly, Nelson-Jones (1997) believed that this type of posture conveys acceptance and receptivity when used in counselling. As with some other nonverbal reinforcers, studies conducted in part to establish the reinforcing effects of a forward leaning posture, have combined it with several other reinforcers. However, there is some research evidence supporting the reinforcing effects that a forward leaning posture *per se* can have (Banks, 1972).

Touch

This literally represents a complete lack of interpersonal distance and, on occasion, can be used to good effect to encourage a partner to continue with a line of conversation. According to Jones and Yarbrough (1985), it can be construed in a number of ways to convey, among other things, affection, appreciation and support. As such, the relevance of touch to care delivery is evident and its effects in the nursing setting have been reviewed by Routasalo (1999). Wheldall *et al.* (1986) found that when teachers of mixed-gender infant classes used positive contingent touch when praising good 'on-task' classroom behaviour, rates of this type of behaviour rose by some 20 per cent. Nevertheless, as with many forms of nonverbal behaviour, 'Touch and the lack of touch are intriguing and complex entities because the meaning of touch can vary from one situation to the next' (Davidhizar *et al.*, 1997: 204). In many contexts, of course, touch is inappropriate, even socially forbidden, and must be used with according discretion. (See Chapter 3 for further information on touch.)

HOW DO REINFORCERS REINFORCE?

Reinforcement modifies the future probability of the behaviour that led to it, as we have seen. There is much less agreement, however, about just how this is brought about. Three main possibilities will be briefly considered here.

Reinforcement as a direct modifier of behaviour

Favoured by the likes of Skinner (1953), this view is that, essentially, reinforcers function directly and automatically to bring about behavioural change. Two important implications stem from this view, each of which will be considered. The first is that the individual's awareness of what is taking place is not a prerequisite for reinforcement. According to Martin and Pear (1999: 37) 'For reinforcement to increase an individual's behaviour, it is not necessary that that individual be able to talk about or indicate an understanding of why he or she was reinforced.' While reporting findings substantiating this proposition, Lieberman (2000) nevertheless concluded that the circumstances in which reinforcement without awareness takes place tend to be rather contrived or extraordinary.

The second concerns the nature of the relationship between the targeted response and the reinforcing event. Does reinforcement depend on the behaviour in question bringing about a positive outcome (*contingency*) or simply being followed in time by it (*contiguity*)? A belief in contiguity as a necessary and sufficient condition for reinforcement to take place is commonly associated with its unconscious operation. Skinner (1977: 4), for instance, wrote that, 'Coincidence is the heart of operant conditioning. A response is strengthened by certain kinds of consequences, but not necessarily because they are actually produced by it.' The precise nature of the relationship between behaviour and subsequent events in respect of contingency and contiguity is not entirely clear. Wasserman and Neunaber (1986) demonstrated how subjects could be influenced to respond in the mistaken belief that it increased the frequency of a light coming on, which was associated with points being earned, even though the effect was in fact the opposite. We can sometimes infer a causal relationship where none exists.

Reinforcement as motivation

A second possibility is that reinforcers serve largely to motivate. The expectation of receiving a reward for succeeding in a task spurs on further efforts in that direction and makes it more likely that this type of task will be undertaken again. Such incentives may be external and represent the projected attainment of a tangible outcome (e.g. money, food, praise, etc.), or as Bandura (1989) stressed, be internal and derivable from anticipated positive self-evaluations at the prospect of succeeding in the task at hand.

Reinforcement as information

The third possibility adopts the cognitive stance that reinforcers function, in the main, by providing information on task performance. Cairns (1997) discussed reinforcement as feedback. Likewise Sarafino (1996: 146) acknowledged that 'Feedback is implicit in many of the types of reinforcer we receive. If we receive praise or a gift for something we did, the reward also tells us we performed well.' According to Dulany (1968), conditioning results can best be explained in terms of subjects trying to figure out the connection between what they do and the outcomes they experience in a sort of puzzle-solving exercise. Conditioning studies with people are often arranged so that response-contingent points are allocated which can then be exchanged for back-up reinforcers like food or money. The material value of these is usually quite small. Wearden (1988), for example, drew attention to the fact that in some instances, subjects work diligently for paltry financial remuneration. Likewise, when food is the reward it is often left unconsumed, indeed sometimes discarded without being tasted, and yet at the same time subjects continue to work for more.

109

These findings are difficult to reconcile in motivational terms if money or food are thought of as the key inducements. A more plausible explanation, offered by Wearden (1988), portrays the conditioning procedure as a problem-solving exercise in the eyes of the subjects. Points received for an appropriate move are prized, not hedonistically through association with money or food, but on account of the information they contribute to finding a solution to the 'puzzle'.

While conclusive proof to resolve these differences in position is lacking, the present consensus of opinion appears to be that, as far as social performance in everyday situations is concerned, probably little instrumental conditioning takes place without at least some minimal level of conscious involvement (Lieberman, 2000). While recognising exceptions, the effects of reinforcement seem to rely more on a contingent than a mere contiguous association between behaviour and reward (Schwartz, 1989). Furthermore, recipients' understanding of why they received a reward also seems to matter (Miller and Hom, 1997).

GUIDELINES FOR THE USE OF THE SKILL OF REINFORCEMENT

Sets of recommendation for enhancing the effectiveness of reinforcing procedures can be found in different sources (e.g. Maag, 1999; Burden and Byrd, 1999; Zirpoli and Melloy, 2001). In this section seven points concerning the use of the skill which tend to promote its effectiveness will be outlined.

Appropriateness of rewards

Throughout this chapter an attempt has been made to stress the fact that stimuli that may have reinforcing properties in some situations may not have the same effects in others. It is, therefore, important that one remains sensitive to the characteristics of the situation, including the other people involved, when choosing the type of reinforcement to use. (This also applies to most of the other skills included in this book.) Thus some forms of praise that would be quite appropriate when used with a child will seem extremely patronising if used with an adult.

Attention should, in addition, be paid to the reinforcement history of the individual. Not all rewards will be prized equally. Not only is it the case that different people may prefer certain reinforcers to others, but the same individual on different occasions may find the same reinforcer differentially attractive.

Reinforcement given should also be appropriate to the task undertaken and the degree of success achieved. A consideration here has to do with the recipient's perception of equity. Lawler (1983) produced evidence that, at least with material rewards, less satisfaction is expressed when there are discrepancies between what is received and what is felt to be deserved, even when the inequity results in higher recompense than was thought to be merited. Furthermore, as mentioned earlier, people who receive praise for completing a relatively easy task may, if they have little else to go on, assume they have low ability at this type of work (Miller and Hom, 1997).

Genuineness of application

It is important that social rewards are perceived as genuinely reflecting the source's reaction to the targeted person or performance. If not, they may come across as sarcasm, veiled criticism or perhaps as bored habit. Complementarity of verbal and nonverbal behaviour is important in this regard. When seen as an attempt at cynical manipulation, rewards are likely to be counterproductive (Aronson, 1999).

Contingency of reinforcement

In order for the various social behaviours reviewed in this chapter to function as effective reinforcers, it is important that their application be made contingent on the particular action which it is intended to modify. Martin and Pear (1999: 38) offered advice to 'be sure that the reinforcers are contingent upon specific behaviours that you want to improve'. This does not mean that the random use of such behaviour will fail to produce an effect. It may well serve to create a particular impression of the provider, interpret the situation in a particular way, or put the other person at ease. It is highly improbable, however, that it will selectively reinforce as desired.

In many situations, it may be prudent to specify, quite precisely, the behavioural focus of attention. Burden and Byrd (1999) recommended that praise by teachers should specify the particulars of the behaviour being reinforced.

Frequency of reinforcement

It is not necessary to reinforce constantly each and every instance of a specific response for that class of response to be increased. It has been found that, following an initial period of continual reinforcement to establish the behaviour, the frequency of reinforcement can be reduced without resulting in a corresponding reduction in target behaviour. This is called *intermittent* reinforcement and many real-life activities are maintained in this way. Not only do frequencies of performance not decline in the face of intermittent reinforcement, they actually increase (Leslie and O'Reilly, 1999) and become more resistant to extinction. Accordingly, Maag (1999) recommended that rewards should be used sparingly to maximise their reinforcing efficacy. A related recommendation is that recipients have access to these only after performing the desired behaviour.

Along similar lines, *gain/loss theory* predicts that when the receipt of a reward is set against a backdrop of a general paucity of positive reaction from that source its effect will be enhanced (Aronson, 1999).

Variety of reinforcement

The continual and inflexible use of a specific reinforcer will quickly lead to that reinforcer losing its reinforcing properties. The recipient will become satiated. If an interviewer responds to each interviewee statement with, for example, 'good', this utterance will gradually become denuded of any evaluative connotations, and consequently will rapidly cease to have reinforcing effects. An attempt should therefore be made to employ a variety of reinforcing expressions and behaviours while ensuring that they do not violate the requirement of appropriateness.

Timing of reinforcement

A broadly agreed recommendation is that a reinforcing stimulus should be applied directly following the target response. As put by Zirpoli and Melloy (2001: 166) 'As the interval between the behavior and reinforcement increases, the relative effectiveness of the reinforcer decreases.' If reinforcement is delayed there is a danger that other responses may intervene between the one to be promoted and the presentation of the reinforcer. Making the individual aware of the basis on which the reinforcer, when it is delivered, is gained may help to reduce the negative effects of delay. This is not to overlook the fact that, from a motivational viewpoint, the availability of immediate payoff is likely to have greater incentive value than the prospect of having to wait for some time for personal benefits to materialise.

Selective reinforcement

In this context selective reinforcement refers to the fact that it is possible to reinforce selectively certain elements of a response without necessarily reinforcing it in total. This can be effected during the actual response. Nonverbal reinforcers such as head nods and verbal reinforcers like 'mm-hmm', are of particular relevance in this respect since they can be used without interrupting the speaker. Selective reinforcement can also be applied following the termination of a response. Thus a teacher may partially reinforce a pupil who has almost produced the correct answer to a question, with, 'Yes, John, you are right, Kilimanjaro is a mountain, but is it in the Andes?' By so doing the teacher reinforces that portion of the answer which is accurate, while causing the pupil to rethink the element which is not.

Allied to this process, *shaping* permits nascent attempts at an ultimately acceptable end performance to be rewarded. By systematically demanding higher standards for rewards to be granted, performances can be shaped to attain requisite levels of excellence. The acquisition of most everyday skills like swimming, driving a car, or playing a violin, involve an element of shaping (Martin and Pear, 1999). If reinforcers were withheld until the full-blown activity was performed in accordance with more advanced criteria of excellence, learning could take a long time and be an extremely thankless task for the learner.

OVERVIEW

As a social skill, reinforcement is central to interpersonal interaction. What people do, what they learn, the decisions that they take, their feelings and attitudes towards themselves and others, indeed the sorts of individuals they become, can be shaped and moulded by the reactions of others.

While the basic notion that people tend to behave in ways that bring about positive outcomes for them is scarcely iconoclastic, it does seem that in many professional circles reinforcement as a social skill is not well used. Brophy (1981), for example, questions whether teachers routinely use praise in the classroom in such a way as to be maximally reinforcing of desired behaviour and achievement.

The sorts of social reinforcers that we have concentrated on in this chapter can be divided, for convenience, into the verbal and the nonverbal. In practice, however, these two channels operate closely together. Verbal reinforcers include such reactions as acknowledging, confirming, praising, supporting and developing the other's responses by a variety of potential means. Nonverbally, gestures such as smiles, head nods, and eye-contact, together with grosser body movements, including reducing interpersonal distance, forward posture leans and touch, have been found to have reinforcing possibilities.

When utilised in accordance with the guidelines outlined above, reinforcement can serve to promote interaction and maintain relationships; increase the involvement of the interactive partner; make interaction interesting and enjoyable; demonstrate a genuine interest in the ideas, thoughts and feelings of the other; create an impression of warmth and understanding; enhance the interpersonal attractiveness of the source; and improve the confidence and possibly the self-esteem of the recipient.

It is worth repeating that there is no implication that any of the verbal or nonverbal behaviours associated here with the skill of reinforcement *must* invariably have the reinforcing effects outlined. Nor is it assumed that only those ways of relating mentioned can have reinforcing potential. Whether or not reinforcement takes place will be determined by a complex of factors including those to do with the source, the recipient, the context, the reward itself and the way in which it is delivered.

Chapter 5

Questioning

INTRODUCTION

THE QUESTION IS A key constituent of the DNA of interactional life. In our communication courses we use an exercise in which we ask four volunteers to come to the front of the class. We then instruct them to carry on a conversation about 'the events of the week'. The only rule is that no one is allowed to ask a question. Two things happen: first, the interaction is very stilted and difficult; second, someone very quickly asks a question. To continue with the above analogy, in the absence of questioning DNA, the communication organism often becomes unstable and eventually dies.

Questioning is perhaps one of the most widely used interactive skills, and one of the easiest to identify in general terms. As we shall see, however, and as stated by Hawkins and Power (1999: 235): 'To ask a question is to apply one of the most powerful tools in communication.' Questions are at the heart of most interpersonal encounters. Information seeking is a 'basic human activity . . . that contributes to learning, problem solving, decision making, and the like' (Mokros and Aakhus, 2002: 299). Indeed, Waterman *et al.* (2001: 477) argued that 'Asking questions is a fundamental part of communication, and as such will be an important factor in the work of many professionals.' In most social encounters questions are asked and responses reinforced – this is the method whereby information is gathered and conversation encouraged.

Society is fascinated by questions and answers. Those involved in public question and answer sessions have become the gladiators of the electronic era. Let us take a few examples. Contestants in TV quiz shows can win fame and fortune just by knowing the answers to questions they are asked. Their 'hosts', or interrogators, on these shows are already household names. TV and radio interviewers also become celebrities because they are good at asking the right questions, albeit in an entertaining fashion. Courtroom dramas, in which lawyers thrust rapier-like questions at innocent and guilty defendants or witnesses, are ubiquitous. So, too, with police films where the skilled detective eventually breaks down the recalcitrant suspect through insightful and incisive questioning. 'Question time' in the UK House of Commons and Senate Investigations in the USA, both of which involve hard and often harsh questioning, have a special type of fascination for viewers.

These examples underline the ultimate power and potential of questions as contributors to success or failure across different contexts. They also reflect the fact that this is a core interpersonal skill. But what exactly is meant by the term? A question can be defined as a request for information, whether factual or otherwise. This request for information can be verbal or nonverbal. As delineated by Stewart and Cash (2000: 79) 'A question is *any statement or nonverbal act that invites an answer.*' For example, a high-pitched 'guggle' such as 'hmmm?' after someone has made a statement is a form of request to the speaker to continue speaking. Similarly, a nod of the head, after asking one member of a group a question, can indicate to another group member that the question is being redirected and a response expected. Questions, then, may be nonverbal signals urging another to respond, or they may even be statements uttered in an inquisitive fashion; for example, 'Tell me more'; or 'You realise what will happen?' Statements which request information are termed *prosodic questions*, and defined as 'declarative sentences containing question cues that may be intonational, or these utterances are marked as questions by means of a variety of contextual cues' (Woodbury, 1984: 203). In the legal context, prosodic questions are widely used by attorneys (e.g. 'You were still in your home at that time?'), especially during the cross-examination of witnesses (Dillon, 1997).

Although a question can be posed nonverbally, most questions in social interaction are verbal in nature. At the same time, there are certain nonverbal signals that should accompany the verbal message if a question is to be recognised as such. One paralinguistic signal is the raising or lowering of the vocal inflection on the last syllable of the question. Other nonverbal behaviours include head movements, rapidly raising or lowering the eyebrows, and direct eye-contact at the end of the question accompanied by a pause. The function of these nonverbal behaviours is to emphasise to the other person that a question is being asked and a response is expected.

The skill of questioning is to be found at every level in social interaction. Young children, exploring a new environment, seem to be naturally inquisitive, always seeking answers to an ever increasing number of questions. At this stage questions play a crucial role in their learning and development process, as they attempt to assimilate information in order to make sense of their surroundings. The importance of the skill of questioning is, therefore, recognised from an early age.

Investigations into the use of questions in various professional contexts have been carried out for decades. An early study was conducted by Corey (1940), in which she had an expert stenographer make verbatim records of all classroom talk in six classes. It was found that, on average, the teacher asked a question once every 72 seconds. Some thirty years later, Resnick (1972) working with teachers and pupils in an infant school (serving 5- to 7-year-old children) in south-east London, found that 36 per cent of all teacher remarks were questions. Furthermore, this figure increased to 59 per cent when only extended interactions were analysed.

In a review of such studies, Dillon (1982) reported results to show that teachers ask about two questions per minute, while their pupils taken as a whole only ask around two questions per hour, giving an average of one question per pupil per month. When the teachers were surveyed about their use of questions, it was found that they actually asked three times as many questions as they estimated they had, and received only one-sixth the number of pupil questions estimated. However, as previously mentioned, reticence at asking questions is not the general norm for children. For example, Tizard *et al.* (1983) radio-recorded 4-year-old girls at home and at school and found that on average per hour the children asked twenty-four questions at home and only 1.4 at school. Interestingly, one major reason given by students for their reluctance to ask questions in class is fear of a negative reaction from *classmates* (Dillon, 1988). Daly *et al.* (1994), in a study in the US, found a significant and negative correlation between question-asking and age in pupils between 13 and 16 years old. As pupils got older they felt *less* comfortable about asking questions in class. Daly *et al.* also found that in terms of question-asking the following felt more at ease:

* males;
* whites;
* higher income groups;
* those with higher self-esteem;
* those who felt accepted by the teacher.

Such findings indicate that teachers need to be aware of the many facets pertaining to classroom questioning.

An analysis of the use of questions by doctors reveals parallel findings. As Brashers *et al.* (2002: 259), in their review of information exchange in the consultation, put it: 'Physicians ask most of the questions and patients provide most of the infor-mation.' Indeed, West (1983) found that, out of a total of 773 questions identified in twenty-one doctor–patient consultations, only sixty-eight (9 per cent) were initiated by patients. Furthermore, when patients did ask questions nearly half of these were marked by speech disturbances, indicating discomfort at requesting information from the doctor. Likewise, Sanchez (2001) cited a study in which, during an average consultation time per patient of 2.1 minutes, doctors asked 27.3 questions. Such a pattern and volume of doctor questions means that patients have little scope to reply, let alone formulate a question. Yet, one of the key elements rated most highly by patients when receiving bad news is the opportunity to ask questions (Hind, 1997).

The difficulties faced by patients in asking questions were highlighted by Skelton and Hobbs (1999), who found that they often prefaced them with the phrase 'I was wondering . . .', whereas doctors never used this expression with patients. Interestingly, the only time they did use it was when they telephoned colleagues. Likewise, Wynn (1996) found that medical students quickly learned how to handle patient-initiated questions – by adopting the strategy of asking unrelated doctor-initiated ones. In this way, they maintained control of the consultation. However, Parrott *et al.* (1992), in a study of paediatrician–patient communication, found that while paediatricians generally asked more questions than patients, during consultations in which they specifically addressed concerns raised by patients more questions were subsequently asked by the latter. It would therefore seem that patient questions can be encouraged (and of course discouraged) by the approach of the doctor.

In relation to community pharmacy, Morrow *et al.* (1993) carried out a study in which they recorded a series of community pharmacist–patient consultations. They found that patients asked on average 2.5 questions per consultation compared with an average of 4.1 for pharmacists. This ratio of patient questions is much higher than that found in doctor–patient consultations. Interestingly, a number of the questions asked by these patients related to requests for clarification about what the doctor had previously told them. This suggests that either they felt more at ease asking questions of the pharmacist than indicating lack of understanding to the doctor, or that they had subsequently thought of questions they would have liked to have been able to ask the doctor. Morrow *et al.* argued that the public may have a view that since pharmacies are readily and easily accessible, pharmacists are probably 'approachable' professionals. Furthermore, the fact that in most instances clients are paying directly for the services they receive may mean that they feel more empowered to ask questions in community pharmacies.

These findings reflect the control differential in relation to questioner and respondent. As noted by Gee *et al.* (1999: 112) 'there is generally a substantial status, power and expertise differential between interviewer and respondent'. Indeed, this power imbalance was noted in a humorous fashion by Lewis Carroll in *Alice's Adventures In Wonderland* where a father responds to his child's questions as follows:

'I have answered three questions and that is enough',
Said his father 'don't give yourself airs!
Do you think I can listen all day to such stuff?
Be off, or I'll kick you down stairs.'

In most contexts it is the person of higher status, or the person in control, who asks the questions. Thus the majority of questions are asked by teachers in classrooms, by doctors in surgeries, by nurses on the ward, by lawyers in court, by detectives in interrogation rooms, and so on. For this reason some counselling theorists have long argued that counsellors should try not to ask *any* questions at all of clients, to avoid being seen as the controller of the interaction (Rogers, 1951). Another aspect is the attitude of the questioner. As noted by Fiedler (1993b: 362), 'The way in which a person is questioned may have a substantial effect on his or her credibility, regardless of what he/she actually says.' For example, witnesses in court or candidates at selection interviews may be treated with the utmost respect when being questioned, or alternatively dealt with in an offhand manner. As well as directly impacting on the respondent's self-esteem and confidence, such treatment is in turn likely to have an impact on how the jury or selection panel respectively evaluate the responses.

A related facet is that the respondent in many instances feels under stress when being questioned. This is certainly true in the above examples where stress and anxiety are often experienced by patients on the ward or in the surgery, by suspects in police stations, by pupils in classrooms, and by defendants in court. Furthermore, in the latter two cases, the person asking the questions already knows the answers, and this makes these situations even more stressful and removed from normal interaction.

In everyday conversation, we do not ask questions to which we already know the answers, or if we do we employ elaborate verbalisations to explain our behaviour ('I was surprised to discover something . . . Let me see if you can guess . . .').

In the courtroom, it is a long-known maxim that lawyers should only ask questions to which they already know the answers. In this context, the creation of stress in witnesses is regarded as a legitimate tactic, and this is developed by a rapid-fire questioning approach. Take the excerpt in Box 5.1, involving a sequence of questions

---

Box 5.1 Excerpt from the OJ Simpson trial

Q: When you entered the home, did you go directly out the front door to view the bodies once again or did you at that time begin to walk around and make observations?

A: No. I was led by Officer Riske.

Q: All right. The purpose in taking that route was to get back to where you had started, but in a different place, right?

A: Yes, sir.

Q: And to get there without walking through the pooling of blood that was around the area, that was your purpose, right?

A: Yes. Yes, sir.

Q: How long would you say you spent at the crime scene from that vantage point up on the steps I believe you told us on that occasion?

A: Once Officer Riske brought us out into the landing? Just long enough to point out a few items of evidence, show us the footprints and then walk us back along the right side of those shoeprints.

Q: Okay. Well, how long do you think you spent there?

A: Couple minutes.

Q: Maybe only two?

A: Two, three minutes.

Q: Okay. And you made the observations you described for us on direct examination about Mr Goldman, the other evidence that was lying around?

A: Officer Riske was pointing them out with his flashlight.

Q: Okay. These are things he had discovered and he was showing them to you. These were not things that you were discovering as a detective, right?

A: I was listening and he was pointing them out, yes, sir, that's correct.

Q: Were you?

A: No. We were quiet listening to his – his lead.

Q: And he told you that he had seen them there when he first came on the scene a little after midnight?

A: Yes.

Q: Now, after spending two, three minutes there, where did you go?

A: We walked down along the pathway that's on the north side of the residence, looked at the gate.

Q = Mr Bailey, Defence Counsel
A = Mark Fuhrman, LAPD Detective

---

posed by Defence Counsel Mr Bailey to Mark Fuhrman, one of the LAPD detectives at the murder scene in the famous OJ Simpson trial. Such a sequence, where one question is asked every few seconds, the respondent does not know what to expect next, and the answers are already known by the questioner, would undoubtedly put most people under pressure.

In the classroom, however, the heightened anxiety of pupils may be dysfunctional, and detrimental both to learning and to pupil–teacher attitudes. Teachers need to bear this in mind when employing this skill.

FUNCTIONS OF QUESTIONS

Stenstroem (1988: 304) pointed out that 'It is difficult to imagine a conversation without questions and responses. They do not only constitute a convenient means of starting a conversation but also make it a great deal easier to carry on and can be used for a variety of purposes.' While 'the essential function of a question is to elicit a verbal response from those to whom the question is addressed' (Hawkins and Power, 1999: 236), in fact questions serve a range of functions, depending on the context of the interaction. Thus questions are asked by:

- salespeople to assess customer needs and relate their sales pitch to the satisfaction of these needs (Heiman and Sanchez, 1999);
- negotiators to slow the pace of the interaction and put pressure on their opponents (see Chapter 13);
- pharmacists to facilitate diagnoses (Morrow and Hargie, 2001).

The main general functions of questions are outlined in Box 5.2.

Box 5.2 Functions of questioning

Questions can be used to:

1   obtain information
2   maintain control of an interaction
3   arouse interest and curiosity concerning a topic
4   diagnose specific difficulties the respondent may have
5   express an interest in the respondent
6   ascertain the attitudes, feelings and opinions of the respondent
7   encourage maximum participation from respondents
8   assess the extent of the respondent's knowledge
9   encourage critical thought and evaluation
10 communicate, in group discussions, that involvement and overt participation by all group members is expected and valued
11 encourage group members to comment on the responses of other members of the group
12 maintain the attention of group members (e.g. by asking questions periodically without advance warning).

However, it should be realised that the type of question asked influences the extent to which each of these various functions can be fulfilled. Indeed it is the responses made to questions that determine whether or not the objective has been achieved. In this sense, a question is only as good as the answer it evokes.

TYPES OF QUESTION

Several different classifications of questions have been proposed. Once again, the context is important – whether it be interviewing, teaching, counselling, interrogating or merely engaging in social conversation – and the type of questions used varies accordingly. Rudyard Kipling (1902) put forward the following early categorisation of questions:

> I keep six honest serving men,
> (They taught me all I knew);
> Their names are What and Why and When,
> And How and Where and Who.

As will be seen, these lines reflect, to a fair degree, the different classifications of questions that have been identified.

Closed/open questions

The most common division of questions relates to the degree of freedom, or scope, given to the respondent in answering. Those that leave the respondent open to choose any one of a number of ways in which to answer are referred to as open questions, while those which require a short response of a specific nature are termed closed questions.

Closed questions

These usually have a correct answer, or can be answered with a short response selected from a limited number of possible options. There are three main types:

1   *The selection question.* Here the respondent is presented with two or more alternative responses from which to choose. As a result, this type is also known as an *alternative question* or *forced-choice question*. Examples include:

- 'Would you rather have Fyfe, Cameron or Rodgers as the next President?'
- 'Do you want to travel by sea or by air?'

2   *The yes–no question.* As the name suggests, this question may be adequately answered by 'yes' or 'no', or by using some equivalent affirmative or negative. Examples include:

- 'Did you go to university?'
- 'Has there been any bleeding?'

3   *The identification question.* This requires the respondent to identify the answer to a factual question and present this as the response. This may involve:

- recall of information, e.g. 'Where were you born?'
- identification of present material, e.g. 'Where exactly is the pain occurring now?'
- queries about future events, e.g. 'Where are you going on holiday?'

Closed questions have a number of applications. They are usually easy to answer, and so they are useful in encouraging early participation in an interaction. In fact-finding encounters, they are of particular value and are often used in a variety of research and assessment type interviews. In the research interview it is the responses of subjects that are of importance, and responses to closed questions are usually more concise and therefore easier to record and code than responses to open questions; this in turn facilitates comparisons between the responses of different subjects. In many assessment interviews, the interviewer has to ascertain whether or not the client is suitable for some form of grant or assistance and so find out whether the person meets a number of specified requirements (e.g. a social welfare official has to ask a client about financial affairs, family background, etc., before deciding on eligibility for state allowances). Here again, closed questions are of value.

Morrow *et al.* (1993) found that almost all pharmacist questions were closed in nature and that 69 per cent of these were of the yes–no variety. They argued that pharmacists were following the clinical algorithm approach of eliminative questioning for diagnosis. While this approach, if carried out expertly, should result in the correct clinical conclusion, it is not without drawbacks in that important information may be missed. For example, one of the clients in their study was suffering from very severe toothache for which the pharmacist had recommended a product and was completing the sale when the client asked 'What about if you've taken any other tablets? I've taken Paracodol.' This unsolicited enquiry provoked further questions and subsequently altered the pharmacist's dosage recommendations.

Closed questions can usually be answered adequately in one or a very few words. They are restricted in nature, imposing limitations on the possible responses that the respondent can make. They give the questioner a high degree of control over the interaction, since a series of such questions can be prepared in advance in order to structure a given social encounter, and the answers that the respondent may give can usually be estimated. Where time is limited and a diagnosis has to be made, or information gathered, closed questions may be the preferred mode.

Open questions

These can be answered in a number of ways, the response being left open to the respondent. Here the respondent is given a higher degree of freedom in deciding which answer to give. Open questions are broad in nature, and require more than one or two words for an adequate answer. In general they have the effect of 'encouraging clients to talk longer and more deeply about their concerns' (Hill and O'Brien, 1999: 113). At the same time, however, some open questions place more restriction on respondents than others, depending on the frame of reference subsumed in the question. Consider the following examples of questions asked by a detective of a suspect:

1   'Tell me about your spare time activities.'
2   'What do you do in the evenings?'
3   'What do you do on Saturday evenings?'
4   'What did you do on the evening of Saturday, 19 January?'

In these examples, the focus of the questions has narrowed gradually from the initial very open question to the more restricted type of open question. This could then lead into more specific closed questions, such as:

5   'Who were you with on the evening of Saturday, 19 January?'
6   'Where were you at 7.00 pm that evening?'

This approach, of beginning an interaction with a very open question and gradually reducing the level of openness, was termed a *funnel sequence* (Kahn and Cannell, 1957) (see Figure 5.1). Such a structure is common in counselling interviews, where the helper does not want to impose any restrictions on the helpee about what is to be discussed, and may begin a session by asking 'What would you like to talk about?' or 'How have things been since we last met?' Once the helpee begins to talk, the helper may then want to focus in on certain aspects of the responses given. Likewise, in the medical interview, Cohen-Cole and Bird (1991: 13) pointed out that:

> A considerable body of literature supports the use of open-ended questioning as an efficient and effective vehicle to gain understanding of patients' problems. To be sure, after an initial nondirective phase ... the doctor must ask progressively more focused questions to explore specific diagnostic hypotheses. This ... has been called an 'open-to-closed cone'.

An alternative approach to this sequencing of questions is to use an *inverted funnel* (or *pyramid*) *sequence*, whereby an interaction begins with very closed questions and gradually opens out to embrace wider issues. Such an approach is often adopted in careers guidance interviews in which the interviewer may want to build up a picture of the client (e.g. academic achievements, family background, interests) before progressing to possible choice of career and the reasons for this choice (e.g. 'Why do you think you would like to be a soldier?'). By using closed questions initially to obtain information, the careers interviewer may then be in a better position to help the client evaluate possible, and feasible, career options.

A third type of questioning sequence is the *tunnel sequence*, also known as a 'string of beads' (Stewart and Cash, 2000). Here, all the questions employed are at the same level and are usually closed. Such a sequence may be used in certain types of

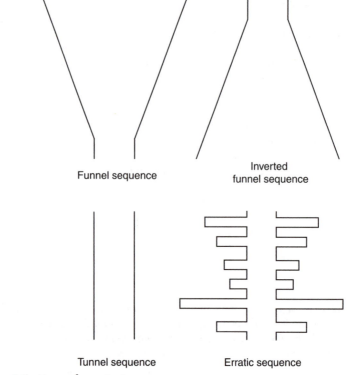

Funnel sequence

Inverted funnel sequence

Tunnel sequence

Erratic sequence

Figure 5.1 Types of questioning sequence

assessment interview, wherein the objective is to establish a set of factual responses. This type of closed tunnelling for information is often characteristic of screening interviews, where the respondent has to be matched against some pre-set criteria (e.g. eligibility for some form of state welfare benefit or grant). A closed tunnel sequence of questions is also used by lawyers in court when they wish to direct a witness along a predetermined set of answers (as can be seen from the transcript in Box 5.1).

There is research evidence to suggest that a consistent sequence of questions facilitates participation and understanding in respondents, whether the sequence be of a tunnel, funnel or inverted funnel nature. On the other hand, an *erratic sequence* of open and closed questions is likely to confuse the respondent and reduce the level of participation. Erratic sequences of questions (also known as rapid variations in the level of cognitive demand) are common in interrogation interviews where the purpose is to confuse suspects and 'throw them off guard' since they do not know what type of question to expect next. Indeed, in courtrooms, Kestler (1982: 156) recommended that when lawyers wish to trap witnesses they should use an erratic sequence, involving 'a quick change of focus designed to catch the witness off-balance, with thoughts out of context'.

Open questions are useful in allowing a respondent to express opinions, attitudes, thoughts and feelings. They do not require any prior knowledge on the part of the questioner, who can ask about topics or events with which they are not familiar.

They also encourage the respondent to talk, thereby leaving the questioner free to listen and observe. This means, of course, that the respondent has a greater degree of control over the interaction and can determine to a greater extent what is to be discussed. It also means that the questioner has to pay attention to what is being said in order to show interest and attentiveness.

Another advantage is that the respondent may reveal information that the questioner had not anticipated. Where a respondent has a body of specialised knowledge to relate, the use of open questions can facilitate the transmission of this knowledge. At the same time, however, where time is limited, or with over-talkative clients, they may be inappropriate. Answers to open questions may be time-consuming, and may also contain irrelevant, or less vital, information.

Comparing open and closed questions

Several research studies have examined the relative effects of open and closed questions in different situations. In an early investigation, Dohrenwend (1965) found that, in research interviews, responses to open questions contained a higher proportion of self-revelation than did responses to closed questions when the subject matter under discussion was objective, and a lower proportion when the subject matter was subjective. This finding suggests that when concerned with self-disclosures, closed questions may be more effective in keeping the respondent to the topic of the question (for more information on self-disclosure see Chapter 9). Dohrenwend also found, however, that responses to open questions were about three times longer than those to closed ones, as measured by amounts of verbalisation. Again, responses to subjective open questions were significantly shorter than responses to objective open questions, whereas length of response to closed questions did not vary with subject matter.

Generalisations about the relative efficacy of open or closed questions are difficult, since the intellectual capacity of the respondent must be taken into consideration. It has long been known that open questions may not be as appropriate with respondents of low intellect. Schatzman and Strauss (1956) compared respondents who had not gone beyond grammar-school level, with respondents who had spent at least one year at college. They found that open questions tended to be more effective with the latter group than with the former, as judged by the questioning behaviour of experienced interviewers who were given a certain degree of freedom about what type of questions to employ. The interviewers used more open questions with the respondents of higher education than with those of lower education. Dohrenwend concluded that closed questions offer more definite advantages than open questions in research interviews because they exert a tighter control over respondents' answers. Open questions, while answered in more detail, tended to result in responses that deviated from the topic of the question, whereas with closed questions the respondent was more likely to answer the question in a direct fashion.

However, although closed questions may facilitate control, they also have disadvantages in research interviews. Dillon (1997) illustrated how both types of question may result in missing or inaccurate information being gathered. He showed how, when asked the open question of what they preferred in a job, only half as many respondents mentioned a 'feeling of accomplishment' as those who selected it when it was presented as one of the alternatives in closed format. On the other hand, good pay was the most frequently volunteered answer to the open question, but the least frequently selected alternative in the closed. Furthermore, some 60 per cent of responses to the open question did not appear in the five main alternatives to the closed. If the factor a respondent considers most important is missing from the list attached to a closed question, it is not likely to be mentioned and instead some of the presented factors will be offered as the answer. This is because the respondent perceives one of the 'rules' of the task to be that of having to make a choice from the presented list. Unless told otherwise, the respondent assumes that the items on the list are the sole focus of the questioner. On the other hand, if only the open question is used, the respondent may simply overlook one or more important factors. Dillon therefore recommended the use of open questions with a range of respondents in order to produce an exhaustive list of alternatives for later inclusion in closed question format in survey interviews.

Research comparing the use of open and closed questions in counselling has found (Dickson *et al.*, 1997) that open questions are more effective in:

- promoting interviewee self-disclosures;
- producing more accurate responses;
- increasing perceived counsellor empathy.

Thus most texts in the area recommend that counsellors should concentrate on asking open questions. For example, Egan (2002: 121) proffered the following advice to helpers: 'As a general rule, ask open-ended questions . . . Counselors who ask closed questions find themselves asking more and more questions. One closed question begets another.'

In a different context, Loftus (1982) found that, in the questioning of eye-witnesses, open questions produced more accurate information, but less overall detail, than specific closed questions. As a result, she recommended that in the questioning of eye-witnesses, questions should be open initially ('Tell me what happened') to obtain accuracy of information, followed by specific closed questions ('What age was he?') to obtain a fuller picture. This recommendation has been widely confirmed in studies of forensic interviewing (see Memon and Bull, 1999).

Another feature that needs to be taken into consideration in any examination of the relative effects of open and closed questions is the length of the question itself. There is evidence to indicate that duration of responses is related to length of questions, in that longer answers tend to be given to longer questions (Wilson, 1990). One explanation for this may be that as the length of a question increases it is likely to contain an increased number of propositions, each of which then needs to be addressed by the respondent.

The linguistic context of questions is also important. For example, Allwinn (1991) demonstrated how closed questions could be elaborated on by skilled people through the use of pre-remarks (e.g. 'I'm not very knowledgeable about this so could I ask you . . .?') to indicate that a detailed response is required, despite the fact that the question could logically be answered in one or a few words. Also, the context and rules of the interaction may mean that although a question has been phrased in a closed fashion, it is clear that an open reply is expected. Thus the perceived purpose of a question is influenced by a range of factors, each of which may affect how it is interpreted.

Recall/process questions

This division of questions refers to the cognitive level at which questions are pitched. Recall questions are also known as lower-order cognitive, and process as higher-order cognitive, questions. The distinction between recall and process questions is most commonly made within education, and can be found primarily in classroom interaction research studies.

Recall questions

As the name suggests, these involve the simple recall of information. They are at a lower level of cognitive demand since they only test the ability of the respondent to recall factual information; for example: 'Where were you born?'; or 'When was the Battle of Waterloo?' Recall questions serve a number of useful purposes in different settings. A teacher may employ recall questions at the beginning of a lesson in order to ascertain the extent of pupil knowledge about the lesson topic. Such questions provide information and also serve to encourage pupil participation at the outset. Similarly, at the end of a lesson a teacher may use this type of question to determine the extent of pupil learning that has taken place as a result of the lesson, and also to highlight to pupils that such learning has occurred.

In interviewing contexts, recall questions may be employed at the beginning of an interview as a form of 'ice-breaker' to get the interviewee talking. As mentioned earlier, they are also important when questioning eye-witnesses to crimes. In medicine, recall questions are also of importance in the diagnosis of an illness. Thus a doctor will use questions such as: 'When did the pain first begin?'; or 'Have you had any dizzy spells?'

Process questions

These are so called because they require the respondent to use some *higher mental process* in order to respond. This may involve giving opinions, justifications, judgements or evaluations; making predictions; analysing information; interpreting situations; or making generalisations. In other words, the respondent is required to think, at a higher-order level, about the answer. For example: 'How do you think you could improve your relationship with your wife?'; or 'What do you believe to be the characteristics of a good manager?' Such questions require the respondent to go beyond the simple recall of information and usually there is no correct answer. Furthermore, they require longer responses and can seldom be answered in one or two words.

Process questions are employed in situations where someone is being encouraged to think more deeply about a topic. For this reason they are often utilised in order to assess the ability of an individual to handle information at a higher-order level. In executive-type selection interviews, they are frequently used in this assessment function, e.g. 'What can you offer this company that other applicants cannot?'; or 'What have been your main strengths and weaknesses as a manager?'

In teaching, they encourage pupils to reflect on the material being presented. Research reviews of questioning in the classroom context have consistently found that teachers ask considerably more recall than process questions (Gall, 1970; Hargie, 1983; Dillon, 1997). These are somewhat disconcerting findings, since the type of question asked by teachers affects the degree of creativity or expressiveness available to pupils, and process questions provide more scope than recall questions. In a world where technological advances move at a rapid pace, facts can rapidly become outdated and the ability to evaluate new information is of great importance. For this reason, Hargie (1983: 190) argued that during training 'attention should be given to means whereby teachers can increase their use of thought-provoking questions as opposed to factual or recall questions'. There is firm research evidence to support such a proposal, since Rousseau and Redfield (1980: 52), in reviewing a total of twenty studies, showed that 'gains in achievement over a control group may be expected for groups of children who participate in programmes where teachers are trained in questioning skills ... gains are greatest when higher cognitive questions are used during instruction'.

However, caution should be exercised in attempting to generalise about the use of process as opposed to recall questions. Research also tends to suggest that process questions are more effective in increasing both participation and achievement of individuals of high intellectual ability, whereas recall questions appear to be more appropriate for individuals at lower ability levels. For teachers with mixed ability classes, this finding poses some obvious difficulties, in that the consistent use of process questions is likely to stimulate pupils with a high IQ but be inappropriate for, or confuse, pupils with a low IQ.

At first sight, there would appear to be little difference between the recall/ process and the closed/open categorisations of questions, and indeed many closed questions are of a recall nature, while many process questions are open. However, it is possible to have closed process questions, and open recall questions. Consider a science teacher who has explained to pupils the properties of water and limestone, and then asks 'Will the water pass through the limestone?' While the question is process, it is also closed. Similarly a question such as 'What did you do during the holidays?' is both open and recall. Thus there are differences inherent in these two classifications of questions and both are useful in varying contexts.

Affective questions

These are questions that relate specifically to the emotions, attitudes, feelings or preferences of the respondent – that is, to the *affective* domain. An affective question can be either recall, process, open or closed, depending on which aspect of feelings is being explored. Where an attempt is being made to ascertain reactions to a past event, a recall question may be employed (e.g. 'Who was your favourite teacher at school?'). On the other hand, when present feelings are being explored, a closed question may be used (e.g. 'Do you feel a little embarrassed talking about this?').

The utilisation of recall or closed questions, however, places restrictions on respondents in terms of what they are expected to relate about their feelings. Where it is important that the client be given time and freedom to discuss emotions, open questions are more advantageous. Open affective questions facilitate the expression of true feelings. These can relate to past emotions (e.g. 'How did you feel when your mother died?') or to the present emotional state ('What are your feelings towards your husband now?').

To encourage a respondent to think more deeply about feelings, and about the underlying reasons for these, process questions may be applicable. Rather than merely asking for feelings to be reported, they further tap into an evaluation of possible underlying causes (e.g. 'What caused you to hate your father so much?'). This type of question encourages the respondent to interpret reasons for feelings and perhaps become more rational in exploring them. Affective questions are therefore particularly relevant in counselling contexts where the discussion of feelings is very important.

While affective questions are clearly relevant in many contexts, in certain situations they seem to be avoided. There is, for example, a growing body of research to indicate that the overwhelming focus of practitioner–patient interaction is task-centred, concerns the discussion of physical symptoms and tends to ignore the emotional aspects of the patient's well-being (Gilmore and Hargie, 2000). Furthermore, Dickson *et al.* (1997: 114) argued that the 'dearth of questions relating to the affective domain is the main reason for the poor rate of detection of psychosocial problems in patients'.

Leading questions

All questions contain assumptions or presuppositions. As a very simple example, if I ask you 'What time is it?' the presuppositions are that (a) you have a watch, (b) you can read the time, and (c) you are willing to give me this information. Likewise you would usually assume that (a) I genuinely do not know the time, and (b) I really wish to find out this information. However, if the interaction is between a pair of young adult strangers, the target might then make the assumption that the questioner is really attempting to open dialogue as the first step in relational development, and respond accordingly. If the target is the spouse of the questioner, both are at a party, and the hour is late, the question might be read as a signal that it is time to go home, as the baby-sitter will be ready to leave. Adler *et al.* (2001) termed these *counterfeit questions* in that they are not what they appear at first sight, since they carry hidden agendas. Question assumptions can also, of course, be true or false. For example, a detective in attempting to trap a suspect who claims to have been at a particular cinema on the evening of a crime, may ask 'What did you do when the power failed in the cinema at 8.45 pm?' There was no power failure, and so this false assumption places the suspect in a difficult position if being deceitful.

Leading questions are assumption-laden. By the way they are worded, they lead the respondent towards an expected response. The anticipated answer is implied or assumed within the question, and may or may not be immediately obvious to the respondent, depending on the phrasing. For this reason, they have also been termed *misleading questions* or *suggestive questions* (Gee *et al.*, 1999). There are four different types.

Conversational leads

As the name suggests, these are used in common parlance. Everyday conversations typically contain comments that anticipate a certain type of response, e.g. 'Isn't it a lovely day?'; or 'Wasn't that a terrible accident yesterday?' These comments lubricate the flow of conversation since they anticipate the response that the other person is likely to give and so demonstrate shared understanding. In interviews, conversational leads convey to respondents the impression of friendliness and interest on the part of the interviewer, providing of course they accurately anticipate the respondent's answer. Correct conversational leading questions create the feeling among respondents that the interviewer is listening carefully and 'in tune' with them. This, in turn, stimulates them to continue developing their ideas, feeling confident that the interviewer is paying attention and understanding what they are saying.

Simple leads

These are unambiguously intended to lead the respondent to give an answer that the questioner expects to receive. Unlike the conversational lead, the simple lead assumes the answer the questioner expects, as opposed to the answer that the respondent would have given in any case. The simple lead, then, takes less cognisance of the respondent's thoughts and feelings, e.g. 'You do, of course, go to church, don't you?' 'Surely you don't support the communists?'

It has been known for some time that the use of simple leads that are obviously incorrect can induce respondents to participate fully in an interview, in order to correct any misconceptions inherent in the question. Beezer (1956), for example, conducted interviews with refugees from the then East Germany in which he found that simple leading questions that were clearly incorrect yielded more information from respondents than did questions that were not leading. Thus when respondents were asked, 'I understand you don't have to pay very much for food in the East Zone because it is rationed?' most replied by trying to correct the interviewer's mistaken impressions about general living conditions.

The blatantly incorrect simple leading question serves to place the respondent in the position of expert *vis-à-vis* the misinformed interviewer. As a result, the respondent may feel obliged to provide information that will enlighten the interviewer. Some of this information may involve the introduction of new and insightful material. While they can be effective in encouraging participation, it is not possible to state how, and in what contexts, simple leading questions can be most gainfully employed. In certain situations, and with particular types of respondent, their use is counterproductive. Most authors of texts on interviewing have eschewed this form of question as being bad practice. Furthermore, in the courtroom, leading questions are not permitted in the direct examination of a witness by the counsel for the side calling the witness, although they are allowed during cross-examination of the other side's witnesses.

Kestler (1982: 59) positively recommended the use of leading questions by lawyers during cross-examination since they 'permit control of the subject matter and scope of the response. The witness is constrained to answer "yes" or "no"'. Likewise, Sear and Williamson (1999) illustrated how they are used by detectives to encourage suspects to confess to crimes. They identified two types.

- *Minimisation theme*. Here, the purpose is to reduce the suspect's perceived responsibility for what happened (e.g. 'She led you on and on and look at the way she was dressed, what else would you have thought?').
- *Justification theme*. The idea here is to give moral justification for the criminal action and allow the suspect to blame the victim (e.g. 'She's a bit of a slag, she was asking for it really, wasn't she?').

In many settings, however, the constraint placed on the respondent by simple leads is not desirable.

Implication leads

These lead the respondent to answer in a specific fashion, or accept a negative implication if the response given is contrary to that anticipated. Implication leads exert a much greater degree of pressure on the respondent to reply in the expected manner than simple leads, and for this reason they are also known as *complex leading questions*. An example of this type of question is: 'Anyone who cared for their country would not want to see it destroyed in a nuclear attack or invaded by a foreign power, so don't you think any expenditure on an effective defensive deterrent is money well spent?' In this case, a negative answer places the respondent in the position of apparently being unpatriotic.

If a respondent disagrees with the assumed response, some type of justification is usually expected by the questioner. For this reason, implication leads are often used by radio and television interviewers when interviewing political, or controversial, individuals. Similarly in arguments and debates they are employed in order to put opponents under pressure, and to emphasise a certain point of view. Loftus (1982) provided another example of an implication lead – namely 'Did you know that what you were doing was dishonest?' Again, the respondent is put under pressure to either accept the negative implication of dishonesty or respond at length. This is a variant of the well-known and oft-cited implication question 'When did you stop beating your wife?'

There are some well-documented instances where leading questions have tripped up politicians. The late Canadian leader Pierre Trudeau was once asked in a TV interview 'If you were shaken awake in the night, would your first words be in English or French?' No matter what his reply he was going to alienate a considerable constituency. Likewise the then UK Labour opposition leader Neil Kinnock, who supported nuclear disarmament, was asked whether he would send soldiers in a nuclear-free Britain into battle against a nuclear power. His dithering response resulted in the Conservatives producing a poster of a soldier with his arms raised in surrender with the caption 'Labour's policy on arms'. Finally, the former leader of the then UK Conservative opposition William Hague was asked in a radio interview the dual-negative implication lead 'You're a grown-up. Do you really expect to win the next election?' Given that he was by stature a small person, the question had a doubly hurtful yet impactful resonance.

Subtle leads

A humorous example of the effects of subtle leads is the old story about the Dominican and Jesuit priests who debated whether it was permissible to say their daily prayers and smoke their pipes at the same time. Unable to reach a definitive conclusion, each agreed to consult his superior for guidance. The Jesuit returned very satisfied saying he had obtained permission. The Dominican bemoaned this saying his superior had refused such permission. 'What did you ask him?' enquired the Jesuit. 'Well obviously, was it OK for me to smoke while praying.' 'Ah' said the Jesuit 'that was your mistake. I asked mine if it was permissible to pray while smoking.'

As this story indicates, subtle leads may not be instantly recognisable as leading questions, but nevertheless they are worded in such a way as to elicit a certain type of response. They are also known as *directional questions* in that the respondent is being directed towards a particular type of answer. Most people when asked 'How many animals of each kind did Moses take on the ark?' will reply 'two' even though they are aware that in the biblical story it was Noah who took animals on the ark. This phenomenon, termed *The Moses Illusion* (Erickson and Mattson, 1981), illustrates how respondents attempt to gauge and anticipate the answer that the questioner is seeking and so demonstrate helpfulness by supplying it. We are not just passive recipients of questions. Rather, we actively search for and interpret the meanings and assumptions behind the inquisitive words being used. Indeed as Gaskell *et al.* (1993: 500) noted 'Respondents often interpret even trivial components of the question as being informative and purposive.'

In the sphere of interviewing suspects of crimes, Buckwalter (1983) illustrated that suspects are more forthcoming when asked to 'tell the truth' rather than 'confess your crime'. Similarly, in cases of murder, motives are given more readily to the question 'Why did you do it?' than to 'Why did you murder him?' Buckwalter advised interviewers to avoid terms such as kill, steal, rape, and replace them with words such as shoot, take, sex. In fact it is a myth that the key to effective interrogation is to accuse, confuse, hurt or embarrass the suspect. Such Gestapo-like techniques just do not work. Rather, they make the person afraid, resentful, reluctant, hostile and defensive – all of which reduces the likelihood of truthful disclosure. Texts on inter-rogation recommend that the best guide is not to think of oneself as asking questions, but as *being questioned*. Put yourself in the position of the respondent and ask what would make *you* tell the truth in this context? Research in interrogation consistently reveals that to be successful the person asking the questions must appear to be non-judgemental (Dillon, 1990). Good interrogators possess qualities such as genuineness, trustworthiness, concern, courtesy, tact, empathy, compassion, respect, friendliness, gentleness, receptivity, warmth and understanding. We disclose to such people – they seem to care and do not judge.

An early example of how the wording of a question can influence the respondent to answer in a particular way was reported by Harris (1973). When subjects were asked either 'How tall was the basket-ball player?' or 'How short was the basket-ball player?' they guessed about 79 inches and 69 inches, respectively. Other questions asked by Harris along the same lines produced similar results – thus the question 'How long was the movie?' resulted in average estimates of 130 minutes, whereas 'How short was the movie?' produced an average of 100 minutes.

Loftus (1975) reported similar findings. When subjects were asked either 'Do you get headaches frequently, and if so, how often?' or 'Do you get headaches occasionally, and if so, how often?' the respective reported averages were 2.2 and 0.7 per headaches per week. Loftus also asked either 'In terms of the total number of products, how many other products have you tried? 1? 2? 3?' or 'In terms of the total number of products, how many other products have you tried? 1? 5? 10?' Responses to these questions averaged 3.3 and 5.2 other products, respectively. Likewise, Gaskell *et al.* (1993) showed how, when asked about annoyance with TV adverts, respondents given high alternatives (every day, most days, once a week, once a month, less often, never) reported significantly higher frequencies than those given low alternatives (once a week or more often, once a month, about every few months, once a year, less often, never). The reason for this is that the values in a given scale are assumed to reflect average, typical, or normative behaviour, and so respondents wishing to be seen as 'normal' choose a figure near the mid-point (Schwarz and Hippler, 1991). It has also been shown that the nature of the given response scale can affect perceived definitions of terms. Thus in one study two groups of subjects were asked to report how often they felt 'really annoyed' (Wright *et al.*, 1997). Subjects either received a set of low response frequencies (from 'less than once a year' to 'more than every three months') or high response frequencies (from 'less than twice a week' to 'several times a day'). Respondents were then asked to define 'annoyed' and it was found that those in the low response frequency group described it as a more severe disturbance than those in the high frequency condition.

Findings such as these have been consistently reported in research investigations. Furthermore, 'researchers have long known that people tend to agree with one-sided statements, and that the same subject may agree to two opposite statements on different occasions' (Kunda and Fong, 1993: 65). This is referred to as the *acquiescence effect* wherein respondents comply or acquiesce to the explicit or implicit direction of the question. Such acquiescence was found by Bless *et al.* (1992: 309), who carried out a series of studies showing that 'respondents report higher behavioural frequencies when the response scale offers high rather than low frequency response alternatives'. They also cited evidence to demonstrate that the more demanding the computation of a requested frequency response, the more likely it is that respondents are led by the alternatives suggested in the question. One practical example of the acquiescence effect occurs in retail contexts, where staff are trained to ask directional questions. For example, in a fast-food outlet if a customer asks for a coke, the person taking the order will use a directional assumptive question: 'A large one?' The customer usually accepts the assumption, and so profits are maximised.

In another classic study Loftus and Palmer (1974) had subjects view films of car accidents, and then questioned them about what they had seen. The question 'About how fast were the cars going when they smashed into each other?' produced higher estimates of speed than when the verb 'smashed' was replaced by 'hit', 'bumped', 'collided' or 'contacted'. One week later those subjects who had been asked the former question were also more likely to say 'yes' to the question 'Did you see broken glass?' even though no glass was broken in the accident.

In a follow-up piece of research Loftus and Zanni (1975) compared the effects of questions containing an indefinite article with the same questions containing a definite article. In this study 100 graduate students were shown a short film of a car accident and then asked questions about this. It was found that questions which contained a definite article (e.g. 'Did you see *the* broken headlight?') produced fewer uncertain or 'I don't know' responses, and more false recognition of events which never in fact occurred, than did questions which contained an indefinite article (e.g. 'Did you see *a* broken headlight?').

This *false recognition* was also reported in the Loftus (1975) study. She conducted four different experiments, each of which highlighted the way in which the wording of questions, asked immediately after an event, influenced the responses to questions asked considerably later. In one of these experiments students were shown a video-tape of a car accident and asked a number of questions about the accident. Half of the subjects were asked 'How fast was the white sports car going when it passed the barn while travelling along the country road?' while half were asked 'How fast was the white sports car going while travelling along the country road?' Although no barn appeared in the film, 17.3 per cent of those asked the former question responded 'yes' when later asked 'Did you see a barn?' as opposed to only 2.7 per cent of those asked the latter question.

In reviewing research findings relating to the use of subtle leads, Dillon (1997: 117) summed up the situation as follows:

> respondents find it easier – even more desirable – to go along with the question as posed than to dispute it and complicate the interchange. Once having been so agreeably incorrect in their answer, respondents then base their answers to subsequent questions upon the truth of the false presupposition that they had affirmed in their previous answer.

The concept of 'recovered memory' has caused much debate in this area. Here, people are interviewed in depth until they eventually recall past experiences, often of abuse, which had previously been repressed. However, it has been argued that such *recovered memory* is often in fact *false memory* planted as a result of biased questioning (Pezdek and Banks, 1996). In particular, questions that encourage respondents to think about an event can lead to a process termed *imagination inflation*. As defined by Loftus (2001: 584), this is 'the phenomenon that imagining an event increases subjective confidence that the event actually happened'. Interestingly, getting people to write down their constructed experiences greatly increases their belief in their veracity of these fictitious events. Loftus further showed that certain people are more susceptible to such inflation, including those who:

- have a tendency to confuse fact with fiction;
- more often experience lapses in attention and memory;
- possess more acute powers of imagery.

How questions are contextualised can also influence responses. For example, Hirt *et al.* (1999) showed that low expectancy conditions (e.g. saying 'If you don't remember it's all right') as compared with high expectancy conditions (e.g. 'Tell me when you get an earlier memory') produced earliest life memories from respondents of 3.45 years and 2.28 years respectively. Furthermore, when college students were initially asked to report their earliest memory the mean recall age was 3.7 years. However, students were then told that most people could recall their second birthday if they were willing to really let themselves go, focus and concentrate. When then asked for memories of their second birthday and earlier, 59 per cent of subjects reported a memory of their second birthday, and the mean recall age fell to 1.6 years. In addition, when fed a piece of false information (i.e. getting lost in a shopping mall) together with three actual events (as supplied by parents or siblings) some 25 per cent then claimed to have memories of this false event.

The implications of the above findings have ramifications for anyone concerned with obtaining accurate information from others, but they are of particular import for those who have to interview children.

Effects of leading questions on children

There is a growing volume of research to show that leading questions have a particularly distorting effect on the responses of children. Milne (1999: 175) showed how children with learning disabilities 'were significantly more likely to go along with misleading questions (i.e. questions which lead the child to the wrong answer).' Likewise, Gee *et al.* (1999: 112) reported that 'younger children are more likely than older children to comply with misleading questions'. As a result, they recommended that those who have to interview children in legal, medical or clinical contexts must be aware of such findings. During the 1990s there was a series of child abuse scandals in which children were clearly subjected to biased interviews. One such scandal was the 'Orkney satanic abuse' inquiry in which social services believed children had been subjected to sexual and satanic ritual abuse. This belief led to some suggestive and insistent interviewing of very young children (see Box 5.3) and the inquiry was eventually discredited.

Leading questions need to be used with caution, or avoided altogether, by those who interview children. For those on the receiving end of such questions, Gee *et al.* (1999) showed how young people could be inoculated against the effects of misleading questions by receiving training in how to deal with them. Endres *et al.* (1999) similarly illustrated how giving children advance warning about 'tricky' questions, and explicitly allowing them to reject a question by saying 'I don't know' when unsure about the answer, led to a reduction in errors in responses to suggestive questions. These findings were confirmed by Ghetti and Goodman (2001), who found that giving children clear prior instructions about how to deal with questions resulted in more accurate recall by them of events.

Box 5.3 Orkney satanic abuse crisis

Excerpt from an interview between a female social worker and 4-year-old child

Q: Where are the dickies and the fannies?

A: Don't know.

Q: Can you write the word?

A: No.

Q: ... a word for when a dickie goes into a fanny?

A: Don't know.

Q: Would you like to whisper?

A: No.

Q: Is it yuckie inside and outside ... is there any other word?

A: (Anxious to please) Gooey?

Q: (Amid childish laughter) Oh that's a good word ... what does gooey feel like?

A: Here, this (puts finger in mouth and pops).

Q: What happened to gooey?

A: Don't know.

Q: Has it got a colour?

A: (Begins to count slowly up to four).

Q: I wonder what this gooey is. Can you tell me?

A: No.

Q: When you put the dickie into the fanny ...

A: No. (Angry) Now can I play? I am going to get my red car. This is boring. (Gets the red car and begins to play) Go and get me some toys.

Q: When you put the dickie into the fanny it's yucky and gooey and disgusting. Who hurt you the most?

A: No one did it to me ...

Q: We won't write it down.

A: No one has been doing it to me (breaks into a scream). NOBODY HAS BEEN DOING IT TO ME.

Q: You can play with the red car. We won't write it down if you want to whisper it ...

A: (Shouting even louder) I AM NOT ... AND I AM NOT GOING TO WRITE IT DOWN.

Q: If it's a name you can see written down you can point to it (She shows child a list of names). Is it a name you see written down?

A: (Still shouting) No. I don't have to tell. No one has been doing that thing to me.

The room falls silent. The child is seen rocking in her chair, staring at her inquisitors.

Source: Sunday Times Magazine (27 February 1994).

In their detailed work in this area, Waterman *et al.* (2001) showed how children were less accurate in reporting events they had experienced when answering closed questions than when answering open ones. They further found that yes–no questions could produce distorted responses. For example, when asked nonsensical yes–no questions (e.g. 'Is a fork happier than a knife?'; 'Is red heavier than yellow?') 75 per cent of 5- to 8-year-olds answered either 'yes' or 'no'. Yet, when later questioned about their responses it was clear that many children who answered 'no' were simply indicating that they did not agree with the assumption inherent in the question. But they did not say so at the time. The problem is that a yes–no question presupposes a predetermined response (either 'yes' or 'no') and the child acquiesces with this (Peterson *et al.*, 1999). Furthermore, the social demands of the situation are such that children assume that adults will ask reasonable questions, and so they feel under pressure to respond to the expectations inherent in these questions (Siegal, 1997). When asked open format nonsensical questions (e.g. 'What do feet have for breakfast?') 95 per cent of children said they did not understand the question. This was particularly the case when children were told that it was OK to say if they did not understand. Waterman *et al.* (2001: 477) concluded that when interviewing children, 'On the basis of our results we suggest that interviewers should use open questions as much as possible.'

These findings have obvious implications for those involved in questioning children in forensic situations, such as child abuse investigations. As summarised by Lamb *et al.* (1999: 261) 'researchers agree that the manner in which children are questioned can have profound implications for what is "remembered"'. The title of a book chapter by Walker and Hunt (1998) neatly sums it up, '*Interviewing child victim-witnesses: how you ask is what you get*'. Yet it has been shown that closed questions predominate in many such interview contexts (Davies *et al.*, 2000), and that children often respond to the assumptions in the questions they are asked without making their real answers clearly known.

Probing questions

These are follow-up questions designed to encourage respondents to expand on initial responses. Stewart and Cash (2000) referred to them as *secondary questions* in that they follow on from the main, or primary, question. They are ubiquitous, so that in group discussions, some 90 per cent of all questions asked have been shown to be probes (Hawkins and Power, 1999). Once a respondent has given an initial answer it can be explored further in a number of ways, using one of the following types of probing question.

Clarification probes

These are used to elicit a clearer, more concisely phrased response, in situations where the questioner is either confused or uncertain about the content or meaning of the initial responses. Since an important purpose here is to obtain more detail, they are also known as *informational probes*. Examples include 'What exactly do you mean?', or 'Could you explain that to me again?'

Justification probes

These require respondents to explain and expand on initial responses by giving a justification and reasons for what they have said, e.g. 'Why did you say that?', or 'How did you reach that conclusion?'

Relevance probes

These give respondents an opportunity to re-assess the appropriateness of a response, and/or make its relevance to the main topic under consideration more obvious. This enables the questioner to ascertain which relationships are being made between objects, people or events, and in addition encourages the respondent to reflect on the validity of these. Examples of relevance probes include 'How does this relate to your home background?', or 'Is this relevant to what we discussed earlier?'

Exemplification probes

These require respondents to provide concrete or specific instances of what they mean by what may, at first, appear to be a rather vague statement. Asking for an example to illustrate a general comment often helps to clarify it and provide further insight into the thoughts of the respondent. Included here are questions such as 'Could you give me an example of that?'; or 'Where have you shown leadership qualities in the past?'

Extension probes

These are used to encourage a respondent to expand on an initial response by providing further information pertinent to the topic under discussion. An extension question is best employed in situations where it is felt that a respondent should be able to make further responses that will facilitate the development of the discussion. Examples include 'That's interesting, tell me more'; or 'Is there anything else that you can remember about it?' The simple, brief, form of this type of question ('And ...?'; 'So ...?'; 'Go on') is referred to as a *nudging probe*.

Accuracy probes

These are questions that draw the respondent's attention to a possible error in fact that has been made. This offers the respondent a chance to adjust or restructure the response where necessary. As they give an opportunity for the person to think about what has just been said they are also known as *reflective probes*. They are most useful in situations where either it is absolutely vital that the respondent is certain about the accuracy of responses (e.g. an eye-witness being cross-examined in court), or where the questioner knows the correct answer and wishes to give the respondent a chance to reflect on an initial response (e.g. a teacher questioning pupils). Accuracy probes include 'Are you quite sure about that?'; or 'It definitely happened before 3.00 pm?'

Restatement probes

These are used to encourage a respondent to give an adequate answer, following either an unrelated answer, or no answer at all, to an initial question. This form of probe is also known as *prompting*. Depending on the hypothesised cause of the respondent's failure, the questioner may prompt in different ways. If it is thought that the respondent did not correctly hear the initial question, the questioner may simply restate it. If it is thought that the respondent did not understand the initial phrasing of the question, it may be rephrased either in parallel fashion, or at a simpler level. It may, however, be deemed necessary to prompt the respondent either by reviewing information previously covered (e.g. 'You remember what we talked about last week?') or by giving a clue that will help to focus attention in the right direction. An example of this latter type of prompt is included in the following excerpt from a radio 'phone-in' quiz:

Q: With what country would you associate pasta?
A: Spain.
Q: No, think of Chianti. (prompt)
A: Oh yes, of course, Italy.

Echo probes

These are so called because they are questions that 'echo' the words used by the respondent in the initial response, by repeating these in the follow-up probe. They are often employed in interpersonal interaction, but if over-used they are counterproductive, since if every answer is echoed the respondent will soon become very aware of this procedure and, in all probability, stop responding. Examples of echo probes are included in the following:

A: After the meal he became very romantic, and told me that he loved me.
Q: He told you that he loved you?
A: Yes, and then he took my hand and asked me to marry him.
Q: He asked you to *marry* him?

Nonverbal probes

These are behaviours employed in such a manner as to indicate to the respondent a desire for further information. Included in these is the use of appropriate paralanguage to accompany expressions such as 'Ohh?!', or 'Never?!', together with inquisitive nonverbal behaviours (e.g. raising or lowering of eyebrows, sideways tilt of the head, and eye-contact). An attentive pause following an initial response can be used as a *silent probe*, indicating a desire for further responses. Indeed, interviewer pauses can put pressure on interviewees to respond in order to fill the silence.

Consensus probes

These give an opportunity for a group to pause in a discussion and for individual respondents to express their agreement or disagreement with an initial response. Asking consensus questions is a useful technique for a group leader to employ in order to gauge the extent of support within the group for any proposed idea or line of action. By asking 'Does everyone agree with that?' or 'Is there anyone not happy with that?' the level of group consensus can be evaluated.

Probes must be used skilfully, and as a result of ineptitude or faulty listening by the questioner this is not always the case (see excerpts 1 and 2 in Box 5.4). The ability to probe effectively is at the core of effective questioning. Fowler and Mangione (1990) illustrated how probing is one of the most difficult techniques for interviewers to acquire, while Millar *et al.* (1992: 131) noted that: 'Novice interviewers often find that they have obtained a wealth of superficial information because they have failed to explore interviewee responses in any depth.' Stewart and Cash (2000) recommended the use of *clearinghouse probes* at the end of interviews. These are very open questions that allow the respondent to answer as they wish. For example, at the end of selection interviews the interviewer may ask the candidate 'Is there anything we haven't asked you that you would like to have been asked, or anything you would like to add before we finish?'

In one study of groups, Hawkins and Power (1999) found that females used more probing questions than males. They speculated that this is because women value connection and co-operation more than men do. Males may be more sensitive to what they see as 'intrusions' into their personal and private life. Indeed, Millar and Gallagher (2000) illustrated how some interviewees may resent interviewers who probe too deeply, especially about sensitive topics, since they then feel an increase in vulnerability and a need to defend themselves. Likewise, Egan (2002) underscored the importance of sensitivity when using probing questions in a helping context, and recommended they be employed as 'gentle nudges' to help keep the interviewee focused, rather than as a way of extorting information from reluctant clients. Probes therefore must be used with care. When skilfully employed they invite elaboration of arguments, sharing of information and opinions, and result in increased respondent participation.

One interesting aspect here is what is known as the *probing effect*. This refers to the fact that a respondent who is probed is rated as being more honest, both by the questioner and by observers, as compared to someone who is not probed. This unusual finding has been well corroborated across a range of conditions and contexts (Levine and McCornack, 2001). There is no consensus about why this probing effect should occur. One explanation is that probing produces in respondents a heightened state of awareness, as they realise they are under scrutiny. As a result, they carefully monitor and adapt their verbal and nonverbal behaviours to make these appear more truthful, and thereby convey a greater impression of honesty. The probing effect has

---

Box 5.4 Examples of questioning by lawyers

Excerpt 1

Q: 'You say the stairs went down to the basement?'
A: 'Yes.'
Q: 'And these stairs, did they go up also?'

Excerpt 2

Q: 'She had three children, right?'
A: 'Yes.'
Q: 'How many were boys?'
A: 'None.'
Q: 'Were there any girls?'

Excerpt 3

Q: Okay, we've talked at length about how the accident happened, what people said as to how the accident happened, is there anything we haven't covered that you can think of, anything in your mind that you're thinking about how the accident happened that I haven't asked you and you're thinking 'he hasn't asked me that' and 'I'm not going to tell him because he hasn't asked me', is there anything?
A: Have you lost your mind?

Source: Massachusetts Bar Association (1996).

---

implications across many situations, not least for lawyers who have to make decisions about the questioning of individuals in the courtroom.

Rhetorical questions

These do not expect a response, either because the speaker intends to answer the question, or because the question is equivalent to a statement (as in 'Who would not wish their children well?' to mean 'Everyone wishes their children well'). In the former case, rhetorical questions are often used by public speakers in order to stimulate interest in their presentation by encouraging the audience to 'think things through' with them. With large audiences, interactive questions are usually not appropriate since only a few people would be given a chance to answer, and the rest may have difficulty in hearing their responses. For this reason, lecturers, politicians and other individuals, when addressing large groups of people, often employ rhetorical questions. As Turk (1985: 75) put it: 'Asking questions is the best way to promote thought . . . We are so conditioned to provide answers to sentences in question form, that our minds are subconsciously aroused towards an answer, even if we remain silent.' In this way, rhetorical questions have been shown to impact on the type of thinking engaged in by listeners (Whaley and Wagner, 2000). However, while they are useful devices for providing variation and generating interest, they do not seem to have any persuasive power in relation to the message being delivered (Gayle *et al.*, 1998).

Multiple questions

These are two or more questions phrased as one. While a multiple question may contain a number of questions of the same type, quite often it comprises an open question followed by a closed one to narrow the focus (e.g. 'How is the project progressing? Did you get the interviews finished?'). Multiple questions may be useful where time is limited and it is important to get some answer from a respondent. For this reason they are often used by radio and television interviewers who have a given (often brief) period of time in which to interview a respondent. In most situations, however, they are wasteful – especially where the questions subsumed within the multiple question are unrelated. They are liable to confuse the respondent, and/or the responses given may confuse the questioner who may be unclear exactly which question has been answered. They can also cause frustration as shown in excerpt 3 in Box 5.4.

In an early classroom study, Wright and Nuthall (1970) found that the tendency on the part of a teacher to ask one question at a time was positively related to pupil achievement, whereas the tendency to ask more than one question at a time was negatively related to pupil achievement. In the field of health, Dickson *et al.* (1997) showed how patients have difficulties in formulating a reply when asked multiple questions. They serve to pressure and confuse the patient and they also decrease the probability of receiving accurate information. Despite this, they are often employed, such as the following example taken from a medical context: 'So how are you feeling? Did the tablets help? Are you able to get some sleep now?'

RELATED ASPECTS OF QUESTIONING

Effective communicators are uniquely concerned with *how* they ask questions. In particular, they pay attention to the following issues.

Structuring

In certain social situations where a large number of questions will be asked, it is useful to structure the interaction in such a way as to indicate to the respondent what questions are likely to be asked, and why it is necessary to ask them (e.g. 'In order to help me advise you about possible future jobs I would like to find out about your qualifications, experience and interests. If I could begin with your qualifications . . .'). By structuring the interaction in this way, the respondent knows why questions are being asked, and also knows what questions to expect. Once the respondent is aware of the immediate goals of the questioner, and recognises these as acceptable, the interaction will flow more smoothly, with the respondent attempting to give adequate answers (see also the skill of set induction in Chapter 10 for a fuller discussion of this type of structuring).

Pausing

The function of pausing as a form of silent probe has already been mentioned. However, as well as pausing after receiving a response, pauses both before and after asking a question can be advantageous. By pausing before asking a question, the attention of the listener can be stimulated and the question given greater impact. By pausing after asking a question, the respondent is given the distinct impression of being expected to give some form of response. The use of pauses after asking a question also reduces the likelihood of the questioner asking multiple questions. Finally, pausing after a respondent gives an initial response encourages the respondent to continue talking.

The importance of pausing was investigated in studies by Rowe (1969, 1974a, b). She found that when teachers increased the average 'wait-time' after pupil responses the length of these responses increased from seven words when the pause was 1 second to twenty-eight words when the pause was 3 seconds. Other positive benefits were that:

- the teacher tended to ask more process questions;
- pupils asked more questions;
- those pupils who did not tend to say much started talking and produced novel ideas.

The benefits of teacher pauses of some 3 seconds were confirmed by Tobin (1987). Yet there is evidence to indicate that the average teacher pauses following a teacher question and a pupil response are 1.26 seconds and 0.55 seconds respectively (Swift *et al.*, 1988). The disadvantages of such a short wait-time were highlighted by Dillon (1990: 221) who, in a review of research into the benefits of pausing across a range of professional contexts, concluded that pauses need to last a minimum of 3 seconds in order 'to enhance the partner's participation and cognition'.

Distribution

In group contexts, leaders should try to involve as many respondents as possible in the discussion (see Chapter 14 for more information on groups). One method whereby this can be achieved is by distributing questions to all members, so that everyone's point of view is heard. This is a useful technique to employ, especially with individuals who may be reluctant to express their views unless specifically given an opportunity to do so. The redirection of a question from one group member to another may be of particular value in achieving a discreet distribution of questions, without exerting undue pressure or embarrassing any one individual in the group. Distribution has also been found to be important in the medical context. For example, in paediatric consultations, research has shown that the recipient of the initial physician question determines the extent to which the child is likely to participate in the encounter (Stivers, 2001). When this is addressed directly to the child (e.g. 'Well Joan and how can I help you today?') rather than to the parent ('Well Mrs Jones and how is Joan today?'), the child is likely to become a more active participant.

Responses

Just as there is a wide variation in types of questions that can be asked, so too is there a broad range of possible responses. For example, Bob Dylan once replied enigmatically to a reporter 'How can I answer that if you've got the nerve to ask?' Likewise, respondents often choose what questions, or parts thereof, to answer. This was exemplified in the following exchange between the journalist Michael Parkinson and Nelson Mandela:

Mandela: 'Mr Parkinson, I have to tell you before we begin that I am deaf.'
Parkinson: 'I hope, sir, that you will be able to hear my questions.'
Mandela: (smiling) 'I will hear the ones I want to answer.'

Dillon (1997) identified a large number of possible answers to questions, the main types of which can be summarised as follows:

1   *Silence*. The respondent may choose to say nothing.
2   *Overt refusal to answer*, e.g. 'I'd rather not say'.
3   *Unconnected response*. The respondent may change the topic completely.
4   *Humour*. For example, to the question 'How old are you?', the respondent may reply 'Not as old as I feel.'
5   *Lying*. The respondent may simply give a false answer.
6   *Stalling*. Again, to the question 'How old are you?' the respondent may reply 'How old do you think I am?' Answering a question with a question is a classic stalling technique.
7   *Evading*. Wilson (1990) discussed several techniques used by politicians to evade having to answer questions directly. These include questioning the question, attacking the interviewer, or stating that the question has already been answered. A good example of evasion occurred when the fiery former miners' union leader Arthur Scargill was being pressed by a TV interviewer to 'answer this important question' and replied: 'Let me answer *my* important questions first, and then I'll answer yours.'
8   *Selective ambiguity*. Thus to the question about age, the respondent may reply 'Don't worry, I'll finish the marathon OK'. In other words, the respondent pretends to recognise the 'real' question, and answers it.
9   *Withholding and concealing*. In this instance, respondents attempt to avoid disclosing information that may be damaging to them or those close to them. This is a problem commonly faced by investigators (criminal, insurance, etc.), but is also applicable to those professionals who have to deal with sensitive or taboo issues such as child abuse, incest, drug abuse and so on.

10   *Distortion*. Respondents in many instances give the answers that they feel are socially desirable, often without consciously realising they are doing so. Thus in survey interviews, respondents tend to overestimate behaviours such as voting, reading books, and giving to charity, and underestimate illnesses, financial status and illegal behaviour.

11   *Direct honest response*. Finally, the respondent may give a direct, truthful answer to a question.

In any interaction, the professional needs to evaluate the responses received, and make decisions about how to follow these up with appropriate probing questions if necessary.

OVERVIEW

Although, at first sight, questioning would seem to be a straightforward interpersonal skill, on further examination it can be seen that, in fact, it is quite complex. While most of us employ a barrage of questions in everyday parlance without giving them a great deal of thought, in professional contexts this is not acceptable. As Dillon (1997: 131) pointed out: 'the professional practice of questioning is nothing like our everyday use of questions, instead requiring of us effortful thought and concentrated behaviour'.

As we have seen in this chapter, there is a large variety of different types of question that can be asked in any given situation, and the answers received are markedly affected by both the wording, and the type, of question asked. When using questions the following points should be borne in mind:

- the person who asks the questions is of higher status or in control of the encounter
- questions can cause stress for the respondent
- closed questions are useful for encouraging initial involvement, for obtaining specific facts, and for controlling responses
- open questions usually educe longer answers and tend to be more effective with people of higher intelligence
- longer answers are given to longer questions
- for conducive encounters there should be a consistent sequence of questions rather than an erratic combination of open and closed ones
- affective questions are useful in encouraging discussions of feelings and emotions
- leading questions often produce misleading answers, and this is especially the case with children
- probing questions allow the interviewer to go deeper and they also show extended listening; although it should be remembered that a respondent who is probed is then rated as being more honest
- multiple questions are confusing and in general should be avoided
- pausing before and after asking a question, and after receiving an initial answer encourages maximum response
- a question is only as good as the response it produces

However, no hard-and-fast rules about which types of question to use in particular social encounters exist, since much more situation-specific research is needed in order to investigate the effects of aspects such as type of respondent and the nature of the social context. Nevertheless, the categorisations of questions contained in this chapter provide a key template for the analysis of the effects of questions in social interaction. Furthermore, the examples given, and the research reviewed, provide the reader with insight into the different modes of usage, and the accompanying effects, of different types of question.

It is clear that questions are powerful tools for finding out about others. However, they can also constitute a useful and subtle method for regulating the participation levels of respondents, maintaining control of the conversation, getting the answers we want, and encouraging conformity. In other words, questions need to be used *skilfully*. There would therefore seem to be a great deal of truth in the advice given by Voltaire that we should 'Judge a man not by his answers but by his questions.'

Chapter 6

Reflecting

INTRODUCTION

IN THE LAST CHAPTER the key characteristics of questioning were outlined as one technique that is commonly employed to gain information and conduct interpersonal exchanges. Here an alternative procedure called 'reflecting' will be introduced. While sharing some of the functional features of questioning, reflecting differs in a number of important respects. To help you begin to appreciate what some of these are, consider the two short fictional scenes in Boxes 6.1 and 6.2.

These two conversations with Karen differ markedly in the approaches adopted by Keith and Kim. In the first situation (Box 6.1), Keith obtained mainly factual information to do with Karen's book, her course, and what she intended to do after university. Keith and his agenda were very much the dominating features of the conversation with Karen doing little more than passively acting as the information source. Questioning was the tactic used exclusively to direct the interchange from one topic to the next, and each question did little to develop the previous response. There was minimal encouragement for Karen to furnish information other than what was directly relevant to Keith's line of enquiry. The second exchange (Box 6.2), in contrast, centred very much on Karen and the difficulties she was experiencing, with Kim staying, conversationally, much more in the background. Rather than directly leading Karen into areas that were not of her choosing, Kim gently guided the conversation in ways that facilitated Karen's discussion of personal issues that seemed important for her, Karen, to ventilate. Unlike the first exchange, in the second there were no

---

Box 6.1 Strangers on a train: scene I

Karen is a first-year student travelling home by train for the weekend. During the journey she falls into conversation at different times with two fellow passengers, both of whom are strangers to her. Let's call the first Keith and look at how the conversation progresses:

Keith: Good book, is it?
Karen: Sorry!
Keith: That book you're reading . . . Good is it?
Karen: No, not really.
Keith: Why're you reading it then?
Karen: I have to, in a way. It's part of my course.
Keith: Oh . . . you a student or something?
Karen: Yes . . . at the university.
Keith: What're you studying?
Karen: English . . . and I must have this novel finished before my tutorial on Monday morning.
Keith: Enjoy it, do you . . . university?
Karen: I suppose so, in a way.
Keith: What do you intend to do then . . . when you finish?
Karen: I don't really know . . .

---

questions asked by Kim, apart from her opening query. Rather, her interjections took the form of statements – these statements were reflections.

While some inconsistencies have been identified by Dickson (1997) among the definitions which exist in the literature, reflections can be regarded as statements in the interviewer's own words that encapsulate and re-present the essence of the interviewee's previous message. Carl Rogers, the founder of client-centred (or person-centred) counselling (Rogers, 1980, 1991), is commonly credited with coining the term, although the technique can, of course, be used in other approaches to counselling (Ivey and Ivey, 1999) and, indeed, in a variety of non-counselling settings (Mills, 1991; Riley, 2000; Hayes, 2002). An overview of definitional issues, together with contrasting theoretical perspectives on reflecting, has been provided by Dickson (1997).

Returning to the two contrasting conversational excerpts involving Karen, apart from contributing examples of the technique of reflecting, they further serve to make two additional points. The first is that it is not always necessary to ask questions to get in-depth information from others. The second more general point is that verbal styles adopted during interaction can differ markedly.

STYLES OF INTERACTING

Style, in this sense, refers to the characteristic manner in which someone handles interpersonal episodes. It can be thought of as *how* what is done is done. Cameron (2000) emphasised its expressive function in creating a particular 'aesthetic' presence

---

Box 6.2 Strangers on a train: scene II

After Keith leaves the train, Kim enters the carriage and joins Karen. Let us now eavesdrop on their conversation:

Kim: You're not really reading it, are you?

Karen: Pardon!

Kim: The book . . . you haven't turned a page in the last ten minutes.

Karen: (smiling) No, I suppose I haven't. I need to get through it though, but I keep drifting away.

Kim: It doesn't really hold your interest.

Karen: No, not really. I wouldn't bother with it, to be honest, but I have to have it read for a tutorial. I'm at the university.

Kim: (smiling) It's a labour of labour then, rather than a labour of love.

Karen: I should say! I don't like Hardy at all, really . . . the author . . . Indeed, I'm getting to like the whole course less and less . . .

Kim: It's not just the book, it's the course as well.

Karen: Yes, in a way . . . although the course itself isn't really bad . . . a lot of it is pretty good, in fact, and the lecturers are fine. It's me, I suppose. You see, I wanted to do Philosophy rather than English . . . but my parents talked me out of it.

Kim: So the course is okay, as such, it's just that, had it been left to you, you would have chosen a different one.

Karen: Oh, they had my best interests at heart, of course, my parents. They always do, don't they? They believed that my job prospects would have been pretty limited with a degree in Philosophy. And they give me a really generous allowance . . . but, I'm beginning to feel that I'm wasting my time . . . and their money. They would be so disappointed, though, if I told them I was quitting.

Kim: They decided on the course that you should do, but now that it's not working out you seem to feel guilty about the money that they've given you, and their disappointment . . .

Karen: Yes, I suppose, I do feel guilty? . . . But when you put it like that, there's a part of me that's angry as well. They had no right to take over and railroad me into something I didn't want to do in the first place. It was a bit my fault as well, I suppose . . . I shouldn't have let them talk me into something I knew wasn't right for me. I should have insisted.

Kim: You are resentful of your parents for making your decision for you but angry with yourself, as well, for not taking a stand.

Karen: You know, I really think that's what's bothering me most . . . not standing up for myself . . .

---

for the other. Conversational style includes the degrees of formality, elaboration or directness adopted (Adler and Rodman, 2000). We will dwell on the latter characteristic, directness, which has been commented on in the contexts of teaching (Brown and Atkins, 1988), social work (Seden, 1999), counselling and psychotherapy (Corey, 1997), and interviewing (Stewart and Cash, 2000). Directness involves the degree of explicit influence and control exercised by, for example, an interviewer and, correspondingly, the extent to which the interviewee is constrained in responding. At one extreme of this dimension, the interviewer following a direct style will determine the form, content and pace of the conversation. At the other extreme these features will depend on the concerns and predilections of the interviewee, with the interviewer staying conversationally much more in the background, guiding and facilitating lines of talk.

According to Benjamin (1987), a direct style is typified by the use of interviewer leads, and an indirect style by responses. Although acknowledging difficulties in producing unambiguous definitions of these two terms, he commented:

> When I respond, I speak in terms of what the interviewee has expressed. I react to the ideas and feelings he has communicated to me with something of my own. When I lead, I take over. I express ideas and feelings to which I expect the interviewee to react.... When leading, I make use of my own life space; when responding, I tend more to utilise the life space of the client. Interviewer responses keep the client at the centre of things; leads make the interviewer central.
>
> (p. 206)

Reflections can be thought of as responses, in this sense, and are contrasted with questions, which are more a way of leading.

The particular style adopted by an interviewer is, in part, dependent on the type of interview being conducted. Different forms that interviews can take are discussed by Keats (2000). A more direct, questioning style is frequently adopted in circumstances where:

- the interviewee has accepted the interviewer's role as interrogator;
- the information required is, basically, factual in nature;
- the amount of time to be devoted to the interview is limited;
- a long-term relationship need not be established;
- the information is directly for the benefit of the interviewer.

In contrast, a more indirect, responsive style is typically used to best advantage when:

- the interviewee is the participant who stands to gain from the encounter;
- the information exchanged is affective;
- the information is confused, fragmented and hazy due, perhaps, to the fact that it involves a problem never fully thought through before.

Despite this distinction it would be inappropriate to assume that a more direct style of operating is never used in the latter set of conditions, or that questions should not form part of the range of skills employed. Equally it would be mistaken to conclude that in the former circumstances a reflective statement should never be contemplated. Additionally, counsellors vary in the directness of their style depending on the particular school of thought about counselling to which they subscribe, so some are likely to be more direct across a range of contexts than others. Nevertheless, as a generality, the above distinction holds.

Some of the disadvantages of relying on questions have been pointed out in both counselling settings (Hough, 1996; Egan, 2001) and during classroom discussion (Dillon, 1990). Questions can:

- socialise the interviewee to speak only in response and merely to reveal information directly requested;
- encourage the interviewee to let the interviewer take complete responsibility for the interaction, and for finding a satisfactory solution to the problems or difficulties presented by the interviewee;
- inhibit the development of a warm, understanding relationship, conducive to the exploration of important, but perhaps intimate and, for the interviewee, potentially embarrassing details;
- direct the conversation in ways that are shaped by the interviewer's underlying assumptions (Hartley, 1999).

As far as promoting pupil discussion is concerned, Dillon (1990: 234) concluded that, 'we see discussion diminish in the face of teacher questions, resurging when alternatives are used, and again receding when the questions resume'. Far from producing the desired outcome, pupils addressed in this way tend to become dependent and passive, reacting only to further teacher questions. The skill of reflecting is a viable alternative in such circumstances. During motivational interviewing while dealing with the client's ambivalence towards change, reflecting has been advocated as a useful way of helping mixed feelings to be recognised and resolved (Terry, 1999).

RESEARCH OUTCOMES OF A REFLECTIVE STYLE

A number of empirical studies have compared the outcomes of an indirect, reflective style with a range of alternatives. Most of this research has had an interviewing or counselling orientation. In some cases attitudes of both interviewees and external judges to interviewers manifesting contrasting styles were sought. In early work by Silver (1970), for example, low-status interviewees were reported to feel much more comfortable with interviewers who displayed a reflective rather than a judgmental approach. Ellison and Firestone (1974) found that subjects observing a reflective interviewer, rather than an intrusive counterpart who controlled the direction and pace of the interview in a particularly assertive manner, indicated a greater willingness to reveal highly intimate details. The reflective interviewer was also perceived as passive, easygoing and nonassertive.

An interrogative approach in which further information was requested, and a predictive style which required the interviewer accurately to predict interviewees' reactions in situations yet to be discussed, were the alternatives to reflecting examined by Turkat and Alpher (1984). Although impressions were based on written transcripts rather than actual interviews, those interviewers who used reflections were regarded as understanding their clients. Empathic understanding and positive regard (two of the core conditions for effective counselling according to the person-centred school of thought) were related to the reflective style of interviewing in a study by Zimmer and Anderson (1968). They drew on the opinions of external judges who viewed a video-taped counselling session. From the painstaking analysis of therapy sessions undertaken by Hill and her colleagues (Hill *et al.*, 1988; Hill, 1989), not only was reflecting discovered to be one of the most common of the identified techniques utilised by therapists, but clients reported that they found it one of the most helpful. They regarded it as providing support and seldom reacted negatively to its use. Such reflections assisted clients in becoming more deeply attuned to their emotional and personal experiences, leading to more profound levels of exploration and greater insights into their circumstances and difficulties. One of the most marked outcomes was an association with significantly reduced levels of anxiety. Incidentally, and by way of comparison, closed questions, in particular, were regarded by clients as decidedly unhelpful when used by therapists. (It should be noted that 'reflecting' in these studies was actually labelled 'paraphrasing'. Since the latter encompassed a range of different types of reflective statement, this general use of the term paraphrasing contrasts with the rather specialised application to be encountered later in the chapter.)

Other researchers, rather than focusing on attitudes, have investigated the effects of reflecting on the actual behaviour of the interviewee. Some form of interviewee self-disclosure has commonly been measured. (For further information on self-disclosure see Chapter 9.) Powell (1968), for instance, carried out a study on the effects of reflections on subjects' positive and negative self-referent statements (i.e. statements about themselves). 'Approval-supportive' and 'open disclosure' were the comparative experimental conditions. The former included interviewer statements supporting subjects' self-references while the latter referred to the provision of personal detail by the interviewer. Reflections were found to produce a significant increase in the number of negative, but not positive, self-references. Kennedy *et al.* (1971), while failing to make the distinction between positive and negative instances, similarly reported an increase in interviewee self-statements attributable to the use of this technique.

Vondracek (1969) and Beharry (1976) looked at the effects of reflecting not only on the amount of subjects' self-disclosure but also on the degree of intimacy provided. More intimate detail was associated with the reflective style of interviewing in both cases. However, the contrasting conditions of interviewer self-disclosure and use of probes were equally effective in this respect. A similar result was reported by Mills (1983) in relation to rates, rather than quality, of self-disclosure. Feigenbaum (1977) produced an interesting finding concerning sex differences of subjects. While females disclosed more, and at more intimate levels, in response to reflections, male subjects scored significantly higher on both counts in response to interviewer self-disclosure.

An investigation of marital therapists and couples undergoing therapy was conducted by Cline *et al.* (1984). A complex relationship emerged involving not only gender but also social status of subjects. Thus therapist reflectiveness was found to correlate positively with subsequent changes in positive social interaction for middle-class husbands but with negative changes for both lower-class husbands and wives. It also related positively to changes in expression of personal feeling for middle-class husbands and wives. When assessed three months after the termination of therapy, a positive relationship emerged between therapist reflections and outcome measures of marital satisfaction but for lower-class husbands only.

There seems to be little doubt now that there is a strong individual difference factor influencing reactions and outcomes to non-directive, reflective versus directive styles of engagement. In addition to demographic variables such as gender and class differences already mentioned, personality characteristics have also been researched. Some evidence reviewed by Hill (1992) suggests that locus of control, cognitive complexity, and reactance of clients may be important. Locus of control, it will be recalled from Chapter 4, refers to a belief in personally significant events deriving from either internal or external sources, while reactance is a pre-disposition to perceive and respond to events as restrictions on personal autonomy and freedom (we will discuss the phenomenon of reactance in more detail in Chapter 12). Cognitive complexity relates to the conceptual differentiation and sophistication with which individuals make sense of their circumstances. Hill (1992) came to the conclusion that those high on internality of control and cognitive complexity, and low on reactance, were more suited to less directive interventions such as reflecting.

In sum, these findings would suggest that attitudes towards interviewers who use a reflective style are largely positive. At a more behavioural level, this technique would also seem capable of producing increases in both the amount and intimacy of information which interviewees reveal about themselves, although it would not appear to be significantly more effective than alternative procedures such as inter-viewer self-disclosures or probes. In the actual therapeutic context there is some evidence linking reflecting with positive outcome measures for certain clients. How-ever, the intervening effects of individual differences in demographic and personality factors should not be overlooked.

FACTUAL AND AFFECTIVE COMMUNICATION

Reflecting has been regarded by some as a unitary phenomenon, while others have conceived of it as encompassing a varying number of related processes. These include *reflection of content* (Manthei, 1997), *reflecting experience* (Brammer *et al.*, 1993), *reflecting meaning* (Ivey and Ivey, 1999) and *restatement* (Hill and O'Brien, 1999). Perhaps the most commonly cited distinction is between *reflection of feeling* and *paraphrasing* (Dickson, 1997). Although sharing a number of salient characteristics, these two skills have one important difference. In order to appreciate this difference fully some preliminary considerations are necessary.

Most of the messages that we both send and receive provide different types of information. This is, of course, an echo of an earlier point made in Chapter 2 when the multi-dimensionality of communication was emphasised. One type of information is basically factual or cognitive concerning things, places, people, happenings, and such like. Another is predominantly feeling or affective concerning our emotional states or attitudinal reactions to ourselves, others or our environment. As explained by Cormier and Cormier (1998: 101):

The portion of the message that expresses information or describes a situation or event is called the *content*, or the cognitive part, of the message. The cognitive part of a message includes references to a situation or event, people, objects, or ideas. Another portion of the message may reveal how the client feels about the content; expression of feeling or an emotional tone is called the *affective* part of the message.

Some messages are strongly factual, others essentially affective. An example of the former would be 'It's 4.30 pm', in response to a request for the correct time (and providing, of course, that the person with the watch does not suddenly realise their lateness for an appointment!). An example of the latter might be 'Oh no!', uttered by someone who has just been informed of some tragic happening. This is obviously an expression of shocked grief, rather than a challenging of the fact that the event has occurred, and is therefore fundamentally affective. The majority of messages, however, contain elements of both types of information. Consider the following statement:

> Mornings could not come soon enough, that summer. I was always up well before the others. I could scarcely wait for them to rise. Breakfast was eaten on the way to the beach as each day made ready to unfold in endlessly exciting possibilities.

The factual parts of the message are that the person got up early, waited for the others, grabbed some breakfast and headed for the beach. The affective part, of course, conveys the sense of excited anticipation and general *joie de vivre*.

The affective component of a message can take three basic forms:

1   *Explicit.* Here the feeling aspect is explicitly stated in the verbal content. For example, 'I was ecstatic.'
2   *Implicit.* In this case feelings are not directly stated but rather the affective information is implicitly contained in what is said. Thus when someone who has recently suffered loss says listlessly, 'Some days I just don't get up . . . I don't have the energy . . . I don't have the energy to do anything. I can't concentrate . . . not even think straight, sometimes . . . I've lost all interest and I keep having these really black thoughts about dying and that . . .', depression, while not mentioned, is a palpable emotional message carried by the words. In other instances, though, the emotional message 'written between the lines', as it were, may be less certain, leading Hill and O'Brien (1999) to caution against making dogmatic but inappropriate assumptions.
3   *Inferred.* The affective component of a message can be inferred from the manner in which the verbal content is delivered – from the nonverbal and paralinguistic accompaniments. Research has shown that when the verbal and nonverbal/ paralinguistic elements of an emotional or attitudinal message conflict as, for example, when someone says glumly, 'I am overjoyed', the latter source of information often holds sway in our decoding (Knapp and Hall, 1997). In the case of inferred feelings, unlike the previous two, the verbal content of the message (i.e. *what* is said) does not play a part.

154

It can be difficult trying to decode affect accurately when it has not been explicitly stated and, in these cases, caution is recommended. This would seem to be particularly good advice in the case of some types of nonverbal behaviour. Indeed the notion of a direct, invariable relationship between an underlying emotion and a particular corresponding facial display has been challenged (Fernandez-Dols, 1999). Reflecting nebulous feelings expressed in these less direct ways can often be difficult and uncertain, but potentially more beneficial if it helps put the other in touch with feeling states of which they may have been largely unaware (Egan, 2001).

We thus convey and receive both factual and affective information. Paraphrasing involves mirroring back, primarily, the factual content of a message, while reflection of feeling, as the name suggests, focuses on the affective element.

FUNCTIONS OF REFLECTING

Reflecting serves a number of functions as outlined by Cormier and Cormier (1998), Brammer and MacDonald (1999) and Hill and O'Brien (1999). These are presented in Box 6.3. While a number of these functions are common to both paraphrasing and reflection of feeling, some are more obviously relevant to one than the other.

Box 6.3 Functions of reflecting

The main functions of reflecting are to:

1 Demonstrate an interest in and involvement with the interviewee.
2 Indicate close attention by the interviewer to what is being communicated.
3 Show that the interviewer is trying to understand fully the interviewee and what the latter is saying.
4 Check the interviewer's perceptions and ensure accuracy of understanding.
5 Facilitate the interviewee's comprehension of issues involved and clarity of thinking on these matters.
6 Focus attention on particular aspects and encourage further exploration. Indeed it has been contended that helping clients to progress towards complete self-awareness and understanding is the primary aim (Manthei, 1997).
7 Communicate a deep concern for that which the interviewee considers to be important.
8 Place the major emphasis on the interviewee, rather than the interviewer.
9 Indicate that it is acceptable for the interviewee to have and express feelings in this situation and to facilitate their ventilation.
10 Help the interviewee to 'own' feelings expressed.
11 Enable the interviewee to realise that feelings can be an important cause of behaviour.
12 Help the interviewee to scrutinise underlying reasons and motives.
13 Operate from within the interviewee's frame of reference and empathise with that person.

PARAPHRASING

Paraphrasing is sometimes also referred to as *reflection of content* or *restatement*. It can be defined as the process of mirroring or feeding back to person B, in person A's own words, the essential content of B's previous statement. The emphasis is on factual material (events, thoughts, ideas, descriptions, etc.) rather than on affect. There may be occasions, of course, when the message received carries little emotion to be dealt with. At other times it may be inappropriately premature to begin to explore the affective undertow in depth. Attending to factual content by paraphrasing may be the better option under such circumstances (Cormier and Cormier, 1998).

There are three important elements of the above definition:

1   The paraphrase should be couched *in the speaker's own words*. As described by Adler and Rodman (2000: 123) it 'involves restating in your own words the message you thought the speaker just sent, without adding anything new'. It is not simply concerned with repeating what has just been said. It will be remembered (from Chapter 5) that one type of probing technique, echoing, involves the repetition of the interviewee's previous statement, or a part of it. This restatement, however, does not constitute a paraphrase. If, when paraphrasing, the interviewer continually repeats the interviewee's words it can quickly lead to the latter becoming frustrated. When counsellors persist in this, Brammer *et al.* (1993: 118) warned, 'they do not convey understanding but merely repeat blindly what has already been said. Their reflections, moreover, are generally met with denial rather than acceptance'. Instead, interviewers should respond using their own terms, perhaps using synonyms, while not violating or misrepresenting the original meaning.

2   The paraphrase should contain the *essential* component of the previous message. This requires the speaker to identify the core of the statement embedded in the verbiage. The key question to consider is: 'What is this person really communicating?' It should, therefore, not be assumed that the paraphrase must encompass everything that has just been said, some of which may well be tangential.

3   Paraphrasing is fundamentally concerned with reflecting the *factual information* received. It largely ignores feelings that may also have been intimated. The word 'largely' is used deliberately, however, since it is often difficult to eliminate affective aspects entirely.

The piece of conversation between Jeremy and Julie to be found in Box 6.4 neatly demonstrates how this skill can be put to good effect. These examples of paraphrasing manifest, 'in action', some defining characteristics of the skill. They also help to illustrate some of the functions of paraphrasing. By demonstrating that she can accurately reproduce the fundamentally important part of what Jeremy has just said, Julie 'proves' that she is attending single-mindedly, feels it important to understand fully what Jeremy is striving to relate, and has, in fact, accurately 'tuned in'. By so doing, Jeremy is also made aware of the fact that Julie is interested in his present difficulty and quite prepared to become involved in helping him explore it further.

Box 6.4 Jeremy, Rebecca and the party that went wrong

Jeremy: I'm not sure whether or not to phone Rebecca, after what happened at the party on Saturday night . . . and the row, and that.

Julie: You had an argument with Rebecca but now want to make up.

Jeremy: I didn't know Vicky would be there. There's nothing between Vicky and me now, but you know the way she always comes on strong . . . trying to make other girls jealous?

Julie: Ah, Rebecca thought that you and Vicky had something going, behind her back.

Jeremy: Yes, and Rebecca started to talk to Andy and one thing led to another. Andy didn't know that we were together . . . and the next thing they were getting cozy on the sofa. Andy couldn't believe his luck! She only did it to get back at me, though.

Julie: Right, Rebecca didn't really fancy Andy, she was simply retaliating, as she saw it . . .

Jeremy: At the time though, I didn't realise what was going on. Andy and I are mates and I *thought* he was trying to make a move on my girl. So I grabbed him by the shirt and dragged him out . . . He thought I had gone mad. So he hit me and I hit him . . . Mind you we were both fairly drunk as well.

Julie: You thought that Andy was taking liberties, so you started a fight . . . being drunk didn't help.

Jeremy: Yeah . . . when I think of it now, I feel so stupid . . . so embarrassed . . . neither Rebecca nor Andy has been in touch since. If I phone they might ring off, but the longer I leave it, the worse it could get. On the other hand, I suppose, waiting until the weekend could give everyone a chance to simmer down and forget it.

Julie: Rebecca and Andy seem to be avoiding you. You are keen to mend fences but are unsure when's best to make a start.

According to Hill and O'Brien (1999: 103–4), responding with this type of reflective statement, in a formal helping setting, has an effect whereby:

> clients typically talk extensively and elaboratively about their thoughts. Rather than just repeating themselves, clients discuss additional facets of their problems. They explain more about their issues so that helpers can obtain a clearer picture of their concerns. Effective [paraphrases] help clients feel understood, especially when they are phrased to capture the essence of what clients are communicating rather than just repeating what the client said.

One of the foremost uses of this type of reflective statement is to let clients know they are being listened to (Cormier and Cormier, 1998). From the interviewer's point of view the subsequent reaction of the interviewee to the paraphrase offered also confirms (assuming that it is accurate) that he or she is on the proper 'wavelength'. Indeed it seems that paraphrases are often used for this very purpose as a check on accurate understanding (Hill, 1989).

Likewise in the classroom, teachers may frequently paraphrase when, in response to a question, a pupil produces a rather involved and, perhaps, disjointed response. By so doing teachers not only establish that they have fully understood what was said, but also clarify the information provided for the rest of the class. Again, it is not uncommon to hear someone who has just received directions to get to a particular place, paraphrase back what was told, e.g. 'So I go to the end of the road, turn right, second on the left, and then right again.' In this case paraphrasing helps both to check accuracy and to promote the memorisation of the information.

By encapsulating, and unobtrusively presenting to the interviewee in a clear and unambiguous manner a salient facet of their previous communication, the speaker also gently guides and encourages the continuation of this theme and the exploration of it in greater depth. Interviewees' thoughts, especially when dealing with an apparently intractable problem, are often inchoate and ambiguous. An accurate paraphrase, by condensing and crystallising what has been said, can often help the interviewee to see more clearly the exigencies of the predicament (Lindon and Lindon, 2000). Paraphrasing also enables interviewers to keep interviewees and their concerns, rather than themselves, in the forefront, by responding and guiding rather than leading and directing. It indicates that interviewers, rather than insisting on imposing their own agenda, are actively trying to make sense of what is being heard from the frame of reference of the interviewee (Hough, 1996). In the sports context, it has often been said that a good referee is one who controls the game while remaining invisible. In many situations the same holds true for a good interviewer. Paraphrasing is one method of accomplishing this. The emphasis is firmly placed on the inter-viewee. Using Benjamin's (1987) terminology, the interviewer uses the interviewee's life space rather than that of the interviewer. By keeping the focus on those issues which the interviewee wants to ventilate, the interviewer also says, metaphorically, that their importance is acknowledged. A tacit commitment to get involved per-sonally with these concerns is also extended by the interviewer, when paraphrasing effectively.

Research related to paraphrasing

Research studies centred on the skill of reflecting in general, and paraphrasing in particular, are limited. The majority of the suggestions and recommendations concerning the skill have been derived from adopted philosophical positions in respect of, for example, counselling. Experiences of those practitioners who have employed and 'tested' the skill in the field have also been influential. Research investigations, however, have been conducted. For the most part these have been experimental in design, conducted in laboratory settings and have sought to establish the effects of paraphrasing on various measures of interviewees' verbal behaviour.

In some cases, though, paraphrases are defined in such a way as to include affective material (e.g. Hoffnung, 1969), while in others affective content is not explicitly excluded (e.g. Kennedy and Zimmer, 1968; Haase and Di Mattia, 1976). These definitional inconsistencies have also been noted by Hill and O'Brien (1999) in reviewing research in the area and should be kept in mind when interpreting the following findings.

Kennedy and Zimmer (1968) reported an increase in subjects' self-referenced statements attributable to paraphrasing, while similar findings featuring self-referenced affective statements were noted by both Hoffnung (1969) and Haase and Di Mattia (1976). According to Citkowitz (1975), on the other hand, this skill had only limited effect in this respect, although there was a tendency for the association to be more pronounced when initial levels of self-referenced affect statements were relatively high. The subjects in this experiment were chronic schizophrenic inpatients and the data were collected during clinical-type interviews.

The distinction between the affective and the factual has been more explicitly acknowledged by others who have researched paraphrasing. Waskow (1962), for instance, investigated the outcome of selective interviewer responding on the factual and affective aspects of subjects' communication in a psychotherapy-like interview. It emerged that a significantly higher percentage of factual responses were given by those subjects who had their contributions paraphrased. Auerswald (1974) and Hill and Gormally (1977) produced more disappointing findings. In both cases, however, paraphrasing took place on an essentially random basis. Affective responses by subjects were also selected as the dependent variable.

The few studies considering the effects of this technique on attitudes towards the interviewer, rather than behavioural changes on the part of the interviewee, have reported largely favourable outcomes. A positive relationship was detailed by Dickson (1981) between the proportion of paraphrases to questions asked by employment advisory personnel and ratings of interviewer competency provided by independent, experienced judges. A comparable outcome emerged when client perceptions of interviewer effectiveness were examined by Nagata *et al.* (1983).

It would therefore seem that when paraphrases are used contingently and focus on factual aspects of communication, recipients' verbal performance can be modified accordingly. In addition paraphrasing seems to promote favourable judgements of the interviewer by both interviewees and external judges. Counselling trainees have also indicated that this is one of the skills which they found most useful in conducting interviews (Spooner, 1976).

REFLECTION OF FEELING

Reflection of feeling can be defined as the process of feeding back to Person B, in Person A's own words, the essence of B's previous communication, the emphasis being on feelings expressed rather than cognitive content. The similarity between this definition and that of paraphrasing will be noted and many of the features of the latter, outlined in the previous section, are applicable. The major difference between the two definitions is, of course, the concern with affective matters peculiar to reflection of feeling. Brammer and MacDonald (1999) regarded the most important elements of the skill to be:

- recognising the feeling being expressed;
- labelling and describing this feeling accurately;

- observing the outcome on the other;
- judging the extent to which the reflection was facilitative or obstructive.

From the research carried out by Hill (1989), reflection of feeling was found to be the type of reflective response mentioned most often as being helpful in six of the eight psychotherapeutic cases examined. A necessary prerequisite for the successful use of this skill is the ability to identify accurately and label the feelings being expressed by the other. Unless this initial procedure can be adequately accomplished, the likelihood that the subsequent reflection of those feelings will achieve its desired purpose will be greatly reduced. A number of relevant distinctions to do with expressing feelings, have been drawn by Nelson-Jones (1997). He pointed out that feelings can be simple or complex. Sometimes what comes across is a jumble of mixed emotions. Two common complexes of affect mentioned by Teyber (1997) are:

1   anger–sadness–shame;
2   sadness–anger–guilt.

In the first, the predominating anger may be a reaction to hurt, invoking sadness, with both then combining to trigger shame. In the second, sadness is the primary emotion, connected to repressed anger and leading to guilt. This multi-dimensionality makes the task of identifying and reflecting feeling that much more demanding. Again, and with respect to the objects of feelings, they may be self-focused, directed towards the interviewer, or be vented on a third party, thing or event. Furthermore, feelings discussed may have been experienced in the past or be current in the here-and-now of the encounter. Ivey and Authier (1978) stressed that present tense reflections of here-and-now states create more powerful experiencing and can often be most useful.

Thinking about inferred emotional states, some are more readily identifiable than others from nonverbal cues such as facial expressions (Ekman and O'Sullivan, 1991; Remland, 2000) and vocal features (Kappas et al., 1991). In an early series of experiments, Davitz (1964) had actors read verbally neutral sentences in such a way as to convey different emotions. Tapes of these were presented to judges for decoding. Fear and anger were most easily recognisable. Research in this area has revealed that members of some social groups are more adept at identifying emotions from nonverbal features than are others. Females tend to be more successful than males (Kirouac and Hess, 1999). It would also seem possible to train individuals to improve their performance. As far as reflecting back feelings based solely on nonverbal cues is concerned, though, Lindon and Lindon (2000) recommended a cautious approach. Until a certain level of familiarity and trust has been established, recipients may be made to feel embarrassingly transparent and quite vulnerable, if treated in this way.

While the terms 'feelings' and 'emotions' are sometimes used synonymously, feelings often refer to more subtle emotional or attitudinal states. For this reason they are typically more difficult to label accurately. It has been suggested that one cause of this difficulty, especially with the novice interviewer, is an insufficient repertoire of feeling terms making fine discrimination and identification problematic. Cormier and Cormier (1998) advocated that interviewers have at their disposal a number of broad categories of feeling words such as anger, conflict, fear, happiness and sadness. Each of these can be expressed at either a mild, moderate or intense level. For example, 'petrified' could accurately describe someone in intense fear; 'alarmed' if that feeling is moderate; and 'uneasy' if only mildly experienced. By initially determining the broad category and then the intensity level, subtle feelings can more easily be deciphered, thereby facilitating the process of reflecting them back. Nelson-Jones (1997) stressed the obvious importance of feelings expressed being reflected at the appropriate level of intensity, in order for the helper to become fully in touch with the client.

Hill and O'Brien (1999: 131–2) contributed some useful examples of the skill of reflection of feeling as employed in a helping interview, and these are presented in Box 6.5.

Compare the helper responses in this excerpt with the examples of paraphrases provided previously. Here the interviewer's primary focus is on the feelings being conveyed by the other. The intent is to encourage further exploration and understanding of them. While the examples in Box 6.5 were drawn from a helping session it should be realised that this skill is not confined to that context. For instance, it has been found to be important in the negotiating process, particularly in 'win–win' situations where both parties have recognised possibilities for mutual gain (Mills, 1991; Hargie *et al.*, 1999). Here reflecting the feelings of the other assists in the process of exploring their needs and, at the same time, builds rapport and mutual respect.

Box 6.5 Examples of reflecting feeling

Client: I had to miss last week because I got a call right before class that my father had been in a serious car accident. He was on the [motorway] and a truck driver fell asleep at the wheel and swerved right into him, causing a six-car pile-up. It was really awful.

Helper: You sound very upset.

Client: I am. All the way to the hospital, I kept worrying about whether he was okay. The worst thing is that he had already had several bad things happen to him. His third wife had recently left him, he lost money in the stock market, and his dog died.

Helper: You're concerned about him because of all the things that have happened lately.

Client: Yeah, he doesn't have much will to live, and I don't know what to do for him. I try to be there but he doesn't really seem to care.

Helper: It hurts that he doesn't notice you.

Client: Yeah, I have always tried to please my father. I always felt like I couldn't do enough to make him happy. I think he preferred my brother. My brother was a better athlete and liked to work in the shop with him. My father just never valued what I did. I don't know if he liked me very much.

Helper: Wow, that's really painful. I wonder if you are angry too?

Client: Yeah, I am. What's wrong with me that my father wouldn't like me?

Source: Hill and O'Brien (1999: 131–2).

(See Chapter 13 for further discussion of this topic.) Reflection of feeling is therefore applicable in a broad range of circumstances as a means of promoting further examination of feelings, emotions and attitudes.

Reflecting feeling shares a number of functions with the skill of paraphrasing. By responding in this way, attention to, and interest in the other is demonstrated. It helps clients to feel understood, to sense that both they and their concerns are important and respected. This skill also acts as a means whereby the speaker can check for accuracy of understanding. Going beyond these common functions, however, reflection of feeling indicates to others that it is acceptable for them to have and express feelings in that situation. This is important, since in many everyday conversations the factual element of communication is stressed to the neglect, and even active avoidance, of the affective dimension. People often need to be 'given permission' before they will reveal emotion-laden detail. When they do unburden themselves the release can heighten energy and promote a sense of well-being (Cormier and Cormier, 1998).

By reflecting the other's feelings, a speaker acknowledges that person's right to both have and disclose such feelings. As pointed out by Albrecht *et al.* (1994: 437), in discussing supportive communication, 'Messages that acknowledge, elaborate, and grant legitimacy to the feelings of a distressed other are perceived to be more sensitive and effective.' When performed accurately the skill further serves to encourage exploration and promote understanding of aspects of the recipient's affective state. Reflecting back the central feeling element of what they have just related enables them to think more clearly and objectively about issues that previously were vague and confused. As explained by Riley (2000: 171),

> When you reflect others' thoughts and feelings, you are like a recording, giving them a chance to hear what they are really saying. When helpers respond with clear, concise, detailed statements about others' concerns it helps the people with problems clarify them.

Another function of reflection of feeling, mentioned by Brammer *et al.* (1993), is to help people to 'own' their feelings – to appreciate that ultimately they are the source, and can take responsibility for their affective states. Various ploys commonly used in order to disown feelings include speaking in the second person (e.g. '*You* get depressed being on your own all the time'), or third person (e.g. '*One* gets pretty annoyed'), rather than in the first person (e.g. '*I* get depressed being on my own all the time' and '*I* get pretty annoyed'). Sometimes a feeling state is depersonalised by referring to 'it' (e.g. '*It's* not easy being all alone', rather than, 'I find it difficult being all alone'). Lindon and Lindon (2000: 136) talked about helping the other to 'find "I"' through reflecting. Since reflective statements make explicit others' affective experiences, and label them as clearly theirs, they help those people to acknowledge and come to terms with their emotion. Recipients are also encouraged to examine and identify underlying reasons and motives for behaviour, of which they previously may not have been completely aware. Furthermore, they are brought to realise that feelings can have important causal influences on their actions.

The use of this skill can also serve to foster a facilitative relationship. It is widely held that interviewers who reflect feeling accurately tend to be regarded as empathic (Lang and van der Molen, 1990; Hough, 1996). That said, it should not be assumed that reflection of feeling and empathy are one and the same. Empathy is a much broader concept and being empathic involves much more than reflecting feeling (Egan, 2001; Hill and O'Brien, 1999). Nevertheless, an appropriate, well-chosen reflection can be one way of manifesting empathic understanding and adopting the other's internal frame of reference. Such interviewees consequently feel deeply understood, sensing that the interviewer is with them and is able to perceive the world from their perspective. The interviewee in such a relationship is motivated to relate more freely to the interviewer and divulge information that has deep personal meaning (Teyber, 1997).

Problems to avoid when reflecting feeling

Reflection of feeling is, therefore, a very useful skill for all interactors, professional or otherwise, to have in their repertoires. It is, however, one which many novices initially find difficult to master. Problems associated with it and highlighted by Brammer *et al.* (1993), Brammer and MacDonald (1999) and Hill and O'Brien (1999) include the following.

1   *Inaccuracy*. Anyone attempting to use the skill should be aware of the dangers of reflecting inaccurately. By reflecting feelings that were neither experienced nor expressed, the other's sense of confusion and failure to be understood can be heightened.

2   *Premature exposure*. This happens when the reflection begins to surface sensed emotion that the listener is not yet ready either to acknowledge or perhaps to discuss in that situation.

3   *Emotional abandonment*. Interviewers should avoid bringing deep feelings to the surface without assisting the interviewee to deal with them. This can sometimes happen at the end of a session when the interviewer leaves the interviewee 'in mid-air'.

4   *Ossified expression*. There is a tendency among many inexperienced practitioners to consistently begin their reflection with a phrase such as 'You feel . . .'. While such a sentence structure may be a useful way of learning the skill, its monotonous use can appear mechanical and indeed 'unfeeling' and can have an adverse effect on the recipient. For this reason a greater variety of types of statement should be developed.

5   *Parroting*. Another malpractice includes over-reliance on the words of the other by simply repeating back what was said. This 'parroting' should be distinguished from reflecting. It tends to stunt conversations (Mills, 1991) and can quickly become irritating and antagonising (Riley, 2000). At the same time, when using their own words, speakers should be careful to ensure that the language chosen is appropriate to the listener and the situation.

6   *Over-inclusion*. This occurs when the reflection goes beyond what was actually communicated by including unwarranted suppositions, or speculations. Conversely, the reflective statement should not neglect any important aspect of the affective message of the other.

7   *Emotional mis-match.* Perhaps one of the most difficult features of the skill is trying to match the depth of feeling included in the reflection to that initially expressed. If the level of feeling of the reflection is too shallow the recipient is less likely to feel fully understood or inclined to examine these issues more profoundly. If it is too deep that person may feel threatened, resulting in denial and alienation. More generally, the reflective statement should mirror the same type of language and forms of expression used by the other, without being outrageously patronising. The latter, together with the other potential pitfalls mentioned earlier, can only be overcome by careful practice, coupled with a critical awareness of one's performance.

Research related to reflection of feeling

As with paraphrasing, the various recommendations concerning the use of reflection of feeling have, for the most part, been based on theory and practical experience rather than research findings. Again, studies featuring this skill can be divided into two major categories:

1   experiments, largely laboratory-based, designed to identify effects of reflecting feeling on subjects' verbal behaviour
2   studies that have attempted to relate the use of the technique to judgements, by either interviewees or observers, of interviewers in terms of such attributes as empathy, warmth, and respect. In many instances both types of dependent variable have featured in the same investigation.

A significant relationship between reflection of feeling and ratings of empathic understanding emerged in a piece of research conducted by Uhlemann *et al.* (1976). These ratings were provided by external judges and were based on both written responses and audio-recordings of actual interviews. Likewise, Ehrlich *et al.* (1979) found that interviewers who reflected feelings that had not yet been named by interviewees were regarded by the latter as being more expert and trustworthy. A similar procedure, labelled 'sensing unstated feelings', by Nagata *et al.* (1983), emerged as a significant predictor of counsellor effectiveness when assessed by surrogate clients following a counselling-type interview.

However, not all findings have been as positive. Highlen and Baccus (1977) failed to reveal any significant differences in clients' perceptions of counselling climate, counsellor comfort or personal satisfaction between clients allocated to a reflection of feeling and to a probe treatment. Similarly, Gallagher and Hargie (1992) found no significant relationships between ratings of counsellors' reflections, on the one hand, and on the other, separate assessments by counsellors, clients and judges, of empathy, genuineness and acceptance displayed towards clients. As acknowledged, the small sample size may have been a factor in the outcome of this investigation.

The effects of reflections of feeling on interviewees' affective self-reference statements have been explored by Merbaum (1963), Barnabei *et al.* (1974), Highlen and Baccus (1977), and Highlen and Nicholas (1978), among others. With the exception of

Barnabei *et al.* (1974), this interviewing skill was found to promote substantial increases in affective self-talk by subjects. Highlen and Nicholas (1978), however, combined reflections of feeling with interviewer self-referenced affect statements in such a way that it is impossible to attribute the outcome solely to the influence of the former. One possible explanation for the failure by Barnabei *et al.* (1974) to produce a positive finding could reside in the fact that reflections of feeling were administered in a random or non-contingent manner. It has already been mentioned that paraphrases used in this indiscriminate way were equally ineffective in producing increases in self-referenced statements. Dickson (1997) and Hill and O'Brien (1999) provide further reviews of research on reflecting feeling and paraphrasing.

OVERVIEW

The following points, which should be remembered when adopting a reflective style, apply to the skills of both paraphrasing and reflection of feeling. Some of them have already been mentioned, but their importance makes it unnecessary to apologise for their repetition. The core guidelines for reflecting are as follows.

1   *Use your own words*. Reflecting is not merely a process of echoing back the words just heard. Speakers should strive rather to reformulate the message in their own words. In addition, Ivey and Ivey (1999) recommended using a sentence stem that includes, as far as possible, a word in keeping with the other's characteristic mode of receiving information. For example, assuming that the other is a 'visualiser' (i.e. someone who relies mainly on visual images as a means of gathering and processing information), it would be more appropriate to begin a reflection, 'I *see* that you ...' or 'It *appears* to me that ...', rather than 'I *hear* you talk about ...' or '*Sounds* to me as if ...'. The latter would be much better matched to someone who prioritises the aural channel.

2   *Do not go beyond the information communicated by the addressee*. Remember, reflecting is a process of only feeding back information already given by the addressee. The speaker should not add or take away from the meaning as presented. For this reason, when using the skill, speakers should not include speculations or suppositions which represent an attempt to impose their own meaning on what was communicated, and while based on it, may not be strictly warranted by it. The speaker, therefore, when reflecting, should not try to interpret or psychoanalyse. Interpretation may be useful on occasion, but it is not reflection. For example:

> A: I suppose I have never had a successful relationship with men. I never seemed to get on with my father when I was a child ... I always had problems with the male teachers when I was at school ...
>
> B: You saw the male teachers as extensions of your father.

Note that this statement by B is not a reflection. It is an interpretation that goes beyond what was said by A.

165

3   *Be concise.* The objective is not to include everything said but to select what appear to be the most salient elements of the preceding message. It is only the core feature, or features, that the speaker should strive to reflect: the essence of what the other has been trying to communicate. Reflections tend to be short statements rather than long, involved and rambling, although the actual length will obviously vary depending on the information provided.

4   *Be specific.* It will be recalled that one of the functions of reflecting is to promote understanding. Frequently interviewees, perhaps due to never having previously fully thought through that particular issue, will tend to express themselves in a rather vague, confused and abstract manner. It is more beneficial if, when reflecting, interviewers try to be as concrete and specific as possible, thereby ensuring that both they, and indeed the interviewees, successfully comprehend what is being said. For example, Riley (2000) has shown the significance of specificity when reflecting patient concern during nurse/patient interaction.

5   *Be accurate.* Accuracy depends on careful listening (see Chapter 7). While person B is talking, person A should be listening single-mindedly, rather than considering what to say next, or entertaining other thoughts less directly relevant to the encounter. The inclusion of a 'check-out' statement as part of the reflective utterance has been advised as a means of assessing accuracy of understanding, when the affective message received has not been explicitly stated (Ivey and Ivey, 1999). For instance, 'Deep down I sense a feeling of relief, would you agree?' In addition to inviting corrective feedback, by offering the opportunity to comment on the accuracy of understanding, the speaker avoids giving the impression of assumed omniscience or of imposing meaning on the other. If a practitioner is frequently inaccurate in reflections proffered, the client will quickly realise that further interaction is pointless, since the practitioner does not seem able to appreciate what is being said. This does not mean that the occasional inaccuracy is disastrous. In such a case the recipient, realising the speaker's determination to grasp meaning, will generally be motivated to provide additional information to rectify the misconception.

6   *Do not over-use reflections.* Manthei (1997) revealed that reflections are frequently misused in this way. Not all contributions have to be reflected. To attempt to do so may restrict rather than help a conversational partner move forward. Reflections can be used in conjunction with the other skills that an interviewer should have available (e.g. questioning, reinforcing, self-disclosure, etc.). In some instances it is only after rapport has been established that reflection of feeling can be used without the interviewee feeling awkward or threatened.

7   *Focus on the immediately preceding message.* Reflections of feeling and paraphrases typically reflect what is contained in the other's immediately preceding statement. It is possible, and indeed desirable on occasion, for reflections to be wider ranging and to cover a number of interjections. The interviewer may wish, for example, at the end of the interview, to reflect the facts and feelings expressed by the interviewee during its entire course. Reflections such as these, that have a broader perspective, are called *summaries of content* and

summaries of feeling, and are a useful means of identifying themes expressed by the interviewee during the complete interview, or parts of it (see Chapter 10 for more detail on closure).

8   *Combining facts and feelings.* Reflection contains two essential component skills – reflection of feeling and paraphrasing. It is, of course, possible to combine both factual and feeling material in a single reflection if it is felt to be the most appropriate response at that particular time. This is often how the skill is used in practice (Brammer and MacDonald, 1999). As such, Hill and O'Brien (1999) suggested that by combining both feelings and facts in a format such as, 'You feel . . . because . . .', one type of information complements the other and enables the recipient to perceive the relationship between them. Moreover, Ivey and Ivey (1999) identified how, in this way, deeper meanings underlying expressed experiences can be located and sensitively surfaced. They referred to this more profound process as *reflecting meaning*.

Chapter 7

Listening

INTRODUCTION

IN SOCIAL INTERACTION THE process of listening is of crucial importance. As Mark Twain observed: 'If we were supposed to talk more than we listen, we would have two tongues and one ear.' In order to respond appropriately to others, we must pay attention to the messages they are sending and link our responses to these. In Chapter 3 it was noted that the average person does not actually speak for long periods in each day, and indeed several studies into the percentage of time spent in different forms of communication have found listening to be the predominant interpersonal activity. Adults spend about 70 per cent of their waking time communicating (Adler *et al.*, 2001). Of this, on average 45 per cent of communication time is spent listening, 30 per cent speaking, 16 per cent reading and 9 per cent writing. In the work context, for the average employee these figures have been calculated as 55 per cent listening, 23 per cent speaking, 13.3 per cent reading and 8.4 per cent writing, but for managers the listening figure increases to 63 per cent (Wolvin and Coakley, 1996).

The importance of listening is now widely recognised across many contexts. For example, in the business sphere, Stewart and Cash (2000: 39) reported how:

> Surveys of hundreds of corporations in the United States have revealed that poor listening skills are a major barrier in nearly all positions from accountants to supervisors; good listening skills are considered critical to entry-level positions, effective performance, high productivity, managerial competency, and promotion within most organizations.

In their review of this field, Wolvin and Coakley (1996) found that some 70 per cent of the top US companies, including corporations such as Ford, Delta Airlines, IBM, Bank of America and Pacific Telephone, regularly provide listening training for their employees. These findings were confirmed by Goby and Lewis (2000) in a study of the insurance industry, where staff at all levels, as well as customers (policyholders), regarded listening as the primary communication skill. Likewise, in a study of 1,000 salespeople, Rosenbaum (2001) found that the ability to listen in depth to client needs was a defining characteristic of success. For professionals in most fields this is therefore a core skill. Knowledge of, and expertise in, listening techniques are central to success in interactions with clients and other professionals. For example, in their empirical investigation of this area, Hargie *et al.* (2000) identified listening as a key skill in community pharmacy practice. Indeed, for those whose job involves a helping or facilitative dimension, it has been argued that the capacity to be a good listener is the most fundamental of all skills (Nelson-Jones, 1997).

In terms of personal well-being, 'Not only is listening a valuable skill, it is also conducive to good health. Studies have shown that when we talk our blood pressure goes up; when we listen it goes down' (Borisoff and Purdy, 1991a: 5). However, this may also depend on the amount of effort we devote to listening. Brilhart and Galanes (1998) reviewed research that showed how those who are actively trying to listen to, remember, and understand, what another person is saying show signs of concerted physical activity including accelerated heartbeat, whereas those not listening at all to the speaker have heart rates that often drop to the level of sleep.

Listening is a central skill at the earliest stage of personal development. The infant begins to respond to a new world by hearing and listening. Wilding *et al.* (2000) illustrated how neonates are able to discriminate between their father's voice and that of a male stranger, and infants prefer to look at their mother's face rather than a stranger's. They showed how babies rapidly develop the ability to combine visual and auditory stimuli, so at age 6–12 weeks they become distressed when shown a video of their mother in which the speech and visual content are discrepant. In fact, listening is at the heart of communicative development, since the child has to learn to listen before learning to speak, learns to speak before learning to read, and learns to read before learning to write.

In this sense, listening is a fundamental skill and the foundation for other communication skills. For this reason, we term listening a *prerequisite skill* on which all other interactive skills are predicated. To ask the right questions, be assertive, give appropriate rewards, employ apposite self-disclosure, negotiate effectively, open and close interactions, and so on, you must engage in concerted listening. As aptly expressed by Robbins and Hunsaker (1996: 35), 'if you aren't an effective listener, you're going to have consistent trouble developing all the other interpersonal skills'. Indeed, many of the problems encountered during social interchange are caused by ineffective listening. Not surprisingly, research studies have shown a range of benefits that accrue from effective listening in both personal and commercial contexts (see Box 7.1 for a summary of these).

Box 7.1 Benefits of effective listening

At work

- Greater customer satisfaction
- Increased employee satisfaction
- Higher levels of productivity
- Fewer mistakes
- Improved sales figures
- More information sharing
- Greater innovation and creativity

Personally

- Better family relationships
- Improved social network
- Greater interpersonal enjoyment
- Improved self-esteem
- Higher grades at school/college
- More close friends
- An enriched life

DEFINING THE TERM

Academic interest in listening is relatively recent in terms of social science research, and can be traced back to the work of Wiksell (1946) and Nichols (1947). Since that time, the volume of literature in this area has expanded rapidly. But what is the exact meaning of 'listening'? In their analysis, Wolff *et al.* (1983: 6) noted that: 'The word "listen" is derived from two Anglo-Saxon words: *hylstan*, meaning hearing and *hlosnian*, meaning to wait in suspense.' However, there is a lack of consensus in the literature with regard to the precise meaning of the term. Thus some theorists regard listening as a purely auditory activity, as 'a deliberate process through which we seek to understand and retain aural (heard) stimuli' (Gamble and Gamble, 1999: 178). In this sense it is 'the process of receiving and interpreting aural stimuli' (Pearson and Nelson, 2000: 99). More specifically, listening is viewed as 'the complex, learned human process of sensing, interpreting, evaluating, storing and responding to oral messages' (Steil, 1991: 203).

In terms of interpersonal interaction, the focus of study for those who hold this perspective has been on 'the process by which spoken language is converted to meaning in the mind' (Lundsteen, 1971: 1). As Bostrom (1997: 236), in his systematic overview of the field, concluded, these 'Definitions and assessment of listening have grown out of the cognitive tradition and have been importantly influenced by an assumption that listening and reading are simply different aspects of a single process – the acquisition and retention of information.' In this paradigm, listening is perceived as being parallel to, and the social equivalent of, reading: when we read we attempt to understand and assimilate the written word; when we listen we attempt to understand and assimilate the spoken word. Both are seen as cognitive, linguistic, abilities.

This cognitive perspective made an important distinction between hearing and listening, in that hearing was regarded as a physical activity, while listening is a mental process. In this sense, we may use our visual pathways to see but we read with our brains (and indeed blind people read using tactile pathways and Braille), and we use our aural pathways to hear but we listen with our brains. We do not need to learn to see but we need to learn to read. Similarly, we do not have to learn how to hear, but we have to learn how to listen. As expressed by Roach and Wyatt (1999: 197) 'Far from being a natural process, listening is clearly a consciously purposive activity for which we need systematic training and supervision to learn to do well.'

However, aural definitions of listening ignore the important nonverbal cues emitted by the speaker. Yet such cues help to determine the actual meaning of the message being conveyed (see Chapter 3). For this reason, researchers in interpersonal communication have highlighted the importance of *all* interactive behaviour in listening, encompassing both verbal and nonverbal responses. Thus Bostrom (1997: 247) asserted that 'the best definition of listening is the *acquisition, processing, and retention of information in the interpersonal context.*' It is 'the process of becoming aware of all the cues that another person emits' (Van Slyke, 1999: 98). As such, it necessitates 'capturing and understanding the messages that clients communicate, either verbally or nonverbally, clearly or vaguely' (Hill and O'Brien, 1999: 83). This is the perspective that is followed in this chapter, where listening is regarded as *the process whereby one person pays careful overt and covert attention to, and attempts to assimilate, understand, and retain, the verbal and nonverbal signals being emitted by another.*

Scholars in this field also distinguish between two other usages of the term. The first sense emphasises the visible nature of the process, and is referred to as *active listening*. This occurs when an individual displays behaviours that signal overt attention to another. The second usage emphasises the cognitive process of assimilating information. This does not imply anything about the overt behaviour of the individual, but rather is concerned with the covert aspects. An individual may be listening covertly without displaying outward signs of so doing, and so is engaged in *passive listening*. In terms of interpersonal skill, it is the former meaning of the term that is utilised, and it is therefore important to identify those verbal and nonverbal aspects of behaviour that convey the impression of active listening.

FUNCTIONS OF LISTENING

The skill of listening serves a number of purposes in social interaction, as summarised in Box 7.2. The specific functions vary depending on interactional context. One recurring problem in relation to the main goal here is that often 'we listen with the intent to respond, instead of listening with the intent to understand' (Van Slyke, 1999: 98). In other words, our main concern is with our own point of view rather than with gaining a deeper insight into the other person's perspective. As shown in Box 7.2, our objectives when listening should include conveying attention and interest, gaining a full, accurate insight into the perspectives held by others, and encouraging an open interchange of views leading to agreed understanding and acceptance of goals.

ASSIMILATING INFORMATION

The processes of feedback, perception and cognition are all of importance in the assimilation of information during listening. As explained in Chapter 2, these processes are central to social action, wherein the individual receives responses,

Box 7.2 Functions of listening

Box 7.2 Functions of listening

1 To focus specifically on the messages being communicated by the other person.
2 To gain a full, accurate, insight into the other person's communication.
3 To critically evaluate what others are saying.
4 To monitor the nonverbal signals accompanying the other person's verbal messages.
5 To convey interest, concern and attention.
6 To encourage full, open and honest expression.
7 To develop an 'other-centred' approach during interaction.
8 To reach a shared and agreed understanding and acceptance with others about both sides' goals and priorities.

assimilates these and in turn responds. In interpersonal interaction a constant stream of feedback impinges on us, both from the stimuli received from other people and from the physical environment. Not all of this feedback is consciously perceived, since there is simply too much information for the organism to cope with adequately. As a result, the individual actively selects information to filter into consciousness. Thus a *selective perception filter* (see Figure 7.1) is operative, and its main function is to filter only a limited amount of information into the conscious, while some of the remainder may be stored at a subconscious level. Evidence that such subconscious storage does occur can be found from studies into *subliminal perception*, which refers to the perception of stimuli below the threshold of awareness. For example, information flashed on to a screen for a split second, so fast that it cannot be read consciously, can influence our behaviour.

Figure 7.1 illustrates how, from the large number of stimuli in the environment, a certain amount is presented as feedback. These stimuli are represented by the arrows on the extreme left of the diagram. Some stimuli are not perceived at all, or are filtered into the subconscious at a very early stage. Within the physical environment, the ticking of clocks, the hum of central-heating systems, the pressure of one's body on the chair, etc., are usually filtered into the subconscious during social encounters, if these are interesting. If, however, one is bored during an encounter (e.g. sitting through a dull lecture) then these items may be consciously perceived, and the social 'noises' filtered into subconscious. Unfortunately, in interpersonal interaction, vital information can be filtered out, in that we may be insensitive to the social signals emitted by others. Where this occurs, effective listening skills are not displayed. In order to listen effectively we must be sensitive to verbal and nonverbal cues, and select the most relevant of these to focus upon. By observing closely the actions and reactions of others, it is possible to improve one's ability to demonstrate concerted and accurate listening.

The listening process begins when our senses register incoming stimuli. The sensory register receives large amounts of information but holds it for a brief period of time. Visual sensory storage is highly transitory, lasting only a few hundred milliseconds. Auditory sensory data is held in the register for slightly longer – up to four seconds. To be retained, stimuli must be filtered from the sensory register into the

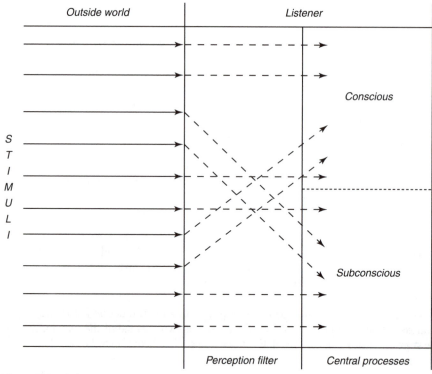

Figure 7.1 Selective perception process

individual's level of consciousness and held in memory. Social encounters can be coded and stored both in semantic memory (remembering what someone said) and episodic memory (remembering what someone did). The short-term memory (STM) store retains stimuli for between 20 seconds and one minute. STM can only cope with seven units, plus or minus two, of information. Thus a new telephone number is retained for only a short period as each digit is assimilated as a separate unit. However, if this number is used frequently, it becomes one single unit of information and is transferred to the long-term memory (LTM) store. LTM is a permanent storage facility that can retain information literally for a lifetime.

Bostrom (1997) reviewed a range of research studies that found a link between capacity for short-term listening (STL) and success in various contexts. Good STLs asked more questions in interviews, performed better in oral presentations, were rated as being better managers, and had a higher rate of upward mobility within their organisation. However, while the importance of STM for the listening process has been illustrated, the exact nature of any causal relationship between STM, listening ability and overt listening behaviour is unclear (Bostrom, 1996; Thomas and Levine, 1996). The latter authors, in an earlier study, found a positive and significant correlation between recall ability and use of head nods, gaze duration and short back-channel behaviours ('uh hu', 'mmm', etc.), but concluded, 'there is more to listening than simply recall. The reverse is also true. There is obviously more to recall than listening' (Thomas and Levine, 1994: 121). Likewise, Bostrom (1997: 243) concluded that although 'research indicates that short-term listening (STL) is closely implicated in interpersonal activities ... just how these abilities relate to one another is not known'. It should be noted that no link exists between long-term memory and listening ability. In other words, there is no relationship between having a good memory for distant events and being an effective listener. Fans of *The Simpsons* TV cartoon series will be aware of the Grandpa Simpson character, who frequently regales the family with detailed memories of days of yore, while blissfully ignoring what others are saying to him in the here-and-now.

TYPES OF LISTENING

There are six different types of listening.

Discriminative listening

This is the most basic form of listening, where the goal is simply to scan and monitor auditory and/or visual stimuli (Wolvin and Coakley, 1996). Examples include listening to hear if the baby is crying upstairs, looking at someone's facial expression to see if what we are saying has caused shock or surprise, or checking to see if a critically ill loved one in a hospital bed is still breathing. In each case the objective is to focus on, or *discriminate*, incoming stimuli for feedback purposes. For some professionals, of course, discriminative listening is vital. This is especially the case with health professionals in a hospital context who have to monitor the well-being of patients on a regular basis, and make crucial discriminative decisions based on the stimuli received.

Comprehension listening

This occurs when we listen to informative or instructive messages in order to increase our understanding, enhance our experience and acquire data that will be of future use to us. We may practise this type of listening while attending lectures, conducting fact-finding interviews or watching radio or TV documentaries or news programmes. The emphasis here is on listening for central facts, main ideas and critical themes in order to fully *comprehend* the messages being received. For this reason, it has also been termed *content listening* (Kramer, 2001).

Evaluative listening

This takes place when a speaker is trying to persuade us, by attempting to influence our attitudes, beliefs or actions. We listen evaluatively to enable us to make appropriate judgements concerning such persuasive messages. As part of this, we listen for the spin or slant that the speaker puts on the message (Egan, 2002). We may practise this type of listening when dealing with sales people, negotiating at meetings, listening to party political speeches, watching TV adverts, or even when deciding with friends which pub to go to for the evening. In all these instances we have to listen to the available evidence and the supporting arguments, weigh these up and *evaluate* them, before making a decision. The emphasis here is therefore on listening for the central propositions being made, and being able to determine the strengths and weaknesses of each. Bostrom (1997) termed this form of listening *interpretive listening*. It has also been referred to as *critical listening* in that it 'challenges the speaker's message by evaluating its accuracy, meaningfulness, and utility' (Pearson and Nelson, 2000: 109).

Appreciative listening

This occurs when we seek out certain signals or messages in order to gain pleasure from, or *appreciate*, their reception. We may listen appreciatively to relax and unwind, to enjoy ourselves, to gain inner peace, to increase emotional or cultural understanding, or to obtain spiritual satisfaction. This type of listening occurs when we play music which appeals to us, when we decide to attend a church service, when sitting in a park or walking in the country while assimilating the sounds of nature, or when we attend a public meeting in order to hear a particular speaker.

Empathic listening

Empathic listening takes place when we listen to someone who has a need to talk, and be understood by another. Here the listener demonstrates a willingness to attend to and attempt to understand the thoughts, beliefs and feelings of the speaker. One in-depth study of listening dyads found that what speakers most wanted was for the listener to understand what they were saying, and to care about and empathise with them – their recommendation was to 'listen with your heart' (Halone and Pecchioni, 2001: 64). As Stewart and Cash (2000: 40) put it 'Empathic listening is total response. You reassure, comfort, express warmth, and show unconditional positive regard for the other party.' While the first four types of listening are intrinsic in that they are for the benefit of the listener, empathic listening is extrinsic in that the listener is seeking to help the speaker. This type of listening is common between close friends and spouses. It is at the core of formal helping situations, and hence has also been termed *therapeutic listening* (Wolvin and Coakley, 1996).

Dialogic listening

The term dialogue comes from the Greek words *dia* ('through') and *logos* ('meaning', or 'understanding'). In dialogic listening, meaning emerges and is shaped from conversational interchange. Here, listening is two-way and of benefit to both sides, as we share views with one another in an attempt to reach a mutually agreed position. For this reason it is also known as *relational listening* (Halone and Pecchioni, 2001). All of us carry large amounts of cultural, national, racial, etc., baggage with us when we enter into discussions. We also bring our own ethnocentric slant, which means that we tend to perceive and judge other viewpoints from the perspective of our own. For effective listening we need to adopt a more cosmopolitan attitude that does not assume that the values and beliefs of any particular group are the only possible alternative. Rather, we must suspend judgement and be open and receptive to the views of others. As Stewart and Logan (1998: 199) expressed it, the 'first step towards dialogic listening is to recognize that each communication event is a ride on a tandem bicycle, and you may or may not be in the front seat'. This type of listening is central to negotiations, where to reach effective outcomes the needs and goals of both sides must be jointly explored (see Chapter 13).

While appreciative listening is not so applicable in the social context, knowledge of discriminative, comprehension, evaluative, empathic and dialogic listening skills are of key import. Bearing these types in mind, a useful acronym for effective interpersonal listening is *PACIER*:

*P*erceive the other person's verbal and nonverbal communication
*A*ttend carefully to gain maximum information
*C*omprehend and assimilate the verbal message
*I*nterpret the meaning of the accompanying nonverbals
*E*valuate what is being said and, where appropriate, empathise
*R*espond appropriately.

THE LISTENING PROCESS

At first sight listening may be regarded as a simple process (Figure 7.2) in which both sides take turns to respond and listen, but in fact this perspective needs to be extended to take full account of all of the processes involved (Figure 7.3). As we talk we also at the same time scan for feedback to see how our messages are being received. When we listen we evaluate what is being said, plan our response, rehearse this, and then execute it. While the processes of evaluation, planning and rehearsal usually occur subconsciously, they are important because they can interfere with the pure listening activity. Thus we may have decided what we are going to say before the other person has actually stopped speaking, and as a result may not really be listening effectively. It is, therefore, important to ensure that those activities which mediate between listening and speaking do not actually interfere with the listening process itself.

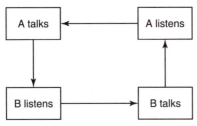

Figure 7.2 Basic model of listening

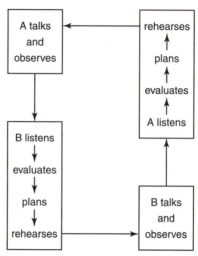

Figure 7.3 Extended model of listening

In terms of the verbal message being received, the listening process is influenced by three main factors.

Reductionism

The human memory is notoriously fallible. On average, we have forgotten about half of what we hear immediately after hearing it, and within 8 hours we remember only 35 per cent of the message (Adler *at al.*, 2001). After 24 hours we have forgotten up to 80 per cent of the information received (Wilson, 1999). Since we can only assimilate a limited amount of data, the messages we receive have to be reduced, sometimes at the expense of vital information. For this reason it is important to attempt to ensure that the central information being conveyed is remembered. The following techniques can help to facilitate retention.

Recording

Obviously, where it is possible to video- or audio-record the interaction this provides verbatim recall. However, this is not always feasible.

Note-taking

Retention can be facilitated by noting the main points emanating from the interaction. As Bostrom (1990: 29) pointed out: 'Notetaking may enhance memory by enabling the receiver to transform the message so that it corresponds more closely with his or her own cognitive structure.' Such transformation involves several sub-processes, including the:

- increased mental activity involved in writing and listening;
- selection and reduction of material;
- repetition of the core features being presented;
- adaptation or translation of the message into more personally meaningful and accessible terminology.

These processes should enable the message to be more readily assimilated. Watson and Barker (1984) reported that note-taking interchanged, rather than concurrent, with listening was more effective in terms of remembering what has been said. It is also socially more appropriate if note-taking does not dominate the interaction, but is rather something that occurs sporadically, and is explained to the speaker ('Can I just note down some details before I forget them?'). Care needs to be taken, since it has been shown that note-taking by doctors is regarded by patients as problematic. In particular, when the doctor consults medical records or makes notes therein, patients have been shown to become unsure about whether the doctor is actually listening or not (Ruusuvuori, 2001).

Memory devices

A range of techniques have been proposed as aids to memory. Dickson *et al.* (1997) highlighted three main mnemonics.

1   *Acronyms*, such as PAIL for the four types of skin cuts Puncture, Abrasion, Incision, Laceration.
2   *Rhymes* to remember names, such as
    'Big Bobby Blair,
    Very fat, red hair'.
3   *Visualisation* whereby the listener creates a mental picture of what the speaker is saying – for example trying to visualise a client's home environment and relationships as they are being described.

In a review of this area, Gellatly (1986) illustrated how mnemonics were a key part of early Greek and Roman education, and pointed out that 'mnemonics work because they impose organization on the material to be remembered' (p. 92). While there is some research evidence to vindicate the use of these memory aids (Gregg, 1986), it would appear that their success is dependent both on the ability of the listener to use them, and on the nature of the message being communicated.

Organising material

Material should be organised into main themes, ideas and categories, and into a chronological sequence where possible. Such organisation must not, of course, interfere with the act of listening, but where time is available during interaction (as is usually the case), then this type of 'conceptual filing' can facilitate later recall.

Rationalisation

As we listen, we assimilate information in such a way as to make it fit with our own situation and experience. If it does not fit immediately we may rationalise what we hear in order to make it more acceptable, but by so doing distort the facts. This occurs in three main ways.

1   We *attribute different causes* to those presented. Thus a patient may attribute a troublesome cough to the weather, or argue that it 'runs in the family', rather than accept a practioner's explanation that it is due to heavy smoking.
2   *Transformation of language* is a common form of rationalisation. This is often due to what Gregg (1986) termed *acoustic confusions*, caused by close similarity in the sounds of certain words. In the medical field products with similar sounding names can be mixed up by doctors, nurses and pharmacists, with potentially tragic consequences (for example, in one case a Belgian patient died after being given the diuretic Lasix® instead of the anti-ulcer drug Losec®).
3   Paradoxically given the aforementioned reductionism, there may be the *addition of material*. A classical instance of this occurs in everyday gossip, whereby a basic story is enlarged and embroidered on during each re-telling, until it eventually becomes a sensational story. Care needs to be taken in professional situations to avoid 'reading too much into' what the client has said.

Change in the order of events

This is a common occurrence in the assimilation of information, whereby data become jumbled and remembered in the wrong order. Thus 'Take two tablets three times daily after meals' is remembered as 'Take three tablets twice daily before meals'; or 'He lost his job and then started to drink heavily' becomes 'He started to drink heavily and then lost his job as a result'. Such mistakes can be avoided by the careful conceptual organisation of material being received.

FACETS OF LISTENING

There are four main facets that need to be taken into consideration. These are the characteristics associated with the listener, the speaker, the message and the environment. From the available evidence, the following conclusions can be adduced (for fuller reviews, see Borisoff and Purdy, 1991b; Burley-Allen, 1995; Wolvin and Coakley, 1996; Bostrom, 1997).

The listener

Galanes *et al.* (2000) distinguished between four main types of listener (see Box 7.3). In addition, several positive correlations have been found between characteristics of the listener and ability to listen effectively.

> *Box 7.3* Four types of listener
>
> 1 *People-oriented listeners.* Their primary concern is for others' feelings and needs. Can be distracted away from the task owing to this focus on psycho-emotional perspectives. We seek them out when we need a listening ear. Are good helpers.
> 2 *Task-oriented listeners.* Are mainly concerned with getting the business done. Do not like discussing what they see as irrelevant information or having to listen to 'long-winded' people or 'whingers'. Can be insensitive to the emotional needs of others.
> 3 *Content-oriented listeners.* These are analytical people who enjoy dissecting information and carefully scrutinising it. They often focus on the literal meaning of what has been said. They want to hear all sides and leave no stone unturned, however long the process. Can be slow to make decisions as they are never quite sure if they have garnered all the necessary information. Are good mediators.
> 4 *Time-oriented listeners.* Their main focus is on getting tasks completed within set time frames. They see time as a valuable commodity, not to be wasted. Are impatient with what they see as 'prevaricators' and can be prone to jump to conclusions before they have heard all the information.

Linguistic aptitude

Those with a wider vocabulary are better listeners, since they can more readily understand and assimilate a greater range of concepts. Academic achievement has also been shown to be associated with listening ability (although as might be expected academic achievement is also usually highly correlated with linguistic aptitude).

Motivation

A listener who is highly motivated will remember more of the information presented. Such motivation can be caused by a variety of factors, ranging from a school pupil's fear of retribution from a harsh teacher, to the desire of a caring professional to help a particular client.

Organisational ability

As mentioned earlier, the ability to organise incoming information into appropriate categories facilitates learning. Good listeners identify the key elements of the messages received, and store these in appropriate conceptual compartments.

Use of special concentration techniques

There are several such techniques employed by effective listeners. One of these is to attempt to put oneself in the speaker's position and try to see the world from this perspective. The memory aids mentioned previously are also useful here. A final approach is the use of intrapersonal dialogue, wherein the listener engages in covert self-talk to heighten receptivity. Egan (2002) referred to this as 'listening to oneself'. This may involve the use of:

- covert coaching ('I'm not paying enough attention. I need to listen more carefully');
- self-reinforcement ('I'm listening well and understanding what he is saying');
- asking covert questions ('Why is she telling me this now?').

There is some evidence that when listening to lectures, the latter technique of self-questioning may be most effective. King (1992) carried out a study in which she found that undergraduates trained to use self-questions (asking themselves questions during the lecture such as 'What is the main idea of . . .?'; 'How is this related to what we studied earlier?') remembered more about the lecture content one week later than either those taught to summarise the lecture in writing or those who simply took notes.

Age

In his review of communication problems when dealing with older individuals, Giordano (2000) noted that a reduced capacity for information processing has been widely reported in this age group. However, he also highlighted how there are wide differences between older people so that some will be more adversely affected than others. Furthermore, age also brings positive changes, such as an increased vocabulary and a wealth of experience of dealing with people in various situations. Thus listening faculties may be reduced or enhanced, depending on the individual.

The reaction to noise is, however, relatively consistent. Most young people enjoy noisy, rapidly changing, environments with lots of stimulation (the so-called 'MTV generation'), and become bored if this is not available. With age, however, our need for such levels of arousal decreases. Older adults in general prefer quiet, peaceful and tranquil surroundings and find noise off-putting. This is because they find it more difficult to cope with the cognitive interference caused by the intrusive stimuli. They are less able to manage divided attention, and so tend to be much more susceptible to distraction from the effects of extraneous noise. So, when dealing with this age group the importance of securing a quiet location should be borne in mind. Likewise, reaction time and speech discrimination decrease with age, so that older people tend to need more time to process information and respond. This means that a slower rate of speech may be desirable. Giordano also recommended the use of periods of silence to allow the older person time for reflection. However, as discussed in Chapter 2, when communicating with this age group, the dangers of *ageism* must be avoided.

Gender

There is now a substantial body of research to substantiate the view that females are more perceptive at recognising and interpreting nonverbal messages. Borisoff and Merrill (1991: 65), after reviewing the available evidence, concluded: 'Numerous studies have established women's superior abilities as both decoders and encoders of nonverbal messages when compared with men.' They suggested that part of the reason for these differences may be attributable to a status factor, in that lower status people spend more time listening to higher status people than vice versa and males may therefore conceptualise the listening role as being of lower status. However, this view is not in line with research findings by Johnson and Bechler (1998). They conducted a study at a Midwestern US university, where undergraduate students met in leaderless groups and were rated on leadership skills and on listening skills by separate teams of raters. Results showed that those rated high in listening behaviours by one set of coders were also rated high in leadership by a different set of coders. Interestingly, no differences were found in recall ability among subjects, and so it was the *display* of listening behaviour that was important. Johnson and Bechler concluded that their results confirm the general finding that 'leaders typically display more effective listening skills than the other members' (p. 452).

What may be the case is that each gender tends to tune in to different aspects of a message, and indeed Adler and Elmhorst (1999: 109) argued that 'Women are more likely to catch the feelings behind a speaker's words, while men tend to listen for the facts'. Another difference is that males tend to use head nods as a sign of *agreement*, whereas females use them more as indicators of *attention* but not necessarily agreement with the speaker (Stewart and Logan, 1998). This can lead to gender confusion if a male takes nods as agreement and then becomes annoyed when the female proceeds to express disagreement. (A similar problem occurs in cross-cultural communication in that people from some cultures – e.g. Asian – also use nods as signs of listening but not necessarily concurring). However, much more research is required in order to chart the precise nature and extent of gender influence on listening ability.

Physical condition

Physical condition is important, in that listening ability deteriorates as fatigue increases. Thus someone who is extremely tired is less capable of displaying prolonged listening. Professionals with a heavy case-load need to attempt to ensure that they do not have to handle their most demanding cases at the end of a tiring day.

Disposition

Introverts are usually better listeners than extroverts, since they are content to sit back and let the other person be the centre of attention. Furthermore, highly anxious individuals do not usually make good listeners, since they tend to be too worried about factors apart from the speaker to listen carefully to what is being said. As noted by Beck (1999: 63) 'Anxiety makes the mind wander from the current communication situation.' Individuals who are high sensation-seekers also perform poorly if they are required to listen for long periods (Bostrom, 1990). Likewise, those who are more susceptible to distractions are not good listeners, an extreme example being the hyperactive child. Finally, what Adler *et al.* (2001) referred to as 'stage hogs' or 'conversational narcissists' are bad listeners. These are dominating, self-centred, egotistical individuals who only want to talk and have no real interest in what others have to say.

The speaker

A number of aspects pertaining to the speaker are of importance.

Speech rate

While the average rate of speech is between 125 and 175 words per minute, the average 'thought rate' at which information is cognitively processed is between 400 and 800 words per minute. The differential between speech rate and thought rate gives the listener an opportunity to assimilate, organise, retain and covertly respond to the speaker. However, this differential may also encourage the listener to fill up the spare time with other unrelated mental processes (such as daydreaming). Listening can be improved by using this spare thought time positively, by, for example, asking covert questions such as:

- 'What are the main points being made?'
- 'What reasons are being given?'
- 'In what frame of reference should this be viewed?'
- 'What further information is necessary?'

Where a speaker drops below the 100 words per minute rate, or far exceeds 300 words per minute, listening can be much more problematic. In the former case, it is difficult to listen to a very slow speaker. Professionals who have to deal with depressed clients will be aware of the problems involved in maintaining concentration with someone who says very little. At the other extreme, it is difficult to listen effectively for an extended period to a very rapid speaker, since we cannot handle the volume of information being received. Wolff *et al.* (1983), in reviewing the literature on speech rate, however, concluded that listeners:

> prefer to listen, can comprehend better, and are more likely to believe a message that is presented at the rate of 190 words or more per minute . . . They demonstrate marked efficiency when listening to a speaker talking at 280 words per minute – twice the rate of normal speech.
>
> (p. 155)

Interestingly, as a result of such findings, television advertisers speeded up the rate of verbal presentation in their adverts, with positive results in terms of viewer comprehension and recall. These findings also suggest that we have problems paying attention for lengthy periods to people who talk at, or below, the normal rate of speech. Thus when long pauses and a slow speech rate are used by a client, concentrated listening is required from the professional.

However, the topic of conversation and its degree of difficulty need to be factored in to the equation. A slow speed may be appropriate with a complex issue whereas with more basic material a faster pace is usually the norm. This was confirmed in a study by Robinson *et al.* (1997), where undergraduates were presented with taped lectures delivered at slow, moderate or fast rates. The results indicated that students receiving the slower speed comprehended the lectures better and rated the material as more important than those receiving the faster delivery. As a result of their findings Robinson *et al.* recommended that for lectures, a speech rate of around 100 words per minute is most appropriate. One reason for this was identified by Dabbs (1985: 191) who observed: 'Long pauses are accepted by the participants in intellectual conversation as a normal result of trying to "figure things out", while long pauses in social conversation indicate things are not going well and will tend to be avoided.'

Speech delivery

The clarity, fluency and audibility of the speaker all have an influence on listener comprehension. Thus it is difficult to listen to, and comprehend, someone who speaks English with a pronounced foreign accent, or who has a strong, unfamiliar, regional dialect. It is also difficult to listen to someone with a severe speech dysfluency, both because the message being delivered is disjointed, and because the listener is preoccupied thinking about how to respond to the dysfluency. Finally, it is difficult to pay attention to an individual who speaks in a dull monotone (as most students will testify), or who mumbles and does not have good voice projection.

Emotionality

If the speaker displays high levels of emotion, the listener may be distracted by this and cease to listen accurately to the verbal message. In situations where individuals are in extreme emotional states, their communication is inevitably highly charged. It is often necessary to sustain an interaction in these circumstances. Sustaining can be defined as the process whereby someone experiencing an extreme emotional state is encouraged to ventilate, talk about, and understand, their emotions. When faced with a person experiencing extreme emotions (e.g. depression or aggression) it is often not advisable either to reinforce positively or to rebuke the individual for this behaviour, since such reactions may well be counterproductive. For example, by rebuking an individual who is displaying aggressive behaviour, it is likely that this will only serve to heighten the aggression. A more reasoned response is to react in a calm fashion, demonstrating an interest in, without overtly reinforcing, the emotional person, but also showing a willingness to listen and attempt to understand what exactly has caused this to occur.

Only when strong emotional feelings begin to decrease can a more rational discussion take place. Someone who is 'too emotional' about something is likely to be 'too worked up about it' to listen to reasoned arguments. When dealing with an individual who is displaying high levels of emotion, it may be necessary to be prepared to wait for a considerable period of time before this is ventilated. During this period the anxiety of the listener may interfere with the ability to listen carefully. Too much attention may be paid to the emotional message being conveyed, and as a result important information of a more factual nature may not be assimilated. Conversely, full concentration may be on the factual content with the emotional message being ignored. In both these cases, message distortion occurs, in that the listener is not perceiving the total message.

Status

If the speaker is regarded as an important person, or a recognised authority on a topic, listening comprehension is increased, as more credence will be attached to what is being said. Also, more attention tends to be paid if the speaker is in a position of superiority. Attention is therefore greater if the listener has admiration and respect for a speaker of high credibility. Interestingly, in a study of interruptions in British and Italian management meetings, Bargiela-Chiappini and Harris (1996: 292) found that 'Participants with lower status rarely interrupt and are rarely interrupted.' Presumably, their relative position in the pecking order means that lower status people feel less able to interrupt their superiors. It may also be that those of higher status consider it rude to interrupt those further down the hierarchy, or that they do not consider them to be rivals in the battle for dominance in meetings and so allow them to speak without intervention.

The message

The following aspects of the message itself need to be borne in mind.

Structure

A message that is unclear and lacking in any coherent structure is more difficult to listen to and comprehend. The speaker may be emphasising the trivial, being deliberately vague and evasive, or speaking for a long time without a break. It is sometimes the goal of the speaker to confuse, distract or mislead the listener by distorting the message being conveyed (many politicians are quite adept in this field), or the speaker may simply be incapable of clarity of expression. In both these cases, it is often necessary to interrupt, by asking questions in an attempt to understand what is being said.

Significance

If the message is of particular interest, or of special significance, comprehension and recall are heightened. In an experimental study in this area, Schneider and Laurion (1993) investigated how well undergraduates listened to and recalled items on radio news. They found greatest recall for 'high-interest' items of particular relevance (e.g. student-related issues, stories about their university). In addition, when the message conveys similar values, attitudes or viewpoints to our own, listening is facilitated, since most of us like to have our beliefs and expectations confirmed. Paradoxically, however, it has also been found that if a message contains a disconfirmation of our expectations, listening is also heightened, as we are then motivated to evaluate this unexpected message. Frick (1992), in an investigation of the concept of 'interestingness', discovered that people find most interesting those statements that change, or challenge confidence in, their existing beliefs. Results also suggested that statements that advance our understanding are attended to with particular interest. An example given by Frick was that: 'a clinician would find most interesting those statements by a client that further the clinician's understanding of the client' (p. 126). In similar vein, a social worker who suspects a parent of child abuse is likely to pay concerted attention to both the parent and the child when they are discussing parent–child relationships. On the other hand, it is also important to pay attention to those areas that a client does not initiate. Indeed, listening theorists often emphasise the importance of listening to what is *not* being said by the speaker. Thus a child who steadfastly avoids or blocks any discussion about a parent may well be sending out an important message.

Complexity

The difficulty of the material being delivered also affects listening. As discussed in relation to speech rate, most people can cope more effectively with basic material delivered at a fast rate, but with complex information a slower speed of speech is required, to allow time for assimilation.

The environment

Three elements of the environment in which the interaction is taking place need to be considered.

Ventilation and temperature

Listening is impaired if the environment is either unpleasantly warm or cold, and optimum listening occurs when the room temperature is at a comfortable level.

Noise

In a study of the impact of music on performance, Ransdell and Gilroy (2001) investigated the effects of music on students' ability to write essays on computer. They found that music disrupted writing fluency. However, in this study the music (slow ballads taken from a Nelson Riddle Orchestra tape) was not self-selected by the students. From our own (admittedly non-scientific) survey of students and colleagues we have found that some people like to work to music while others do not (indeed one of the authors of this book writes while listening to background music, while the other prefers silence). In terms of interpersonal encounters, comprehension deteriorates when there is loud, intrusive noise that interferes with the assimilation process (such as building work going on outside). However, it is unclear whether non-intrusive or self-selected background noise has an adverse effect on listening or indeed facilitates it. For example, most pubs, restaurants and hotel lounges play background music to encourage conversation. The level of noise is important, since background noise may be filtered out whereas intrusive sounds cannot (see Figure 7.1). However, the nature of the interaction is relevant, so that a lecturer would not encourage even background noise if total concentration from students was desired. Dentists, on the other hand, often play background music to encourage patients to relax while in surgery.

Seating

Perhaps not surprisingly, one empirical study of 123 interactive dyads found that being seated was regarded as a facilitator to effective listening (Halone and Pecchioni, 2001). If someone is expected to listen for a prolonged period, suitable seating is important. Yet most schools provide less than comfortable chairs for pupils and expect sustained, concerted attention from them throughout the school day. In group contexts, a compact seating arrangement is more effective than a scattered one. People pay more attention and recall more when they are brought close together physically, as opposed to when they are spread out around the room.

OBSTACLES TO EFFECTIVE LISTENING

The following factors have been identified as obstacles to listening (see Figure 7.4 for a summary of obstacles at the main stages of listening).

Dichotomous listening

This occurs when we attempt to assimilate information simultaneously from two different sources. Examples include trying to listen to two people in a group who are speaking at the same time, and conducting a telephone conversation while carrying on a face-to-face interaction with another person, or when distracted by

Listening stage	Obstacles
Sensing	External noise (e.g. roadworks outside) Physical impairments (e.g. hard of hearing) Information overload
Attending	Poor speaker delivery (e.g. monotone) Overly long messages Lack of message coherence or structure Fatigue Uncomfortable environment Poor attending habits or disposition Negative attitudes to the speaker
Understanding	Low academic or linguistic ability Selective listening Mental set and biases of the listener Inability to emphathise Different speaker/listener backgrounds
Remembering	Poor short-term listening ability Memory store limitations Proactive and retroactive inhibition

Figure 7.4 Obstacles to listening

some form of extraneous noise. In all these instances the dichotomous nature of the listening interferes with the ability of the listener to interact effectively, since messages may be either received inaccurately or not received at all. Effective listening is facilitated by paying attention to only one person at a time, and by manipulating the environment in order to ensure that extraneous distractions are minimised (e.g. by closing doors, switching off television or having telephone calls intercepted).

Inattentiveness

Here the listener for some reason does not give full attention to the speaker. Someone who is self-conscious, and concerned with the personal impression being conveyed, is unlikely to be listening closely to others. In terms of research into memory, two identified problems relate to the process of inhibition (Hayes, 1998). Proactive inhibition occurs when something that has already been learned interferes with attempts to learn new material. A parallel problem is retroactive inhibition, which is where material that has already been learned is impaired as a result of the impact of, and interference from, recent material. In interpersonal encounters inhibition also occurs. *Retroactive listening inhibition* is where the individual is still pondering over the ramifications of something that happened in the recent past, at the expense of listening to the speaker in the present interaction. *Proactive listening inhibition* takes place when someone has an important engagement looming, and their preoccupation with this militates against listening in the present. The main mental focus then tends to be more about how to handle the future encounter than about what the speaker is currently saying.

Individual bias

Our biases are like comfort blankets – we do not like them to be threatened and cannot contemplate losing them. In a study of what individuals wanted from others in terms of listening, two of the key features were that they should put their own thoughts aside and be open minded (Halone and Pecchioni, 2001). Yet as Egan (2002: 90) noted 'It is impossible to listen to other people in a completely unbiased way.' The biases we have developed as part of our upbringing and socialisation are filters that may distort the messages we receive. This can occur in a number of contexts. Someone with limited time may not wish to get involved in lengthy dialogue and therefore may choose to 'hear' only the less provocative or unproblematic part of what was said. Oscar Wilde clearly identified one of the pitfalls of listening when he said 'Listening is a very dangerous thing. If one listens one may be convinced.' Similarly a person who does not want to recognise difficult realities, may refuse to accept these when expressed by another – either by distorting the message or by refusing to listen to the speaker altogether (a common example where this occurs is in bereavement where the bereaved may initially not accept the fact that a loved one has actually died – the *denial stage* of bereavement). At another level, people may not respond accurately to questions or statements, simply because they wish to make a separate point when given the floor. One example of this is politicians who want to ensure, at all costs, that they get their message across, and when asked questions in public meetings frequently do not answer these accurately, but rather take the opportunity to state their own point of view.

Mental set

We are all affected by previous experiences, attitudes, values and feelings, and these in turn influence our mental set for any given situation (see Chapter 10). We evaluate others based on their appearance, initial statements, or what they said during previous encounters. These influence the way the speaker is heard, in that statements may be screened so that only those aspects that fit in with specific expectations are perceived. The process of stereotyping acts as a form of cognitive short-cut that enables us to deal swiftly with others without having to take the effort to find out about them. Here all members of a particular group are regarded as homogeneous and having identical traits and behaviour patterns. By ascribing a stereotype to the speaker (e.g. racist, communist, delinquent, or hypochondriac) we then become less objective. Judgements tend to be based on *who is speaking*, rather than on *what is being said*. As Tourish (1999: 193) noted 'we fail to appreciate the full uniqueness of the whole person, ensuring that our stereotypes sometimes lead us into judgements which are both erroneous and biased'.

While it is often important to attempt to evaluate the motives and goals of the speaker, this can only be achieved by a reasoned, rational process, rather than by an irrational or emotional reaction to a particular stereotype. Galanes *et al.* (2000) used the term *mind raping* to refer to the process whereby the listener enforces ascribed meaning to what the speaker has said. Such people forcefully impose their interpretation on the other, in statements such as 'I heard what you *said*, but I know what you really *mean*.' It is therefore important to listen both carefully and objectively to everything that is being said.

Blocking

The process of blocking occurs when an individual does not wish to pursue a certain line of communication, and so employs various techniques to end or divert the conversation. These blocking techniques are presented in Box 7.4. On occasions, some of these are quite legitimate. For example, a pharmacist would be expected to advise a patient to see a doctor immediately if a serious illness was suspected. However, it is where blocking is used negatively that it becomes a serious obstacle to effective listening.

Box 7.4 Blocking tactics to listening

Tactic	Example
Rejecting involvement	'I don't wish to discuss this with you.' 'That has nothing to do with me.'
Denial of feelings	'You've nothing to worry about.' 'You'll be all right.'
Selective responding	Focusing only on specific aspects of the speaker's message, while ignoring other parts of it.
Admitting insufficient knowledge	'I'm not really qualified to say.' 'I'm only vaguely familiar with that subject.'
Topic shift	Changing the topic away from that expressed by the speaker.
Referring	'You should consult your doctor about that.' 'Your course tutor will help you on that.'
Deferring	'Come back and see me if the pain persists.' 'We'll discuss that next week.'
Pre-empting any communication	'I'm in a terrible rush. See you later.' 'I can't talk now. I'm late for a meeting.'

ACTIVE LISTENING

Research has shown that speakers want listeners to *respond appropriately* to what they are saying rather than 'just listen' (Halone and Pecchioni, 2001: 63). In other words, they desire active listening in the form of both verbal and nonverbal behaviours. Although verbal responses are the main indicators of successful listening, if accompanying nonverbal behaviours are not displayed it is usually assumed that an individual is not paying attention, and *ipso facto* not listening. Thus while these nonverbal signs may not be crucial to the assimilation of verbal messages, they are expected by others. Furthermore, the nonverbal information conveyed by the speaker adds to, and provides emphasis for, the verbal message (see Chapter 3). An early example of this was shown in a study by Strong *et al.* (1971) who asked college students to listen only, or both view and listen, to tapes of counsellors, and rate them on a 100-item checklist. Results indicated that when the counsellors were both seen and heard they were described as more cold, bored, awkward, unreasonable and disinterested than when they were heard only. This study highlighted the importance of attending to both verbal and nonverbal information in judging social responses.

Verbal indicators of listening are discussed in many of the skills reviewed throughout this book. As we noted earlier, listening is a prerequisite skill that is part of all other skills. Within the skill of reinforcement, for example, *verbal reinforcers* are often regarded as being associated with attending (see Chapter 4). In terms of listening, however, it has long been known that caution is needed when employing verbal reinforcement. Thus Rosenshine (1971) found that the curve of the relationship between amount of verbal reinforcement by teachers and degree of pupil participation in classroom lessons was bell-shaped. While verbal reinforcers (e.g. 'very good', 'yes') initially had the effect of increasing pupil participation, if this reinforcement was continued in its basic form, pupils began to regard it with indifference. Rosenshine pointed out that it is simple to administer positive reinforcers without much thought, but to demonstrate genuine listening some reasons have to be given for their use. Pupils need to be told why their responses are good, for the reinforcement to be regarded as genuine.

Another aspect of reinforcement that is a potent indicator of effective listening is *reference to past statements*. This can range from simply remembering someone's name, to remembering other details about facts, feelings or ideas they may have expressed in the past. This shows a willingness to pay attention to what was previously discussed and in turn is likely to encourage the person to participate more fully in the present interaction. This is part of the process of *verbal following*, whereby the listener matches verbal responses closely to those of the speaker so that they 'follow on' in a coherent fashion. If the listener asks related questions, or makes related statements that build on the ideas expressed by the speaker, this is an indication of attentiveness and interest.

However, a distinction needs to be made between *coherent topic shifts*, which occur once the previous topic has been exhausted, and *noncoherent topic shifts*, which are abrupt changes of conversation that are not explained. We often use *disjunct markers* to signal a change of topic ('Incidentally', 'Can I ask you a different question?', 'Before I forget'). In the early stages of a relationship, individuals usually ensure that a disjunct marker is used before making a noncoherent topic shift, whereas once a relationship has been developed the need for such disjunct markers recedes. Thus married couples often use unmarked noncoherent topic shifts during conversation without this unduly affecting their relationship. However, in professional interactions disjunct markers are advisable where verbal following does not take place.

Within the skill of questioning (see Chapter 5) the use of *probing questions* is a direct form of listening, wherein the questioner follows up the responses of the respondent by asking related questions. What Kramer (2001) termed 'verbal door openers' are also useful (e.g. 'Would you like to talk about that a little bit more?'). Similarly, the skill of *reflecting* (see Chapter 6) represents a powerful form of response development. In order to reflect accurately the feeling, or the content, of what someone has said, it is necessary to listen carefully before formulating a succinct reflecting statement. The use of *summarisation* during periods of closure is also evidence of prolonged listening throughout an interaction sequence (see Chapter 10).

Nonverbal responses are also important during listening. A key feature of effective listening is the ability to combine the meaning from body language and paralanguage with the linguistic message (Burley-Allen, 1995). Certain nonverbal behaviours are associated with attending while others are associated with lack of listening. Thus Rosenfeld and Hancks (1980) showed how head nods, forward leaning posture, visual attention and eyebrow raises were all correlated with positive ratings of listening responsiveness. They also found the most prevalent vocalisation to be the guggle 'mm hmm', with the most frequent nonverbal listening indicator being the head-nod. This latter finding was confirmed more recently by Duggan and Parrott (2001) who showed that head nods and smiles were very potent indicators of listening in doctor–patient interchanges. The main nonverbal listening responses are shown in Box 7.5.

Parallel and contrasting nonverbal cues have been identified as signs of inattentiveness or lack of listening (Duggan and Parrott, 2001). The most common of these are:

- inappropriate facial expressions;
- lack of eye-contact;
- poor use of paralanguage (e.g. flat tone of voice, interrupting the speaker, no emphasis);
- slouched or shifting posture;
- absence of head nods;
- the use of distracting behaviours (e.g. rubbing the eyes, yawning, writing, or reading while the speaker is talking).

In fact, an effective technique to induce someone to stop talking is to use these indicators of non-listening. These nonverbal signals can of course be deceiving, in that someone who is assimilating the verbal message may not appear to be listening. Most teachers have experienced the situation where a pupil appears to be inattentive and yet when asked a question is able to give an appropriate response. Conversely, people may engage in pretend listening, or *pseudolistening*, where they show all of the overt signs of attending but are not actually listening at all.

Box 7.5 Nonverbal signs of listening

1   *Smiles* used as indicators of willingness to follow the conversation or pleasure at what is being said.
2   *Direct eye-contact.* In western society, the listener usually looks more at the speaker than vice versa. (In other cultures this may not be the case, and direct eye gaze may be viewed as disrespectful or challenging.)
3   *Using appropriate paralanguage* to convey enthusiasm for the speaker's thoughts and ideas (e.g. tone of voice, emphasis on certain words, lack of interruption).
4   *Reflecting the facial expressions* of the speaker in order to show sympathy and empathy with the emotional message being conveyed.
5   *Adopting an attentive posture,* such as a forward or sideways lean on a chair. Similarly a sideways tilt of the head (often with the head resting on one hand) is an indicator of listening. What is known as *sympathetic communication* involves the mirroring of overall posture, as well as facial expressions. Indeed where problems arise in communication such mirroring usually ceases to occur (see Chapter 6 for a fuller discussion of mirroring).
6   *Head nods* to indicate agreement or willingness to listen.
7   *Refraining from distracting mannerisms,* such as doodling with a pen, fidgeting, or looking at a watch.

Although it is possible to listen without overtly so indicating, in most social settings it is important to demonstrate such attentiveness. Thus both the verbal and nonverbal determinants of active listening play a key role in social interaction. In fact, these signs are integrated in such a fashion that, in most cases, if either channel signals a lack of attention this is taken as an overall indication of poor listening.

OVERVIEW

Listening is a fundamental component of interpersonal communication. In their text on this topic, Wolvin and Coakley (1996: 15) reviewed research to demonstrate how 'the role of listening in interpersonal, group, and public communicative situations has become more significant in the economic, political, social, mental, and spiritual phases of our lives'. It is important to realise that listening is not something that just happens, but rather is an active process in which the listener decides to pay careful attention to the speaker. It involves focusing on the speaker's verbal and nonverbal messages, while at the same time actively portraying verbal and nonverbal signs of listening. The following guidelines should be borne in mind.

1   *Get physically prepared to listen.* If the interaction is taking place in your own environment, provide an appropriate physical layout of furniture, ensure adequate temperature and ventilation, and keep intrusive noise and other distractions to a minimum.

2   *Be mentally prepared to listen objectively.* Try to remove all other thoughts from your mind, and concentrate fully. Be aware of your own biases, avoid preconceptions, and do not stereotype the speaker.

3   *Use spare thought time positively.* Keep your thoughts entirely on the message being delivered by asking covert questions, constructing mental images of what is being said, or employing other concentration techniques.

4   *Do not interrupt.* There is a Native American Indian proverb that advises: 'Listen or your tongue will make you deaf.' Research has shown that interruptions are not well received during interactive episodes (Halone and Pecchioni, 2001). It is important to 'hold your tongue' and let the other person contribute fully. Develop a system of *mental banking*, where ideas you wish to pursue can be cognitively 'deposited' and 'withdrawn' later. This allows the speaker to have a continuous flow, and the fact that you can later refer back to what has been said is a potent indicator of active listening.

5   *Organise the speaker's messages* into appropriate categories and, where relevant, chronological order. Identify the main thrust and any supporting arguments. This process facilitates comprehension and recall of what was said.

6   *Do not overuse blocking tactics.* These are often employed subconsciously to prevent the speaker from controlling an interaction.

7   *Remember that listening is hard work.* It has been said the only place you will find easy listening is a specialist section in a music store. It takes energy to listen actively and this involves a firm initial commitment. Professionals who spend their working day listening will testify that it is an exhausting activity, and one that requires discipline and determination. Indeed, as Figley (2002) has shown, those who work in the therapeutic sphere (counsellors, health professionals, etc.) can suffer from the phenomenon of *compassion fatigue* as a result of concerted listening to accounts of traumatic experiences.

In concluding this chapter, we recommend that you bear in mind one of the precepts proffered by Polonius to his son Laertes in Shakespeare's *Hamlet, Prince of Denmark*: 'Give every man thine ear, but few thy voice.'

Chapter 8

Explaining

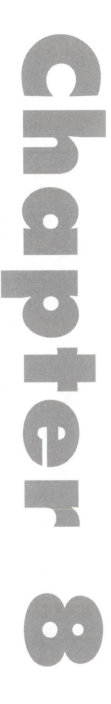

INTRODUCTION

THIS CHAPTER IS DEVOTED to the processes involved in giving information in such a way as to maximise comprehension. We will concentrate essentially on the cognitively based task of sharing detail and bringing about understanding. Presentations that rely more on emotion and are intended primarily to persuade (rather than enlighten) through creating changes in attitude or opinion (rather than knowledge) will be dealt with in Chapter 12, in relation to influencing. Without any shadow of doubt, people have more information available to them now than at any other time in history. We live in a world where the onward march of computer-mediated technology in all its forms and guises is an ever-present reality. The Internet is currently its proudest epitome. Yet being able to access a welter of undigested facts, theories and findings does not automatically make us more enlightened.

Referring to communication within organisations, Clampitt (2001) made a valid distinction between *data, information* and *knowledge*. While recognising difficulties in providing tight definitions of each, data are said to concern particular representations of reality, not all of which may be accurate or relevant to that person at that time. Information is created when certain elements are focused on, isolated from background data, and their potential contribution to decision-making realised. Finally, knowledge relies on recognizing patterns and consistencies in information, making possible the development of theories that can be tested. It is only such knowledge that produces effective action. There is, therefore, a need to give thought to the organisation of material, how it is delivered and to whom, if we are to benefit from what we read and hear, as well as successfully getting our own message across.

Explaining is a standard feature of everyday casual talk and forms the sub-stance of more formal addresses to large gatherings attending lectures or public hearings. It is also a crucial part of skilled professional practice in areas such as education, medicine, nursing, management, technology, and law (Brown and Atkins, 1997; Hayes, 2002). The importance of teachers being able to put across material in such a way that pupils readily grasp it is obvious and has been a concern of educationalists for many years (Thyne, 1963). But patients too have a need for information about diagnosis, prognosis, condition or treatment to be delivered in ways that they can understand. Likewise in the world of law, advice and instruction that may be couched in an equally arcane (indeed archaic) language have to be com-municated clearly if recipients are not to be disadvantaged.

Despite what has just been said, explaining is an activity often performed poorly by many professionals. As put by Gage *et al.* (1968: 3) with reference to teaching:

> Some people explain aptly, getting to the heart of the matter with just the right terminology, examples and organization of ideas. Other explainers, on the contrary, get us and themselves all mixed up, use terms beyond our level of comprehension, draw inept analogies and even employ concepts and principles that cannot be understood without an understanding of the very thing being explained.

But teachers need not be singled out for special attention. Gage's claim unfortunately seems to be equally applicable to other domains of professional practice. Instances of health worker–patient conversation have been pinpointed where deficiencies in information-giving lie at the heart of poor levels of professional communication (Dickson, 1999a, b). Patients criticise not being told enough by doctors and not understanding what is said when they are. The findings were summarised by the Audit Commission (1993: 1) as follows: 'A common complaint is that there is not enough information. Equally, information often exists but the quality is poor.' This chimes with a comment from the Health Services Commissioner who cautioned health care staff that they have a responsibility 'to ensure that information given has been fully and correctly understood' (HMSO, 1995: 8).

Moving from health to law, doubts have been raised about how well the criminal law system is working in some US courts. At the centre of this process of justice is a trial overseen by a judge whose task it is to apply the appropriate law and make the jury familiar with it. The jury in turn is charged with applying that law to the evidence in reaching a verdict. The extent to which this is done successfully is limited by how successfully members fully grasp instructions received. Charrow and Charrow (1979) were among the first to point out that many jurors experienced problems comprehending this material. In a recent review of research in the area, Tiersma (2001) documented different sources of evidence suggesting that jurors frequently fail to properly understand their role. In some instances members have been caught delving into dictionaries in an attempt to clarify their confusion, despite the fact that technically they are not allowed to consult outside sources during the trial. This can have significant consequences. The case is cited of a federal court that set aside the verdict of a man who had spent some twenty years on death row, partly because it came to light that the jury had acted improperly in this way. Specific problems of comprehension have to do with vocabulary and the technical meaning of some terms that can be at odds with everyday interpretations. Additionally, instructional material is 'often poorly organized, lexically quite dense, and expressed in rambling sentences that start with a proviso, state a rule of law, and end with several exceptions' (Tiersma, 2001: 4).

In the world of management, the ability to get facts, ideas and judgements across in a clear and pithy way is no less valued. Managers prefer business communication to be direct, easily understood and succinct (Hamilton and Parker, 1990). Oral briefings mostly fail because they are too long-winded, include too few examples, are unattractively delivered, and have content that is poorly organised and contains too much technical jargon (Mandel, 1987). The need to retain the interest of the audience emerged as the presentation skill ranked top by a variety of professionals, as reported by Engleberg (2002). In a survey of 500 managers in a broad swathe of public and private sector organisations, Maes *et al.* (1997) reported oral communication to be the competency felt to be of most value to graduates entering the workforce. When the actual skills associated with this competency were broken down, those to do with making presentations were ranked highly in terms of both importance and frequency of use. Deficits in presentation skills were also noted by deMayo (1997) among mental health professionals when making psychological findings available at case conferences. It is therefore essential that a broad range of professionals have the skills necessary to proffer explanations that are comprehensible to a variety of audiences. But what exactly is an explanation? We will now address this question.

WHAT IS AN EXPLANATION?

This is a deceptively simple question but one that has occupied philosophers and educationalists for some time (Achinstein, 1983; Brown and Armstrong, 1984). One particular semantic knot to be unravelled is whether 'explaining' is essentially the same as other activities such as 'describing', 'instructing' and 'relating', involving the giving of information, or is in some important characteristic apart from these. A further difficulty centres on whether anything has to be understood for an explanation to have happened. But let us leave this matter aside for the moment and tackle the first issue.

Some take a very broad and inclusive approach to defining what represents an explanation. According to Martin (1970: 59) 'the job of someone who explains something to someone . . . is to fill in the gap between his audience's knowledge or beliefs about some phenomena and what he takes to be the actual state of affairs'. Here we see that what counts is leaving the audience knowing or believing something of which they were previously ignorant. In a sense it does not really matter if information given is strictly accurate provided that the explainer takes what is told to be the case. At the other extreme, explaining has been thought of in a much more restrictive sense as a special type of 'telling'. Here an explanation is different from a description, instruction or speculation. What is peculiar about it is that it goes beyond mere description to give reasons or reveal causes for the facts or events under discussion. In other words answering the question 'why?' is an implicit or explicit feature. This defining characteristic was brought out by, for instance, Pavitt (2000: 379) in discussing scientific explanations when he wrote,

> A question such as, 'Why did she say that?' or 'Why will she say that?' demands a third type of answer, one that increases understanding by giving a reason for the content of her past or future utterance. We call this type of answer an 'explanation'.

One way around this definitional dilemma is to think of categories of explanation rather than just explanations versus non-explanations. Some, but not all of these, may have to do with presenting cause–effect relationships. One of the most pragmatic and robust typologies is that provided by Brown and Armstrong (1984) who teased out *descriptive, interpretive* and *reason-giving* varieties. Gilbert *et al.* (1998) used a similar categorisation.

- *Descriptive explanations* are provided when presenting information about specific procedures, structures, processes or directions. They typically address the question 'how?'
- *Interpretive explanations* define or clarify issues, meanings or statements. Here it is the question 'what?' that is mainly being responded to.
- *Reason-giving explanations* specify the cause–effect relationships that account for a phenomenon or the reasons behind an action or event. They are commonly occasioned by the question 'why?'

Within the latter category, Pavitt (2000) made a finer distinction between *causal* and *functional* explanations.

- *Causal explanations* set out cause–effect relationships and often invoke laws or general principles.
- *Functional explanations* are 'relevant when the audience is confused about the purpose served by some phenomenon or set of phenomena either in the operation of some process or in maintaining the well-being of some object' (p. 389).

Examples of these can be found in Box 8.1.

But we are not quite out of the philosophical thicket yet! The term 'to explain' has two further meanings. As Turney *et al.* (1983b: 14) pointed out in their review of the literature in this area, the verb 'to explain' has 'a meaning that emphasizes the intention of the explainer, and a meaning that emphasizes the success of the explanation'. Adopting the former, it makes sense to say 'I explained it to him but he did not understand'. What matters for Achinstein (1983) in this respect is that:

- The speaker intends to answer the listener's question.
- The speaker believes that what is said is a correct answer to the question.
- The intention is to directly answer the question.
- The listener appreciates the speaker's intentions in these respects.

Note that there is no mention of the listener's consequent levels of comprehension.

Box 8.1 Examples of types of explanation

Descriptive

- Going over the steps of how to bath a baby.
- Outlining how to programme a new model of video.

Interpretive

- Making clear the significance of a white line on an X-ray of a damaged leg.
- Offering the meaning of the word 'oxymoron'.

Reason-giving

- Pointing out why wage rises that are not linked to productivity can trigger inflation.
- Explaining why some trees lose their leaves in winter.

Causal

- Outlining why sunbathing can lead to skin cancer.
- Setting out the sequence of steps leading from turning the key in the ignition to a car engine firing up.

Functional

- Explaining why flamingos have oddly shaped bills.
- Presenting reasons why racing cars have broad tyres and spoilers.

In professional contexts, however, this usage is frequently not sufficient. Rather, when it is said that something has been explained by a teacher or doctor, for example, not only is it an expectation but a requirement that it be understood by the pupil or patient. Not to be so, and particularly in the case of patients, could endanger life and lead to court action. Here, while it may be necessary to give information, this is not sufficient in order to claim that material was explained. An additional requirement is that understanding be brought about. In this case the claim, 'I explained it to them but they did not understand' would be inherently contradictory. We see this stipulation partly reflected in the working definition offered by Brown and Atkins (1997: 184) that 'Explaining is an attempt to provide understanding of a problem to others', although the possibility of failure is also recognised. This way of thinking also sits foursquare with the original meaning of the word as derived from the Latin verb *explanare*, 'to make plain'.

ABOUT EXPLAINING

Any particular explanation may involve elements that are descriptive, interpretive, causal or functional. It may also take place in the context of an impromptu encounter with another, as for instance when a nurse delivers some opportunistic health teaching to a patient. Alternatively it can be a well-prepared, formal presentation to a class or group, such as when the nurse is invited to speak to the local women's association on breast cancer awareness. The coverage in this chapter should be useful in both sets of circumstances.

Explanations can also take contrasting forms. We tend to think of the *monologue* approach with the explainer delivering a 'lecture' while the recipient listens. But the *Socratic technique* can be even more effective on occasion when it comes to creating understanding. Named after the Greek philosopher renowned for his habit of responding with a whole series of questions when asked to explain some abstract idea, such as 'justice', we can often lead others to understanding in a dialogue where we do most of the questioning (see Box 8.2). This approach has the advantage of affording the explainee an active role in the learning process.

Three principal modes of explaining can also be employed as follows:

- *verbal explanations* rely exclusively on the spoken (or written) word to carry meaning and create understanding;
- *illustrations* supplement verbal presentations with pictures, models, graphs, videos, and such like;
- *demonstrations* involve 'explaining by doing'. They are a very practical and applied way of getting information across, usually about some process or technique.

Skilful explaining is difficult to legislate for. Regardless of the particular topic, there is no one proper way of presenting it that guarantees understanding. This is because the perceived adequacy is directly related to the recipient's age, background knowledge and mental ability. Imagine the following situation, so typical of classroom instruction: a social studies teacher is planning to teach a lesson on the concept of 'prejudice'. The problem is how to teach it, given the current level of understanding of the pupils and their perceived degree of interest in the subject. How can the teacher introduce the concept? What activities can the pupils benefit from engaging in? How

---

Box 8.2 The Socratic technique

Why have camels got flat feet?

Mother: Well Jane, where do camels live?
Jane: In the desert.
Mother: That's right. What is the ground like in the desert?
Jane: It's all sandy.
Mother: Where else can sand be found?
Jane: At the beach.
Mother: Yes, do you remember last summer on the beach when we played ball?
Jane: Oh yes!
Mother: What was it like trying to run on the soft sand?
Jane: It was really hard. My feet dug in.
Mother: Yes so did mine. What though if we had large, flat feet like a camel?
Jane: Oh, I see now, why camels have flat feet.

finely should the concept be broken down? At what level should it be pitched? How can it be related to other lessons and other subjects? These are the sorts of decisions faced by teachers on both an hourly and day-to-day basis.

However, it would be mistaken to believe that teachers are the only professional group faced with such dilemmas (McEwan, 1992). Lawyers, accountants, engineers, doctors, nurses, and a host of other groups, also find themselves having to make clients and patients aware of complicated information and involved states of affairs, often to enable informed decisions to be taken. Even restricting recipients to the adult population, what may well work as a clear and concise outline for one individual may merely serve to make a second confused and frustrated, while an indignant third may find it insultingly patronising. Perhaps the most fundamental rule is that explanations, as indeed with communication more generally, must be tailored to the needs, abilities and backgrounds of the audience.

The onus is on the explainer to establish at what level an explanation should be pitched and how it can best be delivered. Gleason and Perlmann (1985), analysing the speech patterns and content of adults speaking to young children, found that adults simplify their speech in terms of pronunciation, grammar and vocabulary, as well as exaggerated intonations. Professionals must also be aware when explaining to children and young adolescents that they process information differently from adults, being much more concrete in their thinking (Bruner *et al.*, 1956). Abstract concepts such as honesty, love, loyalty and duty may be taken for granted when dealing with adults, but with younger children they need to be spelled out in more detail and related where possible to everyday occurrences within the child's experience.

FUNCTIONS OF EXPLAINING

The main functions of explaining are listed in Box 8.3. Some of these purposes take precedence, depending on the context of the interaction. While a teacher may start off a lesson by explaining briefly what the lesson is about and what precisely the class has to do during it, this use would be anathema to, for instance, a non-directive counsellor. Successfully meeting the needs and wants of recipients, particularly in professional contexts, is an important guiding principle. In health care, research reviews demonstrate that many patients positively value and benefit from the presentation of information by health professionals about their condition (Thompson, 1998; Dickson, 1999b). This is particularly so for 'monitors' – patients who actively search out and request such information. 'Blunters', in contrast, deliberately avoid this detail, especially when news may be unpleasant (Miller *et al.*, 1988). Thus Leydon *et al.* (2000) revealed that while all cancer patients in their study wanted basic information to do with diagnosis and treatment, some did not want further extensive detail at all stages of their illness.

Giving adequate and relevant information and explanation can result in tangible benefits to patients in terms of reduced pain and discomfort, anxiety and depression, and earlier recovery (Wilson-Barnett, 1981; Ong *et al.*, 1995; Thompson, 1998). It can also promote patient adherence to treatment regimens (Nobel, 1998) and reduce levels of non-attendance for medical appointments (Hamilton *et al.*, 1999). Nevertheless,

---

Box 8.3 Functions of explaining

The main functions of explaining are to:

1   provide others with information otherwise unavailable;
2   simplify complexity;
3   illustrate the essential features of particular phenomena;
4   clarify uncertainties revealed during social interaction;
5   express opinions regarding particular attitudes, facts or values;
6   reach some common understanding;
7   demonstrate how to execute a specific skill or technique;
8   empower others through giving understanding and increased autonomy;
9   ensure learning.

Wallen *et al.* (1979) reported that less than 1 per cent of total time spent in information exchange between doctor and patient was spent on doctor explanations to patients. Similarly, Fisher *et al.* (1991a) discovered that the time spent by community pharmacists in talking to patients about their medication amounted only to some 3.5 minutes per hour. Deficient explanations also contribute to the finding by Jackson (1992) that patients in general forget about 50 per cent of the information given by practitioners, and that 'at least 50% of patients in Europe, Japan, and North America fail to take their medicines properly' (International Medical Benefit/Risk Foundation, 1993: 14).

Usable information is an important source of social power (Raven and Rubin, 1983) (see also Chapter 12). It follows that informing and training are ways of developing self-empowerment in others through enabling them to make more informed decisions over matters affecting their lives without having to seek help and guidance. Personal autonomy is promoted as a result.

Finally, we have mentioned explaining as a way of creating understanding on behalf of the audience. But having to explain material after being exposed to it can also be an effective way for the explainer to learn it. Indeed, there is an old maxim that asserts: 'The best way to learn something is to have to teach it.' This was demonstrated in an experiment by Coleman *et al.* (1997) who discovered that setting students the task of subsequently explaining Darwin's theory of evolution through natural selection, produced more learning and understanding of that material than asking them to summarise it, or merely listen to it.

THE EXPLAINING PROCESS

We can think of the key features of explaining in terms of the '5-Ps' – *p*re-assessment, *p*lanning, *p*reparation, *p*resentation and '*p*ostmortem'. Each of these will be developed with the aid of a diagram that extends the ideas of French (1994) and Kagan and Evans (1995) (see Figure 8.1). Although the first three are often overlooked in a rush to 'get on with it', when explanations go wrong it is often on account of inadequate forethought. Admittedly the unexpected can sometimes knock off course even the most carefully crafted presentation. In the famous words of Robert Burns:

> The best-laid schemes o' mice an' men
> Gang aft a-gley.

However, studies have shown that competent planning and preparation is linked to clarity of explanations (Brown and Armstrong, 1984). Someone who has a firm grasp of the material to be put across and has given thought to how best to do so is much more likely to explain effectively.

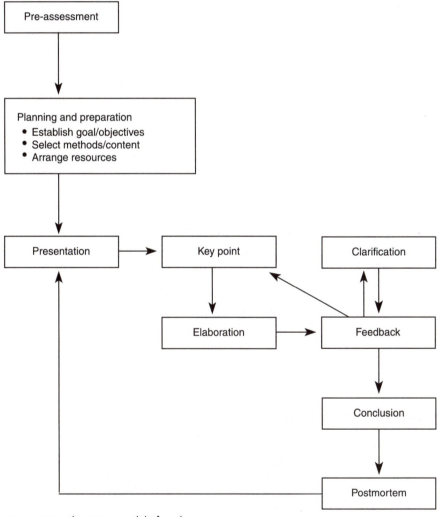

Figure 8.1 The '5-Ps' model of explaining

PRE-ASSESSMENT

Webb (1994: 30) made the claim, in relation to effective health promotion, that 'A prerequisite for effective teaching, whether of the well person or the patient, is adequate assessment.' A quick check-list of things to assess includes:

- what the other wants or needs to know;
- what they already know;
- their ability to make sense of what they are about to hear;
- its potential emotional impact.

Neglecting these considerations can result in much wasted effort – or worse. Referring to scientific explanations, Gilbert *et al.* (1998) claimed that an audience's judgement of the adequacy of an explanation is a feature of the extent to which it meets a need. This will depend on (1) the degree to which prior relevant knowledge and understanding is taken into account, and (2) the use that can be made of the explanation in the future. Professionals such as doctors (Thompson, 1998) and judges (Tiersma, 2001) often make the mistake of over-estimating what patients and jurors already know. Health workers should establish, at the outset, whether what appears to be a request for information is indeed that, rather than a plea for reassurance. Nurses sometimes respond to the former with reassurance and to the latter with a factual explanation (Kagan and Evans, 1995).

Finding out what is already known makes sense not only from the point of view of avoiding needless repetition but also for establishing a suitable starting point from which to launch the explanation. Again, without some appreciation of the audience's linguistic code and cognitive abilities it is highly probable that information will be pitched at entirely the wrong level. Calderhead (1996) indicated that successful teachers build pupil understanding, other pupil characteristics and available resources into their planning. In a way, explaining successfully requires a certain empathic understanding of the other. That person's perspective must be taken into account (McLaughlin *et al.*, 1992). The explainer must develop a feel for how what is being proposed will be received and experienced. This can be particularly challenging for a scientist, for instance, working at the cutting edge of research in some esoteric field when it comes to trying to present ideas to non-scientists. The extent though to which empathy typifies health professionals' relationships with those to whom a service is provided has also been called into question (Reynolds and Scott, 2000).

PLANNING AND PREPARATION

In an investigation by Menzel and Carrell (1994) involving 119 public speaking students, a positive association was found between quality of speech performance and total preparation time. Time available to plan and make adequate preparation will obviously differ depending on settings and circumstances. A nurse called aside by a concerned patient anxious to know more about a pending operation will obviously not have the same luxury of forethought as an influential theoretical physicist invited to appear on a TV programme popularising science. Nevertheless unless some thought is given to what needs to be covered and how best to do so, it is unlikely that much of benefit will be achieved in either case. This seems to be realised by more experienced professionals. Carter (1990) noted that novice teachers tend to jump in without giving adequate thought and planning to the task in hand. The more expert on the other hand develop:

- *cognitive schemata* which rely on the integration of specialised knowledge linked to specific situations;
- *organisational knowledge* in terms of how concepts are related and form a pattern;
- *tacit knowledge* which is constructed or invented from repeated experiences over time.

Planning and preparation comprise several sequenced and interdependent sub-tasks.

Establish goals/objectives

An explanation may be triggered by a direct request from someone who needs or wants to know something. Alternatively it may be the explainer who initiates the exchange. In the latter case, an important first step may be to create a 'felt need' on the part of recipients. They should have a sense that listening to what is to be said will be worthwhile. (For further information see the section on 'Motivational set' in Chapter 10.) Regardless of who initiates the episode, the explainer must have a firm grasp of the issue to be dealt with and what the explanation should achieve. A broad goal may be broken down into specific objectives and thought of in terms of changes brought about in recipients by listening. These may relate to:

- what they should be able to *do* (*behavioural objective*);
- what they should *know and understand* (*cognitive objective*);
- how they should *feel* and their attitudes (*affective objective*).

Identify content and select methods

Here decisions are taken about the content of the explanation (the actual material to be put across) and how best to do this. There is a logic that links this set of judgements with those concerning goals and objectives. Each type of objective will suggest a somewhat different approach to giving information. For example, if the intention is that the explainee should be able to complete some manual task, perhaps involving an element of skill, a demonstration coupled with practice opportunities may be required. A need simply to know, on the other hand, could probably be satisfied with a verbal explanation or illustration.

Linked in turn to the material to be covered are the boundaries that circumscribe it, marking the relevant from the irrelevant. Once the subject matter is firmly located, several other processes were advocated by Brown and Atkins (1997). They included selecting the key elements, determining how these key elements are related, and structuring and linking the explanation to the audience's characteristics.

Any body of information will have key elements that really must be grasped. These require teasing out and their interrelationship clarified. This in turn will suggest a sensible approach to structuring the explanation so that it moves, for instance, from the simple to the complex, and is easy to follow. There is ample evidence from research into teaching to suggest that the teacher's ability to prepare, structure, organise and sequence facts and ideas with the maximum logical coherence is positively related to pupil achievement (Gage *et al.*, 1968; Wragg, 1993).

Finally, as has been previously stated, when selecting, linking and structuring terms and ideas, the age, sex, background, experience and mental ability of the audience should not be forgotten. The length of time available for the task is also relevant.

Arrange resources

This point is particularly applicable in the context of a more formal presentation. Part of preparation is arranging for all the various resources drawn on to be where you need them, when, and in working order. Most presentations benefit from visual aids in one form or another. These can range from physical objects and models, to pictures, tables, charts, graphs, diagrams, etc., shown on video, film, computer, slides, a flip-chart, or an overhead projector (OHP). Downing and Garmon (2002) provided a useful guide to selecting and using equipment of this type. In preparing visual aids, Hargie *et al.* (1999) advised avoiding:

- having too many;
- cluttering each with too much information;
- using a font size for print material that is too small;
- letting the technology take over – remember these are just *aids*.

If possible, it is also worthwhile checking out the location of the presentation in advance and the actual room that has been set aside. The size and position of the room, type of furniture and facilities, and available equipment should be noted (Tierney, 1996). They can all influence levels of comfort and be more or less conducive to learning. They will also shape what it is possible for you to do with the group.

PRESENTATION

Now we move on to the actual communicative part of the process. While the potential of an explanation will be enhanced as a result of the above preparatory processes, effectiveness must ultimately depend on the flow of the discourse and levels of clarity created. According to the model represented in Figure 8.1, sequenced and ordered key points should be presented one at a time. After making the point, it should be elaborated on and understanding checked before moving on to the next. If necessary, clarification can be provided. Although relatively few studies have been concerned with the identification of effective planning and structuring aspects, a great deal of research attention has focused on presentation skills and tactics (Wragg, 1993). An examination of these research findings has revealed a number of crucial features and these are discussed and analysed in the remainder of this chapter.

Clarity

Clear explanations tend to be understood: those that are unclear simply cause confusion. There is little doubt that clarity of speech is one of the most challenging features of effective explaining. Of course explainers need to know their subject, but while this may be necessary it is not a sufficient condition for success (Wragg, 1993). Their knowledge base is only one part of the equation. The topic still has to be communicated to an audience in a clear, unambiguous and structured way. As analysed by Chesebro and McCroskey (2001), instructional clarity encompasses two elements, having to do with the structure of content, and how different elements that make up the body of material are organised and interrelated, and how that content is delivered. These researchers found, with a student group, that teacher clarity was associated not only with lower levels of learner apprehension, but with heightened motivation to learn and greater liking for the teacher together with the course. Moreover, the students also felt that they actually learned more in these circumstances.

Here we will deal with structural aspects of clarity, picking up on issues of delivery later on in this section on presentation. Brown and Atkins (1997) identified four structuring moves associated with clarity.

1   *Signposts.* These are statements setting out a structure for the pending presentation and charting a path through it. As with any signpost, they point the way ahead. In so doing they provide the listener with an advanced framework for organising the information to come. For example a fitness instructor may begin explaining why a pulse monitor is being used by saying:

> You need to know the importance of 'training smart'. Let me first explain what a pulse monitor does in measuring your heart rate, then the importance of knowing how hard you are working when you train. Finally I will go over how this information can be used to work out different training schedules for you.

In essence, these comments take the place of the introduction in a report or essay.

2   *Frames.* These are used to delineate the boundaries of specific topics or sub-topics contained in the explanation. They are words or phrases that sketch beginnings and endings of sections within the body of the talk and are particularly useful when the material is complex, with different embedded sub-elements. An example would be:

Okay, that covers what the pulse monitor does in picking up an electrical signal from the heart, each time it beats. Moving on from there to why that information is useful to you as you train . . .

3   *Foci.* Foci statements highlight or emphasise key features of the explanation and help to make these 'stand out' from a background of lesser material. Such phrases are particularly useful when giving information where safety matters, for example, are at a premium. Examples of foci statements in relation to the ongoing example might be:

Don't forget, you should always make sure someone is with you if you try to check your maximum pulse.
So remember, never turn training sessions into races.
It's very important that you include some recovery sessions in your regime as well.

4   *Links.* Most talks or explanations cover a series of sub-topics each designed to contribute to an audience's overall knowledge of a subject. Clarity of comprehension is improved if the speaker links these sub-topics into a meaningful whole. In addition, however, speakers should try to link their explanation to the experience, previously acquired knowledge, and observations of the audience. For instance:

Now you see, given that the heart adapts to higher levels of demand, why it is important to organise training so that you are continually asking a little more of it each time, if you are to notice improvements in your fitness level. It's just like any other muscle, in that sense. The pulse monitor lets you check accurately how hard your heart is working.

Concision

The old maxim that 'A little remembered is better than a lot forgotten', has much to commend it when it comes to giving information. Ruben (1990) argued that an explanation that carries more detail than is necessary is just as defective as one that does not carry enough. It is well established that 'learning begins to diminish seriously after fifteen minutes' (Verner and Dickinson, 1967: 90). In health care situations where patients may be distracted by pain or have little energy, the crucial time period will be considerably shorter. Providing too much detail is a communication problem in community care, as mentioned by Groogan (1999). Similarly, Clampitt (2001: 71), referring to organisations, likened information to food. He asserted that 'There are far too many managers who have grown fat on information, but are starved for knowledge.' One way to 'diet' strongly advocated by Blundel (1998: 33) is by embracing the KISS principle – 'Keep it Short and Simple'.

Fluency

Verbal presentations should be delivered as fluently as possible. It is not only annoying to listen to 'ums' and 'ers' or garbled, rambling sentences, but this annoyance can very quickly lead to inattention. Wragg (1993) noted that a fluent delivery was associated with explaining effectiveness measured in terms of subsequent pupil achievement. Similarly, Christenfeld (1995), in a study of undergraduates, reported that impressions of quality were affected when speakers used a profusion of 'ums'. Sometime these intrusions can go unnoticed, however, when concentrating on the substance of what is being said. It is easier to appreciate what makes for a fluent presentation by considering the different ways in which dysfluency can creep in (see Box 8.4).

Some of the types of dysfluency noted in Box 8.4, such as a lisp or stammering, require specialised treatment. Others may be occasioned by particular circumstances. As pointed out by Crystal (1997: 280), 'A certain amount of "normal non-fluency" is found in young children . . . and indeed every one is prone to hesitation, especially in situations where they have to speak under pressure.' One of the causes of punctuating speech with sounds such as 'eh' or 'mm' is trying to put too many ideas or facts across in one sentence. It is better to use reasonably short crisp sentences, with pauses in between, than long rambling ones full of subordinate clauses. This will generally tend to eliminate speech hesitancies. Another further cause of dysfluency in speech is lack of adequate planning. The importance of the planning stage has already been outlined.

While the evidence points overwhelmingly to the need for a verbal presentation to be as fluent as possible, one area in which dysfluency might be positively encouraged was outlined by Heath (1984). He noted that when doctors, in the medical interview, explain new technical terms they tend to adopt a speech hesitation or dysfluency which may actually gain the attention of the patient. In fact, doctors often combine an 'umm' or an 'ahh' with frame devices such as, 'what we call' or 'it's

---

Box 8.4 Ten ways to be dysfluent

1 *Filled pauses* – 'umm', 'ah', 'er'.
2 *Sloppy diction* – lack of clear enunciation of word sounds.
3 *Articulation handicaps* – lisp, etc.
4 *Stammering* – difficulty in controlling the rhythm and timing of speech.
5 *False starts* – e.g. 'I must mention . . . well, maybe first I should say . . . of course, you may already know . . .'
6 *Poorly organised sentences* – e.g. 'After that, well we didn't intend when we left, see John had this ticket . . .'
7 *Repetitive phrases* – e.g. 'like I mean', 'sort of'.
8 *Hesitation* – 'Can I . . . say that . . .'
9 *Cluttering* – abnormally fast rate of speech, with syllables perhaps running into each other.
10 *Lack of voice projection* – e.g. mumbling.

something like', thereby helping the patient to locate and attend to the conversational moments in which they introduce medical terms.

Pausing

Pausing briefly to collect and organise thought processes before embarking on the explanation can also improve fluent speech patterns. Added to that, planned pausing can also help to increase understanding of the explanation. Rosenshine (1968), in an early research review of those behaviours related to teacher effectiveness, found that teachers who used pauses following an explanation increased pupils' knowledge by ensuring that not too much material was covered too quickly. Brown and Bakhtar (1983) provided further support for the use of pausing when presenting lengthy explanations, in their study of lecturing styles. One of the five most common weaknesses shown by lecturers was saying too much too quickly.

Appropriate language

Any explanation must contain language appropriate to the intellectual capacity, background and language code of the listener. Professionals are inherently bilingual. They speak the specialised and sometimes highly technical language of their calling in addition to their native tongue. All professionals have a stock-in-trade of jargon. Indeed in many respects it serves them well, as a means of facilitating communication within the group, acting as a very conspicuous marker of group identity, and denying information access to non-group members (Kreps and Thornton, 1992). But professionals sometimes forget that others cannot speak this language. Blocks to communication occur when what linguists call *code switching* takes place and jargon forms part of the dialogue with those such as patients or clients not privy to this lexicon. The problem is further compounded by the fact that the same words sometimes appear in the vocabularies of both but with different meanings. Tiersma (2001) gave examples of everyday words such as 'burglary' and 'assault' that have somewhat different and much more precise legal interpretations as well as common meanings. He stressed the difficulty of displacing the latter with the former among jurors, even when specific instructions are given. Similarly, in medicine there is evidence that terms such as 'risk factor' are not particularly well understood by patients (Turton, 1998). Likewise in gynaecology, expressions such as 'incompetent cervix' can have unintended pejorative connotations (Van Der Merwe, 1995).

Of course, it is sometimes difficult for professionals to eliminate completely all technical terms, and to do so may indeed even jeopardise the client's full grasp of issues. Hopper *et al.* (1992), in an interesting study of naturally occurring telephone conversations between specialists of the Cancer Information Service (CIS) in Houston, Texas, and callers seeking medical information, found that the specialists were encouraged to introduce terminology into the encounters in one of four ways:

1   give a term and (as an aside) ask about the caller's familiarity with it;
2   give a paraphrase with the term (see Chapter 6 for further details regarding the skill of paraphrasing);
3   observe the caller's problems with terminology used and follow with a brief explanation;
4   apply a term to a condition that the caller describes.

Language also reflects the culture of the people who use it. Differences are not only a matter of foreign word usage. Communication styles may additionally be at odds in levels of formality, precision and directness. An emphasis on maintaining harmony and not causing offence sometimes means that members of high-context cultures such as the Japanese and Koreans find elaborate forms of circumlocution to avoid a direct 'No' (Adler and Towne, 1996).

At the sub-cultural level within society, there is well-documented variability, for instance, in morbidity, mortality, health knowledge and uptake of health advice, centred on socioeconomic status (Stroebe, 2000). Throughout the social status continuum, those at higher levels have better health (Sidanius and Pratto, 1999). But status can also be an intruding factor in doctor–patient consultations (Ong *et al.*, 1995). Reviewing the literature, Roter and Hall (1992: 46) concluded that 'It is well known that doctors give more information, in particular, to the higher-class patients, even though, when asked later, patients of different classes do not differ in how much information they say they want.' It is important, therefore, for all those involved in the business of communicating valid and relevant information to be sensitive to the amount and kind of words and phrases they use with people from different social class backgrounds in order for this not to form a barrier between them.

Reducing vagueness

An explanation characterised by vague, indeterminate words and expressions is not as successful as one that employs precise terms to present specific information. Language is inherently ambiguous and prone to confusion. In the infamous 1950s trial in England, Derek Bentley was sentenced to be hanged for the murder of a policeman, although the shooting was carried out by his accomplice. Since the latter was a minor he could not be sentenced to death. The verdict, still controversial, depended on the interpretation of Bentley's directive that night to his younger partner – 'Let him have it, Chris'. The prosecution held that he had ordered the shooting, the defence that he had ordered the gun to be handed over.

This 'slipperiness' of language is captured in the well-known communication euphemism that 'Meanings are in people not in words'. Holli and Calabrese (1998) ventured that some 90 per cent of the misunderstandings and breakdowns that plague communication can be laid at this particular door. In English even simple words can have multiple interpretations: 'fast' has some fifteen dictionary definitions. But confusions and imprecision creep into other languages as well, sometimes with disastrous consequences. Adler and Towne (1996) related how confusion over the Japanese word 'mokusatsu' may have led to the atomic bomb attacks on Hiroshima and Nagasaki in 1945. The word was used by Prime Minister Suzuki to describe cabinet policy on the Potsdam Declaration that would have brought war to an end. 'Mokusatsu' can mean either to ignore or to keep silent on something. Suzuki had the latter in mind. The cabinet was withholding comment, given their difficulties in breaking the news of surrender to the Japanese people. The Allied nations interpreted the broadcast message as the Declaration being ignored by the Japanese, hence precipitating the attack on Hiroshima some eight days later.

Not all imprecision can be totally eliminated from verbal explanations on every occasion. Most people will have experienced a situation when they have groped to find the exact term and, failing to find it, have substituted a less precise, more general alternative. However, attempts should be made to remove vagueness if the goal is to promote understanding. Particular words and phrases to look out for, and first commented on by Gage *et al.* (1968) and Miltz (1972), are noted in Box 8.5. Well-established findings by Hiller *et al.* (1969: 674) into teachers' explanations found that 'the greater the number of words and phrases expressing haziness, qualification and ambiguity ("some", "things", "a couple", "not necessarily", "kind of") the less clear the communication'. From a sample of eighty-four undergraduate student lessons, Land (1984) found that students could accurately distinguish teacher clarity on the basis of presence or absence of vague terms. In particular he noted that high clarity lessons were significantly related to high student ratings on achievement tests along with high student ratings of perception of clarity.

Providing emphasis

Another telling feature when attempting to explain effectively is the need to provide emphasis. This helps to make prominent the key points and crucial features of content. By providing points of emphasis the speaker can direct the listener's attention to the most important or essential information in the presentation, while 'playing down' the inessential parts. Emphasis can be grouped into two categories, nonverbal and verbal. In the former, the speaker uses aspects of nonverbal behaviour

---

Box 8.5 Being precise about vagueness

The following are common forms of vagueness in an explanation.

- *Ambiguous designation* – e.g. 'type of thing', 'all of this', 'sort of stuff'.
- *Negative intensifiers* – e.g. 'was not too', 'was not hardly', 'was not quite', 'not infrequently'.
- *Approximation* – e.g. 'about as much as', 'almost every', 'kind of like', 'nearly'.
- *Bluffing and recovery* – e.g. 'they say that', 'and so on', 'to make a long story short', 'somehow'.
- *Indeterminate numbers* – e.g. 'a couple of', 'bunch', 'some'.
- *Groups of items* – e.g. 'kinds', 'aspects', 'factors', 'things'.
- *Possibility and probability* – e.g. 'are not necessarily', 'sometimes', 'often', 'it could be that', 'probably'.

(such as head-nodding, finger-pointing, loudness of voice), to indicate the salient features. The second, verbal, category includes those aspects of language used to draw attention to important detailed information.

Nonverbal emphasis

Effective public speakers, politicians and television presenters, all versed in the skills of oratory, use deliberate variation in their voice to alert their audiences' attention to key issues. As well as the voice, skilful speakers also employ appropriate speech-related gestures and movements to underline key features of their explanations (Tierney, 1996). In particular, varied movements of the eyes, head, face, fingers, hands and whole body are used purposefully and in a focused manner to suit the information being stressed.

Verbal emphasis

As well as using nonverbal behaviour to accentuate the essential parts of an explanation, speakers employ three main verbal techniques to achieve similar results.

Verbal cueing

This occurs when an individual employs specific verbal 'markers' to preface that part of the message to which attention is being drawn. These verbal markers can be individual words such as 'first ... second ... third', 'important', 'finally', 'major', 'fundamental', or phrases such as 'listen carefully', 'the important point to remember is', 'take time before you answer this question'. Verbal cueing helps to differentiate between the relevant and the irrelevant, the more important and the less important, and between specific detail and general background information.

Mnemonics

Perhaps not as common as verbal cueing but in a sense equally effective in acting as an *aide-mémoire* to the listener is the use of a mnemonic. As pointed out in the previous chapter, these are useful devices to facilitate understanding. An example might take advantage of the fact that key words essential to the explanation all begin with the same letter of the alphabet, making it is easy to recall them when needed. In this chapter we talk about the '5-Ps' of the explaining process. An *acronym*, where the first letter of each point combines to make a word, can also be highly memorable. All beginning music students will remember 'FACE' to help recall each of the 'notes in the spaces' on sheet music (i.e. F for note F, etc.).

Planned repetition

A third technique is that of planned repetition of selected points during the presentation. This is especially useful if a great deal of new or unfamiliar material is being explained. Ley (1988), from a research review of patient compliance with doctors' prescriptions, suggested that one major way a doctor can increase patient compliance is to repeat the important points of the instructions. However, Maguire (1985), in an attempt to identify deficiencies in key interpersonal skills for nurses, warned that overuse of repetition can be wasteful and give insufficient time to assess patients properly. Nevertheless, structured summaries occurring at various points throughout a lengthy explanation appear to be beneficial to the recipient. (See Chapter 10 for a fuller discussion on summarisation.)

Aids to explanation

Where possible, the speaker should plan to include some kind of aid to facilitate the efficiency of an explanation. These aids can be an immensely powerful tool for helping to get the message across in an illuminating and attractive manner. The old adage that 'A picture is worth a thousand words' often holds true. Established devices such as video, slides, and overhead projections are now complemented by the enormous versatility of computer graphics packages. The fact, though, that even the best of these are only aids to assist the speaker must be noted (McDaniel, 1994). They should never be permitted to take centre stage thereby relegating the hapless presenter to the wings.

People take in information using different sensory channels. Some favour listening, others looking. Visual representations can, therefore, support the spoken word and, by introducing greater variety, make for a more attractive experience for the group. They may also aid in the retrieval of information from memory. According to the *dual-coding hypothesis* (Paivio, 1971), audiovisual information is coded in memory in two different but related ways. It is coded both verbally and visually. Textual messages are only coded verbally. Support for this hypothesis was documented by Walma van der Molen and van der Voort (2000) in an investigation where children (1) watched news stories on television, (2) read a printed version, (3) read a printed version together with photographs, or (4) listened to an audio version. The television-mediated material was remembered most successfully.

In an interesting study carried out by Togo and Hood (1992) it was suggested that there might be gender differences in the assimilation of information. One hundred and fourteen students, comprising approximately equal numbers of each sex, on a management accounting course, were randomly assigned to receive information conveyed using a graphic format, or using a text and tabular format. Results significantly showed that women who received the graphics presentation did not perform as well as their male counterparts, or as well as other women and men who received the text and tabular format. These results showed that exclusive use of graphical material should be avoided and that in mixed gender groups a combination of textual and graphic presentations of information should be provided. Further support for integrating text and diagrams is available from a series of experiments designed to examine the consequences of combining these two formats in an instructional package on the learning outcome of students (Chandler and Sweller, 1992). These researchers found that where mental integration between diagrams and text is essential in order to make sense of the material, then integrated formats should be adopted.

Some advantages of presenters using visual aids were noted by O'Hair *et al.* (1998) and include being perceived more favourably by their audiences, taking less time to present concepts, and producing greater retention of what is learned. Likewise, Downing and Garmon (2002) reviewed evidence attesting to the beneficial effects of technology-based presentations on ease of note-taking and grasping the organisation of content material.

Verbal examples

The simplest aid to use in an explanation is the verbal example, analogy, or case study. Like a bridge, a carefully selected example should span the chasm between what the audience already knows and what they are about to learn. To work, it must have a firm foundation in the experiences that the listener brings to the situation. It is best to invoke concrete everyday scenarios whenever possible to make the subject 'come alive' for the listener. Rosenshine (1971) claimed that explanations were more effective when a piece of information, principle or concept was followed by an example or examples, leading to a restatement of the initial detail. Thus a concept should be introduced as follows:

$$\text{Statement} \rightarrow \text{Example} \rightarrow \text{Statement}$$

A nurse might say, 'Your blood pressure is the pressure of the blood against your artery walls as it flows. Anything that prevents that flow will increase the pressure' (statement). 'Think of turning on the garden hose and holding your thumb over the end. You could check the build-up of pressure by trying to press the hose in the middle' (example). 'In the same way the pressure of your blood is increased when a narrowing in the artery hinders the flow' (statement).

However, Brown and Armstrong (1984), in an analysis of forty-eight video-recorded and transcribed lessons, found that the rule/example/rule model was more appropriate to an interpretive type of explanation on an unfamiliar topic than for other types of explanations aiming to restructure ideas. This suggests that the pattern of examples should be related both to the type of explanation given and to the listeners' previous knowledge.

Conclusion

Conclusions are opportunities to draw the various strands of the explanation together in a neat summary statement. This may be particularly important when the material has been gone through on a point-by-point basis, so ensuring that the links binding the various sub-elements are firmly in place and that a successful synthesis has been achieved. On occasion, however, it may be appropriate to leave a 'loose thread' – perhaps an unanswered question, or some seeming inconsistency. This can motivate the group to continue reflecting on the issue and act as a useful lead-in if it is intended to continue with the explanation at a later date. (See Chapter 10 for further information on closure.)

'POSTMORTEM'

So the explanation has been given, but the task is not over yet. Do not forget our definition of an explanation and the importance of achieving understanding. This can never be taken for granted. The explainer must reflect on what took place and evaluate to what extent the identified objectives were successfully achieved. If necessary, and as represented in Figure 8.1, the material may have to be gone over again, once some thought has been given to what when wrong and why.

Obtaining feedback from the explainee is all important in checking both levels of understanding and, by association, the adequacy of the explanation. A comprehensive review of its role in bringing about learning in a training setting is provided by Dickson *et al.* (1997). Completeness of feedback was shown by Schroth (1992) to significantly affect the speed at which complex concepts were initially acquired. Subjects given verbal feedback after each response, irrespective of whether the response was correct or incorrect, did better than subjects receiving feedback only after correct responses or those receiving feedback only after incorrect responses.

There are several ways to check the efficacy of an explanation.

1   Note the nonverbal behaviour of the listener or listeners, since this is a rich source of evidence. Experienced and successful presenters constantly scan the faces and movements of their audience, both during and after the explanation, to detect signs of puzzlement, confusion or disinterest. However, since individuals vary in the amount and kind of behaviour they overtly display it is not always easy, or even possible, to deduce the efficacy of explanations by nonverbal means alone.

2   Another method of obtaining knowledge of comprehension is to ask a series of general questions. Although this can be a direct measure of comprehension, there can be areas of misunderstanding within the listener's mind that specific recall questions may overlook.

3   Alternatively, feedback can be gleaned by inviting listeners to ask questions on any aspect of an explanation they feel requires further clarification. This would appear to be more valid in terms of 'real' problems encountered by listeners, yet there is a danger that they may not respond for fear of seeming slow or stupid. In many situations, therefore, it is important to look out continually for nonverbal signs of discomfort or lack of confidence in a client in an attempt to detect underlying problems of miscomprehension.

4   It is also possible to ask the listener to summarise what has been heard. Although this is often an effective technique with pupils in school it can sometimes be less so in situations with adults where an impression of 'being

tested' would be inappropriate. This possible interpretation can be overcome by phrasing the request so it seems that the explainer is checking on his or her efficacy (e.g. 'I'm not sure how clear I have made that, would you tell me what you understand from it?').

At a broader level, and taking feedback into account, there is advantage in adopting a reflective approach to presentations (Dimbleby and Burton, 1998). This involves setting time aside to think back over what went well and what perhaps badly, together with trying to pinpoint reasons for successes and failures. Why was the audience still confused and unsure at the end? How could this be improved on next time? Are there general lessons to be learned about explaining this type of material to this type of audience? It is only by adopting this approach that ongoing improvement will be brought about.

DEMONSTRATIONS

Illustrations make use of the sorts of audiovisual aids already mentioned to supplement speech. Demonstrations go further. Here an activity or process is explained by being carried out; it is explaining through doing. When the material is of a practical nature (e.g. a new skill or technique) and the learning objective is behavioural or performative (i.e. the audience being able to carry out the skill or technique), then this form of explanation is often called for. If a picture is worth a thousand words, then a demonstration is worth a thousand pictures. 'Hear one, see one, do one', has a long tradition in medical training. The medical student is told about a procedure, sees it carried out and is then expected to attempt it.

If an explanation does require a demonstration there are several specific points that should be borne in mind in order to achieve effective results. They can be examined under three familiar headings: planning and preparation, presenting, and obtaining feedback.

Planning and Preparation

First, before proceeding with the demonstration, it is important to check that all items of equipment needed are prepared and available for use. In addition, the chief steps involved in the demonstration should be listed in the sequence in which they are to be presented.

Presenting

Having devised the procedures to be used in the demonstration the next step is to present it in action. Initially, observers must be alerted to the purpose of the demonstration and what they will be expected to accomplish once it has been completed. When the viewers are prepared for the demonstration they should be guided step by step through the action with accompanying verbal descriptions of the essential features at each stage of the process (e.g. 'The first point to remember is keep your feet shoulder-width apart . . .'). In addition, the linkage between one step and the next should be clearly illustrated so that observers can see how each one fits into the overall action.

Depending on the complexity of the demonstration, it can be worked through completely, followed by a repeat performance emphasising the vital features at each stage. If, however, the skill or technique being explained is more complicated, the complete action can be broken down into coherent segments which the observer can practise in parts. Whichever format is adopted will be dependent on both the task in hand and the knowledge and experience of the observer.

Obtaining feedback

Finally, it is important to assess whether or not the demonstration has been enacted effectively. Feedback can be obtained by a number of methods:

- having the observer or observers repeat the demonstration;
- repeating the demonstration slowly but requesting the onlookers to give the appropriate directions at each stage;
- requesting viewers to verbalise the salient features of the demonstration following the initial enactment.

Again, the particular option selected to assess the effectiveness of the demonstration will be a feature of the experience of the observers, the resources available and the complexity of the task.

OVERVIEW

This chapter has explored the nature, functions and techniques of explaining in a variety of professional and social contexts. Explaining is an attempt to create understanding, thus going beyond the mere giving of information. Different types of explanation were identified including those that reveal causes, reasons, justifications and motives underlying the problem or event being analysed. While the bulk of research into the skill of explaining has its roots in educational settings it is by no means the sole prerogative of that profession. Other professions, both on a group or one-to-one basis, are also involved in providing relevant and interesting explanations for their consumers or colleagues. For example, in recent years the role of explanations in health care settings and in legal circles has attracted considerable research interest (Ley, 1988; Dickson *et al.*, 1997; Tiersma, 1995, 2001). Likewise, the daunting quest of making knowledge of scientific advances accessible to a wider audience has been taken up by the scientific community. For example, Richard Dawkins, the eminent zoologist whose first book *The selfish gene* was an international best seller, became Professor of the Public Understanding of Science, at Oxford University in 1995.

The explaining process can be analysed using the 5-Ps model of pre-assessment, planning, preparation, presentation, and 'postmortem'. Studies have uncovered that well planned or structured explanations result in greater understanding, that clear, unambiguous explanations are highly valued by listeners and that summaries or feedback checks are effective in aiding retention. Remember that the success of an explanation is indicated by the degree of understanding demonstrated by the listener. As such, the activity must be built around the particular needs, capacities and resources of the audience.

Chapter 9

Self-disclosure

INTRODUCTION

THE TERM SELF-DISCLOSURE is an amalgam of two elements. First, there is the intriguing entity of the 'self', and what exactly this comprises. Second, there is the process of 'disclosure' whereby the individual opens up some aspect of self to others. In this chapter we will examine both of these concepts, but with the main focus on the latter. However, before exploring the fascinating world of how, what, when and why people disclose information about themselves, let us begin by examining the notion of self.

Investigations of the self are as old as social science. Well over 100 years ago the psychologist James (1890, 1892), in attempting to map the terrain, made a distinction between two types of self:

1   The 'I' self, which he saw as a knowing self in that it generates all of the knowledge we have of ourselves;
2   The 'me' self, which he viewed as being composed of three dimensions:

- a material self, relating to our evaluations of our physical bodies and possessions (home, car, etc.);
- a social self, concerned with how we see ourselves relating to and with others;
- a spiritual self, which comprises our ideas, thoughts, values and beliefs.

More recently, the concept of self has attracted an enormous

Box 9.1 Dimensions of self: two examples

1 *Reflexive consciousness* – the ability to think introspectively about who we are.
2 *Interpersonal being* – the self as it relates to and with other people.
3 *Executive function* – how the self makes plans and behaves in such a way as to attempt to exert control over the outside world.

Source: Beaumeister (1999).

1 *Personal self.* You as a unique individual – your ideas, emotions, values, beliefs, etc.
2 *Social self.* Your social roles and how you 'fit' with others.
3 *Cultural self.* Your identification with ethnic, religious, gender, social class, or other grouping.

Source: Stewart and Logan (1998).

---

amount of attention. Different conceptualisations have been put forward as to what exactly constitute its main components (see Box 9.1). However, as Beaumeister (1999: 1) pointed out, 'Providing a satisfactory definition of the self has proven fiendishly difficult.' Giles (2000) illustrated how it takes many forms and can be analysed from a myriad of perspectives. As an illustration of this, we present one conceptualisation of the different sides to self in Figure 9.1.

Me as:	*Type of self:*
I am	Actual self
I would really like to be	Ideal self
I used to be	Past self
A new person	Reconstructed self
I should be	Ought self
I hope to become	Expected self
I'm afraid of becoming	Feared self
I could have been	Missed self
Unwanted by one or more others	Rejected self

Figure 9.1 Types of self

Earlier notions about the existence of a self-contained individual, or 'sovereign self', who reveals or leaks information about 'inner reality' through disclosure, have been replaced by the concept of a social or dialogic self. As succinctly summarised by Anderson (2000: 2), 'the self is possible only in the web of connected lives'. How we present our self is adaptable, and varies from situation to situation. Indeed, some would argue that self is directly shaped by others, so that eventually we come to see ourselves as others see us (Lundgren and Rudawsky, 2000). From this perspective, self is constructed and reconstructed through interaction; it is 'fluid and emergent, characterised by fragmentation and multiplicity. Self cannot be separated from other; rather, other helps to construct self in an ongoing dialogue' (Baxter and Sahlstein, 2000: 293).

Thus, self can be thought of as a social construction and self-disclosure is a process between individuals in which selves are shared, shaped, negotiated and altered. As Woodward (2000: 7) put it, 'Identity combines how I see myself and how others see me . . . It is a socially recognised position, recognized by others, not just by me.' For example, when two people get married they do not have given roles to guide their behaviour as wife or husband. Rather, these are formulated, developed, adjusted and agreed, both as a result of interactions within marriage, and following consultations with significant others. Indeed, if unhappiness with the marriage develops, divorce may result and the role of husband or wife will be terminated within that relationship.

There is a considerable volume of research to show that people who have a large number of successful roles (e.g. husband, father, brother, manager, church treasurer, golf club member) enjoy many benefits compared with those with only a few defining identities. The 'role-rich' cope more readily with change and stress, have better physical health, and are more satisfied with their lot in life than the 'role-poor' (McKenna and Bargh, 2000). Given that the self is social, others (family, friends, work colleagues, and so on) are almost always involved or in some way affected by our disclosures. In this sense, information is often co-owned by a relevant circle of people, who need to be considered before it is revealed (Petronio, 2000a).

There are also inner tensions between what Rosenfeld (2000) termed 'integration versus separation' and 'expression versus privacy', in that part of us wants to engage fully with others and another part wishes to hold something back. Thus there is a need to strike a balance between 'revealing and concealing' (Buslig and Burgoon, 2000). We like to have a group identity but at the same time have private aspects of ourselves that we keep from others. There is a unique essence to each person, such that, 'the inner self may well be shaped by social communication, but the self is far from a passive acceptance of feedback. Instead, the self actively processes and selects (and sometimes distorts) information from the social world' (Beaumeister, 1999: 10). Furthermore, the notion of 'place identity' is also recognised as an important part of self (see Box 9.2), since 'questions of "who we are" are often intimately related to questions of "where we are"' (Dixon and Durrheim, 2000: 27).

A great deal of social interaction consists of participants making statements, or disclosures, about a wide variety of issues. These disclosures may be either objective statements about other people, places or events, or subjective disclosures

> *Box 9.2* Three 'sides' to place identity
>
> 1 *Physical insideness.* Knowing one's way around and being familiar with the physical details of one's environment. Having a sense of personal 'territory'.
> 2 *Social insideness.* Feeling a sense of being connected to and part of a place. Knowing other people and being known and accepted by them.
> 3 *Autobiographical insideness.* The idiosyncratic sense of 'having roots' to a place. Knowing 'where you come from' and 'who you are'.

about the self. This latter type of statement, whereby the speaker reveals some personal information to others, is referred to as self-disclosure. Self-disclosure is the cement that binds the parts together in the structure of interpersonal relationships. Without disclosure, the whole relational edifice will collapse, and so knowledge of this field is of key importance for effective interpersonal functioning.

WHAT IS SELF-DISCLOSURE?

There is disagreement about the exact meaning of the term 'self-disclosure'. Some definitions restrict the field of study to verbal disclosures only. Here, self-disclosure is defined as 'what individuals verbally reveal about themselves (including thoughts, feelings, and experiences) to others' (Dindia, 2000a: 148). A similar definition was offered by Rosenfeld (2000: 6), who added the further stipulation that the disclosure must be made to another person (and not one's self, or a pet, etc.): 'For a communicative act to be considered self-disclosing, it must contain personal information about the sender, the sender must communicate this information verbally, and another person must be the target.' Some go even further to restrict the sphere of study to deeper levels of disclosure in terms of 'the revealing of intimate information about the self in conversation' (Cooks, 2000: 199).

Hoffman's definition (1995: 238) added the issues of veracity and accessibility: 'the revelation of information about the self that is verbally delivered, truthful, significantly revealing, and difficult or impossible to attain through other means'. Others highlight the importance of intentionality on the part of the discloser, and indeed Fisher (1984) argued that information disclosed unintentionally, or by mistake, is a *self-revelation* rather than a self-disclosure. Mader and Mader (1990: 210) further emphasised the aspect of relational consequences: 'You self-disclose when you (1) intentionally give another person information about yourself (2) that the other person is not likely to get on his own and (3) that you realize could significantly affect your relationship to this person.' Pearson and Spitzberg (1987: 142) limited the scope even further by defining self-disclosure as 'communication in which a person voluntarily and intentionally tells another person accurate information about himself or herself', thereby excluding disclosures made under any form of threat.

But these definitions tend to exclude the study of nonverbal self-disclosures, which can be an important channel for communicating personal information –

especially about feelings and emotions. In this chapter a wider perspective is held and self-disclosure is defined as the process whereby person A verbally and/or non-verbally communicates to person B some item of personal information that was previously unknown to B. In this sense, telling a close friend your name would not be a self-disclosure since this information would already be known, whereas telling a complete stranger your name would be a self-disclosure. Likewise, nonverbal disclosures, whether intentional or not, are included since these are the main means whereby we provide information about our emotional state (see Chapter 3). One important difference between verbal and nonverbal self-disclosure is that we have greater control over the former than the latter. For this reason, the nonverbal channel provides important information regarding the detection of deceptive communication from others (Vrij *et al.*, 1996).

The recognition of self-disclosure as a central interpersonal skill began with the pioneering work of Sidney Jourard (1964, 1971), who stressed the need for a high degree of openness between individuals in many contexts, and illustrated the potency of self-disclosure as a technique for encouraging deep levels of interpersonal sharing. Since that time, an enormous amount of interest has been generated, to the point where, 'Self-disclosure is one of the most researched topics of the past three decades in the fields of interpersonal communication, social psychology, and social and personal relationships' (Baxter and Sahlstein, 2000: 289). Indeed, 'The pervasiveness and importance of self-disclosure accounts for the intense interest in this phenomenon shown by social scientists. Literally thousands of quantitative studies have been conducted over a period extending forty years' (Tardy and Dindia, 1997: 213).

Self-disclosure has been analysed and measured in various ways. Thus McKay *et al.* (1999), identified four main disclosure categories.

1   *Observations*. Reporting what you have done or experienced: 'I graduated in 1999.'
2   *Thoughts*. These go beyond simple observations to reveal judgements about what has been experienced: 'If I had it to do again I would take the opportunity to study abroad as part of my degree.'
3   *Feelings*. The expression of affect: 'I really loved university – it was probably the happiest period of my life.'
4   *Needs*. Here the focus is on needs and wants: 'I miss the challenges of academic life and feel that I want to take a postgraduate course now.'

Furthermore, there are a large number of pen-and-paper inventories designed to measure different aspects of self-disclosure, including:

*   as a personality trait (Derlega and Chaikin, 1975);
*   as varying across specific situations (Chelune, 1976);
*   as a function of the target person (Miller *et al.*, 1983);
*   specifically within feminist therapy (Simi and Mahalik, 1997);
*   between spouses within marriage (Waring *et al.*, 1998).

An awareness of the nuances of self-disclosure is important in professional communication, for two main reasons. First, it is vital to be aware of contexts in which it is appropriate to self-disclose to clients. Second, professionals need to be aware of the benefits that accrue from, and the methods whereby they can encourage, full, open and honest self-disclosures from clients.

FEATURES OF SELF-DISCLOSURE

There are four key features of self-disclosure. First, verbal self-disclosures involve the use of the personal pronoun 'I', or some other personal self-reference pronoun such as 'my' or 'mine'. While these words may be implied from the context of the speaker's utterances, their presence serves to remove any ambiguity about whether or not the statement being made is intrapersonal (relating to personal experiences). Compare, for example, the statements:

A: Selection interviews can create a great amount of stress.
B: I find selection interviews very stressful.

In A it is not immediately clear whether the speaker is referring to selection interviews in general or to feelings about attending selection interviews. The use of the personal pronoun 'I' in B, however, serves to clarify the nature of the statement as a self-disclosure.

The use of a personal self-reference pronoun as evidence of a disclosure is often the criterion used in research investigations. This is one of the following three methods used to measure the phenomenon:

1   observer or recipient estimates of disclosure;
2   self-report measures such as inventories, self-ratings or sentence completion tasks;
3   objective counts of actual disclosures made during interaction.

One problem is that different research investigations use:

> a variety of measures, many designed specifically for particular studies. Many studies focus only on one dimension of disclosure, usually depth, whereas others examine three or more. It is sometimes difficult, then, to generalize across different programs of research.
>
> (Omarzu, 2000: 175)

Even studies that use the 'objective' approach may not be directly comparable owing to differing definitions about what exactly constitutes a self-disclosure. While the counting of self-reference pronouns is one measurement criterion, another definition of self-disclosure used in research studies is: 'a verbal response (thought unit) which describes the subject in some way, tells something about the subject, or refers to some affect the subject experiences' (Tardy, 1988: 331). This definition obviously requires detailed training on the part of observers to ensure accuracy and agreement about instances of disclosure. Such differences need to be borne in mind when evaluating research findings in this field. Furthermore, much research on self-disclosure has been conducted in the artificial 'laboratory' situation and the results of these studies need to be treated with caution, since the extent to which they generalise to real-life contexts is unclear.

Second, self-disclosures can be about either facts or feelings. When two people meet for the first time, it is more likely that they will focus on factual disclosures (name, occupation, place of residence) while keeping any feeling disclosures at a fairly superficial level ('I hate crowded parties'; 'I like rock music'). This is largely because the expression of personal feelings involves more risk and places the discloser in a more vulnerable position. At the same time, deep levels of disclosure may be made to a stranger providing we feel sure that we will never meet the person again, and that we do not have friends or acquaintances in common. This is discussed later in the chapter in the section on length and commitment of interaction.

A gradual progression from low to high levels of self-disclosure leads to better relationship development. The expression of deep feeling or of high levels of factual disclosure (e.g. 'I was in prison for 5 years') increases as a relationship develops. For this reason, professionals should expect clients to experience difficulties in self-disclosing at any depth at the early stage of an encounter. Even if the client has a deep-rooted need to 'tell someone', such an experience is inevitably embarrassing, or at least awkward, where the disclosures relate to very personal details. The skilled helper is aware of this and employs techniques that help the client to overcome such initial feelings.

Factual and feeling disclosures at a deeper level can be regarded as a sign of commitment to a relationship. Two people who are in love usually expect to give and receive disclosures about their feelings – especially towards one another. They also want to know everything about one another. In such a relationship there is a high level of trust, just as there is in the confession box, a doctor's surgery or a counsellor's office (areas where disclosures are also high). *Social penetration theory* (Altman and Taylor, 1973; Taylor and Altman, 1987) postulates that relationships progress through a number of stages.

- *Orientation*. When people meet for the first time shallow information about self is disclosed more readily than intimate details. For the relationship to develop, disclosures must be reciprocal. Some estimate will be made of the likely rewards and costs of pursuing the relationship, and for progression to occur the anticipated rewards must outweigh the costs.
- *Exploratory affective exchange*. More intimate details, especially at the feeling level, begin to be reciprocated.
- *Affective exchange*. High levels of disclosure are exchanged as people get to know one another in great depth.
- *Stable exchange*. Once a relationship has been firmly established, it should be characterised by continuing openness.
- *Depenetration*. If a relationship starts to fail as the costs start to outweigh the benefits, there begins a gradual process of withdrawal of disclosure, leading to relational termination.

The third aspect of self-disclosure relates to the object of the statement. A self-disclosure can be about one's own personal experience, or it can be about one's personal reaction to the experiences being related by another. Consider the following interaction:

> John: I haven't been sleeping too well recently. I work from early morning until after midnight every day, and yet nothing seems to sink in. I'm really worried about these exams. What would I do if I failed them?
>
> Mary: You know John, I am very concerned about you. It seems to me that you are working too much, and not getting enough rest.

This is an example of a self-disclosure as a personal reaction to the experiences of another person, in which one individual is expressing concern and giving an opinion about the statements made by the other. It is sometimes referred to as a *self-involving* statement, as opposed to a disclosure about one's self (Knox *et al.*, 1997). In the example given, Mary could have chosen to give a parallel self-disclosure about her own personal experience by saying something like 'I remember when I was sitting my final exams. I was worried about them too. What I did was to make sure I stopped working in time to get out of the house and meet other people. This took my mind off the exams.' In this case, while Mary is reciprocating by self-disclosing she is taking the focus away from John and on to herself.

Both of these types of approach are appropriate in different contexts, depending on the nature of the interaction taking place and the goals of the interactors. If it is desirable to give concerted attention to an individual and encourage full disclosure, then concentrating on one's reactions to the feelings or thoughts of the other person would probably be most successful. If, however, the intention is to demonstrate that the person's feelings are not unusual, then the use of a parallel self-disclosure relating one's own experience may be more effective.

Fourth, self-disclosure can be about the past ('I was born in 1984'; 'I was really grief-stricken when my father died'), present ('I am a vegetarian'; 'I am very happy'), or future ('I hope to get promotion'; 'I want to get married and have a family'). One situation in which people are expected to self-disclose in terms of facts and feelings about the past, present and future is in the selection interview. Candidates will be asked to talk about their previous experience or education, to say why they have applied for the job and to outline their aspirations. Not only are interviewees expected to give factual details about themselves, they will more often than not be expected to relate their attitudes and feelings towards these factual experiences.

ELEMENTS OF SELF-DISCLOSURE

There are several important elements of self-disclosure that need to be taken into consideration.

Valence

This is the degree to which the disclosure is positive or negative for both the discloser and the listener. In the early stages of relationship development, disclosures are mainly positive, and negative self-disclosures usually only emerge once a relationship has developed. This is another reason why some clients find difficulty in disclosing negative information to an unfamiliar professional. Negative self-disclosures have been shown to be marked by paralinguistic cues such as stuttering, stammering, repetition, mumbling and low 'feeble' voice quality, whereas positive disclosures tend to be characterised by rapid, flowing, melodious speech (Bloch, 1996).

There is some research evidence to confirm that negative disclosures can be disadvantageous. Lazowski and Andersen (1991) carried out a study in which they had university undergraduates watch video-tapes of an individual self-disclosing to someone off-camera. They found that the use of negative disclosures (e.g. 'I felt like telling him that I practically hated him, that I disliked him more than anyone I'd met in a long time'), when compared with positive disclosures (e.g. 'I felt like telling him that he was really a pretty nice guy'), led both male and female viewers to like the male speaker significantly less and to expect to be less comfortable when interacting with him.

In another study, Miller *et al.* (1992) contrasted the relative effects of negative, positive and bragging disclosures. The latter contained more superlatives (e.g. 'best' rather than 'good'); reference to doing better than others or having power over them; less emphasis on working hard and more on being a 'wonderful' person; and less credit given to group efforts and more to personal achievements. Examples of each of the three categories used in this study were as follows:

Positive: 'I even got the most valuable player award. Boy, was I surprised . . . I was pleased to get the award and the recognition. I was glad to help my team finish the season so well.'

Negative: 'I didn't play well this season. I was embarrassed . . . I tried to look like I was having fun but I kept thinking how lousy I played and that I shouldn't have come.'

Bragging: 'I was the leading player all summer. Actually, I'm the best all-round player this league has ever seen. I could have my choice to play in any team I want next year.'

The results indicated that, to be rated as competent and successful, the use of bragging disclosures was a better strategy than negative disclosures, whereas the latter were seen as being more socially sensitive. However, the highest overall evaluations were given for positive disclosures, which were viewed as being both successful and socially sensitive. Thus the optimum approach would seem to be a mid-point between being self-deprecating at one extreme and boastful at the other. One context where self-promotion and a degree of bragging is the expected social norm is the employment interview. The rules of this form of interview are such that interviewers expect candidates to sell themselves in the best possible light. Here, two particular behaviours are commonly employed:

1   *Entitlements* refer to attempts to associate oneself with successful events or people (e.g. 'I was at EagleAir when we developed the breakthrough XJ521 jet fighter'; 'I took my degree at London when Eysenck was Head of Department'). This technique is also known as 'basking in reflected glory' (Schutz, 1998).

2   *Enhancements* are attempts to enhance or exaggerate the importance of one's achievements (e.g. 'My degree programme was one of the hardest to gain entry to'; 'The senior manager was off ill quite a lot and so in reality I ran the Department').

Another interesting dimension of valence was highlighted by Emler (1992). In his analysis of gossip as a phenomenon worthy of social scientific study, he argued that an important function of self-disclosure is to influence and guide how others talk and gossip about us. Thus we are aware of the wider implications, regarding the valence of our disclosures, beyond the immediate encounter.

Informativeness

Here, self-disclosure is assessed along three main dimensions, namely:

1   *Breadth*. This relates to the total number of disclosures used. It is measured by counts of self-reference pronouns or topics covered, or by self-report instruments.
2   *Depth*. This refers to the level of intimacy of the disclosure. In general, emotionally intense, negative or embarrassing information tends to be rated as higher in intimacy (Omarzu, 2000). Depth is measured either using self-report instruments, or by rating actual disclosures made for intimacy level.
3   *Duration*. This is measured either by the total amount of time the person spends disclosing, or by a word count of disclosing statements.

The Derlega and Chaikin Inventory (1975) was designed to measure breadth and depth of disclosures. Examples of shallow levels of disclosure given in this inventory include: 'How often my aunts and uncles and family get together', 'Whether or not I have ever gone to a church other than my own', and deeper levels such as 'How frequently I like to engage in sexual activity', 'The kinds of things I do that I don't want people to watch'.

In the Lazowski and Andersen (1991) study mentioned earlier, it was found that negative disclosures were seen as more informative than positive ones. They postulated one reason for this finding as being that, since it is less acceptable for people to disclose negative information, such disclosures are likely to be more heartfelt and revealing. Their study also revealed that disclosures about thoughts and feelings were viewed as deeper and more informative than those concerned with actions, and they surmised that this is because: 'it is access to otherwise hidden cognitions and affects that gives listeners the feeling that they have heard something significant about the speaker' (p. 146). One topic that has been found to be difficult for most people to discuss is that of death. For example, a survey carried out by the US National Hospice Foundation found that parents find it easier to talk to their children about sex than to talk to their own parents about dying with dignity (Levy, 1999).

Appropriateness

This is perhaps the most crucial aspect of self-disclosure. Each disclosure needs to be evaluated in the light of the context in which it occurs. While there are no hard and fast rules about the exact appropriateness of self-disclosure in every situation, there are some general indicators. Self-disclosures are more appropriate:

1   From low status to high status individuals but not vice versa. Where there is a high degree of asymmetry in status, disclosure tends to be in one direction (Bochner, 2000). Thus workers may disclose personal problems to their supervisors, but the reverse does not usually happen. This is because for a supervisor to disclose personal information to a subordinate would cause a loss of face which would affect the status relationship. Research findings tend to suggest, however, that self-disclosures are most often employed between people of equal status (Tardy and Dindia, 1997).

2   When the listener is not flooded with them. There would seem to be a relationship between psychological adjustment and self-disclosure in that individuals who are extremely high or low disclosers are regarded as less socially skilled.

3   Depending on the roles of the interactors. We may disclose information to our spouses that we would not disclose to our children. Similarly, clients will often discuss a problem with a 'neutral' counsellor that they would not wish to discuss with their spouses or with close friends. Patients disclose answers to highly personal questions from doctors, such as 'Do you take drugs?' or 'How often do you have sexual intercourse?', that they would be unlikely to tolerate in other contexts. Nor would they expect the doctor to reciprocate with similar information (Greene *et al.*, 1994).

4   Depending on the setting. We would be unlikely to disclose during an intimate dinner on a first date that we are suffering from painful haemorrhoids or athlete's foot, but we would do so in a doctor's surgery.

Flexibility

Self-disclosure flexibility refers to the ability of an individual to vary the breadth and depth of disclosures across situations. Highly flexible disclosers are able to modify the nature and level of their self-disclosures, whereas less flexible disclosers tend to disclose at the same level regardless of context. Miller and Kenny (1986) illustrated how 'blabber-mouths' who disclose in an undifferentiated fashion are not the recipients of high levels of disclosure from others. Such individuals (also known as *talkaholics*), who have a tendency to communicate compulsively, have been the subject of academic enquiry and scales have been designed to measure this characteristic (Long *et al.*, 2000).

Accessibility

This refers to the ease with which self-disclosures can be obtained from an individual. Some people disclose freely while others are much more reluctant to reveal personal information. This may be due to personality, upbringing and culture in that the child may have grown up in a context where the norm is not to disclose too much. It may also be caused by lack of learning about how and what to disclose during social encounters. Quite often clients disclose a 'presenting' problem and only after they have established confidence in the professional will they reveal the real problem. This is particularly true where the problem is of an intimate or embarrassing nature.

Honesty

There is a joke that goes as follows:

Q: What is the difference between Washington, Nixon and Clinton?
A: Washington couldn't tell a lie. Nixon couldn't tell the truth. Clinton couldn't tell the difference!

This joke relates to the veracity of disclosures. The main reasons for making dishonest disclosures have been shown by De Paulo *et al.* (1996) to be:

1   To save face.
2   To avoid conflict.
3   To make interaction run smoothly.
4   To increase or reduce interaction with others.
5   To gain power.

Given the importance of these functions to the preservation of harmonious relationships, it is not surprising that deception of some form has been shown to occur in at least one quarter of all conversations (Buller and Burgoon, 1996). There has been increasing research into what is known as *avoidance–avoidance conflict* (AAC) (Bull, 2002). AAC occurs in a situation where the person has to choose between disclosing a hurtful truth, telling a face-saving lie, or giving an equivocal response (Edwards and Bello, 2001). For example, a close friend produces a painting that her 13-year-old son has just finished and asks for your opinion. You could respond:

*   'I think it's really beautiful. He has an obvious talent and flair for art.' (Lie)
*   'I think it's very poor. The perspective is all wrong and there isn't enough contrast in the shading to give a 3-dimensional feel to the painting.' (Truth)
*   'Oh, so he's interested in art. You must be very proud of him.' (Equivocation)

When faced with AAC, research shows that the overwhelming majority of people opt for equivocation (Rosenfeld, 2000). The truth may be unpleasant for the recipient and damaging for the relationship, a lie can cause stress for the discloser and may cause problems if unveiled later, while an equivocal response often saves face all round.

In specialised circumstances, such as police interviewing, disclosures need to be examined carefully. Gudjonsson (1999) illustrated how confessions made by suspects are disputed in court for one of three reasons:

1   It is claimed that the confession was never actually made, but was fabricated either by the police or by a third party to whom the defendant is alleged to have confessed.
2   The confession is retracted – the defendant claims that although he or she did confess, this was done under some form of duress and is actually false.
3   The defence counsel disputes a confession that the defendant maintains is true, on grounds that the person is not fit to plead because of intellectual impairment or psychological incapacity.

Since deception is widely practised, it becomes rather difficult to detect. A common joke in comedy sketches goes as follows:

A: I always know when you're lying.
B: How?
A: Your lips move!

In reality, deceit is not always so easy to detect. As Vrij (2000: 92) concluded, 'There is no such thing as typical deceptive behaviour – that is, there is no behaviour or set of behaviours that all liars exhibit. Deceptive behaviour depends on someone's personality and on the circumstances under which the lie is told.' For example, the degree of motivation is important. If I tell you (falsely) that the bottle of wine you have brought to my house is one that I like and that I will enjoy drinking it at a later time, the costs associated with being found out are relatively small. On the other hand, a perpetrator trying to convince a detective of personal innocence following a brutal murder has a great deal at stake.

Knowledge of the base-line or 'normal' pattern of individual behaviour has been shown to be crucial before decisions about deviations therein can be made in judging the veracity of disclosures (Malone and De Paulo, 2001). In general terms, however, the following behaviours tend to be associated with deception (Dickson et al., 1997; Vrij, 2000):

*   higher vocal pitch;
*   slower speech rate;
*   longer pauses;
*   larger number of speech errors and hesitations;
*   shorter response length;
*   decreased use of arms, hands, fingers, feet and legs;
*   more indirect answers that do not specifically refer to self (e.g. replying to the question 'Do you drink?' with 'Nobody in my family takes drink');

- increased use of negative statements ('I am not guilty' rather than 'I am innocent');
- greater degree of 'levelling' (use of terms such as 'all', 'every', 'none', 'nobody');
- more general statements with fewer specific details given.

Disclosure avoidance

The corollary of self-disclosure is self-suppression, and Hastings (2000a) illustrated how suppression, or avoidance, of certain talk and actions is culturally universal. She used the term *egocasting* to describe the intrapersonal process whereby the individual decides what side of self to display and portray to others (Hastings, 2000b). She argued that when the person has to decide whether to disclose something that could cause potential personal harm, the self (or 'ego') makes a decision based on the probable reaction of others and how this will in turn impact on self and self-image. In identifying the main general aim of suppression as to protect the individual against harm, Afifi and Guerrero (2000) charted a number of more specific reasons for disclosure avoidance:

- Need for privacy. As expressed by a young female in the Afifi and Guerrero study: 'My mom wants me to tell her everything. She thinks she has to know everything about me all the time. I get sick of it. Sometimes I want to tell her it's just not her business. I am almost an adult. I have my own life. I need my privacy' (p. 176).
- Social inappropriateness of the disclosure (e.g. we do not discuss bowel movements at the dining table).
- Futility (e.g. 'We've discussed this hundreds of times before and got nowhere').
- Wanting to avoid criticism, punishment or embarrassment (this is the primary reason given by children for avoiding disclosure to parents).
- A desire to avoid conflict (so we may not tell aggressive others that we disagree with what they are saying).
- Protection of the relationship (e.g. we would be unlikely to tell our partner that we found someone else more attractive).

The issue of secrecy has also been explored in relation to disclosure avoidance. Secrecy refers to information that one or more persons consciously withhold from one or more others (Finkenauer and Rime, 1998). As well as the *secret-keeper*, there is the person from whom the information is kept (i.e. *secret-target*). For example, a wife (secret-keeper) tells her husband (secret-target) that their 18-year-old daughter is going steady with a boy at college, but does not tell him that they are sleeping together. Those in the secret-keeper position often have a benign attitude to secrecy, yet this usually changes to resentment when they find themselves in the secret-target position. This is because being in the former position tends to give one a feeling of control and power, while being 'kept in the dark' leads to feelings of exclusion, rejection or betrayal (Finkenauer and Hazam, 2000).

While, in general, secrecy can be damaging for relationships, in certain circumstances it is beneficial. For example, Vangelisti and Caughlin (1997) found that, within families, secrets kept to protect family members from hurt or pain were positively related to relational satisfaction, while secrets held as a result of poor intra-family communication or a desire to avoid evaluation had negative effects on familial relationships. However, the distinction is not always easy to make and requires a deeper knowledge of those involved. In the example above, is the wife withholding the secret to protect her husband from pain, because she is afraid of how he will evaluate their daughter, or is it just one more instance of poor communications generally within the family? In their study of marriage, Finkenauer and Hazam (2000) found that both disclosure and secrecy were important potential sources of marital satisfaction, and it was the appropriate use, and goal, of each that was most important.

FUNCTIONS OF SELF-DISCLOSURE

The goals of the discloser appear to be of paramount importance in determining the amount, content and intimacy of disclosure in different contexts (Oguchi, 1991). For example, research has shown (Rosenfeld, 2000) that with friends the top two reasons for self-disclosure are (1) relationship maintenance and enhancement, and (2) self-clarification – to learn more about one's thoughts and feelings. With strangers, however, the top two purposes are (1) reciprocity – to facilitate social interchange, and (2) impression formation – to present oneself in the best light. The skilled use of self-disclosure can therefore facilitate goal achievement for both professionals and their clients. The main functions of self-disclosure by professionals are as follows.

To overcome fear

Many people have a fear of disclosing too much about their thoughts and feelings, since there is the risk of being rejected, not understood, or subjected to ridicule; causing embarrassment or offence to the listener; or expressing and presenting oneself so badly that a negative image of self is portrayed. The fear of disclosure is so great in some people, termed 'inhibitors' or 'suppressors', that they avoid revealing *anything* negative to others (Kowalski, 1999). Indeed, in many sub-cultures self-disclosure is actively discouraged, with the child being told 'Don't let others know your business' or 'Tell people only what they need to know'. This attitude then persists into later life where respect is often given to the person who 'plays cards close to the chest'. While in a game of poker it is wise not to disclose too much, either verbally or nonverbally, the attitude of avoiding self-disclosure can cause problems for people when they may have a need to talk about personal matters. Often, before we make a deep disclosure, there is a strategic process of *testing* (Kelly and McKillop, 1996) or *advance pre-testing* (Duck, 1999), whereby we 'trail' the topic with potential confidants and observe their reactions. If these are favourable, then we continue with the revelations; if not we move on to a new topic.

However, the initial dangers of self-disclosure are such that we expect an equal commitment to this process from people with whom we may wish to develop a relationship. For this reason, reciprocation is expected in the early stages of everyday interaction. In relation to the poker analogy it is a case of the individual wanting to see all of the cards on the table. The fear of self-disclosure can be overcome partially by a self-disclosure from the professional to the effect that this type of problem has been dealt with often, or that it is quite acceptable for the client to have the problem.

To encourage reciprocation

Self-disclosure is contagious. In everyday interaction, reciprocation of self-disclosures is the norm, so that if one person is prepared to reveal personal details this results in the listener also revealing intimate information. As Kowalski (1996) illustrated, this can sometimes take the form of one-upmanship. For example, if I tell you about my experience of being burgled and what I had stolen, you may top this by telling me about how when you were burgled you lost five times as much as I did. In professional situations, clients can often be encouraged to 'open up' by receiving a self-disclosure from the professional. Such a disclosure can have a very potent effect on the client, who will then be more likely to begin to self-disclose more freely. Where reciprocation of self-disclosures does not occur, one of three types of situations prevails:

1   The person making the disclosures is not really interested in the listener. This type of person's need to tell all is so great that the effect this may have on the listener is not considered. The speaker is simply using the listener as a receptacle into which to pour disclosures. This is quite common when someone is undergoing some form of inner turmoil, and needs a friendly ear to encourage the ventilation of fears and emotions. To use another analogy, the listener becomes a 'wailing wall' for the speaker. In certain professional contexts this is acceptable, as in counselling and therapy.

2   The person who is receiving the disclosures does not care about the speaker. In this case the speaker is foolish to continue disclosing, since it is possible that the listener may use the disclosures against the speaker, either at the time of the disclosure or later.

3   Neither one cares about the disclosures of the other. In this case there is no real relationship. If one person discloses, it is a monologue; if both disclose it is a dialogue in which exchanges are superficial. A great deal of everyday, fleeting conversation falls into the latter category.

In many fields there is a need for more self-disclosure from the professional. For example, Hargie *et al.* (2000) found that self-disclosure was recognised by pharmacists as a core skill, but in their study, which involved video-recording community pharmacist–patient interactions, few pharmacist disclosures actually occurred. Likewise, Fisher and Groce (1990) analysed forty-three medical interviews and found that doctors rarely disclosed even the obvious information about themselves. This pattern seems to evolve at an early stage. Thus Ashmore and Banks (2001) also found that student nurses were less willing to disclose to patients than to any other target-person. Yet, the use of some disclosures, however shallow, would help practitioners to present a more 'human' face to patients, and self-disclosure by the professional can be advantageous in other contexts.

Baldwin's (2000) edited text *The use of self in therapy* presented a comprehensive and convincing case in support of disclosures by therapist to client. Likewise, Bochner (2000) illustrated how the use of disclosure by therapists can help to achieve 'mutuality' (a greater degree of equality) with clients. However, Hill and O'Brien (1999) demonstrated that, whereas clients tended to rate disclosures by the therapist as helpful, counsellors rated them as unhelpful. Likewise, Knox *et al.* (1997) found that the majority of clients appreciated, and benefited from, appropriate counsellor disclosures. But in their qualitative study of clients currently in long-term therapy, at one extreme they identified a minority of clients who preferred no counsellor disclosures at all, while at the other some were voracious in their desire to know as much as possible about the helper – even to the extent of seeking out other clients of the same therapist to share information. These studies revealed a number of advantages of counsellor disclosures, as listed in Box 9.3.

Knox *et al.* (1997) found that the most effective therapist disclosures occurred when:

- clients were discussing important personal issues;
- they were personal as opposed to self-involving; they were often about past experiences, and none was concerned with feelings or opinions about the therapy relationship *per se*. Three main categories of disclosure emerged here – (1) *family* (e.g. one therapist revealed having a son), (2) *leisure activities* (one talked about fly-fishing), and (3) *shared difficult experiences* (one revealed the problems she experienced with her family when she came out as a lesbian);
- clients felt that the helper had disclosed to normalise their experiences or offer reassurance.

In noting that helper disclosures can have advantages and disadvantages depending on how they are employed, Egan (2002) recommended that helpers:

- let clients know at the outset if they intend to disclose their own experiences – this should form part of the initial 'contract';

Box 9.3 Advantages of counsellor disclosure

When used appropriately counsellor disclosures:

- act as a role model for clients to make changes in themselves;
- make the helper seem more human and more real;
- serve to balance the power differential between helper and helpee;
- are beneficial for the overall relationship;
- offer new insights to clients;
- give clients a feeling of *universality,* through reassurance that they are not alone in how they feel and that their feelings are neither abnormal nor unexpected;
- show clients that things can and do work out.

- time the disclosures to fit with the flow and content of the interaction;
- ensure that the disclosures are appropriate and for the client's benefit; role reversal is not the purpose here – helpers should not burden the client with their problems;
- do not disclose too much, but be selective and focused; counsellor disclosures should be to the point rather than rambling;
- be flexible – disclosure will be more appropriate with some clients than with others.

To open conversations

When two people meet for the first time they give and receive self-disclosures. Chaikin and Derlega (1976) identified three main stages or levels of relationship development:

1   *Awareness.* Here, people have not actually interacted but are aware of the presence of one another. At this stage, for example, a female may stand close to, or walk slowly past, a male in whom she is interested.
2   *Surface contact.* At this stage individuals give superficial information about themselves, and make judgements about whether or not to pursue the relationship.
3   *Mutuality.* Finally, people begin to disclose and exchange personal feelings, and engage in more intimate self-disclosures as the relationship develops.

Many professionals use self-disclosure to open interactions and establish surface contact. Such disclosures are usually directly related to the job role.

To search for commonalities

At the surface contact stage of a relationship, people give self-disclosures in the hope that the other person may be able to identify with them. At this stage they search for shared interests or experiences in order to identify some common ground on which to build a conversation. This would usually occur in informal meetings between professionals and clients. It is also important in certain business contexts, such as selling, where the professional salesperson may want to establish a common frame of reference with the client, in order to facilitate the development of a relationship (and the likelihood of a successful outcome in terms of sales). On occasions, the professional may want to highlight commonalities. Thus a health professional visiting a young mother who has just had her first child may say 'I know the problems associated with becoming a parent since I have three children myself', thereby establishing a common bond, and providing a good foundation for a discussion of the particular problems faced by this mother.

To express concern for the other person

This is the type of self-disclosure in which the professional expresses feelings about the other person. Such disclosures can serve as a potent form of reinforcement (see Chapter 4). Disclosure is a skill employed by effective negotiators as a way of building trust with their opponents (Thompson, 2001). By making disclosures such as 'I am worried that we are so far apart on this', the negotiator gives an impression of openness and honest concern for the other side, which in turn is usually reciprocated (see Chapter 13).

To share experiences

In certain instances, the professional will have had similar experiences to the client, and can share these to underline the fact that there is a depth of understanding between the two. This also helps to portray the professional as 'human'. For example, one situation where this can be of immense benefit is where a client has recently been bereaved, and the professional has also faced the pain of bereavement. The use of a self-disclosure here can be a valuable reassurance to the client that the pain will pass (e.g. 'I remember when my mother died I thought I would never get over it ...'). However, this type of 'me too' approach needs to be used appropriately and should not be taken to the extreme of what Yager and Beck (1985) termed the 'We could have been twins' level.

To express one's point of view

In many contexts, such as at staff meetings, interviews, case conferences, the professional is expected to put forward personal thoughts, ideas and opinions. The ability to do so confidently and competently is therefore important.

These are the main functions of professional self-disclosure. However, self-disclosure by clients also serves a number of important functions. These will now be explored.

To facilitate self-expression

It can become a burden not being able to tell others about personal matters, and having to keep things 'bottled up'. Self-disclosure can have a therapeutic effect, by enabling us to 'get it off our chest', which is why counselling, the confessional, or discussing something with a close friend can all make us feel better. There is indeed truth in the old maxim that 'A problem shared is a problem halved.' As summarised by McKenna and Bargh (2000: 63):

People have a need to present their true or inner self to the outside world and to have others know them as they know themselves ... When an individual is unable to do this in his or her current relationship, there is likely to be a strong motivation to establish relationships in which those needs and preferences can be expressed and accepted.

Stewart and Logan (1998) referred to self-disclosure as part of a process of social *exhaling* (as opposed to listening which they termed *inhaling*). Professionals should be aware both of the existence of the need for clients to exhale, and of ways to allow them to satisfy it. It is interesting to note that when people are not able to utilise interpersonal channels for disclosure, they often use substitutes such as keeping a personal diary, talking to a pet, or conversing with God. Indeed, this need can be observed at an early stage in young children who often disclose to a teddy bear or doll.

Frequently, after a traumatic event the victim attempts to suppress or inhibit thoughts about it, and avoid discussing it with others. However, the more disturbing the event, the greater is the need to talk about it and ventilate one's feelings. If this process is not facilitated, then adverse health effects are likely to occur, as the person continually ruminates about what has happened (Kowalski, 1999). Trying to keep it inside tends to result in thoughts and visions of the experience beginning to dominate – a phenomenon referred to as the *hyperaccessibility of suppressed information* (Erber and Wegner, 1996). Interestingly, Kowalski (1999) illustrated how, while disclosure after a stressful event provides a necessary catharsis, disclosure before a stressful event may not be beneficial as it can serve to magnify feelings of anxiety.

In a comprehensive review of the research on a range of illnesses (such as cardiovascular diseases, HIV, cancer), Tardy (2000: 121) found considerable evidence to show that self-disclosure has positive effects on health, concluding that: 'self-disclosure facilitates health by not only eliminating the deleterious consequences of inhibition but also organizing thoughts and memories in more productive ways'. One reason for this is that disclosure has been shown to boost immunological functioning (Petrie *et al.*, 1995). These findings are particularly important for health professionals, since it is clear that for patients to fully disclose, the most important prerequisite is the sensitivity shown by health caregivers who must be aware that 'the messages they convey – even when they are saying nothing at all – will guide patients in their decision making about whether to tell the whole truth, or only that part which the caregiver seems most receptive to hearing' (Parrott *et al.*, 2000: 147).

There is evidence that written disclosures can also be beneficial. For example, Greenberg and Stone (1992) had sixty undergraduates (36F; 24M) write about their deepest thoughts and feelings regarding the most traumatic and upsetting experience of their lives which they had not previously discussed in any depth with other people. Students who disclosed more severe traumas reported fewer physical symptoms on a health questionnaire in the months following the study than either those who described low-severity traumas, or a control group not involved in the written exercise. Similarly, Pennebaker and Francis (1996) found that first-year students who were asked to write about their thoughts and feelings about coming to college, in comparison with a control group, had a reduced level of illness visits to the health centre coupled with improved grade point averages. Likewise, Brown (1997) carried out a study in which eighty-five college-aged rape victims wrote about and then read aloud their rape experience. Those who included greater detail, more emotional content and deeper personal insights in their accounts demonstrated a significant decrease in symptoms of post-traumatic stress disorder, depression and social anxiety. Greenberg and Stone (1992) argued that the written expression of feelings has a definite therapeutic effect, which on occasions may even be superior to oral disclosures, since the recipient of interpersonal disclosures may respond inappropriately. They cite the example of how when incest victims tell their mothers about the event a high proportion respond by disbelieving or blaming them.

This also occurs in other areas. Victims of abuse in childhood often face threats about what will happen if they disclose and may not be believed when they do tell (Walker and Antony-Black, 1999). Studies of the gay population reveal difficulties with disclosure or 'coming out', especially to family (Savin-Williams and Dube, 1998). In a study of 194 gay people between the ages of 14 and 21 years, living at home, D'Augelli *et al.* (1998) found that those who had disclosed that they were gay reported verbal or physical abuse from family members, and higher levels of 'suicidality' (feelings and thoughts about suicide).

These findings are interesting for the process of therapy. It would appear that writing about trauma can contribute to the healing process because the written task necessitates the person having to work through the event and come to terms with thoughts and feelings about it. Thus people seem to benefit from discussing or writing about their deepest feelings, and this can be a key step in the process of coping with the trauma. As Tubbs (1998: 229) summarised it: 'Part of returning to mental health involves sharing oneself with others.'

To heighten personal knowledge

This is exemplified by the saying 'How do I know what I think until I hear what I say?' The value of the 'talking cure' in therapy is a good example of how the process of allowing someone freely to express their thoughts, ideas, fears, problems, etc., actually facilitates the individual's self-awareness. The importance of self-disclosure in therapy was aptly summarised by Stricker (1990: 289):

> It is through the self-disclosure of the patient to the therapist that he can begin to recognize previously hidden and unacceptable aspects of himself, to recognize the acceptability of what had been experienced as forbidden secrets, and to grow in a healthier fashion.

Thus self-disclosure can help people to understand their feelings and the reasons for them; in other words it encourages them to know themselves more fully. This view was confirmed in a study of adults (aged 33–48 years) in Japan and the USA, where it was shown that in both countries levels of self-knowledge and self-disclosure were positively correlated (Asai and Barnlund, 1998).

To promote social comparison

A key process in interpersonal interaction is that of *social comparison*, in that we evaluate ourselves in terms of how we compare to others. In particular, we engage in

243

two types of comparison (Adler *et al.*, 2001). First, we decide whether we are *superior or inferior* to others on certain dimensions (attractiveness, intelligence, popularity, etc.) Here, the important aspect is to compare with an appropriate reference group. For example, modest joggers should not compare their performance with Olympic standard marathon runners. Second, we judge the extent to which we are the *same or different* from others. At certain stages of life, especially adolescence, the pressure to fit in with and be seen as similar to peers is immense. Thus wearing the right brand of clothes or shoes may be of the utmost importance. We also need to know whether our thoughts, beliefs and ideas are in line with and acceptable to those of other people.

People who do not have access to a good listener may not only be denied the opportunity to heighten their self-awareness, they are also denied valuable feedback as to the validity and acceptability of their inner thoughts and feelings. By discussing these with others, we receive feedback as to whether these are experiences which others have as well, or whether they may be less common. Furthermore, by gauging the reactions to our self-disclosures, we learn what types are acceptable or unacceptable with particular people and in specific situations. On occasions it is the fear that certain disclosures may be unacceptable to family or friends that motivates an individual to seek professional help. Counsellors will be familiar with client statements such as: 'I just couldn't talk about this to my husband'; 'I really can't let my mother know my true feelings'. Another aspect of social comparison in the counselling context relates to a technique known as *normalising*. This is the process whereby helpers provide reassurance to clients that what they are experiencing is not abnormal or atypical, but is a normal reaction shared by others when facing such circumstances (Dickson *et al.*, 1997).

To develop relationships

The appropriate use of self-disclosure is crucial to the development and maintenance of long-term relationships. Those who either disclose too much or too little tend to have problems in establishing and sustaining relationships. Even in close relationships there can be dangers with deep disclosures, especially of a highly sensitive nature. This is shown in studies of the difficulties faced by those diagnosed with HIV/AIDS in disclosing this to intimate partners (Derlega *et al.*, 2000). Similarly, individuals who disclose at a deep level to relative strangers, or who make only negative disclosures, will find it difficult to make friends. In the therapeutic context, by encouraging clients to self-disclose, and giving sensitive feedback, helpers can provide them with a valuable learning experience about how to use this skill.

To ingratiate and manipulate

Some clients use self-disclosures in an attempt to ingratiate themselves with the professional, for whatever reason. This type of client tends to disclose quite a lot, and say very positive things about the professional ('You are the only person who under-

	Known to self	*Unknown to self*
Known to others	A	B
Unknown to others	C	D

Figure 9.2 The Johari window

stands me'; 'I don't know what I would do without you'). In a sense, the client
is 'coming on too strong', and this can be very difficult to deal with. The purpose may
be to manipulate the professional for some form of personal gain. On the other hand,
if this type of revelation is genuine, it can be a signal that the client is becoming over-
dependent. Either way, it is advisable to be aware of this function of manipulative
disclosure.

These, then, are the main purposes of self-disclosure by both the professional
and the client. A number of them can be illustrated with reference to the Johari
window (Luft, 1970) developed by two psychologists, Joseph Luft and Harry Ingram
(and named after the initial letters of both first names). As depicted in Figure 9.2 this
indicates four dimensions of the self. There are aspects that are:

- known both by self and by others (A), such as statements one has made;
- unknown by the self but known to others (B), including personal mannerisms,
  annoying habits and so on;
- personally known but not revealed to others (C), including embarrassing
  thoughts or feelings;
- unknown both to self and others (D), such as how one would behave in a
  particular crisis context.

One of the effects of self-disclosing is that the size of segment A is increased and
the size of segments B, C and D reduced. In other words by encouraging clients
to self-disclose, not only do they find out more about themselves, but the professional also gains valuable knowledge about them, and thereby understands them
more fully.

FACTORS INFLUENCING SELF-DISCLOSURE

A number of factors pertaining to the nature of the discloser, the recipient, the
relationship, and the context influence the extent to which self-disclosure is employed.

The discloser

The following characteristics of the discloser have been examined.

245

Age

First-born children tend to disclose less than later-born children. This difference may be due to later-borns being more socially skilled, because their parents have more experience of child-rearing, and they have older siblings to interact with. It may also be the case that the eldest child has higher status and is therefore less likely to disclose to lower status siblings. More generally, in a study of 212 undergraduates in the USA, Dolgin and Lindsay (1999) found that there was less disclosure to siblings who were five years younger. They also found that while younger siblings reported disclosure to seek advice and emotional support from older siblings, the latter reported more disclosures aimed at teaching their younger brothers or sisters. Another difference was that females reported making more disclosures for emotional support than did males. One important factor here is the nature of the relationship between siblings. Thus Howe *et al.* (2000), in a study of Canadian 5th and 6th grade children (mean age 11.5 years), found that warmth of the relationship was a key determinant of sibling disclosure.

Disclosure tends to increase with age. As Archer (1979) pointed out, this finding has been reported in studies of children between the ages of 6 and 12 years, and in college students between the ages of 17 to 55 years. However, Sinha (1972), in a study of adolescent females, found that 12–14-year-old girls disclosed most, followed by 17–18-year-olds, with 15–16-year-olds disclosing least. Sinha argued that at this latter stage the adolescent is at a stage of transition, from girl to woman, and may need more time to 'find herself'.

In a study of 174 adolescents in the US, Papini *et al.* (1990) found that self-disclosures about emotional matters to best friends increased from 12 to 15 years of age. They also found that at the age of 12 years adolescents preferred to emotionally disclose to parents, but by the age of 15 years they preferred to disclose to friends. It was further discovered that adolescents with high self-esteem and the esteem of peers were more likely to disclose their emotional concerns to friends, whereas those who felt 'psychosocially adrift' did not communicate such worries in this way. The adolescents in this study disclosed more about their concerns to parents who were perceived to be open to discussion, warm and caring. The above findings have obvious implications for professionals dealing with mid-adolescent individuals.

Coupland *et al.* (1991) conducted a series of studies on 'painful self-disclosure' (PSD) in interactions between women aged 70–87 years and women in their mid-30s. PSD refers to the revelation of intimate information on ill-health, bereavement, immobility, loneliness, etc. They found that the older women revealed more PSDs, initiated more of them and were less likely to close such disclosing sequences. Since older women usually have experienced more painful events simply by virtue of longevity, it is perhaps not surprising that they disclose more of them than younger women. It could also be related to a reduced need for approval from others, in that the older individual may be less concerned with what other people think, and so more willing to voice an opinion. Coupland *et al.* suggested that PSDs can have positive effects for older women in terms of earning credit for having coped success-fully with difficult life events. They speculated that such PSDs can help the older person to 'locate oneself in relation to past experiences, to one's own state of health, to chronological age and perhaps to projectable future decrement and death' (p. 191).

Many older people clearly enjoy, and benefit from, talking about their past and indeed such reminiscence is a positive method of therapy for this age group (Williams and Nussbaum, 2001). The experiences of loss are of particular import at this life stage (Suganuma, 1997). However, their greatest recall (the 'personal memory bump') is for life events that occur between the ages of 10 and 30 (Thorne, 2000). During this span, identity is shaped for adult life. It is also a time of highly charged emotional events, such as going to high school, dating, college, starting employment, finding a partner, setting up home, having children. Hence, many of the memories recalled are of 'firsts' (first love, first job, etc.).

Gender

In summarising findings in this area, Dindia (2000b: 24) concluded that, 'women disclose more than men. However, sex differences in self-disclosure are small and are moderated by the sex of the person being disclosed to.' While, in general, people judge females to be higher disclosers, what Dindia found to be the case is that:

- females do not disclose to males any more than males do to males;
- females disclose more to females than males do to males;
- females disclose more to females than males do to females;
- females disclose more to males than males do to females.

Kowalski (1999: 239) noted another gender difference in that 'whereas men tend to be more vigilant in the content of their self-disclosures, women more closely monitor their target'. There are several impinging variables that interact with gender to determine disclosure levels.

1   *Situational factors*. The topic, gender of recipient and relationship between discloser and recipient are all determinants of disclosure. For example, battered women specifically want to talk to another female about their experiences (Dieckmann, 2000).
2   *Gender role identity*. This refers to how strongly a person feels male or female. It would seem that individuals, either male or female, who regard themselves as possessing female attributes disclose more. Shaffer *et al.* (1992) ascertained that measures of sex role identity were better predictors of self-disclosure to same-sex strangers than was gender *per se* (which failed to predict willingness to disclose). Both males and females high in femininity self-disclosed more. Masculinity had no effect on disclosure levels, while androgynous subjects (high in both male and female traits) demonstrated high levels of intimacy and flexibility in their disclosures across various contexts.
3   *Gender role attitudes*. This refers to how one believes a male or female should behave. We all learn to display what we feel are the appropriate behaviours for our gender role. These will have been influenced by same-sex parent and significant others. Thus if a male believes his role to be the solid, strong, silent type he is unlikely to be a high discloser.

4   *Gender role norms* of the culture or sub-culture. Grigsby and Weatherley (1983) found that women were significantly more intimate in their disclosures than men. It would seem that it is more acceptable in western society for females to discuss personal problems and feelings. Males disclose more about their traits, work and personal opinions while females disclose more about their tastes, interests and relationships. Males also disclose less negative personal information than females (Naifeh and Smith, 1984). It is therefore important to be aware that males may find difficulty in discussing personal matters, and may need more help, support and encouragement to do so.

Ethnic and religious group

Differences in disclosure have been found between different ethnic groups (Asai and Barnlund, 1998; Harris *et al.*, 1999). In the USA, European Americans tend to disclose more than African Americans, who in turn disclose more than Latin Americans. In general, Americans have been found to be more disclosing than similar groups in Japan, Germany, Great Britain and the Middle East. Yet Wheeless *et al.* (1986), in a study of 360 students, found no difference in disclosure levels between American students and students of non-western cultural origin studying in the USA. Likewise, Rubin *et al.* (2000) compared forty-four North Americans with forty Chinese students studying in the USA for less than three years, and found that target person and nature of topic were much more powerful determinants of disclosure than either gender or nationality.

In another study Hastings (2000a) investigated disclosure among Asian Indian postgraduate students at university in the USA. She found clear cultural differences in nature and pattern of disclosure. Role relationships played a very large part in determining disclosure among Asian Indians. Hindus believe that God has decreed the roles occupied by individuals and so the hierarchy is sacred and one's position deserved. Therefore, subordinates should not question those in authority. As a result, the Indians found difficulties with the propensity for US students to make demands of, or challenge, those in authority (their professors). They also disliked perceived American traits of extensive talk, overt expressions of self, and the direct, forcible statement of personal viewpoints. As summarised by Hastings: 'Whereas American friendship is enacted through expressing oneself, Indian friendship is enacted through suppressing oneself' (p. 105).

The traditional Japanese trait of humility has caused difficulties in the operation of effective focus groups (Flintoff, 2001). This is because it is almost impossible to get participants to express strong views, and if someone does so the other group members invariably concur with this opinion. Western companies operating in Japan consider focus groups an integral part of the business process. In an attempt to overcome prevailing disclosure norms they have asked participants to write down their views and then read them out. But this is far from ideal, removing as it does the dynamic interchange of ideas that characterises this method. Flintoff argued that if Japan wants western companies to engage fully, changes may have to take place in their traditional pattern of avoiding disagreements.

There is little evidence regarding the effects of religious affiliation on disclosure levels. One early study was conducted by Jourard (1961) at the University of Florida, in which he investigated differences between affiliates of the Baptist, Methodist, Catholic and Jewish faiths in relation to level of disclosures to parents and closest friends of both genders. No significant differences were found between denominations for females, although Jewish males were significantly higher disclosers than members of the other denominations, none of whom differed from one another. Jourard speculated that this difference may have been due to closer family ties in the Jewish community and therefore could have been a factor of sub-culture rather than religion *per se*.

In another American study, Long and Long (1976) found that attire (presence or absence of a habit) but not religious status (nun versus non-nun) produced significant differences in interviewee responses. Males were more open in the presence of an interviewer not in habit, whereas the opposite was true for females. Thus religious dedication appeared to be less important than the impact of clothing whereby such dedication is usually signalled.

A similar 'identification' effect was reported by Chesner and Beaumeister (1985), in a study of disclosures by clients to counsellors who identified themselves as devout Christians or Jews compared with counsellors who did not disclose religious convictions. It was found that Jewish subjects disclosed significantly less to the counsellor who declared himself a devout Christian. Chesner and Beaumeister concluded that counsellor disclosure of religion does not facilitate client disclosure, and may in fact reduce it.

In the Northern Ireland context, a study of Protestant (P) and Catholic (C) undergraduates revealed that both C and P students were significantly more likely to disclose to those of the same religion than to those of the other religion, as measured by the Miller *et al.* (1983) scale (Dickson *et al.*, 2000). Interestingly, gender differences emerged here, in that females were significantly more likely than males to disclose to those from the opposite religion. In another part of this study, actual interactions between same- and opposite-religion dyads revealed a greater breadth of disclosure (number of topics discussed) in same-religion pairs.

Personality

A number of personality variables have been shown to relate to disclosure level (Reno and Kenny, 1992; Suganuma, 1997; Waldo and Kemp, 1997; Omarzu, 2000; Matsushima *et al.*, 2000). Shy, introverted, types, those with low self-esteem, and individuals with a high need for social approval disclose less, and social desirability is negatively related to depth of disclosure. Also those with an external locus of control (who believe their destiny is shaped by events 'outside' themselves over which they have no control) disclose less than those with an internal locus of control (who believe they can largely shape their own destiny). Lonely individuals have also been found to disclose less (Schwab *et al.*, 1998), while neurotics tend to have low self-disclosure flexibility, in that they disclose the same amount, regardless of the situation. Finally, a significant and positive correlation between machiavellianism and disclosure has been reported for females but not for males (O'Connor and Simms, 1990).

Intoxication level

There is a common conception that alcohol consumption has a positive effect on disclosure level. In fact this has not been consistently shown to be the case. In their review of the area, Monahan and Lannutti (2000: 194) found that: 'studies examining the effects of alcohol consumption on self-disclosure and talk time have produced mixed results, with some studies finding more disclosure, others finding less, and still others finding no effects of alcohol consumption at all'. The context of the interaction is the crucial variable. Thus, for example, Monahan and Lannutti found that, when sober, females with low social self-esteem (SSE) disclosed significantly less than those with high SSE when interacting with a flirtatious male, but, when intoxicated, low SSE females disclosed at the same level as those with high SSE.

The recipient

A number of characteristics of the listener influence the amount of self-disclosure received.

Acceptance/empathy

Accepting/empathic people receive more disclosures. Miller *et al.* (1983) identified certain individuals, whom they term 'openers', who are able to elicit intimate disclosures from others. They developed an 'opener scale' to measure this ability, containing items such as 'I'm very accepting of others' and 'I encourage people to tell me how they are feeling'. The nonverbal behaviour of openers is very important. For example, Duggan and Parrott (2001) found that head nods and appropriate smiles and related facial expressions from physicians encouraged greater levels of disclosure from patients. Stefanko and Ferjencik (2000) identified five dimensions that were characteristic of openers.

1   *Communicativeness and reciprocity.* The ability to readily engage with others and to reciprocate disclosure appropriately.
2   *Emotional stability.* Showing appropriate reactions and avoiding any rapid mood swings.
3   *Perspective taking ability.* Being able to see things from the other person's point of view.
4   *Spontaneity in communication.* Showing acceptance of disclosure, especially about intimate or embarrassing topics.
5   *Sympathetic.* Showing understanding and concern for the other.

In her study of people who had survived a near-death experience, Hoffman (1995) found that the reaction of potential targets was crucial. If the discloser detected listener rejection or disinterest on initially raising the issue, this stymied their future willingness to discuss what had been a pivotal life experience for them.

Furthermore, Yeschke (1987) illustrated how acceptance is important in encouraging self-disclosure in the often stressful context of interrogations, giving the following advice to interrogators: 'Even if dealing with so called rag bottom, puke, scum bag type interviewees, select a positive accepting attitude' (p. 41).

Gender

While females in general tend to receive more disclosures than males, as discussed earlier this is influenced by the gender of the discloser. It is also dependent on topic and context. For example, a male may prefer to discuss embarrassing personal health problems with a male rather than female doctor.

Status

As previously discussed, individuals disclose more to those of the same status than to people of higher status, and disclose least to lower status individuals.

Attractiveness

The attractiveness of the listener is another important element in encouraging self-disclosures. Part of the reason for this is simply that we like attractive people. Dindia (2000b: 32) illustrated in her research review that self-disclosure is related to liking in three ways, 'we like people who self-disclose to us, we disclose more to people we like, and we like others as a result of having disclosed to them'. Not surprisingly, therefore, more self-disclosures tend to be made to individuals who are perceived as being similar (in attitudes, values, beliefs, etc.), since such individuals are usually better liked. Evidence that this is a two-way link was found in a study by Vittengl and Holt (2000), where a positive correlation occurred between self-disclosure and ratings of attractiveness even in brief 'get acquainted' 10-minute conversations between strangers. It is therefore clear that appropriate disclosure is a key element in the establishment of positive relationships.

The relationship

The following features of the relationship between discloser and recipient influence the amount of self-disclosure used.

Trust

As noted by Fitness (2001: 75), in her review of the phenomenon of 'betrayal' in interpersonal relationships, 'Over the course of evolutionary history, humans have become finely attuned to the possibility of betrayal by others.' This means that we need to trust others before we will disclose to them. Interestingly, however, a paradox here is that self-disclosure requires trust, but also creates it (Stewart and Logan, 1998). As the following rhyme, published in *Punch* in 1875, illustrates, if the discloser trusts the recipient to keep disclosures in confidence, and not misuse them, then more self-disclosures will occur.

> There was an old owl liv'd in an oak
> The more he heard, the less he spoke;
> The less he spoke, the more he heard
> O if men were all like that wise bird!

In certain contexts the professional can be faced with an ethical dilemma when receiving self-disclosures. For example, if a client discloses having committed a crime of some sort, there may be a legal requirement for the professional to inform the police, yet to do so could well destroy the relationship of trust that has been developed. How such ethical dilemmas are resolved will, of course, depend on the particular circumstances involved.

There is evidence to suggest that people regard trust as a relative dimension in relation to self-disclosure. Petronio and Bantz (1991) investigated the use of prior restraint phrases (PRPs), such as 'Don't tell anyone' or 'This is only between ourselves', on disclosures. Their study of 400 undergraduates revealed that: 'a substantial percentage of both disclosers and receivers of private information expect recipients to pass on that information' (p. 266). This was confirmed in a survey of 1,500 office workers by the company Office Angels (2000), where some 93 per cent admitted to imparting to others information that they had been asked specifically not to disclose to anyone else. This report, entitled 'Forget kissing . . . everyone's busy telling!' also revealed that over three-quarters (77 per cent) of workers would have told at least two others by the end of the working day in which they received the disclosure. The main reason (36 per cent) given for so doing was the attention and recognition obtained from having 'inside' information, although 20 per cent of staff had a more machiavellian motive, reporting that they would use the new knowledge as a means of demonstrating power.

The use of PRPs is part of what Petronio (2000b) has termed 'communication boundary management', whereby we attempt to place a border around who will have access to private information about self. When one self-discloses information of a highly private nature there is both the possibility and temptation of betrayal by the recipient, while for the discloser there is the external danger of being discovered and the internal danger of giving oneself away. This makes such disclosures particularly fascinating elements of interpersonal encounters.

Interestingly, a gender difference emerged in the Petronio and Bantz (1991) study, in that males were more likely to expect subsequent disclosure when a PRP was not used, whereas females were more likely to expect subsequent disclosure when a PRP was used. It was also found that the five types of people most likely to receive disclosures were (in order and for both genders)

- best female friend;
- non-marital significant other;

- best male friend;
- mutual friend;
- spouse.

Those most unlikely to be told were strangers and the recipient's father. This latter finding is compatible with other research findings, which show that fathers are often the least likely recipients of disclosure (Greene, K., 2000). In addition, one study of parents' disclosures about their own lives and concerns to their late-adolescent children (freshers at university) found that fathers disclosed less than mothers, and the self-stated purpose of their disclosures was more likely to relate to attempts at changing the behaviour of the children. Mothers, on the other hand, cited venting, seeking advice and looking for emotional support as their main reasons for disclosing (Dolgin, 1996). These findings were confirmed by the same author in a parallel survey of freshers themselves, who rated mothers as disclosing more than fathers, especially about their problems and emotions (Dolgin and Berndt, 1997).

Reciprocation

In her review of research, Dindia (2000b: 27) concluded, 'there is overwhelming evidence that self-disclosure is reciprocal'. Thus those who reciprocate with self-disclosures will receive further self-disclosures. Also, in everyday interaction if A makes an intimate self-disclosure, this influences the depth of disclosure reciprocated by B. Indeed, there is evidence that the reciprocation effect holds even when the recipient of disclosure is a computer pre-programmed to respond in specific ways (Moon, 2000). Of course, social rules and norms must be followed for reciprocation to occur – the depth of disclosure needs to be gradual, beginning at a shallow level and slowly becoming more intimate (Aron *et al.*, 1997). People are also more likely to reciprocate fully if they believe they were individually sought out by the discloser to receive the initial disclosure, rather than being just another in a whole line of people being told the story (Omarzu, 2000). If these rules are broken then not only will reciprocation not occur, but the relationship between disclosure and attraction is also broken.

Three main theories have been proposed to explain the reciprocation effect (Archer, 1979).

1 *Trust–attraction.* The argument here is that when A discloses, B perceives this as conveying trust. As a result, B is likely to be more attracted to A and this increased liking in turn leads B to disclose to A.
2 *Social exchange.* Interpersonal encounters have been conceptualised as a form of joint economic activity or social exchange in which both sides seek rewards and try to minimise costs, which may be in the form of money, services, goods, status, love or affection (Kelley and Thibaut, 1978). Thus, when A discloses, this is a form of investment in the relationship and a reciprocal return is expected. There also tends to be a norm of equity between people, which means that we do not like to feel in debt or beholden to others and so B feels under pressure to

reciprocate the initial disclosure at a similar level of intimacy in order to return the investment.

3   *Modelling.* This approach purports that, by disclosing, A is providing B with a model of appropriate and perhaps expected behaviour in that context. B then follows the model as provided and so reciprocates the disclosure.

There is no firm evidence to support one of these theories over the other two and different studies have lent support to one or another. Indeed it is likely that all three explanations can partially account for reciprocation and that the relative importance of each will vary across situations.

Role relationships

In certain professional relationships the reciprocation norm does not hold, and it is the expectation that one person makes almost all of the disclosures. For instance, at a selection interview the candidate is expected to be the discloser.

Anticipated length and commitment

As previously indicated, an awareness of the one-off nature of an interaction can encourage self-disclosure in certain situations. This was initially termed the 'stranger-on-the-train phenomenon' (Thibaut and Kelley, 1959) and, more recently, 'in-flight intimacy' (De Vito, 1993). This phenomenon can also apply to some professional situations. For example, a client may be reluctant to return to a counsellor, following an initial session in which deep self-disclosures may have been made to the counsellor, who is usually in effect a complete stranger. Counsellors should therefore employ appropriate closure skills in order to help overcome this problem (see Chapter 10).

Physical proximity

Johnson and Dabbs (1976) found that there was less intimate disclosure at close interpersonal distances (18 inches), and more tension felt by the discloser, than at a medium distance (36 inches). However, there is some evidence to suggest that it is males, but not females, who find close interpersonal distance a barrier to disclosure (Archer, 1979). A recent example of distal disclosure is via the Internet. Here, the anonymity afforded by the medium tends to result in increased disclosures. Interestingly, this in turn leads to greater liking for the person. Studies show that even when people thought they had met two different people, one on the net and the other face-to-face, but in fact it was one and the same person, they expressed significantly greater liking for the Internet person (McKenna and Bargh, 2000). The Internet also allows people to present a new self to the world without upsetting existing 'off-line' relationships. It can be very difficult for someone to make changes to existing aspects of self when the social environment stays the same. One's family, colleagues and friends may resist these new sides of self. Such problems do not occur on-line.

Voluntary involvement

There is more self-disclosure in relationships where the client has volunteered to talk about some issue. An extreme example of the negative effects of coercion on self-disclosure is the individual who is 'helping police with their enquiries'. However, this can also be a problem where a client has been referred to the professional and is present under some degree of duress. In such a relationship greater efforts need to be made to encourage self-disclosure.

The situation

Finally, the situation in which the interaction is taking place influences the degree of self-disclosure. Thus Wyatt *et al.* (2000) found that the two locations in which disclosure occurred most frequently were at home and at work. Other important dimensions of situation include the following.

Warmth

A 'warm' environment has been found to encourage self-disclosure, so that if there are soft seats, gentle lighting, pleasant décor and potted plants in an office a client is more likely to open up. This finding is interesting, since interrogation sessions stereo-typically take place in 'cold' environments (bare walls, bright lights, etc.). Presumably, the willingness of the person to self-disclose is an important factor in determining the type of environment for the interaction. One piece of research (Jensen, 1996) also found that background classical music had an effect on the choice of topics for disclosure, and promoted self-expression among undergraduates, but more research is needed to chart the exact effects of different types of music on various people across diverse settings.

Privacy

Solano and Dunnam (1985) showed that self-disclosure was greater in dyads than in triads, which in turn was greater than in a four-person group. They further found that this reduction applied regardless of the gender of the interactors and concluded that 'there may be a general linear decrease in self-disclosure as the size of the group increases' (p. 186). Likewise, in an earlier study, Derlega *et al.* (1973) found that when student subjects were informed that their interaction with another subject (a con-federate of the experimenter) was being video-recorded for later showing to an intro-ductory psychology class, their depth of self-disclosures stayed at a superficial level, regardless of the intimacy of disclosures of the confederate subject. However, when no mention was made of being video-taped, the level of intimacy of disclosure from the confederate subject was reciprocated by the 'true' subject. This study highlighted the importance of privacy for encouraging self-disclosure.

One interesting exception to the privacy norm lies in the phenomenon of TV chat or 'shock' shows, when people appear in front of what they know will be huge audiences and disclose sometimes excruciatingly embarrassing and often negative personal information (Peck, 1995). So, why do they do this? Orrego et al. (2000) in researching this area found four main motives:

1   A desire to remedy negative views about themselves or their group, and 'set the record straight'.
2   A forum to enable them to hit back against those whom they feel have victimised them.
3   Wanting '15 minutes of fame'.
4   The opportunity to promote some business venture.

Priest and Dominick (1994) in their study of people who had appeared on such shows found that most were from marginalised groups (gays, AIDS victims, transsexuals, etc.) or were a little on the 'outside' (e.g. plastic surgeons). Most were evangelical in wanting to disseminate their views to a wider audience and to serve as role models for others. There are therefore specific reasons behind this exception to the general rule of privacy and disclosure.

One variant of privacy is that of anonymous disclosure, sometimes achieved through the camouflage of an alternative identity or pseudonym. Anonymity occurs in a range of contexts, such as unsigned letters, leaks and whistle-blowing in organisations, the church confessional, radio call-in shows, police confidential telephone lines, and computer-based bulletin boards and chat rooms. In his review of this field, Scott (using the byline Anonymous, 1998) illustrated how the rapid expansion in communication technologies resulted in a concomitant increase in anonymous messages being sent. In a study of disclosure in computer-mediated communication, Joinson (2001) also found that visually anonymous individuals disclosed significantly more information about themselves than those who could be seen. Anonymity usually results in deeper levels and greater honesty of disclosure – the safety of remaining 'hidden' allows the individual to express intimate information or true feelings more readily. In this way, confidential telephone help-lines, such as the Samaritans, encourage people to discuss very personal problems without undue embarrassment. This is because the physical distance and anonymity in such encounters facilitates the establishment of 'psychological proximity' (Hargie et al., 1999).

Crisis

People are more likely to self-disclose in situations where they are undergoing some form of crisis, especially if this stress is shared by both participants. Thus patients in a hospital ward who are awaiting operations generally disclose quite a lot to one another.

Isolation

If individuals are cut off from the rest of society they tend to engage in more self-disclosure. For example, two prisoners sharing a cell often share a high degree of personal information. Indeed, for this reason the police sometimes place a stooge in a cell along with a prisoner from whom they want some information. Likewise in cults, people are encouraged to fully disclose their most intimate details. As well as fostering a sense of bonding and belonging, this enables the cult leaders to exploit members' expressed weaknesses (Tourish and Wohlforth, 2000).

These, then, are the main findings relating to the influence which the characteristics of the discloser, the recipient, the relationship and the situation have on the extent to which self-disclosure is employed during interpersonal interaction. From this review of research findings, it is obvious that self-disclosure is affected by a wide range of variables, many of which are operative in any particular encounter. It is important for professionals to be aware of the importance of these variables when making decisions about giving and receiving self-disclosures.

OVERVIEW

Self-disclosure is the cement that binds the bricks in any relationship edifice. Without it, relational structures are inherently unstable and prone to collapse. It is an important skill for professionals to be aware of, from two perspectives. First, they need to be aware of the likely effects of any self-disclosures they may make on the clients with whom they come into contact. Second, many professionals operate in contexts wherein it is vital that they are able to encourage clients to self-disclose freely, and so a knowledge of factors which facilitate self-disclosure is very useful. Our impressions of other people can be totally wrong in many cases since we do not know what is 'going on inside them'. As Jourard (1964: 4) pointed out, 'Man, perhaps alone of all living forms, is capable of *being* one thing and *seeming* from his actions and talk to be something else.' The only method of attempting to overcome this problem of finding out what people are really like, is to encourage them to talk about themselves openly and honestly. If we cannot facilitate others to self-disclose freely, then we will never really get to know them.

When giving and receiving self-disclosures Stewart and Logan (1998) argued that three factors are important:

1   *Emotional timing.* Is the person in the right frame of mind to receive your disclosure? (e.g. someone who has just been fired may not be the best person to tell about your promotion).
2   *Relevance timing.* Does the disclosure fit with the purpose and sequence of this conversation?
3   *Situational timing.* Is this environment suitable for discussion of this topic?

In addition, the following factors need to be considered:

*   the total number of disclosures made;
*   the depth of these disclosures;

- the nonverbal, as well as verbal, disclosures;
- the age, gender and personality of the interactors;
- the status and role relationships between the interactors;
- how best to respond to client disclosures;
- when it is best not to disclose.

The general importance of self-disclosure in everyday interaction reflects the fundamental value of this skill in many professional contexts. It is therefore useful to conclude with an early quotation from Chaikin and Derlega (1976: 178), which neatly encapsulates the central role that this aspect has to play:

> The nature of the decisions concerning self-disclosure that a person makes will have great bearing on his life. They will help determine the number of friends he has and what they are like: they will influence whether the discloser is regarded as emotionally stable or maladjusted by others: they will affect his happiness and the satisfaction he gets out of life. To a large extent, a person's decisions regarding the amount, the type, and the timing of his self-disclosures to others will even affect the degree of his own self-knowledge and awareness.

Chapter 10

Set induction
and closure

INTRODUCTION

Sᴇᴛ ɪɴᴅᴜᴄᴛɪᴏɴ ᴀɴᴅ ᴄʟᴏsᴜʀᴇ are the skills we employ to get in to and get out of social encounters. As summarised by Burgoon *et al.* (1996: 340) 'The first task for conversants is knowing how to start and stop interactions. Some conversations begin and end smoothly and effortlessly, others are difficult, uncomfortable, and problematic.' Firsts and lasts seem to be of special importance for us. This is reflected in the host of words we have to describe these periods – beginning and ending, opening and closing, hello and goodbye, salutation and farewell, arrival and departure, introduction and conclusion, alpha and omega, start and finish, etc. In psychological terms, one of the reasons for this is that we are much more likely to remember that which we encounter first (the *primacy effect*) and last (the *recency effect*) in any sequence. Events in between are less clearly recalled. Given that people are more likely to be influenced by what we said or did as they met us and just before they left us, we should give due consideration to how these interactional phases are handled. Not surprisingly, their role in the development and maintenance of relationships has been the subject of serious study for some considerable time (e.g. Roth, 1889).

Greetings and partings are therefore very important parameters within which social interaction takes place. They are structured, formalised sequences during which we have a greater opportunity to make important points or create an effective impact on others. Humans have developed elaborate meeting and leave-taking rituals to mark these occasions, and parents overtly teach their children to engage in appropriate behaviours at both stages ('Say hello ...' 'Wave goodbye . . .'). The greeting auto-pilot kicks in when we meet those that we know, even if we are just passing and do not intend to engage in conversation. As colleagues walk past one another they smile, engage in eye-contact and make *adjacency pair* verbal responses (where an utterance anticipates a related one from the other person), such as: 'Hi. How are you?' followed by the reply 'Good. And you?' and walk on. These responses are so much a part of our everyday lives that in fact we often only notice them when they are absent. Thus if we meet a friend or colleague who does not engage in the process of salutation, or who leaves without any disengaging ritual, we immediately become concerned. Indeed, if we cannot engage fully in greetings and partings, rules of interactional politeness deem that we provide some or all of: an apology ('Sorry . . .'), a justification ('I can't stop now. I'm late for class . . .'), and a *relational continuity indicator* ('I'll phone you this evening').

Although in this chapter set induction and closure are discussed separately, these are complementary skills within any interaction. There is truth in the old adage that to have a good ending you must first have a good beginning. The symbiotic relationship between the two can be exemplified by examining the behaviours initially identified by Kendon and Ferber (1973) as being associated with the three main phases involved in both greetings and partings between friends:

A   *Distant phase.* When two friends are at a distance, but within sight, the behaviours displayed include hand-waving, eyebrow flashing (raising both eyebrows), smiling, head-tossing and direct eye-contact.

B   *Medium phase.* When the friends are at a closer, interim distance, they avoid eye-contact, smile and engage in a range of grooming (self-touching) behaviours.

C   *Close phase.* At this stage the friends again engage in direct eye-contact, smile, make appropriate verbalisations, and may touch one another (shake hands, hug or kiss).

During greetings the sequence is ABC, while during partings the reverse sequence CBA, operates. At the greeting stage the sequence underlines the availability of the participants for interaction, whereas during parting it signals the decreasing accessibility for interaction.

Greetings and partings are important relational events. Relationships have been conceptualised as mini-cultures with their own meanings, values, communication codes, and traditions (Baxter, 1987). Within them, communicative symbols, often comprehensible only to those involved, are used as 'tie signs' to create feelings of 'we-ness'. As part of this, different groups evolve their own special greeting and parting codes. For example:

•   Steuten (2000) illustrated how bikers and rockers developed elaborate greeting rituals relevant to their type of group, which reflected their shared interests and helped to cement the bonds between members.

•   Bell and Healey (1992), in their study of university students in the USA, found a special language of terms used between friends at greeting and parting.

- Williams (1997) charted the unique behaviours used at these stages by Saramakan Bushnegroes in the rain forest in Suriname, South America.

Opening and closing have been identified from a review of research studies in medicine as two of the fourteen core skills that contribute to effective consultations (Lipkin, 1996). Interestingly, in the psychotherapeutic context, Flemmer *et al.* (1996) found that experienced therapists (more than sixteen years experience) rated the opening phase as being significantly more important than did less experienced therapists. This suggests that over time the import of the skill of set induction becomes even more apparent.

SET INDUCTION

Anyone who is familiar with the world of athletics will be aware of the instructions given to the competitors before a race – 'On your marks. Get set. Go!' By telling the athletes to get set, the starter is preparing them for the final signal, and allowing them to become both mentally and physically ready for the impending take-off, which they know is about to follow. This simple example is a good introduction to the skill of set induction.

Set induction is a term coined by psychologists to describe that which occurs when 'an organism is usually prepared at any moment for the stimuli it is going to receive and the responses it is going to make' (Woodworth and Marquis, 1949: 298). In other words, it establishes in the individual a state of readiness, involves gaining attention and arousing motivation, as well as providing guidelines about that which is to follow.

It is a skill that is widely used, in various forms, in social interaction. At a simple level it may involve two people discussing local gossip, where, to stimulate the listener's attention, they may use phrases such as: 'Have you heard the latest . . .?' At another level, on television and at the cinema, there are 'trailers' advertising forthcoming attractions in an exciting and dramatic fashion to arouse interest in what is to follow. Indeed, television programmes usually contain a fair degree of set induction in themselves, employing appropriate introductory music and accompanying action to stimulate the viewer.

The term 'set' has many applications in our everyday lives. For example, how a table is set reveals information about the forthcoming meal – how many people will be eating, how many courses there are and how formal the behaviour of the diners is likely to be. Other uses of the term set include 'It's a set up', 'Are you all set?' and 'Is the alarm set?' In all these instances, preparation for some form of activity to follow is the central theme, and this is the main thrust of the skill of set induction.

In relation to social interaction, the induction of an appropriate set can be defined as the initial strategy employed to establish a frame of reference, deliberately designed to facilitate the development of a communicative link between the expectations of the participants and the realities of the situation. Set induction can therefore be a long, or a short, process depending on the context of the interaction.

261

Functions of set induction

Set induction involves more than simply giving a brief introduction at the beginning of a social encounter. It may involve a large number of different activities, appropriate to the situation in which set is to be induced. The generic functions of the skill in interpersonal interaction are shown in Box 10.1. However, the specific functions need to be tailored to the demands of the immediate interaction, and so different techniques are employed in order to achieve them. Thus a helper opening a counselling session uses different behaviours from a professor introducing a lecture to a large university class. The process can take an infinite variety of forms both between, and within, social settings. The set used is influenced by, among other things, the subject matter to be discussed, the amount of time available, the time of day, the length of time since the last meeting, the location of the encounter and the personality, experience and cultural background of those involved. These factors should all be borne in mind when evaluating the main techniques for inducing set. There is even some research to suggest that the approach used in greetings is influenced by the individual's testosterone level. In an interesting experimental study of greeting behaviour, Dabbs *et al.* (2001) discovered that high-testosterone males and females entered the room more quickly, were more business-like and forward in their manner, focused directly on the other person, and displayed less nervousness. In comparison, low-testosterone individuals were more responsive, attentive and friendly, but also more tense and nervous.

During professional encounters set usually progresses through the four phases of:

MEETING → GREETING → SEATING → TREATING

At the meeting stage the initial *perceptions* gleaned of one another are very important. Greetings represent the *social* phase of welcome and salutation. During the seating stage the professional must demonstrate a *motivation* to become involved with the client. Finally, 'treating' represents the transition to the *cognitive* or substantive

---

Box 10.1 Functions of set induction

1 To induce in participants a state of readiness appropriate to the task to follow, through establishing rapport, arousing motivation and gaining attention.
2 To establish links with previous encounters (during follow-up sessions).
3 To ascertain the expectations of participants.
4 To discover the extent of the participants' knowledge of the topic to be discussed.
5 To indicate to, and agree with, participants what might be reasonable objectives for the encounter.
6 To explain what one's functions are, and what limitations may accompany these functions.

---

business to be transacted. These stages do not always progress in a linear fashion, but rather they overlap and are interdependent. However, it is useful in terms of analysis to examine each separately.

Perceptual set

There is wisdom in the aphorism 'You don't get a second chance to make a first impression.' The initial perceptions received in social situations undoubtedly influence the expectations of participants. As Dickson *et al.* (1997: 124) put it: 'During the first few minutes of an interaction people make judgements which can then influence how they perceive one another and how they interpret each other's behaviour.' These early perceptions impact on subsequent judgements, since we tend to adapt any conflicting information to make it fit in more easily with our existing cognitive frame (Adler *et al.*, 2001). This can take the form of the *halo effect*, whereby if our initial perceptions are positive we then tend to view the person's future behaviour in a benevolent light. The corollary is the *horn effect*, where we form an early adverse opinion and then interpret the person's future behaviour within this negative frame. Although it is often true that first impressions can be deceptive, most people judge a book to some extent by its cover. As Lamb (1988: 103) noted:

> Infants develop fear of strangers at between seven and eight months, when they begin to make the distinction between who they know and who they do not. We never outgrow this uncertainty about people outside our established circle. As adults we worry about the first impressions we make, finding ourselves at the mercy of someone who is bound to form judgments on the basis of very little genuine knowledge about us.

Perceptual set is influenced both by the environment and the participants.

The nature of the environment

When an individual enters a room for the first time, the layout of tables, chairs and other furnishings is translated into a set of expectancies about the format for the interaction to follow (for a full discussion of these aspects of nonverbal communication see Chapter 3). For example, a table and upright chairs usually convey an impression of a business-like environment, whereas a coffee-table and easy-chairs suggest a more social or conversational type of interaction. Thus an individual attending a selection interview may be somewhat taken aback if confronted with the latter type of setting, since this is contrary to expectations.

The nature of the environment in terms of affluence may also affect initial impressions. Dittmar (1992) carried out a study in which she filmed a young male and a young female individually in a relatively affluent and in a fairly impoverished environment. She then showed the five-minute videos of these individuals moving about their home to fifty-six pupils aged 16–18 years at a prestigious public school, and to fifty-six pupils of the same age at a working-class comprehensive school in

England. She found that the 'wealthy' people were seen as more intelligent, successful, educated and in control of their lives than the 'impoverished', whereas the latter were rated as warmer, friendlier and more self-expressive. No significant differences emerged between the two socioeconomic groups of judges on these evaluations.

Personal features of the participants

The age, sex, dress and general appearance of the other person all affect the initial perceptual set that is induced. It has been found that important decisions, such as whether or not to offer someone a job, are affected by initial impressions of the candidate gleaned by the interviewer (Millar and Gallagher, 1997). In their review of this area, Whetzel and McDaniel (1999: 222) concluded: 'interviewers' reactions to job candidates are strongly influenced by style of dress and grooming. Persons judged to be attractive, or appropriately groomed or attired, received higher ratings than those judged to be inappropriately dressed or unattractive.'

Body features

In fact, we are judged on level of attractiveness from early childhood (Hargie, 1997b). Burnham and Phelan (2000) argued that some aspects of attractiveness are universal because they have a biological foundation. For example, clear skin is favoured because it is a sign of health, physical symmetry is viewed as the ideal and so is desirable, and, as pointed out in Chapter 3, males from most cultures find females with a 0.7 ratio between waist and hip measurements most attractive. However, as also noted in Chapter 3, the latter finding has been queried in subsequent studies (Marlowe and Westman, 2001). Thus Furnham *et al.* (2001) found that the female feature most preferred by males was an attractive face. Here, a female with a waist-to-hip ratio (WHR) of 1 and an attractive face was rated as more desirable than an unattractive one with a WHR of 0.7. Finally, one study of females' ratings of attractiveness in males found that their preferences changed across the menstrual cycle (Penton-Voak and Perrett, 2000). When presented with a choice of faces varying in masculinity and femininity, females preferred the masculine face during the follicular (fertile) phase of the cycle (days 6–14) but not at other times. Many of these judgements about attractiveness are, of course, subconscious but they nevertheless influence the way in which we respond. For example, it has been shown that unattractive, when compared with attractive, females are regarded as more deceptive and are less likely to be believed when making a claim of sexual harassment (Seiter and Dunn, 2001).

As discussed in Chapter 3, individuals rated high in attractiveness are viewed more positively by others. They tend to receive more eye-contact, more smiles, closer bodily proximity and body accessibility (openness of arms and legs) than those rated as being unattractive. It is likely that someone rated as being very attractive will also be seen as being popular, friendly and interesting to talk to. This, in turn, influences the way in which the attractive individual is approached, thereby creating a *self-fulfilling prophecy*. However, decisions about interpersonal attractiveness are not just skin deep and involve more than mere physical features (Duck, 1995). Factors that are relevant here include cleanliness, dress, rewardingness, personality, competence and similarity of attitude. A physically unattractive professional may be successful and popular with clients by adopting a good interactive style and a professional approach.

Dress

People are frequently evaluated on the basis of their mode of dress. The reason for this is that the style of dress that one adopts is often a sign of the group with which one identifies. Thus certain professions have become associated with a particular style of dress, with the deliberate intention of conveying a definite public image. This is exemplified by the adoption of uniforms by members of many institutions and organisations, who wish to present a consistent image or be immediately identified in their job function. Policemen, soldiers, nurses, hospital doctors, clergymen and traffic wardens all immediately induce a certain type of set in the observer. At another level, however, business executives, civil servants, salesmen, solicitors and estate agents have a less formal type of 'uniform' – namely, a suit, shirt and tie. Indeed, the notion of 'dressing down days' at work proves the rule that dressing up is the expected norm. Forsythe (1990) found that female job applicants received more favourable hiring recommendations from experienced male and female business personnel when they were wearing more masculine clothing (e.g. a dark navy suit) than when wearing distinctly feminine attire (e.g. a soft beige dress).

Numerous research studies have been conducted into determining the effects of dress, and physical attractiveness, on evaluations of counsellors. In summarising the findings from these studies, Kleinke (1986) concluded that counsellors who dress formally enough to portray an impression of competence and whose attire is in style rather than old-fashioned are preferred to those who dress very formally and are consequently seen as 'stuffy' or unapproachable. Likewise, physically attractive counsellors are preferred to unattractive counsellors.

Age

Judgements are also made in terms of age. Generally, older, more mature professionals are likely to be viewed as being more experienced, while newly qualified professionals are seen as having a more up-to-date knowledge base. In terms of gender, males tend be more positively evaluated if they are regarded as being competent, assertive and rational, whereas females are viewed more positively if they portray traits such as gentleness, warmth and tact (Hargie, 1997b).

These are the main facets of perceptual set linked to personal attributes. However, as discussed in Chapter 3, our evaluations of individuals are influenced by other features, such as height, the use of cosmetics and perfumes, whether a male has a moustache or a beard, and whether or not glasses are worn. In one study into the accuracy of first impressions, first-year undergraduate students were shown a series of people on video for one minute with the sound turned off and were asked to judge a number of attributes and provide reasons for their choices (Hargie and Dickson,

1991). It was found that the students were accurate in estimating age but not in making judgements of marital status, socioeconomic status, personality or religion. One fascinating aspect of this particular study was the fact that the observers believed they *had* the ability to make such judgements; furthermore, they readily gave reasons as to why they believed these to be accurate. Perhaps they believed the view of Oscar Wilde when he argued: 'It is only shallow people who do not judge by appearances'! The findings also underscore the fact that we all readily make judgements about other people whom we have just met.

Social set

Before proceeding with the main business of the interaction, it is desirable to employ a number of social techniques. These serve to humanise the encounter, and often facilitate the achievement of the core task objectives. Indeed, one of the difficulties with telephone communication is what has been labelled the *coffee and biscuits problem* (Hargie et al., 1999). In most business settings when people meet, the first thing that happens is that refreshments are wheeled in. They then begin the process of getting to know one another, as they engage in the universal shared human activity of drinking coffee and eating biscuits. As well as being a sign of basic civility, this has a deeper level of significance. In a sense, coffee can help to lubricate the business machine. Before progressing to the main task, it enables each side to make judgements about the likely formality of the occasion, and how personable and amenable the other is. On the telephone this cannot happen and so the social opportunities are lost.

The induction of an appropriate social set is, therefore, an important preliminary to the more substantive issues to follow, in that it serves to establish a good, amicable, working relationship between the participants at the beginning of the interaction. Three techniques are employed to induce a good social set, namely receptivity, non-task comments, and the provision of creature comforts.

Receptivity

The way in which professionals receive their clients is of considerable importance. Robinson (1998) argued that the first stage is to negotiate a *participation framework* where both sides communicate their availability (or otherwise) to become involved. This is followed by an *engagement framework* where the interactors move on to mutually collaborative communication. In the doctor–patient context, Robinson charted how degree of willingness to be involved was signalled nonverbally by the doctor, from an extreme of not looking at the patient, through eye gaze but not body asymmetry, and on to full engagement with the upper and lower torso and feet oriented towards the patient. As mentioned in Chapter 5, in paediatric encounters the degree of involvement of children is influenced by the physician's first question. This can be directed to the child (e.g. 'Right, James how can I help you?'), parent (e.g. 'So what can we do for James today?'), or open to either (e.g. 'How can I help you today?'). When the opening query is directed to the child, there is a greater likelihood of the child becoming more actively involved in the consultation (Stivers, 2001).

The use of social reinforcement techniques (handshake, smile, welcoming remarks, tone of voice and eye-contact) is important at the outset, since they serve to make the other person feel more at ease and responsive. Axtell (1999) illustrated how, while some form of nonverbal greeting ritual is universal across countries and cultures, there is a huge variation in the exact form this takes. His examples include Maori nose rubbing, Tibetan tribesmen sticking out their tongues at one another, Eskimos banging their hand on the other person's head or shoulders, and East African tribes spitting at each other's feet. These behaviors all serve the same function – that of forming a human bond.

Brown and Sulzerazaroff (1994), in a study of bank tellers, found that words of greeting, a smile and direct eye-contact were all significantly correlated with ratings of customer satisfaction. The importance of smiling was also shown in an experimental study by Monahan (1998), who found that the effect existed even at a subconscious level. Subjects shown slides at a subliminal level of a person smiling gave increased ratings of their likeability and attractiveness. Another important aspect of receptivity is the use of the client's name. This leads to a more favourable evaluation of the speaker (Hargie *et al.*, 1999), and has been shown to be important in the professional context (Hargie *et al.*, 2000). Whether formal or first names are used is a matter for sensitive judgement or negotiation.

An important aspect is *how* greeting behaviours are employed. Let us consider for a moment just one common greeting ritual – the handshake. One feature of the handshake is that it is usually initiated by the person of higher status (Webster, 1984). However, this is not a unitary behaviour, but, as illustrated by Astrom and Thorell (1996) takes many forms (see Box 10.2 for the main ones). In a Swedish study, they investigated the effects of handshakes and associated behaviour (e.g. direction of eye gaze) on a rather eclectic mix of therapists, car salesmen and clergymen – all selected

---

Box 10.2 Handshake variations

The other person:

- Clasps your hand more weakly than 'normal'.
- Clasps your hand more strongly than 'normal'.
- Retains your hand longer than 'normal'.
- Releases your hand immediately after touching it.
- Pulls your hand towards them.
- Pumps your hand up and down several times.
- Performs pumping and clenching movements.
- Proffers only the fingers.
- Proffers the whole hand in a sort of thumb grip.
- Rejects your hand.
- Grasps your hand with both of theirs.
- Clasps your hand from above.
- Clasps your hand from below.
- Clasps your hand with their palm turned downwards.
- Clasps your hand with their palm turned upwards.

because they were professional groups who regularly engage in handshaking. They found that a strong handshake was clearly associated with ratings of extraversion and a weak one with introversion. The most satisfying greeting behaviour was direct eye gaze while a weak handshake was rated as the least satisfying. This latter finding confirmed other research by one of these authors showing that a limp, wet, 'dead fish', handshake is disliked and rated negatively whereas a firm handshake is viewed positively (Astrom, 1994).

This result was also confirmed in a detailed study by Chaplin *et al.* (2000), who noted that the handshake has historically been seen as a male greeting behaviour. They studied the handshake in relation to gender, personality and first impressions. Four trained coders shook hands twice with college undergraduates, and rated each handshake on a five-point scale along eight dimensions:

1   strength (weak–strong);
2   temperature (cold–warm);
3   dryness (damp–dry);
4   completeness of grip (very incomplete–full);
5   duration (brief–long);
6   vigour (low–high);
7   texture (soft–rough);
8   eye-contact (none–direct).

These ratings were then correlated with the other variables. Among the main significant findings to emerge were that five of the above variables (strength, duration, completeness of grip, vigour, and eye-contact) combined to constitute the 'firm handshake', and male handshakes were firmer than females. Those with firm handshakes were more extraverted, and less shy and neurotic, and also created better first impressions. Chaplin *et al.* highlighted the significance of these findings for females in professional contexts, where, 'giving a firm handshake may provide an effective initial form of self-promotion for women that does not have the costs associated with other less subtle forms of assertive self-promotion' (p. 117).

Gender differences have also been noted in greeting rituals. Thus the eyebrow flash (both eyebrows raised briefly) has been found to be rated more positively when it is used with members of the opposite sex, and as a greeting with people we know (Martin, 1997). In a study of 152 greeting dyads at Kansas City International Airport, Greenbaum and Rosenfeld (1980) found that bodily contact was observed in 126 (83 per cent) of the greetings. The types of contact observed were

•   mutual lip-kiss;
•   face-kiss;
•   mutual face contact excluding kiss;
•   handshake;
•   handholding;
•   hand to upper body (touching the face, neck, arm, shoulder, or back);
•   embrace.

Female greeting behaviour was very similar with both males and females, whereas males used markedly different greetings with females as opposed to males. Male same-sex dyads had a significantly higher frequency of handshaking, whereas dyads containing a female had significantly more mutual lip-kisses and embraces. In another study, females were shown to smile more and have closer interpersonal proximity during greetings (Astrom, 1994).

Non-task comments

A seemingly universal way of opening interaction is the empty question regarding the other's well-being. An example is the formal, and slightly ridiculous, 'How do you do?' Variants on this theme proliferate. For example, in inner-city Belfast it is 'How's about you?' often reduced to "bout ye?' In their analysis of *phatic communion*, or small talk, Coupland *et al.* (1992) highlighted how this type of HAY (How are you?) question serves to signal recognition for and acknowledgement of the other person, but is not expected to produce any self-revelations from the respondent. They used the following joke to illustrate this.

A: How are you?
B: I have bursitis; my nose is itching; I worry about my future; and my uncle is wearing a dress these days.

But, although this type of question is linguistically redundant, it is nevertheless expected as a curtain-raiser for the business to follow. To employ another metaphor, non-task comments are employed to 'break the ice' in social encounters and serve as a preliminary to the exchange of information at a more substantive level. Statements relating to the weather or non-controversial current affairs are quite common social openers, as are comments relating to the specific situation (e.g. 'Sorry about the mess. We're having some renovations carried out . . .'). In the health care setting, Holli and Calabrese (1998: 36) emphasised that 'Although it may be time-consuming for the busy professional, the opening exchange of either information or pleasantries is important and should not be omitted.'

While non-task comments are useful in a range of situations, they need to be used judiciously. An early note of caution was sounded by the eminent psychiatrist Sullivan (1954), who warned against the use of non-task comments (which he termed *social hokum*) in the psychiatric interview. He argued that in this particular context it was more important to get into substantive issues as soon as possible. More recently, Millar and Gallagher (1997: 392) noted that in selection interviews: 'Although non-task comments may help to reduce anxiety levels of nervous applicants, it is equally possible that the use of social chit-chat may introduce unwanted variations into the procedures.' Thus, non-task comments need to be appropriate to context.

Provision of 'creature comforts'

Creature comforts refer to those items used to make someone feel more at ease in any given situation. These include a soft or 'easy' chair, an offer of a drink, whether alcoholic or a cup of tea or coffee, and reasonable lighting and temperature in the room. All of these are important for rapport building. This is clearly demonstrated by the fact that they are often taken away in situations where an individual is being subjected to stress, such as in severe interrogation sessions. In some settings professionals have little control over the physical location of the encounter and so have to try to compensate for a less than ideal environment by optimising their use of interpersonal skills.

Motivational set

The skill of set induction can be employed in order to gain attention and arouse motivation at the beginning of an interaction. The way individuals perceive and assimilate information is affected by their initial motivation to attend. To maximise client involvement, the professional must be both motivated and motivating. Thus the two core methods used to induce motivational set are showing personal commitment and dramatic techniques.

Showing personal commitment

A prerequisite to the successful motivation of others is that we show enthusiasm and commitment for the task ourselves. A professional who seems unprepared, uninterested, rushed, or nervous is most unlikely to inspire confidence in, or be able to motivate, clients. The best gospel preachers display evangelical zeal in their performance. Good counsellors adopt a caring style. Successful lawyers exude confidence and expertise. In the service sector, employers use the technique of *mystery shopper*, whereby an assessor pretending to be a client visits the service area, to check that staff are showing motivation when they meet clients (Hargie and Tourish, 2000). Looking and sounding the part are key aspects of motivational set. To fully engage clients, professionals must show concern, commitment, enthusiasm, interest, attention and expertise. These are all core features in the influence process (see Chapter 12).

Dramatic techniques

In many situations, particularly in learning environments, it is very important to gain the attention of participants at the outset, so that the task may proceed as smoothly as possible. All good entertainers know the value of beginning a performance with a 'flash-bang' to immediately grab the attention of the audience – indeed, Munter (2000) used the term *grabbers* to describe such techniques. The following four dramatic techniques can be employed to engage motivational set.

1   *Novel stimuli*. These are effective attention-gaining devices. Magicians have long recognised the power of rabbits being pulled from hats. Producers of TV news programmes, aware of the value of stories involving violence in obtaining the attention of viewers, have a maxim regarding opening items of 'If it bleeds,

it leads.' They also use 'teasers' to trail upcoming items, since it has been found that viewers pay more attention to news stories that have been teased and to commercials immediately following the teaser (Cameron *et al.*, 1991). The implications of these results are fairly obvious. There are many aids (diagrammatic, real objects, audio-visual recordings, etc.) that can be used in order to arouse motivation. By focusing on any of these at the outset, the learning environment can be enhanced.

A word of caution is needed here, however, in that to be effective in the longer term, the novel stimulus must be related to the task in hand. Otherwise this technique will be seen as gimmickry and all it will achieve is literally novelty value. In addition, it has been shown that the use of teasers can lead radio listeners to form premature judgements about culpability in relation to threatening stories (rape, murder, etc.). Dolinski and Kofta (2001) carried out an experiment whereby university students either heard stories as a whole, or as a headline followed by a break (the typical 'more on that story after this short break' approach) and then the full story. They found that listeners were consistently more likely to attribute culpability to the central person (e.g. a male arrested for suspected rape, or a hospital doctor who misdiagnosed a ruptured appendix as inflammation of the ovary after which a patient died) when the story was teased. It seems that we make judgements based on the information available and these then become resistant to change (see the discussion later in the chapter on *need for closure*). Dolinski and Kofta (2001: 255) concluded that 'newspaper readers, radio listeners, and TV viewers should be aware that they are prone to make biased moral judgments on the basis of information provided in the headline part of the message'.

2   *An intriguing problem.* Employed at the beginning of an interaction sequence this can engage listeners' interest immediately, and hold it for a long time if they are required to solve the problem. This technique is equally applicable whether the problem posed is a technical or a social one. Furthermore, it does not really matter whether or not the problem has a correct solution. The idea here is to establish immediate involvement and participation at either an overt or a covert level. The use of case histories can be particularly relevant in this respect. Here, a tutor presents details of a particularly difficult case, and asks trainees how they would have dealt with it.

3   *A provocative statement.* This method of inducing set must be carefully thought out, since the object of the exercise is to provoke comment, rather than aggression, on the part of the listener. With very sensitive topics or volatile audiences, great caution should be exercised!

4   *Behaviour change.* The adoption of unexpected, or unusual, behaviour can be a powerful method for gaining attention. This needs to depart from the normal behaviour pattern to be most effective. For example, a presenter may sit with the audience or move about the room without speaking in order to grab attention. All humans have a basic cognitive structure that strives to accommodate new information of an unexpected nature. It is, therefore, the element of behavioural surprise that is central to the efficacy of this method, since it stimulates the individual's attentiveness, and hence facilitates the process of assimilation.

Cognitive set

The main purpose of many encounters is concerned with substantive issues of fact. Before proceeding to these issues, however, it is important to check that the terms of reference are clearly understood at the outset. In order to achieve this objective, it is necessary to ensure that all parties are in clear agreement as to the nature and objectives of the ensuing interaction. In other words, it is important to induce an appropriate cognitive set in the participants, so that they are mentally prepared in terms of the background to, and likely progression of, the main business to follow. As Millar and Gallagher (2000: 75), in their analysis of interviewing, noted: 'the interviewer must indicate what the objectives are, propose ideas about how the interview will proceed, and give an indication of the structure, content and duration of the interview'.

The functions of cognitive set can be summarised as the process of informing participants where they have been, what stage they are now at, and where they are going. This involves five main components, namely providing prior instructions, reviewing previous information, ascertaining expectations, outlining functions, and goal setting.

Prior instructions

It has long been known that prior instructions, such as techniques to use in solving a problem or special items to be aware of, help to improve performance. In an early study in this field, Reid *et al.* (1960) found that serial learning was speeded up by providing instructions to subjects about how to approach the learning task. In reviewing research into prior instructions, Turk (1985) concluded that telling individuals what they will hear actually biases them to perceive what they have been encouraged to expect, regardless of what message they actually receive. As Turk put it 'Telling people what they are about to perceive will radically affect what they do perceive' (p. 76). The effect of prior instructions was borne out in a classic study by Kelley (1950), who found that when subjects were told to expect a 'warm' or 'cold' instructor they developed a positive or negative mental set respectively. This influenced both their perceptions of instructors and the way in which they interacted with them. More recently, Singh *et al.* (1997) confirmed the importance of 'warm' and 'cold' as central traits, which once ascribed to someone trigger other positive or negative evaluations respectively.

Park and Kraus (1992) had a group of subjects ask one question each to a person they did not know. They found that when the questioners were instructed to obtain as much information as possible about traits of the respondent such as intelligence, honesty, truthfulness and dependability, they were able to do so successfully. Park and Kraus concluded that it is possible to 'obtain a greater amount of verbal information relevant to difficult-to-judge dimensions when instructed to do so' (p. 445). On the basis of their results they recommended that personnel officers and selectors at employment interviews should be instructed in advance to search for specific information about candidates.

Finally, Miller *et al.* (2001) found that our reactions to others in need can be mediated by prior instructions. In a meta-analysis of research studies in this field they found that subjects responded much more sympathetically and empathically when asked either to put themselves in the other person's situation, or to try hard to imagine how that person was actually feeling. Conversely, when asked only to focus objectively on the person's behaviour or the facts of the situation, feelings of empathy and sympathy were greatly reduced.

Reviewing previous information

It is important to ascertain the extent of knowledge which participants may have regarding the subject to be discussed. This information, when gathered at an early stage, enables decisions to be made about the appropriate level for any ensuing explanations and whether or not to encourage contributions. These points are pertinent when addressing a person or persons on a new topic for the first time. The process of linking what is already known with the new material to follow has been shown to be an effective teaching procedure for facilitating the understanding and retention by pupils of new information (Burden and Byrd, 1999).

In many interpersonal transactions, one encounter is influenced by decisions made and commitments undertaken in the previous meeting. Again, it is important to establish that all parties are in agreement as to the main points arising from prior interactions and the implications of these for the present discussion. If there is disagreement or confusion at this stage it is unlikely that the ensuing encounter will be fruitful. This problem is formally overcome in many business settings, where minutes of meetings are taken. The minutes from a previous meeting are reviewed, and agreed at the outset, before the main agenda items for the current meeting are discussed. This procedure ensures that all participants are in agreement about what has gone before, and have therefore a common frame of reference for the forthcoming meeting. In addition, agenda items are usually circulated prior to the meeting, and this in itself is a form of cognitive set, allowing individuals to prepare themselves for the main areas to be discussed.

Dealing with expectations

People approach social encounters with certain explicit or implicit expectations, which they expect to have fulfilled (Tourish, 1999). If expectations are unrealistic, or misplaced, it is important to discover this and make it clear at a very early stage, otherwise the conversation may proceed for quite some time before these become explicit. This may result in frustration, embarrassment or even anger, if people feel their time has been wasted. It can also result in the discussion proceeding at dual purposes, and even terminating, with both parties reading the situation along different, yet parallel, lines. By ascertaining the immediate goals of those involved, such problems can be overcome. This can be achieved simply by asking what others expect from the present encounter. Once goals are clarified, behaviour is more easily understood.

Another factor here is what is termed the *interpersonal expectancy effect* also known as the *Pygmalion effect*. This refers to the way in which our expectations of others influence how we perceive and respond to them. In the words of Baker (1994: 38) 'Expectations are self-fulfilling prophesies. What we expect of people is often what we get.' Hanna and Wilson (1998: 102) gave as an example, 'if you are subconsciously looking for evidence that another person is angry with you, you are likely to find that evidence in the person's behavior'. This process is known as the *perceptual confirmation effect*. In one classic study in the USA, researchers selected pupils at random and informed their teachers that these children had been identified as 'late bloomers' who would soon show marked improvements in their academic performance. Follow-up analyses revealed that these children had indeed out-performed their peers. This was attributed to the increased attention and reward they had received from teachers based on the set expectations (Rosenthal and Jacobson, 1992). A range of follow-up studies confirmed how teacher expectations directly impact on pupil performance (Blanck, 1993). This effect is prevalent in all social contexts. If we are set to perceive others in either a positive or a negative light, our behaviour towards them is likely to provoke the response we expected.

The corollary of the Pygmalion effect is the *Galatea effect*, which refers to the expectations we hold of ourselves, and the fact that we are likely to realise these self-expectations (Gamble and Gamble, 1999). In analysing this area, Kirsch (1999) distinguished between two types of expectancy.

1   *Stimulus expectancy* does not affect the stimulus itself but rather the person's perception of it. For example, if I expect people of a certain race to be aggressive, when I interact with individuals of that race I am more likely to perceive their behaviour as aggressive regardless of whether it really is or not.

2   *Response expectancy* relates to one's anticipated responses in a situation. Thus if I believe that I am going to really enjoy spending time with a particular individual, then when I am with that person I am more likely to behave in a way consistent with this expectation (smiling, laughing, paying attention to the other person, etc.). In fact this example is very pertinent since there is considerable research to show that people tend to behave in such a way as to ensure that their emotional expectations are confirmed (Catanzaro and Mearns, 1999).

Another distinction is between expectation-congruent (*assimilation effect*) stimuli that confirm what we had thought, and expectation-discrepant (*contrast effect*) stimuli that are contrary (Geers and Lassiter, 1999). How the latter are perceived is crucial in shaping final opinions about the experience. The strength of expectation is central here. People spend months or years planning and looking forward to great occasions in their lives such as wedding ceremonies or holidays. The expectations of success and enjoyment are very high, and this in turn is likely to lead to expectation-discrepant (negative) experiences being filtered out of the occasion itself.

Outlining functions

This may involve the outlining of professional job functions. If someone holds false expectations, as was discussed in the previous section, it is vital to make this clear, and to point out what can and cannot be done within the limitation of professional parameters. Once this has been achieved the interaction should flow more smoothly, with both participants aware of their respective roles. Nelson-Jones (1997) used the term *structuring* to refer to the process by which professionals make clients aware of their respective roles, and argued that a key juncture for outlining functions is at the contracting stage of the initial session. At this stage the professional often has to answer the implicit or explicit client question 'How are you going to help me?' Counsellors answer this question in different ways, depending on their theoretical perspectives. A useful general approach for counsellors is to respond to this question by emphasising that their role involves helping and supporting people as they sort out their problems and reach eventual *personal* decisions, rather than offering instant solutions.

Goal setting

As discussed in Chapter 2, goals are at the very epicentre of interaction. They provide direction for action and serve as an interpretation filter through which the behaviour of others is judged. A key goal in new or relatively unfamiliar contexts is that of *uncertainty reduction*, in that 'we want to know what others think of us, what relationship we will have with them, what is expected of us, what the rules of the interaction are, and so on' (Hargie, 1997b: 33). Experienced professionals develop *cognitive schemas* to enable them to deal swiftly and efficiently with a range of persons and situations (see Chapter 2). These schemas, developed after repeated exposure to the same situation, are cognitive structures containing knowledge and information about how to behave in a particular context. They contain *scripts* that are readily enacted – for example, the same greeting ritual is often implemented automatically with every client. As noted by Kellerman *et al.* (1991) we tend to be *cognitive misers*, using established schemas to guide our behaviour across different people and settings. However, for trainee professionals who have not acquired relevant schemas, interaction is much more difficult and uncertain.

Likewise, for clients the visit to a professional may be a one-off in which no schema or script exists. Again, uncertainty will be high and so the stage of goal-setting is crucial in helping the client to better understand what the interaction entails. Thus, in the medical sphere, orientation statements by the physician that explain to the patient the sequence and purpose of forthcoming activities that will be carried out have been shown to facilitate both the communication process and health-related outcomes (Robinson and Stivers, 2001). In the workplace, newly hired employees have been shown to use a range of techniques to decrease their uncertainty (Clampitt, 2001). Similarly, at times of major change the information needs of all employees are heightened. If the organisation itself does not effectively deal with such uncertainty, the grapevine goes into overdrive and rumours proliferate. Interestingly, one exception here is that police interrogators deliberately increase uncertainty when they imply to suspects that they know a lot more about their activities than they are being told, thereby keeping the suspect off-balance and so more vulnerable to 'cracking' under the pressure. This technique, whereby detectives exaggerate to suspects the evidence they have about them, is known as *maximisation* (Gudjonsson, 2001). However, the reduction of uncertainty should usually be a core goal of the opening phase of interaction. If it is not dealt with, the cognitive space of individuals is occupied with attempts to reduce it, often at the expense of what would be more profitable activities.

In many contexts (e.g. in person-centred counselling where the client is allowed to structure the interaction and decide what should be discussed) it is not feasible for the professional simply to state the goals. However, in those situations where it is appropriate, it is helpful to state clearly the goals for the present interaction, and the stages that are likely to be involved in pursuit of these goals. This can be a useful method for structuring the encounter. For example, the ability of teachers to structure lesson material in a logical, coherent fashion has long been shown to be a feature of effective teaching (Rosenshine, 1971). There are other situations where it is desirable to structure interaction by providing guidelines about that which is to be discussed and the stages through which the discussion will proceed. In the medical sphere, Cohen-Cole (1991: 53) pointed out that 'effective interviews begin with an explicit statement or acknowledgement of goals. Sometimes these may need to be negotiated between the doctor and the patient if there are some differences in objectives.'

The importance of negotiating the agenda has been recognised in the counselling context. Lang and van der Molen (1990: 93) noted that as early as possible in the helping interview

> the helper is advised to inform the client straightaway about his way of working, and then see if the client agrees with that, or whether he has other expectations. The helper can then consider these expectations and see if they are realistic and if they fit in with his way of working.

Similarly in the negotiation context, the stage of formulating an agenda is essential to success. One side cannot simply decide on the goals of the encounter and impose them on the other, but rather the first act of the negotiation drama is that of deciding the nature and structure of play (see Chapter 13). In the medical sphere, Kurtz *et al.* (1998) also highlighted the importance of the *screening* process, whereby the doctor checks and confirms the list of problems raised by the patient, giving as an example 'So that's headaches and tiredness. Is there anything else you'd like to discuss today?' (p. 23).

Goal-setting allows participants to prepare themselves fully. They will therefore be mentally prepared for the topics to be discussed, and be thinking about possible contributions they may be able to make. It also means that the individual feels less uncertain and more secure in the situation, knowing in advance what the purpose of the interaction is, what the main themes are likely to be, how the sequence of discussion should proceed, and the anticipated duration of the interaction.

Overview of set induction

In *The Republic* Plato argued, 'The beginning is the most important part of the work.' This also holds for interpersonal encounters. In their analysis of interviewing Stewart and Cash (2000: 57) noted that 'The first few seconds or minutes you spend in the opening are often the most important portion of the interview ... (and) ... often determine whether the interview will continue at all.' Set induction is, therefore, a very important process. It is of particular relevance during first meetings – hence the expressions 'well begun is half done' and 'start off as you intend to go on'. It will vary in length, form and elaborateness depending on the context of the interaction. *Perceptual set* refers to the effects of the initial impression formed by people based on the nature of the environment and the personal attributes of the interactors. *Social set* is the process of welcoming people, providing creature comforts and generally making them feel settled. *Motivational set* is concerned with showing personal commitment and encouraging clients to participate fully. *Cognitive set* involves establishing expectations and outlining goals for the interaction.

The acronymn STEP can be used to describe the four main stages of the skill of set induction, as people step into a relationship.

- *Start.* This involves welcoming others, settling them down, and gaining attention.
- *Transact.* Here, expectations are ascertained, and the functions of the participants outlined. Any links with previous encounters should be made.
- *Evaluate.* An analysis is then carried out of the relationship between the expectations of the participants and the realities of the present situation. Any discrepancies must be clarified before the interaction can progress fruitfully.
- *Progress.* This stage marks the end of the beginning, when the interaction moves on to the main body of the business to be conducted. It involves finalising and agreeing the goals for, and the nature, content and duration of, the forthcoming interaction.

CLOSURE

The expression 'need for closure' has entered the everyday lexicon in relation to ending a particular episode – this could be an argument between colleagues, the completion of a work project, or agreeing a divorce settlement. It is also widely employed to refer to the process of coming to terms with the loss of a loved one. This is especially so where there are problems surrounding the death, and indeed the need for closure is particularly strong where the person's remains have not been located (e.g. following kidnapping, or terrorist offences). The term refers to the strongly felt human need to go through a process that will lead to acceptance of the loss, and at the same time having a feeling of contact and continuity with the memory of the person by being able to visit the location where the remains have been laid to rest. Understanding exactly how and why someone died and being able to go through the normal rituals associated with burial are all involved in this process of 'putting it all to rest' as part of final closure. This psychological phenomenon in many ways underscores and reflects the importance of closure more generally in human relationships.

There has been a considerable amount of research into the psychological phenomenon of *need for closure*, defined as 'the desire for a definite answer to a question and the eschewal of ambiguity' (De Grada *et al.*, 1999: 348). There are individual differences in the degree to which different people need to have issues sorted out and wrapped up quickly. Some can handle large amounts of uncertainty and put off making decisions for as long as possible, while others wish to have things cut-and-dried as swiftly as is feasible. As summarised by Mannetti *et al.* (2002: 140) 'there exists a continuum of motivation for closure, ranging from a strong need to avoid closure to a strong need to obtain closure'. Related dimensions here are the concepts of *seizing* and *freezing*, in that individuals with a high need for closure seize on early information to make judgements and then freeze their decision at that point, closing their minds to any further relevant information (Kruglanski and Webster, 1996). The *confirmation bias* then comes into play as the person with high need for closure actively seeks data that confirm the decision and filters out contradictory stimuli. Thus, in the courtroom context, Honess and Charman (2002: 74) have shown how 'once jurors have made up their mind, they stop thinking about the evidence too hard'.

A *Need for Closure Scale* (Neuberg *et al.*, 1997) has been developed to measure this phenomenon. It includes items such as 'I think that having clear rules and order at work is essential for success' and 'I don't like to go into a situation without knowing what to expect'. However, the situational context is an important moderating variable here, so that as the costs of not making a decision escalate the need for closure increases accordingly (Webster and Kruglanski, 1998). For example, if your child is very seriously ill and you have to make a decision about agreeing to surgery that could save its life, this decision is likely to be expedited regardless of degree of personal need for closure.

This concept has relevance both for interactional set and for closure. Those with a high need for closure are more heavily influenced by first impressions as they search for aspects to seize on in terms of decision-making. They desire clearly structured interactions with transparent goals, and readily accept the need to bring an encounter to an end in a neat and tidy manner. On the other hand, individuals with a low need for closure are less likely to make judgements based on initial information. They prefer interactions that are loosely structured with less clear-cut goals, and they can be difficult to persuade that it is time to terminate an inter-action. As a result, with this type of person closure can be more prolonged and messier.

As mentioned earlier, closure is the parallel side of set induction. However, there are also differences between the two. First, in general social encounters we may think about how we should welcome someone, but we seldom give much thought as to how we will part from them (unless the relationship is not going well and we want to extricate ourselves from it). Generally, closure is more of an impromptu event – it just happens. However, in professional contexts more care and attention needs to be paid to the closing phase. A second major difference, as noted by one of the first academics to seriously study this field, is that 'greetings mark a transition to increased access and farewells to a state of decreased access' (Goffman, 1972: 79). The fact that access is literally being closed down means that the ending of the encounter has to be managed in such a way that the relationship is maintained and no one feels a sense of being rejected.

Burgoon *et al.* (1996: 343) noted how 'It would be very efficient to end conversations by just walking away. But social norms call for balancing efficiency with appropriateness.' In fact, these norms are learned at an early age. First (1994) illustrated how 'The leaving game' is one of the first examples of dramatic play enacted by children (at around the age of 2.3 years). In this game, the child shows knowledge of the ramifications of parting, by giving the twin instructions to the role-playing other: 'I'm leaving. You cry'.

Abrupt closures usually indicate personal or relational dysfunction. For example, one study compared twenty-four autistic individuals with a group of twenty-four nonautistic persons with 'mental retardation' matched for chronological and mental age (Hobson and Lee, 1996). It was found that the autistic individuals were less likely to engage in greeting and parting behaviours. More generally, abrupt closures occur for a variety of reasons, such as:

- *ending an undesired interaction* (including the rejection of sexual advances);
- *testing affinity* (e.g. to see if the other person will come after you as you walk away);
- *when frustration reaches a certain point* ('This is hopeless, I'm leaving');
- *avoiding possible conflict* (if discussion is becoming over-heated it may be better to leave rather than risk verbal or physical abuse);
- *demonstrating power and status* (those with higher status can terminate interactions suddenly – they see their time as more important than anyone else's and so may decide unilaterally how it is used).

The nonverbal behaviours used in these abrupt endings range through breaking off all eye-contact, stopping talking altogether, to the extreme of turning one's back and walking away. Verbal statements fall into three main types.

1   *Rejection remarks* that indicate you do not want the conversation to continue ('Would you please go away?' 'Clear off').
2   *Departure injunctions* that are a sign of higher status and power ('Off you go now' 'I'm stopping it there. Go and work on it').
3   *Exasperation exits* that show you feel any further communication is a waste of time ('This is going nowhere. I've had enough' 'I can't take any more of this').

In linguistic terminology, closure has been defined as a final speech turn that is recognised as such by both parties, involving: 'the simultaneous arrival of the conversationalists at a point where one speaker's completion will not occasion another speaker's talk, and that will not be heard as some speaker's silence' (Schegloff and Sacks, 1973: 295). This is achieved through 'a set of regularly occurring behaviors that provide a normative, mutually agreed-upon process for terminating interactions' (Kellerman *et al.*, 1991: 362). These behaviours, in turn, serve to bring the interaction 'to an orderly ending and pull together the issues, concerns, agreements, and information shared' (Stewart and Cash, 2000: 70). They also shift the perspective from the present to the future. Thus closure involves directing attention to the termination of an encounter, highlighting the main issues discussed, making arrangements for future meetings, and ending the interaction in such a way that the relationship is maintained.

FUNCTIONS OF CLOSURE

The main functions of closure are shown in Box 10.3. Not all of these are relevant in every context, since to be effective, the closure must reflect the tone, tenor and overall purpose of the encounter. In addition, closure, like set induction, depends on a range of variables including location, time available, the type of people involved, and the anticipated duration of separation. Like set induction, closure also progresses through four interrelated and overlapping sequential stages, in this case:

RETREATING → REVIEWING → REINFORCING → RE-BONDING

The retreating phase involves efforts to influence the *perceptions* of others in such a way that they fully realise that you are in the process of leaving. The stage of reviewing relates to *cognitive* issues pertaining to the substantive business conducted, when decisions taken are summarised. Third, clients should be reinforced or *motivated* to carry out certain actions. Finally, re-bonding refers to the *social* dimension of ensuring that a good rapport is maintained as leave-taking occurs.

Perceptual closure

The first stage of closure is that of indicating to the client that it is time to close. This necessitates the use of closure indicators and markers to signal that it is time to wrap-up the interaction. These *preclosing behaviours* and *final closure markers* have been shown to occur in telephone conversations as well as in face-to-face encounters (Placencia, 1997). A wide range of behaviours has been identified for both purposes (Wolvin and Coakley, 1996).

Box 10.3 Functions of closure

1   To signal that the interaction is about to end.
2   To summarise substantive issues covered and agreements reached.
3   To consolidate any new material introduced in the session.
4   To assess the effectiveness of the interaction.
5   To motivate participants to carry out certain courses of action.
6   To provide links with future events.
7   To give participants a sense of achievement.
8   To establish commitment to the future of the relationship.
9   To formally mark the final termination of the encounter.

Preclosing

This involves the use of both verbal and nonverbal behaviours to signal the end of the encounter. These behaviours flag to clients that the time has come to start winding up, and help to steer the discussion gently and smoothly into the final termination. They convey an imminent end to proceedings, and indicate that the introduction of new material is not anticipated. Closing indicators include elongated and emphasised words such as 'Soooo ...' 'OooKaay' 'Riiight ...' These are followed by more direct phrases: 'In the last few minutes that we have ...' 'We're coming to the end of our session ...'. Another tactic here is that of *projection*, where the other person is portrayed as the one really wanting or needing to terminate the interaction, owing to fatigue, other commitments, etc. ('You have worked very hard. I'm sure you've had enough for today' 'I know how busy you are so I don't want to take up any more of your time'). Accompanying nonverbal signals should reinforce the preclosing message (see Box 10.4). O'Leary and Gallois (1999) found that the most common nonverbal signs of preclosing were placing the hands on the arms of the chair in a way that would assist standing up, a forward lean of 30° or more from previous position, smiling, more movement while speaking, and looking away from the other person.

This step of preparing the client for closure is very important. In the context of interviewing, Stewart and Cash (2000: 69) illustrated how, 'an abrupt or tactless closing may undo the relationship established during the interview and agreements reached by making the other party feel like a discarded container – important only as long as you need what is inside'. Using preclosing to shade into the final parting ritual is therefore well advised.

Clients also make closing indicators when they feel that the time has come to end an interaction, and professionals need to be sensitive to these. In certain areas, such as selling and negotiating, this is a key to success. For example, in the former context clients emit buying signals to convey that they are ready to close the interaction. These signals include receptive verbalisations such as 'It looks really nice', acceptance questions such as 'Do you have it in blue?', body language including approving nods and smiles, and physical actions such as handling the sales item lovingly and possessively (Hargie *et al.*, 1999).

Box 10.4 Nonverbal closure indicators

- breaking eye-contact;
- taking out car keys;
- gathering papers together;
- looking at a watch or clock;
- placing both hands on the arms of the chair;
- explosive hand movements on the thighs or desk;
- changing seated posture to a more raised position;
- nodding the head rapidly;
- orientating one's posture and feet towards the exit.

Closure markers

These are used to mark and underscore the final ending of the encounter. They take three forms:

- *formal markers*, usually used in business contexts – 'It was nice to meet you' 'Goodbye';
- *informal markers* used with friends and colleagues – 'Cheers' 'See you later' 'Bye';
- *departure announcements* – 'I've got to go now' 'Right, I'm off'.

Likewise, accompanying nonverbal markers occur along a continuum of formality – on the formal side is the handshake, while at the informal side there may be not much more than a smile. In between there are waves, kisses, and hugs. More formal parting rituals tend to occur in business encounters, with people of higher status, and with those who are not kith and kin. The duration and intensity of closure markers is also greater when the period of anticipated separation is longer.

The success of closure indicators and markers is dependent on the client. Those with a low need for closure may blissfully ignore closure attempts, and very direct methods may then be required (opening the door, walking slowly out of the office, etc.). Indeed Kellerman *et al.* (1991) reported that although much research has focused on mutually negotiated leave-taking, in fact some 45 per cent of all conversations have unilaterally desired endings. They found that when ending an encounter that the other side does not want to close, the most common tactic was the use of external and uncontrollable events, such as third party entrances. For example, where it is known that a particular client will be difficult to get to leave, an *orchestrated intervention* can be arranged. Examples of this include the secretary coming in to announce your next urgent appointment, a colleague calling in to accompany you to a meeting, or someone calling on the telephone at a prearranged time.

Cognitive closure

As defined by Millar and Gallagher (2000: 79) cognitive closure is 'a means of seeking agreement that the main themes of communication have been accurately received and understood'. It involves three main strategies: summarisation, checking out, and continuity links.

Summarisation

Summaries offer both sides the opportunity to check out that they are in agreement about the meaning of what has been discussed. There is now a considerable body of research across a wide range of professional contexts, including community pharmacy (Hargie *et al.*, 2000), university lecturing (Saunders and Saunders, 1993), medicine (Maguire *et al.*, 1986), psychotherapy (Flemmer *et al.*, 1996), physiotherapy (Adams *et al.*, 1994) and negotiating (Rackham, 2003), to attest to the fact that professionals see summarisation as a key part of their role. Interestingly, however, actual practice often differs from the ideal. Thus, in the above studies, university lecturers often closed lectures abruptly, claiming to have 'run out of time'; doctors frequently ended the consultation with the writing and handing over of a prescription; and pharmacists had brief closing statements (e.g. 'Go and see your doctor if it persists'). Time and effort, therefore need to be allowed for summarisation.

Research has clearly shown that an explicit concluding summary increases the listener's comprehension (Cruz, 1998). It should certainly take place at the end of interaction, but in longer meetings *intermittent summaries*, or *spaced reviews*, can be used periodically. In essence, summaries are important at three points:

- *At the end of discussion on a particular issue or topic*. Where there has been a detailed, involved or protracted exchange it is useful to provide a summary of what has been covered. Such transitional reviews help to map out the contours of the relational terrain. They enable both sides to reflect, and hopefully agree, on what was covered. In certain types of encounter (e.g. educational or medical) this also serves the purpose of consolidating learning, by cementing core material in the listener's memory. Another important function is that they enable the professional to bring that part of the discussion to a rational end, and progress on to the next topic.
- *At the end of the session*. At the parting stage, the summary should scan back over the main features of the interaction. The key issues that emerged should be crystallised and linked to previous sessions and to future meetings. On the perceptual side, a session summary is also a very potent closure indicator, signalling that the interaction is now ending. For this reason, they were termed *historicising acts* by Albert and Kessler (1976), since they treated the session as something that was now in the past. Part of this may also involve *contingency planning*. This involves giving advice to the client about coping with unexpected events, what to do if things do not work out according to plan, and when and how to seek help if required. Kurtz *et al.* (1998) emphasised the importance of this part of closure, which they termed *safety netting*, in doctor–patient interactions.
- *At the final termination of the professional relationship*. The summary at this stage must range back over all previous meetings, putting what has been covered into a final perspective. This is one of the most difficult periods of professional communication. Final endings of relationships are never easy. Once human bonds have been formed, we do not like to break them. The impact on clients of final termination has long been recognised within psychoanalytic theory (Ferraro and Garella, 1997). In his analysis of the psychoanalytic context, Schubert (2000) highlighted how clients at this 'mourning' stage of the loss of the relationship can experience separation anxiety and depressive affects. The role of therapist is therefore crucial. An important function of final summarisation is what is known in relational communication theory as *grave dressing* (Duck, 1999). The relationship is dead but its 'grave', or memory, should be presented in a positive light. The relationship is thereby portrayed as having been worthwhile and not a waste of time. Thus the summary at this juncture should give emphasis to client achievements.

Checking out

This is the process whereby the professional ensures that the client fully understands what has been covered, and that both parties are in agreement about what has been agreed. One of the identified weaknesses of health professionals is that they do not always check that patients fully comprehend the information they have been given (Dickson *et al.*, 1997). Indeed, studies have shown that when filling prescriptions community pharmacists are often asked by patients to re-explain what the doctor has already told them about how to use the prescribed medication (Morrow *et al.*, 1993). They had not understood, but this lack of comprehension was not picked up by the doctor.

Checks can be made in two ways. First, the professional can ask questions to test for understanding of the material covered. As discussed in Chapter 5, questions are widely used across every profession. However, while they are expected and accepted by pupils in classrooms or students in seminars, feedback questions need to be used with care in other contexts (see also Chapter 8). It is not normal practice in social exchanges to 'test' others – it can be taken as a sign of being seen as somewhat slow or stupid. For this reason, a useful tactic is to preface such questions with statements like 'I'm not sure if I explained that fully enough, could I just ask you . . .?' Questions can also be used to ascertain how the client feels about how the session went. This type of summative evaluation can provide very useful feedback for future encounters.

Second, the client can be invited to ask questions. Norms of professional–client interaction mean that clients often neither expect nor are encouraged to ask questions (see Chapter 5). This means that time, thought and effort may be needed to facilitate clients as they formulate relevant questions. One exception to this rule is in the employment interview where there is a definite 'invite questions' stage, when candidates are asked 'Is there anything you would like to ask us?' Here, interviewees are well advised to prepare informed questions and to ask these in an appropriate manner (Millar and Gallagher, 1997).

Care also needs to be taken with this tactic of inviting questions. One problem is that the client may take the opportunity to introduce new and potentially vital material. Those with a low need for closure are particularly prone to this tactic. In their oft-quoted study of doctor–patient consultations, Byrne and Long (1976) termed this the *by the way . . . syndrome*, later referred to in the counselling context as the *door handle phenomenon* (Lang and van der Molen, 1990). In the latter context, an extreme example of this is where a client, standing at the door and about to leave, lobs an interactional hand grenade back into the room in the form of a controversial statement (e.g. 'I've been thinking a lot lately about suicide . . .'). The door handle phenomenon causes major problems for the professional in making a decision as to whether to continue with the encounter (not easy where appointments have been booked), or arrange to discuss the issue at a later time.

White *et al.* (1997) carried out a detailed study of audio-recordings of doctor–patient encounters. They found that new problems were introduced by patients at the end of the consultation in 23 per cent of cases. They termed such instances *interrupted closures*, which they defined as occurring when, 'an attempt by one person to shift from present problems to a future orientation was not followed by a corresponding shift on the part of the other' (p. 159). To circumvent such

Box 10.5 Techniques for circumventing the interrupted closure

1 Orient the client at the beginning of the session (see the section on cognitive set) and continue this throughout the encounter, explaining what is going to happen next at each stage.
2 Explicitly ask clients to state all of their concerns early in the encounter, and secure their agreement on the identified list.
3 Address psychosocial and emotional as well as task concerns.
4 Allow the person to talk freely and without interruptions.
5 Do not invite questions during the final closing phase. A common reason for the 'by the way' interjections in the White *et al.* (1997) study was the tendency for doctors to finish with the 'Anything else?' question. This raises new expectations in the client's mind and may negate the closing ritual.
6 When new issues are raised at the end it is generally best to defer exploration of these to a future visit, rather than engage in a hurried discussion at the end.

problems they recommended a number of procedures. Building on these we have identified six strategies to help prevent interrupted closures (see Box 10.5).

Continuity links

Most animals have greeting rituals, some of which are very elaborate. Indeed, nesting birds have greeting displays each time one of them returns to the nest with food. Chimpanzees are most similar to humans in that they touch hands, hug and kiss when they meet. However, in his analysis of greetings and partings Lamb (1988: 103) noted that there is no ritual of parting among other animals, since 'they presumably do not have any conception of the future of their relationships and therefore do not need to reassure each other that there will be such a future or that the past has been worthwhile'. For humans, however, the sense of temporal and relational continuity means that endings of interactions are seen as important. Bridges must be built at this stage to carry the interactors over to their next encounter. Knapp *et al.* (1973) termed this stage of closure *futurism*.

In professional contexts, continuity links include reference to how the work covered in the current encounter will be carried on at the next one. Where agreements by either side have been made about work to be carried out in advance of the next session, these should also be covered at closure. In formal business meetings one aspect of futurism is the very simple task of agreeing or noting the date of the next meeting. At the same time, however, a good chairperson should relate the business transacted in the present meeting to the agenda for the next one. Relational bonds also need to be consolidated at this stage, in the form of social comments about future meetings (e.g. 'I look forward to seeing you again next week').

Motivational closure

By employing this type of closure, individuals can be directed to reflect more carefully, consider in greater depth, and relate any new insights gained from the present encounter to more general issues in a wider context. Three principal methods are employed to effect motivational closure: motivational exhortations, thought-provoking aphorisms and interim tasks.

Motivational exhortations

In many interactions, an important function of this stage of closing is that of minimising the phenomenon of *cognitive dissonance*, initially identified by Festinger (1957). When individuals have to make decisions, they often experience doubts and anxiety – or dissonance – about whether their decision is the right one. The more important the decision the greater will be the dissonance, or discomfort. Eventually, dissonance is overcome in one of two ways. Either by convincing oneself that the decision is indeed a good one and embracing it warmly, or alternatively by abandoning the decision and reverting to the former state of affairs. Motivational exhortations are useful in helping to persuade clients that they have made the correct decision. For example, Hargie *et al.* (1999) illustrated how such exhortations (e.g. 'This is the best deal in the store – and you'll get years of enjoyment from it') are of importance for salespersons in ensuring that clients stay committed to a buying decision. Likewise, after an initial counselling encounter a client may experience dissonance about whether the decision to seek help and reveal personal details to a stranger was justified. Here, again, motivating exhortations can be used to reassure the client about the efficacy of their decision, and so encourage the person to return for another session ('You have taken the first step towards resolving this by coming here today').

Another function of these exhortations is to secure maximum commitment from clients. They are used ubiquitously by sports coaches during 'pep' talks before their players go out to perform. Sometimes the imagery used can be quite violent – and indeed unprintable here! Expressions used include: 'Go out and kill them' 'Give them hell', 'Let them know you mean business' 'You have one chance. Don't blow it or you'll regret it for the rest of your life'. The purpose here is to ensure that the sportspeople are fully geed up to give of their utmost.

In her analysis of motivational interviewing, Terry (1999) illustrated how securing *commitment* from clients to carry out a course of action is crucial. If this commitment is not there, then the behaviour is unlikely to follow. For example, she gives the example of how research has shown that there is no point in explaining to clients the methods that they can employ to stop a certain behaviour (such as smoking or drinking) unless they are fully committed to stopping. There is little advantage in knowing how to do something that you have no intention of doing. Thus time is most gainfully spent in these contexts on gearing motivational exhortations towards commitment. Once a person has fully and irrevocably decided on a course of action, the means will usually be found to effect it (for further discussion on commitment see Chapter 12).

Thought-provoking aphorisms

In certain types of situation, it is useful to end an interaction with a succinct and apt statement that encourages listeners to reflect on the main theme covered. These can be self-produced or quotations from the great and the good. This strategy is very common in public presentations. Let us take two recent examples from the radio programme *Thought For Today*. Here, the presenter has a two- or three-minute slot in which to cover a topical issue. One speaker, discussing the issue of animal rights, finished with, 'When you're dying for a big steak remember that a cow just did', while another talking about third world poverty ended, 'Live simply so that others can simply live'. This strategy is also relevant in other contexts. Interviewers can use it to motivate clients to continue (or change) a certain course of action.

Interim tasks

Homework and assignments have a familiar ring for students. Although not always welcomed, they serve the important purpose of making students think more about the subject in between classes. This technique is used in many settings to motivate clients to carry out tasks relating to the issue under consideration after the interaction has ended. In therapy, clients may be encouraged to try out new techniques that have been discussed. In training, tasks are geared towards the process of optimising transfer from the training environment to the actual organisational setting. To effect maximum motivation, the task set should be one that is challenging but also manageable.

Social closure

If an interaction has been successful, the leave-taking is marked by mixed emotions – happiness with the encounter coupled with sadness at its ending. As aptly expressed by Juliet to Romeo in Shakespeare's *Romeo and Juliet*, this means that 'Parting is such sweet sorrow.' One function of social closure is to underline a 'feelgood' factor in terms of the relationship. How we leave an interaction influences our attitudes to it. If it ends on a relational high, we depart feeling that it has been an enjoyable and worthwhile venture. We are then more likely to contact the person again if required. Social closure encompasses both task and non-task elements.

Task rewards

These are used to underline for the client that they have achieved something of worth, and that this is recognised and valued (for a full discussion of the role of rewards see Chapter 4). They can be employed to reward the person individually using 'you' language ('You achieved a lot today. Well done' 'Your work is really paying dividends. I wish everyone put in as much effort as you'). Alternatively, they can emphasise the sense of 'working together' using 'we' language ('That was a good meeting. We work well together' 'That's great. I think we've nearly cracked it'). Where the interaction has involved a group, then whole-group rewards are appropriate. Thus teachers and lecturers may reward an entire class for their work, or a chairperson in concluding a meeting can point out how well the members worked together. This technique helps to foster a sense of team spirit.

Like summaries, task rewards are important at three stages.

- *At significant points within a session.* When a major part of the work has been completed, statements such as 'We are really getting somewhere' provide participants with a feeling that something is being achieved and encourage further effort. Rewards may also include a 'time-out' ('I think we deserve a break and a coffee') to mark such successes. Negotiators often signal and celebrate interim agreements on particular points in this way.
- *At the end of a session.* Here, the client should be rewarded for major efforts made during the encounter.
- *At the termination of the relationship.* As discussed above, 'grave dressing' is important as the final curtain falls, and so clients must be rewarded for the efforts they made and everything they achieved during the professional relationship.

Non-task comments

The final part of closure should emphasise the human moment. The main business is over, tasks have been completed, and it is time to acknowledge the client as a person. So, personal or welfare aspects of leave-taking enter the fray at this point. These fall into five main types:

1   *The expression of gratitude phase,* as the name suggests, involves thanking the person for their time and efforts ('Thanks for coming along' 'I appreciate you giving up your time').
2   *Social closing niceties.* Here, we owe a considerable debt to the weather and traffic in formulating comments such as, 'Oh dear it's really pouring down. Good thing you brought your umbrella' 'Hope you get home before the rush hour'.
3   *Reference to generic or specific social events.* This is commonplace – ranging from the ubiquitous 'Have a nice day' in the US service sector, to more tailored generalities ('Have a good weekend'), or mention of specific occasions ('Enjoy the wedding').
4   *Reference to future meetings.* These occur during continuity links ('Look forward to seeing you again next week').
5   *Well-wishing comments.* These are statements of concern regarding the other person's well-being ('Look after yourself' 'Take care now').

At final termination, such statements not only reward the client, they also underline the finality of the occasion – 'It was a pleasure working with you. If you need to talk with me at any time in the future, you know where I am.' These statements should of course be accompanied by appropriate nonverbal reinforcers (see Chapter 4).

Overview of closure

In *Julius Caesar*, Shakespeare summarised the over-arching functions of closure:

> 'If we do meet again, why we shall smile!
> If not, why then, this parting was well made.'

Closure serves to leave participants feeling both satisfied with an encounter, and happy to re-engage with one another as and when required. While introductions can be prepared, closures usually cannot. This is because the termination has to be directly related to the interaction that has gone before. However, knowing the stages through which closure progresses can greatly facilitate the implementation of the process.

Perceptual closure is used initially to signal that the encounter is entering the end-zone, and then to mark the final exchange. *Cognitive closure* allows agreements to be ratified regarding the main issues discussed and decisions made, as well as establishing links with the next meeting. *Motivational closure* is employed to encourage clients to continue to consider, and work on, issues further. Finally, *social closure* cements the relational bonds that have been established. It is important to remember that the closure is the last point of contact between interactors and therefore the one they are most likely to remember. The advice of Millar and Gallagher (2000: 78) in their review of interviewing is pertinent here: 'it is important to plan and allocate time for ending the interview as both a business transaction and a social encounter'. Efforts made at this juncture can have very significant import, both on the impact of the current encounter and for the future of the relationship itself.

OVERVIEW

Greeting and parting skills represent the ties that bind interaction. Arrivals and departures are ubiquitous. Across countries and cultures people wish each other a good morning, afternoon, evening or night. We have all been taught the basics of these skills as part of the socialisation process, and so we often take them for granted. So much so, indeed, that we then proceed to ignore them by jumping quickly into and out of social encounters. As Irving and Hazlett (1999: 264–5) noted, the busy professional 'often feels that he or she is pressed for time and it is these very important elements at the beginning and end that are often rushed or overlooked'. But a cheap and clipped hello and goodbye is no substitute for a sincere, focused welcome, and a warm, thoughtful parting. Due to the primacy and recency effects, much of what we do at these two junctures remains imprinted on the minds of those with whom we interact. Time and effort spent at the opening and closing phases should therefore be regarded as a key investment towards the effectiveness of relationships.

Chapter 11

Assertiveness

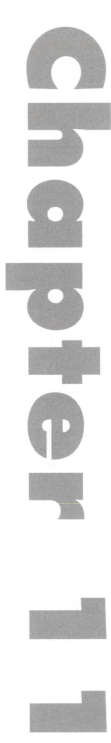

INTRODUCTION

ASSERTIVENESS IS AN AREA of study with a long history. It dates back to the pioneering work in the field of behaviour therapy by Salter (1949) and Wolpe (1958), who recognised that certain individuals in society had specific problems in standing up for their rights. As a result, the skill of assertiveness was introduced during therapy in an attempt to help such people function more effectively in their everyday lives. Since then, the skill has attracted enormous interest, reflecting the importance of this aspect of social interaction across many areas. A huge volume of research has been conducted, and assertion training (AT) programmes are now widespread and at many levels.

Professionals must possess the ability to be assertive, and so AT programmes proliferate in this area (McCartan, 2001). This is because a key feature of assertiveness is that it is an aspect of interpersonal communication that can be developed and improved. As Rakos (1997: 290) pointed out, 'assertion is a *learned skill*, not a "trait" that a person "has" or "lacks"'. It is a skill that is of importance when dealing with family, friends, peers, superiors and subordinates. It is pertinent to interactions between different groups of professionals, especially where differences of power and status exist, and it is of relevance to inter-actions between professionals and clients.

Early definitions of assertiveness were fairly all-embracing in terms of interactional skills. Lazarus (1971), for example, regarded assertiveness as comprising four main components, namely the ability to:

1   refuse requests;
2   ask for favours and make requests;
3   express positive and negative feelings;
4   initiate, continue and terminate general conversations.

It is obvious that this conceptualisation of assertiveness is very broad, encompassing almost all forms of human interaction. Indeed, in the US, as Kelly (1982: 172) pointed out: 'the terms "assertion training" and "social skills training" were often used in interchangeable fashion; it was not recognized that assertiveness represents one specific kind of interpersonal competency'. It would seem that training in this field was introduced and found to be beneficial before the concept of assertiveness was defined with any precision. Dissatisfaction with this state of affairs led to a more focused study of assertion, based specifically on the theme of standing up for one's rights in a sensitive, competent, manner. This latter interpretation is the one given by most dictionaries, and a perspective usually held by lay people, and it is the view adopted in this chapter.

While differing definitions of assertion proliferate within the literature, useful definitions of assertive behaviour can be found in two of the influential texts in this area. Thus Lange and Jakubowski (1976: 38) stated that 'assertion involves standing up for personal rights and expressing thoughts, feelings and beliefs in direct, honest, and appropriate ways which respect the rights of other people'. In like vein, Alberti and Emmons (2001: 6) stated that 'Assertive behavior promotes equality in human relationships, enabling us to act in our own best interests, to stand up for ourselves without undue anxiety, to express honest feelings comfortably, to exercise personal rights without denying the rights of others.' Both of these definitions emphasised an important component of assertion, namely respect for the rights of other people. The skilled individual must therefore achieve a balance between defending personal rights while not infringing the rights of others.

Assertiveness can be conceptualised as comprising two broad response classes – one negative and the other positive (see Box 11.1). However, most research and training efforts have been devoted to the negative, or conflict, components, since this is the aspect of assertion many people find particularly difficult.

FUNCTIONS OF ASSERTIVENESS

The skill of assertion serves nine main purposes (Box 11.2). Most of these relate to the ability of the individual to respond effectively in an assertive manner. However, linked to the behavioural repertoire are functions to do with protection of personal rights (no. 1) and respect for the rights of others (no. 5), as well as the development of feelings of confidence (no. 8) and self-efficacy (no. 9) in being able to respond in a self-protecting fashion. The type of assertiveness used can determine the extent to which each of these functions is fulfilled, and so knowledge of types of assertiveness is of vital importance during social encounters. Furthermore, personal and contextual factors also play a crucial role in determining the effectiveness of assertive responses.

Box 11.1 Negative and positive assertion

Negative, or *conflict*, *assertion* comprises six main components:

- making reasonable requests;
- refusing unwanted or unreasonable requests;
- asking others to change their behaviour;
- giving personal opinions even if unpopular;
- expressing disagreement or negative feelings;
- responding to criticism from others.

Positive assertion also involves six main aspects:

- expressing positive feelings;
- responding to positive feelings expressed by others;
- giving compliments;
- accepting compliments gracefully;
- admitting mistakes or personal shortcomings;
- initiating and sustaining interactions.

Box 11.2 Functions of assertiveness

Assertive responses help individuals to:

1 ensure that their personal rights are not violated;
2 withstand unreasonable requests from others;
3 make reasonable requests of others;
4 deal effectively with unreasonable refusals from others;
5 recognise the personal rights of others;
6 change the behaviour of others towards them;
7 avoid unnecessary aggressive conflicts;
8 confidently, and openly, communicate their position on any issue;
9 develop and maintain a personal sense of self-efficacy.

SEQUENTIAL STAGES IN ASSERTIVENESS

A sequence of stages is involved in the decision-making process with regard to whether or not to implement an assertive approach (see Figure 11.1).

Self-focus

First, the individual must engage in what Kowalski (1996) termed 'self-focused attention'. This process of self-focus involves monitoring and evaluating the behaviour of self and others. Without an awareness of the nuances of interpersonal communication, success in assertion, or indeed in any social skill, is unlikely. As we shall see later

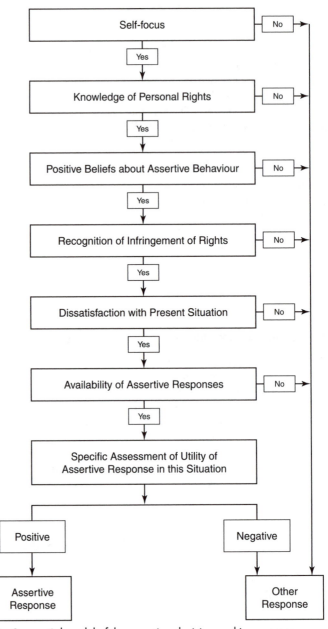

Figure 11.1 Sequential model of the assertion decision-making process

in the chapter, at one extreme some (unassertive) people are blissfully unaware that they are being treated woefully, while at the other there are those (aggressive) who have no idea of how obnoxious they appear to others. As we repeatedly emphasise in this book, skill necessitates acute perceptual acumen.

Knowledge of rights

Given that the individual has the capacity to self-focus, the next prerequisite is knowledge of personal rights. In order to protect our rights we must first know what they are. It is not always clear in many situations exactly what one's rights are, and it is therefore sometimes necessary to consult with others in order to gauge their views about whether personal rights have been infringed. This process of consultation is termed *reality testing*, which may involve asking other people for advice either about what exactly your rights are (e.g. 'Has he the right to ask me to do that?'), or about their perceptions of your behaviour (e.g. 'Have I upset you in some way?' 'Do you mind doing this?'). There is evidence to indicate that assertive individuals may have a greater awareness of what their job role actually entails. In a study of social workers in Israel, Rabin and Zelner (1992) found that assertiveness in the work setting was significantly and positively correlated to both role clarity and job satisfaction. Knowing the parameters of one's job would therefore seem to facilitate the protection of personal rights, which may in turn contribute to increased happiness in the work environment.

In terms of actual rights, Zuker (1983) produced a general Assertive Bill of Rights for individuals, which included the right to:

- be treated with respect;
- have and express personal feelings and opinions;
- be listened to and taken seriously;
- set one's own priorities;
- say no without feeling guilty;
- ask for what one wants;
- get what one pays for;
- make mistakes;
- assert oneself even though it may inconvenience others;
- choose not to assert oneself.

Positive beliefs about assertion

Our beliefs about assertive behaviour are very important. As expressed by Mnookin *et al.* (1996: 221) 'Assertiveness also presupposes the self-esteem or belief that one's interests are valid and that it is legitimate to satisfy them.' Take someone who believes that one should always do what one's superiors say or negative consequences will accrue. Before this person could effectively be assertive, this belief would have to be replaced with a new one, for example that it is always valid to ask for a good reason if requested to do anything that seems unreasonable. Piccinin *et al.* (1998) carried out a study with Canadian undergraduates on their ability to criticise others. They found that high as opposed to low assertives reported more confidence in their ability to criticise the behaviour of others effectively, believed that this was more likely to produce positive outcomes, and were less worried about the possible negative consequences of so doing. From previous research Piccinin *et al.* identified five behaviours as being associated with quality of criticism. We will illustrate these with examples relating to a work situation where one person is too cold.

1   *'I'-language* (e.g. 'I see the window is wide open . . .' rather than 'You have left the window wide open . . .').
2   Clearly *specifying the problem* ('I can't work because I'm freezing' rather than 'It's cold').
3   Showing *empathy* ('I know you like fresh air').
4   *Bidirectionality*, or 'roundedness' ('You are hardy and could survive an arctic expedition, but it's just too cold for me in here').
5   Suggesting *explicit change* ('Please close the window').

Interestingly, using these criteria Piccinin *et al.* found no difference between high and low assertives on *quality* of responses. This result confirmed earlier research that a crucial determinant of assertion is *motivation to act* rather than lack of understanding of how to be assertive.

Those who are very socially anxious are more likely to be nonassertive, as they have a strong desire to make a good impression but also doubt their ability to achieve this desired state (Leary and Kowalski, 1995). This was confirmed in a study by Gudleski and Shean (2000), which found that depressed individuals rated themselves lower than nondepressed people on assertiveness, but significantly higher on measures of submissiveness and the need to please others. Anderson (1997) also found that those who experienced most anxiety were least assertive in terms of both verbal and nonverbal behaviours. Likewise, those high in the personality trait of *agreeableness* are less likely to assert themselves, since such individuals are noncritical, trusting and helpful (Kowalski, 1996).

These research findings illustrated how changes in beliefs and expectations may well be a prerequisite for changes in assertive behaviour. The process of *cognitive restructuring* is important for people with inappropriate beliefs. Such restructuring includes changes in *self-instructions*, i.e. those covert behaviour-guiding self-statements we employ when making decisions about which responses to carry out. Kern (1982) found that nonassertive individuals had a higher frequency of negative self-statements and a greater belief that their behaviour would lead to negative consequences. Thus, submissive individuals use self-statements such as 'She will not like me if I refuse', rather than 'I have the right to refuse'.

In terms of intrapersonal dialogue, there would also seem to be a difference in the use of self-reinforcements, with nonassertive people again being more negative in their self-evaluations of performance. Submissive people are more likely to think 'I sounded terrible, stuttering and stammering. She is probably laughing at me now.' Assertive individuals, on the other hand, tend to be more positive (e.g. 'I'm glad I said no. She is not likely to bother me again'). In reviewing research in this field, Rakos (1991) illustrated how nonassertive individuals emit roughly equal numbers of positive and negative self-statements in conflict situations, whereas assertive people generate about twice as many positive as negative self-statements. He concluded that 'direct training in autonomous self-instruction, apart from any other intervention, has resulted in significant gains in assertiveness' (p. 53).

Recognition of infringement of rights

The individual also has to recognise that personal rights have been infringed. One study found that nonassertive people tend to need more time to perceive and assimilate information and make decisions about how to respond, and concluded, 'If individuals fall behind at this early step in the process of asserting themselves, then they may be more likely to miss opportunities to be assertive' (Collins *et al.*, 2000: 931). Thus by the time submissive individuals realise that their rights have indeed been violated, it is probably too late to rectify the situation. To quote the title of the Collins *et al.* article, it is a case of 'Those who hesitate lose'. Submissive individuals are also more likely to perceive the behaviour of others inaccurately by, for example, perceiving unreasonable requests as being reasonable. Such people are viewed as 'easy touches' in terms of borrowing items, doing extra work, etc., since they are always ready to be helpful. There comes a time when being helpful turns into being used, and people need to learn not only to be able to draw the line between these two, but also to learn to perceive the behaviour of others more accurately, in order to distinguish between reasonable and unreasonable requests. Indeed, on occasions other people point out to us that this has happened – for whatever reason we have accepted unreasonable behaviour as reasonable.

Dissatisfaction with present situation

We must then experience dissatisfaction with this state of affairs. As Lundgren and Rudawsky (2000) noted, two important features in determining an assertive response are the importance of the issue, and the strength of negative feeling. These are related, in that with more important issues we are likely to feel more dissatisfied or aggrieved when our rights are negated. Thus affect is important in assertiveness. For example, when standing in line outside a theatre we may notice someone jumping the queue, but if it is a warm evening and we are chatting happily with our date, our mood may be such that we think 'what the heck' and ignore it. Alternatively if we have had to wait for a long time in the rain and have become annoyed, we may challenge the queue-jumper very assertively.

Availability of assertive responses

In order to be assertive, we must first be aware of what the available response alternatives are, and have learned how to use them. Much of this chapter is devoted to an analysis of assertive response components and their likely effects.

Assessment of response utility

Before we invoke an assertive response, we should assess the utility of so doing. The nature of the situation has been shown to be an important aspect in making a decision to be assertive (Piccinin *et al.*, 1998). If we adjudge that assertion is a legitimate response in this situation, and that it will produce a *long-term* positive benefit for the relationship (as opposed to, for example, merely a short-term behaviour change), then we are likely to choose this alternative. However, assertion is not always the most appropriate choice in every situation. From our own evaluation of a range of professional groups, we have ascertained a number of contexts in which it is more difficult to be assertive. These include:

- in someone else's home or office;
- in a strange country or sub-culture;
- when alone as opposed to being with friends or colleagues;
- with superiors at work;
- with other professionals of higher status and power;
- when promoted to a position of authority over those who were formerly friends and colleagues;
- with the elderly;
- with the seriously or terminally ill and their relatives;
- with those in poverty or in severe social deprivation;
- with friends or close work colleagues;
- with members of the opposite sex;
- with those who are disabled.

The utility of assertion in these situations is more likely to be negatively evaluated. In addition, there are at least three broad contexts in which it may be more skilled to be nonassertive.

1   Interacting with a highly sensitive individual. If as a result of your being assertive someone is liable to burst into floods of tears, or physically attack you, it may be wise to be nonassertive, especially if the encounter is a one-off. Thus, in the example used earlier, if the queue-jumper is a huge, inebriated male, uttering expletives and waving a knife, we may justifiably decide that there is a negative utility for an assertive response.

2   Seeing that someone is in a difficult situation. If you are in a busy restaurant and know that a new waitress has just been employed, you are more likely to overlook certain issues, such as someone who came in later being served before you. Here it is appropriate to be nonassertive, since personal rights are not deliberately being denied, and to be assertive may cause undue stress to the other person. Equally, if the other person is from a different culture, and may not fully understand the norms of the present situation, you may decide not to adopt an assertive stance (issues of culture are discussed later in the chapter).

3   Manipulating others. Some females may deliberately employ a helpless style in order to achieve their goals, for example to encourage a male to change a flat tyre on their car. Equally, males may do likewise. If stopped by police following a minor traffic misdemeanour it is usually wise to be nonassertive ('I'm terribly sorry officer, but I've just bought this car . . .'), since such behaviour is more likely to achieve positive benefits.

STYLES OF RESPONDING

In order to fully understand the concept of assertiveness, it is necessary to distinguish this style of responding from other approaches. Three core styles are of relevance here, namely nonassertion, assertion and aggression.

Nonassertive

Nonassertive responses involve expressing oneself in such a self-effacing, apologetic manner that one's thoughts, feelings and rights can easily be ignored. In this 'cap in hand' style, the person:

- hesitates and prevaricates;
- speaks softly;
- looks away;
- tends to fidget nervously;
- avoids issues;
- agrees regardless of personal feelings;
- does not express opinions;
- values self below others;
- lacks confidence;
- suffers personal hurt to avoid any chance of hurting others.

The objective here is to appease others and avoid conflict at any cost. This can be described as the 'Uriah Heep' style, as epitomised in Charles Dickens' *David Copperfield* in which Uriah explains how he was brought up: 'to be umble to this person, and umble to that; and to pull our caps off here, and to make bows there; and always to know our place, and abase ourselves before our betters'. This style has been referred to as *protective* by Schutz (1998), who noted that such people:

- tend to avoid public attention;
- use minimal self-disclosure or remain silent so as not to receive criticism for what they say;
- are modest and self-deprecating;
- use self-handicapping strategies whereby they underestimate potential future achievements so as to avoid negative evaluation if they fail;
- if they have to engage with others, prefer to play a passive, friendly and very agreeable role.

Assertion

Assertive responses involve standing up for oneself, yet taking the other person into consideration. The assertive style involves:

- answering spontaneously;
- speaking with a conversational yet firm tone and volume;
- looking at the other person;
- addressing the main issue;
- openly and confidently expressing personal feelings and opinions;
- valuing oneself equal to others;
- being prepared to listen to the other's point of view;
- hurting neither oneself nor others.

The objective here is to try to ensure fair play for everyone. Perhaps not surprisingly, Watson *et al.* (1998) found that there was a positive correlation between assertion and self-esteem. Assertive individuals have also been shown to be high in the constructive trait of *argumentativeness*, which is the tendency to present and defend one's position while also challenging opposing views, whereas *verbal aggressiveness* is a destructive trait that involves a tendency to focus one's attacks on the self-concept of others (Martin and Anderson, 1996). A key aspect of assertion is the 'acceptance of the other person's feelings and limitations' (Sanchez, 2001: 64). In emphasising the importance of taking the other person into consideration, Williams and Akridge (1996) developed the *Responsible Assertion Scale* that measures the extent to which assertive responses are coupled with respect for others.

Aggression

Aggression is defined as the delivery by one individual of noxious stimuli intended to cause harm to another (Geen, 1990). In social situations, aggressive responses involve the use of demands, blunt directives, threats, ridicule or abuse – all of which violate the rights of the other person. Here the aggressor:

- interrupts and answers before the other has finished speaking;
- talks loudly and abrasively;
- glares at the other person;
- speaks 'past' the issue (accusing, blaming, demeaning);
- vehemently and arrogantly states feelings and opinions in a dogmatic fashion;
- values self above others;
- hurts others to avoid personal hurt.

The objective is to win, regardless of the other person. It may involve belittling others through the tactic of *downward comparison*, whereby an attempt is made to demean the achievements of those with whom one may be compared (Schutz, 1998). This form of direct aggression, also known as *blasting*, involves 'the act of derogating others in an effort to make oneself look better' (Kowalski, 1996: 186). It clearly violates the rights of others and so should be avoided. A variation of this tactic is a straight verbal attack on the other person. This is a strategy commonly used by politicians. Let us take two examples in relation to critical questions asked of politicians by journalists: the then Bavarian Prime Minister Franz-Josef Strauss replied by asking whether the journalist had finished high school, while the fiery Ulster politician

Rev. Ian Paisley implied a degree of journalist inebriation when he retorted 'Let me smell your breath'. In the cut-throat battle between politicians and journalists these responses may be fair game, but in the general social world they are much less acceptable.

Comparing the three styles

Hargie *et al.* (1999), in their review of the management field, illustrated how in earlier times the aggressive style was often employed by autocratic managers in oppressive organisations. However, as a result of a range of changes, including a better-educated workforce, the flattening of managerial hierarchies, and a recognition by employees of their legal rights not to be bullied or harrassed, an aggressive style is no longer acceptable. Managers must be assertive, not aggressive. The former style should lead to harmony at work, the latter is likely to result in litigation in court.

These three styles can be exemplified in relation to a situation in which you are asked for the loan of a book that you do not wish to lend:

1 'Um . . . How long would you need it for? It's just that . . . ah . . . I might need it for an assignment. But . . . if it wasn't for long . . .' (Nonassertion).
2 'I'm sorry. I'd like to help you out, but I bought this book so I would always have it to refer to, so I never lend it to anyone.' (Assertion).
3 'No. Why don't you buy your own damn books!?' (Aggression).

Although some psychoanalytic perspectives conceptualise assertiveness and aggression as distinct entities belonging to two different types of motivational system (Fosshage, 1998), most theorists see these response classes as differing in intensity rather than in kind (McCartan, 2001). In this sense, they are regarded as points on the same continuum of:

Nonassertion → Assertion → Aggression

Assertiveness forms the mid-point of this continuum, and is usually the most appropriate response. Aggressive individuals tend to be viewed as intransigent, coercive, overbearing and lacking in self-control. They may initially get their own way by brow-beating and creating fear in others, but they are usually disliked and avoided. Alternatively, this style may provoke a similar response from others, with the danger that the verbal aggression may escalate and lead to overt physical aggression. Nonassertive individuals, on the other hand, are often viewed as weak, 'mealy-mouthed' creatures who can be easily manipulated, and as a result they frequently express dissatisfaction with their lives, owing to a failure to attain personal goals. They may be less likely to inspire confidence in others or may even be seen as incompetent. Assertive individuals, however, tend to feel more in control of their lives, derive more satisfaction from their relationships and achieve their goals more often. They also obtain more respect from, and inspire confidence in, those with whom they interact since they tend to be viewed as strong characters who are not easily swayed.

This is evident at an early stage, so that in junior high school, Windschitl (2001) found that assertive pupils were more likely to voice their views, make suggestions, and give directives to peers. Less assertive pupils, in turn, tended to acquiesce to these directives. Leaper (2000) linked the assertive–nonassertive continuum to the affiliative–nonaffiliative continuum (Figure 11.2). This produces four styles of behaviour. Those who are assertive and affiliative are *collaborative* individuals who only use assertion when necessary, but place a high value on having good relationships with others. On the other hand, assertive individuals who are nonaffiliative do not care about being friendly, and use assertive skills to *control* others and get their own way. Nonassertive people who are affiliative are *obliging* by nature and like to fit in and do what others want. Finally, those who are both nonassertive and nonaffiliative tend to *withdraw* from interaction with others and like to keep themselves to themselves.

Several research studies have verified the behavioural responses associated with these three styles. An early investigation by Rose and Tryon (1979) found that assertive behaviour was clearly associated with:

- louder voice (68 decibel (dB) level was viewed as nonassertive; 76 dB level was the assertive ideal; 84 dB level was towards the aggressive end of the continuum);
- reduced response latency (pauses of 16 seconds before responding were seen as nonassertive, whereas pauses of 3–4 seconds were viewed as assertive);
- greater use of gestures (although increased gestures coupled with approach behaviour were seen as aggressive);
- increased vocal inflection.

The relationship between amplitude of voice and perceptions of dominance (high amplitude) and submissiveness (low amplitude) was confirmed in a later study by Tusing and Dillard (2000). They postulated the reason for this relationship as being

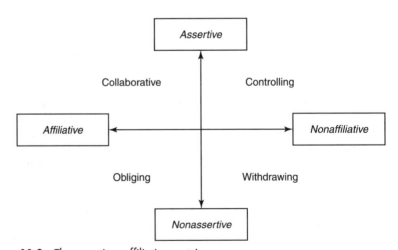

Figure 11.2 The assertion–affiliation matrix

that, 'during the course of evolutionary history, certain vocal cues became associated with dominance because they served as markers of organisms' aggressive potential' (p. 164). In other words, a loud bark was a signal of a deep bite.

McFall *et al.* (1982), in a detailed research investigation identified what they termed *assertive body movements*, the most salient being hands, arms and overall body cues. The nonverbal behaviour of assertive individuals was controlled, smooth, and purposive, whereas nonassertive people displayed shifty, shaky and fidgety body activity. Furthermore, Kolotkin *et al.* (1983) found that duration of eye-contact was greater for assertive, as opposed to nonassertive individuals. They also found that the use of smiles helps to convey that a response is meant to be assertive rather than aggressive. Interestingly, however, there is a relationship between laughter and dominance, in that submissive people laugh much more at the humour of dominant individuals than vice versa (Provine, 2000).

Types of aggression

Although most texts on assertion differentiate between three styles of responding, some theorists have made a distinction between different types of aggression. Buss and Perry (1992) developed an aggression inventory which contains four factors, or sub-divisions, of aggression. These are outlined below, with examples of actual items from the inventory.

1   *Physical aggression*. 'Given enough provocation, I may hit another person' 'If I have to resort to violence to protect my rights, I will'.
2   *Verbal aggression*. 'I tell my friends openly when I disagree with them' 'When people annoy me I may tell them what I think of them'.
3   *Anger*. 'I sometimes feel like a powder keg ready to explode' 'Sometimes I fly off the handle for no good reason'.
4   *Hostility*. 'I am sometimes eaten up with jealousy' 'When people are especially nice, I wonder what they want'.

The relationship between these elements is that they each represent different dimensions of aggression: physical and verbal responses represent the instrumental or behavioural components; anger is the emotional or affective aspect; and hostility the cognitive element.

Another common distinction is that between open, direct aggression and passive, indirect aggression. Del Greco (1983) argued that these two types combine with nonassertion and assertion to form the two continua of coerciveness and directness, as shown in Figure 11.3. The passive, or indirect, aggressive style of responding seems to embrace a range of behaviours including sulking, using emotional blackmail (such as crying in order to get your own way), pouting, and being subtly manipulative. Del Greco (1983) developed an inventory to measure all four response styles. Indirect, or passive, aggressive items include 'When I am asked for my preference I pretend I don't have one, but then I convince my friends of the advantages of my hidden preferences' and 'When my friend asks me for my opinion I state that I have none, then I proceed to make my true preference seem the most

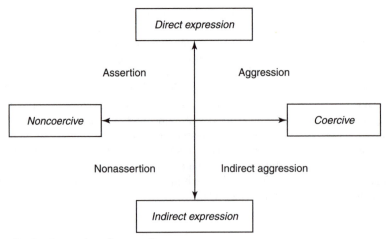

Figure 11.3 Four styles of responding

attractive'. This type of machiavellian approach is one clear example of indirect aggression. Another example is the *deflected aggression* scenario, where for example a person slams drawers and doors shut while refusing to discuss the reason for so doing.

The four response styles can be illustrated with reference to alternative ways of responding to someone smoking in a 'No Smoking' area:

1   'Hey, you, there's no smoking allowed in this area. Either put out or get out!' (Aggressive)
2   'Excuse me, but do you realise that this is a No Smoking area? Cigarette smoke affects me quite badly, so I'd be grateful if you would not smoke here.' (Assertive)
3   Not mentioning your discomfort, and hoping that someone else will confront the smoker. (Nonassertive)
4   Coughing loudly and vigorously waving a hand towards the smoker as if to fan the smoke away. (Indirectly aggressive)

Once again, assertiveness is regarded as the optimum approach. While it is possible to be skilfully manipulative, there is always the danger of being found out, with resulting negative consequences. Similarly in the case of passive aggression, as in the fourth example, this can also lead to a negative evaluation, or may simply be ignored by the other person.

A distinction has also been made between aggression and resort-to-aggression styles. In their study of assertion in relation to consumers' verbal behaviour following a failure of service, Swanson and McIntyre (1998) confirmed the two factors of aggression and assertion as originally measured by the *Consumer Assertiveness and Aggression Scales* (Richins, 1983). They further analysed the aggression factor in relation to aggression *per se* and resort-to-aggression. As illustrated in Figure 11.4 aggressive individuals are high on aggression but low on assertion – they don't use

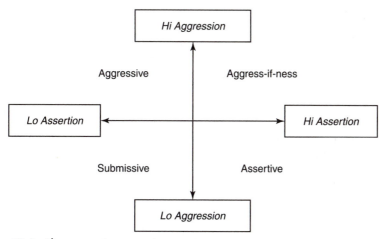

Figure 11.4 The aggression–assertion matrix

the assertive approach at all. By comparison, some individuals are high on both assertion and aggression. They employ an assertive style initially but are prepared to become aggressive if necessary (thus we have termed this the 'aggress-if-ness' style) to get what they want. An example of an item on the Richins Scale relating to the aggress-if-ness style is 'Sometimes being nasty is the best way to get a complaint taken care of'. Swanson and McIntyre (1998) found that the two high assertive groups (assertive and resort-to-aggression) reported a greater likelihood of discussing an incident of poor customer service with family, friends and acquaintances than the low assertive groups (nonassertive and aggressive).

TYPES OF ASSERTIVENESS

There are five key types of assertive behaviour.

1   *Basic assertion.* This involves a simple expression of standing up for personal rights, beliefs, feelings or opinions. For example, when interrupted, a basic assertive expression would be: 'Excuse me, I would like to finish what I was saying.'

2   *Empathic assertion.* This type of assertion conveys sensitivity to the other person, by making a statement that conveys some recognition of the other person's situation or feelings before making the assertive statement. Thus an example of an empathic assertion to an interruption would be: 'I know you are keen to get your views across, but I would like to finish what I was saying.'

3   *Escalating assertion.* Here the individual begins by making a minimal assertive response, and, if the other person fails to respond to this, gradually increases or escalates the degree of assertiveness employed. Someone visited at home by a 'pushy' salesperson may use escalating assertiveness as follows:

Level 1: 'No, I've decided that I don't wish to purchase any of these products.'
Level 2: 'No, as I've already said, I'm not buying any of them.'
Level 3: 'Look, I've told you twice that the answer is no. I'm going to have to ask you to leave now.'

There may come a time when assertion fails, and a stronger response is required. As Rakos (1997) pointed out, if your assertion attempts are repeatedly ignored, it may be necessary to escalate to the level of reasonable threats or actions. For example, someone who has been continually bullied or harassed at work despite assertive attempts to overcome this may then refuse to speak to or deal with the bully, take the matter to higher levels of management, or initiate legal action.

4   *Confrontive assertion.* This is used when someone does not do what had been previously agreed. It involves firmly reminding the person what was agreed, and contrasting this with what actually happened. The speaker then clearly states what the other person must now do (e.g. 'You said you would have the report finished by Tuesday. It is now Thursday and you still haven't produced it. I want you to have it completed by 4.00 pm today.')

5   *I-language assertion.* Here the speaker objectively describes the behaviour of the other person, how this affects the speaker's life or feelings and why the other person should change this behaviour. In the case of being interrupted, an I-language assertive response would be: 'This is the fourth time you've interrupted me in the past few minutes. This makes me feel that you aren't interested in what I am saying, and I feel a bit hurt and annoyed. I would like you to let me finish what I want to say.' This statement also contains *You-language*, which tends to be perceived as blaming or accusing the other person and can result in defensive reactions. Compare the following two utterances.

a   'You are annoying me because you never pay for your fair share of these expenses.'
b   'I feel annoyed because I believe that I am paying more than my fair share of these expenses.'

Statement (b) is much less accusatory than (a) and therefore is less likely to provoke a hostile response. However, there is a danger, especially if overused, of I-language being perceived as selfish, self-centred and unconcerned with the other person. Indeed, I-language statements do not seem to be characteristic of most everyday conversations (Gervasio, 1987). For these reasons, the use of *We-language* can be an effective alternative. The use of We-language helps to convey the impression of partnership in, and joint responsibility for, any problems to be discussed. Continuing with the above exemplar, the We-language response would be:

c   'We need to talk about how we are both contributing to the payment of these expenses. It is important that neither of us feels annoyed about the present arrangement.'

Direct and indirect assertion

Linehan and Egan (1979) distinguished between direct and indirect styles of assertiveness. They argued that a direct, unambiguous assertive style may not always be the most effective, especially for those individuals for whom it is important to be liked and regarded positively by others. Rather, a more ambiguous, indirect style of response seems more appropriate in some instances (despite the fact that many texts recommend a direct style). An example of these two styles can be seen in relation to the following question:

Q: 'Could you lend me that DVD you bought yesterday?'
Direct: 'No, I never lend my DVDs to anyone.'
Indirect: 'Oh, you mean *The Oceans Live* – You know, I'm still trying to get a chance to sit down and watch it myself. I usually take ages with a new DVD.'

Here the direct approach may be seen as brusque or even offensive. In the indirect approach, however, there has been no refusal and so the other person may reply by attempting to obtain a commitment about borrowing the DVD in the future. However, as will be shown later, the direct style can be less abrasive if it is coupled with an embellishment to turn it into a complex-direct style and so soften the impact of direct assertion. Some theorists suggest that little white lies may be used here, but caution is required as, not only does it pose an ethical dilemma, it can backfire if the lie is later unveiled. At the same time, as mentioned in Chapter 9, deception occurs in around one quarter of all conversations. Niikura (1999a) in a study of assertiveness across four cultures found that the option of 'making an excuse' (a euphemism for telling a lie) when having to turn down a request from a senior colleague was very popular in all cultures. Another option was that of 'You tell the boss that you would do it but actually you don't, and tell him/her a lie about why you didn't do it' and again this was a not infrequent selection.

The goal is to lessen the impact of the refusal and so maintain the relationship. Thus, using the complex-direct approach, a response (whether truthful or not) to the above question would be:

Complex-Direct: 'I know you would look after it really well, but I've recently had two DVDs that I lent damaged, so I've just had to make the general decision never to lend my DVDs to anyone again. That way I hope no one will feel personally offended.'

There is consistent research evidence to show that standard, direct assertion is viewed as being as effective as, and more socially desirable than, aggressive behaviour, and more socially competent but distinctly less likeable than nonassertion (Wilson and Gallois, 1993). It seems that assertiveness is evaluated positively in theory, but when faced with the practical reality is rated less favourably than non-assertion (McCartan, 2001). As expressed by Dickson *et al.* (1997: 131) 'One interesting research finding, however, is that while people tend to respect assertive individuals, they often do not like to have to deal with assertive responses.' For example, Harwood *et al.* (1997) carried out a study in which subjects evaluated conversations between a bystander and the driver following a car accident. They found that an assertive style of response from the bystander was perceived to be more competent but less kind and less respectful than a nonassertive style. Equally, we may not like to be in the company of those who are continually assertive. In a review of research on complaining, Kowalski (1996) concluded that people who complain frequently are viewed more negatively than those who seldom do so. A similar dislike for assertion emerged in a Slovakian study, where Bugelova (2000) found an assertive style was perceived as unbecoming or impolite, and regarded as a hindrance to friendship. In fact in their review of this phenomenon, Buslig and Burgoon (2000: 193) noted, 'submissive behavior is often ineffective for reaching instrumental goals, but perceived more positively in terms of interpersonal impressions'. We like, and probably have more empathy for, nonassertive people. Thus assertion needs to be used sensitively.

Assertiveness can provoke a number of adverse reactions. This may especially be the case when a change in style from submissiveness to assertiveness is made. It is useful to be aware of some of the possible negative reactions of others. Alberti and Emmons (2001) identified five main ones:

1   *Back-biting.* Making statements *sotto voce*, which the assertee ensures are overheard by the asserter ('Who does she think she is?' 'All of a sudden he's now Mr Bigfellow').

2   *Aggression.* Others may try to negate the assertion by using threatening or hostile behaviour in an attempt to regain dominance. They may also use apologetic sarcasm as a form of aggression ('I'm so terribly, terribly, sorry. How unforgivably rude of me to even think of asking you').

3   *Over-apologising.* Apologies can also be genuine. Some people may feel they have caused offence and as a result apologise profusely. In such instances reassurance by the asserter is needed, showing that the apology is accepted and the deed now in the past.

4   *Emotionality.* When someone who was formerly submissive becomes assertive, the recipient may react by becoming emotional. This can include temper tantrums, huffing or guilt-based accusations ('You don't love me any more' 'You've become very selfish. Can't you think of me at all?'). In extreme cases, when the new behaviour signals a potential change in the relational power balance, it can also result in assertee psychosomatic reactions (headaches, stomach pains, feeling weak). Again, an assertive response is required to deal with these.

5   *Revenge-seeking.* The assertion may apparently be accepted but the person retains hidden resentment and a desire to 'get their own back'.

Protective assertion

Assertiveness is an important skill when one is coming under pressure from others. This is particularly important in areas such as drug abuse and safe sex. Thus assertion has been shown to be related to a reduced incidence of alcohol abuse

(Epstein *et al.*, 2000), lower chronicity and quantity of alcohol, cocaine and heroin consumption (Torrecillas *et al.*, 2000), and greater condom use to prevent sexually transmitted disease (Zamboni *et al.*, 2000). Three types of protective assertion skills were identified by Fry (1983), as forms of verbal defence to be used against manipulation, nagging or rudeness.

1   *Broken record.* Here the person simply makes an assertive statement, and keeps repeating it (analogous to the needle sticking on a broken record) until it is accepted by the other person. For example, to repeated pleas for a loan the individual may just keep using the refusal assertion response: 'No, I'm not going to give you any money.'

2   *Fogging.* Using this tactic the person verbally accepts negative criticism but clearly has no intention of changing behaviour. The idea here is that eventually the initiator becomes tired of getting no real response to the criticisms and eventually gives up. An example of a fogging sequence is:

    A: 'You always look down in the dumps.'
    B: 'Yes, I probably do.'
    A: 'Could you not try to look a bit happier?'
    B: 'I suppose I could.'
    A: 'If you did, you would be a bit more pleasant to work with.'
    B: 'Yes, you're probably right.'

3   *Metalevel assertion.* As the name suggests, this involves an attempt to widen the perspective rather than sticking to a specific issue. One example of this approach, of moving from the particular to the general, would be where some-one involved in an argument with a colleague says 'We obviously are not going to agree about this, and I think this is typical of what is happening to our whole working relationship.'

COMPONENTS OF ASSERTIVENESS

In order to execute assertiveness skills effectively, three central components need to be mastered: content, process and nonverbal responses.

Content

The actual content of an assertive response should include both an expression of rights, and a statement placing this within the context of socially responsible and appropriate behaviour. A number of accompanying elaboration components, or embellishments, have been identified (Linehan and Egan, 1979; Rakos, 1997). Box 11.3 presents a summary of these in relation to an assertive response to the refusal of an invitation. These content statements can obviously be combined to soften the assertion, and to distinguish the response from aggression. They serve the important purpose of protecting mutual face and so maintaining the relationship: the asserter

---

Box 11.3 Elaboration components in assertion statements

Using the example of a refusal to an invitation from a colleague to go to the bar at lunchtime, the elaborations are:

- A short *delay,* or brief *filled pause* ('Ahh'), before responding, so that the refusal is not seen as abrupt or brusque.
- An *expression of appreciation or praise* for the kindness and thoughtfulness of the other person in making the offer ('It's really nice of you to ask'). The power of praise in conflict assertion was aptly noted by Mark Twain: 'I think a compliment ought always to precede a complaint, where one is possible, because it softens resentment and insures for the complaint a courteous and gentle reception.'
- A *cushioning* of the way the refusal itself is expressed, usually through an expression of regret at not being able to accept ('Much as I'd like to come, I'm afraid I won't be able to').
- An *explanation* for the necessity to assert oneself ('I have work to finish off during the lunch break').
- Showing *empathy* for the other person's situation ('I know you had been looking forward to it').
- A short *apology* for any resulting consequence ('I'm sorry if you are on your own over lunch').
- An attempt to identify a mutually acceptable *compromise* ('I haven't time to go out to the bar, but how about just having a quick bite in the canteen?').

---

achieves the desired personal goal, but at the same time shows concern for the face needs of the assertee (Edwards and Bello, 2001). However, a note of caution was sounded by Rakos (1997), who pointed out that these embellishments are likely to be more consistent with a female than a male approach to, and expectations of, assertion.

One situation that can be difficult to cope with assertively is that of embarrassment. In their discussion of strategies for handling embarrassing predicaments, Cupach and Metts (1990) identified four main types of content responses.

1   *Apology.* This can range from a basic statement ('I'm sorry') to elaborate expressions of remorse and attempts at remediation or restitution (e.g. offering to replace a spilled drink).

2   *Accounts.* These can be either in the form of an *excuse,* which expresses denial of responsibility for an untoward act without negating its severity ('I know it is a mess, but it was an accident'); or a *justification,* which expresses responsibility for the untoward act but denies the pejorative nature of the consequences ('Yes, I did spill it, but there's no real harm done').

3   *Humour.* A joke can be one of the most effective methods for dealing with embarrassment, since it can convert a potential loss of social approval into a positive gain. In this sense 'a well formed joke, especially one reflecting on the unintentional incompetence of the transgressor, can express remorse, guilt, and

embarrassment as an apology would without unduly lowering the individual's status *vis-à-vis* others who are present' (Cupach and Metts, 1990: 329).

4   *Avoidance.* This strategy would include not mentioning sensitive topics to particular people, quickly changing an embarrassing topic, staying silent, or simply leaving the room.

Obviously, two or more of these can be used at the same time. Thus an assertive response might involve giving an excuse, apologising and offering restitution, while at the same time employing appropriate humour.

In her analysis of tactics used by those who are held publicly responsible for an event that has been evaluated negatively, Schutz (1998) identified six possible response strategies.

1   *Denial.* This is summarised by the 'It never happened' response. The veracity and motives of those who claim that it did are then called into question.

2   *Reframing.* Here the essence is 'It was not like that'. The approach is to present the event in a new 'frame' – it did occur but it was not nearly as bad as portrayed.

3   *Dissociation.* This is the 'I was not to blame' strategy. The event did occur but the person did not cause it. It was someone else's fault. One variation of this is in the use of pronominals to associate or dissociate oneself with what happened – here Shutz gave the example of supporters of sports teams when talking about victories saying '*We* won . . .' but when defeated saying '*They* lost . . .'

4   *Justification.* The nub of this approach is 'It was the only thing to do'. Responsibility is accepted but the argument is that nothing else could have been done, or even that the response averted potentially more damaging events and so the public should be grateful.

5   *Excuses.* The typical statement here is 'I could not prevent it'. The main excuse tends to be that of extenuating or extraordinary circumstances – that no one could have forseen the event.

6   *Apologies and remediation.* The response here is 'I accept full responsibility and wish to do whatever I can to compensate'. As Schutz illustrated, when remediation is offered as well as an apology the impact is more positive in terms of public perceptions of the perpetrator's image.

Rose and Tryon (1979) made another important distinction between three general types of assertion content, which can be exemplified in relation to complaining about a meal in a restaurant, as follows:

1   *Description of the behaviour* – 'Excuse me, this meal is cold.'

2   *Description of behaviour plus indication of your noncompliance* – 'Excuse me, this meal is cold. I couldn't eat it.'

3   *Description, noncompliance, plus request for behaviour change* – 'Excuse me, this meal is cold. I couldn't eat it. Could you please replace it?'

Rose and Tryon found that ratings of assertiveness increased as individuals moved from simply giving a description, through to using all three types of content.

Process

The way in which assertive responses are carried out can be crucial to their success. Thus the correct timing of vocalisations and nonverbal responses is vital. Although a slight delay is important in refusing a genuine invitation (Holman, 2000), assertive responses should be given without long hesitations. On occasions, we may have our rights infringed because we are unsure about whether they actually have been violated. If we later discover this to be the case then it is necessary to reconstruct the situation in which the infringement occurred ('Yesterday you asked me to do X. I have since discovered that it is not my job to do X. I would therefore be grateful if you would not ask me to do this again.')

Stimulus control skills are also important. These refer to manipulations of the environment, or other people, to make the assertive response more successful. For example:

- Asking someone to come to your room where you will feel more in charge, rather than discussing an issue in the corridor. Humans, like all animals, are territorial and our sense of *place* is very important to how we respond (Dixon and Durrheim, 2000). We feel more comfortable in our own lairs, with familiar sights, sounds and smells. Conversely we are more uncomfortable when on someone else's patch. To borrow a sporting analogy, it is always harder to get a result when playing away from home. Thus it is easier to be assertive when we are on our own ground.
- Requesting that you seek the opinion of another person to help settle the matter, when you already know that the views of this third person concur with your own.
- Simply asking for time to think over a request, which allows you to think through the ramifications thereof.

The use of reinforcement (see Chapter 4) is also important, for three reasons. First, rewarding another person is actually a positive use of assertion; someone who has performed a task well has the right to expect reward. Second, the reward can help to minimise any negative feelings resulting from the assertion. Third, it encourages the other person to behave appropriately towards you in the future.

Nonverbal responses

The final component of assertiveness relates to the nonverbal behaviour of the asserter. The main nonverbal assertive behaviours are: medium levels of eye-contact; avoidance of inappropriate facial expressions; smooth use of gestures while speaking, yet inconspicuous while listening; upright posture; direct body orientation; medium interpersonal distance; and appropriate paralinguistics (short response latency, medium response length, good fluency, medium volume and inflection, increased firmness).

PERSONAL AND CONTEXTUAL FACTORS

There are several factors that influence the degree, nature and effectiveness of assertion.

Gender

The relationship between gender and assertiveness is both complex and complicated. In an early review, Kahn (1981: 349) suggested that:

> People expect women to behave unassertively. Women may not only accept this judgment of others and behave so as to fulfill prophecies based on stereotyped beliefs, but . . . may avoid behaviors that do not fit 'the feminine role' and when they do engage in 'masculine assertiveness', they are likely to encounter disbelief or even hostility from others . . . A common attack against females is the labeling of women who assert themselves as aggressive.

However, some feminist writers have argued that the entire concept of assertion is androcentric (male-centred) and imbued with demeaning portrayals of women for being 'weak' in this area (Cameron, 1994; Crawford, 1995). Despite such views, the main perspective within the feminist movement tends to be that this is a skill that women should possess (Rakos, 1997). Thus the training programmes of many women's groups include AT as one of their core themes. Likewise, several assertiveness books have been written specifically for women. This is not surprising given that females consistently report difficulties in being assertive (Rakos, 1991). Indeed, the plethora of written material and self-help texts specifically designed for women and the popularity of women's AT programmes is in itself a form of evidence that females feel they need more help in this field.

One specific problem faced by females is that of negotiating sexual activity with a partner (e.g. refusing sexual advances or insisting on condom use). Morokoff *et al.* (1997) identified three specific problems in this context: (1) prevailing social norms that still expect males to initiate overt sexual activity, (2) a high reported level of unwanted intercourse owing to a reluctance to refuse one's male partner, and (3) an increase in the occurrence of sexually transmitted disease (STD) in women. To address such issues, Morokoff *et al.* developed the *Sexual Assertiveness Scale* for females. This measures responses to three areas of sexual activity as follows, with actual scale items given in parenthesis:

- initiation ('I begin sex with my partner if I want to');
- refusal ('I have sex if my partner wants me to even if I don't want to');
- pregnancy/STD prevention ('I refuse to have sex if my partner refuses to use a condom or latex barrier').

In testing this scale with women from both university and the wider community, Morokoff *et al.* (1997) found that:

- the greater a woman's sexual experience the more likely she was to initiate sex;
- the anticipation of a negative partner response reduced the level of assertiveness in refusing a sexual advance or requesting barrier precautions;
- feelings of self-efficacy about how to use condoms were related to self-reported ability to refuse a sexual advance.

In reviewing the field of gender differences in language use, Mulac (1998: 127) concluded, 'There are two abiding truths on which the general public and research scholars find themselves in uneasy agreement: (a) men and women speak the same language, and (b) men and women speak that language differently.' However, he also noted that these differences should be read as *gender-indicative tendencies* since both genders can and do display the same language features. While, overall, women or men may have a higher mean differential level of production of certain linguistic features, their usage varies according to situation. In addition, specific individuals may use gender-opposite language styles. Two theories have been put forward to explain gender differences in language. The first is *gender-as-culture*. This approach, also known as the *two cultures hypothesis*, argues that boys and girls to a large extent inhabit different 'worlds' at the formative stage of development (up to 15 years old). As a result of their repeated exposure to same gender in-group, they adopt a specific type of either 'masculine' or 'feminine' language usage. The second perspective is that of *gender-as-power*, where differences in male and female language use are purported to reflect the relative dominance and submissiveness of the two genders.

Mulac *et al.* (2001) argued that there is truth in both these theories, and that they each reflect one part of the overall process. In their review of research studies of language and gender, they found a number of main difference effects, as shown in Box 11.4. These differences indicate why females may find it more difficult to be assertive. The male-preferred style reflects shorter, more directive, self-opinionated, and explicit, language use. Expressions of direct assertiveness will therefore not be so problematic. On the other hand, the preferred female style of longer and more indirect sentences, coupled with greater expressed uncertainty and qualification, does not lend itself so easily to assertion.

Some research has been carried out to ascertain whether assertion is learned at an early age. One study of 4–6-year-olds in the eastern USA found no difference in assertive behaviour between boys and girls (Beneson *et al.*, 1998). However, confounding variables here included the facts that the study focused almost exclusively on white, middle/upper-class children, the girls were in the presence of friends, and they knew the boys. All of these factors facilitate assertion displays. In contrast, Leaper (2000) analysed the assertion and affiliation behaviours of European American and Latin American girls and boys (mean age 48 months) and their parents in their own homes. Each child played individually with mother or father, with a feminine-stereotyped toy (foods and plates) and a masculine-stereotyped toy (track and cars). It was found that fathers were more assertive (e.g. giving directions, disagreeing) than mothers who, in turn, were more affiliative (e.g. praising, asking for the child's opinion). Furthermore, in general, children were more assertive than their mothers but less assertive than their fathers. Leaper argued that this latter finding may reflect the mother's willingness to let the child take control, but that it could also

Box 11.4 Gender differences in language

Males tend to make greater use of:

- references to quantity ('20 feet high', 'weighed at least a ton');
- judgemental adjectives (giving personal evaluations – 'weak', 'smart');
- directives (telling another what to do – 'Put it over there');
- locatives (these indicate the position/location of objects – 'to the right of . . .');
- elliptical sentences (short or one-word sentences in which either the subject or predicate is understood e.g. 'Awesome!' 'Quite a view');
- self-referenced statements ('My view is . . .').

Females tend to use more:

- intensive adverbs ('terribly', 'so');
- dependent clauses to qualify the primary meaning (e.g. 'in which something . . .');
- reference to emotions ('cheerful', 'angry');
- sentences of greater mean length;
- sentence initial adverbials ('Owing to the background lighting . . .');
- uncertainty verbs ('It seems to be . . .');
- hedges ('sort of . . .' 'a bit like . . .');
- negations (statements of what something is not 'it is not a . . .');
- oppositions ('He looks happy yet also sad . . .');
- questions.

lead to a learned stereotype of women being less powerful than men. Differences also emerged in relation to the play settings, in that the toy food scenario produced higher levels of both assertion and affiliation – in other words it was a more collaborative encounter (see Figure 11.2).

Leaper argued that gender-typed play scenarios mean that girls learn to co-operate from an early age, whereas boys learn to compete. Another finding was that both fathers and mothers demonstrated less assertion than their sons, but not their daughters, in the toy track condition while no such difference emerged in the food play. Leaper summarised these findings as showing a pattern of children being presented with role models of assertive fathers and affiliative mothers, and of boys but not girls being encouraged to be assertive and take control in masculine-stereotyped activities. Overall, this study illustrated how gender differences in assertion can be shaped by a combination of parental role models, and reward for differential behaviours in stereotyped play activities.

Lewis and Gallois (1984) found that both males and females were more assertive towards those of the same gender; that expression of negative feeling was more acceptable from a member of the opposite sex; and that aggressive encounters were more prevalent in same-sex dyads. In another study, Nix *et al.* (1983) concluded that assertiveness is a masculine sex-role characteristic. They found that females achieving high masculinity scores in the Bem Sex Role Inventory scored significantly higher on measures of assertiveness than those high in femininity. This finding is consistent with general trends wherein masculine sex-role characteristics tend to be attributed to assertive individuals; masculine or androgynous females are more likely to be assertive than feminine women; masculinity and conflict assertiveness are positively correlated; and direct assertiveness tends to be viewed as masculine (Rakos, 1991).

The situation in which assertion occurs may also be important. For example, both male and female university students evaluated a female speaker more favourably when she was using an assertive as opposed to a tentative style of speech (Hawkes et al., 1996). Similarly, there is evidence to show that male and female assertiveness is valued equally in business and legal contexts, yet an assertive response by a female police officer is less positively rated than the same response by a male officer (Rakos, 1997). This latter finding may be explained by the stereotypical view that it is not acceptable for females to display conflict assertion. However, even in the professional business situation, one study of higher level managers found that female executives rated displays of warmth and support, and avoiding a direct 'no' in response to requests, higher than males did (Dubrin, 1994). Likewise, Bugelova (2000) found that for both undergraduates and middle managers, levels of assertiveness were higher in males than in females. Other studies in organisations indicate that, while higher level female managers have moderate levels of argumentativeness (an assertive personality trait), female assertiveness is not usually well received by males (Schullery, 1997). A disparity in conflict styles was confirmed in a study by Swanson (1999), which found no difference between males and females on assertion but showed that males were more likely to be verbally aggressive. This latter result was also reported by Archer et al. (1995).

It has been suggested that, when dealing with disputes, males are more likely to operate on a one-up, one-down basis, and so direct confrontation literally gives them the opportunity to achieve one-upmanship. Females, on the other hand, prefer a relational route to conflict resolution; they see the option of openly confronting the other person as leading to likely retaliation and harmful for the overall relationship (Kowalski, 1996; Lundgren and Rudawsky, 2000). However, there is also evidence to indicate that females are more likely to be indirectly aggressive (Bjorkqvist et al., 1994). In recognising this, Owens et al. (2000) carried out a study in Australia on the effects of peer indirect aggression (e.g. exclusion from the group, telling lies about the person) on teenage girls. They discovered that victims suffered a wide range of psychological effects including loss of self-esteem, anxiety and depression. This in turn led to a range of ideas about how to escape the pain, ranging from a desire to leave the school to thoughts of suicide. The most vulnerable girls were those who had few friends, were new to the school, or lacked assertiveness. Some responded by retaliating against the perpetrator. This is interesting, given that another study found that training in physical self-defence actually served to increase women's self-reported levels of assertiveness (Weitlauf et al., 2000).

Overall, however, there is no clear picture as to the exact nature of the relationship between the effects of different types of assertiveness, the situation in which they are employed and the gender of asserter and assertee. One problem here, as with all studies in the field of assertion, is that different investigators use differing measurements and methodologies. For example, subjects may be asked to respond to written, audio or video vignettes of assertiveness, engage in role-plays, complete one of the large number of self-report assertion scales that now exist (see McCartan, 2001 for a review of these), or be confronted with an experimentally contrived assertive encounter they believe to be real. Ratings of assertion may be made by the subjects themselves, by those with whom they have interacted, or by trained observers. These variations make comparisons between studies very difficult.

The final compounding factor here is that the role of women in society has changed rapidly in recent years. In traditional fairy tales, portrayals of females were typically either of 'submissive/beautiful' (e.g. Cinderella, Snow White, Goldilocks) or 'aggressive/ugly' (Ugly Sisters, Wicked Witch, Evil Stepmother). Similarly, in films familiar storylines were of the bold dashing knight in shining armour winning the hand of the shy fair maiden, or of the tough galloping cowboy in the white hat rescuing the defenceless damsel in distress. These stereotypes persisted for quite some time. For example, when the cult TV series *Star Trek* began in the late 1960s, its futuristic interpretation of advanced human civilisation had only one female member as part of the elite group on the bridge of the Enterprise, and she was in essence a glorified telephonist who rarely got 'beamed' anywhere. More recently this has changed. The females on the programme are now centrally involved in the hard action (and indeed one recent captain was female). The concept of 'ladette culture' has also arrived, replete with loud, hard-drinking, self-directed, often sexually predatory, females. Furthermore, female entrants to the traditional professions (medicine, pharmacy, law, etc.) often outnumber males. Within some churches, there are now female priests (interestingly, this is opposed by traditionalists, and so it may be some time before there is a female priest, let alone bishop or Pope, in the Catholic Church). All such changes influence the attitudes of both males and females to assertive behaviour by the latter.

In a fascinating longitudinal meta-analysis of 385 studies dating from the 1920s to the 1990s, Twenge (1998) charted changes in assertiveness across these eight decades. She found no consistent changes in male scores over this period. However, female assertion scores mirrored their social status and roles in each era, showing an increase pre-war (1928–45), a decrease post-war (1945–67), and an increase thereafter. Interestingly, she also found a positive correlation between assertion scores and overall figures for educational attainment for women. This suggests that 'getting on' in society involves standing up for one's rights. It also indicates that female assertive behaviour changes according to shifting societal expectations, whereas male assertion remains constant.

Cultural background

As discussed in Chapter 2, the context within which responses are employed is important. For example, a sub-culture of people with certain strong religious beliefs may actually eschew assertiveness as a valid *modus operandi* and be guided by Biblical maxims of submissiveness such as the following from Matthew 5: 'Blessed are the meek: for they shall inherit the earth'; 'whosoever shall smite thee on thy right cheek, turn to him the other also'; and 'Give to him that asketh thee, and from him that would borrow of thee turn not thou away.' For such groups, obviously AT would not be either relevant or appropriate. One problem with early approaches to the study of cultural differences was that western culture was regarded as 'universal' and other cultures were viewed as having 'special features' (Niikura, 1999a). This perspective no longer prevails, and it is now accepted that no culture should be seen, either explicitly or implicitly, as being universal.

One of the most researched aspects of culture is that of individualism versus collectivism (Cialdini *et al.*, 2001). In North America (Canada and the USA) and some European countries (e.g. Norway and the UK), the emphasis tends to be on the self as an independent entity with needs, wants and goals that are legitimate to pursue individually. As such, standing up for one's rights seems perfectly valid and indeed natural. In collectivist cultures, individual rights are subordinate to those of the group and so assertion is not so appropriate. Thus in many Eastern countries (e.g. China, Japan, Korea) and in Latin America (e.g. Brazil, Mexico), the emphasis is more on an interdependent self. For example, in Hispanic culture the concept of *personalismo* is central. The difference between these two cultural styles, as highlighted in Box 11.5, was neatly summarised by Morris *et al.* (2001: 100) in the example that, 'Brazilians display stronger intentions to do what is expected of them, whereas North Americans display a stronger intention to do what they personally desire.'

It should be noted that the differences between these two cultural styles are not as neat as it may at first seem. Thus collectivist cultures differ in the ways in which they maintain intergroup relations and avoid conflicts. Latin Americans achieve this through open, warm, expressive, emotional displays. On the other hand, the Chinese tradition of *jen* and the Japanese of *amae* emphasise the maintenance of harmony through a more passive, respectful and less overtly emotional approach in their dealings with one another. In addition, as Hargie (1997b) illustrated, aspects of collectivism can be found in individual cultures and vice versa so that 'at different times, in different situations, and with different people, we may adopt either an individualistic or a more collective style of communicating' (p. 58). Reykowski (2001) and Iyengar and Brockner (2001) demonstrated how the individual's own position

---

Box 11.5 Individualist and collectivist cultural differences

Important in individualist cultures:	*Important in collectivist cultures:*
Needs	Duties
Rights	Norms
Concern for self ('I' orientation)	Concern for group ('we' orientation)
Being successful	Being accepted
Innovation	Respect for tradition
Equality	Given role
Privacy	Sharing
Competition	Co-operation
Informality	Formality
Directness	Indirectness
Being up-front	Protecting face
Assertion	Nonassertion

on the individualist–collectivist (I–C) continuum often plays a more influential role in determining responses than the I–C norms of the national or cultural group to which the person belongs. However, it is also clear that cultural differences make attempts to employ assertive behaviour with people from different sub-cultures fraught with difficulty. In particular, assertive responses are not appropriate where values of humility, tolerance or subservience are prevalent.

There is evidence that individuals take culture into account when choosing their style of assertion. Thus a study in Germany of the manner in which Turkish immigrants handled conflict situations found that the preferred style varied depending on target person (Klinger and Bierbraver, 2001). When dealing with someone from the Turkish community a more indirect, nonconfrontational approach, typical of this cultural group, was usually employed. However, when dealing with a German a more direct, instrumental style, again in keeping with the norms of this target group, was used.

Minorities and sub-cultures in the USA with a strong sense of separate identity, such as the Mexican, Japanese, and Chinese communities, tend to report being less assertive than whites. These sub-cultures also emphasise respect for and obedience to elders and in particular parents, so that any form of assertion from child to parent is likely to be frowned on. This again is different from the norm for Caucasians, where open disagreement and negotiated decisions are acceptable between parents and children. In similar vein, in some sub-cultures assertion may be associated with a 'macho' male role model, with females being expected to play an acquiescent or subservient role.

There is evidence to indicate that cultural differences in assertion may be cognitively based, emanating from cultural values and norms rather than from assertive behaviour deficits, since in role-play situations people from these cultures are able to behave as assertively as whites. For example, Sue *et al.* (1990) found that second generation Chinese-American female undergraduates were as assertive as Caucasian females on scores on the Rathus Assertiveness Scale and on role-play tests with either an Asian or a Caucasian experimenter. The only significant difference between the groups was that the Chinese-Americans scored higher on the Fear of Negative Evaluation Scale. It could therefore be the case that in real-life encounters such apprehension of disapproval from others may result in Chinese-American females being less assertive. As Sue *et al.* put it 'Chinese-Americans are able to demonstrate assertiveness in laboratory settings, but do they inhibit this response in other situations?' (p. 161).

Hastings (2000a) investigated the behaviour of Asian-Indian postgraduate students in the USA. She found that this cultural group disliked the 'American traits of extensive use of talk and the expression of direct, extreme viewpoints' (p. 105). The US students were perceived as pushy, verbally aggressive and showing a lack of respect for superiors (their professors). Indian culture places a very high value on acceptance, self-suppression, and concern for the feelings of others. Hindu religion regards the role occupied by an individual as having been designated by God, and as such it has to be respected. The Indians in this study perceived the 'recipients' of their behaviour not to be just those immediately involved, but also their family and wider community that might eventually find out what had been said. Their decisions about assertive responses were guided by these factors. It was not the case that they did not know *how* to use assertive behaviours, but rather they recognised that these were not culturally acceptable.

One study compared assertive responses of African American, Hispanic and European American high school students (Yager and Rotheram-Borus, 2000). It was found that assertive responses were more frequent among European Americans, while aggressive and expressive responses were more common in the Hispanic and African American groups. Yager and Rotheram-Borus argued that these response patterns could be misperceived by the out-group and thus be a potential source of cross-ethnic conflicts. Differences also emerged in a cross-cultural investigation of assertion in low-income 'thirty-something' women in the US (Yoshioka, 2000). Here, African Americans, Hispanic Americans and Caucasians all agreed about appropriate assertive responses towards other females and towards children. However, in relation to assertion with males, the Hispanic group differed from the other two in that they were more affiliative in their reaction to male aggression.

Niikura (1999a, b) carried out an ivestigation which compared the responses of white-collar workers in the USA, Japan, Malaysia and the Philippines on a self-expression questionnaire, and to hypothetical scenarios such as:

> Your boss asks you to do something personal for him/her on a holiday. You have always been on friendly terms with your boss and he/she has helped you in many ways. However, you have already made reservations at a resort hotel for you and your family for that same day.

Similarities were found between workers in Japan, Malaysia and the Philippines in terms of the psychological bonds they felt to relationships with superiors. The Japanese and Malayans showed a much higher reluctance to directly refuse an annoying request from a friend. In contrast, the Americans were more likely to directly turn down unwanted requests from either superiors or friends. The Japanese respondents differed from the other groups in their reluctance to ask questions in a public forum. In Japan there is a sense of shame attached to asking questions about matters one does not understand and indeed it is regarded as a sign of over-assertiveness to ask questions. The Japan, Malaysian and Filipino subjects placed greater importance on group solidarity and respect for senior members of staff than did the Americans. Niikura (1999b) speculated that, 'the differences between the Asian and the U.S. perceptions of assertiveness in interpersonal relations and the conflicting views of how to maintain group harmony would be sources of misunderstanding and friction when such people interact'.

In the study by Leaper (2000) of parent–child interactions described earlier, it was found that there were higher levels of both assertion and affiliation in Latin American than in European American families. While Leaper pointed out that this finding of collaborativeness or *familism* was consistent with other reports of Latino families, he also noted that care is needed in interpreting such findings, since other variables, including parent education and age, socioeconomic status, religion and family size, impact on behaviour patterns. For example, Mexican-descent parents with higher education levels have been shown to hold more gender-egalitarian attitudes (Leaper and Valin, 1996). Furthermore, in his review of this area Rakos (1991: 13) concluded that, 'studies with diverse cultural groups generally find the normative level of self-reported assertive behavior generally approaches that of white Americans as the group's sociocultural similarity to mainstream American norms and values increases'.

These results present an opaque image of the relationship between cultural group and appropriate assertion. While it is clear that culture is a very important variable in the assertion equation, no hard-and-fast guidelines can be offered about how best to respond in any particular cultural context. As Yoshioka (2000) in her review of this area pointed out, a key dimension of AT for sub-cultural groups is that of *message matching*. This involves a careful assessment of both situation and assertee to decide how best to match the specific message being delivered, and whether a sub-cultural or mainstream cultural response is most appropriate.

Situation

It has long been known that the situation in which assertiveness is required is important. Following a detailed research investigation, Eisler *et al.* (1975: 339) concluded that:

> an individual who is assertive in one interpersonal context may not be assertive in a different interpersonal environment. Furthermore, some individuals may have no difficulty responding with negative assertions but may be unable to respond when the situation requires positive expressions.

The old description of a person who is 'a lion inside the home and a lamb outside' is an example of this. Few individuals are assertive across all contexts. Most find it easier to assert themselves in some situations than in others. Attention needs to be devoted to situations in which the individual finds it difficult to be assertive, and strategies devised to overcome the particular problems.

In the context of the work environment, Bryan and Gallois (1992) carried out a study in which people who were all in employment in a variety of occupations ranging from professionals to unskilled labourers, judged written vignettes of supervisors, subordinates and co-workers sending either positive or negative assertive messages to one another. Results indicated that positive messages were more favourably rated than negative ones, especially in relation to judgements concerning the likely outcome of the interaction and the probable effects on the relationship. The expression of a personal limitation was rated least favourably of the positive messages, while expressing displeasure was rated as the most negative message. The only difference to emerge between the status groupings was that subordinates were rated more favourably than supervisors or co-workers when using negative assertions. The judges in this study were also asked to generate rules that would apply to, or govern, these assertive interactions. The most common rules identified, in order of frequency, were maintaining eye-contact, being polite, being friendly, and being pleasant. These findings suggest the importance of using relationship maintenance skills when being assertive.

Certain types of assertiveness may well be more appropriate in some settings than in others. Cianni-Surridge and Horan (1983) found this to be the case in the job interview. They had 276 employers rate the efficacy of sixteen 'frequently advocated assertive job-seeking behaviours' in terms of whether or not each would enhance the applicant's chances of being offered employment. They found that some behaviours were advantageous and some disadvantageous. Thus, for example, 'Following an interview, an applicant writes you a letter thanking you for interviewing him/her and expressing his/her continued interest in the position' was regarded by fifty-four employers as greatly enhancing, by 176 as enhancing, by forty-six as having no effect, and by none as diminishing or greatly diminishing job prospects. On the other hand, 'An applicant feels his/her interview with you went poorly. He/she requests a second interview with another interviewer' was regarded by forty-four employers as greatly diminishing, by 100 as diminishing, by 119 as having no effect, by ten as enhancing, and by three as greatly enhancing job prospects.

Age

This is another important factor in assertiveness. Pardeck *et al.* (1991), in a study of postgraduate students in the US, found a significant and positive correlation between age and assertiveness. This may be because older people have gained more life experience, including of situations where they have to stand up for themselves, and so have developed more confidence in standing up for their rights. However, more research is needed in order to ascertain the exact nature of the relationship between assertiveness and maturation.

Disability

AT has been shown to be of benefit to physically disabled individuals. Glueckauf and Quittner (1992) in a Canadian study found that people confined to wheelchairs who received AT made significant increases in the number of assertive responses and concomitant decreases in passive responses during a role-play test as compared with a control group who received no AT. The AT group also reported significantly higher increases in assertiveness in both general and disability-related situations. This result is of particular interest since previous research has shown that people in wheelchairs often experience discomfort in situations that involve refusing help, managing patronising remarks and giving directives. Furthermore, it has also been shown that nondisabled individuals experience difficulties (e.g. show more motoric inhibition, end interactions sooner and are more likely to express attitudes inconsistent with true beliefs) in interactions with the wheelchair-bound (Glueckauf and Quittner, 1992). There is clearly a need for more research into the possible inhibiting effects of wheelchairs during interpersonal encounters and to ways in which such effects can be overcome.

The assertee

A key aspect of assertion is the target person. From the foregoing reviews, it is clear that the gender and cultural background of the assertee are key determinants of the effectiveness of assertive responses. However, the assertion level of the target person is also important. In two early studies, Gormally (1982) found that assertive behaviour was rated more favourably by assertive individuals, while Kern (1982) discovered that low assertive subjects reacted negatively to assertive behaviour whereas high assertive subjects generally devalued nonassertive behaviour. These findings suggest that decisions about when and how to apply assertion should be moderated by the assertive nature of the recipient.

Thus the relationship with the other person is of vital import in deciding how to be assertive. An interesting dimension of relationships was explored by Alberts (1992) in relation to teasing behaviour (banter). Alberts illustrated how teasing can be interpreted as either playfulness/joking or as derogation/aggression since it usually has both friendly and hostile components. Between friends it is normally the former purpose that is served by banter and the humour is therefore two-way. In other contexts there would seem to be a dominance or control function prevalent, since high status people can tease low status people but not usually vice versa. Alberts points out that decisions about how to react to teasing behaviour are made on the basis of four main elements: the perceived goal of the teaser; background knowledge of and relationship with this person; the context in which the tease is employed; and the paralinguistic tone with which it is delivered. Where banter is used as a form of sarcasm, or 'put-down', it is necessary to assertively indicate that such behaviour is unacceptable. This needs to be done skilfully to avoid accusations of not being able to take a joke.

Lewis and Gallois (1984) investigated the influence of friendship on assertiveness. They found that certain types of negative assertions (expression of anger, or difference of opinion) were more acceptable when made by friends as opposed to strangers. However, refusal of a request from a friend was perceived to be less socially skilled and more hurtful than refusal from a stranger. As a result, they recommend that with strangers it is 'wise to refrain from assertively expressing a difference of opinion or negative feelings, at least until the relationship is well established' (p. 366).

OVERVIEW

The three response styles reviewed in this chapter can be explained succinctly as follows:

* Aggressive – *talking at* others
* Assertive – *talking with* others
* Submissive – *talking little to* others.

Assertiveness is a very important social skill both in professional contexts and in everyday interactions. We feel hurt, aggrieved and upset if our rights have been violated. Yet, some individuals find it very difficult to be assertive. This is often related to upbringing in that they may have been raised under a very strict regime by their parents in which as children they were seen and not heard, and they learned in school that the quiet child who did as he or she was told was most approved of by the teacher. It can then be difficult in later life to overcome this residue of parental and educational upbringing. As summarised by Paterson (2000: 209) in his book on this topic:

> Assertiveness skills can be difficult to learn. Many of us grow up without learning to use them effectively. As well, assertiveness goes against our temptations. Sometimes we want to push other people to do our bidding. Sometimes we are desperately afraid of conflict. Assertiveness may mean holding back from our automatic ways of doing things.

One common pitfall is that individuals move from prolonged nonassertion straight into aggression, feeling they can no longer put up with being used, taken for granted, or having their rights ignored. It is important to employ assertiveness at an early stage during social interaction. Research evidence has clearly shown that assertion skills are not innate – they can be learned and improved. Once they are learned, it becomes easier to protect one's personal rights, to say 'no' without undue concern, to make reasonable requests, and to regard oneself as equal to others. Our self-confidence and sense of self-worth are improved accordingly.

In using assertion the following points should be borne in mind:

- to be assertive it is necessary to know what one's rights are and when they have been infringed
- it is also essential to have positive personal beliefs about the value of and outcomes from assertive responses
- assertion is not always the optimum response in every situation and on occasions it may be better to be submissive or even resort to a degree of verbal aggression
- there are clear nonverbal and vocal styles associated with submissiveness, assertiveness and aggressiveness, with assertion usually the mid-point on the behavioural continuum (e.g. whispering, speaking up for oneself, shouting)
- assertive responses are respected but not necessarily liked, submissive people are better liked but less well respected, while aggressive individuals tend to be neither liked nor respected
- basic direct assertion tends to be dispreferred and so embellishments, such as empathy, praise, apology, etc. should be used to soften the assertive blow
- it is best to begin with the minimal assertive response and then escalate this as required
- the use of *I-language* may be seen as rather self-centred; *you-language* can appear accusatory, while *we-language* emphasises a joint approach to a problem
- assertion is most effective when it combines a description of the behaviour, indication of noncompliance, and request for behaviour change
- issues of gender and culture may make assertive responses problematic

Chapter 12

Influence and persuasion

INTRODUCTION

FORGAS AND WILLIAMS (2001: 7) noted that:

> The sophisticated ability of humans to influence, and be influenced, by each other is probably one of the cornerstones of the evolutionary success of our species, and the foundation of the increasingly complex forms of social organization we have been able to develop.

It is therefore not surprising that persuasion and influence are pervasive in human society. We meet these change agents many times every day, and in different guises. For example, Meyers-Levy and Malaviya (1999) showed how in the USA consumers are exposed to over 1,000 commercial messages daily (TV, radio and newspaper adverts, billboard posters, etc.) all aimed at encouraging the target to adopt a service, idea or product. At this level, the persuasion attempt is directed towards the masses. Consequently, a vast volume of literature has been produced in this field. Research into the effects of TV and radio advertising, health promotion campaigns, posters, PR interventions, and so on, has attracted enormous interest.

However, as noted by Cody and Seiter (2001: 325) 'Scholarly interest in the process of persuasion has changed considerably in the last few decades from a focus on one-to-many influence attempts to the study of interpersonal or one-to-one influence attempts.' The main reason for this is the recognition that almost all exchanges between people involve some element of influence. Even in the most informal encounters, such as when friends meet to 'hang out' together, they behave in such a way as to communicate liking for one another (through smiles, eye-contact, verbal following, etc.). While these behaviours may be carried out without the goal consciously in mind, the purpose is clearly to influence the other person to maintain the friendship. A knowledge of the ways in which we can influence and persuade others is therefore important, since it has also been shown that: 'Individuals vary greatly in their ability to use such tactics. Research findings indicate that such differences are related to success in a wide variety of occupations' (Baron and Markman, 2000: 109). This chapter navigates the large and complex terrain of persuasion, and identifies the central components thereof.

In terms of definition, while the terms 'influence' and 'persuasion' are often viewed as synonyms and used interchangeably, in fact there are three main differences between the two processes.

1   *Resistance.* Sanders and Fitch (2001) argued that persuasion is used to attempt to overcome some level of resistance to the message, and as such 'is a means of influencing resistant others ... to adopt a new conviction that what is being solicited is a desirable or good thing' (p. 263). They argued that persuasion is influence when there is resistance. On the other hand, influence *per se* 'is achieved by offering inducements that make it expedient or self-interested in the moment for that particular target person to do what is being asked, given his or her existing convictions and dispositions' (p. 263). They also made the important point that 'not everything is a *persuadable*' (p. 268). Persuadable actions are those *that are not obligatory*, and as such there may well be resistance to what is being suggested. In similar vein, Johnston (1994: 7) defined persuasion as 'a voluntary change in beliefs, attitudes and/or behaviors'. Another feature here is that for actions to be persuadable *they should not be proscribed*, so that compliance is possible. For example, our head of school at university would not be expected to have to persuade us to come to work – it is part of our contractual obligations. The head would also be unlikely to try to persuade us to carry out a proscribed action, such as robbing a bank in order to obtain finances to help improve our school's financial situation. However, persuasion techniques could be employed to try to encourage us to run a communication consultancy course for businesspersons to bring in additional income.

2   *Conscious awareness.* While influence may take place at a subconscious level, persuasion is carried out with clear and deliberate intent. For example, a film star who wears a certain brand of T-shirt on a TV show may *influence* young people to purchase a similar product, without consciously intending so to do. However, if the same film star had agreed to appear in a TV advert to promote this brand of T-shirt, then it would have been quite clear that a *persuasion* attempt was being made. Given this aspect of intentionality, interpersonal persuasion has been defined as 'the conscious manipulation of face-to-face communication to induce others to take action' (Robbins and Hunsaker, 1996: 110). Taking this line of thought further, persuasion always involves influence, but influence does not always involve persuasion. This distinction was recognised in the definition proffered by Hybels and Weaver (1998: 458):

'*Persuasion* is the process that occurs when a communicator (sender) influences the values, beliefs, attitudes or behaviour of another person (receiver).'

3   *Success*. A final difference between the two terms is that persuasion is successful influence. As O'Keefe (2002: 3) pointed out, 'the notion of success is embedded in the concept of persuasion'. Thus it does not make sense to say 'I persuaded them to do it but they didn't.' However, it is possible to say 'I influenced them but they still didn't do it.' Here, the person is indicating a shift or softening in attitude, but a failure at the behavioural level. In this way, influencing is often incremental, leading to eventual change, whereas persuasion usually refers to a specific change attempt. Thus when parents perceive someone to be a 'bad influence' on their child, they believe that over a period of time this person will effect negative changes and that their son or daughter will eventually be led astray.

A distinction has also been made between 'hard' and 'gentle' persuasion. Pratkanis (2001) illustrated how in democratic societies *deliberative persuasion* is central. This involves debate, discussion, deliberation, argument and analysis – the process is two-way. By contrast in authoritarian or autocratic regimes, leaders assume they know what others should think or want, and persuasion in the form of propaganda is employed to convince them that this is the case. In this latter form of *dictatorial persuasion*, communication is one-way and debate or dissent is discouraged. Deliberative persuasion has been shown to have the benefits of stimulating creative problem-solving, fostering relationships and trust between individuals, and developing greater consent for and commitment to what are regarded as group decisions. Dictatorial persuasion, on the other hand, results in an over-reliance on the leader to make decisions and give guidance, and a reduction in individual initiative. Members have much less commitment to decisions imposed on them to which they feel no sense of ownership. It also leads to hostility and distrust, making long-term group effort and relationships difficult to sustain. These findings have obvious ramifications for organisations, in that employees will respond more favourably to deliberative than to dictatorial forms of persuasion.

FUNCTIONS OF PERSUASION

As noted by Johnston (1994), the goal of persuasion can take many forms. To take but five examples, it may include:

1   The elimination of an existing belief (e.g. that smoking is not bad for one's health).
2   A change in strength of an existing belief (e.g. from the first position to one where it is accepted that heavy smoking can be bad for one's health).
3   The creation of a new belief (e.g. moving further from the second position to believing that smoking is definitely bad for one's health).
4   A change in intention to carry out an action (e.g. saying 'I now definitely intend to stop smoking').
5   A change in actual behaviour (e.g. stopping smoking).

In general terms, the six main functions of persuasion are as shown in Box 12.1.

Box 12.1 The six main purposes of persuasion

1 *Adoption.* Here the aim is to encourage targets to develop new responses – that is to persuade them to *start doing or believing something*. Thus a doctor may encourage an overweight individual to begin a diet or start an exercise regime, and to accept that weight loss will lead to better health.

2 *Continuance.* The objective here is to encourage targets to *keep doing or believing something* at their current level of commitment. For example, if a sports team is top of their league, the main goal of persuasion would be maintenance of performance. Likewise, one goal of a priest should be to encourage devout members of his or her parish to maintain their faith.

3 *Improvement.* The objective here is to get the target to perform at a higher level than at present. In other words, to get them to *do something better or have an increased level of belief.* The former is a common key goal of most educationalists. Thus one reason we give our university students detailed feedback on their coursework is so that their next assignment will improve accordingly.

4 *Deterrence.* Conversely, the objective may be to persuade targets not to develop a particular behaviour, so that they *do not start doing or believing something.* Indeed, this is the aim of many health education campaigns geared towards young people – to encourage them not to take up activities such as smoking, drug taking or drink driving, and not to form the view that such activities are 'cool'.

5 *Discontinuance.* In this instance the goal is to get targets to desist from a current response – to persuade them to *stop doing or believing something.* This can often be the most difficult task for the persuader. Once behaviour patterns and beliefs have been learned they become resistant to change. For example, before new patterns of working can be introduced in an organisation, old practices have to be stopped. This is frequently the most difficult aspect of such change. Humans are creatures of habit, and it is hard to 'unlearn' habituated patterns of behaviour and established belief systems.

6 *Reduction.* Where it is deemed that targets may not be able to completely cease a certain action, the goal may be to encourage them to cut down and *do it less or believe it less strongly.* For example, it would be preferable if someone smoked ten cigarettes a day rather than twenty, or drank three pints of beer as opposed to six. In similar vein, an anorexic may be encouraged to believe that it is not good to be quite so thin.

THE PERSUASION PROCESS

Figure 12.1 illustrates how the process of persuasion involves one person, the influencing 'agent', attempting to alter the beliefs, feelings, knowledge or behaviour of another, the 'target'. This has four main outcomes.

- *Instant success.* It can be immediately effective, resulting in the intended changes to the target's beliefs, feelings, knowledge or behaviour.
- *No change.* The target may simply reject the persuasion attempt and continue with the current response.
- *Increased resistance.* There may not only be no change, but the target may also become very resistant to any future persuasion attempts from this agent. This process is referred to as the *boomerang effect*, which has been defined as 'an unintended situation in which the speaker and the message induce an audience response that is the opposite of what the speaker intended' (Pearson and Nelson, 2000: 441). In this way, a flawed attempt to persuade can backfire by strengthening the original position rather than changing it. Some degree of resistance by the target is a common feature of many persuasion attempts and

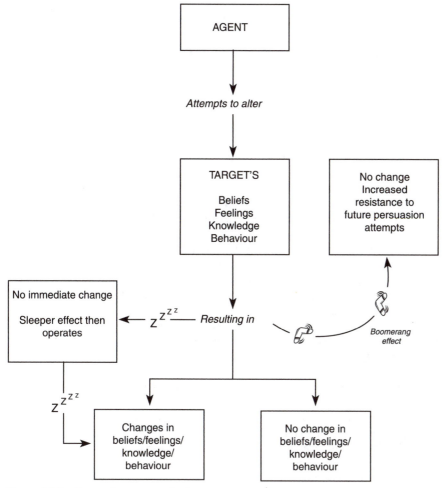

Figure 12.1 Persuasive communication: process and outcomes

ways of overcoming this must be formulated by the agent to ensure success (Knowles *et al.*, 2001).

- *Delayed success.* There may be a time delay before the attempt proves successful. Here, a phenomenon known as the *sleeper effect* occurs. As described by Allen and Stiff (1998: 176), 'The term *sleeper* derives from an expectation that the long-term effect is larger than the short-term effect in some manner (the effect is asleep but awakes to be effective later).' For example, a target may initially reject a persuasion attempt and yet some weeks or months later begin to accept it. This effect often involves a separation between source and message. Thus a message from a low credibility source is likely to be rejected at the outset. With the passage of time, however, the message is further processed and also becomes decoupled from its original source. The message content itself is remembered and becomes important – the source is now irrelevant. The target begins to say things like 'I've changed my mind on that' or 'It's not quite so clear cut as I used to think'. Allen and Stiff (1998), in their meta-analysis of research studies, confirmed the existence of this sleeper effect.

Another important aspect to note here is that even if persuasion attempts are not immediately successful in effecting actual changes in behaviour, they can still have a number of useful benefits. For example, Ohme (2001) itemised five positive effects of media influence attempts.

1   A clearer perception of reality. Thus, although many still smoke, most citizens of western countries (including smokers) are now aware of the health risks associated with smoking as a result of media campaigns.
2   An increased awareness of the issue in general, and possible enhanced receptivity to future messages on this topic. If you are a heavy drinker, messages about possible liver damage may not stop you drinking immediately, but could make you listen more carefully to such messages in the future.
3   Self-initiated information-seeking about the topic – the wish to know more about it. Opportunities to read articles or watch TV programmes about the topic may be more likely to be taken once an initial interest has been stirred.
4   The stimulation of issue-related discussions with significant others. There can be an increased desire to ascertain what family, friends and work colleagues think of the issue.
5   The reinforcement of existing positive behaviour. For instance, health information messages about the importance of regular exercise reward those who currently take such exercise and encourage them to continue.

While the first four of these may not produce instant results, they can contribute to a 'slow burn' effect, resulting in later behavioural change.

Targets can also be encouraged to become more resistant to persuasion messages. There are two main methods whereby this can be achieved.

The first is *forewarning*. This relates to the process wherein the target audience is told something about the person or message they are about to encounter. The forewarning can come (a) from the speaker, or (b) from someone who introduces this person, and so takes one of two forms, respectively:

a *A persuasion intent statement.* This tells the target that a persuasion attempt is about to be made (e.g. 'I am going to present evidence to support the view that all drugs should be decriminalised.').

b *A topic and position statement.* This informs the target about the issue about to be presented and where the speaker stands on this (e.g. 'I now wish to introduce Jo Fleming, a well-known supporter of animal rights, who hopes to convince you of the view that it is not just unethical to kill animals for food, but that it is also wrong to keep them as pets.').

One issue that is linked to forewarning is whether or not there is any delay between warning and message delivery. In a meta-analysis of research in this field, the main conclusion reached by Benoit (1998: 146) was that: 'Forewarning an audience to expect a persuasive message tends to make that message less persuasive ... regardless of type of warning ... (or) presence of delay.' Interestingly, Benoit found that to be effective the warning must come *before* the persuasion attempt. A message does not lose its persuasiveness if the warning is given *after* it has been delivered. Thus it is not the information *per se* that affects persuasiveness, it is the forewarning. In this sense, prevention is essential. It appears that when targets are forewarned they adopt a less receptive frame of mind and become more resistant to the perceived 'interference'. For people who have to address an audience that has been forewarned, Benoit recommended the following five compensatory techniques to attempt to overcome such resistance:

1 be introduced by a credible third person;
2 stress a lack of personal bias on the issue;
3 ask the audience to keep an open mind;
4 emphasise that both sides of the argument have been given due consideration;
5 state that the target's best interests were considered – not just the speaker's.

Two 'reverse psychology' approaches can also be employed in attempting to overcome resistance (Box 12.2). The main lesson, however, is that it is best not to have a forewarned target when making a persuasion attempt.

The second method is *inoculation.* This is a stronger form of forewarning as it actively prepares targets to refute the messages that will be received. Inoculation can be affective or cognitive. Emotional inoculation messages consist of 'affect-laden words, anecdotes, and opinionated statements' whereas cognitive inoculation messages are objective in tone with 'verifiable, falsifiable information, such as statistics, facts, and research findings' (Peau *et al.*, 2001: 217). Inoculation attempts consist of two main components: the first at the affective level and the second at the cognitive.

1 *Threat.* This involves warning the target about the imminent attack on their attitudes or beliefs. All inoculation attempts have been shown to include threat, which in turn acts as a wake-up call for resistance. Thus the objective is to mobilise targets to realise that their beliefs are about to be challenged, and to motivate them to pay attention to ways of dealing with it. This is the *antici-patory warning* stage of inoculation, when the emotions are stirred and the target is motivated towards action.

Box 12.2 Reverse psychology methods for overcoming resistance

1   *Co-opting.* This is a method of attempting to minimise rejection by openly recognising it in advance (e.g. by saying 'Your first reaction is likely to be to reject what I am about to say'). In such instances an appeal for *suppression* is useful. Here, the target audience is asked to suppress the instinctive denial response (e.g. 'I would like you to try to avoid the natural impulse of immediately rejecting what I am about to say to you. Please hear me out and then make a judgement about what I have said').

2   *Paradoxical injunction.* This involves making a suggestion about the target person's future behaviour, but then indicating that perhaps it would be expecting too much and that the person might not be up to the task just yet (e.g. 'I am not sure you have reached the point where you feel you could do this. I'm worried about asking too much of you'). This is a motivational technique in that the goal is to encourage the target to react to the perceived weakness by 'showing' the agent that the apparent lack of faith in their ability is misplaced and becoming motivated to complete the suggested behaviour. The use of paradoxical injunction is best when a relationship has been established, so that the stated lack of belief in the target's ability is seen in a caring light. However, with people of low self-esteem or low self-efficacy this approach needs to be used with care, as they may take the apparent lack of belief in their capability as a confirmation of their low level of worth or ability.

---

2   *Refutational pre-emption.* Here, the likely future arguments with which the target will be faced are detailed, and counter-arguments are provided to refute each of these. This is the *anticipatory coping* stage, and it is at the epicentre of inoculation. It has been shown that the more effort that targets devote to the development of counter-arguments to possible future challenges, by engaging in what has been termed *cognitive work*, the greater is their resistance to later counter-persuasion attempts (Peau *et al.*, 2001). One technique that can be used at this stage is that of *rote learning*. Many religions and cults get members to rote learn sets of beliefs, prayers, and key statements (e.g. Biblical passages) so that they become embedded in their psyche, and as such very resistant to change. As part of this process, it is possible to get individuals to rote learn refutational arguments against future counter-messages. A related tactic here is that of *anchoring*, which involves connecting the forthcoming new message to an already established belief or set of values. It then becomes difficult to change one without the other. For example, a Roman Catholic priest discovers that a student in his parish will later hear a lecture from a pro-choice speaker on the rights of women to decide what to do with their own bodies. He may then attempt to 'anchor' the student by connecting the belief (a) that good and devout Catholics value the sanctity and sacredness of all life, to (b) an opposition to the future message in support of abortion.

Another form of pre-emption has been termed *stealing thunder*, and it involves disclosing incriminating evidence about oneself or one's client, rather than have this revealed by someone else. For instance, defence lawyers in court will tell the jury negative facts about their client rather than giving the prosecuting attorney the opportunity to capitalise on this later. This gives the impression of openness and honesty. It also inoculates the target and so draws much of the poison from the sting of the potentially harmful detail. In their analysis of this phenomenon, Williams and Dolnik (2001) pointed out that stealing thunder is part of the process of *dissuasion*, which involves persuading people not to be swayed by something that could otherwise be influential. Their review of research concluded that: 'Stealing thunder has been shown to be an effective method of minimizing the impact of damaging information in a variety of different contexts' (p. 228).

STEPS TO SUCCESSFUL PERSUASION

A number of what are known as *stage theories* have been put forward to explain the persuasion process (Weinstein and Sandman, 2002). These conceptualise a range of stages or steps that need to be gone through for the overall process to be successful. The most widely employed of these is the *transtheoretical model of change* initially developed by Prochaska and DiClemente (1992). This envisages five main stages.

1   *Precontemplation.* Here the person is not thinking about changing current behaviour or starting a new behaviour. There is no intention to change.
2   *Contemplation.* At this stage the person has been made aware of the issue and thought about the process of change, but is still ambivalent. No decision has been made about whether or not to act. Part of the person may want to change while another part does not. Change is always difficult (and even frightening), and so it does not happen without psychological upheaval.
3   *Preparing.* If the person decides that the benefits of change outweigh the costs, a decision is made to change. Preparations then have to be made to cope with this. Strategies need to be formulated about when, where and how the new response will be carried out. It may also involve publicly informing others about the intention to change.
4   *Action.* This is the implementation phase, when the person is actively involved in an overt attempt to carry out the behaviour. Others may need to be reminded that the new pattern of behaviour has deliberately been adopted, and is not an aberration.
5   *Maintenance.* Once a change has been made there is then the challenge of maintaining it. Behaviour change may meet with resistance from significant others and the person has to deal with this – to the extent of even altering friendship patterns.

A sequential model of the five stages is shown in Figure 12.2. Here it can be seen that the main outcomes of either behaviour change or no behaviour change are dependent on whether or not there is progression through each stage. It is also acknowledged that even after the response has been implemented, relapse can take

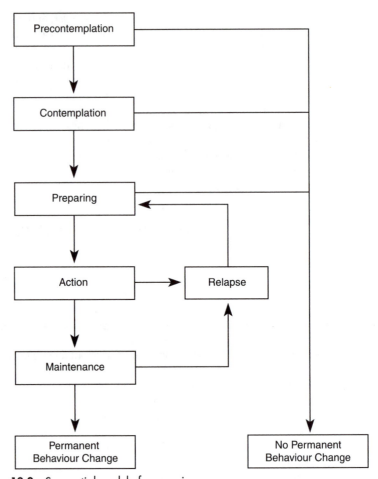

Figure 12.2 Sequential model of persuasion

place. Where relapse occurs the individual either again prepares for action, or reverts to the former response pattern and abandons the new one. As explained in Chapter 10, after making an important decision individuals are affected by the process of *cognitive dissonance*, as doubts and anxiety are experienced about whether the decision was correct. This dissonance is eventually resolved in one of two ways. People can either become convinced that the decision was correct and so stay with it, or alternatively decide that a wrong decision was made and relapse to the former state of affairs. For effective persuasion, the target must be convinced in the long term about the rectitude of the decision taken.

A more fine-grained twelve-step sequential analysis of persuasion was presented by McGuire (1981), involving:

1 exposure to the message;
2 attending to the message;

3   becoming interested in it;
4   understanding it;
5   learning how to process and use it;
6   yielding to it;
7   memorising it;
8   retrieving it when required;
9   using it when making decisions;
10 executing these decisions;
11 reinforcing these actions;
12 consolidating the decision based on the success of the actions.

While each of these stages is important, they can be condensed into five main steps (Figure 12.3). First, the message must be *attended to* if it is to have any impact. However, as summarised by Buller and Hall (1998: 155) in their review of research into this stage:

> attention to persuasive messages is far from guaranteed; it is unstable, fickle, and capricious. Persuasive messages compete for receiver's consideration with other messages, environmental cues, and internal responses. As a result some messages receive detailed examination, whereas others remain ignored or only partially processed.

Buller and Hall investigated two types of distraction.

1   *Communication-irrelevant distractions.* These are stimuli extraneous to the interactive process that shift attention away from the speaker (e.g. intrusive noise). These lessen the power of persuasive appeals.
2   *Communication-relevant distractions.* This refers to stimuli intrinsic to the communication process (e.g. speaker attributes). Buller and Hall found that when the distraction focused on positive aspects (e.g. attractiveness) persuasion was enhanced. However if attention was paid to negative features (e.g. poor speech pattern) persuasibility diminished.

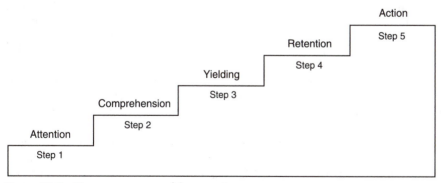

Figure 12.3   Five steps to successful persuasion

The second step in the model shown in Figure 12.3 is that the target person must understand fully what is being said. The importance of message delivery in ensuring *comprehension* will be discussed in more depth later in the chapter. Third, the message must be accepted, in that the person has to *yield* to it. This is at the heart of persuasion, and much of this chapter is concerned with techniques whereby acceptance can be encouraged. Fourth, the target has to *retain* or remember the message. Finally, the acid test is whether the person *carries out the action* and implements the recommended response. As discussed in Chapter 2, attitudes encompass three elements, often referred to as the 'ABC' of attitudes:

- *A*ffect – one's feeling and emotions regarding the object of the attitude.
- *B*ehaviour – how one actually behaves towards the other.
- *C*ognitions – the thoughts beliefs, knowledge, etc. one has concerning that under focus.

Long-term changes in behaviour usually necessitate changes in the other two aspects. An important distinction has been made between *private acceptance*, which produces attitude change, and *public compliance* where the person complies with what is being recommended but does not really change inner beliefs or feelings (Hargie *et al.*, 1999). Retention and implementation of new responses are dependent on private acceptance.

COGNITIVE ROUTES TO PERSUASION

Dual process models of persuasion posit the existence of two cognitive routes in the processing of persuasive messages. The *elaboration likelihood model* (Petty and Cacioppo, 1986) identified these as:

1   *Central route*. Here the target is aware that a persuasion attempt is being made, and consciously examines the advantages and disadvantages of incoming information. The pros and cons are carefully weighed up before a final decision is taken. As summarised by Griffin (1997: 217), 'It's an attempt to process the new information rationally.' The *cognitive-response model* (Wright, 1980) demonstrated how individuals using this rational approach relate incoming material to existing knowledge and beliefs. For a persuasion attempt to be successful the message must receive a favourable evaluation during this cognitive elaboration process.

2   *Peripheral route*. Here, information tends to be processed at a subconscious level, and the target is not aware that a persuasion attempt is being made. There is scant analysis or scrutiny of message content, and the response is more intuitive. The emotional state of the target is important since, as shown in Box 12.3, it has been found that people in a happy or positive mood are less likely to systematically process messages via the central route than are those in a sad or negative state (Mitchell, 2000). Thus establishing a sense of 'feel-good' in the target encourages peripheral processing.

Box 12.3 Negative and positive mood and persuasion

Negative mood is associated with:

- central processing of information;
- a cognitive, systematic style of argument processing;
- more time spent on the evaluation of persuasive appeals;
- stronger arguments being more successful than weaker ones;

Positive mood is associated with:

- peripheral processing of persuasion attempts;
- a passive, less rational approach to the evaluation of information;
- much more rapid processing of incoming information;
- no differential being made between weak and strong arguments.

For example, a television advertisement may sell a particular brand of car by presenting details of its price and features and systematically comparing these with its rivals (central route strategy). An alternative approach would be to show very attractive people having fun as they drive the car past charming locations in bright sunshine under a blue cloudless sky, with a popular soundtrack playing in the background, and ending with a shot of the car and a voice-over stating: 'It's out there' (peripheral route strategy). The latter is an attempt to plant a subconscious association between the car, being happy, and being part of the beautiful people 'set'. If this were processed centrally the viewer would be asking questions such as: 'What does it mean to say that it's out there?' or 'How does buying this car bring with it a guarantee that I will be driving it with a beautiful young person sitting beside me?' However, the fact is that most TV advertisements are not centrally processed, but rather are dealt with through the peripheral route. They are successful because they hit us at the more vulnerable subconscious level.

Message processing is moderated by the cognitive ability and motivation of the target (Mitchell, 2000). To take an example, there is a greater likelihood that those who have undergone third level education will centrally evaluate the arguments being presented by a politician, while those with a basic education may be more influenced by a feeling of whether or not they like this person. However, if the better educated target has no interest whatsoever in politics then the likelihood of peripheral processing is increased. An important difference between the two routes is that attitudes formed via the central route are more persistent over time and more resistant to change (Haugtvedt and Petty, 1992). This is because the individual has thought through the process and made a conscious decision that is then likely to influence behaviour directly over a prolonged period. Attempts to change attitudes that have been formed as a result of a cognitive elaboration process are therefore more easily dealt with, as the counter-arguments will have already been given consideration. By contrast, decisions taken via the peripheral route have been made without careful thought, and so are more vulnerable to counter-arguments. As summarised by Quine *et al.* (2002: 176) '"central route" processing produces attitudes that have temporal persistence and are predictive of behaviour and resistant to change, while peripheral route processing is typified by absence of argument scrutiny and produces only temporary attitude change'.

At the same time, it should be noted that the peripheral route is ubiquitous in human encounters. Cialdini (2001) argued that the fixed-action patterns that guide the behaviour of most animals also occur in humans. In other words, our behaviour becomes hard-wired and we respond without thinking. We do not have the time or cognitive space to analyse and evaluate the hundreds of persuasion attempts that impinge on us every day. As a result we make shortcut decisions to save time and energy. These decisions are, in turn, guided by a set of core processes that directly influence our behaviour and are for the most part based on valid reasoning. Such behaviour-guiding templates are the keys that can unlock the doors to persuasibility in others. To use another metaphor, they are the triggers that fire compliance behaviours. As such, people can be manipulated by their use. For example, the aphorism that 'you get what you pay for' is usually true. The more you pay for a car, a hotel room, or a watch, the better it is likely to be. Thus we expect to pay more for the best. Knowing that this is the case, a sharp operator may take advantage of the 'more-expensive-is-best' short circuit process in potential buyers by inflating the price of goods to make them appear to be of higher quality.

In interpersonal encounters much of what persuades us is processed peripherally. For example, we do not consciously rate others on their level of attractiveness, and are not aware on a moment-by-moment basis whether another person is smiling, is humorous, stands close to us, uses our first name, praises us, and so on. These behaviours are processed via the peripheral route, but they all affect the outcome of persuasion attempts. Likewise, if we go to the bar with someone and they buy us a drink, we do not usually consciously think that we are in debt to this person and must reciprocate. Rather we naturally feel this pressure and so the likelihood is that the reciprocation auto-pilot kicks in and we buy the next round. Indeed, if we become aware that a direct attempt is being made to persuade us to do something, we begin to process information centrally. Then we may become suspicious of the smiles and praise we are receiving or wonder why this person is offering us something with no obligation. In such circumstances a compliance attempt is likely to boomerang.

PERSUASION PROOFS

The study of persuasion has a long tradition. The classical era of scholarship in this field ran from 500 BC to AD 300, and included notable scholars such as Plato, Aristotle, Cicero and Quintellian. It was the Greek philosopher Aristotle who provided the first detailed analysis of persuasion. He identified three main persuasion categories:

1   *Ethos* – Here the credibility of the persuader is highlighted.
2   *Logos* – Here the rationality of the message is focused on.
3   *Pathos* – This involves appeals to the emotions of the target.

These are now known respectively as *personal proofs*, *logical proofs* and *emotional proofs*, although it should be realised that they are not functionally discrete categories as there are areas of overlap between them, and they are interlinked. During persuasion attempts, techniques from each area can be used in combination, and indeed Aristotle believed that the most effective appeals contain a balanced mix of the three. However, for the purposes of analysis we will now examine each separately.

Personal proofs

One of the most important parts of the persuasion equation is the nature of the agent. In order to be persuaded we first have to be convinced of the *bona fides* of the person who is trying to persuade us. There are four main determinants of personal proof: power, the relationship, attractiveness and humour.

Power

The relationship between power and persuasion is reflected in the definition of power as 'the amount of influence that one person can exercise over another' (Georgesen and Harris, 1998: 185). The persuasive force of power has long been recognised. Henry Kissinger famously claimed that 'Power is the great aphrodisiac', but whatever the truth of this particular assertion it is clear that power is a core determinant for gaining compliance in many contexts. As noted by Tourish and Wohlforth (2000: 23) 'human behavior is driven by an impulse to *conform to authority*'. It is therefore hardly surprising that agents are likely to use any power they possess to ensure such conformity. Hargie *et al.* (1999: 34) pointed out that '"The Iron Law of Power" means that people with great power tend to wield it when necessary, to get their own way.' Thus, while power may not be the first shot fired in a battle of wills, it will be brought into play at some stage to ensure compliance. Given its importance, it is not surprising that we are influenced by the power of the source. But how, and in what ways?

This question can best be answered by examining the classic delineation of types of power initially identified by French and Raven (1959), that then became the accepted standard in the field (Raven, 1992). This includes six forms of power. The first three of these (legitimate, reward and coercive) emanate from the ability of the agent to determine and control the target person's outcomes. The last three (information, referent and expert) are purely to do with influence and here the target makes a willing decision to co-operate.

Legitimate power

In essence, the bases of this power are rights and duties. Some people, by virtue of their position, have a legitimate right to request certain types of compliance from others, who in turn have a duty to comply. The power resides in the position. The holder of the power is *in authority*. Thus a police office has considerable power over citizens. If requested by a police officer in uniform to move our car we are much more likely to comply than if asked by someone dressed in casual clothes. But the power only remains while performing the job, so that when the officer is off duty, or has retired, this is relinquished. Legitimate power is attached to the role, not the person. It is also limited to the functions of the role. For instance, the security guard in the building where we work may legitimately ask us for identification, but has no power to request that we work overtime. In addition, this is a two-way street. Both managers and subordinates wield legitimate power. While the former have the authority to direct and control the latter as they perform their job, the latter can insist that set procedures be carried out by the former in accordance with statutory requirements (e.g. selection or appraisal interviews). Indeed the introduction of initiatives such as the Patients' Charter, Citizens' Charter, and Bill of Rights, have empowered those who formerly had little such formal, legitimate, authority. Interestingly, people often excuse their behaviour on the basis that someone with legitimate power told them to carry it out. The ultimate example of this was the defence plea of the Nazi leaders at the Nuremberg war crime trials following the Second World War: 'I was only following orders.'

Reward power

Those who have control over the administration of rewards wield considerable power. There is much truth in the maxim that 'what gets rewarded gets done'. As discussed in Chapter 4, the impact of reinforcement on performance is both far-reaching and ubiquitous. This is learned from a very early age. Young children soon realise that parents have control over valued resources, and that they often have to carry out certain tasks in order to receive these. They also quickly learn that they, too, have similar power over parents and so begin to trade rewards (e.g. 'If I get an A-grade will you buy me a bicycle?'). Throughout life, those who are the controllers of the rewards that we seek have power over us. Thus lecturers have reward power over students, as do employers over employees. However, again this is a two-way process. Employees can reward their employer by working harder, and students their professors by turning up for class and appearing motivated. Social rewards such as praise are potent forms of power (see chapter 4 for a full discussion of rewardingness).

Coercive power

Those who are able to administer punishments also have considerable power. To continue with our earlier example, police officers possess this form of power, and we are therefore likely to obey their request to, for example, move our car from a restricted parking zone. We know that if we do not we are likely to receive a fine. There is a symbiotic relationship between reward and coercive power. Usually someone who can reward us can *ipso facto* also punish us (e.g. by withholding the rewards). Thus, parents can both reward their children (e.g. by allowing them to stay up late to watch a TV programme) and punish them (e.g. by sending them to bed early). However, we tend to like those who reward us and dislike those who threaten or punish us. It is therefore wise to remember the advice proffered by Machiavelli in *The Prince*, written in 1514, that those in power should 'delegate to others the enactment of unpopular measures and keep in their own hands the distribution of favours' (Bull, 1961: 106).

One reason for this is that the norm of exchange means that those who have been punished are likely to seek retribution, while those who have been rewarded seek to reciprocate the favours they have received.

Information power

Here, the content of the message is the basis of the power. Those who are 'in the know' are in a privileged position. The holders of information that is 'inside', 'top secret', 'classified', etc. have considerable power – they can keep this secret or share it with others. Indeed, bribery and blackmail are based on the fact that someone has access to information that they know someone else wishes either to find out or to remain hidden, respectively. Some managers adopt a policy where they inform employees purely on a 'need to know' basis. In other words, they only tell them what they need to know to do their job. The problem here is that staff also have access to vital information (e.g. that a piece of production equipment is about to malfunction) and they may retaliate by withholding this from management who adopt such an approach. Research consistently shows that employees value managers who share as much information with them as they can (Tourish and Hargie, 2000). If information is power, then this power should be used benignly within organisations. Information can be powerful in another way. If I want you to stop smoking, I could give you some material to read that clearly documents the dangers of this practice. This may then persuade you to change your attitude towards smoking. Where the information is perceived to be objective and accurate and includes statistical details (e.g. the percentage of smokers compared with non-smokers who contract serious illnesses) its potency is heightened (Allen *et al.*, 2000).

Referent power

This relates to the power of our reference group. Here, we are influenced by reference to those we identify with, like, and to whose group we aspire. The widely used marketing technique of product endorsement by well-known and popular personalities is a good example of the use of referent power. In many cases the celebrity has no real knowledge of or insight into the product being endorsed, but this does not negatively impact on the power of the message. Sorenson *et al.* (2001) used the term *misplaced authority* to refer to the use of celebrities to endorse specialised products in this way. One example is the use of an actor who plays the role of a doctor in a TV series being used to advertise and recommend a medical product. The actor has no actual medical expertise or authority but there is an implicit or inferred link planted in the target's mind.

In similar vein, hotels and restaurants often have signed photographs of great and good clients prominently displayed. The implication is that to be in such an establishment is to be in with the 'in crowd'. Salespeople use another form of reference power termed *ubiquity technique* when they tell a target that many relevant and significant others are now using a particular item. Research has shown that this process of using *social proof* to validate the acceptability of a product or behaviour, by dint of the fact that it is used by significant others, is a highly effective compliance-gaining technique (Cialdini, 2001). Thus sports stars are paid fortunes just to wear or use a certain product, as the producers know this will trigger enormous referent group sales from those who wish to emulate their hero. This became known as the *wannabe phenomenon*, after the thousands of teenage girls who wanted to be like the pop star Madonna (Hargie *et al.*, 1999).

Among teenagers, referent power in the form of peer pressure is particularly potent. As mentioned in Chapter 9, at this age the need to be accepted by peers is at its strongest, and so certain types of fashion simply *must* be followed. When this is compounded by the fact that the attachment to referent media symbols (music, sports and film stars) is at a high level, the potential for manipulation is huge. Managers of male pop music stars have long realised the value of this human phenomenon. A few planted female fans beginning to scream at a concert sets the example for the rest so that a cacophony of screaming soon ensues. As expressed by Cialdini (2001: 140) 'one important means that people use to decide what to believe or how to act in a situation is to look at what other people are believing or doing there'. Interestingly, this means that the young females then have a high level of involvement in the occasion and so do not evaluate it critically through the central route (e.g. they do not study the extent to which the singers are singing in tune). Peripheral processing is dominant as they enjoy their heightened emotionality, and rate the concert to be a great success. All of this in turn leads to increased merchandising sales (CDs, T-shirts, posters, etc.).

Referent power is most potent under two conditions. First, if we are *uncertain* about how to behave in a situation we tend to look to members of our reference group for guidance, and copy what they do. Second, we are more likely to be influenced by *similar* others. For example, if a female teenager goes to a party where all the females are dancing in a group, while the males are sitting round a table, she is more likely to join the dancing group. This is part of the wider process of *conformity* in groups. While this will be discussed in more depth in Chapter 14, it is worth noting here that when we are in the presence of others, there is strong overt or covert pressure to agree with the views of the majority, and follow group norms. Two needs guide our behaviour in such circumstances – the need to be accepted and the need to know what is the right thing to do (Aronson *et al.*, 2002). These are powerful determinants in shaping our attitudes and behaviour.

In a classic study in this field, Sherif (1936) used the *autokinetic phenomenon* (where a tiny bulb in a pitch black room appears to move if stared at for a few minutes) to study conformity. The bulb does not actually move, since this is an illusion caused by neural processes and unconscious eye movements. Sherif asked subjects to estimate the distance the bulb had moved. Interestingly, two things happened. First, after some discussion, groups eventually reached agreement about the movement distance. Second, different groups differed widely in their estimates. Furthermore, once an estimate had been agreed on it became internalised and resistant to change. Consequently, when a member from a group with a previously 'socially anchored' score was placed in a new group, they persisted with the estimate they had developed in their initial group. In this way, the reference group score was internalised and influenced future behaviour. The fact that the subjects had participated in formulating the norm meant that they were more committed to the decision. An interesting real-life variant of Sherif's experiment occurred in the Republic of Ireland recently when people became convinced that statues outside churches were moving. This 'movement' was caused by the *autokinetic phenomenon*, but interestingly huge crowds gathered each evening and the massed throng convinced one another that a miracle was being witnessed.

In a second famous study on conformity, Asch (1952) had subjects publicly choose which one of three lines matched a fourth 'target' line in length. The task was very simple, so that when it was completed individually few subjects made any errors of judgement. However, by placing a naïve subject next to last in a line of confederates who all concurred on an incorrect choice of line, the pressure to conform could be measured. Asch found that only 25 per cent of subjects did not conform at all to the incorrect majority, while 33 per cent conformed on more than half of the trials. Some conformed on all the blatantly incorrect decisions. When interviewed later, those who conformed admitted that they disagreed with the others but felt under pressure to concur. In other words, the decision was not internalised, and so subjects demonstrated public compliance but not private acceptance. This was confirmed in an interesting reversal of the study procedures, in which Asch ran experiments where there was only one confederate who made the clearly incorrect decision on each trial. In these instances, the group of naïve subjects strongly affirmed the correctness of their decision and treated the single deviating confederate with bemusement and scorn.

Expert power

We live in the age of 'the expert'. In courtrooms, on TV screens, and in newspapers, expert sources are used to give a definitive perspective on issues. This is because people who are perceived to be experts, in that they have specialised knowledge or technical skill, have high persuasive power. Here the basis of the power is the extent to which the agent is seen as *an authority*. As shown in Box 12.4, this type of power is conveyed by what are known as the 'Three Ts' – titles, threads and trappings.

The acid test of expert power is credibility. Indeed, Clampitt (2001: 90) noted that 'every message has a kind of credibility tag attached to it that determines, to a large extent, how that message will be treated'. If the source of the message is regarded as lacking in credibility, then it will have little persuasive power. Thus Schutz (1998) showed how attacks on the credibility of a source who has negatively evaluated someone can serve to weaken the force of the criticism. Credibility in turn is based on two factors: competence and trustworthiness.

We judge competence based on the extent to which people 'know their stuff'. If we go to a store to buy a hi-fi system and the assistant keeps admitting insufficient knowledge of the technical details of the equipment and continually seeks advice from someone in the office, we will not see that person as being an expert, and so their advice will carry little power. Part of this is to do with confidence, in two senses. First, we need to be confident in the person's expertise. Second, the agent must behave in a confident manner. We would never be taken in by a 'no-confidence trickster'. The counter-balance to competence is trust. If someone is perceived to be highly competent but untrustworthy, their credibility rating drops dramatically. Trust may be based on our previous experience of the source, on what others have told us about

---

Box 12.4 The three Ts of expert power

1   *Titles* are ubiquitous across all societies (e.g. King, Chief, President, Emperor). Powerful people use them to set themselves apart from others. The power of titles is illustrated by the way they are sought and used. School children are introduced to them from an early age ('Principal' 'Vice Principal', etc.) and they acquire importance thereafter. In the UK, the 'Honours' system dispenses a huge range of titles every year (Lord, Lady, Sir, Member of the British Empire, etc.). These carry no monetary value but the social cache attached means that there is no shortage of people eager to accept them. Similarly, employees often work much longer hours for little or no more money just by being given a designated title such as 'Unit Co-ordinator'. In organisations, titles often reflect both the job level and expertise of the individual (e.g. 'Chief Technician'). Because we are so accustomed to the role of titles we give respect to those who hold important ones. Thus a 'Professor of Nuclear Physics' is perceived as having a high level of expertise in this field, and so will be more influential when speaking on this topic.

2   *Threads* refer to the specialised clothes worn by experts to set them apart from others. Examples abound – from the fire officer's uniform, to the vicar's black robes and white dog collar, to the 'power' suits worn by business people. While some of these clothes may be functional, for the most part their purpose is that of clearly setting the expert apart from the general populace.

3   *Trappings* are all the paraphernalia used to convey specialised knowledge or know-how. This encompasses framed certificates on the wall, specialist books on shelves, or sophisticated pieces of equipment. For example, for the layperson a visit to the dentist entails an encounter with a baffling array of all kinds of strange apparatus, including a special chair, unusual lights, frightening drills and various implements for probing, drilling, filling and extracting. All of these combine to convey the impression of a high level of expertness.

---

them, or on perceived neutrality. In relation to the latter, we will place more trust in a colleague who tells us that their new *Nevercrash* computer is superb, than in a highly competent salesperson in the *Nevercrash* store who gives us the same story. The former has no personal stake in selling the message and so is more credible.

Thus, in terms of expert power, we give less credence to those whom we regard as honest if they are incompetent, and tend to have lower trust in those with a vested interest regardless of their level of expertise. One highly influential event is when people argue against their own interest. For example, in the following statements we are more likely to be influenced by A than B.

A: I'm a meat eater myself, but I have read the research and it does show that a vegetarian diet is better for your health.

B: As a committed vegetarian I have read the research and it shows that a vegetarian diet is better for your health.

Staying with the vegetarian theme, on one occasion we, the authors, were at a conference and went to the local dining area for an evening meal. We were looking for vegetarian food, and tried a few restaurants without much luck. We then visited an Italian restaurant where, on explaining our requirements, the owner said she could certainly cater for us but she would recommend the Spanish restaurant in the same complex. We explained that we had been there and the waitress we had spoken to had told us they did not really do much in the way of vegetarian food. The owner said that was untrue as she knew the range of food and would commend it. Her demeanour was most helpful and she was knowledgeable about vegetarian cuisine, but she was also arguing against her own interest in terms of losing our business. The result was that we ended up staying in her restaurant for the meal. Our trust in her had increased as a result of her perceived lack of bias.

A meta-analytic review has shown that what is known as 'testimonial evidence' is an effective influencing technique (Reinhard, 1998). This refers to the use of factual statements and opinions of experts that support the speaker's message. A good example is the fact that in this book we have quoted hundreds of scholarly sources to back up our arguments. For this effect to be impactful, the supporting source must have high credibility and the evidence cited has to be believable. Interestingly, Reinhard also found that when people are in the middle of a discussion, the introduction of testimonial evidence serves to make the impact of this technique even more powerful. Thus it is useful to have relevant sources to hand to quote during discussions.

The relationship

We are much more likely to be influenced by those with whom we have developed a close relationship. In fact, the link between relationships and the persuasion process is the focus of one of the best selling popular self-help books in this field (having sold over 16 million copies): *How to win friends and influence people* by Dale Carnegie. It has long been known that the more similar people are the greater will be their liking for one another – this is termed the *law of attraction* (Byrne, 1971). Indeed, the phenomenon of *homophily* has been found to be of central importance in the communication process (Wolvin and Coakley, 1996). Homophily refers to the extent to which people share significant similarity in terms of aspects such as age, dress, appearance, cultural background, religion, political outlook, educational level, social status, habits, interests, beliefs, values, attitudes, etc. Just as birds of a feather flock together, so people who perceive themselves to share significant commonalities tend to form bonds more readily. In highlighting the potency of similarity as a potential influencing weapon, Cialdini (2001: 150–1) noted, 'those who want us to like them so that we will comply with them can accomplish that purpose by appearing similar to us in a wide variety of ways'. The opposite is *heterophily*, where individuals have major differences across these dimensions. In essence, the greater the heterophily the more difficult the influence process becomes.

In a meta-analysis of studies in the field, Miller *et al.* (2001) found that perceived similarity to another was associated with strong feelings of sympathy or empathy for them if they were in a difficult situation. However, this was moderated by whether or not the person was thought to be responsible for their predicament. Thus if an individual's need for help (e.g. money) is regarded as being due to external causes (e.g. being burgled) levels of sympathy and empathy are significantly higher than if the cause seems to be personal (e.g. spending too much on drink or drugs).

In addition to similarity, relational liking is improved by six other main factors.

1   Increased contact under positive circumstances. As we get to know people our liking for them tends to increase, providing this takes place within a conducive context.
2   Physical attractiveness. Beautiful people tend to be better liked than unattractive ones. This is discussed further later.
3   Association with success. Successful people act as a form of social magnet that attracts others. It is as if we are drawn to them in the hope that some of their glitter will rub off on us. We might be able to share in their success or be seen to be successful just by being with them. So powerful is this drive that people visit wax museums to look at and be photographed beside waxwork models of famous people.
4   Praise. We tend to like people who give us valued social rewards (see Chapter 4).
5   Use of less formal name. There is a whole psychology on the use of names, whether titles (Professor), formal address (Mr, Mrs), first name, pet name, or nickname. As relationships deepen, forms of address become less formal. Spouses rarely address one another by title, and more often use pet names (e.g. honey, sweetheart). Salespeople are usually trained to get on first name terms with clients as soon as possible to deepen the relationship. At the other end of the continuum, there is the process of *dehumanisation*. When individuals are not to be treated as humans the labels attributed to them reflect this. Thus terrorists use derogatory terms such as 'legitimate target' 'collaborator' or 'traitor' for those they plan to kill.
6   Eating together. As discussed by Hargie *et al.* (1999) food and drink are essential for human survival and we have an innate drive to seek and protect our sources of sustenance. Although food and drink are plentiful in the western world, the instinct remains. This means that we usually choose to eat, 'have a cuppa', or go for a drink, with people that we like and trust. The ubiquitous business breakfasts and lunches therefore serve a very useful function as part of the process of influence. They help to cement the bonds between people and thereby lubricate the flow of commerce.

As Hargie *et al.* (2000) found, the existence of a good relationship allows for the expression of negative emotions from professional to client (e.g. anxiety, frustration). For example, a patient who is trying to move away from drug abuse, and who perceives the health professional as someone who genuinely cares, is more likely to accept statements such as 'Look, what you are doing to yourself and your family is just awful. You are harming yourself and causing a great deal of grief to everyone who cares about you.' Indeed, when expressed in the context of a positive relationship, such statements of negative affect have been shown to be related to greater adherence to the advice and direction offered. This is because the communication of genuine concern is likely to be reciprocated by the wish of the target person to sustain the balance of the relationship, and so comply. The forceful delivery of negative messages from a liked and respected agent also serves to heighten the person's awareness of the gravity of their behaviour.

Attractiveness

As discussed in earlier chapters, good-looking people are well regarded. We are bombarded every day with images of attractiveness in newspapers, magazines and on cinema and TV screens. The media industry is well aware that beauty is popular and so sells well. Ugly film or pop stars are very much an exception. Furthermore, judgements of beauty are highly and universally consistent. In their review of research in this field, Little and Perrett (2002: 28) concluded 'Across many studies it has been found that there is a high degree of agreement from individuals within a particular culture, and high agreement between individuals from different cultures.' From a very early age, humans show a preference for good-looking others. In reviewing findings in this area, Hargie (1997b) showed how pre-school children have an aversion towards chubby individuals and a liking for physically attractive peers. He also found that those rated high in attractiveness were seen as friendlier, more intelligent, popular and interesting, received higher academic grades, were more likely to be approached for help by strangers, had more dates, better employment prospects and higher earning potential, and were less likely to be found guilty in court. The only down sides were that they were more likely to be viewed as vain, materialistic and prone to have extramarital affairs. Of particular interest here is that they are also rated as more persuasive – they have greater credibility, and are perceived to be higher in expertise, trustworthiness and likeability.

It is small wonder then that the sale of anything that enhances our attractiveness is a huge business. People buy all manner of items, including make-up, wigs and cosmetic surgery, in order to appear more beautiful. However, another reason for the above bonanza of benefits is that from an early age people react positively to physically attractive individuals, who, as a result, develop better interpersonal skills, self-esteem, confidence and optimism. As expressed by Johnston (1994: 155) 'it is not only the beauty, but also the social skills of attractive people that enhance their persuasiveness'. But one thing that the research clearly shows is that for individuals to optimise their persuasiveness they should maximise their attractiveness. It is also the case that initial judgements of physical attractiveness are moderated by psychological, sociological, relational and contextual influences (Duck, 1995). Features such as sense of humour, similarity to the other person, dress, scent, attentiveness, competence, and sensitivity, all affect overall ratings of attractiveness. These aspects can be employed by an influencing agent to make full use of the power of attraction.

Humour

Meyer (2000: 328) pointed out that the 'Use of humor clearly enhances one's leadership and persuasive influence because of the nearly universal admiration of this skill (in moderation – overuse of humor can lower credibility).' Humour has been found to be a

---

Box 12.5 Advantages of humour in persuasion

Humour can facilitate persuasion by:

- Building rapport and making the target more favourably disposed towards the agent – we like people who make us laugh and are therefore more likely to be influenced by them.
- Encouraging the target to attend more closely to the message – humour is engaging and increases our attentiveness.
- Producing in the target a feeling of relaxation and related increased receptivity to the message.
- Increasing retention by making the message more memorable.
- Filling cognitive space – if we are laughing we are not thinking of counter arguments.
- Encouraging peripheral rather than central processing of the message. The feel-good factor inculcated by humour is in itself persuasive.

---

key determinant of interpersonal attraction (Cann *et al.*, 1997). For instance, one study of dating behaviour in college students found that a good sense of humour was rated by both males and females as the most important feature of a member of the opposite sex (Buss, 1988). Humour facilitates persuasion in a number of ways (Bettinghaus and Cody, 1994; Foot, 1997), and these are summarised in Box 12.5. Research studies have found the use of humour by professionals to be effective across a wide range of settings including health care, education and management (Campbell *et al.*, 2001). However, the type of humour used is important, since sarcastic wits are regarded as influential but not popular, while clowning wits are seen as popular but not influential.

Logical proofs

Appeals to reason and logic are potent persuasive devices. Carefully constructed and forcefully delivered arguments, with clear premises leading to logical conclusions, are very persuasive. In this section we examine the six logical proofs that can be used to convince others of the rationality of one's position: message delivery, counter-attitudinal advocacy, case study, sidedness, request size and reciprocation.

Message delivery

In terms of delivery of arguments, these are more persuasive when there is a *powerful* speech style, where the person speaks in a firm, authoritative, tone, and uses intensifiers – i.e. words or phrases that magnify the potency of what is being communicated (e.g. 'definitely', 'absolutely', 'I can say without a shadow of doubt . . .'). By contrast, a *powerless* style is characterised by five main features:

1   hesitations ('Um ... ah ...');
2   hedges or qualifiers ('I sort of think ...' 'It might possibly be ...');
3   disclaimers ('I don't have any real knowledge of this area, however ...' 'I might be wrong, but ...');
4   tag questions ('... don't you think?' '... isn't it?'), and statements made with a questioning intonation;
5   lower voice volume.

If uncertainty has to be expressed, a powerful style employs *authoritative doubt*, which underlines that the dubiety is from a vantage point of expertise (e.g. 'I know the literature very well and the evidence is just not clear on that ...'). A powerless style accepts the blame for the uncertainty ('I'm not very well experienced in this ...'). In their meta-analytic review of research in this area, Burrell and Koper (1998) found that a powerful speech pattern was perceived to be more credible and persuasive. Likewise, in their analysis of this field, Holtgraves and Lasky (1999: 196) concluded: 'a speaker who uses powerless language will be perceived as less assertive, competent, credible, authoritative, and in general evaluated less favorably than a speaker who uses powerful language'. Holtgraves and Lasky also noted that speech power forms a continuum from low to high, so that degree of powerlessness may be important in determining impact. In other words, the occasional hesitation, hedge, tag question or lowered voice may have no impact on persuasiveness but a high number of each will.

While early work in this field suggested that there was a gender difference, in that males used a more powerful speech style whereas females tended to employ powerless speech, later studies refuted this (McFadyen, 1996). What seems to be the case is that females may *choose* to use powerless speech more often if they see this as being in line with the cultural norm or feminine style they wish to portray (Hargie, 1997b).

A related element of language intensity is the extent to which the message contains emotionality and specificity. In terms of the former it can be delivered along a continuum from mild (e.g. 'I am annoyed) to high emotional intensity (e.g. 'I am furious'). With regard to the latter, this again forms a continuum from low ('A few of them came and they stayed for a little while') to high specificity ('Nine of them came and they stayed for 45 minutes'). Hamilton and Hunter (1998a) in a review of research into this aspect found that stress was a moderating variable on the effects of emotional intensity. Relaxed targets are more persuadable as a result of the increased stress/arousal from high intensity messages, whereas with highly stressed receivers the added stress from the emotionality causes a boomerang effect. One other finding was that high emotional intensity had an impact on discrepant messages delivered by credible agents. Presumably the emotionality underlines the importance of what is a discordant message from a believable source.

Another aspect of message delivery, as noted by Bull (2001b) in his analysis of the importance of rhetoric in political persuasion, is use of three-part lists ('we must fight, fight and fight again') and contrasts ('the dark night we have lived through with this government will be transformed into a bright new dawn'). In political speeches these have been shown to attract audience applause – a good indicator of approval and acceptance. The former tactic is part of the *repetition strategy*, whereby the speaker 'stays on message' to ensure that it gets through and people remember it.

Indeed the Nazi leader Goebbels demonstrated the potency of repetition. He argued that, and successfully illustrated how, if you told a lie often enough people would believe it to be the truth.

Another aspect of message delivery is the use of metaphor. This term is derived from the Greek words for over (meta) and carry (pherein), and so the term indicates that an example from one area is carried over to another. For instance, a salesperson may say that the product being sold is 'Like gold dust', to indicate that it has a range of positive properties such as being rare, very valuable, and highly sought after. Sopory and Dillard (2002) carried out a meta-analytic review of research into the use of metaphors (this subsumed analogies, similes and personification), as compared with literal language, in persuasion. Their conclusion was that 'Theorists since Aristotle have proposed that metaphor could be fruitfully used for persuasion. The meta-analytic summary of existing empirical studies affirms this supposition regarding metaphor's suasory effectiveness over literal counterparts' (p. 413). They found that the persuasive power of metaphors was greatest when they were novel, easily understood by the target, used early in the message, single and not extended.

However, a word of caution is required here. Metaphors must be used skilfully, and care needs to be exercised if using them in a negative fashion. One linguistic form that is widely employed by public speakers is that of *rebuttal analogy*. This occurs when a speaker uses an analogy as part of an attack on the position of an opponent. For example an opposition politician might attack the government's policy on health by saying 'They have done too little too late. *What they are doing is the equivalent of giving a patient an aspirin to treat stomach cancer.*' The part in italics is an example of rebuttal analogy. Its purpose is to rebut the other side's arguments by showing them to be ridiculous or absurd. But research has found that this form of message delivery needs to be used with caution, as it often causes a boomerang effect (Whaley and Wagner, 2000). Those who use it are rated as more impolite and less likeable. Furthermore, when compared with non-analogy equivalents, it prompts the target person to formulate more counter-arguments to the message, and to remember fewer of the arguments put forward by the speaker. With partisan listeners, such as at a party political conference, rebuttal analogy, especially when humorous, can be acceptable to the audience. But even here the analogy should not be too insidious, especially if it is likely to be reported by the media to neutral observers (to whom it may seem like a 'smart-ass' comment). Overall, the research findings advise against the use of this tactic. It would be better for our hypothetical politician to reword the previous example as follows: 'They have done too little too late. *They have failed so many seriously ill people in our society, who need and deserve to receive the best possible treatment. Their record is truly shameful.*'

Another question is whether a speaker should have a clear and explicit conclusion at the end of an argument or leave this implicit and allow the audience to draw it out for themselves (see also Chapter 10 for more information on closure skills). In a meta-analysis of research in this field, Cruz (1998: 228) found that the former is advisable, concluding:

> The more explicit the conclusions to a persuasive message, the better the conclusion is comprehended. Greater conclusion comprehension produces perceptions that the source of the message advocates a more extreme position.

Finally, perceptions that the source holds a more extreme position produces more attitude change.

Counter-attitudinal advocacy

It has been found that the act of having to argue for a position that is contrary to one's own point of view can result in modifications to one's original perspective, and a shift towards the other viewpoint. This occurs for two reasons. First, as will be discussed in more depth later, individuals have a desire to portray a consistent sense of self. Consequently, when they publicly espouse an opinion that runs counter to their beliefs, their attitudes tend to move in the direction of the public utterances. This phenomenon has been described as 'saying is believing' (Aronson *et al.*, 2002: 223). Second, the cognitive processes involved in counter-attitudinal advocacy can lead to a positive reappraisal of the arguments involved (Hamilton and Hunter, 1998b). In their review of research in this field, Preiss and Allen (1998) found that when participation in such a task is voluntary, attitude change is highest when a small incentive is offered; if involvement is mandatory there is more change when the incentive is large. They argued that this is likely to be because those who are strongly opposed to the contradictory position will be less likely to volunteer to participate, and so those who do agree to take part may not be so diametrically opposed and hence more willing to change. When participation is compulsory, those who are paid well for completion of the task may feel under an obligation to reciprocate this high reward by working hard at the formulation of arguments for the case they are being employed to advocate. The processes involved in formulating and presenting these arguments are then more likely to impact on personal beliefs and opinions.

Case study

What is known as *the power of exemplary narrative*, or to put it more simply the power of purposive story-telling, has been shown to be effective in persuasive communication (Pinnington, 2001). From childhood we are nurtured on a diet of 'Once upon a time ...' stories, and as adults the inner child in us responds reflexively and positively to case studies about actual people and events. One reason for the success of this tactic is that, as noted by Ohme (2001: 314), 'the vividness and psychological closeness of a single case study is often more relevant to an individual than are scientific data'. While, as mentioned earlier, statistics can heighten the power of evidence, they may appear to be cold and detached, and we can get lost in the detail. Moreover, the oft-quoted remark by Mark Twain that 'There are lies, damned lies and statistics' means that we are often suspicious of statistics. The fact that academics frequently engage in the intellectual equivalent of arm-wrestling over the validity of one another's statistical methods does not help.

On the other hand, we can readily identify with, and indeed enjoy, human-interest stories. The agent can then use such tales to persuade the audience about the importance of the message being delivered. In terms of effectiveness, it does not seem to matter whether the narrative is fictional or true. This technique has a long history.

For example, the early Christian church found that 'the medieval exemplum' (a brief story used to illustrate a particular moral point) was a much more effective tactic for conversion than subtle and learned sermons about doctrine (Scanlon, 1994). As discussed by Pinnington (2001), preachers were therefore encouraged to use relevant examples in order to persuade more easily. This is also shown in the Bible, where Christ made forceful use of 'the parable', which was a case study in the form of a moral tale. A key feature of the potency of persuasive narrative is the extent to which the target becomes engaged with the story. Thus the phenomenon of *absorption* (also known as *transportation*) is important, wherein the 'message recipient is cognitively and affectively invested in a narrative' (Slater and Rouner, 2002: 179). This means that the story should be well told and of interest to the listeners. In terms of cognitive processing, successful narratives tend to be assimilated through the peripheral as opposed to the central route. Those who are engrossed in a story are less likely to employ counter-arguments and to be more affected by the emotional part of the message.

Given its effectiveness, it is not surprising that the case study tactic can be found in the practice of a wide spectrum of persuaders, such as advertisers, politicians and insurance salespeople. Of course it is not an either/or decision with regard to statistics and case studies. Indeed, in a major study involving 1270 participants and fifteen different messages Allen *et al.* (2000) found that a combination of statistics and narrative produced the most potent influencing message.

Sidedness

An important decision is whether to use one-sided or two-sided arguments. In other words, should the disadvantages of what is being recommended also be recognised? Research findings show that one-sided messages are best with those who already support the view being expressed. Accordingly, at party political conferences, the leader should present a partisan perspective, designed to boost the faithful. Likewise, it would be unusual for a clergyman to stand up in church and express doubts about the existence of God. When preaching to the converted it is necessary to target the message in a single direction. One-sided messages are also better with those of a lower IQ, who may become confused if presented with seemingly contradictory arguments.

On the other hand, two-sided arguments are more appropriate with those with a higher IQ. Since they are quite capable of formulating counter-arguments, it is best to openly recognise that there are two sides, rather than attempt to 'insult their intelligence'. It is also better to present the disadvantages as well as advantages to those who are initially opposed to the message, who have heard an opposing perspective earlier, or who will hear one later. In all these instances, of course, while the opposing perspective should be recognised it should also be countered. Allen (1998: 96), in a meta-analysis of research in this area concluded that what is required is that 'a communicator should use a two-sided message with a recognition and refutation of the available counterarguments. This message type receives the most favourable attitude response from the message receivers.' His analysis firmly cautioned against mentioning a counter-position without refuting it.

Request size

Two alternatives exist in relation to the scale of request made in persuasion attempts. The first is *foot-in-the-door* (FITD), where a very small first request is made, and if acceded to, this is followed by a slightly larger request, and so on. To take a simple example, if I want to borrow €20 from a colleague, I could use the FITD approach to say that I had forgotten my wallet and initially ask for €10 to get me through the day. If the person agrees to this, when I meet them later I could then say how really kind it was of them to help but that I have remembered that I had to do some shopping and ask if they could possibly increase the loan to €20.

The second is *door-in-the-face* (DITF), where a very large initial (and usually unacceptable) request is made, and once rejected a much more reasonable one follows. To continue the example of borrowing €20 from a colleague, using DITF I would say how I had forgotten my wallet and ask for a loan of €100, knowing it would probably be refused. I then ask if they could spare €50 or even just €20. Now my target amount seems much more reasonable – and in fact I have made two concessions from the first request.

Both FITD and DITF, which are termed *sequencing requests*, have been shown to be successful tactics when used skilfully, but their effectiveness depends on the circumstances. For example, a cult is unlikely to be successful if it has a DITF strategy of stopping passers-by in the street and asking them to join their group, explaining that this will involve giving all their money to the cult, breaking all contacts with family and friends, wearing strange clothes, accepting new and seemingly weird beliefs, living a frugal existence, and having to recruit strangers. Rather, an FITD strategy is more usual. In their text on cults, Tourish and Wohlforth (2000) termed this tactic the *spiral of escalating commitment*. Here, potential recruits are initially invited to attend an evening meeting to hear more about the group. This is then followed by an increased level of request, such as participation in a weekend conference. In this way, the potential member is slowly 'sucked in' and the level of request escalates gradually, until the person has become a fully fledged cult participant.

One explanation for the success of FITD is *self-perception theory* (Johnston, 1994). This purports that we make inferences about our attitudes, values and beliefs based on how we behave. When we carry out an action we infer that we did so because we are the type of person who would perform such an act. In other words our overt behaviour is seen as reflecting our inner 'self'. Then, when asked to perform a slightly larger action in the same vein, we wish to portray a consistent self and so we also accede to this request. Meta-analytic reviews of FITD have shown it to be effective (Dillard *et al.*, 1984; Fern *et al.*, 1986), provided that the conditions listed in Box 12.6 are met.

DITF is also known as *reciprocation of concessions*. The rationale here is that the target feels bad about having made the initial refusal. Furthermore, the agent has now made a concession in request size and so the target is under pressure to reciprocate. Compliance with the later request serves both to reciprocate the agent's concession and to make the target feel better. DITF also seems to benefit from *perceptual contrast*, wherein the second request is judged in the context of the initial one and, in comparison, is perceived to be smaller than it really is. Many stores use the DITF tactic in this way by placing very expensive items at the entrance,

---

Box 12.6 Foot-in-the-door conditions

For the FITD tactic to be successful, the following conditions must be met:

- *The cause should be pro-social.* If the request is made for purely selfish reasons it can be much more easily resisted; if it is in some way anti-social then it can be rejected with impunity.
- *No incentive should be given for carrying out the initial request.* If a reward is given, this may change the interpreted reason for the action (e.g. 'I did it purely for the money'). This, in turn, can make refusal easier to subsequent requests, especially if there is no concomitant increase in the scale of the reward.
- *The follow-up requests should be related to the initial one.* A later request is more easily rejected by the target without any fear of appearing to be inconsistent if it is unrelated to the issue or theme of the first one.
- *There should not be a huge discrepancy between each subsequent request.* If the disparity is too large the request may be more easily rejected as being 'unreasonable'.

---

so that when customers then encounter comparatively cheaper ones further into the shop these appear to be more reasonably priced than if they had been viewed without the contrast effect. Successive meta-analytic reviews have confirmed the effectiveness of DITF (Fern *et al.*, 1986; O'Keefe and Hale, 1998, 2001). However, they also show that for DITF to be successful the conditions listed in Box 12.7 must be met.

Reciprocation

In our interactions with others there seems to be a need for balance between what we give and what we receive. For example, in the last chapter we highlighted how in social situations when one person discloses to another, the recipient then feels under pressure to make a reciprocal disclosure. Cialdini (2001:50), in noting that 'one of the most widespread and basic norms of human cultures is embodied in the rule for reciprocation', identified three main characteristics of this phenomenon.

1   The expectation of reciprocity is such a potent facet of the human condition that it often supersedes other factors that may influence compliance.
2   The rule applies even to uninvited first favours. Hence companies often offer customers free samples or free trials, so that the recipient then feels under an obligation to return the favour.
3   To relieve ourselves of any lingering feeling of indebtedness we may actually return more to the giver than we received from them.

Reciprocity can be used in two ways, First, by *pre-giving* and so placing the target in the position of indebtness. Then, when a favour is sought in return it is more

---

Box 12.7 Door-in-the-face conditions

For the DITF tactic to be successful the following conditions must be met:

- *The same agent must make both requests.* If a different person makes the second request, the effect disappears. For example, a student approaches the class professor and asks for a large donation to the students' end of term party. This is refused. Later, another student approaches and asks for a smaller sum. Here, no real concession has been made, as it has become a different interaction with new rules. Furthermore, how many more such requests are liable to be made? The effect has been at best compromised and at worst destroyed.
- *The beneficiary should be the same for both requests.* If the recipient is different in the second request the effect is lost. For example, if the agent requests a large sum from the target for one charity initially, and then follows this up by asking for a smaller sum for a different charity, again the concession 'rules' have changed.
- *The requests need to be delivered face-to-face.* When the request is made by telephone the likelihood of success is much weaker. One reason for this is that research has shown that it is easier to refuse requests when they are mediated as opposed to when made in person (Hargie *et al.*, 1999).
- *There is no time delay between the requests.* If there is a delay the power of the effect diminishes. There is truth in the maxim that 'Time changes everything'. When making the second request at a later time, the initial scenario has to be reconstructed and may be difficult to re-create, and the pressure to reciprocate has eased for the target.
- *The requests should be pro-social.* As with FITD, purely selfish or anti-social requests can be readily rejected.

---

likely that the target will comply. If not, debt reminders can be invoked, such as 'I did that for you ... You owe me.' Second, a *promise* can be made that if the target performs a certain action, this will be rewarded by a reciprocal event at a later time. Colloquially this is known as 'you scratch my back and I'll scratch yours'. For example, a manager may say to a member of staff 'If you complete this task I will recommend you for a performance bonus.'

Promises work best when there is a close and trusting relationship between people. There is then less danger of what is known as the *low-ball technique*, where someone gets another to do something by making a promise with no intention of keeping it. For example, in a classic study in Iowa, USA, Pallak *et al.* (1980) investigated methods to persuade natural gas consumers to conserve their usage. They began by just asking a sample of domestic users to be fuel conscious. This had absolutely no effect when usage figures were measured. They then contacted a new sample but this time informed them that those who agreed to take part would later be named in newspaper articles as model citizens. The effect was immediate. Within a month participants had made significant reductions in gas consumption. Then the researchers contacted them to say that it was not going to be possible to publicise their names after all. What happened to energy usage now? Well interestingly it continued to drop even more. Although they had been low-balled into the initial behaviour, once established the new response became resistant to change. There are clear ethical problems about using the low-ball technique but as this study illustrated it certainly can be effective.

Emotional proofs

Emotions have been shown to be a very powerful force in driving and shaping human thoughts and behaviour. Appeals to the heart are as successful in effecting influence as appeals to the head. In their review of research in this field, Dillard and Peck (2001: 38) concluded 'there is a great deal of evidence that affect plays a significant role in the process of opinion change'. There are literally thousands of terms to describe affective states (Hargie, 1997b). However, as discussed in Chapter 3, there are six main categories of emotion – sadness, happiness, surprise, disgust, anger and fear. Each contains a large number of sub-categories (e.g. sadness subsumes *inter alia*, embarrassment, chagrin, guilt, shame, distress, and depression). Given the power and ubiquity of emotions in our lives, they are potent persuasion tools.

The *dual-systems approach* argues that emotions fall into one of two categories. Energetic arousal is seen as positive affect, and experienced as exuberance, vigour, etc. Tense arousal is viewed as negative affect, experienced as anxiety, nervousness, etc. These are in turn linked to two underlying physiological behaviour-guiding systems.

1   The *behaviour approach system* (BAS) is triggered by cues of reward and escape from punishment. The activation of the BAS leads to the experience of positive affect.
2   The *behaviour inhibition system* (BIS) is triggered by cues of punishment and non-reward. The activation of the BIS leads to the experience of negative affect.

The discrete-emotions approach purports that negative emotions arise from a situation where the environment is hindering the achievement of the individual's goals, while positive emotions arise from a situation where the environment facilitates the individual's goals. As discussed earlier, this in turn impacts on the way in which persuasion attempts are processed (see Box 12.3). We will now examine how and in what ways both negative and positive emotions can be invoked to 'move' people to act in certain ways.

Threat/fear

As a core emotion, threatening messages that heighten our sense of fear can be very effective in changing attitudes and behaviour. The *protection motivation model* has shown that there are four main prerequisites for fear to be successful as a weapon of influence (Sutton, 1982).

1   The likelihood and consequences of the threatened outcome must be severe enough to *really frighten* the target. The threat appraisal must be high so that it is perceived as noxious and real and the target must feel vulnerable. This can be difficult to achieve, since the psychological phenomenon of *unrealistic optimism* means that most people believe they are less likely than the average to suffer from negative experiences in life and more likely to experience the positive aspects (Weinstein and Klein, 1999). For example, others are seen as being more likely to get heart disease or cancer than oneself. Young people in particular are often immune to health messages – they believe that it is old people who get sick. For health educators this sense of invulnerability is difficult to overcome in terms of fear induction.

While a sense of vulnerability is essential to the effectiveness of fear appeals, more generally it makes targets susceptible to persuasive messages. Contrary to popular beliefs, research on cults has shown that while about one-third of the people who join these bodies are psychologically disturbed the remaining two-thirds are normal (Tourish and Wohlforth, 2000). However, the latter are more vulnerable to recruitment when they have just undergone a personal trauma, such as bereavement, divorce, job loss or serous illness. Vulnerability is also high when the individual is experiencing a major change of circumstance. For example, young adults who have left home to go to college are often unsettled and confused. Their social anchors have been drawn up and they find they are afloat in a new world having to fend for themselves, often for the first time. Their support network is not at hand, and levels of uncertainty and insecurity can be high. As a result, many cults, religions and various other bodies (sporting, political, etc.), specifically target the college fresher population, seeing this as fertile fishing ground. Furthermore, as intelligent (and often energetic, attractive, and articulate) individuals, once such students join a group they can be great emissaries to further its cause.

2   In relation to fear appeals, the second prerequisite is that there must be *specific recommendations* about how to prevent or remove the danger. The steps needed to remove the threat must be clear and unambiguous.

3   The perceived *response efficacy* has to be high. In other words, the target must believe that what is being recommended will be *effective* in circumventing or overcoming the threat. The remedial actions should be shown to work.

4   The target needs to be *willing to take action* to remove the threat. There should be a high level of *coping appraisal and self-efficacy* so that the target is confident about being able to implement the recommended behaviours. Thus Rimal (2002) showed that a crucial determining factor in the success of fear appeals was how highly individuals rated their own ability to carry out the recommended actions. If the target feels able to implement and maintain these, then fear messages are more likely to be successful.

If all four factors are operative, then threat/fear is a potent tool for persuasion. If one or more is absent then the power of the message is reduced accordingly. For example, someone may accept that being a very heavy drinker is detrimental to health and carries a much higher risk of illness and earlier mortality. They may agree that if they drank less or stopped drinking altogether they would have a drastically reduced rate of risk. However, they may also believe that they need to drink and just could not give it up. Here the power of the threat/fear message begins to dissipate. The target may then either respond with feelings of hopelessness ('I'm going to die anyway so I might as well enjoy my drink'), or reject the threat ('There is no real evidence to show any causal link between alcohol intake and ill health').

Much of the early work on threat and fear appeals was carried out in the field of health, and indeed the *health belief model* emphasised the above four points, as well as a fifth aspect of *cue to action* (Rutter and Quine, 2002). Here, a specific event triggers the entire process. For example, a friend who smoked heavily dies of cancer and this then makes you think seriously about the dangers of smoking. The *parallel response model* (Leventhal, 1970) illustrated how people cope with fear messages by responding at one of two levels.

1   *Fear control.* This is concerned with controlling or reducing internal feelings of fear. Here the person avoids the negative messages that arouse fear. The heavy drinker responding at this level would avoid newspaper articles or TV programmes that highlight the risks of heavy alcohol intake. They may also make a distinction between *general beliefs* ('Heavy drinking is harmful to health'), and *personal beliefs* that either minimise the degree of risk ('I don't really drink that much') or emphasise personal immunity ('Drinking never causes me any problems. I'm built for it'). They may also engage in rationalisations such as generalising from the particular ('I know a man who drank heavily all his life and he lived to be over 80 years old'), or accentuating the positive ('Taking a drink improves my well-being by helping me to relax').

2   *Danger control.* Here the person responds in such a way as to reduce the danger that causes the fear. Thus the person would cut down, or eliminate, alcohol. In other words, the fear message is accepted and acted on.

In a meta-analysis of research into fear-arousal and persuasion, Mongeau (1998: 65) concluded 'Overall, increasing the amount of fear-arousing content in a persuasive message is likely to generate greater attitude and behavior change.' However, he also found that the use of this tactic was not always effective. Fear is more effective with older subjects (i.e. with adults as opposed to school children), and with low anxiety individuals. With highly anxious people it may backfire, so that the heightened anxiety induced by an intense fear scenario can inhibit attention and increase distraction. This in turn reduces comprehension, or results in the message either being ignored completely or rejected. These findings have also been shown in studies of the effects of fear messages in TV advertising (LaTour *et al.*, 1996). Thus Job (1988) illustrated how some health promotion campaigns that use fear appeals (e.g. anti-smoking) may actually boomerang because they raise the stress levels in an already anxious individual, who then responds by actually performing the targeted behaviour (i.e. reaching for a cigarette) to reduce this increased anxiety. The reactions of the target therefore need to be carefully and constantly monitored. The objective is to encourage change, not instil panic and an accompanying 'flight' reaction (where the target just wants to escape from the threatening message).

Moral appeals

Part of the socialisation process in all societies is that individuals are taught the difference between what is 'right' and what is 'wrong'. Behaviour that is upright, ethical, honest, etc. is viewed positively by others and encouraged, while that which is underhand, immoral, deceitful, etc. is disapproved of and discouraged. These societal norms play a powerful role in the development of a personal moral code that in turn shapes our responses. Most people are susceptible to appeals to conscience, in the form of reminders that we have a duty to 'do the right thing', and that if we do not fulfil our moral obligations we will feel bad about ourselves. As shown by Evans and Norman (2002: 157) 'those individuals who anticipate feeling regret after performing a behaviour are less likely to intend to perform the behaviour'. Few people like to be left feeling guilty or ashamed, or to be the subject of opprobrium from significant others, and so messages that target the moral domain can be very potent. One other important aspect here, as summarised by Dillard and Peck (2001: 42), is that 'Guilt may prompt efforts to redress the failure, but only if the transgression can be remedied.' In other words, inducing a sense of guilt is useful in moving someone to act, only if they can do so in such a way as to right the wrong. If the misdemeanour is irreversible or not salvageable, then all that a moral appeal will do at best is make the target feel very bad.

Moral appeals take a number of forms, as shown in Box 12.8. Although these can be effective tactics, there are also drawbacks to their use and so this strategy needs to be treated with some caution (Hargie *et al.*, 1999). Since we do not like to be made to feel guilty, we tend to dislike the person who has caused this to occur, and we are then more likely to avoid them in future. This is especially true when what we have done cannot be easily remedied. Another finding is that an accusation of being uncaring results in the target being more likely to accede to a second moral appeal, providing the follow-up one is made by a different person. This is because the target then wishes to show that they are not uncaring and so the accusation was unfounded. For example, you pass a charity collector shaking a tin in the street without donating, and the person says 'I can see that you really don't care about those a lot less fortunate than yourself. I wouldn't like to have to rely on you for help.' A few streets later you encounter another charity collector waving a tin. There is now an increased probability that you will donate.

Scarcity value

While this aspect of persuasion is sometimes included within logical proofs (e.g. Hargie *et al.*, 1999), there is also a strong element of emotionality involved and so we have incorporated it within emotional proofs. The scarcity principle operates on the basis that once the availability of something is restricted it becomes more valuable and desirable. Items that are hard to get tend to have more value and appeal. There is a perfectly good rationale here – our experience tells us that the best things in life are often in scarce supply. The phenomenon of an increased desire for what is scarce is part of what is known as *reactance theory* (Brehm, 1966). This theory highlighted how when access to something is denied, or when restrictions are placed on an item or

---

Box 12.8 Types of moral appeal

- *Duty calls.* These remind people that they have a moral obligation, or responsibility, to carry out certain actions. For example a parent may be told that it is their duty to provide for their child. In fact, insurance companies use this technique to sell life policies. The person who dies obviously will not benefit financially from the policy, but it is argued that they have a duty to their family to provide for them in the event of their death.
- *Altruism exhortations.* These are direct attempts to trigger a caring or altruistic response in the target person, who has no obligation to help and will receive no tangible benefit from giving assistance. Many charities operate at this level, when they appeal to the population to help others less fortunate than them. Likewise beggars may ask you to give them money 'out of the kindness of your heart'.
- *Social esteem precepts.* Here, social norms are invoked to underline the probability that the reaction of others to a response will either be negative ('You will be shunned if you do that') or positive ('You will be well thought of if you do this'). Most of us care about the reactions of others, and so the danger of being ostracised on one hand, or the likelihood of recognition and social approval on the other, are powerful forces.
- *Self-feeling injunctions.* The concept of self-regard is an important force in driving behaviour. For example, people who donate anonymously to charities do not receive social esteem, but they do have a reward in the form of positive self-feeling. This means that individuals can be influenced by appeals at this level, cast in either a negative manner ('You will find it very difficult to live with yourself if you do not do this') or in a positive frame ('You will feel good if you do this').
- *Altercasting appeals.* This involves encouraging others to 'step outside themselves' and examine their behaviour objectively. The individual is then asked to consider the view that either only a bad, uncaring person would continue with the present behaviour, or that a good and caring person would carry out the recommended action. For example, a heavy gambler whose family was suffering and in severe debt could be asked 'Wouldn't you agree that anyone who cared anything for their family would try to stop this?'

---

activity, our freedom of choice is threatened. We, in turn, react to this threat by experiencing an increased desire for the restricted item. Indeed, the more restricted the item the greater tends to be its appeal. This process first occurs in children at around the age of 2 years, when temper tantrums are often the order of the day if a much wanted toy, snack or activity is not immediately forthcoming. One early study showed that when children at this age were offered access to toys of parallel attractiveness, if one was unavailable (behind a Plexiglas barrier) this was the one on which most attention was focused (Brehm and Weintraub, 1977). Likewise, if teenagers are told by parents not to date a certain person their desire to be with the forbidden individual often becomes much greater. Although the best things in life may be free, we only fully appreciate them if they become less available. In fact, we expect to pay for the best things in life. We know that the best house, car or watch costs more. Shops that sell 'rare artefacts' or 'precious gems' do not 'stack 'em high and sell 'em cheap'.

A key implication of this is that we can persuade others to do something by convincing them that there is scarcity value attached to it. For example, people pay exorbitant fees to join clubs that market themselves as 'exclusive'. There are three important factors attached to scarcity value.

1   Resources attain an even greater value when they are seen to be *newly scarce*. This holds both for items that were once plentiful but have now become rare, and for recently discovered or invented items that are not yet in plentiful supply. Salespeople are able to sell things more easily when they are brand new, and still hard to get hold of (Hargie *et al.*, 1999). Indeed the price of an item usually remains high as long as it is scarce, but tends to drop as availability increases.

2   If we have to *compete* for the scarce resource it attains even greater attraction in our eyes. It is for this reason that auctioneers are delighted when two or more people begin to bid seriously for the same object. The winner is then likely to pay well above the odds to secure it.

3   *Losses are more influential than gains*. Research shows that messages are more effective when scarcity benefits can be presented not as gains but as preventable losses. What is known as *prospect theory* (Tversky and Kahneman, 1981) shows that people are more concerned with minimising losses than maximising gains. In other words, the prospect of something becoming scarce as a result of losing it motivates us more than the thought of gaining something of equal value. For example, smokers are influenced more when told by a physician how many years of life they are likely to *lose* if they do not quit, as opposed to how many years they will *gain* if they do give up (Cialdini, 2001). Likewise, it is more effective to tell them that if they do not stop smoking their lungs will not heal, than to say if they stop their lungs will heal (Ohme, 2001).

Interestingly, in a study into the effects of advertising in Poland, Pietras (2001) showed how the technique of scarcity value that relied on 'limited supply' or 'limited time offer' tactics were less effective as consumer goods became more widely available. She suggested that in affluent societies the deeper psychological principles underlying the scarcity principle (e.g. the uniqueness of the item, competition with others) are more effective, and concluded that 'different compliance-gaining tactics may be best suited to different groups ... their efficacy strongly depends on the demographic and psychological characteristics of consumers' (p. 93).

Consistency and commitment

A powerful human drive is the desire to be regarded as *consistent*. We have a need to show others that we mean what we say and will do what we promise. This means that once we have made a public declaration of *commitment* to a course of action we are more likely to rate it highly and continue with it. A ubiquitous strategy in many organisations and institutions is to get people to make such a declaration. Its potency is reinforced if the person also makes the declaration in writing. Examples of the successful use of this tactic include 'I am an alcoholic . . .' declarations made at Alcoholics Anonymous gatherings, personal testimonies or confessions by members of religious denominations, and statements of devotion to one another made by couples during the marriage ceremony. At another level, performers know that if they can get the audience actively involved (e.g. by clapping, laughing, cheering, chanting, or singing along) their level of perceived enjoyment will increase accordingly. This tactic has been aptly termed the *clap trap* (Huczynski, 1996). Involvement increases enjoyment and so reduces the likelihood of central processing. Such a strategy is used at mass rallies (witness the 'Sieg Heil' roars and Nazi salutes during Hitler's speeches), in church services, and in the best classrooms.

Thus the twin pillars of consistency and commitment can be used to shape and direct the behaviour of others. The principle of *retrospective rationality* means that once people perform a certain behaviour or publicly state a point of view they are then more likely to infer in retrospect that they really believe in what they said or did (Iyengar and Brockner, 2001). In reviewing this area Cialdini (2001: 96) concluded that such 'Commitments are most effective when they are active, public, effortful, and viewed as internally motivated (uncoerced)'. They are also more impactful when the decision taken is final. Let us examine the commitment aspects of persuasion in further depth.

1   *Public declaration.* When the behaviour is enacted publicly rather than privately, the commitment to it is greater. The presence of others has a significant impact – we like to be seen as true to our word. Those who change their mind or renege on what they said are generally perceived as fickle, weak or untrustworthy. Consequently, oaths of allegiance made in public are a key element in the initiation ceremonies of many bodies. Once you have publicly sworn undying allegiance to a cause it becomes more difficult to retract. For example, Islamic suicide bombers usually make a video-taped statement before they go on their mission. This is a very public declaration, as the tape may be seen by millions of people. Having made such a declaration, it then becomes extremely difficult to recant. In fact, members of terrorist organisations who become disillusioned about their organisation may turn informer rather than face the opprobrium of being seen to go back on their sworn oath. More generally, the media love to expose public figures who have broken promises or shown inconsistency, and relish stories involving crooked cops, unfrocked vicars or corrupt politicians. Where someone is inconsistent, the use of *induced hypocrisy* is a powerful force. As noted by Stone *et al.* (1997), this occurs when an individual is: (a) reminded of having publicly espoused a personal position; (b) confronted with evidence of having failed to live up to this position. When both of these events occur, the effect of the induced hypocrisy is powerful. The individual experiences cognitive dissonance and is motivated to be more consistent in future. Having been shown to have broken our word, and as such to be hypocritical, we have a renewed determination to 'put this right' in future.

2   *Implementation intentions.* An important distinction has been made between *goal intentions*, where the individual makes a simple commitment to a particular action ('I intend to do X'), and *implementation intentions*, which involve detailed planning about when, where and exactly how 'X' will be carried out (Gollwitzer,

1999). Research across a wide range of fields has shown that individuals who plan at the implementation level are much more likely to carry out the stated behaviour (Rutter and Quine, 2002).

3   *Level of initial commitment.* The more actively involved the person is in the public declaration process, the more binding their commitment becomes. One way of ensuring that people stay committed to the message they have recently been persuaded to adopt is to get them to proselytise about it. This is a tactic that is used by many religions and cults. In the High Street of most major cities, one meets individuals selling a message either on an individual basis or, as with 'manic street preachers', to all and sundry. Having to 'sell' the message means that it becomes cognitively embedded and resistant to change. It is more difficult to later reject that which you have publicly and vehemently espoused. If individuals have to make sacrifices as part of their commitment they are more likely to 'bond' with the behaviour. Thus many bodies have initiation ceremonies or 'rites of passage' where the initiate may have to endure humiliations before becoming a fully fledged member. Likewise, terrorist leaders recognise the importance of getting volunteers involved in an early 'mission', especially one where targets are killed. The volunteer is then literally 'blooded' and more likely to aver the worth of the cause. People also rate the strength and depth of their belief or attitude based on the extent of effort they have put into it in the past. Thus if you decided to become a vegetarian six months ago but since then have lapsed and eaten flesh at least once a week, you are likely to rate your commitment to vegetarianism lower than if you had never eaten flesh since.

4   *Voluntary act.* If the behaviour has been freely chosen the individual is more committed to it. There is now a huge volume of research to show that freedom of choice is a central factor in the influence equation. In reviewing this area Iyengar and Brockner (2001: 16) concluded, 'The provision of choice seems inherently linked with intrinsic motivation, perceived control and personal commitment.' If we can argue that a public commitment was made as a result of threat or duress, then we do not feel the need to stick to it. For example, some American POWs held by communists in the Korean and Vietnam conflicts made public statements in favour of their captors and against US policy. Interestingly, some stayed committed to what they had said and remained there after the war, while others argued they had been forced by physical or psychological torture to say what they had, and never personally believed in what they were told to say. The reaction of others is similarly mediated by the extent to which they perceive the declaration to be coerced. Snyder and Omoto (2001) identified five key motivations for the phenomenon of *volunteerism*, where individuals volunteer to give time in the service of others. As shown in Box 12.9, the first two of these are other-centred and the last three self-focused. Those who want to encourage others to volunteer need to take cognisance of these different motivations. For example, if producing a publicity video aimed at recruitment, as many of these motivations as possible should be targeted. As expressed by Snyder and Omoto (2001: 295) 'Rather than adopt a *one size fits all* approach to volunteer recruitment and training, organizations may be better served by creating advertisements and recruitment materials that differentially speak to the different motivations.'

Box 12.9 Motivations for volunteerism

1   A general personal system of values and beliefs that includes a felt humanitarian obligation to help others. Self-centred, materialistic, egotists, who believe that 'it's a jungle out there' and that only the fittest will survive, are less likely to become volunteers.

2   Specific concern for or interest in the target group to whom the voluntary work is directed. For example a committed Christian in the developed world may be motivated to go and give practical help to other fellow Christians in the third world.

3   A desire to develop a greater understanding of the field in which one will be working. This is the rationale behind work placement programmes. The person can spend some time in the type of environment that they feel they wish to work in, and gain first hand insight into what is involved.

4   As part of personal development. This may include the motivation to feel a sense of challenge, e.g. volunteering to become a member of the crew of a lifeboat. It may also be a wish to enlarge one's social network – by meeting other volunteers who are of a similar age and likely to hold similar attitudes and beliefs.

5   A need to enhance one's self-esteem and feel better about one's self. Thus, someone who earns a high salary in a very competitive but not socially satisfying job, may stay in the job to earn money but at the same time become involved in charity activities in their spare time.

---

5   *Finality.* We are heavily influenced by commitments that are irrevocable. If there is a possibility that we can change our minds, the alternatives may linger and eventually influence our behaviour. However, if the deed is final, we are more likely to become convinced of its worth. For example, once you have signed the legal contract to sell your house you are more likely to believe that you have made the correct decision. Likewise, some in society argue that because divorce is possible it encourages less of a commitment to marriage.

Commitment to a cause is particularly strong among vociferous minority groups, who maintain their attitudes by using three techniques (Wojciszke, 2001).

1   *Increasing their belief in the subjective validity of their own attitude and the invalidity of opposing perspectives.* This serves to increase the difference between the in-group and the out-group. The minority believe that their views represent the only rational or logical possibility. Those who hold an opposing view are either not thinking straight, do not know the full facts and so must be put right, or are just biased against the minority.

2   *Overestimating the amount of social support for one's position.* Thus the minority group convince themselves that they have huge support for their views. This is part of what is known as the *false consensus effect*, where we believe (erroneously) that our beliefs or behaviours are more prevalent than is actually the case.

3   *Belief in the moral superiority of one's position.* Not only do the minority see their perspective as valid, they also believe that it holds the high moral ground. A good example of this is the militant minority groups who claim to have God on their side, and so are fighting for a 'just cause' or a 'holy war'.

These three perspectives are part of the phenomenon of groupthink (see Chapter 14).

Self-prophecy

The self-prophecy effect occurs when we are requested to predict our future perform-ance. Having made a public prediction, we then feel under pressure to live up to this. There is considerable evidence to support the potency of self-prophecy in guiding future behaviour. In their review of research in this field, Spangenberg and Greenwald (2001: 52) concluded:

> several researchers have shown in multiple contexts that predicting one's own behavior can induce subsequent action consistent with the prediction, yet different than would otherwise have been observed ... its robustness – regarding both the magnitude of the effect size and the variety of contexts in which it has been observed – is compelling.

In well over half a century of joint experience in higher education, we have noted how asking our final year students to predict their degree classification, or dissertation grade, produces remarkably accurate results. In fact, during supervision of their dissertations students, without overtly realising its effect, return to their initial self-prophecy by asking questions such as 'Is the literature review at first class standard?' 'What do I need to do to make sure this is upper second?' One problem with self-prophecy, of course, is that it can be negative as well as positive. Those involved in the therapeutic professions have to deal with clients with poor self-esteem and low expectations of self-efficacy. They, too, are likely to match their projected level of negative performance. As part of the process of goal-setting, the therapists must therefore encourage clients to be as positive as possible in their prophecies, while staying within realistic parameters.

A related perspective here is the *theory of planned behaviour*. As mentioned in Chapter 2, this purports that a person's responses can be predicted from their behavioural intentions, since 'the best predictor of behaviour is the person's intention to perform the behaviour' (Rutter and Quine, 2002: 11). Thus, if a self-prophecy is framed in terms of behavioural intentions, the likelihood of the prophecy being realised is strengthened. The theory of planned behaviour further argues that intentions are determined by two main factors:

1   *Attitude to the behaviour.* This is based on one's beliefs about the consequences (e.g. 'Taking drugs would adversely affect my health') and related evaluations thereof (e.g. 'It would be wrong to risk my health').
2   *Subjective norms*, in the form of perceived social pressure to carry out the behaviour (e.g. 'My parents do not want me to take drugs'), moderated by the

individual's desire to comply with this pressure (e.g. 'I respect my parents and do not want to let them down').

Klinger and Bierbraver (2001) highlighted how three key aspects of the theory of planned behaviour are important. They illustrated these in relation to the processes a Turkish immigrant in Germany may go through in making a decision about whether to attempt to assimilate.

1   *Behavioural evaluation.* The Turkish person has to decide whether it would be good to become a German – would doing so result in positive or negative outcomes?
2   *Normative evaluation.* This involves a consideration of prevailing social norms and pressures in the person's in-group. What would the attitudes and reactions of one's family and friends be?
3   *Competence evaluation.* This relates to perceived ability to perform the necessary behaviours. For example, has the Turkish person a strong belief in the ability to learn to speak fluent German?

These three evaluations are also likely to be influential in the formation of a final self-prophecy. To return to our student example, a student may believe that a first class degree would be very beneficial (behavioural evaluation), and positively acclaimed by family and friends (normative evaluation), but that it is just beyond their ability level or requires more work than they are prepared to expend (competence evaluation). They will therefore predict the more achievable, yet still personally and socially laudable, upper second, and gear their work schedule accordingly.

OVERVIEW

From the review of research presented in this chapter it is clear that persuasion is a multi-faceted and complex area. Success or failure in persuading others is determined by a range of often interlocking elements. As noted by Meyers-Levy and Malaviya (1999: 45) 'the complex process of persuasion is intricately dependent on a myriad of contextual, situational, and individual difference factors'. For example, Rogers (1983) has shown how different people respond in differing ways to innovation. Some people want to be first to have a new gizmo, and warmly embrace all new developments whether in technology, procedures, or processes. Their motto tends to be 'off with the old and on with the new'. Such individuals have been termed *innovators*. At the other end of the scale are those who are extremely reluctant to change their ways at all, and do not want to adopt new approaches or even adapt to them. Their mantra is 'I like things just as they are'. This group of people are called *laggards*. In between the two ends of the continuum, some will react more swiftly than others to change, and as such are more amenable to persuasion.

There is therefore no set of fixed guidelines or magic formula with regard to persuasion. Rather, it is necessary to consider the target, the situation in which the interaction is taking place, and the way in which the persuasion attempt is made. Like all communication, this is a two-way process and so the target makes an evaluation of the agent in considering how to respond. In this chapter we have followed Aristotle's template for analysing persuasion, in terms of ethos (personal proofs), logos (logical proofs), and pathos (emotional proofs). A knowledge of each of the sub-elements of these areas, as summarised in Box 12.10, provides detailed insight into the fascinating world of persuasion.

Box 12.10 Summary of the main persuasion tactics

Personal proofs

- Muster all the *power* you have to good effect.
- Develop a good *relationship* with the target.
- Make yourself as *attractive* as possible.
- Use appropriate *humour.*

Logical proofs

- Deliver the message in a *confident and authoritative* manner.
- Try to get the target to *argue against their own position.*
- Back up your arguments with *case studies* as well as *hard evidence.*
- Give *two-sided arguments with intelligent people,* but refute the counter-arguments.
- Have a *consistent sliding scale of sequential request,* either low gradating to high or vice versa.
- Invoke the norm of *reciprocation.*

Emotional proofs

- Employ *threat/fear,* especially with older and less anxious subjects.
- Introduce *moral appeals* to make the person feel guilty.
- Emphasise the *scarcity value* of the item.
- Get a public declaration of *commitment,* to which the target will then want to be *consistent.*
- Ask the target to make a *self-prophecy* about their performance, as this will then tend to guide their behaviour.

Chapter 13

Negotiating

INTRODUCTION

ONE OF THE GREAT challenges of social life is dealing with difference. Diversity in race, religion, gender or generation leads to people adopting contrasting cultural practices, beliefs, values and ways of doing things. These differences, in turn, can cause problems when people from disparate backgrounds have to attempt to sort out areas of disagreement. Of such is the stuff of wars, communal conflicts and industrial disputes. But even at a more mundane level, among families and friends, there is a frequent lack of concordance when deciding what to do or where to go. Negotiation is one way of overcoming such difference. As Lewicki *et al.* (2003: ix) pointed out, 'negotiation is not only common but also essential to living an effective and satisfying life. We all need things – resources, information, cooperation and support from others. Others have those needs as well, sometimes compatible with ours sometimes not.' This means we inevitably have to enter into regular exchanges of give and take with other people. While many think of it primarily in the context of resolving international disagreements, hostage situations or industrial disputes, in fact we all have to negotiate on a day-to-day basis. It may take place in the context of, for example, agreeing where to eat, what movie to see, what time the children should be home by, where to go on holiday, or more formally the sale and purchase of houses and cars. In this sense, negotiation is pervasive in our lives.

Professionals, of course, have added responsibilities for negotiating with colleagues, managers, clients, and so on, as part of their work role. All jobs necessitate a capacity to negotiate and bargain effectively with a range of others. For some, such as real estate agents or car salespeople, negotiation is of paramount importance. Yet, despite the huge volume of recent literature on the topic, many practitioners receive little or no instruction or training in this dimension of practice. Furthermore, this is a skill that has to be learned. From a developmental perspective, research findings show that as children mature, their capacity for complex negotiation routines becomes more refined and developed (Wilmot and Hocker, 1998). Very young children are totally egocentric. They want what they want and they want it *now*. Learning that others also have needs and wants is an important part of the maturation process, and essential for negotiation.

A main reason why negotiation is a ubiquitous aspect of our everyday experience is that conflict is a pervasive feature of personal and social existence. Were there no clashes of interests or thwarting of objectives (actual or apparent) in a setting where each party is to some extent reliant on the other to do what it wants, there would be no need to negotiate. Conflict has been defined as 'a situation in which interdependent people express (manifest or latent) differences in satisfying their individual needs and interests, and ... experience interference from each other in accomplishing these goals' (Donohue and Kolt, 1992: 3). Such incompatibility is without doubt endemic in many workplaces.

However, conflict is not always negative and – at least in moderation – may actually be productive. An element of competition can start the flow of creative juices, increase the motivation of all parties, and produce improved end results. The secret is to manage it at optimal levels to ensure that it has positive effects. When conflict remains unresolved the results may be very damaging. Failure to ameliorate disputes can have enormous consequences, including relationship breakdown, industrial strikes, lengthy litigation, financial loss, the death of hostages, and civil strife. Mishandled through avoidance, overly aggressive arguments or even recourse to violence or the threat of violence, and the destructive potential can be far reaching. Negotiating is a more positive alternative that has a very important contribution to make to conflict management (Milburn, 1998). But what exactly does negotiation entail, and how can we perform this process more effectively? This chapter attempts to answer these questions by charting the core features of negotiation and delineating the key skills and strategies required for successful outcomes.

DEFINITION OF NEGOTIATION

Negotiation has been conceptualised in many ways (see Morley, 1997 for an overview of these), such as, for example:

- a *game* in which both sides carry out strategic moves (such as making offers);
- an *economic forum* in which resources are exchanged;
- a *cognitive information-processing exercise* in which individuals have to use a range of intra- and interpersonal processes to make decisions;
- a *form of reflexive social action* in which people are concerned with the interpretation of messages and meanings in particular social and historical contexts.

In general terms, for negotiation to occur there has to be some incompatibility of interest, both sides must be interested in seeking a settlement, and the process often involves exchanging concessions in order to reach agreement. The term 'negotiation' has been defined in a variety of ways. Some definitions emphasise the importance of communicating with and eventually influencing the other side. In this sense, 'Negotiation is a highly interdependent process in which each party continuously incorporates information from the other party to develop responses that might lead to resolution of the conflict at hand' (Weingart *et al.*, 1999: 367). The notion of exchange is underscored by Robbins (2001: 396), who defined negotiation as: 'a process in which two or more parties exchange goods or services and attempt to agree upon the exchange rate for them'.

As well as emphasising the relationship element and the search for mutual benefit, negotiation has been viewed as 'an attempt by two parties to change the terms and conditions of their relationship in a situation in which it is to their mutual benefit to do so or in which it is impossible to quit the relationship' (Whitney, 1990: 77). This definition highlights the fact that on occasions people simply *must* negotiate with one another. Parents and their young children negotiate (often passionately) about many issues, but neither can just walk away from the relationship. Similarly, it is difficult for professionals not to negotiate with one another, or with clients, if they are to effectively execute their duties. In large organisations, sub-divisions have to negotiate regularly if the firm is to thrive. For example, the sales, production and delivery departments must all co-ordinate their actions and agree a joint schedule. There is no point in salespeople winning sales that production cannot meet, or agreeing deadlines that delivery cannot make.

The issue of truth-telling was raised by Morley (1981: 86) who defined negotiation as 'an exercise in which parties struggle to exploit asymmetries of interest and power, each knowing that the other may disguise or misrepresent their real position'. Here there is a recognition that, since there are differences in interests and resources, both sides know that the other is likely to be economical with the truth by concealing or distorting their real situation. The reason for this is that: 'There are very few negotiating situations where you can afford to be completely open and honest without risking being exploited by the other side' (Mills, 1991: 2). Continuing with this theme, Morley (1981) viewed negotiation as a type of 'incomplete antagonism' or 'precarious partnership' that allows each participant the opportunity to manipulate perceptions of common interest in an attempt to achieve private goals. In an attempt to move away from such confrontational encounters, many large corporations, such as Ford, Xerox, Whirlpool and Chrysler drastically reduced their number of potential suppliers. The new goal was to develop supply lines based on mutual trust and positive relationships rather than on cut-throat price battles (Jeffries and Reed, 2000).

While the terms 'negotiating' and 'bargaining' are often used synonymously, distinctions have been made between them. For Morley (1986), while parties may enter negotiation with no intention of reaching a settlement (e.g. it may be in their interests to prolong a dispute so as to achieve a better final outcome), when they bargain it is their firm intention to make a deal. In this sense, when we bargain we negotiate for agreement. Thus bargaining has been defined as 'an operative desire to clarify, ameliorate, adjust or settle the dispute or situation' (Lall, 1966: 31), in a process which involves 'making the other side sufficiently content with an agreement to want to live up to it' (Fisher and Ury, 1981: 75).

In reviewing definitional issues, Thompson (1990) identified five defining features of negotiation:

1 There is a conflict of interest on at least one issue.
2 The parties are involved in a voluntary relationship, where communication is emphasised and no one is coerced into being involved in the negotiation.
3 The interaction is concerned with the division or exchange of resources and intermediate solutions or compromises are possible.
4 Discussion centres on the sequential presentation of offers, evaluation of these, and subsequent concessions and counter-offers.
5 Offers and proposals do not determine outcomes until agreed on by both parties.

However, this process does not always run smoothly, and indeed Mnookin *et al.* (1996) noted three core tensions.

1 Maximising one's own personal profit while at the same time attempting to ensure equity and a fair deal for both sides.
2 Standing up for one's own position, yet showing concern for the interests and needs of the other side.
3 Personal interests versus clients' interests. For example, a social worker has to negotiate on behalf of clients and get the best deal possible for them, but is also a government employee who needs to show to line managers an ability to stay within budgetary limits.

In relation to the latter point, Susskind and Mnookin (1999: 282) argued that most people negotiate on behalf of others and not just for personal gain, since 'everyone involved in any kind of negotiation is really an agent of some kind and not just a principal. That is, there are very few negotiators who do not have someone else to whom they are accountable.' For example, when you buy a car, the salesperson is acting on behalf of the garage owner and the motor company, while you may be representing your entire family who will use the vehicle. Indeed, many professionals have jobs in which negotiating on behalf of others is central to their work (agents, lawyers, politicians, union officials, etc.).

FUNCTIONS OF NEGOTIATION

Negotiation serves a number of very important functions (see Box 13.1). In essence, it involves engaging in a structured and reasonably formal process during which each side should be given the opportunity to put forward their arguments, and also show a willingness to listen to the views of the other parties involved. The eventual goal is to attempt to reach a mutually beneficial compromise position that will be acceptable to all those involved.

Box 13.1 Functions of negotiation

To enable people to engage in a process in which parties:

1   present a sequence of arguments to support their case;
2   state their preferences;
3   recognise and acknowledge what the other side sees as important;
4   try to achieve an in-depth understanding of all the issues;
5   ascertain areas of agreement and disagreement;
6   enter into a series of offers and bids relating to personal targets;
7   seek out options to overcome areas of disagreement;
8   engage in a process of mutual concession-making;
9   formally agree and ratify a final deal that is acceptable to both sides, and that can be successfully implemented.

NEGOTIATING STRATEGIES

We have formulated what we term the 'negotiation decision tree' (Figure 13.1), to illustrate the main decisions to be made during a negotiation encounter. The first decision is whether or not to enter into negotiation at all. Sometimes one side will make the decision not to negotiate. As Watkins (1998: 243) put it, 'So long as negotiators believe that the costs of action outweigh the potential benefits of inaction, they cannot be expected to act.' If this is the case, then a *Best Alternative To Negotiated Agreement* (BATNA) should have been formulated. Thompson (2001: 11) pointed out, 'A BATNA is not something that a negotiator wishes for; rather it is determined by harsh reality.' This is because negotiations can and do fail, and when this occurs a party with no BATNA may find itself in serious difficulties. The BATNA comes into operation at various stages (see Figure 13.1).

Two aspects of the BATNA are important. First, the opposing side may attempt to moderate your perceptions of your BATNA in a negative fashion. In other words, they may attempt to persuade you that in fact your BATNA is actually worse than you had thought. It is therefore important to work out your BATNA carefully and objectively, and not to deviate from your belief in this whatever the counter-arguments. Second, you should attempt to ascertain what the other side's BATNA is, and also to remember that people may not tell the truth about this. In one interesting study, Paese and Gilin (2000) found that when one side disclosed their BATNA early in the negotiations, this actually reduced the demands and increased the truthfulness of the other. It would seem that the act of one party stating what their position is if negotiations fail, can give impetus to the other side to try to reach an acceptable settlement.

If negotiation begins, it may be either a short or a long process, depending on how things progress. Indeed, 'time-outs' are often an important part of the scenario, where both sides leave to consult privately with relevant colleagues. These time-outs can be very useful to provide each side with the time, space and distance to take a 'helicopter view' of what is happening. To adapt a well-known analogy, during

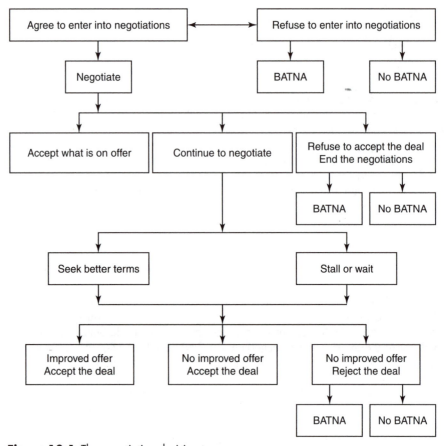

Figure 13.1 The negotiation decision tree

time-outs the solidity of the wood on offer can be separated from the shape of the trees surrounding the deal.

Another possibility is that of stalling, during which one side may engage in *avoidance negotiation*, which is defined as 'an effort to defeat negotiation by mimicking its purpose' (Wallihan, 1998: 267). It may be part of what is an overall avoidance approach, where one side withdraws from any active engagement in negotiation (Taylor, 2002). However, it can also take the form of *demand avoidance* where one side prefers the status quo but is under pressure to be 'seen' to be negotiating. It may also be due to *opportunistic avoidance* where eventual agreement is not ruled out, but one side knows that a delay in reaching settlement is to their benefit. For example, a strike may be costing a factory owner dearly, and so by holding up negotiations the union could get a better eventual deal for its members. Wallihan illustrated how nations, before they declare war on their neighbours, need to be seen to have 'tried to reason' with them, and so negotiate for a time before declaring them to be 'intransigent', 'aggressive' or 'insulting'.

In essence, there are four main strategies that can be employed during negotiations (Hargie *et al.*, 1999).

1   *Unilateral concession.* Using this strategy, one side simply accepts the demands of the other. This can occur where one party has complete power over the other and so debate or resistance is futile. In general, however, it is not a viable long-term strategy, and where it happens the loser is likely to feel rather aggrieved and resentful at the outcome. Weitzman and Weitzman (2000) proposed that suppressed anger held onto after such experiences of poorly resolved conflict could even increase morbidity over the long term.

2   *Individual gain.* Here, one party is interested only in how best to maximise its share, with no thought whatsoever for the other side. There is no concern as to whether others do well or badly, just an all-encompassing focus on self. In one-off negotiations this may work, but the other side will feel alienated, and if further negotiations are required then this approach may well backfire. To adapt the oft-quoted aphorism as espoused by the Gordon Gecko character played by Michael Douglas in the film *Wall Street*, 'Greed is not good'.

3   *Competition.* This usually occurs in what is known as *distributive bargaining* where both parties attempt to obtain a higher share of the distribution of benefits than the other. Competition is also more likely in *zero-sum* payoff situations, so called because the total sum involved in the negotiation equals zero and a gain to one person is a direct loss to the other. For example, if I offer to sell you my watch for €80 and you will only give me €60 then if I accept, you have benefited by €20 and I have lost by the same amount. As a result, this is also referred to as *win–lose* negotiation. It is, of course, possible to reach a compromise by finding some common ground between the initial offers through distributive bargaining – for example in agreeing to split the difference at a price of €70 for the watch. A danger with competition is that the whole negotiation edifice may collapse if neither side is willing to concede what they perceive to be defeat (or surrender), and so it becomes *lose–lose* negotiation.

4   *Co-operation.* Negotiation is viewed as a form of problem-solving exercise, with the goal of achieving the best possible deal for both sides. Here the emphasis is on *integrative bargaining*, in the context of a *variable-sum* payoff in which both sides can benefit from the deal. Unlike distributive bargaining where the focus is on how to 'cut up the cake' with each side intent on getting the bigger share (or even the whole lot), the possibility of both producing a bigger cake is acknowledged when co-operation is countenanced. This transforms the negotiation into a *win–win* encounter. Gatchalian (1998) discussed how this approach can be used constructively in labour relations disputes. There is also some evidence that females do less well than males when negotiating in distributive encounters, and may prefer this more co-operative strategy (Solnick, 2001). Conditions favouring such a strategy are outlined in Box 13.2. A word of caution is warranted, however, since someone who is very co-operative may experience internal pressures to compromise and so may be vulnerable to manipulation by a competitive and deceptive opponent (Murray, 1990).

Box 13.2 The seven rules for 'win–win' negotiations

1 Have a main goal of achieving an outcome that maximises the outcome *for both sides*.
2 Do not view negotiation as simply getting the best for oneself. Likewise, do not see it as a contest in which you have to beat the other side. These strategies are likely to result in conflict and lessen the benefits for everyone.
3 Remain flexible and do not adopt an entrenched position. Remember there are many routes to 'Success City' in negotiations.
4 Develop a good relationship with the other party, founded on mutual trust.
5 Foster the capacity to distinguish the people from the problem – overcoming the latter should be seen as a joint venture.
6 Investigate the needs that may be driving demands – often demands can be adapted in ways that still satisfy the underlying needs.
7 Approach the task on the basis of logic and reason, rather than being swept along on a tide of emotion.

Carnevale and Pruitt (1992) identified four possible outcomes that can emanate from these negotiating strategies.

1 There may simply be *no agreement* and negotiation breaks down.
2 There may be a *victory for one side over the other*. In negotiation parlance, *Pareto superior* agreements occur when the outcome offers benefits to one party without incurring losses for the other. *Pareto inferior* agreements occur when one side ends up worse off while the other does not gain any benefit (Jeffries and Reed, 2000).
3 A *compromise solution* connecting the two offers may be agreed.
4 An *integrative agreement* can occur in which both sides achieve higher joint benefits than in the compromise. Such *Pareto optimal* agreements occur where both sides achieve the best possible gains and the benefits to one side cannot be improved without reducing the gains to the other.

A widely used, if somewhat contrived, example that illustrates the difference between these approaches is that of two sisters arguing over who should have an orange. If negotiation breaks down, neither gets the orange. In unilateral concession, one sister would just give the orange to the other, and in the individual gain approach one sister would try to get the entire orange. In the competitive strategy, a compromise could be reached whereby they agree to divide it in half and distribute the halves equally. However, using the co-operative mode, following discussion they discover that one sister wants the orange to squeeze for juice, while the other just wants the peel for a cake she is baking. As a result, they reach an integrative agreement where one sister gets all the peel and the other gets all the juice. Both benefit more than in any of the other styles. A more realistic example would be where a salesperson offers a supermarket buyer a new product on trial at €4 per unit for 100 units. The buyer in return initially offers €2 per unit. In relation to the four strategies: (1) negotiation may break down and no sale is made; (2) the seller agrees to sell for €2 or the buyer agrees to pay the €4; (3) they split the difference at a price of €3; or (4) they work out a new deal where the supermarket agrees to take not just 100 but 10,000 units of the new product over a set period, if a price of €3 is accepted. In other words, both sides benefit.

Pruitt (1990) highlighted three main reasons why integrative agreements are the most effective negotiating outcome.

1 They are likely to be more stable, whereas compromises are often unsatisfactory to one or both parties, leading to issues not being fully resolved and thus resurfacing in the future.
2 Since they are mutually beneficial, they help to develop the relationship between the two parties. This, in turn, facilitates communication and problem-solving in later encounters. An important feature in negotiation is what is known as the *response-in-kind* (Weingart *et al.*, 1999). This refers to the norm of reciprocity, whereby if we receive something positive from another person we feel obliged to reciprocate by giving something positive back (see Chapter 12 for more information on reciprocation). Alternatively, if we receive negative feedback from others we are likely to return it in kind. Integrative behaviour is likely to beget integrative responses from the other side.
3 Where aspirations are high and both sides are loath to concede, compromise may simply not be possible and an integrative approach, which allows both sides to gain, will be the best solution.

STAGES IN THE NEGOTIATION PROCESS

Negotiations have been conceptualised as typically progressing through, and characterised by, a series of sequential stages (Guirdham, 1996; Holmes, 1997). Kennedy (1998) identified a variety of models, ranging from those specifying a mere three, to more elaborate alternatives outlining eight identifiable phases. However, in essence the five key sequential negotiation stages are as follows: (1) pre-negotiation; (2) opening; (3) exploration; (4) bargaining; and (5) settlement. Each of these will now be explored in turn.

The pre-negotiation stage

Before people meet face-to-face, time and effort should be devoted to preparing for the encounter. Time devoted to planning is time very well spent, and so negotiators should never short-change themselves on making ready. Indeed, preparation is often regarded as the most important part of negotiation (Simons and Tripp, 2003). Thus Cairns (1996: 64), citing the maxim 'Failing to prepare is preparing to fail', cautioned negotiators to 'ignore it at their cost'. In fact, where the negotiation is particularly important it can be useful to have a simulation or rehearsal of the entire process, where some members play the role of the opposition. Rackham (2003) investigated differences in the planning strategies of skilled and average negotiators. As well as interviewing negotiators about their planning techniques, actual planning sessions were observed and recorded. There were actually no differences in amount of planning time *per se*. Rather, it was what they did with the time that mattered. Skilled negotiators considered a much wider range of possible outcomes and options – 5.1 per issue as opposed to 2.6 for average negotiators – and gave over three times as much attention to areas of common ground.

The main aspects of the planning stage have been shown to be goals, the key issues involved in goal achievement, and ways of surmounting any obstacles (Roloff and Jordan, 1992). The key dimensions of the pre-negotiation stage are now examined in more detail.

Formulating realistic goals

To adapt an old maxim: 'If you don't know where you are going, how will you know what direction to take and whether you have arrived?' Before entering into negotiations it is essential to be fully aware in advance as to what exactly your goals are. Indeed, as shown in Figure 13.1, the first decision to be made is whether or not to enter into negotiations at all. For example, the other side may be seen to be completely inflexible and impossible to deal with, your demands may simply not be negotiable, or the goals may be achievable in some other way. If negotiation seems the best option, the next issue to be decided is with which party it is most appropriate to deal. Once this has been worked out, then the serious business of planning really begins. This encompasses three main areas.

1   *Resistance point.* This is the bottom line beyond which a deal will not be done. It has also been termed the *reservation price* (Carnevale and Pruitt, 1992) and the *minimum necessary share* (Morley, 1997). It is also sometimes called the 'walk away' point, for obvious reasons.
2   *Target point* or *target range.* This is also known as the *aspiration level* (Whitney, 1990). It is the ideal point that you hope to achieve. Here, the goal of negotiation may be viewed in terms of achieving an exact amount (target point), or as settling somewhere between an upper and lower limit (target range). Rackham (2003) found that skilled negotiators were significantly more likely to plan in terms of a settlement *range* (e.g. 'I'd like €30 per item but would settle for €24 minimum'), whereas average negotiators planned around a fixed *point* (e.g. 'I want to get €27 per item').
3   *BATNA.* As explained earlier, this is the Best Alternative to a Negotiated Agreement. Formulating a BATNA can help to clarify where exactly the resistance point actually falls. If a settlement is not reached at or above this point, is no agreement then definitely the best option? What exactly are the ramifications of this?

It is important to remember that the other party also has target and resistance points. Settlements usually occur between the two sets of resistance points, as illustrated in Figure 13.2. In this example, the buyer would ideally wish to purchase at a target price of €550, whereas the seller's ideal price is €650. The respective resistance points, which represent the worst deals for each side, are €600 for the buyer

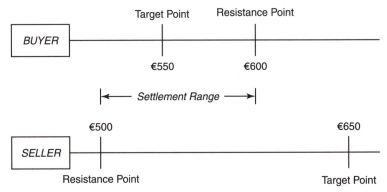

Figure 13.2 Example of target and resistance points in negotiation

and €500 for the seller and this is the range within which any eventual settlement will occur. One of the first things an experienced negotiator attempts to do is to ascertain the target and resistance points of the other side, so a deal can be made that is closer to the opponent's resistance point.

Identifying key issues

When examining issues, a guiding principle is to be as flexible and open as possible. Try not to conceptualise the process as a single-issue debate. Think laterally to identify everything that might be important. Negotiators have been shown to differ in their degree of self-monitoring. High self-monitors are more occupied with situational norms, the impression they create, and how they are being reacted to by others. They then adjust their performance accordingly. Low self-monitors are guided in their behaviour to a greater extent by internal states. Jordan and Roloff (1997), in an analysis of written pre-negotiation plans, discovered that those of high self-monitors were not only more elaborate but that this type of negotiator subsequently achieved a higher percentage of their initial profit goals.

Issues vary widely depending on the context. For example, in an industrial purchasing negotiation they may include aspects such as unit costs, quality of product, guarantees, payment terms and related financing, delivery dates and costs, insurance, installation costs, buy-back agreements and penalty clauses for missed deadlines. Once the main issues have been identified, they should then be prioritised. Which are absolutely essential and which are more peripheral? How, in what ways, and to what extent, are issues linked? In essence, as much information as possible should be gathered about all aspects of the negotiation. For each issue identified, the target, resistance and satisfaction points should also be located. This serves to guide later behaviour as negotiations get under way. While plans may be altered somewhat during the course of negotiations, generally speaking good preparation leads to better outcomes. As Hargie *et al.* (1999: 116) noted 'It is impossible to be too well informed approaching a negotiation.'

Gathering information

Forewarned is definitely forearmed when negotiating. Indeed, large corporations go to great lengths to protect key information from competitors, while some have also been known to use various forms of espionage to ascertain such information from others. It is vital that all members are fully apprised of their own team's perspectives on all of the key issues. The arguments in favour, and likely counter-arguments and how these can be overcome, should all be worked out in advance. Meta-planning is also important, in that Party A should try to see the planning world through the eyes of Party B. It is useful to consider realistically how much they know about your position. Do they have an accurate picture of your true BATNA? Similarly, as much information as possible should be gleaned about the other side's likely position on each issue. As advised by Davies (1998: 128), 'You need to know as much as you can about your opposite number: who they are, what they want, how they are likely to act and react.' For example, what is their BATNA and what are the ramifications thereof for both parties? In addition to the issues *per se*, it is also useful to know something about the interactive style of the other party. Do they tend to play hardball or are they likely to be more co-operative?

This process of information-gathering allows areas of potential agreement and conflict to be formulated. Staking out common ground shared by both sides is always important. This enables the negotiation to be built on a solid foundation of early joint agreement. However, likely areas of disagreement should also be identified, together with possible proposals for overcoming them. This includes an analysis of what and how much you can concede, and what concessions you may realistically seek from the other side in return.

Deciding on the type of negotiation to pursue

The next phase of the pre-negotiation considerations is the decision about how to 'play' the negotiation. As mentioned in relation to strategies to pursue, one option is to view the other side as the enemy, to be engaged in a win–lose macho battle of might in which the purpose is to defeat them in the war of attrition that is negotiation. An alternative is to perceive the activity as a collaborative win–win venture in which the goal is to co-operate so as to achieve the optimum outcome for both sides. The latter strategy has been widely recommended for most negotiating situations (Fisher *et al.*, 1991; LePoole, 1991). It does not benefit either side to become embroiled in a battle of wits and wills, during which they may at best lose potential gains and at worst be damaged or destroyed (Brandenburger and Nalebuff, 1996).

That said, Shapiro (2000), in recommending the more constructive approach, also highlighted the often short-sighted and unnecessary predilection towards 'hard' bargaining in many sections of society. Conditions that promote collaborative negotiations include being involved with the other side in a long-term negotiating relationship and trusting them not to take advantage of one's willingness to co-operate. Cultural background is also a factor here, since 'culture can influence the way in which persons perceive and approach certain key elements in the negotiating process' (Salacuse, 1998: 237). In fact, Salacuse, in a study of 310 negotiators from

North America, Latin America and Europe, across professions such as law, engineering, accounting, the military, teaching and marketing, identified a range of factors that are affected by culture (see Box 13.3). Some studies have found that the Japanese are much more amenable to win–win encounters than are the Russians (LePoole, 1991), and more likely to adopt tactics in line with the other party when involved in intercultural integrative negotiations (Adair *et al.*, 2001). However, Salacuse (1998) also found that professional and occupational culture was as important as national culture in determining negotiation behaviour.

Formulating an agenda

Following on from the considerations just outlined, a proposed agenda for the negotiation can be drawn up, to include the items that you wish to discuss and the preferred order. Of course, the other side will have its own ideas about what should be discussed and when. Indeed agreeing an agenda may form the first part of negotiations – what is sometimes referred to as 'talks about talks'. Where possible, the idea is to collaborate on and jointly agree the agenda, as this sets the tone for the substantive business to follow (Mattock and Ehrenborg, 1996). As part of this, general rules about the process should also be clarified. An important element here may be the actual location for the negotiations. In some settings this may not be a problem – for example in sales negotiations, the salesperson usually visits the buyer. There is an advantage to negotiating on your own 'home ground' where you will tend to feel more relaxed and the opposition may be less settled (Mills, 1991). However, there can also be benefits in visiting the other person's patch to gain some insight into where they are coming from (e.g. their status in the organisation and the nature of the operation *per se*). Negotiations may, of course, take place at a neutral location so that neither side feels disadvantaged. This is often the case in political negotiations, where much of the dispute is about territory.

Flexibility is important in relation to how issues are to be addressed. Rackham (2003) found that average negotiators tended to use sequence planning where each issue had to be dealt with in turn (i.e. Issue 1 → Issue 2 → Issue 3 → Issue 4). The problem is that the other side may wish to discuss Issue 4 first. More successful

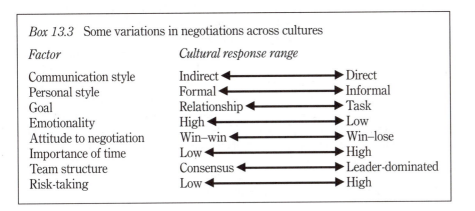

Box 13.3 Some variations in negotiations across cultures

Factor	Cultural response range		
Communication style	Indirect	←→	Direct
Personal style	Formal	←→	Informal
Goal	Relationship	←→	Task
Emotionality	High	←→	Low
Attitude to negotiation	Win–win	←→	Win–lose
Importance of time	Low	←→	High
Team structure	Consensus	←→	Leader-dominated
Risk-taking	Low	←→	High

negotiators therefore simply plan in terms of issues, which they are then willing to discuss in any order. Brett *et al.* (1998b) used the terms *monochronicity* to describe the tendency to deal with information one issue at a time and *polychronicity* to refer to the capacity to deal with many different issues simultaneously. They found that negotiators high in polychronicity were more successful. In their study of simulated negotiation encounters they discovered that joint gains (win–win encounters) were influenced by three key factors: 'a value for information sharing, an ability to deal with multiple issues simultaneously, and the motivation to keep on improving the option on the table' (Brett *et al.*, 1998b: 78).

Planning for settlement

Settlement details can often be forgotten about during the heat of negotiations. The pressure to reach a deal may lead to an unrealistic agreement – one that cannot be implemented – being finalised. There is no point in reaching an unworkable settlement, and so part of the preparatory phase should include an analysis of the extent to which a desired deal will actually work in practice. As part of this phase, thought should be given to how the settlement will be documented, ratified and implemented. For example, who has the authority to sign the agreement, and do they also have the power to make it stick? Who are the *real* key players who must be persuaded that the deal is beneficial for them?

Having said all the above that about the importance of preparation, flexibility must be the key, as things do not always go according to plan. Indeed, Wilson *et al.* (2001: 305) described the negotiation as 'a complex planning environment'. It may sometimes be necessary to formulate multiple goals in circumstances where there are only fuzzy criteria for ordering priorities. Again, while pre-planning is essential, initial decisions typically have to be revisited and revised when the negotiation gets under way.

The opening stage

Here the parties meet face-to-face. As discussed in Chapter 10, the opening phase of any interaction is of key importance, and negotiation is no exception. During the initial meeting, decisions are made about how co-operative or competitive the other party is likely to be, and whether the social relationship will be conducive to the task in hand. As the ideal is the development of a win–win framework, the general advice here is to be co-operative and courteous, but also well organised (Scott, 1988). A significant finding is that negotiators often reciprocate each other's use of strategies and tactics (Brett *et al.*, 1998a). This process, where the approach adopted by one side causes the other to reciprocate, is known as *entrainment*, and it has been shown to be a valuable negotiating tactic (Taylor, 2002). Thus, if one party seems frosty and adopts a rather belligerent opening stance, it is likely that the other will follow suit: threats will provoke counter-threats, demands counter-demands, and so on. On the other hand, a more integrative, co-operative and amenable approach is also likely to be responded to in kind (Weingart *et al.*, 1999).

The first main substantive step is usually agreeing an agenda. This sets the tone for what is to follow, and so should be enacted in a non-confrontational manner and in a spirit of partnership. This can be facilitated by the use of 'we' language to indicate joint responsibility for the process (e.g. 'We seem to agree that our main joint concerns are . . .'). Ideally the negotiation environment should be warm, comfortable, and free from distractions. The location should allow for both formal and informal encounters between parties, and space should be set aside for participants to mingle over coffee and biscuits. Berry (1996) identified a number of factors as being central to the establishment of a good negotiating rapport:

- paying attention to and allowing time for opening rituals such as personal introductions;
- verbally and nonverbally displaying signs of receptivity and enthusiasm;
- ascertaining what issues the other side regard as important and giving recognition to these;
- portraying any identified difficulties as problems to be solved jointly;
- avoiding point-scoring or cheap one-upmanship ploys to gain an early advantage; these can back-fire and cause problems for the entire relationship.

The final act of the opening phase is usually the ratification of an agreed agenda, endorsed by all those present. At this point the negotiation can proceed into the exploration phase.

The exploration stage

Here, parties begin to examine one another's positions. This allows both sides to become familiar with the main proposals being put forward by the other. If these are in complete symmetry and harmony, then an agreement may be possible without further negotiation. If there are areas of disagreement, then these should be fully identified and clarified. Party A can only hope to satisfy the demands of party B, and vice versa, if they know exactly what these are. As mentioned earlier, the opposition may not be completely truthful about their position, and cognisance should be taken of this in evaluating their proposals. For example if they say they need 100 units of 'X' it may be the case that their true target point is closer to 90 units.

An important aspect at this stage is probing in depth beyond the expressed surface-level demands, to explore the needs that may underpin these. What each say they *want* is not always what they really *need* and following concerted discussion and sharing of perspectives this often becomes clear. In addition, the needs may be capable of being met in ways other than expressed in the initial demands. But this realisation usually takes some time and so the exploration stage should not be rushed. Indeed later breakdowns in the negotiation process can often be traced back to a lack of time devoted to initial exploration and clarification of demands, needs and wants.

The goal here is to achieve a panoramic view of the other side and chart the full topography of their needs terrain. The contours of the peaceful valleys where areas of agreement lie, and of the rugged hills of dispute that will have to be climbed, should then be carefully drawn. In addition, ways in which both sides can help one another to climb these hills should also be identified. It is important to remember that the purpose is not to begin bargaining at this juncture. The main goal relates to the exploration and clarification of core areas of each other's position. Central to this is the skill of listening. As explained in Chapter 7 this involves paying attention to the other person's verbal and nonverbal messages, to the slant or emphasis they put on what they say, as well as listening to what is not being said. In her analysis of hostage situations, Dunne (2001: 15) pointed out that 'The best negotiators are good listeners who handle stress well and are able to argue logically and calmly.' If the auguries are good following exploration, then the parties can move on to the next stage, that of bargaining.

The bargaining stage

Once a decision has been made to move from initial explorations to more substantive bargaining, two main processes come into play: making proposals and concession-making.

Making proposals

The opening proposals must be clearly stated. Each party should fully understand precisely what the other is proposing. The generally accepted rule here is that the initial proposal should be high (if you are selling) or low (if buying), but realistically so. For instance, if you apply for a job where the salary is negotiable, and you learn that the average executive in a similar post earns €120,000, it would be inappropriate to ask for a starting salary of €400,000. Initial bids should not be so high or low that they appear to be lacking in credibility, are seen as nonsensical, or the person making them is regarded as highly avaricious. Outrageous opening proposals can quickly lead to a 'take it or leave it' position and negotiation breakdown (Gatchalian, 1998). The first offer should also be stated in a confident manner. If a high/low bid is made in an apologetic fashion it is immediately undermined. It is important to avoid 'one-down' statements such as 'I think this is probably far too much to ask for, but . . .' Realistically high/low opening gambits presented in an assertive fashion serve a number of important functions, in that they:

- influence the opposition's estimate of your target and resistance points and can in turn move their target point more favourably in your direction;
- provide information about the other side's goals; careful scrutiny of their reaction allows insight into their target and resistance points (do they seem stunned at one end of the reaction scale or completely unsurprised at the other);
- allow 'generous' concessions to be made if necessary;
- make the eventual settlement, with your concessions, appear more appealing to the other side.

There can be benefits in linking proposals to other conditions (Mills, 1991). For example, 'We are prepared to accept your offer of €120 per unit if you agree to take at least 10,000 units.' Such proposals are typical in integrative bargaining encounters.

Another decision here is whether or not to make the first proposal. Is it better to get in first or to play a waiting game so that your bid can take advantage of the knowledge gleaned from the other side's opening shot? It seems that there are advantages and disadvantages in both strategies (LePoole, 1991), and so a decision about this issue needs to be based on the specific nature of the negotiation. The side that goes first:

- sets the initial rate;
- is proactive, and the second party then becomes reactive and may be more on the defensive;
- may be able to make the other side revise their target point in the light of the initial demand.

Some of the disadvantages, on the other hand, are that the side that opens may:

- not bid at a sufficiently high (or low) level and so be at an immediate disadvantage;
- be put on the defensive by the other party if they begin to probe the initial offer;
- have to make the first concession after the other party has made a counter-proposal.

Concession-making

When both sides have made their opening pitches, the process moves on to one of trying to formulate mutually acceptable compromises in which each side moves towards the other's position. Positional bargaining has been described by Fisher *et al.* (1991: 3) as happening when 'Each side takes a position, argues for it, and makes concessions to reach a compromise.' A concession is 'a change in offer by party A in the direction of party B's interests that reduces the level of benefit accruing to party A' (Hargie *et al.*, 1999: 122). Concessions lead to *position loss*, which can be interpreted as a willingness to compromise and be co-operative. However, if too much is conceded too quickly this can result in *image loss* where the person is viewed as someone who is weak and easily manipulated. Interestingly, Morris *et al.* (1999) discovered that negotiators often attribute the bargaining behaviour of the other party to personality and personal predispositions (e.g. disagreeableness, truculence) rather than to the circumstances of the negotiation with which they are confronted. Such a misperception can evoke a more hostile response, if a lack of willingness to compromise is attributed to the other party being seen as an obstinate or greedy individual, as opposed to being interpreted as due to the fact that the organisation to which the person belongs has given strict guidelines about what can and cannot be negotiated.

A core dimension of negotiation is the ability to persuade the opposition to make concessions. Pruitt (1981) identified four main tactics in this regard.

1   *Promote a friendly atmosphere*. The goal here is to develop a friendly relation-
     ship between bargainers that is conducive to 'give-and-take'. Friends will not
     want the negotiation to spoil or destroy their relationship and so are more
     concerned with achieving a swift resolution. For example, Halpern (1994) found
     that buyers offered higher opening amounts and sellers made lower initial
     demands when dealing with friends as opposed to strangers. Interestingly, this
     bias to co-operate can have a down side. Friends can actually lose out on a better
     deal for both sides, owing to the fact that they wish to avoid the appearance
     of being awkward. A relational bias towards affiliation means they are liable to
     settle for the first mutually acceptable solution to emerge, when more debate
     and discussion about all the alternatives might have produced a higher, Pareto
     optimal, result (Jeffries and Reed, 2000).

2   *Impose time pressures*. This is a common tactic used in attempts to influence
     others. For example, companies offer bargain discount rates – but only for a
     set time period; time-share salespeople offer a 'special price' which will be
     withdrawn if the prospective buyer leaves without signing a contract; and in
     hostage negotiation, threats may be made to execute hostages at a set time if
     demands are not met.

3   *Increase the impression of firmness*. This may involve making small con-
     cessions, but few of them, as a way of seeking reciprocal concessions from
     the other side. Firmness can be enhanced through emphasising that there are
     specific reasons for the concessions such as:

     •   emphasising that this is a one-off event ('Just this once and just for you –
          do not tell anyone else I gave you it at this price');
     •   stating that the concession is based on special circumstances ('There is a
          new model coming in next month so I want to sell off this one');
     •   seeking a reciprocal concession ('I'll increase my offer for the house if you
          include the carpets in the price'). This latter tactic may involve *logrolling* –
          that is trading off pairs of issues that differ in importance to both parties.
          For example, a car dealer may agree to install a sound system (at small
          personal cost) rather than reduce the price of the car, while the customer
          values this service and sees it as adequate compensation for no price
          reduction.

4   *Reduce the opponent's resistance* to making concessions by using a range of
     techniques including:

     •   face-saving devices that make it easier for the other side to concede
          without appearing to lose or be weak. This can involve some of the
          techniques discussed in point 3 above in relation to perceptions of
          firmness (e.g. explaining that you understand the concession will only
          be a 'one-off'). This is important since 'Sensitivity to the other side's
          face does more than head off resistance: it lays the groundwork for trust'
          (Kolb and Williams, 2003: 213);
     •   being optimistic. In a series of experiments, Bottom and Paese (1999)
          found that when bargainers were optimistic going into a negotiation and

believed that their counterpart had considerable latitude for concession, they tended to come out with a more profitable deal compared with those who actually had a more accurate view of the situation;

- logical arguments (see Chapter 12 for a full review of how such arguments can be persuasive);
- a promise of beneficial outcomes (e.g. a head of a university department may argue that if more staff were allocated to the department the research profile would improve, in turn bringing in more money and greater prestige for the university). Kennedy (1998) termed this tactic 'Sell Cheap, Get Famous', a title derived from the entertainment industry where actors reputedly may be persuaded to lower their fee on the promise that the film will make them famous and open the door to untold fame and fortune;
- highlighting the disadvantages that would befall the other party were the deal to fall through;
- reference to objective criteria (e.g. a trade union may refer to the average percentage pay rise for comparable workers that year);
- 'salami slicing'. This is so called on the basis that if you request a whole salami from someone they may well refuse. However, if you ask for just one slice you are more likely to succeed. If you keep getting more small slices you end up with most of the salami;
- 'good person/bad person'. This is obviously a variant of the soft cop/hard cop routine. Here, one negotiator plays the role of the tough cookie while the other is much more amenable and affiliative. The 'good' negotiator may argue openly with the 'bad' one to give the other side a break. When used skilfully this can encourage the other party to seek to cut a deal with the 'good' person. Sometimes the 'bad person' is a difficult third party outwith the immediate encounter ('My boss would sack me if I accepted this offer');
- indicating the need to refer to a higher authority. The other party will sometimes concede when confronted with a situation in which a negotiator claims not to have the authority to accept the present offer, but were it to be changed ever so slightly the deal could be agreed then and there;
- use of threats. These, however, are not usually recommended since they are invariably viewed as hostile and are dysfunctional for the relationship between the two parties (Putnam and Roloff, 1992a). The threatened side is likely to counter with threats of equal force; will not be committed to any settlement achieved; and will feel resentful, attempting to seek revenge where possible. Research findings clearly show that threats are associated with less successful outcomes (Olekalns and Smith, 2001). As Fisher (1990: 65) put it 'making threats is a particularly expensive and dangerous way of trying to exert influence'. For example, in 1997 the then Chief Executive of British Airways (BA) sent a letter to cabin crews involved in an industrial dispute with the company. In it he threatened that anyone who went on strike risked being sacked. As a result some 2,000 staff simply called in sick instead, disrupting the airline's schedule

at a huge financial cost to BA. If threats are used these should be portrayed as emanating from a third party ('There is no way my union members would accept that. If I go back and put it to them I know they will want to go on strike');

- fait accompli. Under certain conditions a pre-emptive strike may force the other side's hand. Terrorists may set off a large bomb explosion so that they are then seen to be negotiating from a position of strength (with the threat potential of further such bombs also ever-present). A spouse may buy a new dining room suite and have it delivered arguing that it can be sent back within ten days if the partner so desires;

- use of power. People who control resources have been found to have a definite advantage in negotiations (Cai *et al.*, 2001). An extreme example is that a shop-owner is unlikely to cede to a polite request to give all the money in the cash register to a stranger, whereas if the stranger is wielding a handgun then the request is likely to be granted. In this case the gun represents greater power. Imbalances of power have a marked influence on negotiating encounters, in that those who have power will tend to use it and so be less open to making concessions or listening to counter-arguments. Thus Kipnis and Schmidt (1990: 49) found that: 'The more one-sided the power relationship at work, the more likely managers are to demand, get angry and insist with people who work for them, and the more likely they are to act humble and flatter when they are persuading their bosses.' However, it is hardly surprising that people are happier with the outcomes of bargaining encounters when both sides have equal power (Mastenbroek, 1989).

Garko (1992) carried out an investigation into the influencing strategies employed by physician executives (those carrying out managerial roles) when attempting to gain compliance from superiors. They found that with superiors who interacted in an attractive fashion (were attentive, friendly, relaxed) reason was used most frequently. On the other hand, with superiors who interacted in an unattractive style, assertiveness, bargaining, coalition formation with others, and reference to higher authority were more likely to be used. Thus it would seem that, with people of higher power or status, the negotiating tactics of subordinates are influenced by the interactive approach of the former.

Concessions are an integral part of negotiations. Where differences exist, without concessions there can be no mutual agreement. It is important, though, that concession-making is guided by the pointers shown in Box 13.4.

The settlement stage

Catching the settlement moment is a key aspect of negotiation. There comes a time when the other side is receptive and a deal can be struck. If this is missed, problems can arise. When a settlement attempt is made too early the other party can feel pressured and resentful. Conversely if the opportunity is missed further issues may

---

Box 13.4 Pointers for making concessions

Bargainers should:

- not concede too readily;
- make concessions as small as possible;
- monitor the extent and rate of concession-making;
- link concessions to an image of firmness;

Bargainers should not:

- concede too soon in the negotiations;
- make the first main concession;
- make unilateral concessions;
- make large initial concessions – this is likely to give an impression of weakness;
- concede without due consideration of the positive and negative consequences *for both parties;*
- always engage in reciprocal concessions. A concession by the other side may be justified in its own right – it may bring their bid down to what is a reasonable level.

---

then be raised and more concessions sought by the opposition. The closing stage is important in all interactions (see Chapter 10) and negotiation is no exception. A number of central elements have been identified as being crucial to agreeing a settlement (e.g. Cairns, 1996; Kennedy, 1998), and these will now be considered. For the most part, however, the advice offered has been based on experiential rather than empirical evidence.

Trial closure

Here, one side behaves as if a deal has been agreed and so is moving beyond this to the fine-grained implementation issues. It includes what are known as 'assumptive questions' where the assumption of a deal is inferred in the question. An example would be 'Do you intend to pay by cheque or credit transfer?' Linked to this is what is termed 'summary closure'. This involves providing a summary of what the other side has gained in the way of concessions, what the benefits are for them of the deal as it stands, and outlining the potential dangers of failing to agree this deal.

Looking for settlement signals

Positive closure signals include the following.

- Implementation questions: 'You could definitely deliver at that price?'
- Confirmatory statements: 'That seems like a good deal.'

- Physical actions: tidying up papers, bringing out a contract.
- Nonverbal responses: smiling, looking relaxed or excited, clasping the hands enthusiastically.
- Overt settlement verbalisations: 'OK. Can we agree on this . . .?' 'Right, let's get the papers signed.'

The end of the line

At some stage there comes a point beyond which it is not possible to concede any further. The secret is to convince the opposition that in all honesty this point has been reached and any deal must be struck at this limit. In some cases negotiators may hold back a small concession to use as a final inducement to settlement. One potential shortfall of this strategy, however, is that a reputation can be gained of always having something else to concede if the other side bargains long and hard enough.

Split-the-difference

This is quite common in sales negotiations as a way of cutting a deal. You offer €600, I ask for €550 and we finally settle for €575. It is fine in this type of fairly basic negotiation, but where issues are more complex it is not always applicable. In addition, if one side has already conceded a considerable amount and the other has conceded little, then the 'difference' is not just what is left.

Celebrate success

Both sides need to feel that the agreement has been a good one from their point of view. This cements the relationship and facilitates future encounters. It also helps to ensure that the deal will not unravel, but will actually be implemented. Celebrations may include smiles, handshakes and hugs; breaking open the bubbly; or having a meal out together.

Document the agreement

Formal agreements are typically enshrined in a written legal contract, although the actual drafting and signing may take place at a later date (Guirdham, 1996). Settlements that cannot be enforced are of little value. Likewise pursuing disputes through the courts is an expensive and messy business. It is important, therefore, that all parties are agreed on the exact terms of the settlement. Time spent jointly reviewing and agreeing the precise nature of what has been negotiated can avert substantial difficulties at a later date. For example, the ongoing confusions and uncertainties among political parties that plagued subsequent development in Northern Ireland in the aftermath of the Belfast Agreement can be traced back to areas of the settlement that were left (deliberately) vague. Thus one party to this Agreement later used the interesting semantic argument that while what was negotiated was an (interim) agreement it was not a (final) settlement (of the political situation). Paying attention to detail and ensuring that this is contained in the written documentation can pay dividends when it comes to implementing the resolution.

Implementation considerations

To negotiate an agreement that will later hit the buffers is merely to construct a future disagreement. But in more complex bargaining contexts, the devil is in the detail. For this reason, it is worth spending time discussing how, and in what ways, the deal will actually be implemented in practice. Who will do what, when will it be done, and how will it be carried out? Also, what are the ramifications if what has been agreed is not implemented? What penalties and costs will be incurred by either side, and how are these to be included in the contract?

NEGOTIATING SKILLS

There is general agreement that negotiation is a higher-order skill, involving a range of other sub-skills (Fisher *et al.*, 1991b; Taylor, 2002). As expressed by Lewicki (1997: 265) 'effective negotiation is not a single skill; rather it is a complex collection of elements that entail aspects of strategizing, advocacy, communication, persuasion, and cognitive packaging and repackaging of information'. Similarly, McRae (1998: 2) likened negotiation to 'a symphony orchestra of skills. Each instrument (subskill) must be used together with all the others in a harmonious and congruent manner. If one instrument (subskill) is off, the whole orchestra will be off.'

While there is general agreement in most texts about what good negotiators should do, and a host of laboratory studies have been conducted in this area, there is not a great deal of empirical research into the behaviour of negotiators in real encounters. The main reason for this is that conducting such research necessitates obtaining the agreement of both parties to the negotiation, and this is obviously difficult to arrange – especially given the delicate nature of such encounters. One major empirical study was carried out by Rackham and his co-workers (Rackham, 2003), in which they studied forty-eight successful negotiators over a total of 102 separate negotiating sessions, and compared their behaviour with that of a similar number of average negotiators. They used three criteria to select the effective negotiators, namely: they should be rated as effective by *both* sides; should have a track record of significant success over time; and should have a high incidence of implementation success in reaching agreements that proved to be viable. They found that skilled negotiators showed significant differences from average negotiators on a range of behaviours. We now review these, and other key negotiating behaviours.

Leadership

One feature of many professional negotiation encounters is that they are group phenomena: more than two people are involved. Indeed, even if only two individuals engage face-to-face, they will be reporting to and liaising with a range of members, colleagues and/or superiors in their organisation. This means that the skilled negotiator must have the capacity to organise and co-ordinate a group of individuals. Each group in a negotiation is rarely a homogeneous entity. Many groups suffer from divisions and disagreements between members. A minority may not concur with the majority view as to the way ahead, so much so that, as Morley (1997: 346) noted, 'differences within parties are just as important as differences between parties ... (and) ... internal negotiations may affect external negotiations and vice versa'. Intragroup disharmony has to be dealt with in such a way that it does not jeopardise the negotiation effort and outcomes. This means that care and attention need to be devoted to decisions about who is to be part of the overall team, and exactly who should be involved at the negotiating table (Wood, 2001). There should be a designated leader – someone who is both a recognised content expert in the field within which the negotiation is taking place, and who has successful experience of bargaining. This individual, who should have skills in consensus building, will then co-ordinate and direct the team effort in preparing for, conducting, and evaluating the effectiveness of the bargaining encounters (see Chapter 14 for more information on leadership skills).

Empathising and problem-solving

It is clear that the ability to be empathic is a characteristic of effective negotiators (Mnookin *et al.*, 1996). This capacity to see the world through the eyes of the other is very important. People are unlikely to readily accept *your* view of *their* situation, but rather need to be reassured that you appreciate their perspective. Thus efforts should be made to understand where the other side is coming from, and to communicate this understanding overtly. It is often said that in negotiation the cheapest (and often most warmly received) concession that you can make is to show that you are paying attention to what the other side is saying. You need to ascertain what their concerns are and why they have them. Why might they accept or reject your proposals? Linked to this, when presenting a proposal, skilled negotiators frame this as a problem to be solved. The golden rule is to 'Present your proposals as solutions to problems. State the problem before you give your answer' (Morley, 1997: 348). Bald proposals are often seen as selfish moves and as the other side listens they formulate counter-arguments as a way of obstructing them. When cast as a joint problem with a suggested solution, the listening perspective changes and the encounter becomes more co-operative.

Controlling emotionality

The most effective negotiators are those who can think logically, and who do not get involved in a war of words with the opposition. Adler *et al.* (1998a) illustrated how the two most intense emotions in negotiation are fear and anger. The former may be caused by anxieties such as the deal falling through, being told untruths, losing out unnecessarily, or not achieving all that one should. The development of a good trusting relationship helps to reduce such fear-arousing thoughts. High levels of anger have been shown to be destructive to the negotiation process (Taylor, 2002), and so must be controlled. Anger is caused by one side:

- being found to have given misleading or untrue information;
- insisting on discussing unimportant details;
- not listening to what the other has to say;
- making unreasonable or excessive demands;
- being rude or overtly aggressive;
- querying the other person's ability or authority to negotiate;
- overstepping their authority;
- going over the other person's head to deal with their superior.

While expressing concern for the feelings of the other party is important in all negotiations, in crisis situations, where this dimension has been shown to be of particular import, 'detecting and controlling emotional arousal is one of the primary concerns of negotiators' (Rogan and Hammer, 1995: 554). As a result, in these contexts (e.g. suicide attempts, criminal barricades, hostage taking or prison revolts) the tactics used include:

- communicating empathy and concern for the other;
- using an encouraging and agreeing style to calm the other person;
- making appeals to the person ('Please, please do not hurt anyone');
- giving frequent reassurance;
- protecting and saving the perpetrator's face;
- slowing the pace of negotiation;
- emphasising that the interaction is one of problem-solving (as opposed to crisis).

Rackham (2003) identified two negative emotional facets of negotiation that can be dysfunctional for the process, and so need to be curbed. The first of these is *irritators*. As the name suggests, irritators are words or phrases used by one side that irritate, annoy or offend the other. Examples include:

- 'unreasonable demand' (this is doubly irritating – the proposal may have been put forward as being perfectly reasonable, and the term 'demand' suggests aggression);
- 'very fair offer' (again this is annoying as it is up to the other side to decide what is fair and what is not);
- 'you are being unhelpful' (such an accusation is likely to cause problems for the relationship as it is an attack on the other party's interactive style).

Rackham (2003) found that less skilled negotiators used about five times as many irritators when compared with the skilled ones. Often these irritators are used without too much conscious thought. When caught up in the emotional heat of the occasion, they can slip out. Thus negotiators need to take care with their forms of expression. There is little point in describing an offer as a 'good deal' if the other side does not think it is.

The second facet is *defend/attack spirals*. This occurs when one side accuses or attacks the other and this is responded to in kind, leading to a spiral of retaliation with the result that emotions become heated and the entire relationship begins to disintegrate. As summarised by Lytle *et al.* (1999: 32):

> the reality is that negotiations, especially in the dispute context, often become ugly and difficult ... parties may find themselves drawn to respond to threats with counter-threats, escalating the negotiations to a standoff from which it is difficult or embarrassing to retreat.

For example:

A: You don't seem to want to resolve this, as you keep raising objections to every reasonable proposal we make. We may have to pull out of these talks.

B: On the contrary, you have done everything to prevent an agreement and we are the ones who have had to deal with your ridiculous demands. So don't try to threaten us, as we may be ahead of you out of the door.

A: You think that *we're* the problem? I don't believe I'm hearing this.

B: That's exactly been the problem. You just don't listen.

Given the potential relationship damage that can emanate from such encounters, not surprisingly Rackham (2003) found that skilled negotiators were significantly less likely to get entangled in emotional defend/attack spirals.

Building trust

Trust is at the heart of relationships, and negotiation is no exception. We rarely develop or maintain positive relationships with people of whom we are suspicious or wary. Trust has been defined as 'the extent to which a person is confident in, and willing to act on the basis of, the words, actions, and decisions of another' (McAllister, 1995: 25). It can be divided into three separate components (Jeffries and Reed, 2000):

- *Cognitive trust* refers to the extent to which we believe someone has sound technical know-how or a solid knowledge base.
- *Affective trust* is rooted in the degree of emotional feeling of attachment, and of mutual care and concern for one another's well-being, that exists.
- *Organisational trust* encompasses both intra-organisational (the extent to which staff trust others in their own organisation), and inter-organisational (the degree to which staff in two corporations trust one another) dimensions.

Where all three types of trust are present at high levels, negotiations are enhanced. The skill of self-disclosure is central to such relationship development and trust (see Chapter 9). Rackham (2003: 179) called this 'giving internal information', which he defined as 'any reference by negotiators to his/her internal considerations such as feelings and motives'. His results showed that effective negotiators used this skill more than average negotiators, especially in relation to their feelings about the way the negotiation was progressing. He pointed out that 'This revelation may or may not be genuine, but it gives the other party a feeling of security because such things as motives appear to be explicit and aboveboard' (Rackham, 2003: 179). As a result, the use of self-disclosure is likely to contribute to the establishment of trust in the negotiator. This technique can also serve as an alternative to disagreeing, e.g. 'I'm very worried that we seem to be so far apart on this . . .'; 'I'm uncertain how to react to what you've just said. I like most of it, but I feel some doubts . . .'.

Providing focus

A key aspect of negotiation is the ability to keep the discussion focused on the main issues at hand. Two sub-skills are important here.

1   *Questioning.* Given the fundamental importance of this skill in social encounters (see Chapter 5), it is not surprising that questioning is central to effective negotiation. Rackham (2003) found that skilled negotiators demonstrated very significant differences from average negotiators on the amount of questions asked. Questions serve several important functions in negotiations. A primary purpose is to gather detailed information about the other side and their aspirations and concerns. They also allow the questioner to control the focus and flow of the interaction since the opposition have to answer the questions and in so doing have less space for contemplation. This, in turn, gives one's own side a breathing space to reflect on the current state of affairs. Finally, questions can act as an alternative to an overt statement of disagreement. Compare the following:

A   'No. Our members would never accept that proposal.'
B   'You know our members fairly well. How do you think they would react to this proposal?'

The approach used in B is much less abrasive and more likely to produce a receptive response.

2   *Behaviour labelling.* Skilled negotiators have been shown to signal the behaviour they are about to use, by labelling it (Rackham, 2003). For example, rather than asking a question outright (e.g. 'How many can it produce per day?') they are more likely to announce it in advance (e.g. by saying 'Can I *ask you a question*? How many can it produce per day?') Other examples of behaviour labelling include:

*   'I would like to *make a proposal* . . .'
*   'It would be useful for me to *listen* to your views . . .'
*   'Could I *suggest a compromise* here . . .'
*   'If I could just *explain* to you why we see this as so important . . .'

This process of labelling is beneficial in that it reflects a formal and rational approach to bargaining, and subtly puts pressure on opponents to reciprocate in a logical fashion (Morley, 1997). Since it flags the behaviour that is about to follow, it provides focus, reduces ambiguity and clarifies the purpose of the next comment. It also helps to ensure that the negotiation is conducted at a moderate pace. Part of this labelling process also involves the acknowledgement of *joint progress* (e.g. 'We are getting on really well here . . .'). Effective negotiators are twice as likely to make statements labelling joint progress as their less effective counterparts (McRae, 1998).

However, one behaviour which average negotiators were more likely to label was that of expressing disagreement (e.g. 'I disagree with that because . . .') By comparison, the skilled negotiators gave reasons which in themselves were expressions of disagreement, but tried to avoid overt statements of dissent. Rackham argued that the order in which our thought processes occur involves deciding that an argument is unacceptable and then assembling the reasons to show why. He posited that average negotiators follow this tendency overtly, whereas those who are more skilled are able to stifle this initial impulse. When one side has put forward an argument it is likely that a blunt statement of disagreement will increase their antagonism and aggression and make them less likely to give in. Indeed, Dunne (2001: 15) illustrated how in hostage contexts the general advice is that 'the negotiator should never reply "no" to any question posed by the kidnapper'. The calm presentation of counter-arguments, without a public statement of negation, encourages logical debate, such that the eventual acceptance of alternative proposals then involves much less loss of face. It is therefore a useful general rule to always give reasons before (or as an alternative to) expressing disagreement. Furthermore, what has been termed *process labelling* has been shown to be effective in resolving disagreements (Lytle *et al.*, 1999). This involves openly stating and recognising that both sides simply cannot agree about an issue, and that it may be more productive to move on to discuss other aspects first and return to the contentious issue later.

Testing understanding and summarising

As discussed earlier in the chapter, it is crucial for both parties in a negotiation to be fully cognisant with what has been discussed and agreed. It is not unusual for a negotiation to end with each side holding differing views about what has been agreed. The primary concern among the less skilled negotiators was to achieve agreement, and so they tended to ignore rather than confront areas of potential ambiguity or misunderstanding. Rackham (2003) found that to circumvent such confusion, skilled negotiators checked for agreement on all the issues to ensure that the deal could be fully ratified and implemented. Thus they used *summaries* at the end of key points in the negotiation, to check that both sides were in full agreement about precisely what had been decided. A linked skill here was that of *reflection*, and indeed this skill has been shown to have a number of advantages in encounters where clarification of communication is important (see Chapter 6). Examples of reflections in negotiating include:

- 'So delivery times are absolutely vital . . .'
- 'In essence you are saying that if we can move on volume you could move on price.'
- 'You are clearly concerned about this . . .'

This type of reflective statement helps to portray concern for the other side.

Reasoned argument

As explained in Chapter 12, the use of logic can be very persuasive. In negotiations, the image of rationality is desirable. Rackham (2003) identified two aspects that should be avoided to ensure that arguments are used to maximum effect.

Retaliatory counter-proposals

A mistake made by inexperienced negotiators is to respond to a proposal with an immediate counter-proposal, e.g.:

A: We will offer you this at a price of €10 per unit providing we are your sole supplier for the next 12 months.

B: Well what we want is for you to pay all delivery costs and guarantee delivery times.

Here, while delivery and guarantees may be important to B, these could have been addressed after responding to A's initial proposal. Rackham (2003) found that skilled negotiators used about 50 per cent fewer counter-proposals than average negotiators. Counter-proposals are not recommended in negotiation, for three reasons.

1   They muddy the waters. One side has put forward a proposal and suddenly a different one is introduced by the opposition. Which should be discussed? One at a time? Both together? In some instances the first side retaliates to the counter-proposal by introducing a third proposal and this immediately throws the entire process completely out of kilter.
2   They are annoying. One side has made what they regard as a valid proposal and they want this to be fully considered. A counter-proposal completely ignores their bid, and so they in turn are less likely to treat this with respect or consideration.
3   They are regarded as blocking tactics rather than serious proposals *per se*, and so counter-proposals tend to get lost in the negotiation mists that follow. Arguments then begin to become emotional rather than logical.

Argument dilution

Less skilled negotiators tend to give more reasons to justify their bids. This is not good practice, since the more reasons that are proffered the better chance the opposition has of finding and highlighting a weakness in at least one of them. This then puts the first party on the back foot. As Rackham (2003: 180) put it: 'The poorest reason is the lowest common denominator: a weak argument generally dilutes a strong one.' Interestingly, Rackham also found that an unexpectedly high proportion of skilled negotiators had little formal higher education and suggested that graduates, having been steeped in a culture of devising numerous reasons to defend and justify a case, then suffer from the dilution effect in negotiation encounters. Skilled negotiators tended to put forward one reason at a time and would only introduce another reason if they were in danger of losing ground.

OVERVIEW

This review of negotiation has examined the nature of the activity and charted its defining features. The relationship between negotiating and bargaining has been explained. There is a burgeoning literature in this field and this vast body of research findings has identified a range of strategies and skills central to effectiveness. The alternative strategies of negotiation were charted and the likely outcomes of each discussed. The typical process of negotiation was outlined and the role of concession-making therein highlighted, and tactics for producing concessions from the other party itemised. Finally, the key skills employed by effective negotiators were discussed in concert with the behaviours that they tend not to employ.

In the mind of the layperson, negotiation is often perceived as a game of hardball played by tough-minded, hard-boiled, aggressive individuals. Here, the objective is seen as winning at all costs and if the other party is singed in the process, well then they should avoid the heat of the negotiating kitchen in future. But this win–lose perspective is both short-sighted and mistaken. The focus in negotiation should not be on how to divide up the spoils but rather on how to improve the spoils for both parties. The objective is not victory for one side, but for both. To achieve such win–win outcomes the following points need to be borne in mind:

- view negotiation in a co-operative frame;
- identify all the issues at the outset;
- these issues should be re-interpreted as necessary;
- be flexible as to how your goals are to be achieved;
- identify and highlight areas of agreement and common interest;
- begin with these to establish initial rapport;
- show a concern for partnership through the use of 'we' language;
- always listen carefully to the other side;
- use questions to understand their perspective;
- overtly recognise and acknowledge what they see as important;
- never lose sight of the total picture when single issues are being discussed;

- think laterally about new options that might be introduced to overcome disagreements;
- treat differences as challenges to be overcome;
- separate the people from the problem – be kind to the former and work hard on the latter;
- use gentle persuasion techniques rather than threats or coercion;
- formally review, agree and ratify the final settlement.

Chapter 14

Groups and group

interaction

INTRODUCTION

G ROUPS ARE COMMONPLACE IN social life. We are born into a social group (the family) and, as we grow, come to play a more active part in an increasing number and range of others. Branching out from the family, children find themselves in playgroups, school classes, sports teams, and youth organisations. Later these may give way to (in no particular order) staff groups, quality circles, seminar groups, choirs, appreciation societies, leisure classes, trade union committees, parent–teacher associations, and political party executives, to mention but a very few of the vast number of possibilities. Small wonder it has been claimed that, 'Most of our waking hours are spent in, and the bulk of our work-related productivity occurs within, settings consisting of . . . [groups]' (Simpson and Wood, 1992: 1).

Heath and Bryant (2000) likewise drew attention not only to the plethora of small groups of which we may be part but also to how these change and are reconfigured over time as members leave and others join. They concluded that 'groups are a vital part of peoples' life spans' (p. 333). Not only do they variously make it easier for us to do our job, they provide companionship, support and even a sense of identity (Ellemers *et al.*, 1999; Abrams and Hogg, 2001). If someone is asked to write about who they are, it is not long before they begin to anchor a sense of self in some particularly salient group membership/s.

Increasingly the contemporary workplace is structured to opti-mise the potential dynamic of small groups, especially when moulded into teams (Yeatts and Hyten, 1998). Focusing on healthcare delivery, Northouse and Northouse (1998) made the point that many functions that were previously performed by an individual are now team-based: 'Groups are also being used more and more among health professionals in acute care and community-based settings' (p. 195). This is perhaps particularly true of mental healthcare where Yalom (1995) has discussed a whole diversity of group involvement.

Shifting the setting from the workplace to the community, again groups play a prominent role. They may include volunteer, civic or church groups that meet the needs of different sections of the community, and in different ways, and give it a certain vibrancy. The phenomenal rise in popularity of various forms of self-help group can be included here. In this regard, Napier and Gershenfeld (1999: 64) referred to 'an explosion of self-help groups: groups organized to help members deal with grieving, illness, divorce, low self-esteem, being a woman, being a man, and numerous other concerns'. They estimated some half a million variants in the USA alone, with a collective membership of approximately six million people.

Different attempts have been made to impose order on the myriad possibilities that exist by developing a typology that places groups in categories (e.g. Argyle, 1983a; Garrison and Bly 1997). Perhaps the simplest and most basic distinction, as noted by Darley (2001), is between *task groups* – to do essentially with achievement and output; and *affinity groups* – that emphasise contact, friendship and interests shared with convivial company.

Northouse and Northouse (1998) also referred to *task* and what they called *process* (rather than 'affinity') alternatives. Drawing on the essential nature of the communication shared by members, they identified a continuum of involvement relying on *content* at one extreme and *process* messages at the other. The former is primarily concerned with substantive issues, quality of decisions reached, amount of output, etc. In task groups, such as committees or boards of directors' meetings, most of the interaction is at this level. Process messages, by contrast, address relational matters, the internal workings of the group and the well-being of its members. Process groups rely strongly on such contact: examples include those delivering a therapeutic service. (This content/process distinction is an echo of an earlier one encountered in Chapter 2 when the multi-dimensionality of communication was discussed. It will also be revisited shortly and is echoed throughout the chapter.) Most groups share elements of both; it is the relative proportion that serves to locate them at some point on a task/process continuum and provides a distinct identity. *Midrange groups* is the name given to those where content and process exchanges are roughly balanced. A more differentiated list of group types can be found in Box 14.1.

While many of the communication skills that form part of dyadic interaction can also be used when people get together in groups, there are added complexities associated with the latter which must be appreciated. These are not just a matter of scale. As Rosengren (2000: 87) pointed out:

> as the number of communicating units (n) in a communicative system grows, the number of potential direct relations (R) between the units of the system also grows. ... In parallel with this increasing complexity of group structure (this *quantitative change*), the communicative system of the group undergoes some qualitative change. Individual communication rapidly turns into group communication.

Box 14.1 Common types of small group

1   Family – this is our first group.
2   Friendship/leisure – meet needs for affiliation, emotional expression and relaxation.
3   Work – facilitate productivity.
4   Self-help/action – mobilise individual and community support for courses of action.
5   Training/therapy groups – promote personal awareness and growth.
6   Spiritual – meet transcendent needs.
7   Laboratory/focus – short-term groups whose purpose is to provide research data.

It is with such factors that this chapter is concerned. We will begin by considering what exactly is meant by 'a group', and a number of basic features associated with the concept. This will be developed further by concentrating on the characteristics and skills associated with a rather special and particularly important position within the group – that of leader.

WHAT IS A GROUP?

As with several of the concepts introduced in this book, agreeing on a crisp, formal definition of 'group' is more difficult than it might initially seem. Most would probably agree that a group necessarily involves a plurality of individuals – but how many? While four or five people would probably be acceptable would forty or fifty – and what about 4,000 or 5,000? Is a group the same as a gathering, a crowd, or a mob? What about an audience, is it necessarily a group? Can a group be thought of as any social category – e.g. all Portuguese women over 2 metres tall? Have groups special characteristics and qualities that set them apart from other social aggregates? Indeed, does the word 'group' refer to a specific entity at all? Cartwright and Zander (1968) concluded that it merely marks an area of study whose boundaries are altogether blurred and uncertain.

A common distinction is that between *small groups* and larger collectives. This chapter is concerned with the former. Describing a group in this way suggests that a quite precise numeric specification should be possible. While figures can be found suggesting membership of from two to five at the lower end, to fifteen to twenty at the upper, there is little agreement on precise numbers (Bormann, 1990), leading many to abandon attempts to define small groups purely in terms of size *per se*. Size alone does not seem to be what really counts. Rather the telling factor is its ability to facilitate or inhibit other interactive processes. A number of more significant small group features have been teased out by, for example, Hartley (1997), Johnson and Johnson (1997) and Hogg and Vaughan (1998) and will now be considered.

Interaction

To belong to a group, members must be able to interact with others who also belong. Until relatively recently the importance of face-to-face interaction was stressed. This requirement is conspicuous in an early definition by Homans (1950: 1) who defined a group as:

> a number of people who communicate with one another often over a span of time, and who are few enough so that each person is able to communicate with all the others, not at secondhand, through other people, but face-to-face.

Face-to-face communication is, of course, more media rich than alternative forms. This characteristic also forms the basis of the distinction between *primary* and *secondary* groups, first drawn by Cooley (1929). Primary groups are typified by the potential for close and frequent face-to-face association. But do people have to be in each other's presence for groupness to occur? What about those who regularly keep in contact via the Internet? There is now a growing acceptance that people who make use of technologically mediated interaction should not be denied group status on that count alone (Beebe and Masterson, 2000). Indeed, the effects of introducing additional personal information in these circumstances to those who have never met would seem to be more complex than might have been anticipated. Walther *et al.* (2000) discovered that short-term, unfamiliar computer-mediated groups expressed higher levels of affinity and affection when photographs of partners were made available before and during conferencing. The opposite, however, was the case with the introduction of this extraneous information to those who had already established a long-term online relationship.

Influence

Extending the previous point, members should not only interact, but should also be subjected to mutual influence in the process. Each should be able, to some extent, to make a difference to the way that others think, feel and behave and be influenced in return. Indeed this is one of the most important stipulations. Shaw (1981: 8) wrote that, 'two or more persons who are interacting with one another in such a manner that each person influences and is influenced by each other person', constitutes a group. More recently Brown (1996) regarded this attribute as an essential criterion of groupness.

Shared goal/s or common interest/s

The fact that groups are typically formed for some identifiable purpose and that those who belong share at least one common goal, is a long established characteristic regarded as essential by many (Hare, 1976). Furthermore, having a common goal, vision and sense of mission were found by Hare and O'Neill (2000) to be very important sources of influence in focusing the group's energies and shaping its processes and procedures, thereby promoting effectiveness and efficiency of operation. In the case of a formal group, its goal is often reflected in the name (e.g. Eastham Branch of the Animal Rights Movement; Eastham Photographic Society; Eastham Miners' Welfare). Interestingly, when a group's goal has been attained (or rendered obsolete), members may channel their energies in other directions, thereby ensuring the continued existence of the group. Eastham Miners' Welfare may still meet to have a drink and play snooker even though the Eastham pit has long since closed and the miners found alternative employment. New goals can come to dominate group activities. In other cases the achievement of the group goal or goals results in the group's demise.

Apart from acting to maintain the group and direct its activities, goals also influence the development of particular structures and procedures within it. Such considerations will be dealt with more fully in a later section of the chapter.

Interdependence

In addition to interacting with and influencing each other, the interdependence of group members has been noted. Indeed it is central to the definition offered by Northouse and Northouse (1998: 196): 'a small group refers to a set of three or more individuals whose relationships make them in some way *interdependent*'. Members share a *common fate*. If the group fails to achieve the set goal no member is successful. Thus events that affect one person will have a bearing on the rest of the group and group outcomes will affect each individual member.

Shared group identity

While interaction and interpersonal influence, interdependence, and the pursuit of a common goal or goals are commonly accepted as the quintessence of the concept, various other defining features of groups can be found in the literature. Campbell (1958), for example, pointed out that groups are reasonably enduring units and that any aggregate, in order to be so regarded, must have a certain permanency. But how long must it last? As with questions of size, no easy, absolute or commonly accepted answer can be given.

More important is the requirement that members see themselves as belonging to a group: that they share a sense of group identity. This type of more subjective criterion has been advocated by Turner *et al.* (1987), among others, in invoking the concept of people's self-categorisations. As such, a group exists to the extent that two or more individuals consider themselves to belong to the same social category. Brown (1996: 44) stressed that as well as influencing each other, individuals to be a group should 'think of themselves as being group members ("we" rather than "I" and "they") experiencing a sense of belongingness and a common sense of identity'.

The corresponding perceptions of non-group members have also been held to be important (Feldman, 1985). Members must be seen by outsiders to belong to this collective.

Shared social structures

When individuals join a group they begin to function in terms of a system of expectations that shapes what they do as members and their contribution to the collective. They begin to take on a *role* and abide by a set of *norms* that specify appropriate conduct. They will also slot into a particular *status* structure, according to which prestige and a sense of value are bestowed. These pivotal elements of group structure will be returned to shortly.

Various definitions combine sets of these key characteristics. For example Johnson and Johnson (1997: 12) wrote:

> A small group is two or more individuals in face-to-face interaction, each aware of positive interdependence as they strive to achieve mutual goals, each aware of his or her membership in the group, and each aware of the others who belong to the group.

Along similar lines, Beebe and Masterson (2000: 2) delineated small group communication as, 'interaction among a small group of people who share a common purpose or goal, who feel a sense of belonging to the group, and who exert influence on one another'.

WHY DO PEOPLE JOIN GROUPS?

Why are groups so common? What factors can account for this predilection to gravitate towards and associate with others within such social units? One reasonable attempt at explanation suggests that individuals rely on group membership in order to achieve goals and satisfy certain felt needs that would be either more difficult or impossible to satisfy alone. As expressed by McGrath *et al.* (2000: 98), 'All groups act in the service of two generic functions: (a) to complete group projects and (b) to fulfill member needs.' These needs may be broadly material, interpersonal, or informational.

Material needs

It may be to the benefit of all for a number of individuals to pool their various resources in order to complete a task and gain some tangible goal. Each will differ in the knowledge, skills and physical attributes as well as possible tools and equipment they are able to contribute. Indeed the gregarious nature of *Homo sapiens* is thought to stem from the advantages of hunting in groups and sharing the kill. Trade union and co-operative movements (including collective purchasing online) are some of the more contemporary examples of aggregates being formed to further the material well-being of members. The group may *directly* provide advantages or be *indirectly* instrumental in bringing them about. For instance, a person may join the local golf club to avail of the related business contacts that come with membership.

We may, therefore, become attracted to a group on account of the sorts of things the participants do and the outcomes they achieve. This attraction is strongest when those outcomes coincide with what we want for ourselves and when membership is believed to enhance our opportunities for success.

Interpersonal needs

By their very nature these, to be successfully met, require some form of group contact. Individuals on their own cannot assuage them. Such needs, according to Schutz (1955) in a seminal work, may be for varying degrees of: (1) *inclusion* – to want to belong or feel part of a social entity; (2) *control* – to dominate or be controlled; and (3) *affection* – at the extremes, to love (and be loved), or to hate.

Argyle (1995) also proposed that much of interpersonal behaviour is in response to social drives for affiliation, dominance, dependency, ego-identity or aggression. But, of course, being able to dominate depends on one or more others who are prepared to be submissive. Likewise it is impossible to be dependent if there is no one to depend on. The sense of identity that membership affords has already been mentioned and is additionally included by Baron and Byrne (2000) among the advantages of being part of a collective.

In sum, we gravitate towards groups whose members we find attractive, and where we feel that we will fit in and be well received.

Information needs

While we (arguably) may not have to join a group in order to gain knowledge of aspects of our physical environment, it is only through association with others that we come to an understanding of the social world that we inhabit and, indeed, of ourselves. As discussed in Chapter 9, social comparison is an important phenomenon. According to *Social Comparison Theory* (Festinger, 1954: Suls and Wheeler, 2001) individuals make judgements about the quality of their abilities, or accuracy and justifiability of beliefs and opinions, by watching others perform similar tasks, or listening to what they have to say on relevant topics. In this way we frame a picture of where they stand in these respects. For example, it is only possible to decide if you are a good, average or poor student by comparing your marks with others on your course. By so doing you gradually create an impression of yourself, including your strengths and weaknesses. Darley (2001: 348) outlined the implications for self-esteem of such comparative processes. Feelings of self-worth are heightened when the individual compares favourably with others on tasks valued by other members (and diminished when the opposite is the case).

Social comparison processes can have pronounced effects for the group as well. A common finding is that collectives often take more extreme decisions than individuals on their own. One explanation of this *group polarisation* effect makes use of social comparison (Hogg, 2001). Members obtain insights into the stances taken by others in the group in relation of the issue as it is discussed. Being seen to be 'middle of the road', or 'sitting on the fence', tends to be unattractive, so initial positions are shifted to be more extreme in the direction of the prevailing pole. As a result the group takes up a position more strongly in favour of a course of action, let's say, than members would as individuals.

To conclude this line of thought, to be a loner is not only to be denied potential material benefit and fellowship, but also an understanding of ourselves and our social worlds. Little wonder that small groups are so prevalent.

HOW ARE GROUPS ORDERED AND REGULATED?

Given that groups are made up of individuals, each with particular, and perhaps contrasting, personalities, opinions and preferences, it seems reasonable to ask how they manage to become sufficiently organised and co-ordinated for goals to be pursued efficiently and effectively. Here, we will explore how order within the group is made possible through the creation of structure in respect of *norms*, *roles* and *status*, and the related processes of *conformity* and *cohesion*.

Norms

The emergence of *norms* is of crucial importance in regulating the activities of members. As groups evolve, regularities of operation begin to emerge, reflecting the creation of expectations on the part of members. Such norms can be thought of as, 'those behaviours, attitudes, and perceptions that are approved of by the group and expected (and, in fact, often demanded) of its members. Such norms will generally have powerful effects on the thoughts and actions of group members' (Baron *et al.*, 1992: 11). It should be noted that it is not only overt behaviour that is subject to a normative influence but also the characteristic perceptions, thoughts and feelings that members entertain.

Napier and Gershenfeld (1999) teased out four main types of norm, differing in levels of formality and explicitness.

1   *Documented*. These sets of prescriptions are explicit and written down in a formal code of conduct. They are typically communicated directly to those in the group, together with the consequences of violation (Wilke and van Knippenberg, 1996). A case in point would be giving a newcomer the members' handbook of rules and regulations governing club activities, or a new student a list of the terms and conditions of residence in the university's halls of accommodation.

2   *Explicit*. Although drawn to the attention of a member, these expectations would not typically be codified or documented. As such they are slightly less formal, but certainly not to be disregarded.

3   *Implicit*. Many rules are tacit and realised sometimes only when broken. Requirements are not stated directly but have to be assimilated more discreetly by, perhaps, watching what established members do and following their example. It is only when a violation occurs that one realises the existence

of the norm in the first place. This information is often conveyed by subtle verbal and nonverbal cues.

4   *Invisible*. Here the norms are so tightly woven into the fabric of group life that they can no longer be identified as separate threads: they have become virtually invisible. No one is aware of them but simply and automatically acts in accordance. These 'rules' sometimes have to do with standards of politeness or decorum, such as acknowledging the presence of another.

Not all aspects of group life are governed to the same extent by norms. Those most stringently subjected to this type of influence include activities:

*   directly concerned with the achievement of group goals and the satisfaction of members' needs, especially the needs of the most powerful in the group;
*   commonly associated with group membership both by those within and outwith the group;
*   amenable to public scrutiny. Thus strict norms govern the physical examination of patients but not the colour of underwear the doctor should have on while doing it!

On the other hand, behaviours that have a strong physiological basis and those that can only be performed at considerable personal cost to the individual are less likely to come under strong normative control.

Apart from facilitating goal achievement, norms serve to increase regularity and predictability in the operation of the group (Brown, 2000). Members can determine, with reasonable accuracy, what is likely to happen in most situations. This sets down guidelines as to the nature and extent of their own involvement. For the individual they also provide a clear picture of social reality together with a firm sense of belonging (Smith and Mackie, 2000). Personal needs for status and esteem can also be satisfied through the operation of norms. Thus many of the tacit rules of everyday conversation are intended to avoid causing offence or embarrassment in public. A further advantage of having certain actions norm-governed is that it obviates the necessity of frequently having to rely on personal influence. It can be pointed out, for example, that new recruits are expected to behave in a deferential manner to *all* commanding officers: it's not just me – it's the system, the way things are done around here. Furthermore, the fact that certain norms have to do with the maintenance and integrity of the group must not be overlooked. Their importance is reflected in the disapprobation associated with terms such as traitor, scab, etc., levelled at those who violate them.

Regardless of how they are communicated, whether in writing or by disapproving look, norms as discussed here are decidedly *prescriptive*. They stipulate what should and should not be done. Members, to a greater or lesser extent, are required to comply. Marques *et al.* (2001) took this a step further by highlighting a *proscriptive* element involving evaluation. Those who contravene norms can be labelled 'bad' or morally flawed and deserving of punishment by the rest of the group. This may even take the form of exclusion from the group.

Roles

Norms, as we have seen, apply to all group members, although not necessarily to the same extent. In any group, however, it would be highly undesirable for everyone to act in *exactly* the same way. A committee where everyone acted as secretary would get little done (although what was, might be well documented). Against a backdrop of shared norms, it is important that individuals take on different tasks if the group is to make the most of its resources and maximise productivity. A differentiation of function is required. Specific sets of expectations concerning the behaviour of those in particular positions in the group are referred to as *roles*. Bormann (1990: 161), put it as follows, 'Role, in the small group, is defined as that set of perceptions and expectations shared by the members about the behaviour of an individual in both the task and social dimension of group interaction.'

Particular roles that evolve are a function of a number of determinants, including the nature of the specific group and its tasks. Nevertheless it would seem that there are certain roles that typify small group interaction. Some of these were identified and labelled in an important piece of early work by Benne and Sheats (1948), and confirmed by Mudrack and Farrell (1995). This encompassed three categories of role:

1 *Group task roles* (e.g. information giver, information seeker, opinion giver, opinion seeker, evaluator-critic, and energiser). These contribute to the ability of the group to successfully accomplish its objective.
2 *Group-building and maintenance roles* (e.g. encourager, harmoniser, compromiser, follower and gatekeeper). Here the focus is on promoting good internal relations, a strong sense of solidarity, and a congenial social atmosphere.
3 *Individual roles* (e.g. aggressor, blocker, recognition seeker, playboy, and dominator). Unlike the previous two categories, these tend to be self-serving and dysfunctional to the smooth and successful operation of the group.

Additionally, some groups have a member who tends to be much more reticent than the rest, who interacts minimally with others and fails to participate fully in group activities. This individual is commonly labelled the *isolate* and, indeed, in larger groups may, for the most part, go unnoticed. The fact that such individuals do not become fully involved does not mean that they have nothing to offer, as tactful handling by an adroit leader can often demonstrate.

Again, when a group is dogged by setback and failure it is not uncommon for some member to be singled out as the cause and accused of not 'pulling his/her weight' or 'letting the group down'. This poor unfortunate becomes the *scapegoat*. By 'identifying' the source of failure members can have their flagging beliefs in the worth of the group reaffirmed and redouble their efforts to achieve the goal. The projection of unacceptable personal feelings or tendencies on to the scapegoat can also mitigate feelings of guilt among others.

In many respects a role can only be properly appreciated as it fits in with that of others in a system or network. For example, to fully grasp what a teacher does requires some understanding of pupils and perhaps principals. Likewise, nurses operate in a context of patients, doctors, consultants, etc. To add a further level of complication, we all take on a number of roles to be played out, although not necessarily in the same situation. A teacher may also be a mother, daughter, wife, captain of the local ladies' rugby team, joker of the evening art class, etc. This can on occasion lead to *role conflict* when the demands of one are incompatible with those of another. Given that members do not invariably slip smoothly into well-moulded roles in the first place, it is small wonder problems often arise to disrupt group life. Some of these, it has been suggested (Shaw, 1981; Burton and Dimbleby, 1995), stem from differences between the *perceived role* – what the recipient understands is required; the *expected role* – what others in the group expect; and the *enacted role* – what the person actually does. When a member is no longer sure what the demands are, that person is said to be in a state of *role confusion*.

Status

Roles, in part, reflect status differences that exist between various positions in the group. Status refers to the evaluation of a position in terms of the importance or prestige associated with it, and represents a further structuring of the group. Most groups are hierarchically organised in this respect with high-status positions affording greater opportunities to exercise social power and influence. Although status and power are usually closely associated, this need not necessarily be the case. Baron *et al.* (1992: 7) cited the example of the British monarchy as having, 'exceptional status but relatively little power'. As shall be seen in the following section, one facet of intra-group communication has to do with the acknowledgement and confirmation of status differences. This frequently operates at a covert level; for example, the chairperson *directs* the secretary while the secretary *advises* the chairperson.

Conformity

Despite what has just been said about norms, roles and status, none would make much contribution to ordering and structuring group existence if members disregarded them. They must conform: there must be pressures to fit in. The origins of these influences may be internal. From an informational point of view, it can be personally comforting for members to be able to enjoy a sense of surety derived from accepted group norms: from being able to buy into a shared sense of social reality. In addition, feelings of shame or guilt welling up from within may be sufficient to force miscreants to mend their ways. What counts most for Turner (1999) though is that a group provides members with a social identity. It becomes tied up in their sense of who they are: its ways are their ways. They comply because they have accepted a particular group-based self-categorisation.

On the other hand, external pressures in the form of positive and negative group sanctions may be brought to bear to force compliance. Praise and other forms of reward may be bestowed for behaving appropriately: ridicule for failing to do so. Extreme cases of recalcitrance may result in boycott or indeed expulsion from the group.

Conformity to the commonly held views and practices of the majority has a number of advantages for the group. It tends to increase efficiency and facilitate group maintenance as well as reduce uncertainty and confusion among members and project a strong group image to the rest of society. Factors identified by Napier and Gershenfeld (1999) that promote conformity include:

- an extreme norm;
- strong pressure to conform;
- member self-doubt;
- large group;
- reinforcement of appropriate behaviour;
- members' need to self-ingratiate;
- strong sense of group identity.

In circumstances where a number of these factors apply, the forces generated to conform to the ways of the group should never be underestimated. They can lead to young people dressing in strange ways and sporting peculiar haircuts. More seriously, drug abuse and anti-socal behaviour may be promoted. In the extreme, examples of soldiers, paramilitary groups and street gangs behaving with unbelievable brutality towards victims have been attributed to group pressures to abide by the ways of the group. Destructiveness can also be turned in on the group itself. In March 1997, thirty-nine men and women belonging to the Heaven's Gate cult committed group suicide in the belief that they would make contact with a spacecraft flying in the tail of a passing comet. The spacecraft was believed to be their passport to paradise.

Cohesion

Some groups are tight-knit teams, while others tend to be rather loosely made up of individuals, many of whom may have only a weak sense of affiliation to fellow members or the work of the group. Cohesiveness has been thought of as the bonding agent that holds the group together. It refers to the degree of attraction between those who belong to the group and to each other as members. Cohesion also tends to further concentrate the influences to conform. One of the most significant developments in thinking about the concept, according to Dion (2000), is the distinction between task and social cohesion, where *Task cohesion* refers to commitment to the goals, tasks and activities of the group; and *Social cohesion* refers to the attraction towards, and liking among, group members.

A number of advantages of belonging to a cohesive group have been identified (Johnson and Johnson, 1997). The main ones are listed in Box 14.2.

However, pressures against dissent within the group can have a down-side, resulting in less desirable outcomes through flawed decision-making. One of these tendencies is *groupthink* (Janis, 1982, 1997) brought about by an internal dynamic to prematurely concur with some suggested group position. Groupthink is a beguiling seductress – but the consequences can be grave for those falling under her spell. In a mad dash to reach consensus and avoid potential differences of opinion and internal conflict, a group also denies itself the crucial element in decision-making of exploring

---

Box 14.2 Advantages of group cohesion

Cohesive groups are typified by:

1   Ease of goal setting.
2   Commitment to goal attainment.
3   Heightened productivity.
4   Reduced absenteeism.
5   Willingness of members to endure greater hardships and difficulties.
6   Increased morale and satisfaction.
7   Resolute defence against external criticism or attack.
8   Participants listening to and accommodating other members.
9   Less anger and tension.
10 More support.

---

differences of opinion and critically scrutinising options. Several reviews of group-think and studies investigating conditions in which it flourishes have been carried out (e.g. Paulus, 1998; Esser, 1998). It tends to be fostered in conditions where:

- minority dissent is stifled;
- the group is in crisis;
- the group is under external threat;
- the group is under time pressures to reach a decision;
- levels of cohesiveness are high;
- there is a sense of group infallibility or moral superiority;
- the group is insulated from outside influence;
- the group is dominated by a leader who vigorously champions a specific group option to the denigration of others.

The Bay of Pigs incident and the Watergate scandal are two often-cited examples of faulty political decision-making attributed to groupthink (Raven, 1998). In the case of the former, during the Kennedy presidency in the USA, an elite governmental advisory group backed an abortive attempt by Cuban exiles to invade Cuba and wrestle political control from President Castro. It was, in reality, an ill-conceived piece of adventurism doomed to fail from the start, but at the time of planning there was no significant dissenting voice capable of bringing a meaningful dimension of realism to the deliberations. (Kramer, 1998, though, has questioned whether groupthink was indeed the primary cause of this fiasco.) The Watergate scandal centred on the illicit surveillance of political opponents and led to the eventual resignation of President Nixon. Again it seems that the internal dynamics of the group taking the decision to sanction the operation and the subsequent cover-up militated against the raising of objections.

Hargie *et al.* (1999) recommended steps that can be taken to help avoid group-think, as outlined in Box 14.3.

In sum, through the establishment and operation of norms, status and roles, together with pressures to act accordingly, regular and predictable patterns of activity

413

Box 14.3 Avoiding groupthink

Groupthink is less likely to beset group decision-making when:

1 Tasks are established that involve everyone.
2 Clear performance goals are set for the group.
3 Individual contributions are capable of being identified, evaluated and rewarded.
4 The expression of minority opinion and the dissenting voice is cherished, not punished or ignored.
5 The leader avoids adopting a particular stance in relation to the issue, especially at an early stage in the discussion.
6 The expression of a range of viewpoints is promoted.
7 Each member is given responsibility for critically examining views put forward.
8 Three questions are posed of any major decision – What's wrong with it? How can it be improved? What other possibilities have we not considered?
9 Sub-groups are assigned the task of independently developing solutions.
10 Independent parties are brought in from outside the group, from time to time, to review its deliberations.
11 One member is given the role of 'devil's advocate'
12 After arriving at a decision, a 'second chance' meeting is held during which all members, including the leader, express residual concerns and uncertainties.
13 Members are made aware of the insidious operation of groupthink.

---

come to characterise much of group life. For many, this process evolves through identifiable stages as the group changes from being little more than a gathering of relative strangers at initial meetings, to eventually becoming a properly functioning unit. We will now look more closely at how groups develop over time.

GROUP FORMATION

The most popular model presenting a picture of groups evolving through fixed stages following a progressive and predictable path is that proposed by Tuckman (1965). He identified four such stages, later extended to become five (Tuckman and Jensen, 1977), based on reviews of over fifty investigations of mostly short-term therapy and training groups. These stages have become known as forming, storming, norming, performing and adjourning.

- *Forming*. Initially group life is characterised by a good deal of uncertainty and confusion. Individuals are essentially strangers and there is a need to get to know each other both at a social level and also in terms of who does what. A clear picture of group goals and how they can best be achieved may also be missing. This tends to increase the dependence of members on a leader where one is present. Despite this uncertainty, there may be a good deal of optimism in the group and, in this 'honeymoon' period, little explicit conflict.

- *Storming*. According to Kelly (2001: 166) 'the majority of studies and theories about group development highlight the importance of the group dealing with emotional issues'. This second stage is typified by a great deal of negative emotion stemming from conflict and intense disagreement. Initial individual uncertainty over what to do and how to do it, now gives way to individuals' attempts to impose their interpretations on the group. Cliques and temporary sub-groups can form as those with shared views or agendas come together. Again with a poorly formed role structure, individuals disagree vehemently over who should be doing what. One member may feel aggrieved that someone else has suddenly begun to do the tasks that they had taken on. Lacking a recognised status structure, there can also be considerable resentment and hostility over what are seen as illegitimate attempts by some to impose authority on others.

- *Norming*. Assuming that the group makes it through to the calmer waters of this next stage, we now find conflict ebbing as a growing consensus, unity of purpose and shared sense of identity begin to take hold (Wheelan, 1994). Group structures become established, differentiating roles, norms and status. Members how begin to form a clearer vision of the group, what it is about and where they, as well as others, fit in. While conflict may not be banished for good, at least the group is better prepared to handle it.

- *Performing*. Now members are much better placed to begin working smoothly, efficiently and productively to achieve goals. They synchronise effort and harmonise contributions, co-operating with each other to meet challenges, solve problems, reach decisions and implement agreed strategies.

- *Adjourning*. Finally, most groups reach the adjourning phase when specific goals are achieved and there is nothing left to do. In other instances a set lifespan may have been envisaged when the group was created, and that time has now arrived. Alternatively, the end may come when members leave through lack of continued commitment or for other reasons (Smith and Mackie, 2000). Once more, there may be a marked emotional dimension to what takes place during this valedictory phase. If strong social cohesion has been created, members may have become close friends. A deep sense of loss, loneliness and grief can develop at the prospect of social bonds being broken as participants go their separate ways. This is sometimes partly mitigated by vows to remain in contact, plans for reunions, etc. Additionally, much talk at this time is usually devoted to reflecting on the group and what it accomplished. There is typically an effort to complete any outstanding business.

Do all groups go through these same stages? If so, do they invariably follow the same sequence? Is progress always as ordered as suggested by this model? For others who have reflected on group development, the answers to these questions are 'no'. Doubt has been cast on the traditional, single fixed-sequence view of group development (Chidambaram and Bostrom, 1997). Wheelan (1994) proposed phases not unlike those identified by Tuckman and Jensen (1977). She accepted, though, that a group can become 'stuck' at a stage and fail to progress further. Regression to an earlier phase is another possibility. Worchel (1994), on the other hand, argued that a group moves through re-emerging cycles during its existence. Six identified stages are:

1   Discontent – the individual has minimal engagement with the group.
2   A precipitating event brings members together.
3   Group identification is created and forces to conform are established.
4   The group agrees goals and strategies to enhance productivity.
5   Individuation – the achievement of goals is associated with a growing focus by members on personal needs.
6   Disintegration – as members' contributions become more self-serving, conflict and division increases leading to decay and group disintegration. Disintegration produces discontent, and another cycle commences.

For others, group life is typified by efforts to cope with recurring themes or issues. For Bion (1961), who brought a psychodynamic stance to bear, these centred on unconscious assumptions that create an emotional climate and influence members to satisfy unconscious needs and control anxiety (Morgan and Thomas, 1996). Three basic assumptions concern:

- *Dependency* – the search for someone to take control of, protect and deliver the group.
- *Fight/flight* – a united effort to repel or evade attack from within or outside the group and thereby control anxiety.
- *Pairing* – bringing pairs of members together, unconsciously motivated by the desire to create a solution to the difficulties of the group.

TEAMS

Teams are a special type of group that have become extremely popular where people come together to complete tasks, such as in the workplace. Many organisations have responded to ever-present pressures to increase quality production in a more efficient way by turning to teams as core operational units charged with delivering success (Guirdham, 1996). This strategic move has often been associated with a flattening of the organisational structure, reducing status differentials and devolving power to lower levels. There is good evidence that more is achieved by having staff pool their efforts in well-managed, self-directed and committed units of this type rather than either striving on their own or being at odds with others (Chaudhry-Lawton *et al.*, 1992; O'Hair *et al.*, 1998). Hewlett-Packard discovered that efficiency improved by some 50 per cent when the company restructured around quality teams. Declines in absenteeism reported by Xerox headquarters and by the Nissan UK plant in Sunderland were attributed in part to structural changes that placed greater emphasis on teamwork, increased autonomy and responsibility.

But what sets teams apart from the sort of small group that we have already been exploring? When embedded in an organisational setting, Cohen and Bailey (1997) pointed to issues such as task interdependence among members, a shared sense of being an intact social entity, and being seen to be so by others, as being crucial. For Kinlaw (1991) teams are cohesive, develop their own ways of doing things and are largely self-managing with motivation and leadership coming from within. Katzenbach and Smith (1993) highlighted the tendency for teams to achieve more than would have been expected from considering the contributions of members as mere individuals. Extending some of these ideas, Wilson (1999: 8) defined a team as 'a mature group of three or more individuals who interact on an ongoing basis about some common problem or interdependent goal (task), provide their own leadership for development and performance, and exert mutual influence over one another'. More particularly, Guirdham (1996) and Hargie *et al.* (1999) characterised this type of group as outlined in Box 14.4.

INTRA-GROUP COMMUNICATION

Regardless of how groups develop and the stages through which this occurs, communication among members is the growth hormone that makes it happen. It is a necessary prerequisite for the emergence and perpetuation of norms and roles, conformity and coherence, and for the achievement of outcomes. Frey (1999: ix) pointed to both the constitutive and the functional nature of the phenomenon: groups emerge through communication and it is in this way that they achieve their objectives. At the same time, the communication process is heavily influenced in turn by the internal structures that are created, as will be seen in the next section.

Box 14.4 How to spot a team

Teams have:

- highly specific task objectives that are clearly understood and accepted by all members;
- a high level of ownership of and commitment to group tasks;
- a great deal of mutual trust and respect for members;
- a culture of inclusivity;
- strong support within the unit;
- a firm sense of collective accountability;
- quality communication that is honest and open with participants feeling listened to and understood;
- self-control, self-motivation and self-direction;
- interaction and socialising outside the strict work setting;
- conflicts accepted and worked through;
- an emphasis on positive, constructive feedback to members;
- collective success or failure and a reliance on all members to create and maintain an acceptable image;
- members whose skills, knowledge and abilities complement each other and enhance the group.

The importance of communication in the group cannot therefore be overestimated. Nowhere is this more so, as we have seen, than with teams. For Brilhart and Galanes (1998: 44): 'Communication is like the nerve network of a small group; it is the verbal and nonverbal process by which individuals forge themselves into a group, maintain the group, and coordinate their efforts. No communication, no group.' Thus communication makes it possible for those belonging to the group to organise themselves, pool resources and through co-operative action solve common difficulties or reach a desired goal. But, in addition, the resolution of interpersonal and indeed personal difficulties within the group and the creation and maintenance of harmonious relationships relies on effective communication. These two types of communication should, by now, be familiar. In relation to groups, they have been referred to as *content* and *process* dimensions, or alternatively, as *task* and *socio-emotional* or *relational* communication (Littlejohn, 1999; Frey, 1999). Task communication, as the name suggests, concerns substantive group activities and typically operates in accordance with reason and logic. Relational communication, on the other hand, 'refers to the verbal and nonverbal messages that create the social fabric of a group by promoting relationships between and among group members' (Keyton, 1999: 192). This does not necessarily mean, as will be recalled from earlier in the book, that each communicative act must be either task or relational in function. It is not a question or 'either–or'. While ostensibly discussing how to solve a task issue, members may, contemporaneously, be forming impressions of where they stand in relation to the others in terms of status, positive regard, and so on.

Interaction processes

In early but still pertinent work, Bales (1950, 1970) teased out task and socio-emotional (roughly comparable to relational communication) aspects of group communication using a system that he developed, known as *Interaction Process Analysis*. He found that specific contributions of participants to small group interaction could be analysed and assigned to some one of twelve distinct categories. They are briefly presented in Box 14.5. Six are concerned with task functions. Of these, three involve, first, giving suggestions and directions; second, opinions and points of view; and third, orientation and clarification. These are mirrored in three more task functions, this time with a focus on *asking for* (rather than giving) suggestions, opinions or orientation. The remaining six categories relate to socio-emotional reactions with a neat symmetry between the positive and the negative. The three positive include, first, showing solidarity, helping or rewarding; second, showing tension release (e.g. joking, laughing) or satisfaction; and third, showing agreement, acceptance, understanding, etc. The final three categories, also in the socio-emotional area, but negative in character are, first, showing antagonism; second, showing tension, withdrawing, or asking for help; and, third, disagreeing or rejecting.

By analysing the communication between members in this way interesting insights can be gained into the type of group and how it operates. It can be established, for example, whether most of what takes place is concerned with task or relational issues and, if the latter, the relationships that seem to predominate in the group. Different sorts of difficulty are detectable. As explained by Poole (1999), a

Box 14.5 Interaction process analysis categories

Socio-emotional: positive

1   Shows solidarity, supports, rewards.
2   Shows tension release, jokes, laughs, defuses.
3   Agrees, shows passive acceptance, concurs, complies.

Task: neutral

4   Gives suggestions, directions, implying autonomy for the other.
5   Gives opinion, evaluation, analysis, expresses wishes and feelings.
6   Gives orientation, information, clarification, confirmation.
7   Asks for orientation, information, clarification, confirmation.
8   Asks for opinion, evaluation, analysis, expresses wishes and feelings.
9   Asks for suggestions, directions, possible ways of doing things.

Socio-emotional: negative

10   Disagrees, shows passive rejection, acts formally, withholds help.
11   Shows tension, asks for help, withdraws.
12   Shows antagonism, undermines other's status, defends or asserts self.

group sometimes struggles to achieve a compromise between task and socio-emotional concerns. As it devotes all its energies to completing the task, disagreements and friction may be experienced among members. This places a demand on the group to pay greater heed to relational needs or risk becoming dysfunctional or even fragmented. However, if the balance tips too much towards relational matters, the task may not get done, hence a need for readjustment. At the level of the individual, the extent and nature of the contribution of members, reflecting the roles taken up, can also be profiled through observation systems such as Interpersonal Process Analysis.

A common finding to emerge from this sort of detailed observation and analysis is that some members participate markedly more than others in discussion. This seems to be a function of several factors including:

1   Position and status in the group – high status members, particularly group leaders, tend to contribute extensively.
2   Knowledge – those with relevant information are frequently vociferous and indeed may be encouraged to be so by other group members.
3   Personality – extroverts, almost by definition, are more communicative than their introverted colleagues. There is some evidence to suggest that individuals have their characteristic levels of participation across groups, although these are not immutable.
4   Physical location – those centrally located in the group frequently take a more active part.
5   Group size – it has been found that differences between members in the amount of contribution to group interaction increase in relation to increases in overall group size.

As well as quantitative differences existing between high and low participants, contrasts in the typical form of their communications have also been identified. While high participators tend to provide information, give opinions and make suggestions, low participators, when they do contribute, are more likely to ask questions or express agreement. Again the target of such communication is frequently different. Low contributors, for the most part, direct contributions to individual members, but high contributors are more inclined to address their remarks to the group. This is frequently associated with attempts to exert influence and exercise power. Those who contribute most are also likely to be the recipients of frequent messages from others.

Communication networks

As participants interact with one another, regularities begin to emerge in the form of identifiable patterns of communication. Restrictions on member access that may develop as group structures emerge, help shape such networks (Brown, 2000). Researchers have investigated the effects of these patterns, or communication networks, on a number of variables, including group efficiency and member satisfaction. As initially described in experiments by Bavelas (1950), five subjects were each given a number of cards, each containing several symbols. Their task was to identify the symbol common to each member's card. Since the subjects were located in separate booths, channels of communication between them could be carefully controlled by the experimenter, creating the four networks outlined in Figure 14.1.

In each of the four diagrams in Figure 14.1, the circles represent particular group members and the adjoining lines are available channels of communication. Thus in the circle arrangement, for example, (a) and (b) could communicate but not (a) and (e) – at least not directly. Beyond the rather special circumstances of the experiments conducted by Bavelas, it should be appreciated that members in other group situations do not necessarily have to bear the particular spatial relationship to each other depicted in the diagrams in Figure 14.1 for that specific network to pertain. It is rather the pattern of communication channels in each case that is the telling feature. In other words, people may be physically sitting in a circle but typify a wheel communication network as they direct their contributions for the most part to one particular member who in turn reciprocates. This person becomes the hub in the wheel through which communication is channelled to the rest of the group.

Networks differ in two important respects. The first is in terms of *connectivity* – i.e. the number of channels available to members in the network; and the second, *centrality* – a function of the number of channels from a given position to each other's position. The circle in Figure 14.1 contains five channels and is therefore a more highly connected structure than any of the others. Of the four alternatives in Figure 14.1, the circle, although the most highly connected, is the least centralised structure, followed by the chain, Y and wheel, in order. With the wheel it can be seen that one person (c) can communicate directly with a total of four others.

Results from a number of research studies suggest that these networks have a significant impact on group efficiency and member satisfaction (Wilke and Wit, 2001). Group productivity in terms of the number of tasks completed, and efficiency measured by time taken to complete each task together with the number of messages

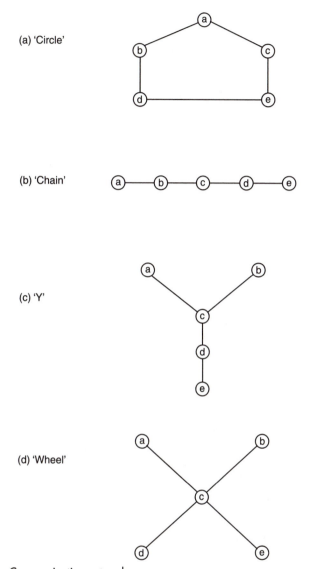

(a) 'Circle'

(b) 'Chain'

(c) 'Y'

(d) 'Wheel'

Figure 14.1 Communication networks

needed, were found to increase with increases in group centrality. The wheel was, therefore, more productive and efficient followed by the Y, the chain and the circle. The likelihood of emerging as group leader was also found to be directly related to the centrality of that person's position in the arrangement. The increased productivity and efficiency of more centralised structures is probably due to organisational and informational factors – it is easier to control what takes place without at the same time overwhelming the key person with information. As tasks become more complex, though, this may not be so. Highly centralised networks may be less, rather than more, effective due to the unreasonable data processing demands placed on the individual at 'the hub'. Indeed, for Hartley (1997) most everyday tasks that groups face are much less straightforward than those set in the laboratory by researchers such as Bavelas.

While more centrally organised groups tend to be more productive and efficient (especially when dealing with simple problems), members frequently manifest low morale and express little satisfaction with group activities. Subjects operating in the circle typically express much greater satisfaction with their involvement in the group than those in the wheel, in spite of the fact that they may not, collectively, achieve as much. This is likely to be a result of the greater independence of action enjoyed by members in the former type of group.

As well as more elaborate tasks being tackled in naturally operating groups, the communication channels between members are not limited in the contrived fashion described by Bavelas, nor are they unchanging. Networks are typically completely connected, in principle, with each individual free to communicate with every other. In practice, however, those patterns that actually emerge frequently resemble one of the more restricted configurations that we have looked at. A range of factors, including the roles being played by different individuals, may serve to reduce the number and sequence of channels typically used. Physical arrangements determining visual accessibility of certain members to others may also play a part (Johnson and Johnson, 1997). The likelihood of initiation of conversation, for instance, depends on those individuals being able to readily engage in eye-contact.

What the group is essentially about will also dictate the most accommodating network for the task. As pointed out by Northouse and Northouse (1998) a completely connected pattern typified by openness and high connectivity would best suit a therapy group. The wheel, in contrast, would better serve the purposes of a group where the intention is for one member to disseminate information to the others in a limited space of time.

Having considered the defining characteristics of groups, some of the reasons for their existence, the mechanisms by which they become ordered and regulated, and the types and patterns of communication between members, we next examine a particularly influential position within the group – that of leader – and the characteristics and skills associated with leadership.

LEADERS AND LEADERSHIP

The related topics of *leader* and *leadership* are among the most widely explored in the fields of group structure and dynamics and indeed of larger social aggregates. Opinions differ however on a range of issues to do with why certain members become leader, the exceptional qualities (if any) that set them apart, the special nature of their contribution to collective life, even the defining features of leadership that may be provided. One thing that is agreed, however, is that all these matters are centrally important in shaping groups, their functioning and effectiveness.

Providing neatly manicured definitions of 'leader' and 'leadership' is not an easy task. Alternatives abound for each. While the terms are related they should not be confused. The former pre-dates the latter. From the dawn of history scholars have been fascinated by the powers bestowed on certain individuals to govern the lives of others. In the Chinese book of wisdom *Tao Te King*, dating from 600 BC, it was written that most leaders are despised, some leaders are feared, few leaders are praised, and the very good leader is never noticed. A *leader* refers to a person who occupies a certain high-status position and fulfils an associated role in the group. That person, according to Brilhart and Galanes (1998), may be leader by dint of the fact that he or she:

- exerts a positive influence on the group to achieve the group goal;

and/or

- has been placed in a position to lead (e.g. chairperson, supervisor, co-ordinator);

and/or

- is perceived by the others as a leader.

In some situations a *designated* leader may be formally appointed to organise the group, perhaps by an outside person or body. While carrying the title of leader confers legitimate power, the respect and acceptance of the membership may still have to be earned in order to tap other resources, such as referent power, and function effectively. When accepted in this way, having a designated leader can be a tremendously facilitative resource, acting as a catalyst to organise and regulate activities, siphon off internal tensions, assuage potential power struggles and maximise productivity. But not all leaders are put in place in this formal way. Others emerge from within the group to take on a leadership role. It is often they, rather than the titular head, who wield the real power and to whom the rest look for guidance and support. One big advantage that *emergent* leaders have is that they are known to members, are one of them and have risen to the top through association with them. Issues of acceptance, allegiance and respect are therefore less likely to surface.

Not all leaders provide leadership, neither does the fact that a group lacks a conspicuous leader mean that leadership is lacking. All who are part of the collective can make a contribution in this direction and, Bertcher (1988) advocated, should recognise this obligation. But what exactly is leadership? Concurring with Baker (2001: 475), most would agree that, 'We all know what leadership is until someone asks us to define it specifically.' He goes on to observe that not all scholars in the field have felt compelled to oblige in this respect. In any case, the word 'leadership' did not appear in the English language until about 1800 and as such is much more recent than 'leader'. Since then, Johnson and Johnson (1997) reckon, in updating an earlier observation by Stogdill (1974) in a seminal review of leadership research, that there are as many definitional variants as there are contributors who have proffered a meaning for the term. Drawing on a classificatory scheme proposed by Bass (1990), Northouse (1997) identified several foci among available sets of definitions.

- *Leadership as group process.* The emphasis here is on the leader at the centre of group operation and acting as a catalyst for change. The mechanisms through which influence comes to be channelled in this way and the relationship between leader and led, has also been a topic of enquiry. After all, leaders can only adopt and continue to fulfil their role with the consent of the rest of the membership. From this point of view, leadership can be thought of as 'the process of being perceived by others as a leader' (Lord and Maher, 1991: 11).

- *Leadership as personality*. Here the focus is on the unique complement of personality traits and personal qualities by dint of which some member comes to attain a dominant position and exercise influence over the rest. We will return to this way of thinking shortly.

- *Leadership as power*. Those who have taken this line accentuate the issue of power at the heart of leadership and how it is handled in the relationship with followers. Is it concentrated in the personification of an authoritarian tyrant or distributed in a more egalitarian fashion? In the world of the modern organisation, Bennis (1999) argued that traditional practices of top-down leadership are not only outdated but quite dysfunctional. Simply ordering others to do one's will is no longer effective. Rather it must be recognised that the workforce is the fulcrum for change in a creative partnership with the person 'at the top'. Issues of power can be further extended by introducing political and ideological dimensions into thinking about leadership. The idea is put forward by Gemmill and Oakley (1992: 114) that what leadership ultimately provides is a 'social defense whose central aim is to repress uncomfortable needs, emotions and wishes that emerge when people attempt to work together'.

- *Leadership as goal achievement*. We have already recognised earlier in the chapter the importance of goals to the formation and functioning of groups. This sentiment has found its way into attempts to distil the essence of leadership. After all, if goals figure prominently in group life, if success is measured in terms of goal output, and if leadership is to have any real significance as a group-based concept, then it must in some way serve to facilitate goal achievement. Such reasoning is reflected in the definition given by Andriessen and Drenth (1998: 323):

> Leadership is that part of the role of a (appointed or elected) leader that is directly linked to influencing the behaviour of the group, or of one or more members of the group, and is expressed through the direction and coordination of activities that are important in connection with the tasks of the group.

Furthermore, De Souza and Klein (1996) reported that those individuals to emerge as group leaders in an experimental task-completion setting were more committed to the group goal and had higher task ability.

THEORIES OF LEADERSHIP

Fascination with the role of leader has not merely been confined to the investigations of social scientists. Although not studied extensively and scientifically until the second half of the last century, leadership has intrigued philosophers and historians for much longer. But even restricted to the social sciences, a range of theories and perspectives has been advanced to account for why or how leaders emerge and with what effects. As put by Gessner *et al.* (1999: xiii) 'Leadership theories are like fingerprints: everyone has them and no two are alike.' A comprehensive review of alternatives is well beyond the reach of this chapter. Rather we will confine our coverage to several of the better known.

Trait approach

What is proposed here is that leaders possess certain personality traits and capacities that set them apart from the rest and make it possible for them to lead. Without this unique advantage, any attempt to fill this role is doomed to failure. In its earliest form, it was furthermore believed that these crucial predispositions were innate – that leaders were born, not made. Proponents of this *Great Person (invariably Man) Theory* pointed to colossal heroic figures as 'proof' of their views. Alexander the Great was an even greater leader than his father Philip II. From Biblical times there is a long tradition of chosen ones having the hand of God placed on them and a divine right to rule conferred. Indeed Machiavelli in the early sixteenth century provoked the wrath of the Church by audaciously setting out principles by which a commoner could *learn* to exert the influence of leadership.

The belief that leadership is inborn would receive little contemporary support from serious social scientists. This still leaves open the possibility that predisposing attributes can be acquired, perhaps early in life. Considerable research effort has been put into their identification and isolation. At best a handful of weak associations have emerged with leaders tending to be more attractive, healthy, intelligent, confident, talkative, as well as higher in need for dominance, and taller (Hogg and Vaughan, 1998). As far as height is concerned, Young and French (1996) drew attention to the fact that American presidents polled as the greatest were almost four inches taller than those regarded as failures. More disappointingly, though, an extensive and frequently cited review by Stogdill (1974) failed to unearth a distinct set of general qualities or abilities of leadership. Indeed while Alexander the Great, Mahatma Gandhi, Winston Churchill, and Nelson Mandella all share the accolade of being towering global figures, it is probably their differences that impress rather than their similarities. If given a battery of personality tests, would a common leadership factor emerge?

That said, however, Kirkpatrick and Locke (1991) listed six basic traits that distinguish leaders from non-leaders in management:

- drive;
- desire to lead;
- honesty/integrity;
- self-confidence;
- cognitive ability;
- knowledge of the business.

It is readily acknowledged, however, that these operate at the level of preconditions and are not in themselves sufficient for success (Van Yperen and Van de Vliert, 2001).

Still, interest in this line of research keeps being rekindled. In the mid-1970s, House (1976) reintroduced the notion of the charismatic leader, originally mooted by Weber (1947). Charismatic leaders are those who 'by force of their personality are capable of having a profound and extraordinary effect on followers' (Schermerhorn, *et al.*, 1995: 171). Several alternate versions of this theory now exist. While inconsistencies and ambiguities persist, as reviewed by Yukl (1999), their major impact has been in addressing the behavioural manifestations of charismatic leadership rather than weeding out underlying personality factors *per se*. Again the fact that leaders can lose charisma poses questions for a strict personality-based explanation.

For others the quest to isolate a leader personality type, or elements thereof, has become transmogrified into a search for behavioural skills and competencies that seem crucial, at least in some situations.

Situation approach

If we cannot explain why certain people come to prominence through concentrating on those individuals and dissecting their personalities, then perhaps we can do so by shifting the direction of enquiry on to the circumstances of their rise to power. In its most extreme form, the situational approach attributes leadership, not to the person, but to the particular demands of the situation. Here there are no universally important traits of leadership, nor does it follow that a person who becomes leader in one situation will do so in another, as trait theory would predict. Winston Churchill scarcely covered himself in glory during his military service during the First World War, but the perilous situation that Britain faced when he became Prime Minister during the later world conflict made him an ideal person to lead the nation on that occasion. Once circumstances changed, with the advent of peace, however, he lost power at the next general election. But mustn't the individual be factored into the equation in some way? Isn't his or her unique contribution, in whatever form that may take, still important? Churchill coming to power when he did was a feature of the situation faced and the special qualities that he could bring to tackling it.

Contingency approach

Theories that can be listed here have in common the assumption that effective leadership is a function of situational variables, including task demands, and the approach adopted by the leader in tackling them. Perhaps the best known is that proposed by Fiedler (1967, 1986). Using a variety of group situations, ranging from sports groups through to military and industrial settings, Fiedler's starting point was that some leaders were more committed to the nature or structure of the task and reaching a goal. Others were more oriented to achieving good personal relationships within the group. He concluded that it was unusual to find individuals who were equally oriented to both group socio-emotional needs and task completion.

Turning attention to the situational context, three factors seemed important:

1 the relationship between leader and members;
2 the degree to which the task was clearly structured;
3 the amount of power enjoyed by the leader to reward and punish members.

Fiedler found evidence that the type of leader required in order for group performance to be enhanced was contingent on the nature of the situation defined in terms of these three factors. For instance, task-oriented leaders appear to be most effective when they are on very good terms with group members, the task is clearly structured and they are in a powerful position within the group. Such leaders are also effective when on poor terms with group members, the task is ambiguous and they have limited power. However, it would appear that when moderate relationships exist between leader and group members, when the task is moderately clear and when the leader has an intermediate position of influence, the leader who emphasises good relationships within the group is the most effective at achieving member participation and productivity. Effectiveness therefore depends on a proper match between elements of the situation and the type of leadership provided.

While much research has been produced in broad support of Fiedler's findings, criticisms have also been levelled. One source stems from the fact that the theory provides little explanation for the patterns of relationship between personal and situational variables (Northouse, 1997). Another major criticism is that group performance is measured in terms of task or goal completion. Output is only one measure of a group's value, however. Individual group members' satisfaction may be equally important yet not contribute to the achievement of the extrinsic goal. It will be recalled from earlier in the chapter that the most satisfied members do not necessarily belong to the most productive groups. Furthermore, the validity of the instrument used to measure leadership orientation (task vs. relation) has been brought into question (Fiedler, 1993a).

Transformational approach

As part of a more recent way of thinking about the topic, 'transformational leadership' can be traced back to the work of Burns (1978). He focused on the relationship between leaders and followers and distinguished between its *transactional* and *transformational* characterisations.

- *Transactional leadership* – concentrates on the exchange nature of the relationship between leaders and led. Each makes a contribution in return for some reciprocating input from the other party. Leaders provide expertise and direction; followers contribute effort and compliance. Leaders dispense rewards; followers meet their production targets. This attitude has typified much traditional thinking.
- *Transformational leadership* – focuses on the process by which the leader engages with members in such as way as to raise to new heights the levels of motivation, aspiration and commitment of the whole group. As part of this

transmogrification, a new way of thinking and feeling is brought about such that the greater good of the collective takes precedence over the separate needs of individuals, creating a different set of moral values that they all share. Mahatma Gandhi is a good example of this type of leader who did much more than merely offer political direction to the Indian people in exchange for, let's say, their recognition and patronage. He offered them a new vision of independence to which they could aspire together with a sense of hope, belief and commitment to its achievement.

This early contribution by Burns (1978) has since been extended perhaps most noticeably by Bass (1985, 1996) and his colleagues. Leaders who provide this sort of influence are thought to raise members to new levels of achievement by:

1   heightening their consciousness about actual and potential goals;
2   having them promote the greater interests of the group over narrow personal agendas;
3   bringing attention to bear on higher-order needs.

Transformational leadership is therefore provided when the leader induces members to see beyond their own limited personal interests, recognising and embracing the mission of the group (Schermerhorn *et al.*, 1995). Followers, in turn, tend to respond with a sense of trust, loyalty and mutual respect towards the leader and are sufficiently motivated to accomplish more than they would initially have thought possible. As a corollary, they experience conditions conducive to the maximisation of their full potential. According to Bass (1985), four factors lie behind this effect.

1   *Charisma or idealised influence*. Bass (1996) proposed that charisma was a necessary but not sufficient condition of transformational leadership – a leader could be charismatic but not necessarily transformational. For him, it was important that the transformational leader be someone that the rest can look up to and wish to emulate, capable of commanding confidence, allegiance, and unwavering loyalty, and encapsulating a vision to be shared by all. On the other hand, it has been proposed that a leader can be transformational but not charismatic: even that these two concepts have little in common (Yukl, 1999).
2   *Inspirational motivation*. This factor is about instilling a strong sense of will to achieve for the good of the group. It is created through developing ownership of a collective vision of the group and what it is going to achieve, together with an appreciation of the part that the individual member has to play in bringing this to fruition. Team spirit and collaboration for the good of the organisation are important. Emotion, dynamism and symbolism are often tools at the disposal of the transformational leader in this regard.
3   *Intellectual stimulation*. It should not be thought, however, that transformational leadership is merely a more sophisticated way of brainwashing followers to do the bidding of the leader – but now with a smile. When truly implemented, this approach stimulates followers to challenge their established ways of thinking,

evaluating and reacting, as well as those of the leader and the organisation. Members should be both encouraged to and facilitated in considering innovative approaches to tackling problems and bringing these to the attention of the group.

4   *Individualised concern.* Transformational leaders should also be capable of dealing with members on an individual basis, listening to their concerns, acknowledging their needs and taking an interest in their personal development and actualisation.

The transformational approach to explaining leadership can rightly claim a number of advantages. It offers a broader perspective than some of the alternatives and emphasises not only the relationship between leader and follower, but introduces a moral dimension to the process. In addition to a certain intuitive appeal, a considerable body of empirical research has now been generated, particularly in organisations. In a meta-analysis of thirty-nine studies, Lowe *et al.* (1996) discovered that the central components of this form of leadership were positively associated with member performance and satisfaction. Focusing specifically on the global organisational setting, Church and Waclawski (1999) reported that transformational, when compared with transactional leaders, were rated higher by co-workers on all accounts, including managing change and relationships.

However, concerns have also been mooted about this way of thinking of leadership (Northouse, 1997; Yukl, 1999; Tourish and Pinnington, 2002). There is a tendency to assume inappropriately that certain traits and personal qualities set transformational leaders apart. Perhaps more compellingly though, conceptual confusions and a lack of clarity have been voiced surrounding, for instance, transformational and charismatic leadership. The underlying mechanisms of influence on which transformational leaders depend also remain obscure. Furthermore, the primary level of analysis tends to be pitched at the dyad between the leader and individual followers, rather than at the organisation. Tourish and Pinnington (2002) also drew attention to the inordinate levels of power necessitated by transformational leadership, the lack of associated checks and balances, and the misconception and mishandling of dissent among followers, as problematic areas for proponents of this approach. As characterised by Tourish and Pinnington (2002: 152), in the context of corporate management, 'the leader may be able to impose his or her vision on recalcitrant followers, however erroneous it is. The edge of a cliff might seem the starting point of an adventurous new journey.'

Behavioural approach

The final approach to be considered here shifts the focus from the traits and aptitudes that may set leaders apart, and places it on how leaders actually conduct themselves when providing leadership in different situations. What do effective leaders do that their ineffective counterparts fail to, and vice versa? Of course, performance can be analysed at different levels from the coarse-grained examination of styles of leadership to the higher resolution identification of skills and actions that express them.

Leadership styles

Style generally can be thought of, 'as *how* what is done is done, with the characteristic manner in which someone handles an interactive episode' (Dickson, 1997: 160). Differences have been reported in this respect between leaders of more and less successful teams (Kolb, 1998). Leadership style has been linked to levels of member job satisfaction, organisational commitment and evaluation of leader competence (Skogstad and Einarsen, 1999), enjoyment (Fox *et al.*, 2000b), creativity (Sosik *et al.*, 2000), and even mental health (Gardiner and Tiggemann, 1999). We have already mentioned how leaders can be mainly task-oriented or relation-oriented. But perhaps the best known variants of style are those introduced by Lewin *et al.* (1939). In what is now considered a classical study involving groups of juvenile boys in a recreational youth centre, they distinguished three types:

1   *Autocratic* – the leader was instructed to be totally authoritarian, directing others and making all decisions.
2   *Democratic* – the leader was asked to encourage participation, help group members to interact, and consult them when taking decisions.
3   *Laissez-faire* – the leader had to more or less leave the boys to get on with it.

The results revealed that members were more dependent on the leader and lacking in co-operation with their peers when led by an autocratic leader. When the leaders adopted a democratic approach, the same boys showed more initiative and responsibility for the progress of the group and were friendlier towards each other, even when the leader left the room. In the laissez-faire or leaderless group, the boys lacked interest in their tasks and failed to complete successfully any that had been set. Aggressive acts were more frequent under autocratic and laissez-faire leaders. Finally, it was found that the democratic leader was the most liked, the autocratic leader the least so. Transferred to a 'real-life' working environment, Packard and Kauppi (1999) found, among employees in rehabilitation agencies, that those who recorded their immediate supervisor's style as democratic, rather than autocratic or laissez-faire, also reported that they enjoyed greater support, less work pressure, and more job satisfaction.

Muczyk and Reimann (1987) suggested that such styles actually involve two separate dimensions.

1   *Autocratic–democratic* – charts the extent to which leaders allow members to become actively involved in the decision-making process.
2   *Permissive–directive* – determines the degree to which leaders tell members what to do.

When these two dimensions are put together, four possibilities exist.

1   *Directive autocrat* – members are permitted little autonomy in organising their work and the leader makes all significant decisions.
2   *Permissive-autocrat* – members have considerable autonomy in organising their work, but the leader makes all significant decisions.

3   *Directive democrat* – members are permitted little autonomy in organising their work but are actively involved in the decision-making process.
4   *Permissive democrat* – members have considerable autonomy in organising their work and are actively involved in the decision-making process.

Related to these four options, *directive* and *participative* styles (House and Mitchell, 1974; Larson *et al.*, 1998) are two further contrasting possibilities, commonly referred to, that derive from the same underlying issues of the management of power and members' involvement.

1   *Participative leaders* – share power with members, actively involve them in decision-making, and seek their views and suggestions, taking these into account rather than trying to impose personal opinions.
2   *Directive leaders* – give instructions, clarify regulations, make their preferences known and seek to influence others to their way of thinking when reaching decisions. Two sub-components have been proposed by Peterson (1997):

- *Outcome directiveness* has to do with advancing a solution favoured by the leader.
- *Process directiveness* concerns the degree to which steps taken to reach an outcome (but not the outcome itself) are shaped by the leader. In the study undertaken by Peterson this element emerged as a significant predictor of the quality of both decisions reached by groups and the processes they used.

A much more elaborate system for identifying leadership styles and one of the most popular was first introduced in the 1960s by Blake and Mouton (1964). Since then it has undergone several revisions (Blake and Mouton, 1985; Blake and McCanse, 1991). According to this model a range of leadership patterns can be plotted on a grid formed from the intersection of two basic dimensions:

1   *Concern for people* relates to the leader's commitment to members, their levels of satisfaction, working conditions, sense of being valued, loyalty to the organisation, etc.
2   *Concern for production* has to do with the leader's dedication to achieving organisational goals and maximising quality output.

Each of these dimensions can be plotted on an axis and scored from low to high on a nine-point scale. Various styles can be identified in the resulting matrix, characterised by a combination of a certain level of concern for people on the one hand, and for production on the other. Five principal styles to emerge are as follows:

1   *Impoverished management* – low on concern for people and production. This person simply goes through the motions but provides no meaningful influence (similar to the laissez-faire leader already mentioned).

2   *Country club management* – high concern for people but low for production. Here leaders concentrate narrowly on relationships within the workforce and the needs of its members, to the neglect of output.

3   *Middle-of-the-road management* – medium concern for people and for production. In this case, a balance is struck between relational and task matters.

4   *Authority-compliance* – low concern for people but high concern for production. Members' concerns here only count to the extent that they may hamper output. Achievement and the processes that promote it are all important.

5   *Team management* – high on people and high on production. This style integrates the importance of both factors. Members are treated as important, their ideas and contributions valued and their active involvement encouraged. This boosts morale and satisfaction, as well as promoting high level production.

While the 'team manager' would appear to win the best style award hands down, there is some concern that this potent combination of high production coupled with high care for people may not be pertinent to all situations (Quinn and McGrath, 1982). The maturity of the group (i.e. whether newly formed or existing) can have a major influence on optimal leadership style. The best style for a newly formed group, for instance, may be one where task issues are promoted over those of group members. While leaders are thought to have a preferred style and a fallback alternative when this customary approach fails, *opportunism* describes a person who makes use of any combination of these five styles as circumstances require.

It is not only in relation to the work of Blake and Mouton, and their leadership grid, that questions are raised as to which style is best. While democratic, participative options have much to commend them and fit neatly into a broader western political ideology, the answer is that no one style is 'right' or 'best'. As expressed by Paulus *et al.* (1996: 308) 'no single style of leadership is best under all conditions and in all situations'. Napier and Gershenfeld (1999: 229) contended that 'it is the ability of leaders to first identify the most appropriate behavioral response called for in a particular situation and then to actually use it as needed that separates those who are successful from the rest'.

Groups under directive leadership have been criticised for being prone to flawed decision-making. Larson *et al.* (1998), however, found that where such leaders possess information favouring the best choice alternative, they can actually outperform their participative counterparts. In a study by Surinder *et al.* (1997) the degree of structure of the task also played a part. With moderately structured tasks, participative leadership was conducive to proposing solutions, but this advantage was lost as the level of structure increased. Likewise, gender has been found to be related to ideal leadership style, with females preferring a more relational approach (Boatwright, 1999). Interestingly, Gardiner and Tiggemann (1999) discovered that it was only in female-dominated industries that females were more interpersonally oriented than males. The cultural background of participants should also be taken into account. Different cultures have contrasting perspectives on leadership and what it means. Thus Torres (2000) found that Brazilians had a general preference for less participative styles of leadership than did Americans. On the other hand, Den Hartog *et al.* (1999) produced evidence that aspects of charismatic/transformational leadership are strongly endorsed across a broad range of cultures and have some claim to universality.

In sum, Hargie *et al.* (1999) listed a set of four considerations that are central to decisions about which leadership style may be most effective, namely the:

1   task faced by the group;
2   nature, abilities and characteristics of the members;
3   past history of the group and its members;
4   pressures and demands of the external environment.

Leadership skills

Leaders are required to fulfil a range of functions, thereby making considerable demands on the complement of skills, competencies and tactics that they must have at their disposal. Being a potent agent of influence, building teams, making effective presentations, negotiating and bargaining, selecting and appraising are just some of the sets of skills explored by Hargie *et al.* (1999) in a management context. Indeed the number of diverse and varied actions demanded of a leader when trying to accomplish a task and maintain good internal relations in contrasting sets of circumstances makes the task of defining specific skills a daunting one. Perhaps this is one reason behind the observation by Morley and Hosking (1985: 2) that 'the literature on leadership has not been informed by attempts systematically to articulate the nature of the skills which make leaders effective'. More recent empirical investigations into leadership skills and competencies can, however, be found (e.g. Kolb, 1998; Atkinson, 1997). Still, it is true to say that the majority of contributions to this literature are based on conceptual analysis and experiential insights rather than systematic research (e.g. Clark and Matze, 1999; Zaccaro, 1999).

Providing leadership is undoubtedly a multi-faceted process. In the workplace, meetings are typically valued by members of staff, especially when they provide an opportunity for face-to-face contact with immediate and senior management (Tourish and Hargie, 1998). For the workforce, they offer an important avenue into the decision-making process. People, in turn, are more likely to comply with decisions reached in circumstances affording some level of ownership (Doucouliagos, 1995). One of the common functions expected of leaders by most groups, therefore, involves taking charge of discussions (Galanes *et al.*, 2000). This service is particularly significant in the sort of small group interaction focused on in this chapter. Several publications (e.g. Johnson and Johnson, 1997; Brilhart and Galanes, 1998; Hanna and Wilson, 1998; Wilson, 1999; Hargie *et al.*, 1999; Galanes *et al.*, 2000) have teased out taxonomies of skills and tactics involved in this activity. These sources will be drawn on in the following outline of the major requirements demanded of those leading group discussions. Additionally, most of the skills already covered in this book have a role when applied to this particular enterprise.

Preparation

The work of leading a productive discussion doubtlessly begins in advance of members coming together. Tasks to be taken on board by (or on behalf of) the leader include:

- Researching the issue/s fully, if knowledge is lacking.
- Identifying the purpose of the meeting and formulating an agenda, if appropriate. In formal meetings, this may be distributed in advance for agreement by members.
- Selecting a suitable location and making all necessary physical arrangements including seating, equipment, materials, refreshments, etc.
- Deciding when best to hold the meeting and how long it should last.
- Deciding who should be present, including particular people not part of the group who may be usefully invited on account of their relevant expertise.

Getting started

Much of relevance here has already been covered in relation to set induction (see Chapter 10). Many of the ways of effecting perceptual, social, cognitive, and motivational sets discussed there can be tailored to this particular situation and will not be repeated. Briefly, the leader should:

- *Introduce all present.* If members are meeting for the first time, it is particularly important that time be taken to ensure that each is known to the rest and that all begin to feel at ease with the company. Ice-breaking chit-chat can help people relax and assuage primary tension before moving on to meaningful discussion of more substantive issues.
- *Identify roles.* Where people have been brought along for a particular reason, this should be made known. Alternatively, the leader may invite a participant to take on a special role, e.g. secretary, observer, devil's advocate, etc.
- *Establish the agreed aim of the meeting and what it is designed to accomplish.*
- *Agree procedures to follow.* Where an agenda has been drawn up, the leader may want to agree the order in which items are taken. Additionally, the 'ground rules' to be followed as well as strategic steps to achieve the goal may need to be dealt with. If the task to hand is essentially to solve a problem, it may be prudent to suggest:

  1 spending some time analysing the problem and its causes;
  2 agreeing the criteria that an acceptable solution would have to meet;
  3 brainstorming possible solutions;
  4 critically evaluating suggestions;
  5 selecting an agreed option;
  6 considering implementation issues.

- *Direct a clear question at the group.* This is a way of getting the discussion going and focusing the group's attention on the first of the issues to be tackled.

Structuring and guiding discussion

Once the discussion has been initiated, the leader has a role in keeping it on target. Here a judicious balance has to be struck between, on the one hand, allowing the discussion to run amuck and on the other perpetrating a slow strangulation by forcing it into a strait-jacket of the leader's choosing. The style of leadership selected (e.g. directive vs. participative) will influence how this delicate task is carried out. Structuring and guiding the discussion can be achieved in different ways.

- *Be alert to digression and cul-de-sacs*. When suspected, point out this may be an interesting issue for another occasion, but right now it may divert the group from its goal in the limited time set aside to achieve it.
- *Clarify*. It is essential that participants fully appreciate what is happening. Where it is felt that some issue has not been fully grasped or has been misunderstood, the leader may clarify the point (see Chapter 8 for further discussion on this aspect of explaining) or invite the person who made it to do so.
- *Elaborate*. Certain contributions may be thought more worthy of having greater attention paid to them than others. Here the leader may elaborate directly by offering further information or encourage extended discussion by using techniques such as probing questions (see Chapter 5) and paraphrases (see Chapter 6).
- *Summarise*. In addition, it is useful for the leader or chairperson to provide transitional summaries at the end of each phase of the meeting or discussion before introducing the next issue. These act as signposts, reminding members where they have been, where they are now, and where they are going. This can be a very effective way of guiding the discourse.

Managing conflict

Conflict during discussion is sometimes mistakenly regarded as invariably destructive and to be avoided at all costs. While it may heighten tension in the group and challenge the skill of the leader in dealing with it, having members express different views and opinions can be to the advantage of the group outcome. The perils of groupthink will be recalled from earlier in the chapter. It is controlling conflict that counts. Tactics to consider include:

- *Focusing on issues, not on personalities*. When conflict becomes personalised it tends to shift from being potentially productive to invariably counterproductive. In this form, internal group relations can suffer.
- *Make all contributors feel that their suggestions have at least some merit*. The leader should avoid creating a situation of 'winners' and 'losers', or having some stakeholders feel humiliated. Ways of giving face to those whose line of argument is ultimately not taken up should be found. Likewise all should feel that they have received a 'fair hearing'.

- *Highlight broader areas of agreement.* If discussion reaches loggerheads, taking the group back to a point where all were in agreement on some broader matter can ease tension.
- *Emphasise 'we' and 'us'.* Constantly re-establishing a sense of group unity prevents factionalism and damaged morale. Even in a situation where the views of one member or faction prevail over those of another or others, the contribution of all to the quality of the decision reached by the *group*, should be stressed.

Regulating participation

The following set of tactics addresses the task of conducting the discussion so that everyone has an opportunity to contribute, thereby ensuring an orderly meeting.

- *Encourage contributions.* Here some of the techniques of reinforcement discussed in Chapter 4 can be employed. Members who feel rewarded for their contributions, or who see others rewarded, are more likely to contribute further. In particular, the leader should pay special attention to the more reticent member who may have an important input to make but may only be prepared to so if directly invited in a tactful way. It is a mistake, though, to assume that the leader must comment on each contribution received. Frequently a more useful response is simply silence, or inviting the group or individual members to respond, if no reaction is immediately forthcoming.
- *Discourage contributions.* On the other hand the garrulous member has to be prevented from monopolising the proceedings. Decisions as to how much one person is permitted to hog the floor will be taken based on the value of their input, among other considerations. It may be necessary to thank some diplomatically for their commitment to the discussion, while reminding them that they have already spoken twice on the issue and others still have not been heard, and to say that if there is time remaining at the end they will be returned to.
- *Prevent over-talk.* While all members should be encouraged to contribute to the discussion, if they all insist in doing so at the same time then the effect will be lost. Regulating contributions by bringing individuals in and out of the conversation at particular times is something that effective chairpersons are particularly skilled at doing. Much of it can be conducted nonverbally (see Chapter 3).

Closing

Much of what was said in Chapter 7 on closure is directly applicable here. In drawing the discussion to a close, the leaders can:

- Ensure that there is general agreement on the decision/s taken and that no remaining doubt or confusion exists.

- Identify any outstanding business still to be taken care of.
- Establish how the outcome of the meeting is to be taken forward. If certain members have been tasked with doing certain things, this should be re-established. It is always advisable to have this committed to paper, in the form of a minute, as quickly as possible.
- Deal with any residual tension that may exist, perhaps from an earlier disagreement. It may be sufficient perhaps to mention the contribution of a member still 'smarting', without of course appearing to patronise that person. Taking time personally to have a few informal words before leaving may also be appreciated.
- Thank all participants for their efforts in achieving the aims of the discussion.

OVERVIEW

This chapter has been concerned with small groups, how they operate and the manner in which leaders emerge and leadership is exercised within them. Groups, in this sense, can be thought of as involving a plurality of individuals who influence each other in the course of interaction and share a relationship of interdependence in pursuit of some common goal or goals. Members also characteristically develop a sense of belonging to this particular social entity. People come together to form groups to satisfy needs which may be interpersonal, informational or material. In so doing they become part of an ordered and regulated system which evolves through the establishment of, for example, norms, or commonly expected and accepted ways of perceiving, thinking, feeling and acting; the enactment of roles including that of leader; and the creation of identifiable forms and patterns of communication between members.

Additionally, an attempt has been made to show leadership as virtually synonymous with the act of influencing others in a range of group contexts. However, it is important to bear in mind the distinction between leadership and leader. While specific individuals may occupy the position of leader, acts of leadership can be manifested by any group member.

Theories of leadership offer contrasting explanations about the emergence of leaders and their functioning. Focusing on the actual performance of leaders, their behaviour can be examined on two levels: leadership styles at the macro level and leadership skills and tactics at the micro level. While different styles have been suggested, the three most commonly mentioned are autocratic, democratic and laissez-faire. Underlying dimensions for these and other stylistic variants have to do with the extent to which the leader takes all important decisions single-handedly; directs what subordinates should do and denies them autonomy; and concentrates on group task or relational issues. Leading discussions is one particular facet of leadership. Particular sets of skills involved in leading group discussions and conducting meetings were outlined in terms of getting started; structuring and guiding discussion; managing conflict; regulating participation; and closing.

Chapter 15

Concluding comments

HUMANS SEEM TO HAVE an innate predisposition to commune with one another. Our ability to develop sophisticated methods for communicating both within and between generations is the core dimension that separates us from all other species. As illustrated in Chapter 1, the better able we are to communicate, the more successful we will be in all walks of life. Effective interpersonal skills allow us to develop and maintain relational bonds so that, as noted by Ryff and Singer (2000: 30), 'Quality ties to others are universally endorsed as central to optimal living.'

This book has been concerned with an examination of the central components of interpersonal communication, namely the skills that individuals employ in order to achieve their goals in social encounters. The theory behind the skills approach to the study of interpersonal behaviour, as outlined in Chapters 1 and 2, has provided a key conceptual framework that has been successfully applied across numerous settings and in a wide range of research studies (Dickson, 1999b; Hargie and Tourish, 1999).

Thus there is a solid theoretical base underpining the skills perspective. In his historical overview of this field, Argyle (1999: 142) noted, 'One of the implications of looking at social behaviour as a social skill was the likelihood that it could be trained.' This proved to be the case, and there has been an enormous explosion of interest in communication skills training (Dickson *et al.*, 1997). When individuals receive systematic skills tuition, their social performance has been shown to improve (Hargie, 1997c). Not surprisingly, there has been a concomitant and exponential growth in publications pertaining to interpersonal skills, within a variety of social and professional contexts. As evidenced by the references in this text, research in this field has been voluminous.

439

It has not been our intention, however, to offer a cook-book approach to the study of interpersonal interaction. There are no 'right' or 'wrong' ways to communicate with others. One dimension we have mentioned throughout is that most skills have a 'happy medium' in terms of usage. For example, someone who bombards us with questions, continually self-discloses, or reinforces every single thing we say or do, would not be regarded as skilled. In this sense, a measured combination of skills is preferable. Indeed, two important elements of goals were highlighted by Shah and Kruglanski (2000). The first is that of *multi-finality*, wherein any one means of achieving a goal may serve more than one purpose. For example, a negotiator who demonstrates an interest in and pays attention to the other side may achieve the twin goals of (a) building a good relationship and (b) making the chances of a successful negotiation more likely. The second is *equifinality*, whereby the same goal can be attained in a variety of equally effective ways. Thus there are alternative approaches that can be employed in any particular interactive episode to achieve a desired outcome, and it is up to the individual to select what is deemed to be the most appropriate mix. Such selection, however, demands an extensive knowledge of the range of alternatives available and their likely effects in any given context. It is at this level that the present book has been geared.

The model of the interpersonal process outlined in Chapter 2 provides a conceptual framework that can be used as a basis for making such strategic decisions. Awareness of the skills covered, and of their behavioural determinants, as presented in the remaining chapters, will contribute to the increased understanding of the process of interpersonal communication. These furnish the reader with a language with which to study, and interpret, this process more fully. Fiske (2000: 77) pointed out that for the most part: 'people do not know how they coordinate, plan, construct their action, or interpret each other's action'. While for much of the time we operate at this subconscious level, it is also necessary to have insight into, and understanding of, the skills and strategies that underpin human intercourse. Such knowledge enables us to operate swiftly and effectively without always having to think consciously about what we should do. When problems arise it also allows us to analyse possible underlying reasons, and make alternative responses.

COMMUNICATION ETHICS

Before ending this book, we want to say a little about communication ethics. When people have information, they can use it for good or ill. It is the same with interpersonal skills. It is possible to use the information contained in this book in ethical or unethical ways. For example, the influencing techniques reviewed in Chapter 12 could be used in a manipulative and machiavellian manner to get others to do what we want. Alternatively, they can be employed for the greater good of everyone. In the business world there have long been criticisms of the lack of communication ethics (Stewart, 2001). The ethical manager is seen as being something akin to the Yeti. Several people claim to have seen one in the distance, there is some circumstantial though not very convincing evidence that one exists, but no one has actually encountered the beast face-to-face, and we would be rather taken aback if we saw it in all its glory. But it is clear that in the end an unethical style of operating will be costly for both relational and more material goals (Clampitt, 2001). A code for communication professionals, put forward by Montgomery *et al.* (2001), included the following guidelines.

- *Tell the truth.* As discussed in Chapter 9, harmless white lies (like telling someone their new suit is lovely when you really don't like it) can sometimes be conducive to relationships, but as deceit increases the potential for dysfunctional outcomes escalates.
- *Do not harm others.* The autonomy of others should be recognised and their independent decisions encouraged. Using interpersonal skills in a devious fashion (e.g. persuading people to act against their best interests) is not good practice. Selling others something they don't need at an inflated price is an example of a breach of this moral code; spreading false and malicious rumours is another.
- *Treat others justly.* Being aggressive, bullying or demeaning is not part of any decent moral code. Other people should be treated honourably and with respect. As discussed in Chapter 11, a 'soft' form of assertiveness is the best policy. Here the rights of both sides are protected equally, and there is concern for the relationship.
- *Act professionally at all times.* Respect information given in private and treat it confidentially. Behave in such a way as to inspire confidence. For example, listen carefully, respond in a manner that is apposite to the other person's emotional needs, and do not use inappropriate humour. Recognise that communication must be worked at. Attend professional development courses to update and sharpen your interpersonal skills.
- *Treat others as equals.* In most professional–client encounters there is asymmetry, in that the former often has knowledge and status that the latter does not possess. This can cause *dysfunctional discordance* in the relationship (Morrow and Hargie, 2001). The concept of *concordance* is therefore important as a way of trying to achieve greater balance, whereby professional inter-actions are conceived of as a meeting between equals. It is possible to behave in a power-crazed fashion by, for example, asking all the questions and only rewarding responses that suit your intentions for the other person. This is not good practice. Rather, it is better to empower others to participate as fully as possible. Explain to them what your goals are throughout the interaction, and check these for agreement. Concordance necessitates adopting a more reflective than directive style.

OVERVIEW

Success in most walks of life is predicated on communicative ability. As shown in this book, we now know a great deal about the key constituents of effective social performance. The areas selected for inclusion were: nonverbal communication, reinforcement, questioning, reflecting, listening, explanation, self-disclosure, set induction, closure, assertiveness, influencing, negotiating, and group interaction. It is recognised that this selection is not exhaustive, since other specialised skills may be employed in particular settings. Nevertheless, we believe that these represent the core behavioural elements of skilled interpersonal communication. For this reason, the practising professional needs to have a sound working knowledge of them.

However, in the final analysis, improvements in performance necessitate practical action. In other words, it is only by converting knowledge of skills into actual behaviour that increments in social competence can occur. This may necessitate changes in one's existing behavioural repertoire, and this is not always easily achieved. The most difficult part of learning new responses is often the unlearning of old ones. Thus we would encourage readers to experiment with various social techniques in order to develop, refine, maintain or extend their existing repertoire of skills. Once a wide repertoire has been developed, the individual thereby becomes a more effective communicator with the ability to adjust and adapt to varying social situations. For most professionals, this is an essential prerequisite to effective functioning.

References

Abrams, D. and Hogg, M. (2001) 'Collective identity: group membership and self-conception', in M. Hogg and S. Tindale (eds) *Blackwell handbook of social psychology*, Malden, MA: Blackwell.

Achinstein, P. (1983) *The nature of explanation*, Oxford: Oxford University Press.

Adair, W.L., Okumura, T. and Brett, J.M. (2001) 'Negotiation behaviour when cultures collide: the United States and Japan', *Journal of Applied Psychology* 86: 371–85.

Adams, N., Bell, J., Saunders, C. and Whittington, D. (1994) *Communication skills in physiotherapist–patient interactions*, Jordanstown: University of Ulster Monograph.

Adler, R. and Elmhorst, J. (1999) *Communicating at work*, Boston: McGraw-Hill.

Adler, R. and Rodman, G. (2000) *Understanding human communication* (7th edn), Fort Worth: Harcourt College Publishers.

Adler, R., Rosen, B. and Silverstein, E. (1998a) 'Emotions in negotiation: how to manage fear and anger', *Negotiation Journal* 14: 161–79.

Adler, R., Rosenfeld, L. and Proctor, R. (2001) *Interplay: the process of interpersonal communicating* (8th edn), Fort Worth, TX: Harcourt.

Adler, R., Rosenfeld, L., Towne, N. and Proctor, R. (1998b) *Interplay: the process of interpersonal communication* (7th edn), Fort Worth: Harcourt Brace.

Adler, R. and Towne, N. (1996) *Looking out, looking in* (8th edn), Fort Worth: Harcourt Brace.

Adler, T. (1993) 'Congressional staffers witness miracle of touch', *APA Monitor* (Feb): 12–13.

Afifi, W. and Guerrero, L. (2000) 'Motivations underlying topic avoidance in close relationships', in S. Petronio (ed.) *Balancing the secrets of private disclosures*, Mahwah, NJ: Lawrence Erlbaum.

Ajzen, I. (1991) 'The theory of planned behaviour', *Organizational Behavior and Human Decision Processes* 50: 179–211.

Akande, A. (1997) 'Determinants of personal space among South African students', *Journal of Psychology* 131: 569–71.

Alavosius, M., Adams, A., Ahern, D. and Follick, M. (2000) 'Behavioural approaches to organisational safety', in J. Austin and J. Carr (eds) *Handbook of applied behaviour analysis*, Reno: Context Press.

Albert, S. and Kessler, S. (1976) 'Processes for ending social encounters', *Journal of the Theory of Social Behaviour* 6: 147–70.

Alberti, R. and Emmons, M. (2001) *Your perfect right: assertiveness and equality in your life and relationships* (8th edn), Atascadero, CA: Impact.

Alberts, J.K. (1992) 'An inferential/strategic explanation for the social organisation of teases', *Journal of Language and Social Psychology* 11: 153–78.

Albrecht, T., Burleson, B. and Goldsmith, D. (1994) 'Supportive communication', in M. Knapp and G. Miller (eds) *Handbook of interpersonal communication* (2nd edn), Thousand Oaks, CA: Sage.

Algoe, S., Buswell, B. and DeLamater, J. (2000) ' Gender and job status as contextual cues for the interpretation of facial expression of emotion', *Sex Roles* 42: 183–208.

Allen, K. and Stokes, T. (1987) 'Use of escape and reward in the management of young children during dental treatment', *Journal of Applied Behaviour Analysis* 20: 381–9.

Allen, M. (1998) 'Comparing the effectiveness of one- and two-sided messages', in M. Allen and R. Preiss (eds) *Persuasion: advances through meta-analysis*, Cresskill, NJ: Hampton Press.

Allen, M., Bruflat, R., Fucilla, R., Kramer, M., McKellips, S., Ryan, D. and Spiegelhoff, M. (2000) 'Testing the persuasiveness of evidence: combining narrative and statistical forms', *Communication Research Reports* 17: 331–6.

Allen, M. and Stiff, J. (1998) 'An analysis of the sleeper effect', in M. Allen and R. Preiss (eds) *Persuasion: advances through meta-analysis*, Cresskill, NJ: Hampton Press.

Allwinn, S. (1991) 'Seeking information: contextual influences on question formulation', *Journal of Language and Social Interaction* 10: 169–84.

Altman, I. and Taylor, D. (1973) *Social penetration: the development of interpersonal relationships*, New York: Holt, Rinehart & Winston.

Anderson, J. (2000) 'The organisational self and the practices of control and resistance', *Australian Journal of Communication* 27: 1–32.

Andersen, P. and Guerrero, L. (1998) 'Principles of communication and emotion in social interaction', in P. Andersen and L. Guerrero (eds) *Handbook of communication and emotion: research, theory, applications, and contexts*, San Diego: Academic Press.

Andersen, P., Guerrero, L., Buller, D. and Jorgensen, P. (1998) 'An empirical comparison of three theories of nonverbal immediacy exchange', *Human Communication Research* 24: 501–35.

Anderson, D., Ansfield, M. and DePaulo, B. (1999) 'Love's best habit: deception in the context of relationships', in P. Philippot, R. Feldman, and E. Coats (eds) *The social context of nonverbal behavior*, Cambridge: Cambridge University Press.

Anderson, R. (1997) 'Anxiety or ignorance: the determinants of interpersonal skill display', *Dissertation Abstracts International: The Sciences and Engineering* 57 (9-B): 5959.

Andriessen, E. and Drenth, P. (1998) 'Leadership: theories and models', in P. Drenth, H. Thierry and C. de Wolff (eds) *Handbook of work and organizational psychology, volume 4: organizational psychology*, Hove: Psychology Press.

Anonymous (1998) 'To reveal or not to reveal: a theoretical model of anonymous communication', *Communication Theory* 8: 381–407.

Archer, J., Kilpatrick, G. and Bramwell, G. (1995) 'Comparison of two aggression inventories', *Aggressive Behavior* 21: 371–80.

Archer, R. (1979) 'Role of personality and the social situation', in G. Chelune (ed.) *Self-disclosure*, San Francisco: Jossey-Bass.

Argyle, M. (1983a) 'Five kinds of small social group', in H.H. Blumberg, A.P. Hare, V. Kent and M.F. Davies (eds) *Small groups and social interaction*, Vol. 1, Chichester: Wiley.

Argyle, M. (1983b) *The psychology of interpersonal behaviour* (4th edn), Harmondsworth: Penguin.

Argyle, M. (1988) *Bodily communication* (2nd edn), New York: Methuen.

Argyle, M. (1994) *The psychology of interpersonal behaviour*, London: Penguin.

Argyle, M. (1995) 'Social skills', in N. Mackintosh and A. Colman (eds) *Learning and skills*, London: Longman.

Argyle, M. (1999) 'Why I study social skills', *The Psychologist* 12: 142.

Argyle, M. and Cook, M. (1976) *Gaze and mutual gaze*, Cambridge: Cambridge University Press.

Argyle, M., Furnham, A. and Graham, J. (1981) *Social situations*, Cambridge: Cambridge University Press.

Aron A., Melinat, E., Aron, E., Valone, R. and Bator, R. (1997) 'The experimental generation of interpersonal closeness: a procedure and some preliminary findings', *Personality and Social Psychology Bulletin* 23: 363–77.

Aronson, E. (1999) *The social animal* (8th edn), New York: W.H. Freeman.

Aronson, E., Wilson, T. and Akert, R. (2002) *Social psychology* (4th edn), Upper Saddle River, NJ: Prentice Hall.

Asai, A. and Barnlund, D. (1998) 'Boundaries of the unconscious private and public self in Japanese and Americans: a cross-cultural comparison', *International Journal of Intercultural Relations* 22: 431–52.

Asch, S. (1952) *Social psychology*, Englewood Cliffs: Prentice Hall.

Ashmore, R. and Banks, D. (2001) 'Patterns of self-disclosure among mental health nursing students', *Nurse Education Today* 21: 48–57.

Astrom, J. (1994) 'Introductory greeting behaviour: a laboratory investigation of approaching and closing salutation phases', *Perceptual and Motor Skills* 79: 863–97.

Astrom, J. and Thorell, L. (1996) 'Greeting behaviour and psychogenic need: interviews on experiences of therapists, clergymen and car salesmen', *Perceptual and Motor Skills* 83: 939–56.

Atkinson, D. (1997) 'Rehabilitation management and leadership competencies', *Journal of Rehabilitation Administration* 21: 249–61.

Audit Commission (1993) *What seems to be the matter: communication between hospitals and patients*, London: HMSO.

Auerswald, M.C. (1974) 'Differential reinforcing power of restatement and interpretation on client production of affect', *Journal of Counseling Psychology* 21: 9–14.

Augoustinos, M. and Walker, I. (1995) *Social cognition*, London: Sage.

Austin, J.T. and Vancouver, J.B. (1996) 'Goal constructs in psychology: structure, process and content', *Psychological Bulletin* 120: 338–75.

Axtell, R. (1991) *Gestures: the do's and taboos of body language around the world*, New York: Wiley.

Axtell, R. (1999) 'Initiating interaction: greetings and beckonings across the world', in L. Guerrero, J. DeVito and M. Hecht (eds) *The nonverbal communication reader: classic and contemporary readings disclosures* (2nd edn), Prospect Heights, IL: Waveland.

Baker, R.A. (2001) 'The nature of leadership', *Human Relations* 54: 469–94.

Baker, W. (1994) *Networking smart: how to build relationships for personal and organizational success*, New York: McGraw-Hill.

Baldwin, M. (ed.) (2000) *The use of self in therapy* (2nd edn), New York: The Haworth Press.

Bales, R.F. (1950) *Interaction process analysis: a method for the study of small groups*, Cambridge, MA: Addison-Wesley.

Bales, R.F. (1970) *Personality and interpersonal behaviour*, New York: Holt, Rinehart and Winston.

Bandura, A. (1986) *Social foundations of thought and action: a social cognitive theory*, Englewood Cliffs, NJ: Prentice Hall.

Bandura, A. (1989) 'Self-regulation of motivation and action through internal standards and goal systems', in L. Pervin (ed.) *Goal concepts in personality and social psychology*, Hillsdale, NJ: Lawrence Erlbaum.

Bandura, A. (1997) *Self-efficacy: the exercise of control*, New York: W.H. Freeman.

Bangerter, A. (2000) 'Self-presentation: conversational implications of self-presentational goals in research interviews', *Journal of Language and Social Psychology* 19: 436–62.

Banks, D.L, (1972) 'A comparative study of the reinforcing potential of verbal and non-verbal cues in a verbal conditioning paradigm', unpublished doctoral dissertation, University of Massachusetts.

Bardine, B. (1999) 'Students' perceptions of written teacher comments: what do they say about how we respond to them?', *High School Journal* 82: 239–47.

Bargh, J.A., Gollwitzer, P.M., Lee Chai, A. and Barndollar, K. (1999) 'Bypassing the will: nonconscious self-regulation through automatic goal pursuit', unpublished manuscript.

Bargiela-Chiappini, F. and Harris, S. (1996) 'Interruptive strategies in British and Italian management meetings', *Text* 16: 269–97.

Barnabei, F., Cormier, W.H. and Nye, L.S. (1974) 'Determining the effects of three counselor verbal responses on client verbal behavior', *Journal of Counseling Psychology* 21: 355–9.

Baron, R. and Byrne, D. (2000) *Social psychology* (9th edn), Boston: Allyn & Bacon.

Baron, R., Cowan, G., Ganz, R. and McDonald, M. (1974) 'Interaction of locus of control and type of reinforcement feedback: considerations of external validity', *Journal of Personality and Social Psychology* 30: 285–92.

Baron, R., Kerr, N. and Miller, N. (1992) *Group process, group decision and group action*, Buckingham: Open University Press.

Baron, R. and Markman, G. (2000) 'Beyond social capital: how social skills can enhance entrepreneurs' success', *Academy of Management Executive* 14: 106–16.

Bass, B.M. (1985) *Leadership and performance beyond expectations*, New York: Free Press.

Bass, B.M. (1990) *Bass and Stogdill's handbook of leadership: a survey of theory and research*, New York: Free Press.

Bass, B.M. (1996) *A new paradigm of leadership: an inquiry into transformational leadership*, Alexandria, VA: US Army Research Institute for the Behavioral and Social Sciences.

Bavelas, A. (1950) 'Communication patterns in task-oriented groups', *Journal of the Acoustical Society of America* 22: 725–30.

Bavelas, J.B. (1992) 'Research into the pragmatics of human communication', *Journal of Strategic and Systemic Therapies* 11: 15–29.

Baxter, L. (1987) 'Symbols of relationship identity in relationship cultures', *Journal of Social and Personal Relationships* 4: 261–80.

Baxter, L. and Sahlstein, E. (2000) 'Some possible directions for future research', in S. Petronio (ed.) *Balancing the secrets of private disclosures*, Mahwah, NJ: Lawrence Erlbaum Associates.

Beaumeister, R. (1999) 'The nature and structure of the self', in R. Beaumeister (ed.) *The self in social psychology*, Philadelphia: Psychology Press.

Beck, C. (1999) *Managerial communication: bridging theory and practice*, Upper Saddle River, NJ: Prentice Hall.

Beebe, S.A. and Masterson, J.T. (2000) *Communication in small groups: principles and practice* (6th edn), New York: Longman.

Beezer, R. (1956) 'Research on methods of interviewing foreign informants', George Washington University, Hum RRO Technical Reports, No. 30.

Beharry, E.A. (1976) 'The effect of interviewing style on self-disclosure in a dyadic interaction', *Dissertation Abstracts International* 36: 4677B.

Beier, E. and Young, D. (1998) *The silent language of psychotherapy*, New York: Aldine De Gruyter.

Bell, R. and Healey, J. (1992) 'Idiomatic communication and interpersonal solidarity in friends' relational cultures', *Human Communication Research* 18: 307–35.

Beneson, J., Aikins-Ford, S. and Apostoleris, N. (1998) 'Girls' assertion in the presence of boys', *Small Group Research* 29: 198–211.

Benjamin, A. (1987) *The helping interview with case illustrations*, Boston: Houghton Mifflin.

Benne, K.D. and Sheats, P. (1948) 'Functional roles of group members', *Journal of Social Issues* 4: 41–9.

Bennis, W. (1999) 'The end of leadership: exemplary leadership is impossible without full inclusion, initiatives, and cooperation of followers', *Organizational Dynamics* 28: 71–80.

Benoit, W. (1998) 'Forewarning and persuasion', in M. Allen and R. Preiss (eds) *Persuasion: advances through meta-analysis*, Cresskill, NJ: Hampton Press.

Bente, G., Donaghy, W. and Suwelack, D. (1998) 'Sex differences in body movement and visual attention: an integrated analysis of movement and gaze in mixed-sex dyads', *Journal of Nonverbal Behavior* 22: 31–58.

Berger, C. (1994) 'Power, dominance and social interaction', in M. Knapp and G. Miller (eds) *Handbook of interpersonal communication* (2nd edn), Beverly Hills: Sage.

Berger, C. (1995) 'A plan-based approach to strategic communication', in D. Hewes (ed.) *The cognitive basis of interpersonal communication*, Hillsdale, NJ: Lawrence Erlbaum Associates.

Berger, C. (2000) 'Goal detection and efficiency: neglected aspects of message production', *Communication Theory* 10: 135–8.

Berry, W. (1996) *Negotiating in the age of integrity: a complete guide to negotiating win/win in business*, London: Nicholas Brealey.

Bertcher, H. (1988) 'Effective group membership', *Social Work with Groups* 10: 57–67.

Bettinghaus, E. and Cody, M. (1994) *Persuasive communication* (5th edn), Orlando, FL: Harcourt Brace.

Billing, M. (2001) 'Arguing', in W.P. Robinson and H. Giles (eds) *The handbook of language and social psychology*, Chichester: John Wiley & Sons.

Bion, W.R. (1961) *Experiences in groups and other papers*, London: Tavistock Publications.

Birdwhistell, R. (1970) *Kinesics and context*, Philadelphia: University of Pennsylvania Press.

Bixler, S. (1997) *The new professional image*, Holbrook, MA: Adams Media.

Bjorkqvist, K., Osterman, K. and Lagerspetz, K. (1994) 'Sex differences in covert aggression among adults', *Aggressive Behavior* 20: 27–33.

Blairy, S., Herrera, P. and Hess, U. (1999) 'Mimicry and the judgment of emotional facial expressions', *Journal of Nonverbal Behavior* 23: 5–41.

Blake, B.R. and McCanse, A.A. (1991) *Leadership dilemmas – grid solutions*, Houston: Gulf Publishing.

Blake, B.R. and Mouton, J.S. (1964) *The managerial grid*, Houston: Gulf Publishing.

Blake, B.R. and Mouton, J.S. (1985) *The managerial grid III*, Houston: Gulf Publishing.

Blanck, P. (ed.) (1993) *Interpersonal expectations: theory, research and applications*, Cambridge: Cambridge University Press.

Bless, H. (2001) 'The consequences of mood on the processing of social information', in A. Tesser and N. Schwarz (eds) *Blackwell handbook of social psychology: intraindividual processes*, Malden, MA: Blackwell.

Bless, H., Bohner, G., Hild, T. and Schwarz, N. (1992) 'Asking difficult questions: task complexity increases the impact of response', *European Journal of Social Psychology* 22: 309–12.

Bloch, C. (1996) 'Emotions and discourse', *Text* 16: 323–41.

Blundel, R. (1998) *Effective business communication: principles and practice for the information age*, London: Prentice Hall.

Boatwright, K.J. (1999) 'Women and men's ideal leadership style preferences within the workplace', *Dissertation Abstracts International: Section B: The Sciences & Engineering* 59(10-B): 5606.

Bochner, D. (2000) *The therapist's use of self in family therapy*, Northvale, NJ: Jason Aronson.

Boddy, J., Carvier, A. and Rowley, K. (1986) 'Effects of positive and negative verbal reinforcement on performance as a function of extroversion-introversion: some tests of Gray's theory', *Personality and Individual Differences* 7: 81–8.

Bohner, G. (2001) 'Attitudes', in M. Hewstone and W. Stroebe (eds) *Introduction to social psychology* (3rd edn), Oxford: Blackwell.

Borisoff, D. and Merrill, L. (1991) 'Gender issues and listening', in D. Borisoff and M. Purdy (eds) *Listening in everyday life*, Maryland: University of America Press.

Borisoff, D. and Purdy, M. (1991a) 'What is listening?', in D. Borisoff and M. Purdy (eds) *Listening in everyday life*, Maryland: University of America Press.

Borisoff, D. and Purdy, M. (eds) (1991b) *Listening in everyday life*, Maryland: University of America Press.

Bormann, E. (1990) *Small group communication: theory and practice*, New York: Harper and Row.

Borrego, J. and Urquiza, A. (1998) 'Importance of therapist use of social reinforcement with parents as a model for parent–child relationships: an example with Parent–Child Interaction Therapy', *Child and Family Behavior Therapy* 20: 27–54.

Bostrom, R. (1990) *Listening behavior: measurement and applications*, New York: Guilford Press.

Bostrom, R. (1996) 'Memory, cognitive processing and the process of "listening": a reply to Thomas and Levine', *Human Communication Research* 23: 298–305.

Bostrom, R. (1997) 'The process of listening', in O. Hargie (ed.) *The handbook of communication skills* (2nd edn), London: Routledge.

Bottom, W. and Paese, P. (1999) 'Judgment accuracy and the asymmetric cost of errors in distributive bargaining', *Group Decision and Negotiation* 8: 349–64.

Bradford, L. and Petronio, S. (1998) 'Strategic embarrassment', in P. Andersen and L. Guerrero (eds) *Handbook of communication and emotion: research, theory, applications, and contexts*, San Diego: Academic Press.

Brammer, L. and MacDonald, G. (1999) *The helping relationship* (7th edn), Boston: Allyn and Bacon.

Brammer, L., Shostrom, E. and Abrego, P. (1993) *Therapeutic psychology: fundamentals of counselling and psychotherapy*, Englewood Cliffs, NJ: Prentice Hall.

Brandenburger, A. and Nalebuff, B. (1996) *Co-opetition*, New York: Doubleday.

Brashers, D., Goldsmith, D. and Hsieh, E. (2002) 'Information seeking and avoiding in health contexts', *Human Communication Research* 28: 258–71.

Brehm, J. (1966) *A theory of psychological reactance*, Academic Press: New York.

Brehm, J. and Weintraub, M. (1977) 'Physical barriers and psychological reactance: two-year-olds' responses to threats to freedom', *Journal of Personality and Social Psychology* 35: 830–6.

Brett, J., Adair, W., Lempereur, A., Okumura, T., Shikhirev, P., Tinsley, C. and Lytle, A. (1998b) 'Culture and joint gains in negotiation', *Negotiation Journal* 14: 61–86.

Brett, J.M., Shapiro, D.L. and Lytle, A.L. (1998a) 'Breaking the bonds of reciprocity in negotiation', *Academy of Management Journal* 41: 410–24.

Brigham, J. (1991) *Social psychology* (2nd edn), New York: HarperCollins.

Brigman, G., Lane, D., Switzer, D., Lane, D. and Lawrence, R. (1999) 'Teaching children school success skills', *Journal of Educational Research* 92: 323–9.

Brilhart, J. and Galanes, G. (1998) *Group discussion* (9th edn), Boston: McGraw-Hill.

Brodsky, S., Hooper, N., Tipper, D. and Yates, S. (1999) 'Attorney invasion of witness space', *Law and Psychology Review* 23: 49–68.

Brooks, W. and Heath, R. (1993) *Speech communication*. Dubuque, IA: W.C. Brown.

Brophy, J. (1981) 'Teacher praise: a functional analysis', *Review of Educational Research* 51: 5–32.

Brown, C. and Sulzerazaroff, B. (1994) 'An assessment of the relationship between customer satisfaction and service friendliness', *Journal of Organizational Behavior Management* 14: 55–75.

Brown, E. (1997) 'Self-disclosure, social anxiety, and symptomatology in rape victim-survivors: the effects of cognitive and emotional processing', *Dissertation Abstracts International: The Sciences and Engineering* 57(10-B): 6559.

Brown, G. and Armstrong, S. (1984) 'Explaining and explanations', in E. Wragg (ed.) *Classroom teaching skills*, Beckenham, Kent: Croom Helm.

Brown, G. and Atkins, M. (1988) *Effective teaching in higher education*, London: Methuen & Co.

Brown, G. and Atkins, M. (1997) 'Explaining', in O. Hargie (ed.) *The handbook of communication skills*, London: Routledge.

Brown, G. and Bakhtar, M. (1983) 'Styles of lecturing: a study and its implications', *Research Papers in Education* 3: 131–53.

Brown, H. (1996) 'Themes in experimental research on groups from the 1930s to the 1990s', in M. Wetherell (ed.) *Identities, groups and social issues*, London: Sage in association with the Open University.

Brown, P. and Levinson, S. (1978) 'Universals in language usage: politeness phenomena', in E. Goody (ed.) *Questions and politeness: strategies in social interaction*, Oxford: Basil Blackwell.

Brown, R. (2000) *Group processes* (2nd edn), Oxford: Blackwell.

Brownell, J. (1995) 'Responding to messages', in J. Stewart (ed.) *Bridges not walls: a book about interpersonal communication* (6th edn), New York: McGraw-Hill.

Bruner, J., Goodnow, J. and Austin, G. (1956) *A study of thinking*, New York: Wiley.

Bryan, A. and Gallois, C. (1992) 'Rules about assertion in the workplace: effects of status and message type', *Australian Journal of Psychology* 44: 51–9.

Buck, R. (1994) 'Facial and emotional functions in facial expression and communication: the readout hypothesis', *Biological Psychology* 38: 95–115.

Buckmann, W. (1997) 'Adherence: a matter of self-efficacy and power', *Journal of Advanced Nursing* 26: 132–7.

Buckwalter, A. (1983) *Interviews and interrogations*, Stoneham: Butterworth.

Bugelova, T. (2000) 'Comparative analysis of communication skills of university students and median level executives in relation to career orientation', *Studia Psychologica* 42: 273–7.

Bull, G. (1961) *Machiavelli: the prince* (trans. G. Bull), Harmondsworth: Penguin.

Bull, P. (2001a) 'Nonverbal communication', *The Psychologist* 14: 644–7.

Bull, P. (2001b) 'Massaging the message', *The Psychologist* 14: 342–3.

Bull, P. (2002) *Communication under the microscope: the theory and practice of micro-analysis*, London: Routledge.

Bull, P. and Frederikson, L. (1995) 'Nonverbal communication', in M. Argyle and A. Colman (eds) *Social psychology*, London: Longman.

Buller, D. and Burgoon, B. (1998) 'Emotional expression in the deception process', in P. Anderson and L. Guerrero (eds) *Handbook of communication and emotion: research, theory, applications, and contexts*, San Diego: Academic Press.

Buller, D. and Burgoon, J. (1996) 'Interpersonal deception theory', *Communication Theory* 6: 203–42.

Buller, D. and Hall, J. (1998) 'The effects of distraction during persuasion', in M. Allen and R. Preiss (eds) *Persuasion: advances through meta-analysis*, Cresskill, NJ: Hampton Press.

Burden, P. and Byrd, D. (1999) *Methods for effective teaching* (2nd edn), Boston: Allyn & Bacon.

Burgoon, J. (1980) 'Nonverbal communication in the 1970s: an overview', in D. Nimmo (ed.) *Communication yearbook 4*, New Brunswick, NJ: Transaction Publishers.

Burgoon, J. (1994) 'Nonverbal signals', in M. Knapp and G. Miller (eds) *Handbook of interpersonal communication* (2nd edn), Thousand Oaks, CA: Sage.

Burgoon, J., Birk, T. and Pfau, M. (1990) 'Nonverbal behaviours, persuasion, and credibility', *Human Communication Research* 17: 140–69.

Burgoon, J., Buller, D. and Woodall, W. (1996) *Nonverbal communication: the unspoken dialogue*, New York: McGraw-Hill.

Burgoon, J. and Langer, E. (1995) 'Language, fallacies, and mindlessness-mindfulness in social interaction', in B. Burleson (ed.) *Communication yearbook 18*, Thousand Oaks: Sage.

Burgoon, J., Walther, J. and Baesler, E. (1992) 'Interpretations, evaluations, and consequences of interpersonal touch', *Human Communication Research* 19: 237–63.

Burley-Allen, M. (1995) *Listening: the forgotten skill*, New York: Wiley.

Burnham, T. and Phelan, J. (2000) *Mean genes: from sex to money to food: taming our primal instincts*, Cambridge, MA: Perseus Books.

Burns, J.M. (1978) *Leadership*, New York: Harper & Row.

Burrell, N. and Koper, R. (1998) 'The efficacy of powerful/powerless language on attitudes and source credibility', in M. Allen and R. Preiss (eds) *Persuasion: advances through meta-analysis*, Cresskill, NJ: Hampton Press.

Burton, G. and Dimbleby, R. (1995) *Between ourselves*, London: Arnold.

Buslig, A. and Burgoon, J. (2000) 'Aggressiveness in privacy-seeking behavior', in S. Petronio (ed.) *Balancing the secrets of private disclosures*, Mahwah, NJ: Lawrence Erlbaum.

Buss, A. (1983) 'Social rewards and personality', *Journal of Personality and Social Psychology* 44: 553–63.

Buss, A.H. and Perry, M. (1992) 'The aggression questionnaire', *Journal of Personality and Social Psychology* 63: 452–9.

Buss, D. (1988) 'The evolution of human intersexual competition: tactics of mate attraction', *Journal of Personality and Social Psychology* 54: 616–28.

Butler, J., Pryor, B. and Grieder, M. (1998) 'Impression formation as a function of male baldness', *Perceptual and Motor Skills* 86: 347–50.

Buttny, R. and Morris, G.H. (2001) 'Accounting', in W.P. Robinson and H. Giles (eds) *The new handbook of language and social psychology*, Chichester: Wiley.

Byrne, D. (1971) *The attraction paradigm*, New York: Academic Press.

Byrne, P. and Long, B. (1976) *Doctors talking to patients*, London: HMSO.

Cai, D., Wilson, S. and Drake, L. (2001) 'Culture in the context of intercultural negotiation: individualism–collectivism and paths to integrative agreements', *Human Communication Research* 26: 591–617.

Cairns, L. (1996) *Negotiating skills in the workplace: a practical handbook*, London: Pluto Press.

Cairns, L. (1997) 'Reinforcement', in O. Hargie (ed.) *The handbook of communication skills*, London: Routledge.

Calderhead, J. (1996) 'Teachers: beliefs and knowledge', in D. Berliner (ed.) *The handbook of educational psychology*, New York: Macmillan.

Cameron, D. (1994) 'Verbal hygiene for women: linguistics misapplied?', *Applied Linguistics* 15: 382–98.

Cameron, D. (2000) *Good to talk? Living and working in a communication culture*, London: Sage.

Cameron, G., Schleuder, J. and Thorson, E. (1991) 'The role of news teasers in processing TV news and commercials', *Communication Research* 18: 667–84.

Cameron, J. and Pierce, W. (1994) Reinforcement, reward and intrinsic motivation: a meta-analysis, *Review of Educational Research* 64: 363–423.

Cameron, J. and Pierce, W. (1996) 'The debate about rewards and intrinsic motivation: protests and accusations do not alter the results', *Review of Educational Research* 66: 39–51.

Campanella Bracken, C.M. (2001) 'Children and social responses to computers: praise, intrinsic motivation, and learning', *Dissertation Abstracts International: A (Humanities and the Social Sciences)* 61(10-A): 3812.

Campbell, D.T. (1958) 'Common fate, similarity and other indices of the status of aggregates of persons as social entities', *Behavioural Science* 3: 14–25.

Campbell, K., Martin, M. and Wanzer, M. (2001) 'Employee perceptions of manager humor orientation, and assertiveness, responsiveness, approach/avoidance strategies, and satisfaction', *Communication Research Reports* 18: 67–74.

Campbell, R., Benson, P., Wallace, S., Doesbergh, S. and Coleman, M. (1999) 'More about brows: how poses that change brow position affect perceptions of gender', *Perception* 28: 489–504.

Cann, A., Calhoun, L. and Banks, J. (1997) 'On the role of humour appreciation in interpersonal attraction: it's no joking matter', *Text* 10: 77–89.

Cannell, C.F., Oksenberg, L. and Converse, J.M. (1977) 'Striving for response accuracy; experiments in new interviewing techniques', *Journal of Marketing Research* 14: 306–21.

Caris-Verhallen, W., Kerkstra, A. and Bensing, J. (1999) 'Nonverbal behaviour in nurse–elderly patient communication', *Journal of Advanced Nursing* 29: 808–18.

Carnevale, P. and Pruitt, D. (1992) 'Negotiation and mediation', *Annual Review of Psychology* 43: 531–82.

Carter, K. (1990) 'Teacher's knowledge and learning to teach', in W.R. Houston (ed.) *Handbook of research on teacher education*, New York: Macmillan.

Cartwright, D. and Zander, A. (1968) *Group dynamics* (3rd edn), New York: Harper & Row.

Carver, C. and Scheier, M. (1999) 'Themes and issues in the self-regulation of behaviour', in R.S. Wyer (ed.) *Advances in social cognition*, Mahwah, NJ: Lawrence Erlbaum Associates.

Carver, C. and Scheier, M. (2000) 'On the structure of behavioral self-regulation', in M. Boekaerts, P. Pintrich and M. Zeidner (eds) *Handbook of self-regulation*, San Diego: Academic Press.

Catanzaro, S. and Mearns, J. (1999) 'Mood-related expectancy, emotional experience, and coping behavior', in I. Kirsch (ed.) *How expectations shape experience*, Washington, DC: American Psychological Association.

Chaikin, A. and Derlega, V. (1976) 'Self-disclosure', in J. Thibaut, J. Spence and R. Carson (eds) *Contemporary topics in social psychology*, New Jersey: General Learning Press.

Chandler, P. and Sweller, J. (1992) 'The split-attention effect as a factor in the design of instruction', *British Journal of Educational Psychology* 62: 233–46.

Chaplin, W., Phillips, J., Brown, J., Clanton, N. and Stein, J. (2000) 'Handshaking, gender, personality, and first impressions', *Journal of Personality and Social Psychology* 79: 110–17.

Charrow, R. and Charrow, V. (1979) 'Making legal language understandable: a psycholinguistic study of jury instructions', *Columbia Law Review* 79: 1306.

Chaudhry-Lawton, R., Lawton, R., Murphy, K. and Terry, A. (1992) *Quality: change through teamwork*, London: Century Business.

Chelune, G. (1976) 'The self-disclosure situations survey: a new approach to measuring self-disclosure', *JCSAS Catalog of Selected Documents in Psychology* 6 (Ms. No. 1367); 111–12.

Chesebro, J.L. and McCroskey, J.C. (2001) 'The relationship of teacher clarity and immediacy with student state receiver apprehension, affect, and cognitive learning', *Communication Education* 50: 59–68.

Chesner, S. and Beaumeister, R. (1985) 'Effects of therapist's disclosure of religious beliefs on the intimacy of client self-disclosure', *Journal of Social and Clinical Psychology* 3: 97–105.

Chidambaram, L. and Bostrom, R. (1997) 'Group development (I): a review and synthesis of development models', *Group Decision and Negotiation* 6: 159–87.

Chovil, N. (1997) 'Facing others: a social communicative perspective on facial displays', in J. Russell and J. Fernandez-Dols (eds.) *The psychology of facial expression*, Cambridge: Cambridge University Press.

Christenfeld, N. (1995) 'Does it hurt to say um?', *Journal of Nonverbal Behavior* 19: 171–86.

Church, A. and Waclawski, J. (1999) 'The impact of leadership on global management practices', *Journal of Applied Social Psychology*, 29: 1416–43.

Church, R., Kelly, S. and Lynch, K. (1999) 'Immediate memory for mismatched speech and representational gesture across development', *Journal of Nonverbal Behavior* 24: 151–74.

Cialdini, R. (2001) *Influence: science and practice*, Boston: Allyn & Bacon.

Cialdini, R., Wosinska, W., Barrett, D., Butner, J. and Gornik-Durose, M. (2001) 'The differential impact of two social influence principles on individualists and collectivists in Poland and the United States', in W. Wosinska, R. Cialdini, D. Barrett and J. Reykowski (eds) *The practice of social influence in multiple cultures*, Mahwah, NJ: Lawrence Erlbaum.

Cianni-Surridge, M. and Horan, J. (1983) 'On the wisdom of assertive jobseeking behavior', *Journal of Counseling Psychology* 30: 209–14.

Cipani, E. (1990) 'The communicative function hypothesis: an operant behavior perspective', *Journal of Behavior Therapy and Experimental Psychiatry* 21: 239–74.

Citkowitz, R.D. (1975) 'The effects of three interview techniques – paraphrasing, modelling, and cues – in facilitating self-referent affect statements in chronic schizophrenics', *Dissertation Abstracts International* 36: 2462B.

Clampitt, P. (2001) *Communicating for managerial effectiveness* (2nd edn), Thousand Oaks, CA: Sage.

Clark, B.D. and Matze, M.G. (1999) 'A core of global leadership: relational competence', in W. Mobley, M.J. Gessner and V. Arnold (eds) *Advances in global leadership*, Vol. 1, Stamford, CT: JAI Press.

Cline, V.B., Mejia, J., Coles, J., Klein, N. and Cline, R.A. (1984) 'The relationship between therapist behaviors and outcome for middle and lower class couples in marital therapy', *Journal of Clinical Psychology* 40: 691–704.

Clore, G. and Byrne, D. (1974) 'A reinforcement–affect model of attraction', in T.S. Huston (ed.) *Perspectives on interpersonal attraction*, New York: Academic Press.

Coates, L. and Johnson, T. (2001) 'Towards a social theory of gender', in W. P. Robinson and H. Giles (eds) *The new handbook of language and social psychology*, Chichester: Wiley.

Cody, M. and McLaughlin, M. (1988) 'Accounts on trial: oral arguments in traffic court', in C. Antakis (ed.) *Analysing everyday explanations: a casebook of methods*, London: Sage.

Cody, M. and Seiter, J. (2001) 'Compliance principles in retail sales in the United States', in W. Wosinska, R. Cialdini, D. Barrett and J. Reykowski (eds) *The practice of social influence in multiple cultures*, Mahwah, NJ: Lawrence Erlbaum.

Cohen, S. and Bailey, D. (1997) 'What makes teams work: group effectiveness research from the shop floor to the executive suite', *Journal of Management* 23, 239–90.

Cohen-Cole, S. (1991) *The medical interview: the three-function approach*, St Louis: Mosby Year Book.

Cohen-Cole, S.A. and Bird, J. (1991) 'Function 1: gathering data to understand the patient', in S. Cohen-Cole (ed.) *The medical interview: the three-function approach*, St Louis: Mosby Year Book.

Coleman, E., Brown, A. and Rivkin, I. (1997) 'The effects of instructional explanations on learning from scientific texts', *The Journal of the Learning Sciences* 6: 347–65.

Collins L., Powell, J. and Oliver, P. (2000) 'Those who hesitate lose: the relationship between assertiveness and response latency', *Perceptual and Motor Skills* 90: 931–43.

Cook, M. (1970) 'Experiments on orientation and proxemics', *Human Relations* 23: 61–76.

Cooks, L. (2000) 'Family secrets and the lie of identity', in S. Petronio (ed.) *Balancing the secrets of private disclosures*, Mahwah, NJ: Lawrence Erlbaum.

Cooley, C.H. (1929) *Social organization*, New York: Scribner.

Coover, G. and Murphy, S. (2000) 'The communicated self: exploring the interaction between self and social context', *Human Communication Research* 26: 125–47.

Corey, G. (1997) *Theory and practice of counselling and psychotherapy*, Pacific Grove, CA: Brooks/Cole.

Corey, S. (1940) 'The teachers out-talk the pupils', *School Review* 48: 745–52.

Cormier, S. and Cormier, B. (1998) *Interviewing skills for helpers: fundamental skills and cognitive behavioural interventions*, Pacific Grove, CA: Brooks/Cole.

Corts, D. and Pollio, H. (1999) 'Spontaneous production of figurative language and gesture in college lecturers', *Metaphor and Symbolic Activity* 14: 81–100.

Coupland, J., Coupland, N. and Grainger, K. (1991) 'Integrational discourse: contextual variations of age and elderliness', *Ageing and Society* 11: 189–208.

Coupland, J., Coupland, N. and Robinson, J. (1992) 'How are you? Negotiating phatic communion', *Language in Society* 21: 207–30.

Craig, K., Hyde, S. and Patrick, C. (1997) 'Genuine, suppressed, and fake facial behaviour during exacerbation of chronic low back pain', in P. Ekman and E. Rosenberg (eds) *What the face reveals: basic and applied studies of spontaneous expression using the Facial Action Coding System (FACS)*, Oxford: Oxford University Press.

Craig, R. (1999) 'Communication theory as a field', *Communication Theory* 9: 119–61.

Craighead, L., Wilcoxon, L., Heather, N., Craighead, W. and DeRosa, R. (1996) 'Effect of feedback on learning rate and cognitive distortions among women with bulimia', *Behavior Therapy* 27: 551–63.

Crawford, M. (1995) 'Gender, age and the social evaluation of assertion?', *Behavior Modification* 12: 549–64.

Crocker, J. and Wolfe, C. (1998) 'Contingencies of worth', cited in A. Tesser (2001) 'Self-esteem', in A. Tesser and N. Schwarz (eds) *Blackwell handbook of social psychology: intraindividual processes*, Oxford: Blackwell Publishers.

Crusco, A. and Wetzel, C. (1984) 'The Midas touch: effects of interpersonal touch on restaurant tipping', *Personality and Social Psychology Bulletin* 10: 512–17.

Cruz, M. (1998) 'Explicit and implicit conclusions in persuasive messages' in M. Allen and R. Preiss (eds) *Persuasion: advances through meta-analysis*, Cresskill, NJ: Hampton Press.

Crystal, D. (1997) *The Cambridge encyclopaedia of language* (2nd edn), New York: Cambridge University Press.

Cupach, W. and Canary, D. (1997) *Competence in interpersonal conflict*, New York: McGraw-Hill.

Cupach, W. and Metts, S. (1990) 'Remedial processes in embarrassing predicaments', in J. Anderson (ed.) *Communication yearbook Vol. 13*, Newbury Park: Sage.

Dabbs, J. (1985) 'Temporal patterns of speech and gaze in social and intellectual conversation', in H. Giles and R. St Clair (eds) *Recent advances in language, communication and social psychology*, London: Lawrence Erlbaum Associates.

Dabbs, J. (1997) 'Testosterone, smiling, and facial appearance', *Journal of Nonverbal Behavior* 21: 45–55.

Dabbs, J., Bernieri, F., Strong, R., Campo, R. and Milun, R. (2001) 'Going on stage: testosterone in greetings and meetings', *Journal of Research in Personality* 35: 27–40.

Daly, J., Kreiser, P. and Roghaar, L. (1994) 'Question-asking comfort: explorations of the demography of communication in the eighth grade classroom', *Communication Education* 43: 27–41.

Darley, J. (2001) 'Social comparison motives in ongoing groups', in M. Hogg and S. Tindale (eds) *Blackwell handbook of social psychology*, Malden, MA: Blackwell.

Darwin, C. (1872/1955) *The expression of emotions in man and animals*, London: John Murray.

D'Augelli, A., Hershberger, S. and Pilkington, N. (1998) 'Lesian, gay and bisexual youth and their families: disclosure of sexual orientation and its consequences', *American Journal of Orthopsychiatry* 68: 361–71.

Davidhizar, R., Giger, F. and Giger, J. (1997) 'When touch is not the best appproach', *Journal of Clinical Nursing* 6: 203–6.

Davies, G., Westcott, H. and Horan, N. (2000) 'The impact of questioning style on the content of investigative interviews with suspected child sexual abuse victims', *Psychology, Crime and Law* 6: 81–97.

Davies, J. (1998) 'The art of negotiating', *Management Today* (Nov): 126–8.

Davitz, J.R. (1964) *The communication of emotional meaning*, New York: McGraw-Hill.

De Grada, E., Kruglanski, A., Mannetti, L. and Pierro, A. (1999) 'Motivated cognition and group interaction: need for closure affects the contents and processes of collective negotiations', *Journal of Experimental Social Psychology* 35: 346–65.

De Paulo, B., Kashy, D., Kirkendol, S. and Wyer, M. (1996) 'Lying in everyday life', *Journal of Personality and Social Psychology* 70: 779–95.

De Souza, G. and Klein, H. (1996) 'Emergent leadership in the group goal-setting process', *Small Group Research* 26: 475–96.

De Vito, J. (1993) *Essentials of human communication*, New York: Harper Collins.

Deci, E. (1992) 'On the nature and function of motivation theories', *Psychological Science* 3, 167–71.

Del Greco, L. (1983) 'The Del Greco assertive behavior inventory', *Journal of Behavioral Assessment* 5: 49–63.

deMayo, R. (1997) 'How to present at case conference', *Clinical Supervisor* 16: 181–9.

Demirbas, O. and Dermirkan, H. (2000) 'Privacy dimensions: a case study in the interior architecture design studio', *Journal of Environmental Psychology* 20: 53–64.

Den Hartog, D.N., House, R.J., Hanges, P.J. *et al.* (1999) 'Culture specific and cross-culturally generalizable implicit leadership theories: are attributes of charismatic/transformational leadership universally endorsed?', *Leadership Quarterly* 10: 219–56.

Derevensky, J. and Leckerman, R. (1997) 'Teachers' differential use of praise and reinforcement practices', *Canadian Journal of School Psychology* 13: 15–27.

Derlega, V. and Berg, J. (eds) (1987) *Self-disclosure; theory, research and therapy*, New York: Plenum Press.

Derlega, V. and Chaikin, A. (1975) *Sharing intimacy: what we reveal to others and why*, Englewood Cliffs, NJ: Prentice Hall.

Derlega, V., Winstead, B. and Folk-Barron, L. (2000) 'Reasons for and against disclosing HIV-seropositive test results to an intimate partner: a functional perspective', in S. Petronio (ed.) *Balancing the secrets of private disclosures*, Mahwah, NJ: Lawrence Erlbaum.

DeVito, J. (1995) *The interpersonal communication book* (7th edn), New York: HarperCollins.

DeVito, J.A. (1998) *The interpersonal communication book* (8th edn), New York: Longman.

Di Blasi, Z., Harkness, E., Ernst, E., Georgiou, A. and Kleijnen, J. (2001), 'Influence of context effects on health outcomes: a systematic review', *Lancet* 357: 752–62.

Dickson, D. (1997) 'Reflecting', in O. Hargie (ed.) *The handbook of communication skills*, London: Routledge.

Dickson, D. (1999a) 'Barriers to communication', in A. Long (ed.) *Interaction for practice in community nursing*, Basingstoke: Macmillan.

Dickson, D. (1999b) 'Communication skills and health care delivery', in D. Sines, F. Appleby and E. Raymond (eds) *Community health care nursing* (2nd edn), Oxford: Blackwell Science.

Dickson, D. (2001) 'Communication skill and health care delivery', in D. Sines, F. Appleby and B. Raymond (eds) *Community health care nursing* (2nd edn), London: Blackwell Science.

Dickson, D., Hargie, O. and Morrow, N. (1997) *Communication skills training for health professionals* (2nd edn), London: Chapman and Hall.

Dickson, D., Hargie, O. and Rainey, S. (2000) 'Communication and relational development between Catholic and Protestant students in Northern Ireland', *Australian Journal of Communication* 27: 67–82.

Dickson, D., Saunders, C. and Stringer, M. (1993) *Rewarding people: the skill of responding positively*, London: Routledge.

Dickson, D.A. (1981) 'Microcounselling: an evaluative study of a programme', unpublished PhD thesis, Ulster Polytechnic.

Dieckmann, L. (2000) 'Private secrets and public disclosures: the case of battered women', in S. Petronio (ed.) *Balancing the secrets of private disclosures*, Mahwah, NJ: Lawrence Erlbaum.

Dillard, J. (1990) 'The nature and substance of goals in tactical communication', in M. Cody and M. McLaughlin (eds) *The psychology of tactical communication*, Cleveland: Multilingual Matters.

Dillard, J. (1997) 'Explicating the goal construct: tools for theorists', in J.O. Greene (ed.) *Message production: advances in communication theory*, Mahwah, NJ: Lawrence Erlbaum Associates.

Dillard, J. (1998) 'The role of affect in communication, biology, and social relationships', in P. Andersen and L. Guerrero (eds) *Handbook of communication and emotion: research, theory, applications, and contexts*, San Diego: Academic Press.

Dillard, J., Hunter, J. and Burgoon, M. (1984) 'Sequential-request strategies: meta-analysis of foot-in-the-door and door-in-the-face', *Human Communication Research* 10: 461–88.

Dillard, J. and Peck, E. (2001) 'Persuasion and the structure of affect: dual systems and discrete emotions as complementary models', *Human Communication Research* 27: 38–68.

Dillon, J. (1982) 'The multidisciplinary study of questioning', *Journal of Educational Psychology* 74: 147–65.

Dillon, J. (1988) 'The remedial status of student questioning', *Journal of Curriculum Studies* 20: 197–210.

457

Dillon, J. (1990) *The practice of questioning*, London: Routledge.

Dillon, J. (1997) 'Questioning', in O. Hargie (ed.) *The handbook of communication skills* (2nd edn), London: Routledge.

Dimberg, U., Thunberg, M. and Elmehed, K. (2000) 'Unconscious facial reactions to emotional facial expressions', *Psychological Science* 11: 86–9.

Dimbleby, R. and Burton, G. (1998) *More than words: an introduction to communication*, London: Routledge.

Dindia, K. (2000a) 'Self-disclosure, identity, and relationship development', in K. Dindia and S. Duck (eds) *Communication and personal relationships*, Chichester: Wiley.

Dindia, K. (2000b) 'Sex differences in self-disclosure, reciprocity of self-disclosure, and self-disclosure and liking: three meta-analyses reviewed', in S. Petronio (ed.) *Balancing the secrets of private disclosures*, Mahwah, NJ: Lawrence Erlbaum.

Dion, K. (2000) 'Group cohesion: from "field of forces" to multidimensional construct', *Group Dynamics: Theory, Research, and Practice* 4: 7–26.

Dittmar, H. (1992) 'Perceived material wealth and first impressions', *British Journal of Social Psychology* 31: 379–92.

Dixon, J. and Durrheim, K. (2000) 'Displacing place-identity: a discursive approach to locating self and other', *British Journal of Social Psychology* 39: 27–44.

Dohrenwend, B. (1965) 'Some effects of open and closed questions on respondents' answers', *Human Organization* 24: 175–84.

Dolgin, K. (1996) 'Parents' disclosure of their own concerns to their adolescent children', *Personal Relationships* 3: 159–69.

Dolgin, K. and Berndt, N. (1997) 'Adolescents' perceptions of their parents' disclosure to them', *Journal of Adolescence* 20: 431–41.

Dolgin, K. and Lindsay, K. (1999) 'Disclosure between college students and their siblings', *Journal of Family Psychology* 13: 393–400.

Dolinski, D. and Kofta, M. (2001) 'Stay tuned: the role of the break in the message on attribution of culpability', in W. Wosinska, R. Cialdini, D. Barrett and J. Reykowski (eds) *The practice of social influence in multiple cultures*, Mahwah, NJ: Lawrence Erlbaum.

Donohue, W.A. and Kolt, R. (1992) *Managing interpersonal conflict*, Newbury Park, CA: Sage.

Doucouliagos, C. (1995) 'Worker participation and productivity in labor-managed and participative capitalist forms: a meta-analysis', *Industrial and Labor Relations Review* 49: 58–77.

Dovidio, J.F., Ellyson, S.L., Keating, C.F., Heltman, K. and Brown, C. (1988) 'The relationship of social power to visual displays of dominance between men and women', *Journal of Personality and Social Psychology* 54: 233–42

Downing, J. and Garmon, C. (2002) 'A guide to implementing PowerPoint and overhead LCD projectors in communication classes', *American Journal of Communication* 5: http://www.acjournal.org/holdings/vol5/iss2/articles/guide.pdf.

Dubrin, A. (1994) 'Sex differences in the use and effectiveness of tactics of impression management', *Psychological Reports* 74: 531–44.

Duck, S. (1995) 'Repelling the study of attraction', *The Psychologist* 8: 60–3.

Duck, S. (1999) 'Expressing meaning to others', in J. Stewart (ed.) *Bridges not walls* (7th edn), Boston: McGraw-Hill.

Duggan, A. and Parrott, R. (2001) 'Physicians' nonverbal rapport building and patients' talk about the subjective component of illness', *Human Communication Research* 27: 299–311.

Dulany, D. (1968) 'Awareness, rules and propositional control: a confrontation with S-R behavior theory', in T. Dixon and D. Horton (eds) *Verbal behavior and general behavior theory*, Englewood Cliffs, NJ: Prentice Hall.

Duncan, S. and Fiske, D.W. (1977) *Face-to-face interaction: research, methods and theory*, Hillsdale, NJ: Lawrence Erlbaum Associates.

Dunne, H. (2001) 'One wrong word and we lose him', *Daily Telegraph* (29 October): 15.

Dweck, C. (2000) *Self-theories: their role in motivation, personality and development*, Philadelphia, PA: Psychology Press.

Edwards, R. and Bello, R. (2001) 'Interpretation of messages: the influence of equivocation, face concerns, and ego-involvement', *Human Communication Research* 27: 597–631.

Egan, G. (2001) *The skilled helper: a problem-management and opportunity development approach* (7th edn), Belmont, CA: Brooks/Cole.

Egan, G. (2002) *The skilled helper* (7th edn), California: Brooks/Cole.

Eggen, P. and Kauchak, D. (1999) *Educational psychology: windows on classrooms*, Upper Saddle River, NJ: Prentice Hall.

Ehrlich, R., D'Augelli, A. and Danish, S. (1979) 'Comparative effectiveness of six counselor verbal responses', *Journal of Counselling Psychology* 26: 390–8.

Eisler, R., Hersen, M., Miller, P. and Blanchard, D. (1975) 'Situational determinants of assertive behavior', *Journal of Consulting and Clinical Psychology* 43: 330–40.

Ekman, P. (1985) *Telling lies*, New York: Norton.

Ekman, P. and Friesen, W. (1969) 'The repertoire of non-verbal behaviour: categories, origins, usage and coding', *Semiotica* 1: 49–98.

Ekman, P. and Friesen, W. (1975) *Unmasking the face: a guide to recognising emotions from facial cues*, Englewood Cliffs, NJ: Prentice Hall.

Ekman, P. and Keltner, D. (1997) 'Universal facial expressions of emotion', in U. Segerstrale and P. Molnar (eds) *Nonverbal communication: where nature meets culture*, Mahwah, NJ: Lawrence Erlbaum Associates.

Ekman, P. and O'Sullivan, M. (1991) 'Facial expression: methods, means and moues', in R. Feldman and B. Rime (eds) *Fundamentals of nonverbal behaviour*, Cambridge: Cambridge University Press.

Ekman, P., O'Sullivan, M., Friesen, W. and Scherer, K. (1991) 'Invited article: face, voice and body in detecting deceit', *Journal of Nonverbal Behavior* 15: 125–35.

Ellemers, N., Spears, R. and Doosje, B. (1999) 'Introduction', in N. Ellemers, R. Spears and B. Doosje (eds) *Social identity*, Oxford: Blackwell.

Ellis, A. and Beattie, G. (1986) *The psychology of language and communication*, London: Weidenfeld & Nicolson.

Ellis, K. (2000) 'Perceived teacher confirmation: the development and validation of an instrument and two studies of the relationship to cognitive and affective learning, *Human Communication Research* 26: 264–92.

Ellison, C.W. and Firestone, I.J. (1974) 'Development of interpersonal trust as a function of self-esteem, target status and target style', *Journal of Personality and Social Psychology* 29: 655–63.

Elwell, W. and Tiberio, J. (1994) 'Teacher praise: what students want', *Journal of Instructional Psychology* 21: 32–8.

Emler, N. (1992) 'The truth about gossip', *BPS Social Psychology Section Newsletter* 27: 23–37.

Emmons, R. (1989) 'The personal striving approach to personality', in L. Pervin (ed.) *Goal concepts in personality and social psychology*, Hillsdale, NJ: Lawrence Erlbaum Associates.

Endres, J., Poggenpohl, C. and Erben, C. (1999) 'Repetitions, warnings and video: cognitive and motivational components in preschool children's susceptibility', *Journal of Legal and Criminological Psychology* 4: 129–49.

Engleberg, I. N. (2002) 'Presentations in everyday life: linking audience interest and speaker eloquence', *American Journal of Communication* 5: http://www.acjournal.org/holdings/vol5/iss2/articles/guide.pdf.

Epstein, J., Griffin, K. and Botvin, G. (2000) 'Role of general and specific competence skills in protecting inner-city adolescents from alcohol use', *Journal of Studies on Alcohol* 61: 379–86.

Erber, R. and Wegner, D. (1996) 'Ruminations on the rebound', in R. Wyer (ed.) *Advances in social cognition*, Mahwah, NJ: Lawrence Erlbaum.

Erickson, T. and Mattson, M. (1981) 'From words to meaning: a semantic illusion', *Journal of Verbal Learning and Verbal Behavior* 20: 540–51.

Erwin, P. (1993) *Friendship and peer relations*, Chichester: Wiley.

Esser, J. (1998) 'Alive and well after 25 years: a review of groupthink, *Organizational Behavior & Human Decision Processes* 73: 116–41.

Esteves, F. (1999) Attentional bias to emotional facial expressions', *European Review of Applied Psychology* 49: 91–7.

Evans, D. and Norman, P. (2002) 'Improving road safety among adolescents: an application of the theory of Planned Behaviour' in D. Rutter and L. Quine (eds) *Changing health behaviour*, Buckingham: Open University Press.

Eysenck, M. (1998) 'Perception and attention', in M. Eysenck (ed.) *Psychology: an integrated approach*, Harlow: Addison Wesley Longman Ltd.

Faraone, S. and Hurtig, R. (1985) 'An examination of social skill, verbal productivity, and Gottman's model of interaction using observational methods and sequential analyses', *Behavioural Assessment* 7: 349–66.

Feeney, J., Noller, P., Sheehan, G. and Peterson, C. (1999) 'Conflict issues and conflict strategies as contexts for nonverbal behaviour in close relationships', in P. Philippot, R. Feldman and E. Coats, (eds) *The social context of nonverbal behavior*, Cambridge: Cambridge University Press.

Feigenbaum, W.M. (1977) 'Reciprocity in self-disclosure within the psychological interview', *Psychological Reports* 40: 15–26.

Feldman, R., Philippot, P. and Custrini, R. (1991) 'Social skills, psychopathology, and nonverbal behavior', in R.S. Feldman and B. Rime (eds) *Fundamentals of nonverbal behaviour*, Cambridge: Cambridge University Press.

Feldman, R.S. (1985) *Social psychology: theories, research and applications*, New York: McGraw-Hill.

Fern, E., Monroe, K. and Avila, R. (1986) 'Effectiveness of multiple request strategies: a synthesis of research results', *Journal of Marketing Research* 23: 144–52.

Fernandez-Dols, J.-M. (1999) 'Facial expression and emotion: a situationist view', in P. Philippot, R. Feldman and E. Coats (eds) The social context of nonverbal behaviour, Cambridge: Cambridge University Press.

Ferraro, F. and Garella, A. (1997) 'Termination as a psychoanalytic event', International Journal of Psycho-Analysis 78: 27–41.

Festinger, L. (1954) 'A theory of social comparison processes', Human Relations 7: 117–40.

Festinger, L. (1957) A theory of cognitive dissonance, Stanford: Stanford University Press.

Feyereisen, P. and Havard, I. (1999) 'Mental imagery and the production of hand gestures while speaking in younger and older adults', Journal of Nonverbal Behavior 23: 153–71.

Fiedler, F. (1967) A theory of leadership effectiveness, New York: McGraw-Hill.

Fiedler, F.E. (1986) 'The contribution of cognitive resources and leader behaviour to organizational performance', Journal of Applied Social Psychology 16: 532–48.

Fiedler, F.E. (1993a) 'The leadership situation and the black box in contingency theories', in M. Chemers and R. Ayman (eds) Leadership, theory and research: perspectives and directions, New York: Academic Press.

Fiedler, K. (1993b) 'Constructive processes in person cognition', British Journal of Social Psychology 32: 349–64.

Fiedler, K. and Bless, H. (2001) 'Social cognition', in M. Hewstone and W. Stroebe (eds) Introduction to social psychology (3rd edn), Oxford: Blackwell.

Figley, C. (ed.) (2002) Treating compassion fatigue, New York: Brunner/Mazel.

Finkenauer, C. and Hazam, H. (2000) 'Disclosure and secrecy in marriage: do both contribute to marital satisfaction?', Journal of Social and Personal Relationships 17: 245–63.

Finkenauer, C. and Rime, B. (1998) 'Socially shared emotional experiences vs. emotional experiences kept secret: differential characteristics and consequences', Journal of Social and Clinical Psychology 17: 295–318.

First, E. (1994) 'The leaving game, or I'll play you and you play me: the emergence of dramatic role play in 2-year-olds', in A. Slade and D. Wolf (eds) Children at play: clinical and developmental approaches to meaning and representation, New York: Oxford University Press.

Fisch, H., Frey, S. and Hirsbrunner, H. (1983) 'Analysing nonverbal behavior in depression', Journal of Abnormal Psychology 92: 307–18.

Fisher, C., Corrigan, O. and Henman, M. (1991a) 'A study of community pharmacy practice', Journal of Social and Administrative Pharmacy 8: 15–23.

Fisher, D. (1984) 'A conceptual analysis of self-disclosure', Journal for the Theory of Social Behaviour 14: 277–96.

Fisher, R. (1990) 'Negotiating power: getting and using influence', in I. Asherman and S. Asherman (eds) The negotiating sourcebook, Amherst, MA: Human Resource Development Press.

Fisher, R. and Ury, W. (1981) Getting to yes: negotiating an agreement without giving in, London: Hutchinson.

Fisher, R., Ury, W. and Patton, B. (1991) Getting to yes: negotiating agreement without giving in (2nd edn), Boston: Houghton Mifflin.

Fisher, S. and Groce, S. (1990) 'Accounting practices in medical interviews', *Language in Society* 19: 225–50.

Fiske, A. (2000) 'Complementarity theory: why human social capacities evolved to require cultural complements', *Personality and Social Psychology Review* 4: 76–94.

Fiske, J. (1990) *Introduction to communication studies* (2nd edn), London: Routledge.

Fiske, S.T. and Taylor, S.E. (1991) *Social cognition* (2nd edn), New York: McGraw-Hill.

Fitness, J. (2001) 'Betrayal, rejection, revenge, and forgiveness: an interpersonal script approach', in M. Leary (ed.) *Interpersonal rejection*, Oxford: Oxford University Press.

Flack, W., Laird, J. and Cavallaro, L. (1999) 'Separate and combined effects of facial expressions and bodily postures on emotional feelings', *European Journal of Social Psychology* 29: 203–17.

Flemmer, D., Sobelman, S., Flemmer, M. and Astrom, J. (1996) 'Attitudes and observations about nonverbal communication in the psychotherapeutic greeting situation', *Psychological Reports*, 78: 407–18.

Flintoff, J. (2001) 'Sayonara to ceremony', *Financial Times Weekend* (May 5/6): I.

Follette, W., Naugle, A. and Callaghan, G. (1996) 'A radical behavioural understanding of the therapeutic relationship in effecting change', *Behavior Therapy* 27: 623–41.

Foot, H. (1997) 'Humour and laughter', in O. Hargie (ed.) *The handbook of communication skills* (2nd edn), London: Routledge.

Ford, M.E. (1992) *Motivating humans: goals, emotions, and personal agency beliefs*, Newbury Park, CA: Sage.

Forgas, J.P. (1994) 'Sad and guilty? Affective influences on the explanation of conflict in close relationships', *Journal of Personality and Social Psychology* 66: 56–68.

Forgas, J. and Williams, K. (2001) 'Social influence: introduction and overview', in J. Forgas and K. Williams (eds) *Social influence: direct and indirect processes*, Philadelphia: Psychology Press.

Forsythe, S.M. (1990) 'Effect of applicant's clothing on interviewer's decision to hire', *Journal of Applied Social Psychology* 20: 1579–95.

Fosshage, J. (1998) 'On aggression: its forms and functions', *Psychoanalytic Inquiry* 18: 45–54.

Fowler, F.J. and Mangione, T.W. (1990) *Standardised survey interviewing: minimising interviewer-related error*, Newbury Park: Sage.

Fox, E., Lester, V., Russo, R., Bowles, R., Pichler, A. and Dutton, K. (2000a) 'Facial expressions of emotion: are angry faces detected more efficiently?', *Cognition and Emotion* 14: 61–92.

Fox, L., Rejeski, W.J. and Gauvin, L. (2000b) 'Effects of leadership style and group dynamics on enjoyment of physical activity', *American Journal of Health Promotion* 14: 277–83.

French, J. and Raven, B. (1959) 'The bases of social power', in D. Cartwright (ed.) *Studies in social power*, Ann Arbor, MI: Institute for Social Research.

French. P. (1994) *Social skills for nursing practice* (2nd edn), London: Chapman and Hall.

Frey, L. (1999) 'Introduction', in L. Frey, D. Gouran and M.S. Poole (eds) *The handbook of group communication theory and research*, Thousand Oaks, CA: Sage Publications.

Frick, R. (1992) 'Interestingness', *British Journal of Psychology* 83: 113–28.

Fridlund, A. (1997) 'The new ethology of human facial expressions', in J. Russell and J. Fernandez-Dols (eds) *The psychology of facial expression*, Cambridge: Cambridge University Press.

Friesen, W. (1972) 'Cultural differences in facial expression: an experimental test of the concept of display rules', PhD thesis, University of California, San Francisco.

Friesen, W., Ekman, P. and Wallblatt, H. (1980) 'Measuring hand movements', *Journal of Nonverbal Behavior* 4: 97–113.

Fry, L. (1983) 'Women in society', in S. Spence and G. Shepherd (eds) *Developments in social skills training*, London: Academic Press.

Furnham, A., Lavancy, M. and McClellenad, A. (2001) 'Waist-to-hip ratio and facial attractiveness: a pilot study', *Personality and Individual Differences* 30: 491–502.

Furst, D. and Criste, A. (1997) 'Students as consumers: using "satisfaction surveys" in the classroom', *Reaching Today's Youth: The Community Circle of Caring Journal* 2: 11–13.

Fussell, S. and Kreuz, R. (1998) 'Social and cognitive approaches to interpersonal communication: introduction and overview', in S. Fussell and P. Kreuz (eds) *Social and cognitive approaches to interpersonal communication*, Mahwah, NJ: Lawrence Erlbaum Associates.

Gable, S. and Shean, G. (2000) 'Perceived social competence and depression', *Journal of Social and Personal Relationships* 17: 139–50.

Gage, N.L., Belgard, M., Dell, D., Hiller, J.E., Rosenshine, B. and Unruh, W.R. (1968) *Explorations of the teachers' effectiveness in explaining*, Technical Report 4, Stanford: Stanford University Centre for Research and Development in Teaching.

Galanes, G., Adams, K. and Brilhart, J. (2000) *Communicating in groups: applications and skills* (4th edn), Boston: McGraw-Hill.

Gall, M. (1970) 'The use of questions in teaching', *Review of Educational Research* 40: 709–21.

Gallagher, M. and Hargie, O. (1992) 'The relationship between counsellor interpersonal skills and core conditions of client-centred counselling', *Counselling Psychology Quarterly* 5: 3–16.

Gamble, T. and Gamble, M. (1999) *Communication works* (6th edn), Boston: McGraw-Hill.

Gao, G. (1996) 'Self and OTHER: a Chinese perspective on interpersonal relationships', in W. Gudykunst, S. Ting-Toomey, and T. Nishida (eds) *Communication in personal relationships across cultures*, Thousand Oaks: Sage.

Gardiner, M. and Tiggemann, M. (1999) 'Gender differences in leadership style, job stress and mental health in male- and female-dominated industries', *Journal of Occupational and Organizational Psychology* 72: 301–15.

Garko, M. (1992) 'Physician executives' use of influence strategies: gaining compliance from superiors who communicate in attractive and unattractive styles', *Health Communication* 4: 137–54.

Garrison, M. and Bly, M.A. (1997) *Human relations: productive approaches for the workplace*, Boston: Allyn & Bacon.

Garven, S., Wood, J., Malpass, R. and Shaw, J. (1998) 'More than suggestion:

consequences of the interview techniques from the McMartin Preschool Case', paper presented at the American Psychology and Law Association Biennial Conference, Redondo Beach.

Gaskell, G., Wright, D. and O'Muircheartaigh, C. (1993) 'Reliability of surveys', *The Psychologist* 11: 500–3.

Gatchalian, J. (1998) 'Principled negotiation – a key to successful collective bargaining', *Management Decision* 36: 222–25.

Gayle, B., Preiss, R. and Allen, M. (1998) 'Another look at the use of rhetorical questions', in M. Allen and R. Preiss (eds) *Persuasion: advances through meta-analysis*, Cresskill, NJ: Hampton Press.

Gee, S., Gregory, M. and Pipe, M. (1999) 'What colour is your pet dinosaur? The impact of pre-interview training and question type on children's answers', *Journal of Legal and Criminological Psychology* 4: 111–28.

Geen, R. (1990) *Human aggression*, Milton Keynes: Open University.

Geers, A. and Lassiter, G. (1999) 'Affective expectations and information gain: evidence for assimilation and contrast effects in affective experience', *Journal of Experimental Social Psychology* 35: 394–413.

Gellatly, A. (1986) 'How can memory skills be improved?', in A. Gellatly (ed.) *The skilful mind: an introduction to cognitive psychology*, Milton Keynes: Open University.

Gemmill, G. and Oakley, J. (1992) 'Leadership: an alienating social myth?', *Human Relations* 45: 113–29.

Georgesen, J. and Harris, M. (1998) 'Why's my boss always holding me down? A meta-analysis of power effects on performance evaluations', *Personality and Social Psychology Review* 2: 184–95.

Gervasio, A.H. (1987) 'Assertiveness techniques as speech acts', *Clinical Psychology Review* 7: 105–19.

Gessner, M.J., Arnold, V. and Mobley, W. (1999) 'Introduction', in W. Mobley, M.J. Gessner and V. Arnold (eds) *Advances in global leadership, Volume 1*, Stamford, CT: JAI Press.

Ghetti, S. and Goodman, G. (2001) 'Resisting distortion', *The Psychologist* 14: 592–5.

Giacolone, R. and Rosenfeld, P. (1987) 'Impression management concerns and reinforcement interventions', *Group and Organizational Studies* 12: 445–53.

Gilbert, J., Boulter, C. and Rutherford, M. (1998) 'Models of explanations, part 2: Whose voice? whose ears?' *International Journal of Science Education* 20: 187–203.

Giles, D. (2000) 'The self in the future', *Social Psychological Review* 2: 12–21.

Giles, H. and Street, R. (1994) 'Communicator characteristics and behaviour', in M. Knapp and G. Miller (eds) *Handbook of interpersonal communication* (2nd edn), Thousand Oaks: Sage.

Gilmore, K. and Hargie, O. (2000) 'Quality issues in the treatment of depression in general practice', *International Journal of Health Care Quality Assurance* 13: 34–41.

Giordano, J. (2000) 'Effective communication and counseling with older adults', *International Journal of Aging and Human Development*, 51: 315–24.

Gleason, J. and Perlmann, R. (1985) 'Acquiring social variation in speech', in H. Giles and R. St Clair (eds) *Recent advances in language, communication and social psychology*, London: Lawrence Erlbaum.

Glueckauf, R.L. and Quittner, A.L. (1992) 'Assertiveness training for disabled adults in wheelchairs: self-report, role-play, and activity pattern outcomes', *Journal of Consulting and Clinical Psychology* 60: 419–25.

Goby, V. and Lewis, J. (2000) 'The key role of listening in business: a study of the Singapore insurance industry', *Business Communication Quarterly* 63: 41–51.

Goffman, E. (1959) *The presentation of self in everyday life*, Garden City, NY: Doubleday.

Goffman, E. (1972) *Relations in public: micro-studies of the public order*, Harmondsworth: Penguin.

Golden, N. (1986) *Dress right for business*, New York: McGraw-Hill.

Goldin-Meadow, S. (1997) 'When gestures and words speak differently', *Current Directions in Psychological Science* 6: 138–43.

Goldman, M. (1980) 'Effect of eye-contact and distance on the verbal reinforcement of attitude', *Journal of Social Psychology* 111: 73–8.

Gollwitzer, P. (1999) 'Implementation intentions: strong effects of simple plans', *American Psychologist* 54: 493–503.

Good, T. and Brophy, J. (1997) *Looking in classrooms* (7th edn), New York: HarperCollins.

Gormally, J. (1982) 'Evaluation of assertiveness: effects of gender, rater involvement and level of assertiveness', *Behavior Therapy* 13: 219–25.

Gouran, D. (1990) 'Introduction: speech communication after seventy-five years, issues and prospects', in G. Phillips and J. Wood (eds) *Speech communication: essays to commemorate the 75th anniversary of the Speech Communication Association*, Carbondale and Edwardsville, IL: Southern Illinois University Press.

Grainger, K. (1995) 'Communication and the institutionalised elderly', in J. Nussbaum and J. Coupland (eds) *Handbook of communication and ageing research*, Mahwah, NJ: Lawrence Erlbaum Associates.

Green, T. and Knippen, J. (1999) *Breaking the barriers to upward communication: strategies and skills for employees, managers and HR specialists*, Westport, CT: Quorum Books.

Greenbaum, P. and Rosenfeld, H. (1980) 'Varieties of touching in greetings: sequential structure and sex-related differences', *Journal of Nonverbal Behavior* 5: 13–25.

Greenberg, M.A. and Stone, A.A. (1992) 'Emotional disclosure about traumas and its relation to health: effects of previous disclosure and trauma severity', *Journal of Personality and Social Psychology* 63: 75–84.

Greene, J. (1995) 'An action-assembly perspective on verbal and nonverbal message production: a dancer's message unveiled', in D. Hewes (ed) *The cognitive basis of interpersonal communication*, Hillsdale, NJ: Lawrence Erlbaum Associates.

Greene, J. (2000) 'Evanescent mentation: an ameliorative conceptual foundation for research and theory on message production', *Communication Theory* 10: 139–55.

Greene, K. (2000) 'Disclosure of chronic illness varies by topic and target: the role of stigma and boundaries in willingness to disclose', in S. Petronio (ed.) *Balancing the secrets of private disclosures*, Mahwah, NJ: Lawrence Erlbaum.

Greene, M., Adelman, R., Rizzo, C. and Friedmann, E. (1994) 'The patient's presentation of self in an initial medical encounter', in M. Hummert, J. Wiemann and J. Nussbaum (eds) *Interpersonal communication in older adulthood: interdisciplinary theory and research*, Thousand Oaks, CA: Sage.

Greenspoon, J. (1955) 'The reinforcing effect of two spoken sounds on the frequency of two responses', *American Journal of Psychology* 68: 409–16.

Gregg, V. (1986) *Introduction to human memory*, London: Routledge & Kegan Paul.

Gress, J. and Heft, H. (1998) 'Do territorial actions attenuate the effects of high density? A field study', in J. Sanford and B. Connell (eds) *People, places, and public policy*, Edmond, OK: Environmental Design Research Association.

Griffin, E. (1997) *A first look at communication theory* (3rd edn), New York: McGraw-Hill.

Griffin, E. (2000) *A first look at communication theory* (4th edn), Boston: McGraw-Hill.

Grigsby, J. and Weatherley, D. (1983) 'Gender and sex-role differences in intimacy of self-disclosure', *Psychological Reports* 53: 891–7.

Groogan, S (1999) 'Setting the scene', in A. Long (ed.) *Interaction for practice in community nursing*, Basingstoke: Macmillan Press Ltd.

Grove, T. (1995) 'Regulating conversation: relationships', in J. Stewart (ed.) *Bridges not walls: a book about interpersonal communication* (6th edn), New York: McGraw-Hill.

Gudjonsson, G. (1999) 'Police interviewing and disputed confessions', in A. Memon and R. Bull (eds) *Handbook of the psychology of interviewing*, Chichester: Wiley.

Gudjonsson, G. (2001) 'False confession', *The Psychologist* 14: 588–91.

Gudleski, G. and Shean, G. (2000) 'Depressed and nondepressed students: differences in interpersonal perceptions', *Journal of Psychology* 134: 56–62.

Gudykunst, W. (1991) *Bridging differences: effective intergroup communication*, Newbury Park: Sage.

Gudykunst, W. and Matsumoto, Y. (1996) 'Cross-cultural variability of communication in personal relationships', in W. Gudykunst, S. Ting-Toomey and T. Nishida (eds) *Communication in personal relationships across cultures*, Thousand Oaks: Sage.

Gudykunst, W. and Ting-Toomey, S. (1996) 'Communication in personal relationships across cultures: an introduction', in W. Gudykunst, S. Ting-Toomey and T. Nishida (eds) *Communication in personal relationships across cultures*, Thousand Oaks: Sage.

Gudykunst, W., Ting-Toomey, S. and Nishida, T. (eds) (1996) *Communication in personal relationships across cultures*, Thousand Oaks: Sage.

Guirdham, M. (1996) *Interpersonal skills at work* (2nd edn), Hemel Hempstead: Prentice Hall.

Gupta, S. and Shukla, A. (1989) 'Verbal operant conditioning as a function of extraversion and reinforcement', *British Journal of Psychology* 80: 39–44.

Gupton, T. and LeBow, M. (1971) 'Behavior management in a large industrial firm', *Behavioral Therapy* 2: 78–82.

Haase, R.F. and Di Mattia, D.J. (1976) 'Spatial environment and verbal conditioning in a quasi-counseling interview', *Journal of Counseling Psychology* 23: 414–21.

Hall, E. (1966) *The hidden dimension*, Garden City: Doubleday.

Hall, J. (1984) *Nonverbal sex differences: communication accuracy and expressive style*, Baltimore: John Hopkins University.

Hall, J. (1996) 'Touch, status, and gender at professional meetings', *Journal of Nonverbal Psychology* 20: 23–44.

Halone, K. and Pecchioni, L. (2001) 'Relational listening: a grounded theoretical model', *Communication Reports* 14: 59–71.

Halpern, J. (1994) 'The effect of friendship on personal business transactions', *Journal of Conflict Resolution* 38: 647–64.

Hamilton, C. and Parker, C. (1990) *Communicating for results*, Belmont: Wadsworth.

Hamilton, M. and Hunter, J. (1998a) 'The effect of language intensity on receiver evaluations of message', in M. Allen and R. Preiss (eds) *Persuasion: advances through meta-analysis*, Cresskill, NJ: Hampton Press.

Hamilton, M. and Hunter, J. (1998b) 'A framework for understanding meta-analyses of persuasion', in M. Allen and R. Preiss (eds) *Persuasion: advances through meta-analysis*, Cresskill, NJ: Hampton Press.

Hamilton, W., Round, A. and Sharp, D. (1999) 'Effects on hospital attendance rates of giving patients a copy of their referral letter: randomised control trial', *British Medical Journal* 318: 1392–5.

Hammen, C. (1997) *Depression*, Hove: Psychology Press.

Hancock, D. (2000) 'Impact of verbal praise on college students' time spent on homework', *The Journal of Educational Research* 93: 384–9.

Hanna, M.S. and Wilson, G.L. (1998) *Communicating in business and professional settings* (4th edn), New York: McGraw-Hill.

Hare, A.P. (1976) *Handbook of small group research*, New York: Free Press.

Hare, L. and O'Neill, K. (2000) 'Effectiveness and efficiency in small group academic peer groups: a case study', *Small Group Research* 31: 24–53.

Hargie, O. (1983) 'The importance of teacher questions in the classroom', in M. Stubbs and H. Hiller (eds) *Readings on language, schools and classrooms*, London: Methuen.

Hargie, O. (1997a) 'Communication as skilled performance', in O. Hargie (ed.) *The handbook of communication skills* (2nd edn), London: Routledge.

Hargie, O. (1997b) 'Interpersonal communication: a theoretical framework', in O. Hargie (ed.) *The handbook of communication skills* (2nd edn), London: Routledge.

Hargie, O. (1997c) 'Training in communication skills: research, theory and practice', in O. Hargie (ed.) *The handbook of communication skills* (2nd edn), London: Routledge.

Hargie, O. and Dickson D. (1991) 'Video-mediated judgements of personal characteristics based upon nonverbal cues', *Journal of Educational Television* 17: 31–43.

Hargie, O. and Marshall, P. (1986) 'Interpersonal communication: a theoretical framework', in O. Hargie (ed.), *A handbook of communication skills*, London: Croom Helm.

Hargie, O., Dickson, D. and Tourish, D. (1999) *Communication in management*, Aldershot: Gower.

Hargie, O., Morrow, N. and Woodman, C. (2000) 'Pharmacists' evaluation of key communication skills in practice' *Patient Education and Counseling* 39: 61–70.

Hargie, O. and Tourish, D. (1999) 'The psychology of interpersonal skill', in A. Memon and R. Bull (eds) *Handbook of the psychology of interviewing*, Chichester: Wiley.

Hargie, O. and Tourish, D. (eds) (2000) *Handbook of communication audits for organisations*, London: Routledge.

Harris, J. (1973) 'Answering questions containing marked and unmarked adjectives and adverbs', *Journal of Experimental Psychology* 97: 399–401.

Harris, P. and Brown, B. (1998) 'The home and identity display: interpreting resident territoriality from home exteriors' *Journal of Environmental Psychology* 16: 187–203.

Harris, S., Dersch, C. and Mittal, M. (1999) 'Look who's talking: measuring self-disclosure in MFT', *Contemporary Family Therapy* 21: 405–15.

Hartley, P. (1997) *Group communication*, London: Routledge.

Hartley, P. (1999) *Interpersonal communication* (2nd edn), London: Routledge.

Harwood, J. (2000) 'Communication media use in the grandparent–grandchild relationship', *Journal of Communication* 50: 56–78.

Harwood, J., Ryan, E., Giles, H. and Tysoski, S. (1997) 'Evaluations of patronizing speech and three response styles in a non-service-providing context', *Journal of Applied Communication* 25: 170–95.

Hastings, S. (2000a) 'Asian Indian "self-suppression" and self-disclosure: enactment and adaptation of cultural identity', *Journal of Language and Social Psychology* 19: 85–109.

Hastings, S. (2000b) '"Egocasting" in the avoidance of dialogue: an intercultural perspective', in S. Petronio (ed.) *Balancing the secrets of private disclosures*, Mahwah, NJ: Lawrence Erlbaum.

Hatfield, E., Cacioppo, J. and Rapson, R. (1994) *Emotional contagion*, Cambridge: Cambridge University Press.

Haugtvedt, C. and Petty, R. (1992) 'Personality and attitude change: need for cognition moderates the persistence and resistance of persuasion', *Journal of Personality and Social Psychology* 63: 308–19.

Hawkes, K., Edelman, H. and Dodd, D. (1996) 'Language style and evaluation of a female speaker', *Perceptual and Motor Skills* 83: 80–82.

Hawkins, K. and Power. C. (1999) 'Gender differences in questions asked during small decision-making group discussions', *Small Group Research* 30: 235–56.

Hayes, J. (2002) *Interpersonal skills at work* (2nd edn), London: Routledge.

Hayes, N. (1998) *Foundations of psychology: an introductory text*, Surrey: Nelson.

Heath, C. (1984) 'Talk and recipiency: sequential organization in speech and body movement', in J.M. Atkinson and J. Heritage (eds) *Structures of social actions*, Cambridge: Cambridge University Press.

Heath, R. and Bryant, J. (2000) *Human communication theory and research: concepts, contexts, and challenges*, Mahwah, NJ: Lawrence Erlbaum Associates.

Hecht, M. and LaFrance, M. (1998) 'License or obligation to smile: the effect of power and sex on the amount and type of smiling', *Personality and Social Psychology Bulletin* 24: 1332–42.

Heiman, S. and Sanchez, D. (1999) *The new conceptual selling*, New York: Warner Books.

Heller, M. (1997) 'Posture as an interface between biology and culture', in U. Segerst-rale and P. Molnar (eds) *Nonverbal communication: where nature meets culture*, Mahwah, NJ: Lawrence Erlbaum Associates.

Henderlong, J. (2001) 'Beneficial and detrimental effects of praise on children's motivation: performance versus person feedback', *Dissertation Abstracts International: Section B: The Sciences & Engineering* 61(9-B): 5028.

Henry, S.E., Medway, F.J. and Scarbo, H.A. (1979) 'Sex and locus of control as determinants of children's responses to peer versus adult', *Journal of Educational Psychology* 71: 604–12.

Hensley, W. and Cooper, R. (1987) 'Height and occupational success: a review and critique', *Psychological Reports* 60: 843–49.

Henss, R. (1996) 'Waist-to-hip ratio and attractiveness. Replication and extension', *Personality and Individual Differences* 19: 479–88.

Heslin, R. and Alper, T. (1983) 'Touch: a bonding gesture', in J. Wiemann and R. Harrison (eds), *Nonverbal interaction*, London: Sage.

Hess, U., Philippot, P. and Blairy, S. (1999) 'Mimicry: facts and fiction', in P. Philippot, R. Feldman, and E. Coats (eds) *The social context of nonverbal behavior*, Cambridge: Cambridge University Press.

Hewes, D. (1995) 'Cognitive interpersonal communication research: some thoughts on criteria', in B. Burleson (ed.) *Communication yearbook 18*, Thousand Oaks: Sage.

Hewes, D. and Planalp, S. (1987) 'The individual's place in communication science', in C. Berger and S. Chaffee (eds) *Handbook of communication science*, London: Sage.

Highlen. P. and Nicholas, R.P. (1978) 'Effects of locus of control, instructions, and verbal conditioning on self-referenced affect in a counseling interview', *Journal of Counseling Psychology* 25: 177–83.

Highlen. P.S. and Baccus, G.K. (1977) 'Effects of reflection of feeling and probe on client self-referenced affect', *Journal of Counseling Psychology* 24: 440–3.

Hill, C. (1989) *Therapist techniques and client outcomes*, Newbury Park: Sage.

Hill, C. (1992) 'Research on therapist techniques in brief individual therapy: implica-tions for practitioners', *The Counseling Psychologist* 20: 689–711.

Hill, C. and Gormally, J. (1977) 'Effects of reflection, restatement, probe and nonverbal behaviors on client affect', *Journal of Counseling Psychology* 24: 92–7.

Hill, C., Helms, J., Tichenor, V., Spiegel, S., O'Grady, K. and Perry, E. (1988) 'Effects of therapist response modes in brief psychotherapy', *Journal of Counseling Psychology* 35: 222–33.

Hill, C. and O'Brien, K. (1999) *Helping skills: facilitating exploration, insight and actions*, Washington, DC: American Psychological Association.

Hiller, J., Fisher, G. and Kaess, W. (1969) 'A computer investigation of verbal charac-teristics of effective classroom lecturing', *American Educational Research Journal* 6: 661–75.

Hind, C. (1997) *Communication skills in medicine*, London: BMJ Publishing Group.

Hinde, R. (1997) *Relationships: a dialectical perspective*, Hove: Psychology Press.

Hinton, P. (1993) *The psychology of interpersonal perception*, London: Routledge.

Hirt, E., Lynn, S., Payne, D., Krackow, E. and McCrea, S. (1999) 'Expectations and memory: inferring the past from what must have been', in I. Kirsch (ed.)

How expectations shape experience, Washington, DC: American Psychological Association.

HMSO (1995) *Health Services Commissioner for England, for Scotland and for Wales, Annual Report for 1994–5*, London: HMSO.

Hobson, R. and Lee, A. (1996) 'Hello and goodbye: a study of social engagement in autism', *Journal of Autism and Developmental Disorders* 28: 117–27.

Hoffman, R. (1995) 'Disclosure needs and motives after a near-death experience', *Journal of Near-Death Studies* 13: 237–66.

Hoffnung, R.J. (1969) 'Conditioning and transfer of affective self-references in a role-played counseling interview', *Journal of Consulting and Clinical Psychology* 33: 527–31.

Hofstede, G. (1980) *Culture's consequences: international differences in work-related values*. Beverly Hills, CA: Sage.

Hogg, M. (2001) 'Social categorization, depersonalization, and group behavior', in M. Hogg and S. Tindale (eds) *Blackwell handbook of social psychology: group processes*, Malden, MA: Blackwell.

Hogg, M. and Vaughan, G. (1998) *Social psychology*, London: Prentice Hall Europe.

Holli, B. and Calabrese, R. (1998) *Communication and education skills for dietetics professionals* (3rd edn), Baltimore: Williams & Wilkins.

Hollinger, L. and Buschmann, M. (1993) 'Factors influencing the perception of touch by elderly nursing home residents and their health caregivers', *International Journal of Nursing Studies* 30: 445–61.

Holman, D. (2000) 'A dialogical approach to skill and skilled activity', *Human Relations* 53: 957–80.

Holmes, M.E. (1997) 'Optimal matching analysis of negotiation phase sequences in simulated and authentic hostage negotiations', *Communication Reports* 10: 1–8.

Holtgraves, T. and Lasky, B. (1999) 'Linguistic power and persuasion', *Journal of Language and Social Psychology* 18: 196–206.

Homans, G. (1950) *The human group*, New York: Harcourt, Brace.

Honess, T. and Charman, E. (2002) 'Members of the jury – guilty of incompetence?', *The Psychologist* 15: 72–5.

Honeycutt, J., Cantrill, J., Kelly, P. and Lambkin, D. (1998) 'How do I love thee? Let me consider my options: cognitive, verbal strategies, and the escalation of intimacy', *Human Communication Research* 25: 39–62.

Hooper, C. (1995) 'A behavioral analysis of clinical performance discriminating novice from expert nurses', *Dissertation Abstracts International Section A: Humanities and Social Sciences* 56(6-A): 2098.

Hopper, R., Bosma, J. and Ward, J. (1992) 'Dialogic teaching of medical terminology at the Cancer Information Service', *Journal of Language and Social Psychology* 11: 63–74.

Hough, M. (1996) *Counselling skills*, Harlow: Addison Wesley Longman Ltd.

House, R. (1976) 'A 1976 theory of charismatic leadership', in J.G. Hunt and L.L. Larson (eds) *Leadership: the cutting edge*, Carbondale: Southern Illinois University.

House, R.J. and Mitchell, R.R. (1974) 'Path–goal theory of leadership', *Journal of Contemporary Business* 3: 81–97.

Howe, N., Aquan-Assee, J., Bukowski, W., Rinaldi, C. and Lehoux, P. (2000) 'Sibling self-disclosure in early adolescence', *Merrill Palmer Quarterly* 46: 653–71.

Huang, L. (2000) 'Examining candidate information search processes: the impact of processing goals and sophistication', *Journal of Communication* 50: 93–114.

Huczynski, A. (1996) *Influencing within organizations*, London: Prentice Hall.

Hummert, M., Shaner, J., Garstka, T. and Henry, C. (1998) 'Communication with older adults: the influence of age stereotypes, context, and communicator age', *Human Communication Research* 25: 124–51.

Huxley, A. (1954) *The doors of perception*, New York: Harper & Row.

Hybels, S. and Weaver, R. (1998) *Communicating effectively* (5th edn), Boston: McGraw-Hill.

International Medical Benefit/Risk Foundation (1993) *Improving patient information and education on medicines. Report from the Foundation's Committee on Patient Information*, Geneva: International Medical Benefit/Risk Foundation.

Irving, P. and Hazlett, D. (1999) 'Communicating with challenging clients', in A. Long (ed.) *Interaction for practice in community nursing*, Basingstoke: Macmillan.

Ivey, A. and Authier, J. (1978) *Microcounseling: innovations in interviewing, counseling, psychotherapy and psychoeducation*, Springfield, IL: C.C. Thomas.

Ivey, A. and Ivey, M. (1999) *Intentional interviewing and counseling: facilitating client development in a multicultural society*, Pacific Grove, CA: Brooks/Cole.

Iyengar, S. and Brockner, J. (2001) 'Cultural differences in self and the impact of personal and social influences', in W. Wosinska, R. Cialdini, D. Barrett and J. Reykowski (eds) *The practice of social influence in multiple cultures*, Mahwah, NJ: Lawrence Erlbaum.

Izard, C. (1997) 'Emotions and facial expressions: a perspective from Differential Emotions Theory', in J. Russell and J. Fernandez-Dols (eds) *The psychology of facial expression*, Cambridge: Cambridge University Press.

Jackson, L. (1992) 'Information complexity and medical communication: the effects of technical language and amount of information in a medical message', *Health Communication* 4: 197–210.

Jacobson, R. (1999) 'Personal space within two interaction conditions as a function of confederate age and gender differences', *Dissertation Abstracts International: Section B: The Sciences and Engineering* 59(7-B): 3743.

James, W. (1890) *Principles of psychology*, Chicago: Encyclopaedia Britannica.

James, W. (1892) *Psychology: the briefer course*, New York: Henry Holt.

Janis, I. (1982) *Groupthink* (2nd edn), Boston: Houghton-Mifflin.

Janis, I. (1997) 'Groupthink', in R. Vecchio *et al.* (eds) *Leadership: understanding the dynamics of power and influence in organizations*, Notre Dame: University of Notre Dame Press.

Jeffries, K. and Reed, R. (2000) 'Trust and adaptation in relational contracting', *Academy of Management Review* 25: 873–82.

Jensen, K. (1996) 'The effects of selected classical music on writing and talking about significant life events', *Dissertation Abstracts International: Humanities and Social Sciences* 56(12-A): 4602.

Job, R. (1988) 'Effective and ineffective use of fear in health promotion campaigns', *American Journal of Public Health* 78: 163–7.

471

Johnson, C. and Dabbs, J. (1976) 'Self-disclosure in dyads as a function of distance and the subject–experimenter relationship', *Sociometry* 39: 257–63.

Johnson, D.W. and Johnson, F.P. (1997) *Joining together: group theory and group skills* (6th edn), Boston: Allyn & Bacon.

Johnson, S. and Bechler, C. (1998) 'Examining the relationship between listening effectiveness and leadership emergence: perceptions, behaviors and recall', *Small Group Research* 29: 452–71.

Johnston, D. (1994) *The art and science of persuasion*, Boston: McGraw-Hill.

Joinson, A. (2001) 'Self-disclosure in computer-mediated communication: the role of self-awareness and visual anonymity', *European Journal of Social Psychology* 31: 177–92.

Jones, S., Collins, K. and Hong, H. (1991) 'An audience effect on smile production in 10 month old infants', *Psychological Science* 2: 45–9.

Jones, S.E. (1999) 'Communicating with touch', in L. Guerrero, J. DeVito and M. Hecht (eds) *The nonverbal communication reader: classic and contemporary readings*, Prospect Heights, IL: Waveland Press.

Jones, S.E. and Yarbrough, A.E. (1985) 'A naturalistic study of the meanings of touch', *Communication Monographs* 52: 19–56.

Jones. W.H., Hobbs, S.A. and Hockenbury, D. (1982) 'Loneliness and social skill deficits', *Journal of Personality and Social Psychology* 42: 682–9.

Jordan, J. (1998) 'Executive cognitive control in communication: extending plan-based theory', *Human Communication Research* 25: 5–38.

Jordan, J.M. and Roloff, M.E. (1997) 'Planning skills and negotiator accomplishment: the relationship between self-monitoring and plan generation, plan enhancement, and plan consequences', *Communication Research* 24: 31–63.

Jourard, S. (1961) 'Religious denomination and self-disclosure', *Psychological Bulletin* 8: 446.

Jourard, S. (1964) *The transparent self*, New York: Van Nostrand Reinhold.

Jourard, S. (1966) 'An exploratory study of bodily accessibility', *British Journal of Social and Clinical Psychology* 26: 235–42.

Jourard, S. (1971) *Self-disclosure*, New York: Wiley.

Justine, A. and Howe, B. (1998) 'Player ability, coach feedback, and female adolescent athletes' perceived competence and satisfaction', *Journal of Sport and Exercise Psychology* 20: 280–99.

Kadunc, T. (1991) 'Teacher's nonverbal skills and communication research', *The Global Educator* 11: 2–4.

Kagan, C. and Evans, J. (1995) *Professional interpersonal skills for nurses*, London: Chapman and Hall.

Kahn, R. and Cannell, C. (1957) *The dynamics of interviewing*, New York: Wiley.

Kahn, S. (1981) 'Issues in the assessment and training of assertiveness with women', in J. Wine and M. Smye (eds) *Social competence*, New York: Guilford Press.

Kaiser, S. (1999) 'Women's appearance and clothing within organizations', in L. Guerrero, J. DeVito and M. Hecht (eds) *The nonverbal communication reader: classic and contemporary readings*, Prospect Heights, IL: Waveland Press.

Kalma, A. (1992) 'Gazing in triads: a powerful signal in floor apportionment', *British Journal of Social Psychology* 31: 21–39.

Kang, Y. (1998) 'Classroom context, teacher feedback and student self-effiacy', *Dissertation Abstracts International Section A: Humanities and Social Sciences* 59(2-A): 0419.

Kappas, A., Hess, U. and Scherer, K. (1991) 'Voice and emotion', in R. Feldman and B. Rime (eds) *Fundamentals of nonverbal behaviour*, Cambridge: Cambridge University Press.

Katz, D. and Stotland, E. (1959) 'A preliminary statement of a theory of attitude theory and change', in S. Koch (ed.) *Psychology: a study of a science, Vol. 3*, New York: McGraw-Hill.

Katzenbach, J. and Smith, D. (1993) *The wisdom of teams: creating the high-performance organization*, Boston: Harvard Business School Press.

Kaya, N. and Erkip, F. (1999) 'Invasion of personal space under the condition of short-term crowding: a case study on an automatic teller machine', *Journal of Environmental Psychology* 19: 183–9.

Kazdin, A. (1994) *Behavior modification in applied settings*, Pacific Grove, CA: Brooks/Cole.

Keats, D. (2000) *Interviewing: a practical guide for students and professionals*, Buckingham: Open University Press.

Kellermann, K. (1992) 'Communication: inherently strategic and primarily automatic', *Communication Monographs* 59: 288–300.

Kellerman, K., Reynolds, R. and Chen, J. (1991) 'Strategies of conversational retreat: when parting is not sweet sorrow', *Communication Monographs* 58: 362–83.

Kelley, H. (1950) 'The warm–cold variable in first impressions of persons', *Journal of Personality* 18: 431–9.

Kelley, H.H. and Thibaut, J.W. (1978) *Interpersonal relations: a theory of interdependence*, New York: Wiley.

Kelly, A. and McKillop, K. (1996) 'Consequences of revealing personal secrets', *Psychological Bulletin* 120: 450–65.

Kelly, F. and Daniels, J. (1997) 'The effects of praise versus encouragement on children's perceptions of teachers', *Individual Psychology* 53: 331–41.

Kelly, J. (1982) *Social skills training: a practical guide for interventions*, New York: Springer.

Kelly, J. (2001) 'Mood and emotion in groups', in M. Hogg and S. Tindale (eds) *Blackwell handbook of social psychology: group processes*, Malden, MA: Blackwell.

Keltner, D. (1997) 'Signs of appeasement: evidence for the distinct displays of embarrassment, amusement, and shame', in P. Ekman and E. Rosenberg (eds) *What the face reveals: basic and applied studies of spontaneous expression using the Facial Action Coding System (FACS)*, Oxford: Oxford University Press.

Kendon, A. (1967) 'Some functions of gaze direction in social interaction', *Acta Psychologica* 26: 22–63.

Kendon, A. (1984) 'Some use of gestures', in D. Tannen and M. Saville-Troike (eds) *Perspectives on silence*, Norwood, NJ: Ablex.

Kendon, A. (1989) 'Gesture', in *International encyclopaedia of communications*, Vol. 2, New York: Oxford University Press.

Kendon, A. and Ferber, A. (1973) 'A description of some human greetings', in R. Michael and J. Crook (eds) *Comparative ecology and behaviour of primates*, London: Academic Press.

Kennedy, G. (1998) *Kennedy on negotiation*, Aldershot: Gower.

Kennedy, J.J. and Zimmer, J.M. (1968) 'Reinforcing value of five stimulus conditions in a quasi-counseling situation', *Journal of Counseling Psychology* 15: 357–62.

Kennedy, T.D., Timmons, E.O. and Noblin, C.D. (1971) 'Nonverbal maintenance of conditioned verbal behavior following interpretations, reflections and social reinforcers', *Journal of Personality and Social Psychology* 20: 112–17.

Kennelly, K.J. and Mount, S.A. (1985) 'Perceived contingency of reinforcements, helplessness, locus of control and academic performance', *Psychology in the Schools* 22: 465–9.

Kern, J. (1982) 'Predicting the impact of assertive, empathic-assertive and non-assertive behavior: the assertiveness of the assertee', *Behavior Therapy* 13: 486–98.

Kestler, J. (1982) *Questioning techniques and tactics*, Colorado: McGraw-Hill.

Keyton, J. (1999) 'Relational communication in groups', in L. Frey, D. Gouran and M.S. Poole (eds) *The handbook of group communication theory and research*, Thousand Oaks, CA: Sage Publications.

King, A. (1992) 'Comparison of self-questioning, summarizing and notetaking-review as strategies for learning from lectures', *American Educational Research Journal* 29: 303–23.

Kinlaw, D. (1991) *Developing supervised work teams: building quality and the competitive edge*, Lexington, MA: Lexington Books.

Kipling, R. (1902) 'The elephant child', in *Just-So Stories*, London: Macmillan.

Kipnis, D. and Schmidt, S. (1990) 'The language of persuasion', in I. Asherman and S. Asherman (eds) *The negotiating sourcebook*, Amherst, MA: Human Resource Development Press.

Kirkpatrick, S. and Locke, E. (1991) 'Leadership: do traits matter?', *Academy of Management Executive* 5: 48–60.

Kirouac, G. and Hess, U. (1999) 'Group membership and the decoding of nonverbal behaviour', in P. Philippot, R. Feldman and E. Coats (eds) *The social context of nonverbal behaviour*, Cambridge: Cambridge University Press.

Kirsch, I. (1999) 'Response expectancy: an introduction', in I. Kirsch (ed.) *How expectations shape experience*, Washington, DC: American Psychological Association.

Kleck, R.E. and Strenta, A.C. (1985) 'Physical deviance and the perception of social outcomes', in J.A. Graham and A.M. Kligman (eds) *The psychology of cosmetic treatments*, New York: Praeger.

Kleinke, C. (1977) 'Compliance to requests made by gaze and touching experimenters in field settings', *Journal of Experimental Social Psychology* 13: 218–23.

Kleinke, C. (1986) *Meeting and understanding people*, New York: W.H. Freeman.

Klinger, E. and Bierbraver, G. (2001) 'Acculturation and conflict regulation of Turkish immigrants in Germany: a social influence perspective', in W. Wosinska, R. Cialdini, D. Barrett and J. Reykowski (eds) *The practice of social influence in multiple cultures*, Mahwah, NJ: Lawrence Erlbaum.

Klinger, E., Barta, S. and Maxeiner, M. (1981) 'Current concerns: assessing therapeutically relevant motivation', in P. Kendall and S. Hollon (eds) *Assessment strategies for cognitive behavioral interventions*, New York: Academic Press.

Knapp, M. and Hall, J. (1997) *Nonverbal communication in human interaction* (4th edn), Forth Worth: Harcourt Brace College Publishers.

Knapp, M., Hart, R., Friedrich, G. and Schulman, G. (1973) 'The rhetoric of goodbye: verbal and nonverbal correlates of human leave-taking', *Speech Monographs* 40: 182–98.

Knapp, M. and Vangelisti, A. (2000) *Interpersonal communication and human relationships* (4th edn), Boston: Allyn & Bacon.

Knowles, E., Butler, S. and Linn, J. (2001) 'Increasing compliance by reducing resistance', in J. Forgas and K. Williams (eds) *Social influence: direct and indirect processes*, Philadelphia: Psychology Press.

Knowlton, S. and Berger, C. (1997) 'Message planning, communication failure and cognitive load: further explorations of the Hierarchy Principle', *Human Communication Research* 24: 4–30.

Knox, S., Hess, S., Petersen, D. and Hill, C. (1997) 'A qualitative analysis of client perceptions of the effects of helpful therapist self-disclosure in long-term therapy', *Journal of Counseling Psychology* 44: 274–83.

Kolb, D. and Williams, J. (2003) 'Breakthrough bargaining', in R. Lewicki, D. Saunders, J. Minton and B. Barry (eds) *Negotiation: readings, exercise and cases* (4th edn), New York: McGraw-Hill.

Kolb, J. (1998) 'A comparison of leadership behaviours and competencies in high and average-performance teams', *Communication Reports* 9: 173–83.

Kolotkin, R., Wielkiewicz, R., Judd, B. and Weisler, S. (1983) 'Behavioral components of assertion: comparison of univariate and multivariate assessment strategies', *Behavioral Assessment* 6: 61–78.

Komaki, J. (1982) 'Managerial effectiveness: potential contributions of the behavioural approach', *Journal of Organizational Behaviour Management* 3: 71–83.

Korda, M. (1975) *Power! How to get it, how to use it*, New York: Random House.

Kowalski, R. (1996) 'Complaints and complaining: functions, antecedents, and consequences', *Psychological Bulletin* 119: 179–96.

Kowalski, R. (1999) 'Speaking the unspeakable: self-disclosure and mental heath', in R. Kowalski and M. Leary (eds) *The social psychology of emotional and behavioral problems*, Washington, DC: American Psychological Association.

Kramer, M. (2001) *Business communication in context*, Upper Saddle River, NJ: Prentice Hall.

Kramer, R. (1998) 'Revisiting the Bay of Pigs and Vietnam decisions 25 years later: how well does the groupthink hypothesis stand the test of time?', *Organizational Behavior & Human Decision Processes* 73: 236–71.

Krasner, L. (1958) 'Studies of the conditioning of verbal behaviour', *Psychological Bulletin* 55: 148–70.

Krause, R., Steimer, E., Sanger-Alt, C. and Wagner, G. (1989) 'Facial expression of schizophrenic patients and their interaction partners', *Psychiatry* 52: 1–12.

Kreps, G. (1988) 'The pervasive role of information in health and health care: implications for health care policy', in J. Anderson (ed.) *Communication yearbook 11*, Beverly Hills, CA: Sage.

Kreps, G. and Thornton, B. (1992) *Health communication: theory and practice*, Prospect Heights, IL: Waveland Press.

Kruglanski, A. and Webster, D. (1996) 'Motivated closing of the mind: "seizing" and "freezing"', *Psychological Review* 103: 263–83.

Kunda, Z. and Fong, G. (1993) 'Directional questions direct self-conceptions', *Journal of Experimental Social Psychology* 29: 63–86.

Kupperbusch, C., Matsumoto, D., Kooken, K., Loewinger, S., Uchida, H., Wilson-Cohen, C. and Yrizarry, N. (1999) 'Cultural influences on nonverbal expressions of emotion', in P. Philippot, R. Feldman and E. Coats (eds) *The social context of nonverbal behavior*, Cambridge: Cambridge University Press.

Kurtz, S., Silverman, J. and Draper, J. (1998) *Teaching and learning communication skills in medicine*, Abingdon: Radcliffe Medical Press.

La Tourette, T. and Meeks, S. (2000) 'Perceptions of patronising speech by older women in nursing homes and in the community: impact of cognitive ability and place of residence', *Journal of Language and Social Psychology* 19: 463–73.

LaFrance, M. and Hecht, M. (1999) *Option or obligation to smile: the effects of power and gender on facial expression*, in P. Philippot, R. Feldman and E. Coats (eds) *The social context of nonverbal behavior*, Cambridge: Cambridge University Press.

Lall, A. (1966) *Modern international negotiation: principles and practice*, New York: Columbia University Press.

Lamb, M., Sternberg, K., Orbach, Y., Hershkowitz, I. and Esplin, P. (1999) 'Forensic interviews of children', in A. Memon and R. Bull (eds) *Handbook of the psychology of interviewing*, Chichester: Wiley.

Lamb, R. (1988) 'Greetings and partings', in P. Marsh (ed.) *Eye to eye: your relationships and how they work*, London: Sidgwick and Jackson.

Land, M. (1984) 'Combined effect of two teacher clarity variables on student achievement', *Journal of Experimental Education* 50: 14–17.

Lang, G. and van der Molen, H. (1990) *Personal conversations: roles and skills for counsellors*, London: Routledge.

Lange, A. and Jakubowski, P. (1976) *Responsible assertive behavior*, Champaign, IL: Research Press.

Langer, E., Blank, A. and Chanowitz, B. (1978) 'The mindlessness of ostensibly thoughtful action', *Journal of Personality and Social Psychology* 36: 635–42.

Larson, J.R., Foster-Fishman, P. and Franz, T. (1998) 'Leadership style and the discussion of shared and unshared information in decision-making groups', *Personality and Social Psychology Bulletin* 25: 482–95.

LaTour, M., Snipes, R. and Bliss, S. (1996) 'Don't be afraid to use fear appeals: an experimental study', *Journal of Advertising Research* 36: 56–67.

Laver, J. and Hutcheson, S. (eds) (1972) *Communication in face-to-face interaction*, Harmondsworth: Penguin.

Lawler, E. (1983) 'Reward systems in organisations', in J. Lorsch (ed.) *Handbook of organizational behavior*, Englewood Cliffs, NJ: Prentice Hall.

Lawler, J. (1991) *Behind the screens*, Melbourne: Churchill Livingstone.

Lawrence, J. (2001) 'Does academic praise communicate stereotypic expectancies to Black students?', *Dissertation Abstracts International: Section B: The Sciences & Engineering* 61(10-B): 5622.

Lazarus, A. (1971) *Behavior therapy and beyond*, New York: McGraw-Hill.

Lazowski, L. and Andersen, S. (1991) 'Self-disclosure and social perception: the impact of private, negative and extreme communications', in M. Booth-Butterfield (ed.) *Communication, cognition and anxiety*, Newbury Park: Sage.

Leakey, R. (1994) *The origin of mankind*, London: Weidenfeld and Nicolson.

Leaper, C. (2000) 'Gender, affiliation, assertion, and the interactive content of parent–child play', *Developmental Psychology* 36: 381–93.

Leaper, C. and Valin, D. (1996) 'Predictors of Mexican-American mothers' and fathers' attitudes towards gender equality', *Hispanic Journal of Behavioral Sciences* 18: 343–55.

Leary, M. (1996) *Self-presentation: impression management and interpersonal behaviour*, Boulder, CO: Westview Press.

Leary, M. (2001) 'Towards a conceptualisation of interpersonal rejection', in M. Leary (ed.) *Interpersonal rejection*, Oxford: Oxford University Press.

Leary, M. and Kowalski, R. (1995) *Social anxiety*, New York: Guilford Press.

Leathers, D. (1979) 'The impact of multichannel message inconsistency on verbal and nonverbal decoding behavior', *Communication Monographs* 46: 88–100.

LePoire, B., Hallett, J. and Erlandson, K. (2000) 'An initial test of inconsistent nurturing as control theory: how partners of drug abusers assist their partners' sobriety', *Human Communication Research* 26: 432–57.

LePoole, S. (1991), *Never take no for an answer: a guide to successful negotiating*, London: Kogan Page.

Lepper, M., Keavney, M. and Drake, M. (1996) 'Intrinsic motivation and extrinsic reward: a commentary on Cameron and Pierce's meta-analysis', *Review of Educational Research* 66: 5–33.

Leslie, J. and O'Reilly, M. (1999) *Behavior analysis: foundations and applications to psychology*, Amsterdam: Harwood Academic Publishers.

Leventhal, H. (1970) 'Findings and theory in the study of fear communications', in L. Berkowitz (ed.) *Advances in experimental social psychology*, Vol. 5, New York: Academic Press.

Levine, T. and McCornack, S. (2001) 'Behavioral adaptation, confidence, and heuristic-based explanations of the probing effect', *Human Communication Research* 27: 471–502.

Levy, D. (1999) 'The last taboo', *Time* 28 June: 77.

Lewicki, R. (1997) 'Teaching negotiation and dispute resolution in colleges of business: the state of the practice', *Negotiation Journal* 13: 253–69.

Lewicki, R., Saunders, D., Minton J. and Barry B. (2003) 'Preface', in R. Lewicki, D. Saunders, J. Minton and B. Barry (eds) *Negotiation: readings, exercises and cases* (4th edn), New York: McGraw-Hill.

Lewin, K., Lippitt, R. and White, R.K. (1939) 'Patterns of aggressive behaviour in experimentally created social climates', *Journal of Social Psychology* 10: 271–99.

Lewis, P. and Gallois, C. (1984) 'Disagreements, refusals, or negative feelings: perception of negatively assertive messages from friends and strangers', *Behavior Therapy* 15: 353–68.

Ley, P. (1988) *Communicating with patients*, London: Chapman & Hall.

Leydon, G., Boulton, M., Moynihan, C. *et al.* (2000) 'Cancer patients' information needs and information seeking behaviour: in depth interview study', *British Medical Journal* 320: 909–13.

Lieberman, D. (2000) *Learning: behaviour and cognition* (3rd edn), Belmont, CA: Wadsworth.

Lieberman, P. (1998) *Eve spoke: human language and human evolution*, London: Picador.

Lindon, J. and Lindon, L. (2000) *Mastering counselling skills*, Basingstoke: Macmillan.

Linehan, M. and Egan, K. (1979) 'Assertion training for women', in A. Bellack and M. Hersen (eds) *Research and practice in social skills training*, New York: Plenum.

Lipkin, M. (1996) 'Physician–patient interaction in reproductive counseling', *Obstetrics and Gynecology* 88: S31-S40.

Little, A. and Perett, D. (2002) 'Putting beauty back in the eye of the beholder', *The Psychologist* 15: 28–32.

Littlejohn, S. (1999) *Theories of human communication*, Belmont, CA: Wadsworth Publishing.

Locke, E.A. and Latham, G.P. (1990) *A theory of goal setting and task performance*, Englewood Cliffs: NJ, Prentice Hall.

Loftus, E. (1975) 'Leading questions and the eyewitness report', *Cognitive Psychology* 7: 560–72.

Loftus, E. (1982) 'Interrogating eyewitnesses – good questions and bad', in R. Hogarth (ed.) *Question framing and response consistency*, San Francisco: Jossey-Bass.

Loftus, E. (2001) 'Imagining the past', *The Psychologist* 14: 584–7.

Loftus, E. and Palmer, J. (1974) 'Reconstruction of automobile destruction: an example of the interaction between language and memory', *Journal of Verbal Learning and Verbal Behavior* 13: 585–9.

Loftus, E. and Zanni, G. (1975) 'Eyewitness testimony: the influence of the wording of a question', *Bulletin of the Psychonomic Society* 5: 86–8.

Long, K., Fortney, S. and Johnson, D. (2000) 'An observer measure of compulsive communication', *Communication Research Reports* 17: 349–56.

Long, L. and Long, T. (1976) 'Influence of religious status and religious attire on interviewees', *Psychological Reports* 39: 25–6.

Lord, R. and Maher, K. (1991) *Leadership and information processing: linking perceptions and performance*, Winchester, MA: Unwin Hyman.

Lowe, K., Kroeck, K. and Sivasubramaniam, N. (1996) 'Effectiveness correlates of transformational and transactional leadership: a meta-analysis of the MLQ literature', *Leadership Quarterly* 7: 385–425.

Luft, J. (1970) *Group processes: an introduction to group dynamics*, Palo Alto, CA: National Press Books.

Lundgren, D. and Rudawsky, D. (2000) 'Speaking one's mind or biting one's tongue: when do angered persons express or withhold feedback in transactions with male and female peers?', *Social Psychology Quarterly* 63: 253–63.

Lundsteen, S. (1971) *Listening: its impact on reading and other language acts*, New York: National Council of Teachers of English.

Lytle, A., Brett, J. and Shapiro, D. (1999) 'The strategic use of interests, rights, and power to resolve disputes', *Negotiation Journal* 15: 31–51.

Maag, J. (1999) *Behaviour management: from theoretical implications to practical applications*, San Diego: Singular Publishing Group.

Mader, T. and Mader, D. (1990) *Understanding one another: communicating interpersonally* (2nd edn), Madison: WCB Brown & Benchmark.

Maes, J., Weldy, T. and Icenogle, M. (1997) 'A managerial perspective: oral communication competency is most important for business students in the workplace', *Journal of Business Communication* 34: 67–80.

Maes, S. and Gebhardt, W. (2000) 'Self-regulation and health behaviour: the Health Behaviour Goal model', in M. Boekaerts, P. Pintrich and M. Zeidner (eds) *Handbook of self-regulation*, San Diego: Academic Press.

Maguire, P. (1985) 'Deficiencies in key interpersonal skills', in C. Kagan (ed.) *Interpersonal skills in nursing*, London: Croom Helm.

Maguire, P., Fairburn, S. and Fletcher, C. (1986) 'Consultation skills of young doctors', *British Medical Journal* 292: 1573–8.

Major, B. and Heslin, R. (1982) 'Perceptions of same-sex and cross-sex touching: it's better to give than to receive', *Journal of Personality and Social Psychology* 6: 148–62.

Malone, B. and De Paulo, B. (2001) 'Measuring sensitivity to deception', in J. Hall and F. Bernieri (eds) *Interpersonal sensitivity: theory and measurement*, Mahwah, NJ: Lawrence Erlbaum.

Mandel, S. (1987) *Effective presentation skills: a practical guide for better speaking*, Los Altos, CA: Crisp Publications.

Mannetti, L., Pierro, A., Kruglanski, A., Taris, T. and Bezinovic, P. (2002) 'A cross-cultural study of the Need for Cognitive Closure Scale: comparing its structure in Croatia, Italy, USA and The Netherlands', *British Journal of Social Psychology* 41: 139–56.

Manthei, R. (1997) *Counselling: the skills of finding solutions to problems*, London: Routledge.

Margo, A. (1997) 'Why Barbie is perceived as beautiful', *Perceptual and Motor Skills* 85: 363–74.

Marisi, D.Q. and Helmy, K. (1984) 'Intratask integration as a function of age and verbal praise', *Perceptual and Motor Skills* 58: 936–9.

Markham, R. and Wang, L. (1996) 'Recognition of emotion by Chinese and Australian children', *Journal of Cross-Cultural Psychology* 27: 616–43.

Marlowe, F. and Westman, A. (2001) 'Preferred waist-to-hip ratio and ecology', *Personality and Individual Differences* 30: 481–9.

Marques, J.M., Abrams, D., Paez, D. and Hogg, M. (2001) 'Social categorisation, social identity, and rejection of deviant group members', in M. Hogg and S. Tindale (eds) *Blackwell handbook of social psychology*, Malden, MA: Blackwell.

Martin, D. (1997) 'Slaughtering a sacred cow: the eyebrow flash is not a universal social greeting', *Dissertation Abstracts International: The Sciences and Engineering* 58(5-B): 2751.

Martin, G. and Pear, J. (1999) *Behavior modification: what is it and how to do it*, Englewood Cliffs, NJ: Prentice Hall.

Martin, J. (1970) *Explaining, understanding and teaching*, New York: McGraw-Hill.

Martin, M. and Anderson, C. (1996) 'Argumentativeness and verbal aggressiveness', *Journal of Social Behavior and Personality* 11: 547–54.

Maslow, A. (1954) *Motivation and personality*, New York: Harper & Row.

Mastenbroek, W. (1989) *Negotiate*, Oxford: Basil Blackwell.

Matarazzo, J.D. and Wiens, A.N. (1972) *The interview: research on its anatomy and structure*, Chicago: Aldine-Atherton.

Matsumoto, D. (1990) 'Cultural similarities and differences in the display rules', *Motivation and Emotion* 14: 195–214.

Matsushima, R., Shomi, K. and Kuhlman, D. (2000) 'Shyness in self-disclosure mediated by social skill', *Psychological Reports* 86: 333–8.

Mattock, J. and Ehrenborg, J. (1996) *How to be a better negotiator*, London: Kogan Page.

McAllister, D. (1995) 'Affect- and cognition-based trust as foundations for inter-personal cooperation in organizations', *Academy of Management Journal* 38: 24–59.

McCann, K. and McKenna, H. (1993) 'An examination of touch between nurses and elderly patients in a continuing care setting in Northern Ireland', *Journal of Advanced Nursing* 18: 838–46.

McCartan, P. (2001) 'The identification and analysis of assertive behaviours in nurses', unpublished PhD thesis, University of Ulster, Jordanstown.

McClave, E. (2000) 'Linguistic functions of head movements in the context of speech', *Journal of Pragmatics* 32: 855–78.

McCowan, R., Driscoll, M. and Roop, P. (1995) *Educational psychology: a learning-centred approach to classroom practice*, Needham Heights, MA: Allyn & Bacon.

McDaniel, R. (1994) *Scared speechless: public speaking step by step*, Thousand Oaks, CA: Sage.

McEwan, H. (1992) 'Teaching and the interpretation of texts', *Educational Theory* 42: 59–68.

McFadyen, R. (1996) 'Gender, status and "powerless" speech: interactions of students and lecturers', *British Journal of Social Psychology* 35: 353–67.

McFall, M., Winnett, R., Bordewick, M. and Bornstein, P. (1982) 'Nonverbal components in the communication of assertiveness', *Behavior Modification* 6: 121–40.

McGinniss, J. (1969) *The selling of the President 1968*, New York: Simon and Schuster.

McGrath, J., Arrow, H. and Berdahl, J. (2000) 'The study of groups: past, present, and future', *Personality and Social Psychology* 4: 95–105.

McGuire, W.J. (1981) 'Theoretical foundations of campaigns', in R. Rice and W. Paisley (eds) *Public communication campaigns*, Newbury Park: Sage.

McKay, M., Davis, M. and Fanning, P. (1999) 'Expressing', in J. Stewart (ed.) *Bridges not walls* (7th edn), Boston: McGraw-Hill.

McKenna, K. and Bargh, J. (2000) 'Plan 9 from cyberspace: the implications of the internet for personality and social psychology', *Personality and Social Psychology Review* 4: 57–75.

McLaughlin, M., Cody, M. and Read, S. (eds) (1992) *Explaining one's self to others*, New Jersey: Lawrence Erlbaum.

McNeil, D. (1995) *Hand and mind: what gestures reveal about thought*, Chicago: University of Chicago Press.

McNeil, N., Alibali, M. and Evans, J. (2000) 'The role of gesture in children's com-prehension of spoken language: now they need it, now they don't', *Journal of Nonverbal Behaviour* 24: 131–50.

McRae, B. (1998) *Negotiating and influencing skills*, Thousand Oaks, CA: Sage.

Meerabeau, L. (1999) 'The management of embarrassment and sexuality', *Journal of Advanced Nursing* 29: 1507–13.

Mehrabian, A. (1972) *Nonverbal communication*, Chicago: Aldine-Atherton.

Mehrabian, A. and Blum, J. (1997) 'Physical appearance, attraction, and the mediating role of emotions', *Current Psychology: Developmental, Learning, Personality, Social* 16: 20–42.

Melamed, J. and Bozionelos, N. (1992) ' Managerial promotion and height', *Psychological Reports* 71: 587–93.

Memon, A. and Bull, R. (eds) (1999) *Handbook of the psychology of interviewing*, Chichester: Wiley.

Menzel, K. and Carrell, L. (1994) 'The relationship between preparation and performance in public speaking', *Communication Education* 43: 17–26.

Merbaum, M. (1963) 'The conditioning of affective self-references by three classes of generalized reinforcers', *Journal of Personality* 31: 179–91.

Merrett, F. and Thorpe, S. (1996) 'How important is the praise element in the pause, prompt and praise tutoring procedures for older low-progress readers?', *Educational Psychology* 16: 193–206.

Messer, D. (1995) *The development of communication: from social interaction to language*, Chichester: Wiley.

Metts, S. and Bower, J. (1994) 'Emotion in interpersonal communication', in M. Knapp and G. Miller (eds) *Handbook of interpersonal communication* (2nd edn), Thousand Oaks: Sage.

Meyer, J. (1997) 'Cognitive influences on the ability to address interaction goals', in J.O. Greene (ed.) *Message production: advances in communication theory*, Mahwah, NJ: Lawrence Erlbaum Associates.

Meyer, J. (2000) 'Humor as a double-edged sword: four functions of humor in communication', *Communication Theory* 10: 310–31.

Meyer, W.V., Miggag, W. and Engler, U. (1986) 'Some effects of praise and blame on perceived ability and affect', *Social Cognition* 4: 293–308.

Meyers-Levy, J. and Malaviya, P. (1999) 'Consumers' processing of persuasive advertisements: an integrative framework of persuasion theories', *Journal of Marketing* 63: 45–60.

Miczo, N., Segrin, C. and Allspach, L. (2001) 'Relationship between nonverbal sensitivity, encoding, and relational satisfaction', *Communication Reports* 14: 39–48.

Milakovich, J. (1999) 'Differences between therapists who touch and those who do not', in E. Smith, P. Clance and S. Imes (eds) *Touch in psychotherapy: theory, research, and practice*, New York: The Guilford Press.

Milburn, T. (1998) 'Psychology, negotiation and peace', *Applied Psychology and Preventive Psychology* 7: 109–19.

Millar, R., Crute, V. and Hargie, O. (1992) *Professional interviewing*, London: Routledge.

Millar, R. and Gallagher, M. (1997) 'The selection interview', in O. Hargie (ed.) *The handbook of communication skills* (2nd edn), London: Routledge.

Millar, R. and Gallagher, M. (2000) 'The interview approach', in O. Hargie and D. Tourish (eds) *Handbook of communication audits for organisations*, London: Routledge.

Miller, A. and Hom, H. (1997) 'Conceptions of ability and the interpretation of praise, blame and material rewards', *The Journal of Experimental Education* 65: 163–77.

Miller, J. and Eller, B.F. (1985) 'An examination of the effect of tangible and social reinforcers on intelligence test performance of middle school students', *Social Behaviour and Personality* 13: 147–55.

Miller, K., Cooke, L., Tsang, J. and Morgan, F. (1992) 'Nature and impact of positive and boastful disclosures for women and men', *Human Communication Research* 18: 364–9.

Miller, L., Berg, J. and Archer, R. (1983) 'Openers: individuals who elicit intimate self-disclosure', *Journal of Personality and Social Psychology* 44: 1234–44.

Miller, L., Cody, M. and McLaughlin, M. (1994) 'Situations and goals as fundamental constructs in interpersonal communication research', in M. Knapp and G. Miller (eds) *Handbook of interpersonal communication skills* (2nd edn), Thousand Oaks, CA: Sage.

Miller, L. and Kenny, D. (1986) 'Reciprocity of self-disclosure at the individual and dyadic levels: a social relations analysis', *Journal of Personality and Social Psychology* 50: 713–19.

Miller, P. (2000) *Nonverbal communication in the classroom*, New York: Miller and Associates.

Miller, P., Kozu, J. and Davis, A. (2001) 'Social influence, empathy, and prosocial behavior in cross-cultural perspective', in W. Wosinska, R. Cialdini, D. Barrett and J. Reykowski (eds) *The practice of social influence in multiple cultures*, Mahwah, NJ: Lawrence Erlbaum.

Miller, S., Brody, D. and Summerton, J. (1988) 'Styles of coping with threat: implications for health', *Journal of Personality and Social Psychology* 54: 142–8.

Mills, H. (1991) *Negotiate: the art of winning*, Aldershot: Gower.

Mills, M.C. (1983) 'Adolescents' self-disclosure in individual and group theme-centred modelling, reflecting and probing interviews', *Psychological Reports* 53: 691–701.

Milne, R. (1999) 'Interviewing children with learning disabilities', in A. Memon and R. Bull (eds) *Handbook of the psychology of interviewing*, Chichester: Wiley.

Milne, R. and Bull, R. (1999) *Investigative interviewing: psychology and practice*, Chichester: Wiley.

Miltz, R. (1972) *Development and evaluation of a manual for improving teachers' explanation, Technical Report 26*, Stanford: Stanford University Center for Research and Development in Teaching.

Mitchell, M. (2000) 'Able but not motivated: the relative effects of happy and sad mood on persuasive message processing', *Communication Monographs* 67: 215–26.

Mizes, J. (1985) 'The use of contingent reinforcement in the treatment of a conversion disorder: a multiple baseline study', *Journal of Behavior Therapy and Experimental Psychiatry* 16: 341–5.

Mnookin R., Peppet S. and Tulumello, A. (1996) 'The tension between empathy and assertiveness', *Negotiation Journal* 12: 217–30.

Mokros, H. and Aakhus, M. (2002) 'From information-seeking behavior to meaning engagement practice: implications for communication theory and research', *Human Communication Research* 28: 298–312.

Molloy, J. (1975) *Dress for success*, New York: Peter H. Wyden.

Monahan, J. (1998) 'I don't know it but I like you: the influence of nonconscious affect on person perception', *Human Communication Research* 24: 480–500.

Monahan, J. and Lannutti, P. (2000) 'Alcohol as social lubricant: alcohol myopia theory, social self-esteem, and social interaction', *Human Communication Research* 26: 175–202.

Mongeau, P. (1998) 'Another look at fear-arousing persuasive appeals', in M. Allen and R. Preiss (eds) *Persuasion: advances through meta-analysis*, Cresskill, NJ: Hampton Press.

Montepare, J., Koff, E., Zaitchik, D. and Albert, M. (1999) 'The use of body movements and gestures as cues to emotions in younger and older adults', *Journal of Nonverbal Behavior* 23: 133–52.

Montgomery, D., Wiesman, D. and DeCaro, P. (2001) 'Towards a code of ethics for organizational communication professional: a working proposal', *American Communication Journal* 5(1): http://www.acjournal.org/holdings/index.htm.

Moon, Y. (2000) 'Intimate exchanges: using computers to elicit self-disclosure from consumers', *Journal of Consumer Research* 26: 323–39.

Morgan, H. and Thomas, K. (1996) 'A psychodynamic perspective on group processes', in M. Wetherall (ed.) *Identities, groups, and social issues*, London: Sage Publications in association with The Open University Press.

Morley, I. (1981) 'Negotiating and bargaining', in M. Argyle (ed.) *Social skills and work*, London: Methuen.

Morley, I. (1986) 'Negotiating and bargaining', in O. Hargie (ed.) *A handbook of communication skills*, London: Routledge.

Morley, I. (1997) 'Negotiating and bargaining', in O. Hargie (ed.) *The handbook of communication skills* (2nd edn), London: Routledge.

Morley, I.E. and Hosking, D.M. (1985) 'The skills of leadership', paper presented at the West European Conference on the Psychology of Work and Organization, Aachen, FRG, 1–3 April.

Morokoff, P., Quina, K., Harlow, L., Whitmire, L., Grimley, D., Gibson, P. and Burkholder, G. (1997) 'Sexual Assertiveness Scale (SAS) for women: development and validation', *Journal of Personality and Social Psychology* 73: 790–804.

Morris, M., Larrick, R. and Su, S. (1999) 'Misperceiving negotiation counterparts: when situationally determined bargaining behaviours are attributed to personality traits', *Journal of Personality and Social Psychology* 77: 52–67.

Morris, M., Podolny, J. and Ariel, S. (2001) 'Culture, norms, and obligations: cross-national differences in patterns of interpersonal norms and felt obligations toward coworkers', in W. Wosinska, R. Cialdini, D. Barrett and J. Reykowski (eds) *The practice of social influence in multiple cultures*, Mahwah, NJ: Lawrence Erlbaum.

Morrison, T., Conaway, W. and Borden, G. (1994) *Kiss, bow, or shake hands: how to do business in 60 countries*, Holbrook, MA: Adams Media Corporation.

Morrow, N. and Hargie, O. (2001) 'Effective communication', in K. Taylor and G. Harding (eds) *Pharmacy practice*, London: Taylor and Francis.

Morrow, N., Hargie, O., Donnelly, H. and Woodman, C. (1993) 'Why do you ask? A study of questioning behaviour in community pharmacist–client consultations', *International Journal of Pharmacy Practice* 2: 90–4.

Motley, M. (1992) 'Mindfulness in solving communicators' dilemmas', *Communication Monographs* 59: 306–13.

Muczyk, J.P and Reimann, B.C. (1987) 'The case of directive leadership', *Academy of Management Executive* 1: 301–11.

Mudrack, P. and Farrell, G. (1995) 'An examination of functional role behaviour and its consequences for individuals in group settings', *Small Group Research* 26: 542–71.

Mueller, C. (1997) 'Praise for intelligence can undermine children's motivation and performance', *Dissertation Abstracts International: Section B: The Sciences and Engineering* 58(3-B): 1596.

Mueller, C. and Dweck, C. (1998) 'Praise for intelligence can undermine children's motivation and performance', *Journal of Personality and Social Psychology* 75: 33–53.

Mulac, A. (1998) 'The gender-linked language effect: do language differences really make a difference?', in D. Canary and K. Dindia (eds) *Gender, power, and communication in human relationships*, Mahwah, NJ: Erlbaum.

Mulac, A., Bradac, J. and Gibbons, P. (2001) 'Empirical support for the gender-as-culture hypothesis: an intercultural analysis of male/female language differences', *Human Communication Research* 27: 121–52.

Munter, M. (2000) *Guide to managerial communication* (5th edn), Upper Saddle River, NJ: Prentice Hall.

Murray, J. (1990) 'Understanding competing theories of negotiation', in I. Asherman and S. Asherman (eds) *The negotiating sourcebook*, Amherst, MA: Human Resource Development Press.

Nagata, D.K., Nay, W.R. and Seidman, E. (1983) 'Nonverbal and verbal content behaviors in the prediction of interviewer effectiveness', *Journal of Counseling Psychology* 30: 83–6.

Naifeh, S. and Smith, G. (1984) *Why can't men open up?* New York: Clarkson N. Potter.

Napier, R. and Gershenfeld, M. (1999) *Groups: theory and experience*, Boston: Houghton Mifflin Company.

Nelson-Gray, R., Haas, J., Romand, B., Herbert, J. and Herbert, D. (1989) 'Effects of open ended versus close ended questions on interviewees' problem related statements', *Perceptual and Motor Skills* 69: 903–11.

Nelson-Jones, R. (1996) *Effective thinking skills*, London: Cassell.

Nelson-Jones, R. (1997) *Practical counselling and helping skills* (4th edn), London: Cassell.

Neuberg, S., Judice, T. and West, S. (1997) 'What the Need for Closure Scale measures and what it does not: toward differentiating among related epistemic motives', *Journal of Personality and Social Psychology* 72: 1396–1412.

Newton, M. (2002) *Savage girls and wild boys: a history of feral children*, London: Faber.

Ng, S. and Bradac, J. (1993) *Power in language: verbal communication and social influence*, Newbury Park: Sage.

Nichols, R. (1947) 'Listening: questions and problems', *Quarterly Journal of Speech* 33: 83–6.

Niikura, R. (1999a) 'The psychological processes underlying Japanese assertive behavior: comparison of Japanese with Americans, Malaysians and Filipinos', *International Journal of Intercultural Relations* 23: 47–76.

Niikura, R. (1999b) 'Assertiveness among Japanese, Malaysian, Filipino, and U.S. white-collar workers', *The Journal of Social Psychology* 139: 690–9.

Nix, J., Lohr, J. and Mosesso, L. (1983) 'The relationship of sex-role characteristics to self-report and role-play measures of assertiveness in women', *Behavioral Assessment* 6: 89–93.

Nobel, L. (1998) 'Doctor–patient communication and adherence to treatment', in L. Myers and K. Midence (eds) *Adherence to treatment in medical conditions*, Amsterdam: Harwood Academic Publishers.

Noller, P. (1980) 'Gaze in married couples', *Journal of Nonverbal Behavior* 5: 115–29.

Northouse, L. and Northouse, P. (1998) *Health communication: strategies for health professionals*, Stamford, CT: Appleton & Lange.

Northouse, P. (1997) *Leadership: theory and practice*, Thousand Oaks, CA: Sage.

Nussbaum, J. and Coupland, J. (eds) (1995) *Handbook of communication and ageing research*, Mahwah, NJ: Lawrence Erlbaum Associates.

Oakes, P., Haslam, A. and Turner, J. (1994) *Stereotypes and social reality*, Oxford: Blackwell.

O'Brien, J.S. and Holborn, S.W. (1979) 'Verbal and nonverbal expressions as reinforcers in verbal conditioning of adult conversation', *Journal of Behaviour Psychiatry* 10: 267–9.

O'Connor, E. and Simms, C. (1990) 'Self-revelation and manipulation: the effects of sex and machiavellianism on self-disclosure', *Social Behaviour and Personality* 18: 95–100.

Oettingen, G. and Gollwitzer, P. (2001) 'Goal setting and goal striving', in A. Tesser and N. Schwarz (eds) *Blackwell handbook of social psychology: intraindividual processes*, Malden, MA: Blackwell.

Office Angels (2000) *Forget kissing . . . everyone's busy telling!*, London: Office Angels.

Oguchi, T. (1991) 'Goal-based analysis of willingness of self-disclosure', *Japanese Psychological Research* 33: 180–7.

O'Hair, D. and Friedrich, G. (1992) *Strategic communication in business and the professions*, Boston: Houghton Mifflin.

O'Hair, D., Friedrich, G. and Shaver, L. (1998) *Strategic communication in business and the professions* (3rd edn), Boston: Houghton Mifflin Company.

Ohme, R. (2001) 'Social influence in media: culture and antismoking advertising', in W. Wosinska, R. Cialdini, D. Barrett and J. Reykowski (eds) *The practice of social influence in multiple cultures*, Mahwah, NJ: Lawrence Erlbaum.

O'Keefe, D. (2002) *Persuasion: theory and research* (2nd edn), Thousand Oaks, CA: Sage.

O'Keefe, D. and Hale, S. (1998) 'The door-in-the-face influence strategy: a random effects meta-analytic review', in M. Roloff (ed.) *Communication yearbook 21*, Thousand Oaks, CA: Sage.

O'Keefe, D. and Hale, S. (2001) 'An odds-ratio-based meta-analysis of research on the door-in-the-face influence strategy', *Communication Reports* 14: 31–8.

O'Leary, M. and Gallois, C. (1999) 'The last ten turns in conversations between strangers', in L. Guerrero, J. DeVito and M. Hecht (eds) *The nonverbal communication reader: classic and contemporary readings disclosures* (2nd edn), Prospect Heights, IL: Waveland.

Olekalns, M. and Smith, P. (2001) 'Understanding optimal outcomes: the role of strategy sequences in competitive negotiations', *Human Communication Research* 26: 527–57.

Omarzu, J. (2000) 'Disclosure decision model: determining how and when individuals will self-disclose', *Personality and Social Psychology Review* 4: 174–85.

Omata, K. (1996) 'Territoriality in the house and its relationship to the use of rooms and the psychological well-being of Japanese married women', *Journal of Environmental Psychology* 15: 147–54.

Ong, L., de Haes., J., Hoos, A. and Lammes, F. (1995) 'Doctor–patient communication: a review of the literature', *Social Science and Medicine* 40: 903–18.

O'Reilly, C. and Puffer, S. (1989) 'The impact of rewards and punishments in a social context: a laboratory and field experiment', *Journal of Occupational Psychology* 62: 41–53.

Orrego, V., Smith, S., Mitchell, M., Johnson, A., Yun, K. and Greenberg, B. (2000) 'Disclosure and privacy issues on television talk shows', in S. Petronio (ed.) *Balancing the secrets of private disclosures*, Mahwah, NJ: Lawrence Erlbaum Associates.

Oster, H., Hegley, D. and Nagel, L. (1992) 'Adult judgements and fine-grained analysis of infant facial expressions: testing the validity of a priori coding formulas', *Developmental Psychology* 25: 954–62.

O'Sullivan, P. (2000) 'What you don't know won't hurt me: impression management functions of communication channels in relationships', *Human Communication Research* 26: 403–31.

Owens, L., Slee, P. and Shute, R. (2000) 'It hurts a hell of a lot . . . the effects of indirect aggression on teenage girls', *School Psychology International* 21: 359–76.

Packard, S.H. and Kauppi, D.R. (1999) 'Rehabilitation agency leadership style: impact on subordinates' job satisfaction', *Rehabilitation Counselling Bulletin*, 43: 5–11.

Paese, P. and Gilin, D. (2000) 'When an adversary is caught telling the truth: reciprocal cooperation versus self-interest in distributive bargaining', *Personality and Social Psychology Bulletin* 26: 79–90.

Paivio, A. (1971) *Imagery and verbal processes*, New York: Holt.

Pallak, M., Cook, D. and Sullivan, J. (1980) 'Commitment and energy conservation', *Applied Social Psychology Journal* 1: 235–53.

Pansa, M. (1979) 'Verbal conditioning of affect responses of process and reactive schizophrenics in a clinical interview situation', *British Journal of Medical Psychology* 52: 175–82.

Papini, D., Farmer, F., Clark, S., Micka, J. and Barnett, J. (1990) 'Early adolescent age and gender differences in patterns of emotional self-disclosure to parents and friends', *Adolescence* 25: 959–76.

Papousek, H. and Papousek, M. (1997) 'Preverbal communication in humans and the genesis of culture', in U. Segerstrale and P. Molnar (eds) *Nonverbal communication: where nature meets culture*, Mahwah, NJ: Lawrence Erlbaum Associates.

Pardeck, J., Anderson, C., Gianino, E. and Miller, B. (1991) 'Assertiveness of social work students', *Psychological Reports* 69: 589–90.

Park, B. and Kraus, S. (1992) 'Consensus in initial impressions as a function of verbal information', *Personality and Social Psychology Bulletin* 182: 439–49.

Parrott, R., Duncan, V. and Duggan, A. (2000) 'Promoting patients' full and honest disclosure during conversations with health caregivers', in S. Petronio (ed.) *Balancing the secrets of private disclosures*, Mahwah, NJ: Lawrence Erlbaum.

Parrott, R., Greene, K. and Parker, R. (1992) 'Negotiating child health care routines during paediatrician–parent conversations', *Journal of Language and Social Psychology* 11: 35–46.

Paterson, R. (2000) *The assertiveness workbook: how to express your ideas and stand up for yourself at work and in relationships*, Oakland: New Harbinger.

Paulus, P. (1998) 'Developing consensus about groupthink after all these years', *Organizational Behavior & Human Decision Processes* 73: 362–74.

Paulus, P.B., Seta, C.E., and Baron, R.A. (1996) *Effective human relations: a guide to people at work* (3rd edn), Boston: Allyn & Bacon.

Paunonen, S., Ewan, K., Earthy, J., Lefave, S. and Goldberg, H. (1999) 'Facial features as personality cues', *Journal of Personality* 67: 555–83.

Pavitt, C. (2000) 'Answering questions requesting scientific explanations for communication', *Communication Theory* 10: 379–404.

Pavlov, I. (1927) *Conditioned reflexes*, New York: Dover Reprint.

Pearson, J. and Nelson, P. (2000) *An introduction to human communication: understanding and sharing* (5th edn), Boston: McGraw-Hill.

Pearson, J. and Spitzberg, B. (1987) *Interpersonal communication: concepts, components, and contexts* (2nd edn), Madison: WCB Brown & Benchmark.

Peau, M., Szabo, E., Anderson, J., Morrill, J., Zubric, J. and Wan, H. (2001) 'The role and impact of affect in the process of resistance to persuasion', *Human Communication Research* 27: 216–52.

Peck, J. (1995) 'TV talk shows as therapeutic discourse: the ideological labor of the televised talking cure', *Communication Theory* 5: 58–81.

Penman, R. (2000) *Reconstructing communicating: looking to a future*, Mahwah, NJ: Lawrence Erlbaum.

Pennebaker, J. and Francis, M. (1996) 'Cognitive, emotional, and language processes in disclosure', *Cognition and Emotion* 10: 601–26.

Penton-Voak, I. and Perrett, D. (2000) 'Female preference for male faces change cyclically: further evidence', *Evolution and Human Behaviour* 21: 39–48.

Perrett, D., Burt, D., Penton-Voak, I., Lee, K., Rowland, D. and Edwards, R. (1999) 'Symmetry and human facial attractiveness', *Evolution and Human Behavior* 20: 295–307.

Pervin, L. (1978) 'Definitions, measurements and classifications of stimuli, situations and environments', *Human Ecology* 6: 71–105.

Peterson, C., Dowden, C. and Tobin, J. (1999) 'Interviewing preschoolers: comparisons of yes/no and wh- questions', *Law and Human Behavior* 23: 539–55.

Peterson, R. (1997) 'A directive leadership style in group decision making can be both virtue and vice: evidence from elite and experimental groups', *Journal of Personality and Social Psychology* 72: 1107–21.

Petrie, K., Booth, R., Pennebaker, J., Davison, K. and Thomas, M. (1995) 'Disclosure of trauma and immune response to a hepatitis B vaccination program', *Journal of Consulting and Clinical Psychology* 63: 787–92.

Petronio, S. (2000a) 'Preface', in S. Petronio (ed.) *Balancing the secrets of private disclosures*, Mahwah, NJ: Lawrence Erlbaum.

Petronio, S. (2000b) 'The boundaries of privacy', in S. Petronio (ed.) *Balancing the secrets of private disclosures*, Mahwah, NJ: Lawrence Erlbaum.

Petronio, S. and Bantz, C. (1991) 'Controlling the ramifications of disclosure: "don't tell anybody but . . . "', *Journal of Language and Social Psychology* 10: 263–70.

Petty, R. and Cacioppo, J. (1986) *Communication and persuasion: central and peripheral routes to attitude change*, New York: Springer-Verlag.

Pezdek, K. and Banks, W. (eds) (1996) *The recovered memory/false memory debate*, San Diego: Academic Press.

Phillips, E. (1978) *The social skills basis of psychopathology*, New York: Grune and Stratton.

Piccinin, S., McCarrey, M., Fairweather, D., Vito, D. and Conrad, G. (1998) 'Impact of situational legitimacy and assertiveness-related anxiety/discomfort on motivation and ability to generate effective criticism responses', *Current Psychology: Developmental, Learning, Personality, Social* 17: 75–92.

Pietras, M. (2001) 'Social influence principles in Polish advertising and consumer decision making', in W. Wosinska, R. Cialdini, D. Barrett and J. Reykowski (eds) *The practice of social influence in multiple cultures*, Mahwah, NJ: Lawrence Erlbaum Associates.

Pilkington, C. and Smith, K. (2000) 'Self-evaluation maintenance in a larger social context', *British Journal of Social Psychology* 39: 213–29.

Pinnington, A. (2001) 'Charles Handy: the exemplary guru', *Reason in Practice* 1: 47–55.

Pitts, M. and Roberts, M. (1997) *Fairweather Eden*, London: Century.

Placencia, M. (1997) 'Opening up closings – the Ecuadorian way', *Text* 17: 53–81.

Planalp, S. (1998) 'Communicating emotion in everyday life: cues, channels and processes', in P. Andersen and L. Guerrero (eds) *Handbook of communication and emotion: research, theory, applications, and contexts*, San Diego: Academic Press.

Planalp, S. (1999) *Communicating emotion: social, moral and cultural processes*, Cambridge: Cambridge University Press.

Poling, A., Dickinson, A., Austin, J. and Normand, M. (2000) 'Basic behavioural research and organisational behaviour management', in J. Austin and J. Carr (eds) *Handbook of applied behaviour analysis*, Reno: Context Press.

Pollack, B. (1998) 'The impact of the sociophysical environment on interpersonal communication and feelings of belonging in work groups', in J. Sanford and B. Connell (eds) *People, places, and public policy*, Edmond, OK: Environmental Design Research Association.

Poole, M.S. (1999) 'Group communication theory', in L. Frey, D. Gouran and M.S. Poole (eds) *The handbook of group communication theory and research*, Thousand Oaks, CA: Sage.

Porter, R. and Samovar, L. (1998) 'Cultural influences on emotional expression: implications of intercultural communication', in P. Andersen and L. Guerrero (eds) *Handbook of communication and emotion: research, theory, applications, and contexts*, San Diego: Academic Press.

Powell, W.J. (1968) 'Differential effectiveness of interviewer interventions in an experimental interview', *Journal of Consulting and Clinical Psychology* 32: 210–15.

Pratkanis, A. (2001) 'Propaganda and deliberative persuasion: the implications of Americanized mass media for established and emerging democracies', in W. Wosinska, R. Cialdini, D. Barrett and J. Reykowski (eds) *The practice of social influence in multiple cultures*, Mahwah, NJ: Lawrence Erlbaum Associates.

Preiss, R. and Allen, M. (1998) 'Performing counterattitudinal advocacy: the persuasive impact of incentives', in M. Allen and R. Preiss (eds) *Persuasion: advances through meta-analysis*, Cresskill, NJ: Hampton Press.

Premack, D. (1965) 'Reinforcement theory', in D. Levine (ed.) *Nebraska Symposium on Motivation*, Vol. 13, Lincoln: University of Nebraska Press.

Priest, P. and Dominick, J. (1994) 'Pulp pulpits: self-disclosure on "Donohue"', *Journal of Communication* 44: 74–96.

Prkachin, K. (1997) 'The consistency of facial expressions of pain', in P. Ekman and E. Rosenberg (eds) *What the face reveals: basic and applied studies of spontaneous expression using the Facial Action Coding System (FACS)*, Oxford: Oxford University Press.

Prochaska, J. and DiClemente, C. (1992) 'Stages of change in the modification of problem behaviors', in M. Hersen, R. Eisler and P. Miller (eds) *Progress in behavior modification*, Sycamore, IL: Sycamore Press.

Proctor, R. and Dutta, A. (1995) *Skill acquisition and human performance*, Thousand Oaks, CA: Sage.

Provine, R. (2000) *Laughter: a scientific investigation*, London: Penguin.

Prue, D. and Fairbank, J. (1981) 'Performance feedback in organizational behavior management: a review', *Journal of Organizational Behavior Management* 3: 1–16.

Pruitt, D. (1981) *Negotiating behavior*, New York: Academic Press.

Pruitt, D. (1990) 'Achieving integrative agreements', in I. Asherman and S. Asherman (eds) *The negotiating sourcebook*, Amherst, MA: Human Resource Development Press.

Putnam, L. and Roloff, M. (1992a), 'Communication perspectives on negotiation', in L. Putnam and M. Roloff (eds) *Communication and negotiation*, Newbury Park, CA: Sage.

Putnam, L. and Roloff, M. (eds) (1992b) *Communication and negotiation*, Newbury Park, CA: Sage.

Quine, L., Rutter, D. and Arnold, L. (2002) 'Increasing cycle helmet use in school age cyclists: an intervention based on the theory of planned behaviour', in D. Rutter and L. Quine (eds) *Changing health behaviour*, Buckingham: Open University Press.

Quinn, R.E. and McGrath, M.R. (1982) 'Moving behind the single solution perspective', *Journal of Applied Behavioral Science* 18: 463–72.

Rabin, C. and Zelner, D. (1992) 'The role of assertiveness in clarifying roles and strengthening job satisfaction of social workers in multidisciplinary mental health settings', *British Journal of Social Work* 22: 17–32.

Rackham, N. (2003) 'The behavior of successful negotiators', in R. Lewicki, D. Saunders, J. Minton and B. Barry (eds) *Negotiation: readings, exercises and cases* (4th edn), New York: McGraw-Hill.

Ragan, S. (1990) 'Verbal play and multiple goals in the gynaecological exam interaction', *Journal of Language and Social Psychology* 9: 67–84.

Rakos, R. (1991) *Assertive behavior: theory, research and training*, London: Routledge.

Rakos, R. (1997) 'Asserting and confronting', in O. Hargie (ed.) *The handbook of communication skills*, London: Routledge.

Ransdell, S. and Gilroy, L. (2001) 'The effects of background music on word processed writing', *Computers in Human Behavior* 17: 141–8.

Raven, B. (1988) 'Social power and compliance in health care', in S. Maes, C. Spielberger, P. Defares and I. Sarason (eds), *Topics in health psychology*, New York: Wiley.

Raven, B. (1992) 'A power/interaction model of interpersonal influence: French and Raven thirty years later', *Journal of Social Behavior and Personality* 7: 217–44.

Raven, B. (1998) 'Groupthink, Bay of Pigs and Watergate reconsidered', *Organizational Behavior & Human Decision Processes* 73: 352–61.

Raven, B. and Rubin, J.Z. (1983) *Social psychology* (2nd edn), New York: Wiley.

Rector, M. and Neiva, E. (1996) 'Communication and personal relationships in Brazil', in W. Gudykunst, S. Ting-Toomey and T. Nishida (eds) (1996) *Communication in personal relationships across cultures*, Thousand Oaks: Sage.

Reid, D. and Parsons, M. (2000) 'Organisational behavioural management in human service settings', in J. Austin and J. Carr (eds) *Handbook of applied behaviour analysis*, Reno: Context Press.

Reid, L., Henneman, R. and Long, E. (1960) 'An experimental analysis of set: the effect of categorical instruction', *American Journal of Psychology* 73: 568–72.

Reinhard, J. (1998) 'The persuasive effects of testimonial assertion evidence', in M. Allen and R. Preiss (eds) *Persuasion: advances through meta-analysis*, Cresskill, NJ: Hampton Press.

Remland, M. (2000) *Nonverbal communication in everyday life*, Boston: Houghton Mifflin.

Reno, R. and Kenny, D. (1992) 'Effects of self-consciousness and social anxiety on self-disclosure among unacquainted individuals: an application of the social relations model', *Journal of Personality* 60: 79–95.

Resnick, L. (1972) 'Teacher behaviour in an informal British infant school', *School Review* 81: 63–83.

Reykowski, J. (2001) 'Principles of social influence across cultures', in W. Wosinska, R. Cialdini, D. Barrett and J. Reykowski (eds) *The practice of social influence in multiple cultures*, Mahwah, NJ: Lawrence Erlbaum Associates.

Reynolds, W. and Scott, B. (2000) 'Do nurses and other professional helpers normally display much empathy?', *Journal of Advanced Nursing* 31: 226–34.

Rice, R. (1993) 'Media appropriateness: using social presence theory to compare traditional and new organisational media', *Human Communication Research* 19, 451–84.

Richins, M. (1983) 'An analysis of consumer interaction style in the marketplace', *Journal of Consumer Research* 10: 73–82.

Richmond, V. and McCroskey, J. (2000) *Nonverbal behaviour in interpersonal relations* (4th edn), Boston: Allyn & Bacon.

Riggio, R. (1992) 'Social interaction skills and nonverbal behaviour', in R. Feldman (ed.) *Applications of nonverbal behavioral theory and research*, Hillsdale, NJ: Lawrence Erlbaum Associates.

Riggio, R. and Friedman, H. (1986) 'Impression formation: the role of expressive behavior', *Journal of Personality and Social Psychology* 50: 421–7.

Riley, J. (2000) *Communication in nursing*, St Louis: Mosby.

Rimal, R. (2002) Perceived risk and self-efficacy as motivators: understanding individuals' long-term use of health information', *Journal of Communication* 51: 633–54.

Riseborough, M. (1981) 'Physiographic gestures as decoding facilitators: three experiments exploring a neglected facet of communication', *Journal of Nonverbal Behavior* 5: 172–83.

Roach, C. and Wyatt, N. (1999) 'Listening and the rhetorical process', in J. Stewart (ed.) *Bridges not walls* (7th edn), Boston: McGraw-Hill.

Robbins, S. (2001) *Organizational behavior* (9th edn), New Jersey: Prentice Hall.

Robbins, S. and Hunsaker, P. (1996) *Training in interpersonal skills: tips for managing people at work* (2nd edn), New Jersey: Prentice Hall.

Robinson, J. (1998) 'Getting down to business: talk, gaze, and body orientation during openings of doctor–patient consultations', *Human Communication Research* 25: 97–123.

Robinson, J. and Stivers, T. (2001) 'Achieving activity transitions in physician–patient encounters: from history taking to physical examination', *Human Communication Research* 27: 253–98.

Robinson, S., Sterling, C., Skinner, C. and Robinson, D. (1997) 'Effects of lecture rate on students' comprehension and ratings of topic importance', *Contemporary Educational Psychology* 22: 260–7.

Roese, N., Olson, J., Borenstein, M., Martin, A. and Shores, A. (1992) 'Same-sex touching behaviour: the moderating role of homophobic attitudes', *Journal of Nonverbal Behavior* 16: 249–59.

Rogan, R. and Hammer, M.R. (1995) 'Assessing message affect in crisis negotiation: An exploratory study', *Human Communication Research* 21: 553–74.

Rogers, C.R. (1951) *Client-centred therapy*, Boston: Houghton Mifflin.

Rogers, C.R. (1980) *A way of being*, Boston: Houghton Mifflin.

Rogers, C.R. (1991) *Client-centred therapy*, London: Constable.

Rogers, E. (1983) *Diffusion of innovations*, Free Press: New York.

Rogers, W. (1978) 'The contribution of kinesic illustrators toward the comprehension of verbal behavior within utterances', *Human Communication Research* 5: 54–62.

Roloff, M. and Jordan, J. (1992) 'Achieving negotiation goals: the "fruits and foibles" of planning ahead', in L. Putnam and M. Roloff (eds) *Communication and negotiation*, Newbury Park, CA: Sage.

Rose, Y. and Tryon, W. (1979) 'Judgements of assertive behavior as a function of speech loudness, latency, content, gestures, inflection and sex', *Behavior Modification* 3: 112–23.

Rosenbaum, B. (2001) 'Seven emerging sales competencies', *Business Horizons* 44: 33–6.

Rosenblum, N., Wetzel, M., Platt, O., Daniels, S., Crawford, J. and Rosenthal, R. (1994) 'Predicting medical student success in a clinical clerkship by rating students' nonverbal behaviour', *Archives of Pediatric and Adolescent Medicine* 148: 213–19.

Rosenfarb, I. (1992) 'A behaviour analytic interpretation of the therapeutic relationship', *The Psychological Record* 42: 341–54.

Rosenfeld, H. (1987) 'Conversational control functions of nonverbal behavior', in A. Siegman and S. Feldstein (eds), *Nonverbal behavior and communication*, Hillsdale, NJ: Lawrence Erlbaum Associates.

Rosenfeld, H. and Hancks, M. (1980) 'The nonverbal context of verbal listener responses', in M. Kay (ed.) *The relationship of verbal and nonverbal communication*, The Hague: Mouton.

Rosenfeld, L. (2000) 'Overview of the ways privacy, secrecy, and disclosure are balanced in today's society', in S. Petronio (ed.) *Balancing the secrets of private disclosures*, Mahwah, NJ: Lawrence Erlbaum Associates.

Rosenfeld, L., Kartus, S. and Ray, C. (1976) 'Body accessibility revisited', *Journal of Communication* 26: 27–30.

Rosengren, K.E. (2000) *Communication: an introduction*, London: Sage.

Rosenshine, B. (1968) *Objectively measured behavioural predictors of effectiveness in explaining, Technical Report 4*, Stanford: Stanford University Center for Research and Development in Teaching.

Rosenshine, B. (1971) *Teaching behaviour and student achievement*, Windsor: National Foundation for Educational Research in England and Wales.

Rosenthal, R. and Jacobson, L. (1992) *Pygmalion in the classroom*, New York: Irvington.

Roter, D. and Hall, J. (1992) *Doctors talking to patients/patients talking to doctors: improving communication in medical visits*, Westport, CT: Auburn House.

Roth, H. (1889) 'On salutations', *Journal of the Royal Anthropological Institute* 19: 164–81

Rousseau, E. and Redfield, D. (1980) 'Teacher questioning', *Evaluation in Education* 4: 51–2.

Routasalo, P. (1999) 'Physical touch in nursing studies: a literature review', *Journal of Advanced Nursing* 30: 843–50.

Rowe, M. (1969) 'Science, silence and sanctions', *Science and Children* 6: 11–13.

Rowe, M. (1974a) 'Pausing phenomena: influence on the quality of instruction', *Journal of Psycholinguistic Research* 3: 203–33.

Rowe, M. (1974b) 'Wait-time and rewards as instructional variables, their influence on language, logic, and fate control. Part one – wait-time', *Journal of Research in Science Teaching* 11: 81–94.

Rozelle, R., Druckman, D. and Baxter, J. (1997) 'Nonverbal behaviour as communication', in O. Hargie (ed.) *The handbook of communication skills*, London: Routledge.

Ruback, R. and Juieng, D. (1997) 'Territorial defence in parking lots: retaliation against waiting drivers', *Journal of Applied Social Psychology* 27: 821–34.

Ruben, D.-H. (1990) *Explaining explanation*, London: Routledge.

Rubin, D., Yang, H. and Porte, M. (2000) 'A comparison of self-reported self-disclosure among Chinese and North Americans', in S. Petronio (ed.) *Balancing the secrets of private disclosures*, Mahwah, NJ: Lawrence Erlbaum Associates.

Ruffner, M. and Burgoon, M. (1981) *Interpersonal communication*, New York: Holt, Rinehart and Winston.

Russell, J. (1997) 'Reading emotions from and into faces: resurrecting a dimensional-contextual perspective', in J. Russell and J. Fernandez-Dols (eds) *The psychology of facial expression*, Cambridge: Cambridge University Press.

Russell, J. and Fernandez-Dols, J. (1997) 'What does a facial expression mean?', in J. Russell and J. Fernandez-Dols (eds) *The psychology of facial expression*, Cambridge: Cambridge University Press.

Russell, J.L. (1971) *Motivation*, Dubuque, IA: W.C. Brown.

Rutter, D. and Quine, L. (2002) 'Social cognition models and changing health behaviours', in D. Rutter and L. Quine (eds) *Changing health behaviour*, Buckingham: Open University Press.

Ruusuvuori, J. (2001) 'Looking means listening: coordinating displays of engagement in doctor–patient interaction', *Social Science and Medicine*, 52: 1093–1108.

Ryan, R. and Deci, E. (1996) 'When paradigms clash; comments on Cameron and Pierce's claim that rewards do not undermine intrinsic motivation', *Review of Educational Research* 66: 33–8.

Ryan, R., Sheldon, K., Kasser, T. and Deci, E. (1996) 'All goals are not created equal: an organismic perspective on the nature of goals and their regulation', in P. Gollwitzer and J. Bargh (eds) *The psychology of action: linking cognition and motivation to behaviour*, New York: Guilford Press.

Ryff, C. and Singer, B. (2000) 'Interpersonal flourishing: a positive health agenda for the new millennium', *Personality and Social Psychology Review* 4: 30–4.

Saigh, P.A. (1981) 'Effects of nonverbal examiner praise on selected WAIS subtest performance of Lebanese undergraduates', *Journal of Nonverbal Behavior* 6: 84–8.

Salacuse, J. (1998) 'Ten ways that culture affects negotiating style. Some survey results', *Negotiation Journal* 14: 221–39.

Salter, A. (1949) *Conditioned reflex therapy*, New York: Capricorn Books.

Samp, J. and Solomon, D. (1998) 'Communicative responses to problematic events in close relationships I: the variety and facets of goals', *Communication Research* 25: 66–95.

Sanchez, M. (2001) 'Effects of assertive communication between doctors and patients in public health outpatient surgeries in the city of Seville', *Social Behavior and Personality* 29: 63–70.

Sanders, R. and Fitch, K. (2001) 'The actual practice of compliance seeking', *Communication Theory* 11: 263–89.

Sarafino, E. (1996) *Principles of behavior change: understanding behavior modification techniques*, New York: Wiley.

Saunders, C. and Caves, R. (1986) 'An empirical approach to the identification of communication skills with reference to speech therapy', *Journal of Further and Higher Education* 10: 29–44.

Saunders, C. and Saunders, E. (1993) 'Expert teachers' perceptions of university teaching: the identification of teaching skills', in R. Ellis (ed.) *Quality assurance for university teaching*, Buckingham: Open University Press.

Saunders, P. (1998) '"You're out of your mind!": humour as a face-saving strategy during neuropsychological examinations', *Health Communication* 10: 357–72.

Savin-Williams, R. and Dube, E. (1998) 'Parental reactions to their child's disclosure of a gay/lesbian identity', *Family Relations: Interdisciplinary Journal of Applied Family Studies* 47: 7–13.

Scanlon, L. (1994) *Narrative, authority and power: the medieval exemplum and the Chaucerian tradition*, Cambridge: Cambridge University Press.

Schatzman, L. and Strauss, A. (1956) 'Social class and modes of communications', *American Journal of Sociology* LX: 329–38.

Scheflen, A. (1974) *How behavior means*, Garden City, NJ: Anchor.

Schegloff, E. (2000) 'Overlapping talk and the organization of turn-taking for conversation', *Language in Society* 29: 1–63.

Schegloff, E. and Sacks, H. (1973) 'Opening-up closings', *Semiotica* 8: 289–327.

Scherer, K. (1979) 'Acoustic concomitants of emotional dimensions: judging affect from synthesized tone sequences', in S. Weitz (ed.) *Nonverbal communication: readings with commentary* (2nd edn), New York: Oxford University Press.

Schermerhorn, J., Hunt, J. and Osborn, R. (1995) *Basic organizational behaviour*, New York: John Wiley & Sons.

Schiavo, R., Kobashi, K., Quinn, C., Sefscik, A. *et al.* (1995) 'Territorial influences on the permeability of group spatial boundaries', *Journal of Social Psychology* 135: 27–9.

Schlundt, D. and McFall, R. (1985) 'New directions in the assessment of social competence and social skills', in L. L'Abate and M. Milan (eds) *Handbook of social skills training and research*, New York: Wiley.

Schneider, S. and Laurion, S. (1993) 'Do we know what we've learned from listening to the news?', *Memory and Cognition* 21: 198–209.

Schroth, M. (1992) 'The effect of delay of feedback on a delayed concept formation transfer task', *Contemporary Educational Psychology* 17: 78–82.

Schubert, J. (2000) 'Give sorrow words: mourning at termination of psychoanalysis', *Scandinavian Psychoanalytic Review* 23: 105–17.

Schullery, N. (1997) 'Communication behaviors of employed females: a survey focusing on argumentativeness and women's supervisory roles in organizations', *Dissertation Abstracts International: Humanities and Social Sciences* 58(3-A): 0647.

Schultz, C.B. and Sherman, R.H. (1976) 'Social class, development and differences in reinforcer effectiveness', *Review of Educational Research* 46: 25–59.

Schutz, A. (1998) 'Assertive, offensive, protective, and defensive styles of self-presentation: a taxonomy', *The Journal of Psychology* 132: 611–28.

Schutz, W.C. (1955) 'What makes groups productive?', *Human Relations* 8: 429–65.

Schwab, S., Scalise, J., Ginter, E. and Whipple, G. (1998) 'Self-disclosure, loneliness and four interpersonal targets: friend, group of friends, stranger, and group of strangers', *Psychological Reports* 82: 1264–6.

Schwartz, B. (1989) *Psychology of learning and behaviour*, New York: Norton.

Schwarz, N. and Hippler, H. (1991) 'Response alternatives: the impact of their choice and presentation order', in P. Biemer, R. Groves, L. Lyberg, N. Mathiowetz and S. Sudman (eds) *Measurement errors in surveys*, New York: Wiley.

Scofield, M.E. (1977) 'Verbal conditioning with a heterogeneous adolescent sample: the effects on two critical responses', *Psychology* 14: 41–9.

Scott, B. (1988) *Negotiating: constructive and competitive negotiation*, London: Paradigm Press.

Scott, M., McCroskey, J. and Sheahan, M. (1978) 'The development of a self-report measure of communication apprehension in organizational settings', *Journal of Communication* 28: 104–11.

Sear, L. and Williamson, T. (1999) 'British and American interrogation strategies', in D. Canter and L. Alison (eds) *Interviewing and deception*, Aldershot: Ashgate.

Seden, J. (1999) *Counselling skills in social work practice*, Buckingham: Open University Press.

Segerstrale, U. and Molnar, P. (1997) 'Nonverbal communication: crossing the boundary between culture and nature', in U. Segerstrale and P. Molnar (eds) *Nonverbal communication: where nature meets culture*, Mahwah, NJ: Lawrence Erlbaum Associates.

Segrin, C. (1992) 'Specifying the nature of social skill deficits associated with depression', *Human Communication Research* 19: 89–123.

Segrin, C. (2000) 'Interpersonal relationships and mental health problems', in K. Dindia and S. Duck (eds) *Communication and personal relationships*, Chichester: Wiley.

Segrin, C. and Flora, J. (2000) 'Poor social skills are a vulnerability factor in the development of psychological problems', *Human Communication Research* 26: 489–514.

Seiter, J. and Dunn, D. (2001) 'Beauty and believability in sexual harassment cases: does physical attractiveness affect perceptions of veracity and the likelihood of being harassed', *Communication Research Reports* 17: 203–9.

Shaffer, D., Pegalis, L. and Cornell, D. (1992) 'Gender and self-disclosure revisited: personal and contextual variations in self-disclosure to same-sex acquaintances', *The Journal of Social Psychology* 132: 307–15.

Shah, J. and Kruglanski, A. (2000) 'Aspects of goal networks: implications for self-regulation', in M. Boekaerts, P. Pintrich and M. Zeidner (eds) *Handbook of self-regulation*, San Diego: Academic Press.

Shannon, C. and Weaver, W. (1949) *The mathematical theory of communication*, Illinois: University of Illinois Press.

Shapiro, D. (2000) 'Supplemental joint brainstorming: navigating past the perils of traditional bargaining', *Negotiation Journal* 16: 409–19.

Shaw, M.E. (1981) *Group dynamics: the psychology of small group behavior*, New York: McGraw-Hill.

Sherif, M. (1936) *The psychology of social norms*, New York: Harper & Row.

Sherman, W. (1990) *Behavior modification*, New York: Harper & Row.

Showalter, J.T. (1974) 'Counselor nonverbal behavior as operant reinforcers for client self-references and expression of feelings', *Dissertation Abstracts International* 35: 3435A.

Sidanius, J. and Pratto, F. (1999) *Social dominance: an intergroup theory of social hierarchy and oppression*, Cambridge: University of Cambridge Press.

Siegal, M. (1997) *Knowing children: experiments in conversation and cognition*, Hove: Psychology Press.

Siegel, J. (1980) 'Effects of objective evidence of expertness, nonverbal behavior and subject sex on client-perceived expertness', *Journal of Counseling Psychology* 27: 117–21.

Silver, R.J. (1970) 'Effects of subject status and interviewer response program on subject self-disclosure in standardized interviews', *Proceedings of the 78th Annual Convention*, APA 5: 539–40.

Simi, N. and Mahalik, J. (1997) 'Comparison of feminist versus psychoanalytic/ dynamic and other therapists on self-disclosure', *Psychology of Women Quarterly* 21: 465–83.

Simon, B. (1999) 'A place in the world: self and social categorization', in T. Tyler, R. Kramer and O. John (eds) *The psychology of the social self*, Mahwah, NJ: Lawrence Erlbaum Associates.

Simons, T. and Tripp, T. (2003) 'The negotiation checklist', in R. Lewicki, D. Saunders, J. Minton and B. Barry (eds) *Negotiation: readings, exercises and cases* (4th edn), New York: McGraw-Hill.

Simpson, J. and Wood, W. (1992) 'Introduction: where is the group in social psychology?', in S. Worchel, W. Wood and J. Simpson (eds), *Group process and productivity*, Newbury Park, CA: Sage.

Singh, D. and Young, R. (1996) 'Body weight, waist-to-hip ratio, breasts, and hips: role of judgements of female attractiveness and desirability for relationships', *Ethology and Sociobiology* 16: 483–507.

Singh, R., Onglatco, M., Sriram, N. and Tay, A. (1997) 'The warm–cold variable in impression formation: evidence for the positive–negative asymmetry', *British Journal of Social Psychology* 36: 457–78.

Sinha, S., Alka, R. and Parul, V. (1999) 'Selective attention under conditions of varied demands, personal space and social density', *Journal of the Indian Academy of Applied Psychology* 24: 105–8.

Sinha, S. and Mukherjee, N. (1996) 'The effect of perceived co-operation on personal space requirements', *Journal of Social Psychology* 136: 655–7.

Sinha, V. (1972) 'Age differences in self-disclosure', *Developmental Psychology* 7: 257–8.

Skelton, J. and Hobbs, F. (1999) 'Concordancing: use of language-based research in medical communication', *The Lancet* 353: 108–11.

Skinner, B.F. (1953) *Science and human behaviour*, London: Collier Macmillan.

Skinner, B.F. (1957) *Verbal behavior*, New York: Appleton-Century-Crofts.

Skinner, B.F. (1977) 'The force of coincidence', in B. Etzel, J. Le Blanc and D. Baer (eds), *New developments in behavioral research: theory, method and applications*, Hillsdale, NJ: Lawrence Erlbaum Associates.

Skogstad, A. and Einarsen, S. (1999) 'The importance of a change-centred leadership style in four organizational cultures', *Scandinavian Journal of Management* 15: 289–306.

Slater, M. and Rouner, D. (2002) 'Entertainment-education and elaboration likelihood: understanding the processing of narrative persuasion', *Communication Theory* 12: 173–91.

Smith, E. (1999) 'Traditions of touch in psychotherapy', in E. Smith, P. Clance and S. Imes (eds) *Touch in psychotherapy: theory, research, and practice*, New York: Guilford Press.

Smith, E. and Mackie, D. (2000) *Social psychology* (2nd edn), Philadelphia, PA: Psychology Press.

Smith, R. and Smoll, F. (1990) 'Self-esteem and children's reactions to youth sport coaching behaviours: a field study of self-enhancement processes', *Developmental Psychology* 26: 987–93.

Snyder, M. (1987) *Public appearances, private realities*. New York: Freeman Press.

Snyder, M. and Omoto, A. (2001) 'Basic research and practical problems: volunteerism and the psychology of individual and collective action', in W. Wosinska, R. Cialdini, D. Barrett and J. Reykowski (eds) *The practice of social influence in multiple cultures*, Mahwah, NJ: Lawrence Erlbaum Associates.

Solano, C. and Dunnam, M. (1985) 'Two's company: self-disclosure and reciprocity in triads versus dyads', *Social Psychology Quarterly* 48: 183–7.

Solnick, S. (2001) 'Gender differences in the ultimate game', *Economic Inquiry* 39: 189–200.

Sommer, R. (1969) *Personal space*, Englewood Cliffs, NJ: Prentice Hall.

Sopory, P. and Dillard, J. (2002) 'The persuasive effects of metaphor', *Human Communication Research* 28: 382–419.

Sorenson, R., De Bord, G. and Ramirez, I. (2001) *Business and management communication: a guide book* (4th edn), Upper Saddle River, NJ: Prentice Hall.

Sosik, J., Kahai, S. and Avolio, B. J. (2000) 'Leadership style, anonymity and creativity in group decision support systems: the mediating roe of optimal flow', *Journal of Creative Behavior* 33: 227–56.

Spangenberg, E. and Greenwald, A. (2001) 'Self-prophecy as a behavior modification technique in the United States', in W. Wosinska, R. Cialdini, D. Barrett and J. Reykowski (eds) *The practice of social influence in multiple cultures*, Mahwah, NJ: Lawrence Erlbaum Associates.

Spooner, S.E. (1976) 'An investigation of the maintenance of specific counseling skills over time', *Dissertation Abstracts International* (February) 5840A.

Stefanko, P. and Ferjencik, J. (2000) 'Identification of dimensions of opener ability' *Studia Psychologica* 42: 279–82.

Steil, L. (1991) 'Listening training: the key to success in today's organizations', in D. Borisoff and M. Purdy (eds) *Listening in everyday life*, Maryland: University of America Press.

Stenstroem, A. (1988) 'Questions in conversation', in M. Meyer (ed.) *Questions and questioning*, New York and Berlin: de Gruyter.

Sternberg, R. (1988) *The triangle of love*, New York: Basic Books.

Steuten, U. (2000) 'Rituals among rockers and bikers', *Soziale Welt-zeitschrift fur Sozialwissenschaftliche Forschung und Praxis* 51: 25.

Stewart, C. and Cash, W. (2000) *Interviewing: principles and practice* (9th edn), Boston, MA: McGraw-Hill

Stewart, J. and Logan, C. (1998) *Together: communicating interpersonally* (5th edn), Boston, MA: McGraw-Hill.

Stewart, L. (2001) 'The importance of addressing issues of applied ethics for communication scholars and consultants', *American Communication Journal* 5(1): http://www.acjournal.org/holdings/index.htm.

Stivers, T. (2001) 'Negotiating who presents the problem: next speaker selection in pediatric encounters', *Journal of Communication* 51: 252–82.

Stogdill, R.M. (1974) *Handbook of leadership: a survey of theory and research*, New York: Free Press.

Stone, J., Wiegand, A., Cooper, J. and Aronson, E. (1997) 'When exemplification fails: hypocrisy and the motive for self-integrity', *Journal of Personality and Social Psychology* 72: 54–65.

Straub, D. and Karahanna, E. (1998) 'Knowledge worker communications and recipient availability: towards a task-closure explanation of media choice', *Organisational Science* 9: 160–75.

Street, R. (2001) 'Active patients as powerful communicators', in W.P. Robinson and H. Giles (eds) *The handbook of language and social psychology*, pp. 541–60, Chichester: John Wiley & Sons.

Stricker, G. (1990) 'Self-disclosure and psychotherapy', in G. Stricker and M. Fisher (eds) *Self-disclosure in the therapeutic relationship*, New York: Plenum Press.

Stroebe, W. (2000) *Social psychology and health*, Buckingham: Open University Press.

Strong, S., Taylor, R., Branon, J. and Loper, R. (1971) 'Nonverbal behavior and perceived counselor characteristics', *Journal of Counseling Psychology* 18: 554–61.

Sue, D., Sue, D. and Ino, S. (1990) 'Assertiveness and social anxiety in Chinese-American women', *Journal of Psychology* 124: 155–64.

Suganuma, M. (1997) 'Self-disclosure and self-esteem in old age', *Japanese Journal of Psychology* 45: 12–21.

Sullivan, H. (1953) *The interpersonal theory of psychiatry*, New York: Norton.

Sullivan, H. (1954) *The psychiatric interview*, New York: Norton.

Suls, J.M. and Wheeler, L. (eds) (2001) *Handbook of social comparison: theory and research*, New York: Plenum.

Surinder, S.K., Sosik, J.J. and Avolio, B.J. (1997) 'Effects of leadership style and problem structure on work group process and outcome in an electronic meeting system environment', *Personnel Psychology* 50:121–36.

Susskind, L. and Mnookin, R. (1999) 'Major themes and prescriptive implications', in R. Mnookin and L. Susskind (eds) *Negotiating on behalf of others*, Thousand Oaks, CA: Sage.

Sutherland, K., Wehby, J. and Copeland, S. (2000) 'Effect of varying rates of behaviour-specific praise on the on-task behavior of students with EBD', *Journal of Emotional and Behavioral Disorders* 8: 2–8.

Sutherland, K.S. and Wehby, J.H. (2001) 'The effect of self-evaluation of teaching behaviour in classrooms for students with emotional and behavioural disorders', *Journal of Special Education* 35: 161–71.

Sutton, S. (1982) 'Fear arousing communication: a critical examination of theory and research', in J. Eiser (ed.) *Social psychology and behavioral medicine*, New York: Wiley.

Swann, W. (1997) 'The trouble with change: self-verification and allegiance to the self', *Psychological Science* 8: 177–80.

Swann, W., Hixon, J., Stein-Seroussi, A. and Gilbert, D. (1990) 'The fleeting gleam of praise: cognitive processes underlying behavioral reactions to self-relevant feedback', *Journal of Personality and Social Psychology* 59: 17–26.

Swanson, S. (1999) 'Re-examination of assertiveness and aggressiveness as potential moderators of verbal intentions', *Psychological Reports* 84: 1111–14.

Swanson, S. and McIntyre, R. (1998) 'Assertiveness and aggressiveness as potential moderators of consumers' verbal behavior following a failure of service', *Psychological Reports* 82: 1239–47.

Swift, J., Gooding, T. and Swift, P. (1988) 'Questions and wait time', in J. Dillon (ed.) *Questioning and discussion: a multidisciplinary study*, Norwood, NJ: Ablex.

Tannen, D. (1995) 'Asymmetries: women and men talking at cross-purposes', in J. Stewart (ed.) *Bridges not walls: a book about interpersonal communication*, New York: McGraw-Hill.

Tannen, D. (1998) *The argument culture*, London: Virago.

Tardy, C. (1988) 'Self-disclosure: objectives and methods of measurement', in C. Tardy (ed.) *A handbook for the study of human communication*, Norwood, NJ: Ablex.

Tardy, C. (2000) 'Self-disclosure and health: revisiting Sidney Jourard's hypothesis', in S. Petronio (ed.) *Balancing the secrets of private disclosures*, Mahwah, NJ: Lawrence Erlbaum Associates.

Tardy, C. and Dindia, K. (1997) 'Self-disclosure', in O. Hargie (ed.) *The handbook of communication skills* (2nd edn), London: Routledge.

Taylor, D. and Altman, I. (1987) 'Communication in interpersonal relationships: social penetration processes', in M. Roloff and G. Miller (eds) *Interpersonal processes: new directions in communications research*, Newbury Park, CA: Sage.

Taylor, O. (1997) 'Student interpretations of teacher verbal praise in selected seventh- and eight-grade choral classes', *Journal of Research in Music Education* 45: 536–46.

Taylor, P. (2002) 'A cylindrical model of communication behavior in crisis negotiations', *Human Communication Research* 28: 7–48.

Taylor, S., Neter, E. and Wayment, H. (1995) 'Self-evaluation processes', *Personality and Social Psychology Bulletin* 21: 1278–87.

Tedeschi, J. (ed.) (1981) *Impression management theory and social psychological research*, New York: Academic Press.

Temple, L. and Loewen, K. (1993) 'Perception of power: first impressions of a woman wearing a jacket', *Perceptual and Motor Skills* 76: 339–48.

Terry, A. (1999) 'Motivational interviewing', in A. Memon and R. Bull (eds) *Handbook of the psychology of interviewing*, Chichester: Wiley.

Terry, D., Hogg, M. and McKimmie, B. (2000) 'Attitude–behaviour relations: the role of in-group norms and mode of behavioural decision-making', *British Journal of Social Psychology* 39: 337–61.

Tesser, A. (2001) 'Self-esteem', in A. Tesser and N. Schwarz (eds) *Blackwell handbook of social psychology: intraindividual processes*, Oxford: Blackwell Publishers.

Teyber, E. (1997) *Interpersonal processes in psychotherapy* (3rd edn), Pacific Grove, CA: Brooks/Cole.

Thibaut, J. and Kelley, H. (1959) *The social psychology of groups*, New York: Wiley.

Thomas, A. and Bull, P. (1981) 'The role of pre-speech posture change in dyadic interaction', *British Journal of Social Psychology* 20: 105–11.

Thomas, L. and Levine, T. (1994) 'Disentangling listening and verbal recall. Related but separate constructs?', *Human Communication Research* 21: 103–27.

Thomas, L. and Levine, T. (1996) 'Further thoughts on recall, memory, and the measurement of listening: a rejoinder to Bostrom', *Human Communication Research* 23: 306–8.

Thompson, C.D. and Born, D.G. (1999) 'Increasing correct participation in an exercise class for adult day care clients', *Behavioral Interventions* 14: 171–86.

Thompson, L. (1990) 'Negotiation behavior and outcomes: empirical evidence and theoretical issues', *Psychological Bulletin*, 108: 515–32.

Thompson, L. (2001) *The mind and heart of the negotiator*, Upper Saddle River, NJ: Pearson.

Thompson, T. (1998) 'The patient/health professional relationship', in L. Jackson and B. Duffy (eds) *Health communication research: a guide to developments and directions*, Westport, CT: Greenwood Press.

Thorne, A. (2000) 'Personal memory telling and personality development', *Personality and Social Psychology Review* 4: 45–56.

Thyne, J. (1963) *The psychology of learning and techniques of teaching*, London: University of London Press.

Tierney, E. (1996) *How to make effective presentations*, Thousand Oaks, CA: Sage.

Tiersma, E. (1995) 'Dictionaries and death: do capital jurors understand mitigation?', *Utah Law Review* 1: 20–69.

Tiersma, P. (2001) 'The problem of jury instructions', paper presented at the Annual Meeting of the American Association for the Advancement of Science, San Francisco, February.

Timberlake, W. and Allison, J. (1974) 'Response deprivation: an empirical approach to instrumental performance', *Psychological Review* 81: 146–64.

Tizard, B., Hughes, M., Carmichael, H. and Pinkerton, G. (1983) 'Children's questions and adult answers', *Journal of Child Psychology and Psychiatry* 24: 269–81.

Tobin, K. (1987) 'The role of wait time in higher cognitive learning', *Review of Educational Research* 57: 69–95.

Togo, D. and Hood, J. (1992) 'Quantitative information presentation and gender: an interaction effect', *The Journal of General Psychology* 119: 161–7

Torrecillas, F., Martin, I., De la Fuente, E. and Godoy, J. (2000) 'Attributional style, self-control, and assertiveness as predictors of drug abuse', *Psicothema* 12: 331–4.

Torres, C.V. (2000) 'Leadership style norms among Americans and Brazilians: assessing differences using Jackson's return potential model', *Dissertation Abstracts International: Section B: The Sciences & Engineering* 60(8-B): 4284.

Tourish, D. (1999) 'Communicating beyond individual bias', in A. Long (ed.) *Interaction for practice in community nursing*, Basingstoke: Macmillan.

Tourish, D. and Hargie, O. (1998) 'Communication between managers and staff in the NHS: trends and prospects', *British Journal of Management* 9: 53–71.

Tourish, D. and Hargie, O. (2000) 'Communication and organisational success', in O. Hargie and D. Tourish (eds) *Handbook of communication audits for organisations*, London: Routledge.

Tourish, D. and Pinnington, A. (2002) 'Transformational leadership, corporate cultism and the spirituality paradigm: an unholy trinity in the workplace', *Human Relations* 55: 147–72.

Tourish, D. and Wohlforth, T. (2000) *On the edge: political cults right and left*, Armonk, NY: Sharpe.

Tracy, K. and Coupland, N. (1990) 'Multiple goals in discourse: an overview of issues', *Journal of Language and Social Psychology* 9: 1–13.

Trees, A. and Manusov, V. (1998) 'Managing face concerns in criticism: integrating nonverbal behaviour as a dimension of politeness in female friendship dyads', *Human Communication Research* 24: 564–83.

Trenholm, S. and Jensen, A. (2000) *Interpersonal communication* (4th edn), Belmont, CA: Wadsworth.

Tubbs, S. (1998) *A systems approach to small group interaction* (6th edn), Boston, MA: McGraw-Hill.

Tuckman, B.W. (1965) 'Developmental sequence in small groups', *Psychological Bulletin* 63: 384–99.

Tuckman, B.W. and Jensen, M. (1977) 'Stages in small group development revisited', *Group and Organizational Studies* 2: 419–27.

Turk, C. (1985) *Effective speaking*, London: E. & F.N. Spon.

Turkat, I.D. and Alpher, V.S. (1984) 'Prediction versus reflection in therapist demonstrations of understanding: three analogue experiments', *British Journal of Medical Psychology* 57: 235–40.

Turner, J. (1999) 'Social identity and self-categorisation', in N. Ellemers, R. Spears and B. Doosje (eds) *Social identity*, Oxford: Blackwell.

Turner, J., Hogg, M., Oakes, P., Reicher, S. and Wetherell, M. (1987) *Rediscovering the social group: a self-categorisation theory*, Oxford: Blackwell.

Turney, C., Ellis, K.J., Hatton, N., Owens, L.C., Towler, J. and Wright, R. (1983a) *Sydney micro skills redeveloped: series 1 handbook*, Sydney: Sydney University Press.

Turney, C., Ellis, K.J., Hatton, N., Owens, L.C., Towler, J. and Wright, R. (1983b) *Sydney micro skills redeveloped: series 2 handbook*, Sydney: Sydney University Press.

Turton, J. (1998) 'Importance of information following myocardial infarction: a study of the self-perceived needs of patients and their spouse/partner compared with the perceptions of nursing staff', *Journal of Advanced Nursing* 27: 770–8.

Tusing, K. and Dillard, J. (2000) 'The sounds of dominance: vocal precursors of perceived dominance during interpersonal influence', *Human Communication Research* 26: 148–71.

Tutton, E. (1991) 'An exploration of touch and its uses in nursing', in R. McMahon and A. Pearson (eds) *Nursing as therapy*, London: Chapman and Hall.

Tversky, A. and Kahneman, D. (1981) 'The framing of decisions and the rationality of choice', *Science* 211: 453–8.

Twenge, J. (1998) 'Assertiveness, sociability, and anxiety', *Dissertation Abstracts International: The Sciences and Engineering*, 59(2-B): 0905.

Uhlemann, M.R., Lea, G.W. and Stone, G.L. (1976) 'Effect of instructions and modeling on trainees low in interpersonal communication skills', *Journal of Counseling Psychology* 23: 509–13.

Van Der Merwe, J. (1995) 'Physician–patient communication using ancestral spirits to achieve holistic healing', *American Journal of Obstetrics and Gynecology* 1172: 1080–7.

Van Harreveld, F., Van der Pligt, J. and de Vries, N. (2000) 'The structure of attitudes: attribute importance, accessibility and judgment', *British Journal of Social Psychology* 39, 363–80.

Van Slyke, E. (1999) *Listening to conflict: finding constructive solutions to workplace disputes*, New York: AMACOM.

Van Yperen, N. and Van de Vliert, E. (2001) 'Social psychology in organizations', in M. Hewstone, and W. Stroebe (eds) *Introduction to Social Psychology* (3rd edn), Oxford: Blackwell.

Vangelisti, A. and Caughlin, J. (1997) 'Revealing family secrets: the influence of topic, function, and relationships', *Journal of Social and Personal Relationships* 14: 679–705.

Verner, C. and Dickinson, G. (1967) 'The lecture, an analysis and review of research', *Adult Education*, 17: 85–100.

Vittengl, J. and Holt, C. (2000) 'Getting acquainted: the relationship of self-disclosure and social attraction to positive affect', *Journal of Social and Personal Relationships* 17: 53–66.

Vondracek, F.W. (1969) 'The study of self-disclosure in experimental interviews', *Journal of Psychology* 72: 55–9.

Vrij, A. (2000) *Detecting lies and deceit: the psychology of lying and the implications for professional practice*, Chichester: Wiley.

Vrij, A. (2001) 'Detecting the liars', *The Psychologist*, 14, 596–8.

Vrij, A., Edward, K., Roberts, K. and Bull, R. (2000) 'Detecting deceit via analysis of verbal and nonverbal behavior', *Journal of Nonverbal Behavior* 24: 239–63.

Vrij A., Semin, G. and Bull, R. (1996) 'Insight into behavior displayed during deception', *Human Communication Research* 22: 544–62.

Wagner, H. and Lee, V. (1999) 'Facial behavior alone and in the presence of others', in P. Philippot, R. Feldman, and E. Coats (eds) *The social context of nonverbal behavior*, Cambridge: Cambridge University Press.

Waldo, C. and Kemp, J. (1997) 'Should I come out to my students? An empirical investigation', *Journal of Homosexuality* 34: 79–94.

Waldron, V., Cegala, D., Sharkey, F. and Teboul, B. (1990) 'Cognitive and tactical dimensions of conversational goal management', *Journal of Language and Social Psychology* 9: 101–18.

Walker, J. (2001) *Control and the psychology of health*, Buckingham: Open University Press.

Walker, M. and Antony-Black, J. (eds) (1999) *Hidden selves: an exploration of multiple personality*, London: Routledge.

Walker, N. and Hunt, J. (1998) 'Interviewing child victim-witnesses: how you ask is what you get', in C. Thompson, D. Herrmann, J. Read, D. Bruce, D. Payne and M. Toglia (eds) *Eyewitness memory: theoretical and applied perspectives*, Mahwah, NJ: Lawrence Erlbaum Associates.

Wallach, J. (1986) *Looks like work*, New York: Viking Penguin.

Wallen, J., Waitzkin, H. and Stoeckle, J. (1979) 'Physicians' stereotypes about female health illness: a study of patients' sex and the information process during medical interviews', *Women and Health* 4: 135–46.

Wallihan, J. (1998) 'Negotiating to avoid agreement', *Negotiation Journal* 14: 257–68.

Walma van der Molen, J. and van der Voort, T. (2000) 'The impact of television, print, and audio on children's recall of the news: a study of three alternative explanations for the dual-coding hypothesis', *Human Communication Research* 26: 3–26.

Walther, J., Slovacek, C. and Tidwell, L. (2000) 'Is a picture worth a thousand words? Photographic images in long-term and short-term computer-mediated communication', *Communication Research* 28: 105–34.

Waring, E., Holden, R. and Wesley, S. (1998) 'Development of the marital self-disclosure questionnaire', *Journal of Clinical Psychology* 54: 817–24.

Warren, L. and Hixenbaugh, P. (1998) 'Adherence and diabetes', in L. Myers and K. Midence (eds), *Adherence to treatment in medical conditions*, Amsterdam: Harwood Academic Publishers.

Washburn, P. and Hakel, M. (1973) 'Visual cues and verbal content as influences on impressions formed after simulated employment interviews', *Journal of Applied Psychology* 58: 137–41.

Waskow, I. (1962) 'Reinforcement in a therapy-like situation through selective responding to feelings or context', *Journal of Consulting Psychology* 26: 11–19.

Wasserman, E. and Neunaber, D. (1986) 'College students' responding to and rating of contingency relations: the role of temporal contiguity', *Journal of the Experimental Analysis of Behavior* 46: 15–35.

Waterman, A., Blades, M. and Spencer, C. (2001) 'Is a jumper angrier than a tree?', *The Psychologist* 14: 474–7.

Watkins, M. (1998) 'Building momentum in negotiations: time-related costs and action-forcing events', *Negotiation Journal* 14: 242–55.

Watson P., Morris, R. and Miller, L. (1998) 'Narcissism and the self as continuum: correlations with assertiveness and hypercompetitiveness', *Imagination, Cognition and Personality* 17: 249–59.

Watson, K. and Barker, L. (1984) 'Listening behavior: definition and measurement', in R. Bostrom and B. Westley (eds) *Communication yearbook 8*, Beverly Hills, CA: Sage.

Watzlawick, P., Beavin, J., and Jackson, D. (1967) *Pragmatics of human communication*, New York: W.W. Norton.

Wearden, J. (1988) 'Some neglected problems in the analysis of human operant behavior', in G. Davey and C. Cullen (eds) *Human operant conditioning and behavior modification*, New York: Wiley.

Webb, P. (1994) 'Teaching and learning about health and illness', in P. Webb (ed.) *Health promotion and patient education*, London: Chapman & Hall.

Weber, M. (1947) *The theory of social and economic organizations*, New York: Free Press.

Webster, D. and Kruglanski, A. (1998) 'Cognitive and social consequences of the need for cognitive closure', in W. Stroebe and M. Hewstone (eds) *European review of social psychology*, Vol. 8, Chichester: Wiley.

Webster, P. (1984) 'An ethnographic study of handshaking', unpublished doctoral dissertation, Boston University.

Weingart, L.R., Prietula, M.J., Hyder, E.B. and Genovese, C.R. (1999) 'Knowledge and the sequential processes of negotiation: a Markov chain analysis of response-in-kind', *Journal of Experimental Social Psychology* 35: 366–93.

Weinstein, N. and Klein, W. (1999) 'Unrealistic optimism: present and future', *Journal of Social and Clinical Psychology* 15: 1–8.

Weinstein, N. and Sandman, P. (2002) 'Reducing the risks of exposure to radon gas: an application of the Precaution Adoption Process Model', in D. Rutter and L. Quine (eds) *Changing health behaviour*, Buckingham: Open University Press.

Weitlauf, J., Smith, R. and Cervone, D. (2000) 'Generalization effects of coping-skills training: influence of self-defense training on women's efficacy beliefs', *Journal of Applied Psychology* 85: 625–33.

Weitzman, P. and Weitzman, E. (2000) 'Interpersonal negotiation strategies in a sample of older women', *Journal of Clinical Geropsychology* 6: 41–51.

West, C. (1983) 'Ask me no questions . . . an analysis of queries and replies in physician–patient dialogues', in S. Fisher and A. Todd (eds) *The social organization of doctor–patient communication*, Washington, DC: Center for Applied Linguistics.

Westmyer, R. and Rubin, R. (1998) 'Appropriateness and effectiveness of communication channels in competent interpersonal communication', *Journal of Communication* 48: 27–48.

Wetherell, M. (1996) 'Life histories/social histories', in M. Wetherell (ed.) *Identities, groups and social issues*, London: Sage.

Whaley, B. and Wagner, L. (2000) 'Rebuttal analogy in persuasive messages: communicator likability and cognitive responses', *Journal of Language and Social Psychology* 19: 66–84.

Wheelan, S. (1994) *Group process. A developmental perspective*, Boston: Allyn & Bacon.

Wheeless, L., Erickson, K. and Behrens, J. (1986) 'Cultural differences in disclosiveness as a function of locus control', *Communication Monographs* 53: 36–46.

Wheldall, K. and Glynn, T. (1989) *Effective classroom learning: a behavioural interactionist approach to teaching*, Oxford: Basil Blackwell.

Wheldall, K., Bevan, K. and Shortall, A. (1986) 'A touch of reinforcement: the effects of contingent teacher touch on the classroom behaviour of young children', *Educational Review* 38: 207–16.

Whetzel, D. and McDaniel, M. (1999) 'The employment interview', in A. Memon and R. Bull (eds) *Handbook of the psychology of interviewing*, Chichester: Wiley.

White, B. and Sanders, S. (1986) 'The influence on patients' pain intensity ratings of antecedent reinforcement of pain talk or well talk', *Journal of Behaviour Therapy and Experimental Psychiatry* 17: 155–9.

White, C. and Burgoon, J. (2001) 'Adaptation and communicative design patterns of interaction in truthful and deceptive conversations', *Human Communication Research* 27: 9–37.

White, J., Rosson, C., Christensen, J., Hart, R. and Levinson, W. (1997) 'Wrapping things up: a qualitative analysis of the closing moments of the medical visit', *Patient Education and Counseling* 30: 155–65.

Whitney, G. (1990) 'Before you negotiate: get your act together', in I. Asherman and S. Asherman (eds) *The negotiating sourcebook*, Amherst, MA: Human Resource Development Press.

Wigboldus, D., Spears, R. and Semin, G. (1999) 'Categorisation, content and the context of communicative behaviour', in N. Ellemers, R. Spears and B. Doosje (eds) *Social identity*, Oxford: Blackwell.

Wiksell, W. (1946) 'The problem of listening', *Quarterly Journal of Speech* 32: 505–8.

Wilding, J., Cook, S. and Davis, J. (2000) 'Sound familiar', *The Psychologist* 13: 558–62.

Wilke, H. and Wit, A. (2001) 'Group performance', in M. Hewstone, and W. Stroebe (eds) *Introduction to social psychology* (3rd edn), Oxford: Blackwell.

Wilke, H.A.M. and van Knippenberg, A. (1996) 'Group performance', in M. Hewstone, W. Stroebe and G. Stephenson (eds), *Introduction to social psychology* (2nd edn), Oxford: Blackwell.

Willemyns, M., Gallois, C., Callan, V. and Pittam, J. (1997) 'Accent accommodation in the job interview: impact of interviewer accent and gender', *Journal of Language and Social Psychology* 16: 3–22.

Williams, A. (1999) 'Behavior modification', in B. Holli and R. Calabrese (eds) *Communication and education skills for dietetics professionals*, Baltimore: Williams & Wilkins.

Williams, A. and Nussbaum, J. (2001) *Intergenerational communication across the life span*, Mahwah, NJ: Lawrence Erlbaum Associates.

Williams, C. (1997) 'A cross-cultural participant-observer description of intra-cultural communication behaviors: the greetings and partings of the Saramakan Bushnegroes', *Dissertation Abstracts International: Humanities and Social Sciences* 58(3-A): 0648.

Williams, E. and Akridge, R. (1996) 'The Responsible Assertion Scale: development and evaluation of psychometric qualities', *Vocational Evaluation and Work Adjustment Bulletin* 29: 19–23.

Williams, K. and Dolnik, L. (2001) 'Revealing the worst first: stealing thunder as a social influence strategy' in J. Forgas and K. Williams (eds) *Social influence: direct and indirect processes*, Philadelphia, PA: Psychology Press.

Williams, K. and Zadiro, L. (2001) 'Ostracism: on being ignored, excluded, and rejected', in M. Leary (ed.) *Interpersonal rejection*, Oxford: Oxford University Press.

Willis, F. and Briggs, L. (1992) 'Relationship and touch in public places', *Journal of Nonverbal Behavior* 16, 55–63.

Willis, F. and Hamm, H. (1980) The use of interpersonal touch in securing compliance', *Journal of Nonverbal Behavior* 5: 49–55.

Wilmot, W. (1995) 'The transactional nature of person perception', in J. Stewart (ed.) *Bridges not walls: a book about interpersonal communication*, New York: McGraw-Hill.

Wilmot, W. and Hocker, J. (1998) *Interpersonal conflict* (5th edn), Boston: McGraw-Hill.

Wilson, G. (1999) *Groups in context: leadership and participation in small groups* (5th edn), Boston: McGraw-Hill.

Wilson, G. and Nias, D. (1999) 'Beauty can't be beat', in L. Guerrero and J. DeVito (eds) *The nonverbal communication reader: classic and contemporary readings*, Prospect Heights, IL: Waveland Press.

Wilson, J. (1990) *Politically speaking: the pragmatic analysis of political language*, Oxford: Basil Blackwell.

Wilson, L.K. and Gallois, C. (1993) *Assertion and its social context*, Oxford: Pergamon.

Wilson, S., Aleman, C. and Leatham, G. (1998) 'Identity implications of influence goals: a revised analysis of face-threatening acts and applications to seeking compliance with same-sex friends', *Human Communication Research* 25: 64–97.

Wilson, S., Greene, J. and Dillard, J. (2000) 'Introduction to the special issue on message production: progress, challenges and prospects', *Communication Theory* 10: 135–8.

Wilson, S., Paulson, G. and Putnam, L. (2001) 'Negotiating', in W. P. Robinson and H. Giles (eds) *The handbook of language and social psychology*, Chichester: John Wiley & Sons.

Wilson-Barnett, J. (1981) 'Communicating with patients in general wards', in W. Bridge and J. MacLeod Clark (eds) *Communication in nursing care*, London: Croom Helm.

Windschitl, M. (2001) 'Using simulations in the middle school: does assertiveness of dyad partners influence conceptual change?' *International Journal of Science Education* 23: 17–32.

Wojciszke, B. (2001) 'The consequences of being an influential minority in the context of social controversies in the emerging Polish democracy', in W. Wosinska, R. Cialdini, D. Barrett and J. Reykowski (eds) *The practice of social influence in multiple cultures*, Mahwah, NJ: Lawrence Erlbaum Associates.

Wolff, F., Marsnik, N., Tacey, W. and Nichols, R. (1983) *Perceptive listening*, New York: Holt, Rinehart and Winston.

Wolff, K. (1950) *The sociology of Georg Simmel*, New York: Free Press.

Wolpe, J. (1958) *Psychotherapy by reciprocal inhibition*, Stanford, CA: Stanford University Press.

Wolvin, A. and Coakley, C. (1996) *Listening* (5th edn), Boston, MA: McGraw-Hill.

Wood, T. (2001) 'Team negotiations require a team approach', *The American Salesman* 46: 22–6.

Woodbury, H. (1984) 'The strategic use of questions in court', *Semiotica*, 48: 197–228.

Woodward, K. (2000) 'Questions of identity', in K. Woodward (ed.) *Questioning identity: gender, class, nation*, London: Routledge.

Woodworth, R. and Marquis, D. (1949) *Psychology: a study of mental life*, London: Methuen.

Woolfolk, A. (1998) *Educational psychology* (7th edn), Needham Heights, MA: Allyn & Bacon.

Worchel, S. (1994) 'You can go home again. Returning group research to the group context with an eye on developmental contexts', *Small Group Research* 25: 205–23.

Worland, P. (1998) 'Proctor feedback in a modified PSI course format: the effects of prasie, encouragement and group information', *Dissertation Abstracts International: Section B: The Sciences and Engineering* 59(6-B): 3107.

Wragg, E. (1993) *Primary teaching skills*, London: Routledge.

Wright, C. and Nuthall, G. (1970) 'Relationships between teacher behaviors and pupil achievement in three experimental elementary science lessons', *American Educational Research Journal* 7: 477–93.

Wright, D., Gaskell, G. and O'Muircheartaigh, C. (1997) 'How response alternatives affect different kinds of behavioural frequency questions', *British Journal of Social Psychology* 36: 443–56.

Wright, P. (1980) 'Message-evoked thoughts: persuasion research using thought verbalizations', *Journal of Consumer Research* 7: 151–75.

Wyatt, R., Katz, E. and Kim, J. (2000) 'Bridging the spheres: political and personal conversation in public and private spaces', *Journal of Communication* 50: 71–92.

Wyer, R. and Gruenfeld, D. (1995) 'Information processing in interpersonal communication', in D. Hewes (ed.) *The cognitive basis of interpersonal communication*, Hillsdale, NJ: Lawrence Erlbaum Associates

Wynn, R. (1996) 'Medical students, doctors – is there a difference?', *Text* 16: 423–48.

Yager, G. and Beck, T. (1985) 'Beginning practicum: it only hurt until I laughed', *Counselor Education and Supervision* 25: 149–56.

Yager, T. and Rotheram-Borus, M. (2000) 'Social expectations among African American, Hispanic, and European American adolescents', *Cross-Cultural Research* 34: 283–305.

Yalom, I. D. (1995) *The theory and practice of group psychotherapy* (4th edn), New York: Basic Books.

Yeatts, D. and Hyten, C. (1998) *High performing self managed work teams*, Thousand Oaks, CA: Sage.

Yeschke, C. (1987) *Interviewing: an introduction to interrogation*, Illinois: CC Thomas.

Yik, M.S.M. and Russell, J.A. (1999) 'Interpretation of faces: a cross-cultural study of a prediction from Fridlund's theory', *Cognition and Emotion* 13: 93–104.

Yoshioka, M. (2000) 'Substantive differences in the assertiveness of low-income African American, Hispanic, and Caucasian women', *The Journal of Psychology* 134: 243–59.

Young, T. and French, L. (1996) 'Height and perceived competence of U.S. presidents', *Perceptual and Motor Skills* 82: 1002.

Yukl, G. (1999) 'An evaluation of conceptual weaknesses in transformational and charismatic leadership theories', *Leadership Quarterly* 10: 285–305.

Zaccaro, S. (1999) 'Social complexity and the competencies required for effective military leadership', in J.G. Hunt, G.E. Dodge *et al.* (eds) *Out-of-the-box leadership: transforming the twenty-first-century army and other top-performing organizations. Monographs in leadership and management*, Vol. 1, Stamford, CT: JAI Press.

Zahn, G.L. (1991) 'Face-to-face communication in an office setting: the effects of position, proximity and exposure', *Communication Research* 18: 737–54.

Zamboni, B., Crawford, I. and Williams, P. (2000) 'Examining communication and assertiveness as predictors of condom use: implications for HIV prevention', *AIDS Education and Prevention* 12: 492–504.

Zimmer, J.M. and Anderson, S. (1968) 'Dimensions of positive regard and empathy', *Journal of Counseling Psychology* 15: 417–26.

Zimmerman, B. (2000) 'Attaining self-regulation: a social cognitive perspective', in M. Boekaerts, P. Pintrich and M. Zeidner (eds) *Handbook of self-regulation*, San Diego: Academic Press.

Zirpoli, T. and Melloy, K. (2001) *Behavior management: applications for teachers*, Upper Saddle River, NJ: Prentice Hall.

Zuker, E. (1983) *Mastering assertiveness skills*, New York: AMACOM.

Name index

Subject index

management 46, 93, 199, 301, 341, 433;
conflict 370; country club 432; ethical 440;
impoverished 431; middle-of-the-road 432;
pecking order 55; team 432
manipulation 97, 99, 244–5, 298, 309, 312;
cynical 111; potential for 342
Maori nose rubbing 267
marasmus 56
marital status 266
markers 69, 78; closure 280, 282; disjunct
192–3; gender 74; nonverbal 282; verbal
215
marriage 225, 227; commitment to 364
married couples 55, 65
masculine assertiveness 313
masculinity 32, 68, 74, 247, 264, 315, 316
massage 56
Masters and Johnston 58
mastery 26
material: addition of 180; instructional 199;
organising 179; television-mediated 216
material needs 406–7
maximisation 276
meaning(s) 14, 15, 32, 78, 156, 171, 200, 201,
213; common 212; conveying 61; diverse
68; message 172; obscene 60; reflecting
153, 167; shared 17, 40; technical 199;
underlying 167
media 347; influence attempts 330; richness
14
mediating processes 37–9
medical students 117
memory 135, 189, 216; aids to 179, 182;
devices 179; fallibility of 178; false 134;
long-term 175; short-term 174
mental health 243, 430; disorders 95;
'retardation' 279
mental images 61
mental processes 184; higher 127
mental set 190–1; positive or negative 272
merchandising sales 342
messages 14–15, 46; affective part of 154;
anonymous 256; cognitive part of 154;
complexity 187; contradictory 51; delivery
348–51; disjointed 185; emotional 51, 57,
186; extreme 51; factual parts/content of
154, 155; health 357; how presented and
how received 78; important 187;
informative or instructive 175; linguistic
193; low credibility 330; matching 321;
meaning of 172; negative 321, 347;
nonverbal 13, 30, 49, 79, 106, 183;
persuasive 175, 331, 335; positive 321;
process 402; processing 337; propositional

51; significance 187; structure 186; textual
216; threatening 358; unclear 186;
unexpected 187; verbal 13, 47, 51, 60
metacognitions 38
metagoals 35
metalevel assertion 309
metaperception 40
meta-planning 380
Methodist faith 249
Mexico 318; communities in USA 319, 320
micromomentary expressions 66
Middle East 58, 59, 248
midrange groups 402
mimicking 68
mind raping 191
mindlessness 19
minimisation theme 131
minimum necessary share 378
miracles 343
mirroring 63, 155, 156
miscommunication 22, 30, 40
misconceptions 130
misleading questions 130, 135
mistakes 180
misunderstandings 16, 40, 213, 320
mnemonics 179, 215
moaning 78
modelling 7, 254
'monitors' 203
monochronicity 382
monologue approach 202
moral appeals 359
moral superiority 365
mortality rates 56
Moses Illusion, The 132
mother and child 48
motivation 6, 27, 82, 235, 296, 382, 417;
arousing 261; group 427; heightened 209;
inspirational 428; intrinsic 103, 104, 363;
listener 180; maximum 287; protection
356; reinforcement as 109; rewards can
influence 94
motivational closure 286–7, 289
motivational set 270–1, 277
motives 18, 26–7, 35, 47, 132, 191, 256;
machiavellian 252; social 67
motor skills 7
motoric inhibition 322
mouth movements 50
multi-dimensionality 19–20, 34, 153, 160, 402
multi-finality 440
multiple questions 142
murder 132
music 188, 255

54, 79; projection 185; *see also* tone of voice
voluntary acts 255, 326, 363
vulnerability 104, 140, 357

waists *see* WHR
'wannabe' phenomenon 342
warmth 55, 76, 106, 255, 316
Watergate 413
waves 282
We-language 306–7
'wealthy' people 264
well-being 3, 129, 162, 170; maintaining 200; material 406; psychological and biological 56
well-wishing comments 288
white knuckles 61
WHR (waist-to-hip ratio) 74, 264
win–lose negotiation 375
win–win encounters 382

withdrawal 52, 59
withholding 144
women 30, 65–6, 69, 75, 78; battered 247; older 246; role in society 317; 'thirty-something' 320
words 20, 45, 47; actions can speak louder than 54; affect-laden 331; ambiguous 61; everyday 212; exact choice of 5; pauses between 51; sounds of 180; speaker's own 156; vague, indeterminate 213; *see also* spoken word
worthlessness 97

Xerox 416

'yes–no' question 121–2
Yorkshire men 78
young people 182

zero-sum payoff situations 375